Selected Titles in This Series

THE HISTORY OF GREENLAND

THE HISTORY OF GREENLAND

GREENLAND

II

1700 – 1782

by

FINN GAD

MONTREAL

McGILL–QUEEN'S UNIVERSITY PRESS

1973

© C. Hurst & Co. (Publishers) Ltd., 1973

This is a translation from the Danish edition
Grønlands Historie II, 1700–1782, 1969,
published by Nyt Nordisk Forlag/Arnold Busck, Copenhagen.
Translated by Gordon C. Bowden

ISBN 0 7735 0156 8

Library of Congress Catalog Card Number: 73–152067
Legal Deposit 4th Quarter 1973

Printed in Great Britain by Billing & Sons Limited,
Guildford and London

CONTENTS

PLATES

vi

ILLUSTRATIONS IN TEXT

MAPS

PREFACE

This volume narrates the history of developments in and about Greenland in the eighteenth century, in so far as the sources allow. It is thus confined geographically to the history of West Greenland, i.e. the West coast from Cape Farewell to Melville Bay, and confined in time from the dawn of Danish–Norwegian colonization until 1782, a year of fundamental change. Only a few glimpses of the population of the southernmost part of the East coast come into the picture; this is all we are able to tell of the history of the East Greenlanders and of the Polar Eskimos, the sources being only archaeological. It is to be hoped that these sources, as well as cultural-historical source material, extremely scarce as it is from this period, will be included in a subsequent volume in a wider context. Since there is a fairly large amount of source material relating to the history of West Greenland, it has been our main concern here to deal with this. It is justifiable, moreover, because West Greenland is to a large extent a separate entity, largely cut off, culturally and economically, from the other regions.

The reason why the subject has been treated here in such detail is because, first, a great deal of the source material has lain unused in archives and libraries – some of it seeming as though it has never been read since being consigned to the archives or catalogued in the libraries. Secondly (and to some extent as a consequence of the above) there are many problems and questions which have never been dealt with. It has therefore been necessary to go into detail and to include these studies partly in order to build up the picture, and partly to lead properly to the conclusions. Thirdly, it has seemed necessary here and there to take a critical look at the views, opinions and accounts of previous writers on special items, which means that some individual problems have been examined in detail.

In the Danish original (Copenhagen 1969) every statement and all quotations are referred to the sources and their location. Most of these references are to unprinted letters, reports, diaries, government papers, etc. As I wrote in the preface to Volume I: "The student who wants to study the documents and the special literature must have a good knowledge of the Danish language, and it is therefore rational to refer him to the Danish edition", a remark which is even more pertinent to this volume. The notes and references are therefore kept here to a minimum. However, all statements, terms, single words or phrases which have quotation marks in the text are translated into modern English from the Danish used in the actual documents. These may have the function of substantiation.

Instead of having broad references, I have made for this English edition a short survey of the source material, including some of the literature in non-Scandinavian languages. The few notes in the text sometimes refer to titles not mentioned in this survey. For the sake of easier reading, Hans Egede's often-cited *Relations* (see p. 431) are referred to in the text as "Reports".

My wish to synchronize the events in my narrative has led to a number of repetitions, which are made solely to maintain contact with the overall picture. If this has been overdone, it is regretted, but the principle has been that several repetitions too many are preferable to even one too few.

The intention throughout has been to penetrate behind the source material and to record the reactions of the Greenland population on the influences from outside the country. Only very seldom did the eighteenth-century Greenlander express himself, but where the slightest opportunity occurs to catch, directly or indirectly, some evidence of the Greenlander's reactions, I have, as far as lay within my capabilities, squeezed the source material for information. Whether or not I have succeeded in giving an impression of the early cultural changes in West Greenland is for others to judge.

Cultural influences and the background of those who exerted them had of course to be included in the account. As the source material for that aspect of Greenland's history was more plentiful, the descriptions of this development and background have occupied considerable space. This is also due, in my view, to so many of the problems not having been dealt with and the true facts not being established previously. The historical evolution of both the Mission and trade, and the cultural, economic, geographical and political background necessarily had to be included. In doing so, it also became necessary to describe the phases in the growth of the whole complex of international and constitutional problems. The interplay between isolation and integration is not the least interesting side of the history of Greenland society. Everything is carried forward, anticipating a continuation in future volumes; these, however, are not yet written.

Material for illustrating this period of Greenland's history is not only extremely limited, especially for the period after 1750, but much of the little available does not permit of even tolerable reproduction. Eighteenth-century Greenland obviously did not appeal to the artistically gifted. The poor-looking European houses, tarred brown or mouldy grey, or the roughly plastered and starkly constructed stone houses, were not immediately inspiring; nor, strangely enough, did the unique natural features call forth any display of artistic ability. This should be remembered in considering our choice of illustrations.

The translation of this volume has been a difficult and rather lengthy task, and has had to be thoroughly revised and checked by the publisher, Mr. Christopher Hurst, as well as by myself. It is always questionable how special terms and titles are to be translated. It has been my wish to avoid translating the geographical, institutional and administrative names and titles. In my opinion it implies a wrong feeling to "translate" a name that is well established in Danish–Norwegian society to an English name that may be similar, but is not identical; for example, it is inaccurate to "translate" three different institutions by the same term (*Rigsraad, Conseil* and *Cabinet* by "Privy Council"). As in Volume I, I have included a glossary of these "official terms" (see pp. 433–5). This and the glossary in Volume I can be referred to.

In conclusion I want to express my thanks to the translator who did the basic job, to Mr. Hurst who himself had the task of balancing the English style, besides running the risk of the edition itself, and above all to the Danish State's Rask–Ørsted Fond for its financial grant towards the cost of translating this second volume of my work.

Gentofte, Denmark   FINN GAD
1972

MAPS

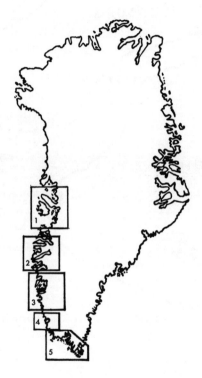

Key to Maps 1–5

1. Area of Disko Bay, and Ûmánaq.

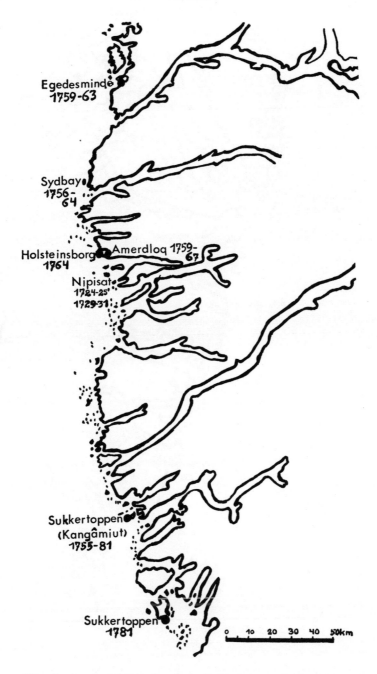

2. The district south of Egedesminde, Holsteinsborg and Sukkertoppen.

3. Godthåb and Fiskenæsset.

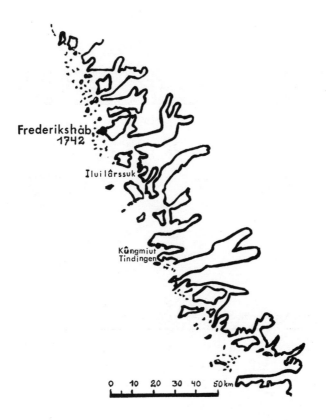

4. Frederikshåb.

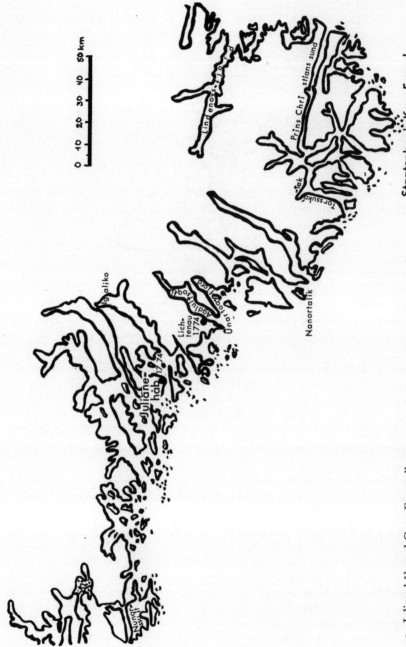

5. Julianehåb and Cape Farewell.

I

PLANS, PROJECTS AND NAVIGATION
OF THE DAVIS STRAIT
1700–1720

Men's thoughts and deeds throughout the centuries give the appearance of a vast sea stretching to infinity. Prominent crests heave skywards and dark troughs reset down into the depths. All is movement. Measurements in terms of time are only a device to arrest the eternal motion for a while in order to observe it. It is humanly possible to follow the movement of only a few waves, perhaps but a single one. The thoughts which circulated about Greenland and the actions affecting that once remote land were only a wave motion in time, seen from a Danish–Norwegian viewpoint, and a scarcely visible ripple, seen from continental Europe. So although Torfæus' thoughts and ideas, as expressed in the 1680s (*see* I, p. 317) seem to have held sway in the early eighteenth century, after the change of sovereign in 1699, this is but a minor feature in the picture of the Danish–Norwegian monarchy in the first decade of the new century. It formed only a part of what happened, what was thought and what was done. But it was important in maintaining the continuity that can be traced in the special development which brought Denmark–Norway closer to the ancient North Atlantic dominions.

In the royal library the various accounts of Greenland gradually came to form quite a comprehensive collection. Arngrimur Jónsson's Latin description dating from the early seventeenth century and Bishop Thorlacius' *Description of Greenland* of 1668–9 were probably not very widely known, nor were the maps drawn by learned Icelanders in the seventeenth century, most lately by Bishop Thorlacius. In his map the Eastern Settlement is clearly sited at the southern end of the East Greenland coastline. About the beginning of the eighteenth century there was keen interest in ancient Norse Greenland. Apart from the Rector of Kerteminde, Matthias Henriksen Schacht, those concerned with this period of Greenland's history were mainly Icelanders. Thormod Torfæus was still active. In Lolland another Icelander, Arngrimur Thorkelsson Vídalín, was Rector first of Maribo and later of Nakskov.

He was the grandson of Arngrimur Jónsson, whose tales of the Norse settlements in Greenland he had heard as a child. The idea of the Danish–Norwegian crown's western dependency had always haunted him. He discussed the matter with Torfæus and finally set down his ideas and opinions in a document, which was never printed,[1] although a few manuscript copies still exist. It was in Latin, and entitled *De veteri et nova Gronlandia diatribe* and is dated 1 July 1703. Of its three parts, the first two give an uninteresting description of Norse Greenland based on Arngrimur Jónsson's manuscript and the Norse literature available to Vídalín, followed by a description of Greenland and the later voyages from Frobisher onwards, based on the literature of the seventeenth century. The third part, which he himself translated into Danish, and of which there are several copies, was regarded by Vídalín as the most important part of his work. It contains a proposal that the connection with Greenland be renewed. Referring to Peder Claussøn's description of Norway, dated 1632, he stated that the Davis Strait should be used if the Western Settlement were to be found, and that to discover the Eastern Settlement it was necessary to travel round Cape Farewell. Peder Hansen Resen had suggested this in 1664,[2] but Vídalín does not mention it. It would be in the King's interest to allow circumnavigation of Greenland to be resumed, he wrote; the country's merchants would also benefit. He referred to "the Dutchman who never lets anything go by which might be useful to him", and who had given up whaling off Iceland and headed for the Davis Strait. He described the abundance which, according to Ivar Bardson's description, existed in Greenland – as opposed to Iceland – and referred to Thormøhlen's voyage which started in 1673.[3] Vídalín had discussed the matter with Thormøhlen and other shipowners in Nakskov, Copenhagen and Flensborg, and was sure that much profit and pleasure would be derived from the resumption of whaling, "which nowhere in these Dominions is given the consideration it deserves".

Vídalín's idea of resuming sailings round Greenland from the north had very different aims from earlier sailings – namely, benefits for the kingdoms and honour and glory for the King. Colonization could be resumed, and thus would consolidate the kingdoms' power in the northwest and either re-establish the Christian Church or send a mission to the heathens he knew to exist on the west coast of Greenland, and who were probably involved in the disappearance of the Norse settlement. Vídalín was sure that "remains of His Royal Majesty's subjects" would be found.

He then went into details of how the matter was to be tackled. It was important to obtain information before actually setting out, so the services of English or Dutch seafarers acquainted with the passage

should be obtained; there were also thought to be Davis Strait navigators in Hamburg and Holstein. (He was probably thinking of Friesians
who had already proved themselves expert whalers.) Two ships with
engineers on board would then be despatched. They would sail close
inshore and seek out the best site for founding the first colony. Not only
would the site have to be suitable in every way for settlement, but
military considerations were also to have their place. During this
preliminary reconnaissance, relations with the "natives" must be such
that they could be welcomed there again in the future, so the expedition
members would have to treat them in such a way as to win their friendship and "trust". Then they must, above all else, beware of kidnapping
any of the natives and carrying them off to Denmark, as had occurred
formerly, such conduct being "both foolish and as harmful to trading
as it could possibly be . . .". This was the opinion expressed by Torfæus
in his memorandum of 18 January 1683.

There are many similarities between Vídalín's and Torfæus' proposals, but Vídalín's are far more detailed. Like Torfæus, Vídalín
tempted the King with the short distance to the promised Vinland,
which he even suggested the King should conquer. However, this was
a digression amid the host of details aimed at the reconquest of Greenland.

When the first reconnaissance had been carried out and the ships
were safely home, there was to be no delay in executing the well-
prepared operation. To provide financial backing, "all merchants
and indeed all other persons of means, whatever their station, should
at first jointly finance a small party, and if their venture were successful,
they might derive great use and benefit from it, especially in the future;
should it unexpectedly fail, they would not suffer any great or serious
harm thereby". Vídalín hit upon the well-tried idea of a company,
but he gave it wide scope, perhaps because he was aware of how much
capital an undertaking of this nature called for. This company or
"association or community of interests", should have a royal charter
and permission to carry to Greenland some 500 families, together with
the materials required for their settlement and defence.

Vídalín wanted formal colonization, on a much bigger scale than
Torfæus had proposed with the Icelandic "vagrants". It was common
sense, he said, "that it is far better to have people in those regions who
can fish both winter and summer and to collect goods from them annually than to send ships out to those waters once a year at great expense for the purpose of whaling or fishing". This colonization was to
be organized with head men, priests, barber-surgeons and physicians
as necessary; Vídalín took this for granted and did not discuss it
further.

Both sides of the Davis Strait were to be settled and then the expedition was to continue down the west coast to Cape Farewell and round it to where riches and wonderful remains were to be found. Only by such a reconnaissance voyage, which would have to set out from the west coast (cf. Resen's proposal'), could it be discovered whether descendants of the old Norse community still existed and whether they "have been driven farther inland or completely destroyed by the natives, for I cannot conceive of their having intermingled. . . ."

Vídalín then described in greater detail the merchandise to be taken which was the same as that mentioned by Frobisher: mirrors, needles, knives, scissors, bells "and other trifles which dazzle the eyes somewhat". Perhaps it would be possible later to sell clothes. "Even though the Greenlanders would reject wine, I can imagine they will drink mead, and possibly brandy too in time. . . . It is probably to be expected that they will, as elsewhere in the world, gradually derive some instruction from the countries with which they come into contact." Vídalín saw no harm in alcohol, an obvious article of commerce, as he also wrote that one must "show them that we have come to their land to do them good, not harm".

Once trade had been established with the "barbarians" it would be time to convert them to Christianity and to bring about their voluntary acceptance of the national government. Some of them should be taught Danish, but their language had to be learnt too. . . "until this has been done, it will be impossible to accomplish anything properly". No force must be exerted on the savages "since force seldom succeeds". On the contrary, an attempt should be made to get on such terms with a few of them that they themselves would wish to accompany a ship back to Denmark. There they were to be given the best possible treatment, by which Vídalín probably meant that they were to learn all about the country and its customs and be given education and skills. They were then to be sent back to Greenland where their reports would be beneficial to trade and also make it possible for the Greenlanders to accept the Christian faith.

Kidnapping only made the Greenlanders hostile, as Frobisher's report suggested. The same had been the experience of the Danish expeditions to Greenland. Some people might have thought this savagery would make commerce impossible. Yet to Vídalín: "No people is so barbaric that, if treated wisely, it is still to be feared and dreaded. The fact that our people were ill-received by the Greenlanders once and were unable to accomplish their mission was their own fault and not that of the Greenlanders. . . ."

The long, elaborately-reasoned report closed with a rousing exhortation to implement the proposal to resume the Greenland voyages and colonization. Vídalín pointed out that not only Thormøhlen, but Peter Klauman, the Copenhagen brewer and merchant, and others among the "wisest and most prominent" merchants in Copenhagen, Lolland and especially Flensborg were interested in putting the thought into action if the King would give his permission and support.

Vídalín's proposals contained all the main features of the subsequent colonization which actually took place on a far smaller scale than he had imagined. Because of the many points on which his ideas coincided with the subsequent reality as regards company formation, mission, colonization and methods of reconnaissance, the question has been raised as to whether his document could have influenced Hans Egede and his colonization plans. It is unlikely that Hans Egede had read the document in 1704–5; however it was brought to his attention in 1718 by the Norwegian missionary among the Lapps, Thomas von Westen[4]. Nowhere does Hans Egede himself mention that he read it. He had, as many as seven years before, submitted to the King his first proposal for a mission to Greenland, and that certainly had nothing in common with the Vídalín document.

Vídalín was in Copenhagen late in 1703 to deliver his document to the King and work on his plans. On 8 February 1704, however, he died, and his scheme was shelved. In 1704 it may have formed an element in the controversy going on in certain circles about resuming the Greenland voyages. Rumours circulated concerning these discussions or plans, and even reached Iceland and the learned Árni Magnusson.[5] In September 1704 he wrote to the president of the *Rentekammer*, Joachim von Ahlefeldt, that he had heard what the King contemplated and that Ahlefeldt was gathering information on Greenland for this purpose. He therefore enclosed a lengthy historical account of events to date as far as he knew them. This is a sober account, in which he sought to demolish the exaggerated idea of the riches to be found in Greenland – this struck at Vídalín. Unlike Torfæus and Vídalín, Árni Magnusson did not believe in the wonders of Vinland. The reports he said, were filled with so many fabulous circumstances as to make the whole story scarcely credible.

Torfæus is said to have refused to collaborate with Vídalín because he himself was engaged on similar work. His manuscript must have existed in its Latin form simultaneously with or perhaps even before Vídalín's. Just as the latter had translated the third part of his document into Danish, Torfæus now began translating his *Gronlandia antiqva*, which, unlike Vídalín's document, found its way into print. This was arranged by his pupil and good friend Jacob Rasch, a brilliant linguist and theologian from Stavanger, near Torfæus' usual place of residence. Rasch was in Copenhagen from 1698 onwards, when he studied geometry, astronomy and navigation, including cartography. Shortly after the turn of the century he had sent King Frederik IV copies of the old Norse itineraries to Greenland collected by Bishop Erik Valkendorf at the beginning of the sixteenth century, which were in Copenhagen.[6] Joachim von Ahlefeldt had been in touch with Rasch, and it was his idea that Rasch should take part in the planned expedition to Greenland, as a linguist and "expert" on Greenland affairs.

Rasch published Torfæus' *Gronlandia antiqva* in 1706, with amendments and cartographic material added. He also drew a map based on Torfæus' additions to Thorlacius' map of 1668; this shows the Frobisher Strait within the southern island, distinct from Greenland itself. The Eastern and Western settlements are located along the strait, on the east and west sides respectively.[7] This map provided a basis for the exploration of Greenland in the years up to 1723 and its influence still lingered on up to the early nineteenth century. Torfæus' work was a link in a series of writings intended to remind the crown of its obligations towards the former Norwegian dependencies, of which Iceland and the Faroe Islands alone now remained. *Gronlandia antiqva* was thus an element in a wider concept.

Joachim von Ahlefeldt's plans for the resumption of Greenland navigation came to nothing, due partly to the tense situation in Scandinavia. Denmark–Norway's first participation in the so-called great Scandinavian war had ended abruptly with the peace of Travendal in 1700. The humiliating situation of the kingdom was not conducive to activity in other sectors of foreign politics, especially as the rest of Europe was engaged in the war of the Spanish Succession. Danish communications with Norway were so uncertain that a government committee in Christiania had been given far-reaching authority. In 1706 the situation looked particularly menacing for Denmark–Norway. There were fears of a Swedish invasion, but the immediate danger passed. However, from 1709 to 1720 Denmark–Norway were again at war with Sweden. Up to 1709 the government had to tread warily regarding the resumption of contact with Greenland, not least for economic reasons. Jacob Rasch left Copenhagen in 1706 for Christiana, but never forgot his interest in Greenland.

During this same time, from July 1704 to August 1705, the Norwegian student Hans Poulsen Egede was in Copenhagen, where he completed his theological studies in record time. He cannot have been unaware of the rumours about the Greenland expedition, but in 1705 he returned to Norway. In April 1706 his father died, and Hans who had acted as tutor to his brothers, had to find a living. In 1707 he was appointed pastor at Thorsken, only to exchange this appointment shortly afterwards for the pastorate of Vågan in the Lofoten Islands.

In the same year he married the thirteen-year-old Giertrud Rasch. Although she was distantly related to Jacob Rasch, this relationship is not significant here.

In the third part of his document, Vídalín had mentioned the Copenhagen merchant Peter Klauman as a willing participant in the proposed Greenland expedition. He had not, however, the means to undertake anything on his own account and it was difficult to get anything organized from Copenhagen. No more is known of the Lolland and Flensborg merchants mentioned by Vídalín, who took no initiative during these years. Christian V's charters of 1697 to the Greenland Companies in Bergen and Copenhagen (I, p. 316) had already been confirmed by his successor in April 1700.

(This apparently had no effect on the initiatives taken south of the Skagerak.)

Behind this confirmation of the charters lay the action on 23 January 1700 of ten Bergen shipowners, who applied successfully for the charter to be confirmed. It is unknown to what extent ships from Bergen sailed to Greenland in the years immediately after 1700; in 1702 the town was razed to the ground by a fire, the second within twenty years. By February 1703 whaling was again being undertaken. It was, however, still uncertain what was meant by "Greenland" in the shipping lists (cf. I, pp. 313, 315). It is frequently recorded that the vessels were going whaling "off Greenland, Iceland or Finnmark". In 1711 the two vessels belonging to the Danish-born Bergen whaler Hans Mathias, the St. Arianne and St. Peter, were mentioned for the first time as having sailed to the Davis Strait. Mathias had been one of the founders of a Greenland company in Bergen in 1697.[8] There is no evidence that he or any other shipowner used the charters to sail to West Greenland. Thormøhlen's business seems to have declined during the years after the fire, and he died in Copenhagen in 1708.

In 1707 the 1697 charters expired, and in the next year Hans Mathias sent a ship on a trading and fishing expedition in the Davis Strait, i.e. West Greenland. In Bergen whaling circles it was he alone who had any interest in West Greenland sailings, or sent ships there. He mentioned this in a petition to be exempted from customs duty, consumption tax and tolls on goods shipped to and from West Greenland. He continued, nevertheless, to send ships there at his own expense and risk. The vessel he sent out in 1708 caused him a loss of nearly 400 rigsdaler, yet in 1720 he sent another ship out on a whaling and trading expedition. In 1708, he and fifteen other shipowners had petitioned the King for the renewal of the 1697/1700 charters. They received no answer, and petitioned again in 1709 and 1710. The petition mentioned that in the first few years only one or two ships could be sent out, but later six and in 1710 as many as ten were mentioned. Whether these vessels ever sailed, and if so to West Greenland, is unknown.

During the war of 1709–10, the enlistment of seamen for service in the Navy made inroads into the whaling owners' skilled labour force. Their petitions, therefore, also sought permission to get such men exempted from war service. However, since the petitions were shelved with other similar requests, we must assume that the application was not granted, an assumption supported by Mathias' renewed petition in 1711 for exemption from duty, consumption tax and excise on the goods shipped on the vessel he had sent to West Greenland in 1710, and which were now being claimed from him because, as expected, royal permission had not been received.

At the same time Mathias announced that he had had two ships fitted out to sail to West Greenland. In time of war, whether in national or in distant waters, it was risky to allow them to sail without the royal sea-pass, which had not arrived in time. He declared that he had spent the greater part of his fortune on fitting out these two vessels. Yet in 1712, 1713 and 1714 he again had vessels sailing to the west, which, in his various petitions concerning charters and exemptions, he stated he had fitted out at his own expense – to encourage other Bergen citizens to undertake similar trading expeditions. In the early years no one followed his example, but from 1711 the names of other Bergen shipowners occur in connection with Davis Strait sailings. Thormøhlen's son-in-law, Nicolaus Christoph Bärenfels Edler von Warnau, took over his late father-in-law's shipping business and sent a ship to the Davis Strait in 1711 and in the three years that followed.

Other names like Magnus Schiøtte and L. Fasting, which were to become well known later in connection with Greenland sailings from Bergen, appear in 1712 as owners of ships sailing to the Davis Strait. There is no doubt that these were trading expeditions, for it is expressly stated that the vessels carried merchandise, including catchpenny goods, for trading on the coast.

In his various petitions to the King, Hans Mathias revealed a fair knowledge, especially about mediaeval Norse Greenland. Like Vídalín, he had fantastic notions of the riches to be found there and had gained his ideas about "the savages" from Olearius; he also referred to the activities of the Dutch.

This Dutch "Davis Strait trade" became more intensive in the years after the Peace of Utrecht in 1713, so much so that the Bergen shipowners felt themselves crowded out and practically gave up the sailings.

In the latter half of the seventeenth century – after Nicolas Tunes' voyage in 1656 (see I, pp. 256 ff.) – Dutch navigation of the Davis Strait was not extensive, and the yield from whaling dropped at the same time. This indicates a reduction in the catch itself in the grounds between Greenland, Spitsbergen and Jan Mayen Island. The decline may have resulted from over-exploitation or migration of the whales due to a change in climate, or from Dutch involvement in several wars during this period, so that vessels and crew were required elsewhere. This fall in the yield and the apparent return of the whales to the Davis Strait no doubt accounted for the interest shown in the Strait at the beginning of the eighteenth century. That Dutch navigation of the Davis Strait became more general towards the end of the century is apparent from both Vídalín's papers and Hans Mathias' petitions. Vídalín mentioned that while in the Faroe Islands a leading merchant in Nakskov, Hans Pederson Top, had several times spoken to Dutchmen who had sailed the Davis Strait. The reason why they did not establish colonies on the West Greenland coast, stated Vídalín, was their awareness that the land belonged to the Danish–Norwegian crown; but they were well satisfied with the whaling there and the trade with the inhabitants, out of which "they can make a good profit". The Dutch had moved from the waters around Iceland to the Davis Strait as their whaling grounds. Although the figures given by Vídalín in connection with the Dutch sailings to the Davis Strait are probably imagined, he was never in doubt about the name "Davis Strait navigators".

The scope of this Dutch traffic around the beginning of the eighteenth century is suggested by Hans Mathias' petition of 1710, which mentioned five Dutch vessels; he said that the Dutch had begun trading with West Greenland some years before and that, after reconnoitring the country and the trade, "they sailed there year after year, making a great profit. . . ." In 1710 the five ships had done their buying before Mathias' vessels arrived and sailed home fully laden with all kinds of goods acquired by barter. Hans Mathias' petition also reveals that the Dutch ships seldom sailed alone and that there were always at least two in view of the hazards at sea and on shore. During the period 1719–28 there were on average seventy-five vessels each year plying between the Netherlands and the Davis Strait, a high figure at that time for waters and a coast so far from the normal shipping routes. The bold Dutch captains had good reason to regard these waters and coasts as virgin territory. No serviceable charts or descriptions of the sea-ways existed, let alone sailing directions or landmarks. Experience was accumulated, and on this basis servicable charts were produced. On these charts the Dutch continued to show the former English nomenclature as well as the Dutch names which they had introduced. Cape Farewell had already been named Staatenhoek. The naming of places was continued up the west coast, being densest along the stretch from where Godthåb now stands to the Ũmánaq area and later farther northwards. These place-names survived for a long time and some are still in use. This has occurred in many parts of the world where the Dutch sailed, and even in Danish home waters Dutch place-names have been perpetuated (e.g. Kattegat and Drogden). Dutch names retained in Greenland, either in the original language or in translation, include Skinderhvalen, Sukkertoppen (a translation of Zuikerbrood), Vester Ejland, Skansen, Rodebay, Vaigat, Hareøen, Svartenhuk and Ubekendt Ejland.

Before sailing home the Dutch Davis Strait navigators met at Sydbay, by Ukîvik Island, just to the north of Nordre Isortoq fjord in the northern Holsteinsborg district.[9] It would seem that this custom was already well-established when Feykes Haan mentioned Sydbay in the title of his 1719 pilot's manual, as the most southerly point of the stretch of coast covered by the manual. In his description of "Straat Davids" or "Outgroenlandt" (Old Greenland), he took his examples from the stretch north of Holsteinsborg and presumably from Disko Bay. The Dutch did not leave the coast to the south unvisited, but because of the ice – vividly described by Feykes Haan – they avoided going too close inshore to Cape Farewell. In his own time, he wrote, no one had landed anywhere along the stretch from Cape Farewell up to latitude 62–63°N., i.e. as far as present-day Fiskenæsset. This excludes those cases where the seafarers were caught in the ice and so had to head south for land. Pack-ice is a hazard today, but at that time seafarers made long detours round those waters where it was known to exist. The Dutch did not put in to land much farther south than the Godthåb area during these years, yet they possessed a detailed knowledge of the coast to the north of it.

The prime motive of the Dutch was probably the search for whales. Feykes Haan stated that the best whaling was to be found in the bay south of Disko which is probably why the region around Godthåb and as far as Holsteinsborg attracted their attention less although certain places were known: Delftshavn (Atangmik), Baals Revier (Godthåb Fjord), Skinderhvalen, Brielse Haven (Fiskenæsset) and Kap Briel (Frederikshåb). If they did their best to avoid these less hazardous stretches, it was probably because they knew that these regions were navigated by Englishmen, Danes and Norwegians, and came under the Danish–Norwegian crown. The more northerly stretches of coast were regarded by the Dutch as a "no man's land". Here they went whaling and bought the fishing and hunting products of the Eskimo population. At first this trade seems to have been extremely profitable, but Feykes Haan was already complaining of its decline. He regarded the trading opportunities as poor, because competition between the various Dutch Davis Strait navigators and the shipowners who backed them had become fierce. In 1720 it had become necessary to pay 75–100 per cent more for the Greenlanders' produce than in his early days.

Trade between the Dutch and the Greenlanders was on a barter basis. The Dutch offered shirts, hose, woollen gloves, brassware, knives, sword blades, sundry tools, pewterware, fish-hooks and, not least, glass beads and pottery. Small wooden chests and specially made blades for women's knives (*ulos*), and later coarse woollen fabrics, were carried by the Dutch ships for bartering. Everything that the Greenlanders could supply was purchased, but fox skins, blubber and whalebone were specially sought after. An ordinary shirt fetched two fox skins or one and a half barrels of blubber, for which the Dutch obtained considerably more than the cost of the shirt at the auctions in their home country. The trade must have been profitable for a long time, as the Dutch Davis Strait sailings continued, and only declined during the latter half of the century.

This relatively intensive commerce over a fairly confined stretch of the West Greenland coast was bound to exert an influence on the economic conditions of the local Greenland population, hence on social and cultural conditions as well. Compared with the rather isolated existence of former times, when contact with the outside world was rare, the West Greenland Eskimo now found himself annually in contact with foreigners, who brought to the small society articles which had previously been difficult to obtain, but which could now be had for as little as a pair of fox skins. Beads, which they otherwise laboriously made themselves, could now be obtained easily, and the imports were much more shiny and attractive. Cutting tools, knives and *ulo*-blades were now available through barter, and there was no longer any need to laboriously hammer out the blade from metal that had been found or acquired accidentally. The same applied to harpoon blades, iron tips for bird javelins, etc. Small sword blades were ideal for the latter purpose. In the way of domestic utensils, it was now possible to obtain pots and pans, kettles, cups and spoons. Metal sewing needles replaced the old bone needles. Iron fish-hooks were now used instead of the home-made ones made of bone or consisting of bent nails. It is probable that woven fabrics also came into use, as they were among the classes of goods which the Dutch seafarers carried with them to sell. All these articles began to appear in various conditions in the middens. The picture of the material culture changed appreciably, so that we now speak of the eighteenth-century Eskimo whaling-season culture, where numerous imported articles appeared alongside the purely Eskimo locally produced objects. The latter underwent no changes, except for the not insignificant fact that the cutting edge of hunting implements was now nearly always made of iron.

Naturally, it is in the middens on derelict sites along the coastal stretch, where the Dutch did most of their trading, that this whaling-season culture is most strongly represented. However, it spread to the whole west coast and merged imperceptibly into the colonization period (post-1721). This spread was linked with two circumstances. First, barter trading, as already mentioned, was carried on among the West Greenlanders themselves, and secondly the West Greenlanders under-took lengthy journeys from both north and south to the areas where the Dutch called to obtain blubber, whalebone and skins by barter. With fully laden *umiaks* they headed for these regular markets where their surplus production was exchanged for bargains. Such extensive journeys were probably not made every year by one family, but they were enough to affect the conditions to which they were accustomed, not least the hunting cycle. The latter was also disturbed by the Dutch-men's interest in fox skins. Greater importance was attached to these skins than previously, although the hunting of other animals was not abandoned on that account.

The Dutch were only in the country for about three months of each year – between April and August. For the rest of the year the Eskimos were left to themselves, and during that time they were able to "lick their wounds" – for the encounter with the Dutch seldom passed off peacefully. Dutch *genever* took its toll. More than one Eskimo awoke from a drunken stupor on board the Dutch vessel in the open sea on the way back to the ship's home port, and later found himself being sold to a travelling showman who exhibited him at fairs. Families in West Greenland might thus find themselves deprived of their bread-winner in this way and having to scrape a living as best they could. It also happened that later in the year families would see their numbers increased by a newborn child with features that were not quite those of an Eskimo. At the "markets" in northern West Greenland the same thing occurred as it does everywhere when men hungry for women gather together and there is plenty to drink. It is also probable that diseases of European origin entered West Greenland during these years (hence presumably tuberculosis, which is mentioned in later eighteenth-century reports). Women were sometimes raped, and de-liberate kidnapping and fights took place with fatal consequences for both Dutchmen and Greenlanders. This caused the Dutch States-General in November 1720 to proclaim it an offence for Davis Strait navigators to assault Greenlanders, rob them of their possessions or use force against them. The inhabitants were to be treated properly, and captains and ships' officers were to ensure that this was done. The orders given referred not only to what was fitting for civilized men, but also to the adverse affects on whaling and trade since the Greenlanders had become hostile. Feykes Haan in his description of West Greenland illustrated these attacks and gave dreadful accounts of Greenlanders' acts of revenge against Davis Strait navigators in distress.

There were similar reports from the Norwegian side. In about 1718, a vessel belonging to the Bergen shipowner Bärenfels became stuck in the pack-ice in fog close to present-day Ivigtut. The ship was crushed to pieces by the ice, but the crew escaped on ice floes with two boats, though only one boat's crew succeeded in reaching the mainland. There they saw the huts of "the savages" but no people. Only after a few days did they encounter people, who shot at them with arrows. After one of the ship's crew was mortally wounded, a Greenlander was shot in self-defence, whereupon the others disappeared and nothing was seen of them for several more days. After many days' wandering they found a Dutch ship which took them home. There are several recorded examples of the belligerent attitude of the West Greenlanders living in the south. Perhaps their aggressiveness was founded in an inherited fear of revenge for their attacks on the old Norse farmers; the tradition of the avenger lives on to this day among the East Greenlanders.

Sailings to Greenland from Bergen were resumed in 1713 after an interval of about five years. In 1718 three Bergen captains sailed to Greenland probably to trade in the Davis Strait, whence they returned home at the beginning of July. Bärenfels stated that he had ten years' navigating experience and that a few years before he had lost his ship off Cape Farewell after trading in the Davis Strait for several years. However, the Bergen trade with Greenland up to 1721 cannot have been widespread.

In the decade between 1708 (when he was twenty-two years old) and 1719 the curate in Vågan, Hans Poulsen Egede,[10] developed the idea of establishing a mission in Greenland. He wrote in his first account: "In October 1708, shortly after I arrived in the parish of Vogen in the north, as I was walking alone one evening in pitch darkness, it occurred to me that in *Norgis Beskrifvelse* I had long ago read about Greenland, that there were Christians as well as churches and convents, etc., but those who have travelled there for whaling have not been able to discover anything, so I became curious to know how things stood in the present time." The following spring he wrote about this to his brother-in-law in Bergen, Niels Rasch, who had been to Greenland with Hans Mathias. Rasch replied that what had been called Greenland was in fact Svalbard "but in Greenland to the south . . . which begins at 60 degrees and is known as far as 74 degrees . . . there are wild people and men. . . . The eastern side of Greenland which faces towards Iceland, where Norsemen are said to have lived long ago, cannot be explored now on account of drift ice which has come to rest along the shore".

Hans Egede had no doubt that among the people who lived on the west coast of Greenland were descendants of the old Norse settlers. He tells how he was seized with compassion for those people, who had once been Christians but who, for lack of priests, had reverted to paganism. It would be the utmost happiness for him to preach Christianity to them again – and in the pure Lutheran form which could not have reached those far-off people. Egede hoped all his life to discover people of "pure Norwegian extraction" in Greenland, but he realized from the outset that the existing West Greenlanders were "savages" who spoke a language difficult for Europeans to understand. We have seen that it is uncertain whether Hans Egede knew Vídalín's writings; for example, he does not refer at all to Olearius, who doubted the Norse descent of the West Greenlandic population (I, pp. 250–1.) Probably on the basis of Caspar Bartholin's 1675 glossary of 300 West Greenlandic words, including Olearius' 114 terms (I, pp. 245 ff.),[11] Egede believed, as did some contemporaries, that he could recognize certain Scandinavian words among the terms in this list. In his *Short Report on Greenland*[12] he mentioned the same supposedly Norwegian words as Olearius, along with some personal names which were said to resemble contemporary Norwegian ones.[13] From this he concluded that "these people must be of old Norse extraction", adducing the possibility that the "Norwegians" on the west coast had at the same time mixed with the people who lived there "called *skraellings*". Thus Hans Egede held the opinion that the population of the west coast was of mixed race. Hoping and believing that he would find descendants of the mediaeval Norse population still alive, he wanted to establish the mission on the west coast where the mixed population lived. The urge to establish the mission is attributed by Hans Egede himself to Peder Claussøn's *Norges Bescriffuelse* of 1632 (see I, p. 236 and above p. 13), but this extremely short and not very informative description could not have been solely responsible for arousing Hans Egede's interest. As mentioned above, there was talk of an expedition to Greenland during 1704–5, when Hans Egede was in Copenhagen; the mission to the King's Indian domain, Trankebar, was under discussion at the same time.

The idea of the mission itself aroused little enthusiasm in those days. The theological climate at the University of Copenhagen, and thus in the state-controlled Danish–Norwegian Church, bore the stamp of pure Lutheranism, which was regarded as a massive bulwark of orthodoxy surrounding the Church under the absolute monarch as its supreme authority; the Church was part of the autocratic centralized administration, and its pastors were appointed by the King to work within the Church's clearly defined terms of reference in the parish where they had been granted a living. Hans Egede had been trained as a theologian fully within this tradition. His mental conflict was thus all the greater when he was fired with the idea of a mission to West Greenland, which must involve his abandoning the call that had brought him to Vågan. Since the Danish–Norwegian Church was a self-contained institution with no competence beyond the borders of the kingdoms, the idea of a mission meant a fundamental break, not to be undertaken lightly. He therefore later stressed that Greenland was a part of the kingdoms, and that the inhabitants were subjects of the King.

Almost as soon as he took up his living at Vågan in 1707, he was involved in a dispute with the neighbouring pastor over the right to the foreshore fishing tithe there. The foreshore fish were those that the extraparochial fishermen landed at Vågan and to which the neighbouring pastor had long been entitled. To Hans Egede this seemed unreasonable, and the dispute led to distressing episodes, in which Egede and his opponent did not spare each other. Egede was summoned by his adversary before the deanery court, where the verdict went againt him; but the dispute continued with undiminished fury with Egede petitioning to the King. His adversary then attempted to find a compromise solution, but Egede was not a man to compromise: when the neighbouring pastor appeared at Egede's church to assert his right, he was turned away by Egede's sympathizers in the congregation. Another verdict of the deanery court was given against Egede in March 1714. This dispute arose from Hans Egede's determination that old regulations should not cut his extremely limited income from the living. His family had grown: between 1709 and 1714 three of his and Giertrud Rasch's four children were born. Concern for them was a contributory factor in his struggle, which in turn affected his conflict over undertaking the Greenland mission.

Between 1709 and 1711 Egede became acquainted with some of the contemporary literature dealing with the idea of a mission—e.g. the writings of Heinrich Müller, Christian Schriver and Christian Gerber, all these authors being connected with pietism and with one of its leaders, Philip Jacob Spener. Egede diligently made use of all the works of these German theologians and preachers, and later took them with him to Greenland. All of them stressed that the mission concept was in keeping with the New Testament.

At odds with the neighbouring pastor and apparently deeply concerned about his wife and children, Hans Egede submitted his proposal

C

for a mission to Greenland in July 1710 to Bishop N. E. Randulf of the Bergen diocese. After this elderly bishop had replied to Egede with a polite refusal but praise for his initiative, Hans Egede must, later in the year, have sent a similar proposal to his own bishop, Peder Krog in Trondheim. Bishop Krog's reply was favourable, but geographically confused. Hans Egede's family attempted to dissuade him, but they agreed, after serious consideration, that he should pursue the course on which he had now decided.

In December 1711 he submitted his petition to the King, elaborating his plan with many theological arguments. Because of the prevailing opinions about missionary work, Egede felt obliged to use his strongest arguments in favour of the idea, quoting from the Gospels and the Epistles, as well as from other literature, including the authors mentioned above. But to these he added his own view, with strong effect. "It is impossible to be a Christian and not bring souls to Christ", he wrote, adding: "Nature compels us to take the sufferer unto us." It was the solemn duty of the Church to take up the mission, a duty which it had neglected, as Gerber and Spener had both proclaimed.

Missions had, indeed, been sent to foreign parts, but mainly by the Roman Catholic Church. New and rich lands had been discovered and explored. On the Danish–Norwegian side, too, voyages of discovery had been undertaken to Greenland; "but if we consider their purpose, it is everywhere for personal profit and advantage, but God's purpose is undoubtedly quite different – I mean the conversion and enlightenment of the heathen".

In 1710 Hans Egede had read of the progress made by Danish missionaries in Trankebar, and rejoiced at it. At a time when the University was complaining that there were too many theologians and the bishops had difficulty in finding posts for them, he thought it would be good if these young men could be assigned to the mission field. Towards the end of his petition Hans Egede went into more practical arrangements. He believed that conditions on the west coast around 64°N. were similar to those in Norway – also as regards climate. It would be possible to grow corn, and the fishing was good. Trade with "the savages" would more than cover the costs, for Norwegian merchants had earned 300 per cent on produce imported from West Greenland. Reminiscent of Vídalín here are the list of produce and the desire for a small fort to be built to protect the settlers on the coast. Egede thought that financial backing for the whole operation should be in the form of an ordinary collection, to be made annually to maintain the missionaries. No contribution could be expected from the heathens.

Hans Egede chose the worst possible moment to submit his proposal. Politically and economically the situation in the Danish–Norwegian monarchy was tense. Nevertheless, his case came quickly before the King's Council, the *Conseil*, but then delays ensued and again in January 1713, a year after it was first considered, the proposal came before the *Conseil*, who forwarded it to the Faculty of Theology at Copenhagen University for their opinion. Hans Egede was informed some time later that the moment was not favourable and that he must wait for better times. This disappointment – together with a further flare-up of his dispute with the neighbouring pastor – depressed him. Friend and foe alike tried to deflect him from his purpose, and this cost him further struggles. By 1715 it seems that he had summoned up fresh resolution. In that year he published a written defence (now lost). The situation had developed into a gordian knot and Egede saw no alternative but to cut through it, although he first tried to remind the King of the matter by sending him a "memorandum". Meanwhile, in December 1714 the Missionskollegium had been set up as the central administrative body to administer the Danish–Norwegian Church's mission operations in India and among the Lapps in northern Norway. The head of the mission to the Lapps was Thomas von Westen, who was appointed assistant professor in Trondheim in 1716 with responsibility for leading the mission. Hans Egede addressed a memorandum to the Missionskollegium through von Westen, but this "spiritual brother" held the memorandum back, and only sent it to the Missionskollegium in June 1718 – it seems clear that he regarded Hans Egede's proposal as competing with his own undertaking for the limited funds available.

The eternal waiting was too much for Hans Egede, and he and his wife now decided to cut the knot and give up his living in Vågan so that he could personally take a hand in matters. He had now given up his family's sole financial base, meagre though the living had been. He was on good terms with most of the congregation, who had backed him in his long-standing dispute with the neighbouring pastor. But this did nothing to mitigate the leanness of the living.

Hans Egede resigned his living in 1717, but was not able to leave until July 1718, when he travelled with his wife and four children to Bergen, which was to be his home for the next three years. How they lived during those years remains a mystery. He himself stated that he frequently helped the pastors in Bergen without being paid for it; it was not in his nature to be idle and apparently he still had to wait. His need for activity led him to study chemistry, perhaps because of the shortage of money: – it was still thought possible to make gold, and with his lively imagination Egede, then as later, dreamed of creating the financial backing for his project by means of alchemy.

It proved more difficult than Egede had imagined to find interested people who would give material and moral support to the mission plan. The influential merchants of Bergen were discouraging; they talked of the difficult times and of the taxes they had to pay in war time. Egede's interpretation of this was that they would probably be willing if the undertaking received royal support. We have suggested above that it was during these years that the Bergen shipowners resumed sailings to Greenland, but not on a large scale, so they hardly dared to provide financial backing for an extremely risky plan. Even when Egede made a public appeal to Bergen citizens of all classes on 26 November 1718 he obtained no more support than before.[14] Indeed, there were signs that people were beginning to find him a nuisance. In this appeal, he went further into the practical side of the project than before; his plans had become more mature. After a lengthy introduction on missions in general and the Greenland mission in particular, he proposed a reconnaissance by a limited number of people, after which an expedition could be made on a larger scale. To back the project he proposed forming a company with support from the churches in Norway and Denmark, and a voluntary collection. He drew a comparison with the Finnmark mission, to which, from January 1720, the surplus church revenues from the deaneries of Vesterålen, Lofoten and Salten were devoted. He ended this open letter with a long account of what missions were doing elsewhere in the world. Not even this rousing appeal had any effect. No progess was made, and no one offered financial support.

However, the great Scandinavian war was nearing its end. The political situation was more relaxed, and it might now be possible to gain the King's ear. Hans Egede travelled to Copenhagen, arriving there shortly after Frederik IV had left for Norway. Finally, on 10 September 1719, he handed his memorandum to the King. Meanwhile, he had had a hearing at the Missionskollegium, where he was well received and promised support by the *Conseil* for his application to the King. This memorandum was clearer and more concise than his petition of 1710 or the open letter of 1718. In it he referred to the fact that he had worked on this plan for many years to no avail, and to the information which Captain Bärenfels and Captain Christen Hansen had submitted to the Missionskollegium. He described his unsuccessful attempts to interest people in Bergen in the establishment of a "colony and trading post" in West Greenland; although various individuals were prepared to participate, they had felt that their resources were insufficient. He noted that it would be easier if the King were to give his aid in the form of a charter and concessions similar to Christian V's arrangements of 1697, ban foreign nations from trading with Greenland and make a collection of voluntary contributions throughout the King's realms and territories. An initial capital of *c.* 20,000 rigsdaler was required and no one in Bergen was in a position to contribute or collect such a large amount.

Hans Egede's 1719 memorandum revealed to the *Conseil* how little hard thought had been given to the details of the whole plan. Before any further action could be taken, information had to be obtained from the only people with any experience of Greenland – Bergen's ship-owners. On 8 November a resolution was passed by the *Conseil* (on 17 November it was embodied in a royal edict) requesting the governor of the Bergenhus district and the town council of Bergen to convene a meeting of the ships' captains at which something would be learned about sailings to Greenland and trading in those regions. Egede was now asked to put a number of questions to Christen Hansen and Bärenfels, of whom the latter was informative except on those points where Egede's petition to the King required most support. Bärenfel wrote that it would be possible to establish trading posts at places on the same latitude as inhabited sites in Norway, the Faroes and Iceland. If the King would first grant rights to a company, an estimate of the cost could be drawn up, but the time was not yet ripe. He enumerated the inexpensive merchandise that could be used for trading and the produce for which it could be bartered. There was abundant whaling and fishing; his men had obtained excellent "smoked" salmon as a gift from "the savages".[15] To the question whether the Dutch trade was an obstacle to Bergen traders, Bärenfels replied that this was the crucial point; a competent trader might well create a good situation for himself if only he had the assurance of "higher assistance", but the matter was too important, delicate and far-reaching for an immediate answer to be given. He knew nothing of the east coast, but concluded by recounting the experience described above (p. 19) in another context.

Bärenfels and Christen Hansen were among the eight "experts" summoned to the meeting at the Bergen town hall. Bärenfels was the only shipowner and merchant, the others being ships' captains or chief officers who had been to Greenland. Since so few attended the meeting, the results were scanty and did little to enlighten the King – or Hans Egede. The description of the land and climate contained in the brief statements was not inviting. The land was well populated – in one place two of the seafarers had seen three or four hundred people. "Otherwise the people are much inclined to mischief, robbing and stealing from foreigners whenever they can." Only one of the men questioned thought he knew of a place where a colony could be located; none could suggest any way of promoting trade on the west coast of Greenland. Bärenfels refused to give his opinion at the meeting, but was willing to submit his views in writing, so the meeting closed and further action was postponed until these views were known. Evidently disappointed, Hans Egede "resolved to try to find people who would participate". In the meantime, he applied all his "efforts to getting the merchants interested in this Greenland trade, and although it was quite difficult and slow, nevertheless, with God's aid, I persuaded one or two people who were willing, with royal authority, to resolve upon it.". These people were a fresh group of eight Bergen merchants and shipowners, of whom Jens Andersen Refdahl and Jens Fæster later came to play an active part in the mission work; Bärenfels was not among this group, and thereafter withdrew from the venture.

On 4 June 1720, in accordance with the royal edict of 17 November 1719, these eight men reported that they had resolved to contribute to and collaborate in carrying out the proposal, but since they estimated the initial capital required at 12,000 to 16,000 rigsdaler, they could not undertake it without the King's help. It was impossible to raise the necessary capital in Bergen because so little interest had hitherto been shown in the scheme. They therefore suggested – pointing out that Greenland was an old Norwegian dependency – some points on which royal help would be needed. First, since those landed must be protected against "the savages", a garrison of thirty men was essential; however, the joint venturers could not afford to equip, transport, pay and maintain them and their officers. Secondly, royal intervention was necessary to ban the Dutch trade and sailings along the west coast of Greenland, otherwise the new trading company could not pay its way. Thirdly, they wanted a monopoly of the Greenland trade and they should be able to trade freely. Fourthly, the company should be exempted from duty and taxes on goods exported to Greenland and on the cargoes brought back.

Hans Egede followed up this proposal with a letter to the King, in which he commented briefly and with surprising frankness on the scheme. The garrison was necessary, but the costs involved were high and if the plan miscarried and had to be abandoned, the loss would be too great. Referring to Thormod Torfæus' *Gronlandia antiqua* and the maps contained in it, he pointed out that from 60°N. "right up to the North Pole" Greenland was the King's land; he recalled Christian V's proclamation of 1691 which banned foreign whaling. Even if the navigation of the Davis Strait could not be banned, it must nevertheless be possible to prohibit foreign trading on the coast and whaling within a limit of 22·5–30 km.; the English, through the Hudson's Bay Company, exercised a similar monopoly. If any progress was to be made in the venture and people were to be persuaded to participate, the King must grant these privileges, and give some assurance of royal aid. Hans Egede requested some form of remuneration for himself: he had been living off his own private resources for two years.

Although the letter from the eight merchants was received in Copenhagen at the end of June 1720, no reply reached Bergen that year.

REFERENCES

1. The manuscript of the third part of Vídalín's work in his complete conception and his own translation into Danish has been edited (in Danish) by the author in The Danish Greenland Society's Series (*Det grønlandske Selskabs Shrifter*) XXI, 1971.

2. Bobé, MoG 55, 1, p. 20, gives him the title of bishop. Peder Hansen Resen (1625–88) was the grandson of the bishop of Zeeland, Hans Poulsen Resen (I, pp. 220–1), and was a professor of history and jurisprudence at the University of Copenhagen.

3. Cf. I, pp. 312 *et seq.*

4. Thomas von Westen (1682–1727) was parish rector at Vedøen, northern Norway, but was attached to the cathedral of Trondheim as lecturer in Lapp language, and was the head of the Lapp mission in Finnmarken. He was called "the Apostle of the Finns".

5. Árni Magnússon (1663–1730), the Iceland-born philologist and historian, who was especially concerned with collecting all kinds of Icelandic manuscripts. He bequeathed his comprehensive collection to the University of Copenhagen, where it still remains (The Arnimagnæan Institute). Most of it will be returned to Iceland in the coming years.

6. Cf. I, p. 183,

7. This map has been reprinted along with older ones in the edition of Thormod Torfæus' book *Det gamle Grønland*, Oslo 1927.

8. Cf. I, p. 216. According to L. Bobé, MoG 55, 1, p. 42, and Bobé, *Hans Egede*, 1952, p. 32, Hans Mathias was from Kerteminde, a little town in the north-eastern part of the island of Funen, Denmark. He became citizen of Bergen in 1684.

9. This island's name Ukîvik means "the wintering place". Until about 1750 it seems to have been called *Tullukune* (in modern West Greenlandic spelt *Tulúkune*), meaning "the place where *tuluit* are". Until about 1750 the first part of the name *tuluk* (plural *tuluit*) meant Dutchman, hence the full translation of the place-name is "the place where the Dutch are". Later on *tuluk* means Englishman, and the Dutch received other sobriquets such as "those with ample trousers" or "foreigners who are trading illegally". These sound as if they were extemporized and are not used any more. *Tuluk* constantly means Englishman; the intrinsic sense of the word is unfathomable.

10. There are several biographies and papers on Hans Egede, *vide* the list of literature. In the following some facts have been taken from the most outstanding of the biographies, Dr. Louis Bobé's *Hans Egede Colonizer and Missionary of Greenland*, Copenhagen, 1952, with its obvious faults corrected. Most of the facts about Hans Egede are derived from his own books and letters, printed and unprinted.

11. Casper Bartholin (1618–70) was an officer, a doctor of law and owner of an estate. In his country house lived the three Greenlandic women of 1654 (I, p. 242). His brother Thomas Bartholin (1616–80), the learned professor of medicine, listed 300 of the Greenlanders' words, perhaps helped by the barber-surgeon Reinhold Horn. This little glossary was printed in Thomas Bartholin's *Acta Medica* II, pp. 70 *et seq.*, Copenhagen, 1675.

12. This short report is printed in Danish in MoG 54, pp. 30–40.

13. It has been said (1958) that the interpretation of these words as of Norse origin should receive scholarly confirmation. From a special point of view—perhaps propaganda—it is "confirmed", but this has no scholarly backing. Only one word must be recognized as non-Eskimo, and obviously of Norse origin, *viz. Qvaun: kvan: Angelica*, in West Greenland dialect now spelled *kuáneq*. Incorporated in the dictionaries of the Labrador Eskimo dialect, it may have been imported by the Moravian Brethren. All the other words in Olearius' and Bartholin's lists and of supposed Norse origin have disappeared from the West Greenland Eskimo dialect in spite of the influence from Danish and Norwegian.

14. That is Dr. Louis Bobé's interpretation, in MoG 129, p. 24, deleted in his Hans Egede monograph of 1952, p. 35.

15. It has never been recounted elsewhere that Eskimos prepared fish or meat by smoking. It sounds here more like a traveller's tale.

2

THE ADVANCEMENT OF THE HOLY WORK NOVEMBER 1720 TO JULY 1722

In November 1720 Hans Egede wrote a letter to the Missionskollegium, making the point that time was running short and that certain formalities would have to be dispensed with if the undertaking was to begin in the spring of 1721. He referred again to his efforts in furthering his proposal; he had persuaded people, especially in Bergen, to support the venture – "even some who were at first against it". But no one would start the preparations until there was an assurance that the King would support the work with the privileges suggested. To Hans Egede all his labours seemed in vain, and he had only succeeded in bringing himself and his family "to ruin and destruction".

There was still no answer to this cry for help, and it was not until mid-January 1721 that the matter came before the *Conseil*, who forwarded it to the *Politi-commerce kollegium* (legal and trade department) which replied a month later that it did not object to the privileges, which could be conferred by order of the Government and were only effective within the realm, but it had misgivings about a ban on sailings to Greenland by foreign nations. Until both the military and political positions were assured, no steps should be taken which might affect foreign policy. Peace had only just been concluded after the great Scandinavian war and there was no desire to risk fresh entanglements with unforeseeable consequences.

Meanwhile, the Bergen Greenland Company had become a reality. A total of 5,100 rdl. was subscribed as the first instalment on 13 February[1] and among the subscribers Hans Egede was down for 300 rdl., equivalent to the annual stipend for an ordinary church living. Only one other individual contributed as much. Most subscribed 100 rdl., a few 200 and 150, and several, mainly poor clergy, 50 rdl. Already in January 1721 four of the shareholders had already been elected directors – Robert Faye, Magnus Schiøtte, J. Van der Lippe and Jens Fæster – and a letter had been sent out by the Company undertaking to cover

23

any expenses arising from the first year's operations using up to 25 per cent of each share. In this way shareholders' liability was limited and any further liabilities fell on the directors.

Also in January, the Company acquired the vessel *Haabet* ("pink"), and chartered a hooker for whaling and a galliot as an escort ship for the *Haabet*. Hans Egede's confidence was revived. The Company was a reality, even before the privileges they desired had been granted.

On 10 March, 1721, a report on the steps decided on was submitted, in belated response to the royal edict of November 1719 and the question put by Bärenfels and Christen Hansen. Two ships were to sail, one with Hans Egede and his family together with the necessary personnel, building materials and provisions, the other to go whaling at a latitude of 69°N. and later to look for the first ship in order to take home letters and the produce purchased. It was expected that one ship would be despatched within a few days, and the other at the end of March. A request was, therefore, made to the King to exempt the Company from customs duty, excise tolls and freight charges in respect of the ships and the goods exported and imported in them; but only when information had been received regarding the country, its nature and the conditions there (by which local business possibilities were probably meant) was it requested that "the necessary and appropriate privileges" be granted. It was reported, moreover, that copies of Lourens Feykes Haan's description (1720) of the Davis Strait and its coastline had been obtained and other books and maps sent for from the Netherlands.

As for himself, Hans Egede had written to the Missionskollegium on 11 February that he had applied to the King to receive a *call* to his future work as a missionary. He asked the Kollegium to support his application and explained that he sought no compensation for his expenses over the years of preparation, but that he must now be granted a sum of money (unspecified) "so that I can equip myself for the forthcoming journey and pay some of what I have come to owe good folk in the meantime". For less than 300 rdl. a year he would not be able to support himself and his family, since his household consisted of eight persons. He would have liked his brother Christian to come with him as a missionary, but his brother had meanwhile taken up a living in the north because of the long delay in deciding about the Greenland mission. Hans therefore asked the Missionskollegium for an eligible theological assistant. "There is no one else here whom I find suitable . . ." wrote Hans Egede.

The feeling that a great risk was involved in the Greenland plan emerged clearly in the report which Jens Andersen Refdahl submitted to the King from Copenhagen in March 1720. While its contents were largely the same as those of the report of 10 March, it mentioned the second vessel's purpose, which was "to sail along the coast to see what Almighty God will grant the Company to help the work forward". In view of the risk and expense of the whole venture, he too asked on behalf of the Bergen Company for the transfer of Greenland from latitude 60°N. as a permanent monopoly, together with a charter to this effect, a ban on foreign trade and navigation with enforcement of a 30 km. limit at sea, except in emergencies; and exemption from customs duty, excise, tolls, and all other imposts. "Since this trade is quite foreign to the Company and it is impossible to know now exactly how everything in this venture is to be organized and arranged", he begged the King for confirmation of his support for "whatever may occur hereafter". It was a bold demand.

It is not clear whether Refdahl and the Bergen Company wanted these privileges granted at once before sailing, but he requested the King to make his will known as soon as possible. If this first venture fared well and more investors came forward, it could be extended for another year. The expedition's departure was planned for March; the hooker, which was to go whaling, sailed on 28 March, while the *Haabet* and the galliot were ready to sail a month later.

Without the letter of appointment, which he needed before beginning his missionary work, Hans Egede and his family were in the same situation as many travellers to Greenland after him – obliged to see his departure date postponed again and again. On 15 March, however, Egede was informed unofficially of the remuneration he would receive; 300 rdl. per annum and 200 rdl. equipment allowance – exactly what he had asked for.

As was the custom, the directors of the Bergen Company had drawn up a number of articles which everyone had to observe. Apart from some special regulations called for by the unusual nature of the undertaking, these first articles resembled ordinary ships' articles, but extended to apply on land in the settlement once it had been established. Just as it was the practice on board ship to form a ship's council consisting of the captain, mates, steward and boatswain together with the cook, a council was formed to act on board the *Haabet*, and later ashore. This council was headed by Hans Egede with, under him, the ship's captain Berent Hansen Wegner, the mate Selgen Dahl, the steward Cornelius Seehusen, the book-keeper and trader Hartvig Jentoft, and the boatswain and cook. It was unusual to have a clergyman in charge.

The articles were handed to Hans Egede by the directors of the Bergen Company on 28 April with a covering letter, which reveals something of the unusual nature of the whole undertaking. It also contained somewhat vague instructions. Hans Egede was to be (tacitly)

in charge of house-building and to initiate the fishery and trading when
land was reached. The galliot was to be sent off immediately to trade
and carry out reconnaissance – apparently in Godthåb fjord – and then
return so that it could reach home before the onset of winter. It was
Egede's task to see that the men were kept at their work and that discipline was maintained, also to send home a report.

At the ceremony held on 30 April on board the *Haabet*, Hans Egede,
together with the others, had to swear an oath by these ship's articles
to both the King and the Company. By this action he emphasized the
unusual character of the whole situation; even before departing, a dual
obligation and multiple responsibility lay on his shoulders. The mission work, which was his calling, stood in juxtaposition to all the practical duties, especially anything that might serve the Company's interests and help to finance the mission. He was also to be responsible
for the many people who, through his initiative, had become involved
in the venture; everything that might be needed to maintain everyday
life now and in the future down to the smallest details had to be planned. With this unwonted burden of responsibility, aware of the risk
that the venture might miscarry and of the obviously hazardous voyage immediately ahead, Hans Egede went on board.

According to Egede's "Reports", the *Haabet* and the galliot cast off on
2 May, but had to put into Gelmevågen outside Bergen because of head-
winds.[2] Here they lay until the 12th when the wind was at last fair.
On 4 June they sighted Cape Farewell but then came the pack-ice,
in which they were stuck so fast by 23 June that Hans Egede thought
their last hour had come. However, on the following day a strong wind
scattered the ice and they were able to steer free into open water. On
2 July they met a Dutch ship, which they approached to within hailing
distance. The foreign captain left one of his men with them as a pilot.
On 3 July the *Haabet* and the galliot made for land and reached harbour. Where this first landing took place is not known for certain but
it was presumably the old Dutch anchorage, now called Faltings Havn,
on one of the large islands to the east of Kangeq, on the northern side
of the entrance to Godthåb fjord.

Immediately on arrival they were concerned to find a suitable
building site and a safe winter anchorage for the ship. However, they
could not find these things close enough together on the mainland
before it had become urgent to send the galliot home, and it was
therefore decided to build a house close to a good anchorage on one of
the islands on the north side of the fjord entrance not far from Faltings
Havn. On 9 July work started on building a winter dwelling of turf
and stone, with internal walls of board. The house was about 16 metres
long and 5 metres wide with walls at least 2·5 metres high. It was divi-

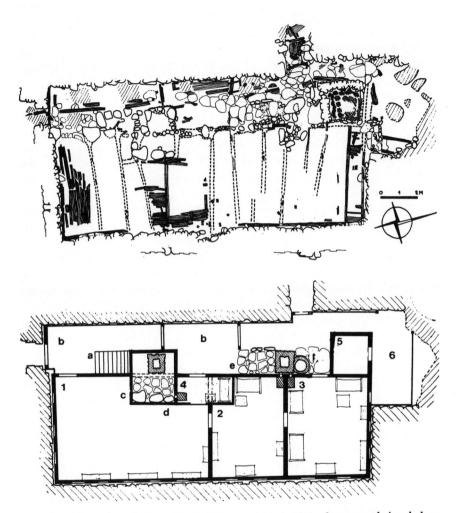

Hans Egede's house, Haabets Øe, built 1721. Above, plan of excavated site; below, a reconstruction. Key: 1, room for "the men"; 2, book-keeper's room; 3, Hans Egede's room; 4, A. Top's room (?); 5, pantry(?); 6, cellar; a, stairs to loft; 6, ventilation area; c, baking oven; d, open hearth; e, fireplace; f, brewing cauldron.

ded into three rooms, of which one was occupied by Hans Egede and his family, another by the book-keeper and some others, and the third and probably the largest room by "the men". In all there were about thirty-seven people.

Hans Egede called the island where the house was built "Haabets Øe" (both the place and the island are now called "Igdluerúnerit", "the place from which the houses have been removed"). The sites of the first house and those built subsequently can still be seen. Consideration of the anchorage and a safe and easily recognizable seaward approach was the deciding factor in locating "the colony" on this bleak island among hundreds of other rounded rocky islands in the skerries north of Godthåb fjord. There was relatively easy access to fresh water, and the islands can be a pleasant place in the sunshine, but generally they are covered in dense fog, and often battered by wind and weather. It is not surprising that Hans Egede later complained that it was difficult to get the peat turves to dry out – burning them would eke out the fuel supplies. The vegetation on the island is extremely sparse, and firewood could be obtained only by collecting driftwood. In the ensuing period right up to September, a search was made for better sites. On one of these trips they entered a fjord, which Hans Egede named Præste fjord, where there were rivers, scrub and areas which he judged good for grazing and cultivation. There was apparently good hunting too, but only on the first few visits.

On these exploratory expeditions both Hans Egede and the others encountered Greenlanders. The first ones they saw were kayak men who met the ship about 15 km. from the coast on the way in to Faltings Havn. These men showed particular interest in the European women and children; presumably it was their first realization that foreigners had such things as wives and children. Once the local Greenlanders had overcome their initial curiosity and helped in the house-building, they apparently became suspicious: the Dutch usually sailed away in June or July but at the beginning of August it still did not look as though Hans Egede and his companions would go. One day about a hundred Greenlanders swarmed around the newly erected house and Hans Egede gathered that they were trying to persuade him and his party to leave before the ice closed in. In December, some of Hans Egede's people, on the way home from hunting up the fjord, wanted to spend the night with some Greenlanders. The Greenlanders were reluctant, but as the people had no choice but to spend the night there, the Greenlanders kept watch all night long. The guests were obliged to stay for three days before they could move on, and by then a Greenlander had attached himself to one of Hans Egede's men, Aron Augustinussen. Egede thought this was due to a certain similarity of name, for the

Greenlander was called Aroch. Thus a relationship had been established between the new arrivals and the country's ancient population. In the period that followed, visitors often settled on Haabets Øe for a time, and an exchange of gifts had the melting effect of a *föhn* wind.

Hans Egede had no doubt that the Greenlanders were afraid of his own people. Possibly experience had taught them to fear foreigners. For the Greenlanders, this settlement which they saw growing up was an encroachment on their hunting rights and indeed they saw the foreigners fishing and hunting in their domain; for that reason alone, the newcomers were a disturbing and thus hostile element. However, when it was seen that their success at hunting and fishing was mediocre, less anxiety was felt; they apparently did not try to shoot seals or catch whales, but made unsuccessful attempts to catch birds. Their hunting on land also yielded little. When they came to the Greenlanders or the latter passed by Haabets Øe, the foreigners were eager to buy things from them, including seal-meat. However, trading was not usually done at this time of the year but in the spring, and seals caught on the site of the settlement belonged to that settlement. There was nothing to prevent the foreigners from visiting them and eating with them, but to trade the catches at all times of the year was something new which gradually became established custom. Trading was poor, even poorer than the hunting and fishing, if that was possible. Only small quantities were purchased. It was late in the year, and, besides being unaccustomed to trading then, the Greenlanders had nothing to sell, as they had sold what they wanted to the Dutch and it was now the autumn and winter hunting season. Sixteen boat-crews, on their way home past Haabets Øe in August, had nothing to sell. It boded ill for the future.

The galliot had set course for home on 21 July. The intention was that the captain, Jens Falck, should try to purchase something on his way south along the coast. The result was a half-barrel of blubber, and with this as her cargo the ship arrived at Bergen. Off Cape Farewell Lorentz Fæster had suffered serious damage to the hooker, which was to have gone whaling, but by good luck it reached Bergen, later than the galliot, less its mast, sail and boats. After that the hooker represented only a heavy liability to the Bergen Company. The biggest vessel, the *Haabet*, stayed for the winter in Greenland and was not due to sail home until it had carried out a purchasing expedition in Greenland. Thus the Bergen Company had to be content with this half-barrel of blubber as the sole merchandise for the year. The Government's previous scepticism regarding the Company's applications for support seemed justified.

However, on 26 May the *Rentekammer* gave its opinion on the question of special privileges for the Bergen Company. Like the Commerce-kollegium, it had no objection to granting the Company the rights it had requested in relation to foreign nations, but there were divergent opinions concerning this part of the desired privileges, it did not venture to make any proposal and suggested that the matter be dealt with by the *Conseil*. However, since the Company had already reached the stage where vessels had been fitted out, it could be proposed that the Company should be granted provisional exemption from customs duty and taxes on the exports to and imports from Greenland. In early June the matter was discussed by the *Conseil*, where King Frederik IV decided that such exemption should be granted to the Bergen Company, for a number of years "until we deem otherwise and until we can agree with you on a fair contract."

The *Rentekammer* showed a positive attitude in this case, by the consideration and speed with which the provisional resolution was communicated. The disappointment of the Bergen Company overshadowed the provisional nature of the arrangement and the prospect of a "fair contract" contained in the resolution. It was not possible in the *Rentekammer's* communication to explain why the "reasonable contract" could not come into existence immediately. This was a political matter and therefore delicate, especially as the government departments concerned could not agree amongst themselves. Among the shareholders in the Bergen Company, only one Bärenfels, had expressed his comprehension of the delicate aspect of the monopoly and the consequent exclusion of foreign traders, he was not at that time involved in the affairs of the Company, apart from having a 50-rigsdaler share.

After the galliot's homecoming the Company's accounts looked miserable; the half-barrel of blubber was sold for 8 rdl. 1 mrk., 10 sk. To cover the expenses, it was recommended to the shareholders that they put in 35 per cent of their first subscription, which was more than their commitment when the Company was formed. By November the 35 per cent was paid in, making the capital 6,885 rdl. The cost of the vessels and their repair, victualling and insurance, of building materials and merchandise, and finally the men's wages and salaries totalled 6,862 rigsdaler 1 mark 14 skillinger. Thus almost the whole of the shareholders' subscriptions had been used up.

However, no official balance-sheet was prepared. As was the custom, cash wages were not paid out immediately for instance, a book-keeper was never paid until his accounts had been audited and found in order. The directors of the Bergen Company were unpaid because, like the shareholders, they had their own businesses. For the Company an additional advantage lay in the fact that the biggest ship and most of the staff were in Greenland, and so any settlement of wages and salaries was a far-off contingency. As a capital asset, the *Haabet* was insufficient to cover the subscriptions. Nor could the building and other materials in Greenland be counted as healthy assets. To continue operations, it was necessary to draw on the initial capital and to refrain from paying outstanding debts. These were the contemporary ways of doing business, no distinction being made between fixed assets and working capital. The accounts themselves, for which Jens Andersen Refdahl, a director of the Company, had undertaken to be responsible, were kept in an extremely primitive way; it was no more than a cashbook. Another director, Magnus Schiøtte, later complained about this situation. expressing surprise that no ledger was kept.[3]

The Bergen Company continued operating with this form of "credit", but as it was not enough, the directors of the Company sent a communication to the King in December 1721 describing the Company's position. Even though the shareholders had now subscribed about 7,000 rdl., which some found onerous, especially when they realized that "the work" required a large amount of capital and no new shareholders were coming forward, they nevertheless resolved to fit out an expedition for the following year. The directors reckoned that this would cost the same as in the first year, so they lived "between hope and fear in risking their funds". The directors therefore enclosed an account of what had happened in 1721, a proposal for "some items of exemption" which would afford greater security for the future, and finally a submission for royal approval of draft ship's articles. Both the items of exemption and a large part of the ship's articles were later included unaltered in the final charter, but it was a long time before any further progress was made in the matter.[4] The proposals of course had the immediate purpose of restoring the current financial situation and strengthening the possibility of fitting out ships for 1722 but as they remained unanswered, it was necessary to proceed with the payment of the subscription approved by the shareholders the previous year – this time 40 per cent of the first instalment, amounting to 2,040 rdl. This was followed by the fourth instalment, fixed at 25 per cent of the first instalment and paid on in August 1722, yielding 1,275 rdl.

Ten days previously the *Haabet* had returned to Bergen after being laid up for the winter, and besides a small cargo, had brought news of how Hans Egede and the others who had wintered there were faring. The cargo consisted of fourteen *cordeler* of blubber, 160 fox and seal skins and a few whalebones, the value of which was estimated at 250 rdl. According to subsequent accounts, expenditure for 1722 amounted to 7,005 rdl. 2 mrk. Thus the combined expenditure for the first two

D

years was 13,867 rdl., 4 mrk., 2 sk. The small cargo brought home by
the *Haabet* probably contributed to the decision to call up the fourth
instalment.

Support for the whole operation was badly needed and it was ventured to press the King for a decision on the proposals submitted in
December 1721. Completion of the work already embarked on now
depended on various factors: mastery of the Greenlandic language,
availability of a capital sum of about 60,000 rdl., the Company obtaining good privileges, keeping out the Dutch, and finally on acting quickly to forestall the Dutch. For the rest, the directors were confident
regarding the future and expressed their belief that trading would
enable the expenses to be met. This was probably wishful thinking.
The *Haabet's* small cargo, together with the reports reaching Bergen
from Greenland, strengthened the wish of the directors and shareholders
for help in driving out the Dutch. Hans Egede had complained to the
directors of the competition which the trade had to endure from "traders of foreign nations". Not only did they have more and better merchandise than the Company had sent out, but they sold it at a reasonable price; "therefore, as long as the foreigners are allowed to travel
and trade freely near our colony we certainly cannot make any progress in trading. On this point too most gracious aid must be sought
. . ." He was expressing his views on the trading problems with increasing confidence.

Hans Egede's letters and Reports over the years are not only the
first detailed descriptions of conditions in Greenland, but describe
the inward struggles of a man of great depth of thought and strong
emotions in an unfamiliar situation and with the special task of bringing
into existence both mission and trading company. He had no source
in contemporary knowledge or thought on which to draw for guidance,
nor had he any conception of the cultural and social process set in
motion through him. For him the main object was to bring the
Christian faith in its evangelical Lutheran form to the people he met
on the coast and in the fjords; for this the trade was to form the sub-
ordinate financial basis.

Hans Egede's practical nature saw to it that the two aspects of his
aim were co-ordinated from the outset. This was due primarily to the
demands made on him from the first settlement onwards. All operational
decisions in Greenland were his responsibility. As those who helped him
to carry on the trading, organize hunting, keep the accounts and supervise the men's work changed often in the early years, Hans Egede
and his family came to personify the continuity of the work and the
responsibilities thus continued to rest on his shoulders, with an inevitable
restrictive effect on the mission.

Within the Lutheran Church generally and the Danish–Norwegian State Church in particular, a foreign mission was unusual and methods as such were unknown. Hans Egede could certainly have read of the work of the Trankebar missionaries, who seem to have attached great importance to use of the local language. For Hans Egede this method had seemed the obvious one from the outset. However, the language had been regarded by Bishop Randulf in Bergen as a serious obstacle when he replied to Egede's first proposal in 1710; he had said it was barbaric and incomprehensible. Hans Egede was optimistic, although this may have been because he regarded the few terms that were known as variations of Norse. He was soon to learn that Bishop Randulf was nearer the truth.

As early as August 1721, Egede wrote that whenever Greenlanders came to Haabets Øe he endeavoured to learn something of their language. However, he had quickly realised that it would take a long time to master it even moderately, because the Greenlanders only knew a few European terms related to trade goods. He could only establish a tenuous contact with the visitors through signs. Occasionally, he managed to pick up some word, but then he brushed aside the whole problem with the optimistic statement: "The whole question of learning the language is a matter of time and daily association, before one can deal with the savages fruitfully and effectively to convert them, for which God himself must grant both the gift and the understanding." At many points in his first report he returned to the language. During the winter Aron Augustinussen had stayed with Greenlanders, and more and more visits by Greenlanders to the low, long dwelling out in the skerries created some contact.

"Ibli Pelleste Angekau" (*Ivdlit palase angákoq*) "You, pastor, *angákoq*" said a visiting Greenlander, who was evidently sick. Presumably misled by the printed glossary and the similarity with the word *angisôq*, Hans Egede misinterpreted the last word as "You, pastor are a great man". That was in May 1722. The extent of the linguistic contact was such that there had been added to the West Greenlandic tongue the words *palase* or *pelleste*, as the spelling was conceived and reproduced throughout the 1700s. It is a clear Greenlandicizing of the word *praest* (pastor), and was the name given to Hans Egede by the local Greenlanders and borne by kayaks and *umiaks* up and down the coast. *Qavdlunât* had come who did not just want to trade but who were behaving most unusually. They had built a house in which they had lived throughout the winter, and it did not seem as if they intended to leave for some time. They were poor hunters, but nevertheless lived on what they had brought from home. They had some women with them and four children. Most of them wore clothes like the other *qavdlunât* but the women's dresses certainly caused some astonishment, impractical as they were in snow and rain.

With his clerical garb Hans Egede looked very different from the others. A pastor then wore his official costume every day – the learned man's gown – not with a ruff, but with the less uncomfortable dog-collar. It is also said that he wore a wig, although this must have been difficult to look after. Hans Egede's special status could also be noted by the Greenlanders from his obvious superiority relative to those with whom he lived. By the end of January 1722 he realized this himself. In his report he wrote that they could probably conclude from his person and his office that there was something special about him. They could see this at his church services and prayer meetings, where every-one listened to him devoutly and he administered Holy Communion. The visiting Greenlanders clearly saw him as wielding authority, but of an unusual kind, since he did not concern himself with hunting. His authority must therefore be founded on inner strength and he must be regarded as an *angákoq* with special powers. Hence a sick Greenlander called him *angákoq* and asked him, like any other *angákoq*, to blow on his stomach where it hurt. Hans Egede did so, and justified his action by saying that he wanted the Greenlander to continue to think well of him.

This account is illustrative of Hans Egede's work. From his never-ending sympathy for these "poor, ignorant" people – who were "good-natured", respected his authority, but also apparently had an open "affection and liking" for him – there arose a practical approach which cannot be called a method. It was Egede's frequent spontaneous actions based on his deep Christian faith, his great charity and his compassionate nature that cleared the way for him. But this would not have sufficed had his authority not prevailed first and foremost over those of his own kind who accompanied him. Hans Egede's concept of religion and the Church largely conditioned his missionary work. He was deeply impressed by the ideas of pietism, yet maintained the form and content of the authoritative evangelical Lutheran State Church. He had with him pietistically inclined books which he used both for prayer meetings and to show to the Greenlanders for whom the illustrations were important. His strongly emotional, active devout-ness bore the imprint of pietism. At the same time he maintained the dignity of his office and performed all the functions incumbent on the Church – including decisions in cases relating to marriage and forni-cation. By seeking a royal call to this ministry he underlined his desire for the mission to be linked with the national Church and State. This call was issued on 4 July 1721 although it did not come to Egede's knowledge until later. However, from August 1721 onwards he called himself the Royal Danish Missionary.[5]

Hans Egede and the others lived through a hard winter. The unsuccessful hunting and indifferent fishing, the few opportunities for obtaining fresh food, poor trade, the language barrier, death and scurvy and difficulties with the people who stayed on Haabets Øe – everything devolved on Hans Egede and his wife. When, in addition, there was no sign of the ships from Bergen, it was decided on 26 May to allow the *Haabet* to leave with most of the people, leaving behind only fourteen, including Hans Egede and his family, to manage on what remained of the provisions. But eight days later Egede felt he could not stay in Greenland any longer: he was overwhelmed with problems and anxieties. He decided to accompany the ship to Bergen with all his companions, and continue the battle for the financial solvency of the venture there. On 6 June it was decided to postpone departure for a fortnight, and two days later contact was made with vessels sent out from home. Morale changed rapidly for the better.

REFERENCES

1. Bobé mentions in his monograph *Hans Egede*, etc., 1952, p. 45, that forty-eight persons had committed themselves to participating in the expedition at the meeting on 8 February 1720. Documentation of this statement is lacking. In the Bergen town council's minute-book these forty-eight persons are not mentioned at all. Forty-eight persons, among them Hans Egede himself, are first registered in the Company's book of accounts under 13 February, 1721. That is why we state here that the Bergen Company had become a reality by that date.

2. Bobé in *Hans Egede*, p. 48, only has the date for the final departure (12 May), but in the Danish, first edition, 1944, MoG 129, 1, p. 40, he referred without any documentation to 3 May as the day of departure from the harbour of Bergen. Hans Egede's own "Reports" have 2 May, MoG 54, p. 7. The "problem" is of course not important, but this is an example of Dr. Bobé's lack of accuracy in details.

3. Magnus Schiøtte's critical remarks were advanced several times in 1725, cf. p. 71 in the text. As co-director he never made any criticism before.

4. As late as 11 November 1722, the First Secretary of Danske Cancelli, Frederik Rostgaard, endorsed the petition and referred it to the Commercekollegium, which 11 January 1723 returned it with its remarks. Rostgaard's dilatoriness is incomprehensible as he was otherwise a good spokesman for the Bergen Company and the Greenland Mission.

5. It is said by some missionary historians that the "vocation" was not so important in Egede's mind that he felt this to be an absolute condition for his taking up the work of a missionary. It may be true, but if so his motive for getting a royal call must be his wish to get support from the Crown, the Church and the parishes at home.

3

THE BERGEN COMPANY AND THE MISSION 1722–1724

The directors of the Bergen Company managed in the spring of 1722 to get two vessels, a hooker and a pink, fitted out. Orders were issued to the captains on 11 April, and the ships reached a point north of Haabets Øe about 1 June.

In their letter to the Council in Greenland the directors of the Company expressed the hope that the *Haabet* had already set out, carrying home more detailed instructions about what the colony needed; the ship would be sent out again with the required cargo towards the autumn. The letter urged haste in unloading and loading the vessels now being sent, and in loading the *Haabet* if she had not already left. "If the ships do not bring good cargoes back with them, all interest in the project will be lost." This message depressed Hans Egede and the others left behind when the ships sailed for Bergen. The ships once again started out too late. As early as mid-April, vessels sailing north had been observed from Haabets Øe, and on 22 May Hans Egede was on board a Dutch vessel which was about to sail for home. The captain had traded successfully, and thought he would earn 3,000 gulden at home for two or three voyages. The Bergen Company were not ignorant of the fact that to send the ships off so late was disastrous for trading; they knew that the Dutch ships set out as early as March. Financial troubles and difficulty in obtaining crews were doubtless to blame but the directors were dilatory as well.

In a letter written in July 1721, Hans Egede had already mentioned the goods most in demand among the Greenlanders: "various wooden articles and wooden platters . . . likewise hose and gloves, ordinary blue-striped fabrics and other flowered linen for shirts. . . . They are always asking for *uglemicher*, which are blades of this shape, and they also want forks; the Dutchman here can give more information about this". It was the latter who had piloted the *Haabet* and the galliot into Faltings Havn. Thus the directors could have obtained all the information they wanted; nevertheless, not enough merchandise was sent out, nor of the kind that Hans Egede had ordered. In a letter which he sent to Bergen in July 1722, he repeated and expanded the list, mentioning long thin sawn timber, long square lathing, shirts – white, striped and variegated – stockings and mittens, good knives, *ulos* (or *uglemicher* – women's knives [see I, plate 35]); coopers, knives, hand-saws, painted wooden platters, chests and boxes, fine polished brass kettles, etc., etc. These had not been sent on the two recently arrived vessels.

In the same letter Hans Egede suggested that the ironware required for bartering with the Greenlanders should be produced in Greenland. If there had been enough coal, the capable local smith could have produced a lot more, but "he will go on working for as long as the coal lasts out". No more is heard of this production. It is characteristic that among the goods requested no "luxury article" is mentioned, but only workaday items, such as tools or useful materials. Egede did however mention subsequently that he had beads and "trinkets" with him to give away. So some "luxuries" were sent out.

Apart from this the post brought Hans Egede one encouraging letter from the Missionskollegium and one from the Bishop of Bergen, Clemens Schmidt. The latter informed him that on 14 November 1721 the King had instructed that prayers be said in church for the conversion of the heathen Greenlanders. This was all the support the authorities offered during the year. No decision had yet been taken on the Bergen Company's petitions made in December 1721.

The two vessels fitted out in mid-April 1722 sailed from Haabets Øe on 11 and 18 July respectively, and reached Bergen sometime in September with the very modest cargo of 9½ *cordeler* of blubber, 16 fox skins and 4 seal skins. Together with the *Haabet* cargo, the Bergen Company obtained at auction a return of 591 rdl., 2 mrk. 11 sk. In the account for the year, expenses were shown as 7,005 rdl. 2 mark., 4 sk. Still nothing was paid to the creditors. Had they been paid, there would have been a deficit of about 2,069 rdl., apart from the capital represented by the ships and stocks of goods.

The directors must have had an inkling of the desperate situation, but there were still hopes of a favourable decision on their petition to the King. When nothing had been heard from Copenhagen by the new year, a long and bitter letter was written to the Missionskollegium, which began thus: "The last thing to be expected and the very last to be believed was that the plans for Greenland initiated by the shareholders of the Greenland Company here in Bergen should, as is now happening, be left in suspension". A shareholder's meeting of the Company took place during New Year's week to discuss the situation. Since there appeared no hope of Government support and their own resources were insufficient to make further contributions, they decided

Bergen, 1750. Engraving by O. H. Lode, after an illustration by P. Cramer, in Erik Pontoppidan's *Norges Naturlige Historie*, 1752. (Royal Library, Copenhagen.)

to call a halt. They would rather write off their investments as lost than go in deeper and ruin themselves. The Company's people in Greenland were to be brought home. It was up to the Missionskollegium to decide whether Hans Egede should return home or stay, and to make arrangements accordingly. In conclusion, the directors stated that they could perhaps still manage to get ships fitted out if something positive came of their petitions.

At the same time as this letter was despatched, the shareholders decided to subscribe a fifth instalment of 40 per cent (2,040 rdl.) to pay the debts for 1722. It was very nearly the amount of the deficit, but it would not have covered the debts in full. Where the money to bring the people home from Greenland was to come from was not mentioned.

Membership of the board of the Bergen Company must have been a thankless task. During its relatively short life the Company limped along on the verge of bankruptcy, and the directors, especially Jens Andersen Refdahl, clutched at any straw for temporary respite. What was most distressing about the Bergen Company's shortage of capital was its effect on the Company's twofold objectives, which were unusual at that time. The directors and shareholders were undoubtedly in earnest in emphasizing the Company's Christian aims time and again in correspondence with Greenland, the Missionskollegium and the King. The Company was formed in 1720–1 with the mission to the Greenlanders as its main object and the creation of a financial base for the mission as a subsidiary object. Driven by the idea of a mission, the shareholders agreed to form the Company, fully aware that it required capital, though they doubted whether their own capital resources were sufficient. The difficulty of attracting shareholders confirmed their doubts. They knew that they would meet with fierce competition from the Dutch, and it would be difficult to get any return from the capital invested, let alone cover it. Experience had shown them that the Bergen whalers and "Greenland traders" were no match for the foreigners. The Dutch were still at that time one of the strongest trading nations in Europe, and were still the masters of whaling.

Competition was bound to force the Company to seek state support – so mercantilists argued "but in order to obtain it the case for a Christian mission had to be put in the strongest terms to the state authorities – the Danish–Norwegian autocracy. Church and Crown identified themselves with each other; indeed, the King was on the throne by divine right and was head of the ecclesiastical hierarchy. The monarchy and the Lutheran evangelical state church were one, as set out in the constitution. Consequently religion, as taught by the state Church, was a natural and inevitable feature of every undertaking. A letter from the directors of the Bergen Company stated that the shareholders and directors "with a good conscience, as true Christians and the King's loyal subjects", had done their duty. After reporting the winding up of the Company and the decision to bring the Company's people in Greenland home, the workers made this spontaneous outburst: "It is lamentable, both for God and the nation, that such a great and holy work – which in God's inscrutable wisdom is already so far advanced that it now only needs human help and succour – should be so utterly abandoned and brought to nought, whereas had the assistance of outsiders been sought, it would in time have been completed with great honour." Future generations would surely resume the work, since it has "its true origin in God". They added: "The Dutch, who are glad to see this happen, will do everything they can to bring the Company down". However, considerable experience of Dutch competition had been gained during the past two seasons. Hans Egede often reported that the Greenlanders would not sell anything, either because they had already obtained what they needed from the Dutch or because they wanted to keep their products for trading with the Dutch later on. From long distances away the fully-laden *umiaks* passed Haabets Øe, obviously bound for the "market" at Sydbay, and then passed by again on their way home, fully laden with their purchases. Hans Egede noted this in his journal with a resigned indignation. It was vital to find ways of stifling this Dutch competition, and there were two ways of doing it. One was to have the right merchandise for bartering and the other was to exclude the Dutch from the coast with support from the state. As the latter would probably be the more effective, the decision on the petition of 16 December 1721 was eagerly awaited both in Greenland and in Bergen.

The directors' impression that some progress had been made in their case in the government departments proved right. While their letter was on its way to Copenhagen, the Commercekollegium belatedly issued its reply to the Bergen Company's various petitions. On most of the points in the petition relating to privileges, the Commercekollegium had no objections, but on other points amendments were suggested. The Commercekollegium was still reluctant to ban foreign trading on the coast of Greenland, as it could be said to enjoy certain prescriptive rights; nor could they agree to draw a limit of 4 Danish miles (30 km.) along the coast. If a ban on trading and navigation on the coast and a four-mile-limit at sea were enforced against the King's own subjects, the Commercekollegium could agree to it, but they could not do so where foreign nations alone were concerned. Hence they envisaged an internal monopoly on the lines of those relating to Iceland and Finnmark.

On 5 February 1723, Frederik IV issued the final charter of the Bergen Company for "the glory of God and the propagation of the Christian gospel", the restoration of trade between Greenland and Norway and thus the improvement of the welfare of his subjects. This charter is politically significant: not only did the King call Greenland "our land" but in the first paragraph he granted the Bergen Company a concession for twenty-five years for "the whole of Greenland with all the lands, coasts, harbours and islands appertaining thereto, from Cape Farewell or Printz Christian, located at latitude 60°N. and as far as it extends in length and breadth, east and west, south and north. . . ." The King only reserved for himself and his successors "our sovereignty, absolute dominion and right of succession". The Danish–Norwegian king thus established his rule over Greenland, known or unknown, and however far it extended. In its contest with the Dutch, the Government had gone as far as possible.

The Company obtained its exemption from customs duty, consumption taxes and town tolls on imports and exports to and from Greenland, together with exemption from tonnage dues and other charges in connection with the ships, and it was granted the right to auction the goods brought home. The ban proposed by the Commercekollegium on other Danish–Norwegian subjects trading and sailing along the coast of Greenland was issued. The Company was free to set up military establishments in Greenland. The sailors needed by the Company would, within reason, be exempted from being called up in the event of war, and the directors, book-keeper and officials at the Company's office in Bergen were to be exempted from civic duties. The Company was exempted from stamp duty and granted the right to appoint any of its employees to dispense justice in Greenland and to set up a court of justice there. The King reserved his rights when the twenty-five years had expired.

At the same time the Company was given permission to organize a lottery of 100,000 tickets, each at 1 rdl., with 219 prizes, some consisting of a share in the Company. In their original proposal the directors had envisaged that almost everyone should be compelled to participate in this lottery with at least one ticket, but the Commercekollegium would not agree to this, as it would then be more like a tax than a lottery; so, in its final form, the lottery was voluntary. This permission must have been given, for on 3 March 1723, the Company issued a prospectus inviting applications for shares with a minimum investment of 100 rigsdaler. This brought in only one application for 200 rdl. from the chief secretary of the Danske *Cancelli*, Frederik Rostgaard.

The directors received the charter with mixed feelings. It was satisfactory as far as it went, but there was no promise of a ban on foreign trading and navigation in relation to Greenland. They regarded this as one of the principal items of their petition, and now petitioned the King to issue such a ban. They referred to Christian V's ban in 1691 – without mentioning that it had been partly lifted the following year. They set their hopes on the lottery selling out. Not a word was said about the resolution to wind up the Company.

Nevertheless, a mood of optimism took hold of the directors. Before the end of March they had purchased office premises,[1] and this, together with the expenses of fitting out the ships, obliged them to raise a loan against debentures. In 1722 and 1723, 8,577 rdl. was borrowed, probably in the hope that the lottery would bring them in new funds and that new investors would come forward. It was impossible to get the present shareholders to invest more, but some of them were in a position to make quite considerable loans.[2] A general optimism had been prevalent for some time, which also encouraged the directors. As early as 19 April letters were written to the council in Greenland and orders were issued to Jens Falck, master of the Company's newly acquired ship *Cron Printz Christian*, which arrived at Haabets Øe on 22 June.

The ship carried some sheep and goats and a message that some cows would be sent out later. Hans Egede had written to the directors asking for animals to be sent out. Most of them died on the way, and Egede had to report that only five sheep, one goat and four cows were left and there was no grazing for them. The request had been made prematurely at a time when he was thinking of a move to a place with more vegetation. At the same time, he had asked for squared and rough-hewn timber for a house, as the building method they had used previously had not been successful. The turves and earth piled against the outside of the woodwork had caused it to rot. Hence the *Cron Printz Christian* carried such a timber house.

Hartvig Jentoft, the book-keeper and trader, wanted to return to Bergen, but he was not allowed to, and instead was promoted chief trader for his services. He was allocated as an assistant Jacob Geelmuyden, whose nineteenth birthday was a few days after his arrival in Greenland.

It was intended that the *Cron Printz Christian* should sail north to Disko Island and try to discover where could best be started. Nothing came of this voyage for, after waiting for the second vessel, *Fridericus Quartus*, captained by Berent Hansen Wegner, Jens Falck left for home with the *Cron Printz Christian* on 1 August 1723. Wegner had set out from Bergen immediately after 7 June with Selgen Dahl, in charge of the small vessel *Printz Friderich*, intending to head for south-east Greenland; the small vessel would try to sail inshore along the

coast to discover if there were any Norse settlements with their inhabitants still alive. At the same time the bigger ship was to hunt for
whales. However great or small their success, both vessels were to go
to Haabets Øe and remain there for the winter. The small vessel
would stay in Greenland permanently while the larger one would be
made ready to sail north and go whaling as early in the spring as
possible.

Although they had received no reply to their petition to the King
to ban foreign trading, the directors issued orders to Captain Wegner
to seize any vessels found within 4 Danish miles (30 km.) of the coast,
unless they carried a Royal Danish *laissez-passer* or were trading with
the country's inhabitants. The directors found a dubious sanction for
this in the charter, where the ban on trading was directed only against
Danish–Norwegian subjects, also in a proclamation of 1691, banning
whaling by the Hanseatic towns. They were unaware that the latter
had been revoked. They informed the council in Greenland accordingly.
It was the directors' good fortune that no situation arose which would
have compelled the Captain or the Council in Greenland to try to
enforce the ban.

The East Greenland venture came to nothing. The small ship *Printz
Friderich* lost contact with the *Fridericus Quartus* in a storm off Cape
Farewell and went down with all hands. The *Fridericus Quartus* reached
Haabets Øe on 30 July, after making no very great effort to land on the
east coast. The future of Danish–Norwegian whaling in Greenland
seemed bleak. For the time being the Company had to be content with
what seal and whale blubber and whalebone could be obtained from
the Greenlanders by barter. We know little of the trading methods
used during these early years. However, in August 1722 Hans Egede
wrote in his "Reports" that twenty-five *cordeler* of blubber had been
bought during the summer after the ships left in July. Few trading
expeditions to the surrounding Greenlandic settlements are described;
the "Reports" only mention one throughout 1722–23 besides that
mentioned above. He deplored the lack of merchandise and the difficulties in bartering them for Greenland products. On the other hand,
several cases are mentioned of people being sent hunting or fishing to
obtain fresh food. Only after 1722–3, it seems, did they begin to visit
the Greenlanders' settlements on trading expeditions and, owing to
lack of the right merchandise, abandon any idea of wasting their energy
on strenuous expeditions by open boat in the inhospitable climate.
Before he learned of the monopoly, Hans Egede bartered eight old
shirts for twenty-five fox skins and some whalebones, which he had sent
to Bergen on his own account to be auctioned. The directors regarded
this as an encroachment on their monopoly, and would not settle the

account until they heard further from Egede. The individual colonists therefore had goods suitable for bartering. Altogether, 76 barrels of blubber, 370 fox skins, 56 seal skins and four whalebones were auctioned for 1,117 rdl. 3 mrk. and 4 sk., which was rather more than the directors had expected. Nevertheless, the financial position was bad, as the lottery and prospectus had been a disappointment. The accounts show that in 1722 the directors raised a total of 3,431 rdl. They felt obliged to disclose their troubles to the King: "One and all agree that it is a very godly and Christian work, and would like to see it encouraged, but when it comes to people being asked for a small trifle so that the work can continue, it is as though all their wealth were being taken away. . . ." They asked that everyone in the King's realms and dominions should take up at least one ticket. Once again considerable difficulties in preparing and supplying provisions for the next year's expedition seemed certain.

In 1723 the directors permitted a change in the lottery, so that the number of prizes should be increased; it was thus hoped to speed up sales. Frederik Rostgaard, chief secretary of the *Cancelli*, wrote personally to the diocesan authorities in the two kingdoms, pleading for support for the lottery, but it was difficult to get people to buy lottery tickets, since there was a general shortage of money. Despite the continued lack of funds, and because of the defective accounting system which failed to give a true picture of the Company's financial position, the 1724 plans again reveal a surprising optimism. What had not been achieved in 1723 would be achieved in the coming year. After a meeting with shareholders, it was "resolved" in February 1724 that Jens Falck with the *Cron Printz Christian* should go on a trading voyage direct to Disko and explore the coast between Disko Island and Haabets Øe, i.e. part of the Disko Bay and the stretch from Egedesminde to the mouth of the Godthåb fjord. The ship *Haabet*, under Captain Claus Hartsen, was to sail direct to Haabets Øe, unload its cargo, and sail from there across the Davis Strait, to the "American coast". No doubt this meant Labrador, although 69°N. was indicated. The captain was to take on a cargo of timber and transport it to Haabets Øe,[3] which was assumed to be cheaper and easier than bringing timber from Bergen. It was finally decided to purchase a galliot or a hooker, and equip it with whaling tackle. Apart from whaling, this ship was to cruise in the waters between Greenland and Iceland "in order to look for the fjords and places once occupied by the ancient Norsemen, as well as anything else they could find in this connection". The Company therefore intended to carry out the 1723 plan in 1724.

The *Cron Printz Christian* and the *Haabet* sailed at the end of March. The hooker *Egte Sophia* sailed about a month later. Around 30 May the

Cron Printz Christian passed Haabets Øe on her way north, and on 23 May the *Haabet* arrived at the colony on the island. The *Egte Sophia* returned to Bergen with her mission unaccomplished, but brought home so much that it was possible at the auction to sell 13 barrels of whale oil and 48 seal skins. This was for a lower price than was obtained earlier the same year for a consignment of 42 barrels of whale oil. This expedition with the *Egte Sophia* was regarded by the subsequent critics of the Bergen Company as ill-timed and wasteful of its limited resources. While the negative result may warrant criticism, it was nevertheless one of the Company's tasks to discover the Norse settlements and bring back any who were still alive into contact with Norway and, through Hans Egede, with the true Christian religion. The directors had to accomplish this with the means at their disposal.

Hans Egede, for his part, undertook an expedition with a similar aim. On 9 August 1723, he sailed south from Haabets Øe in an open boat. Following Vídalín's idea, he wished to make his way through the Frobisher Strait to the east coast and discover the Eastern Settlement. He possibly reached the island Nagtoralik approximately 60°10′N. but found no trace of the Frobisher Strait, and the Greenlanders whom he met on the way knew nothing of a strait. They did mention what is now Prins Christians Sound, but earnestly advised Egede not to attempt to sail through it at that time of the year. After this voyage, Egede doubted whether the strait existed at all and thought it was more likely to be found in America. At several points on this journey south, which took thirty-six days, Egede had been into fjords and visited Norse ruins, in particular Hvalsey church. He believed that all these places belonged to the Western Settlement and that his real objective had not been achieved. He continued to hope that the descendants of the ancient Norsemen would be found.

A more immediate problem for Hans Egede, however, was dissatisfaction with the site on which the colony had been established in 1721. He and the others often went reconnoitring for a better place in which to settle. Godthåb fjord, Præste fjord and places farther into the Ameralik fjord had all seemed attractive. In the sheltered valley at the bottom of Præste fjord he had experimented with growing barley, but with little success. He also looked around north of Haabets Øe, and there was a possibility of settling near the present-day Atangmik in the Sukkertoppen region. He had also heard of a place even farther north where whaling opportunities were said to be good. This place was called by the Greenlanders Nepisene, and was the present-day Nipisat – an island in the Holsteinsborg area on about 66° 50′, barely 50 km. south of the Dutch anchorage, Sydbay. In a journey which lasted most of March, Hans Egede tried to reach it but was prevented by ice and

the bitter cold. He did however make fruitful contact with the Greenlanders living there.

Although nothing further was known about the place, the Council
in Greenland decided that Captain Claus Hartsen should sail there
with an enlarged crew when he returned from his timber-collecting
expedition to America. Hartsen sailed with the *Haabet* on 6 June on
this expedition in search of timber. Barely a month later he was back
with his mission incomplete. He had been unable to penetrate the
tremendous barrier of ice surrounding the coast and had therefore
sailed straight to Nipisat (Nepisene), looked for a good harbour and
enquired about the local whaling. He had been in touch with five
Dutch vessels lying there and they had given him good advice. As
had been decided, Claus Hartsen and the *Haabet* were sent to Nipisat
to establish a colony and prepare for whaling when the opportunity
offered. With the ship went Albert Top, the assistant appointed by
Hans Egede the previous year, so that the station should not be without a pastor and missionary work could be carried on among the local
Greenlanders. In September, Jacob Geelmuyden moved to Nipisat
as trader and book-keeper. Thus before winter a colony similar to the
one on Haabets Øe had been established.

Berent Hansen Wegner sailed north for whaling with the *Fridericus
Quartus* at the end of April. Two months later he returned, having
caught only one whale, but there was some comfort in the fact that
both the Greenlanders and the Dutch had also been unsuccessful.
The solitary whale gave the ship a cargo of a good 49 *cordeler* of blubber,
393 large whalebones, 120 small ones and 36 of the smallest. On arrival
in Bergen 104 barrels of whale oil were realized from refining the blubber. All but a single barrel were auctioned in August, together with
thirteen barrels refined from the blubber cargo brought home by the
Egte Sophia.

Jens Falck, aboard the *Cron Printz Christian*, made an expedition
north to the Greenlanders' settlements and returned home in August
with 59 *cordeler* and 30 barrels of blubber, 771 whalebones, 811 fox
skins and 462 sealskins. In Bergen, refining of the blubber yielded 130
barrels of oil. Of these, 42 barrels were auctioned in September at
barely 8 rdl. per barrel, and 89 barrels had to be put into store. As an
experiment, six barrels were sent to Hamburg, where they were sold
in 1725 at 7 rdl. per barrel. In Copenhagen during the autumn of 1724
a further six barrels were sold at the good price of 9½ rdl. each. This
left 77 barrels which auctioned in Bergen only about 7 rdl. per barrel.
The market for whale oil was not particularly favourable either in
Bergen, Copenhagen or Hamburg. Demand was soon satisfied. The
situation was similar with the sale of pelts, although not to the same

extent. Of the 811 fox skins brought home 631 were sold by auction in Bergen immediately and 20 in Copenhagen. The remaining 157 were not sold till 1725, eleven being sold, as an experiment, in Danzig.

The whalebones were sold without difficulty. All the 549 which Berent Hansen Wegner brought home and Jens Falck's cargo of 771 went at the first auction. However, there was a big difference in the prices obtained for the two consignments. For Wegner's cargo an average price of over 2 rdl. per whalebone was obtained, whereas Falck's barely fetched 11 sk. each. Wegner's cargo weighed four times as much as Falck's. In his trading with the Greenlanders, Falck had only been able to purchase the small whalebones which were evidently of no use to the Greenlanders. Wegner, on the other hand, had obtained the full yield from the one whale caught. The sale of these products brought in 3,314 rdl. 2 mrk., 15 sk. in 1724. The Bergen Company's difficulties concerned not only the trading and hunting in Greenland but also the sale of the products it purchased and obtained from hunting in the narrow and unreceptive market of Denmark–Norway. While the Company had no power to influence the market, it could ease the difficulties in Greenland. Among other things, it was essential to overcome Dutch competition, and the best way to do this was to establish more trading stations in the country.

In March 1724 the directors sent Hans Egede and the council in Greenland a letter assenting to the establishment of a more northerly trading station and whaling base. If the lottery and the various expeditions during the year succeeded, they would possibly establish four colonies between Haabets Øe and Disko, situated as Hans Egede had visualized, 75–90 km. apart. But if the plans for the year went awry, "then we shall be compelled against our will to make another change in the work for the coming year".

Hans Egede sent a rather cautious reply. These high-flying plans would cost too much, and he considered three colonies enough for the time being – one at Nipisat, a second one being transferred from Haabets Øe to a better site nearby, and a third farther to the south at 61–62°N., i.e. somewhere between present-day Ivigtut and Frederikshåb. He probably reasoned that it would thereby be possible to prevent the Greenlanders from the south from travelling to Sydbay. The idea had also occurred to him of stationing a couple of men in well-populated settlements from spring to autumn; this was the origin of the idea of "stations" or "outposts" later put into practice. Gradually, "the work" took shape. Egede's contact with the Greenlanders also began to bear fruit. A considerable number of Greenlanders stayed for varying lengths of time at the Haabets Øe colony. One of these, named Pôq, allowed himself to be persuaded to accompany the ship *Cron Printz Christian*

E

to Europe, but with the definite promise that he would return the following year. He had reached the point of being able to read – in Danish,
of course – part of a particular book, which he took with him on the
voyage. So that he should not feel too lonely, another Greenlander,
called Qiperoq, was persuaded to go with him.

When this vessel arrived in Bergen, the two Greenlanders aroused
great interest. On 8 September, a meeting of the Bergen Company
decided that Hartvig Jentoft, the chief trader (who had left Greenland
by the same vessel) and a director, J. A. Refdahl, should take them
aboard the newly-arrived ship to Copenhagen to be presented to the
King. This visit was the sensation of the year in Copenhagen, where
they arrived at the beginning of October. On 11 October, when Frederik IV was celebrating his birthday at Frederiksborg Castle, Pôq
and Qiperoq were presented to the Court. On 26 October Prince
Carl's birthday[4] was celebrated at Fredensborg, and the two Greenlanders there had an opportunity of demonstrating some of their skills
on Lake Esrum. They paddled about in kayaks, overturned in them
and hunted ducks with bird javelins while the King, the Royal Family
and the court looked on from the shore. This entertainment was not
to be reserved for the King alone. Frederik Rostgaard – perhaps in
collaboration with Refdahl – must have seen the Greenlanders as a
means of stimulating the sale of lottery tickets. On 9 November the
so-called "Greenland Pageant" was launched and this was possibly
the first colonial exhibition in history; among other things, Greenland
products were put on display. The idea and its execution had much in
common with modern sales promotion, but the sale of lottery tickets
was not substantially greater after the pageant than before, although
everyone in Copenhagen thronged the moats around the castle to
watch it. The long procession set out from the "Old Royal Holm [islet]
and went under Holmens Bridge, past the Royal Castle under High
Bridge, Red Bridge and Storm Bridge, past the Crown Prince's palace,
under Prindzens Bridge, round the Royal Brewery and from there under Christianshavns Bridge back to the islet. . . ." The regatta thus
followed the narrow canal-like waters around the island where the old
castle of Copenhagen was situated. First, a barge manned by sailors
cleared the canal for the procession proper. Then followed a second
barge, carrying a brass band. In its wake came the Admiral of the
Fleet in a canopied barge, accompanied by, among others, Refdahl
and Jentoft. Then came another barge, this time with a string orches-
tra and a singer. Finally came Pôq and Qiperoq in their kayaks from
which they shot at the ducks which had been released on to the canal.
The procession ended with six barges containing the products from
Greenland. In front was the Greenland device, the polar bear sejant,

and behind it a polar bear skin was spread out; then came one reindeer skin with the pelage untouched and another which had been
treated, and finally a pair of blue fox skins, a walrus skin and some whale
bones, together with a big picture representing a whaling expedition.
A large poster hung on an upright narwhal tusk depicted a narwhal
above and a walrus below. The fifth barge in the display of products
carried two processed seal skins and pictures of salmon and cod. The
sixth and last barge was decorated with bunting and flags. From this
last barge salutes were fired in front of the castle and the Crown Prince's
palace.

In front of Copenhagen castle, between Holmensbro and Højbro,
the singer gave a rendering of the first two verses of the "aria", as it
was called, which Frederik Rostgaard had composed. The next two
verses were sung in front of the Prince's Palace. This aria was no master-
piece, and the music was not recorded in manuscript. The words of a
second "aria", however showed the real purpose of the pageant:

> Thou godly and virtuous Queen of the North,
> Our hope is mingled with sheer delight.
> When we humbly and diligently consider
> That thou canst not disdain thy possession:
> Greenland has served the Queen's table
> To her shall our rent be tendered.
> If the trade can but be set on its feet,
> There will be rejoicing throughout the Kalaler's
>   land.

The produce from the land of the Kalaler – the land of the Greenlanders – was at one time reserved for Queen Margaret's pantry – just
as the other Norwegian dependencies seem to have been; hence the
allusion to "the Queen's table". The main object, however, was to
promote the trading company.

The pageant provided a topic of conversation for some time. A song
was published to commemorate it and a broadsheet was issued, illustrating the whole procession and containing a three-verse poem,
probably by the Bishop of Ribe, Laurids Thura. Even in 1749 Holberg[5] referred to the visit of Pôq and Qiperoq to Copenhagen and
their questions and reasoning. Holberg had met them and described
each of them vividly. He related Qiperoq's fate – that he had died on
the way to Bergen, where he was buried. In fact he died on 11 February
1725, everyone having returned safe and well from Copenhagen before
Christmas.

REFERENCES

1. This house in Baugaarden, now called Bugården, which is a passage or narrow street in the so-called Tyskebryggen (Germans' Wharf) in Bergen, remains. The fire in 1955 stopped short of the houses in this passage.

2. One shareholder was able to lend 4,000 rigsdaler but would not advance more than 360. One of the directors of the Bergen Company advanced 2,000 rigsdaler as a loan, another 800. All were considerable amounts. The merchants of Bergen obviously did not lack ready funds, but they did not want to risk too deep an involvement in a single business.

3. It appears from the instruction to the captain of the *Haabet* that he was to head for the "south-easternmost point of America, between 69 and 70 degrees, as there according to certain reliable reports shall be found forests in abundance. He shall then do his best to cut timber for a cargo." So it must be Labrador. The "reliable reports" may be the earlier medieval descriptions of Markland, or Peder Claussøn's and Vídalín's accounts. The directors of the Bergen Company seem also to have had some knowledge of the activities of the Hudson's Bay Company in Canada; perhaps in this connection they knew something of the well-timbered Labrador.

4. Prince Carl was the youngest brother of King Frederik IV. He died in 1729. The King's white summer residence had just been rebuilt and called Fredensborg. It lies near Esrum Lake, about 16 km. S.W. of Elsinore in Zeeland.

5. Holberg is the Danish–Norwegian poet, author and historian Ludvig Holberg (1684–1754). Among his many books is a description of his home town Bergen and one of Denmark and Norway, besides five volumes of so-called Epistler (500 fictional letters) concerning all sorts of items for discussion, all more or less of topical interest to his contemporaries. In the descriptive works he several times touches on Greenland matters, and in his letter no. 350 he describes Pôq and Qiperoq. The broadsheet mentioned has been reproduced in Birket-Smith, *Eskimoerne*, Copenhagen 1961.

4

THE BERGEN COMPANY:
ITS HOPES AND DECLINE
1724–1726

Jens Andersen Refdahl did his best to keep alive the interest aroused by the Greenlanders' visit and the pageant, especially the interest of the King and the Government. On 20 October he once again petitioned the King on the subject of the lottery. He gave his assurance that the directors of the Bergen Company still wanted to continue the work, but that they had no great pleasure in it; if the King did not come forward with aid, they would be forced to abandon the Company's operations in 1725. As it was capital that was lacking, he therefore suggested again that every household should be compelled to take up one lottery ticket and that employees receiving 200 rdl. in wages should also take one ticket, those receiving 400 rdl. two tickets, and so on.

This letter remained unanswered, but the King presented a number of cannons and gun-carriages to the Company "for the defence of the colony in Greenland"; and loaded them aboard the *Cron Printz Christian.* As it was subsequently expressed, he was resolved to "support and arm the aforesaid company for the advancement of the godly work already begun". The Company had at one time asked for soldiers for the colony's defence.

During November, Refdahl drew up a lengthy account of the Bergen Company position – and hence that of the mission – and presented it to the King. Refdahl not only reviewed the years from 1721 to date, and the financial situation, but set out plans for the future. The directors' plan, after they had received Hans Egede's letter of 2 August, was to establish five colonies – one near the ruins of Hvalsey church, to transfer the colony on Haabets Øe, to proceed with the settlement at Nipisat, and to establish two new colonies on latitude 67–8°N. and around 69°N. respectively. After that they wanted to establish one or two fishing and trading posts between each colony, and a pair of smaller vessels would have to be bought to ply between the colonies and trade during the summer. By employing the right pastors and traders at each place, both trade and mission would benefit, as there would be every possibility of discouraging the Dutch from trading in Greenland, if only the King would delete the words "Hanseatic towns" from the proclamation of 1691 and replace it by "all foreigners". If and when that happened, real progress could be made and churches could be set up and built. The latter idea is astonishing as the reasoning of a businessman of that time, but it accorded well with the views of Frederik IV and the Government. Refdahl quickly left this subject and turned to the hapless lottery, referring again to his petition of 20 October.

If this plan did not meet with the King's approval, Refdahl suggested that a "collection book", should be opened in each diocese to encourage contributions to "the work". He reveals a somewhat pessimistic psychological view of those collections, to which people contributed on the principle of "what is the other fellow giving and how little can I get away with?" Refdahl therefore suggested that the King thought it better to fix a quota for each diocese, the diocesan authorities should have the right to enforce payment if it were not made voluntarily. If the King did not approve any of these schemes, Refdahl suggested that a joint-stock company, like the East India Company in Amsterdam, should be set up with shares of a low nominal value so that anyone could afford to buy them. However, Refdahl still did not believe that this could be carried out voluntarily in the case of the Danish–Norwegian company, so he proposed a compulsory order basing contributions on rank. But he knew that the King was not given to taking coercive measures, and therefore concluded his proposals: "For either adequate capital must be procured with great speed or the whole work must be given up, and the sooner the better."

Refdahl anticipated any misgivings that the Company's shareholders or directors might be trying to line their own pockets, by describing the organization of the Company and its activities in Bergen. He stated that if the King wished to continue the operations on behalf of the Crown, the shareholders would renounce their investments, once new capital had been procured, and would not ask for any interest. However, matters could be so arranged that the shareholders' investment of 28,000 rdl. remained. Finally he sowed the seed of what happened subsequently, suggesting that an inspectorate be set up to control the company's finances, though adding that it would be impractical and cause dissension if such an inspecting authority had greater power than the directors. The Government's reply to this report and the earlier petition was brief. On 15 December the King promised the Company his continued support without defining what form it would take. The cannon and gun-carriages were all he provided for the time being. Whether the continued support was to be by adding something to the lottery, a collection or some other means would be considered. The Company was wished all success in its preparations for 1725. Refdahl was not slow to take the hint and, in a letter to the *Danske Cancelli* on 20 December, he set out his own and the Company's wishes. Both for information and to provide publicity for the venture, he asked that the "Seven Diary Reports" received each year might be published – on the understanding that the printing expenses would be paid – and repeated his wish for a ban on foreigners trading with Greenland. To supply capital he wanted the diocesan authorities empowered to collect contributions from individuals, if necessary with military aid.

Early in February 1725 Refdahl was informed by the directors of the *Cron Printz Christian*'s successful return; this was the first news to come from Bergen in the new year. A few days later Refdahl felt obliged to send a memorandum to the King regarding his report of December the previous year. February was the month in which all preparations for the annual expedition and the shipment of supplies to the colonies should be made. He reminded the King of the advances contributed hitherto by directors and shareholders; if help did not come soon, "this noble work of the Lord will certainly, lamentable as it may be, perish and be lost". His petition was backed up by one from the directors, stating that they would make arrangements for at least one ship to go to Greenland, to prevent the people there dying of hunger.

But Refdahl gave his opinion that this would not contribute to the advancement of the work, and he repeated his keywords for the Company's salvation – "Sufficient Capital". He mentioned that the King had appointed a commission to deal with the matter but that he had no knowledge of its conclusions. However, there is no trace of this commission's activities. On the other hand, Refdahl's various petitions and memoranda were dealt with by the *Cancelli* and, finally, by the *Conseil* where his suggestion regarding an authority to control the sums allocated to the Bergen Company came under consideration. The *Conseil* wanted security for the large amounts of money involved by having the Governor and Bishop in Bergen ensure that the capital was used to continue the work. From this stemmed the sad end of all the Bergen Company's activities.

The *Conseil* disapproved of Refdahl's suggestion that the amount be divided up among the individual classes and dioceses nor how it should be collected "for it exceeds a tax of 20 sk. on every bushel of corn; the towns are in a poor state through the decline in trade and so are the farmers through a bad harvest and the slump in the cattle trade".[1] The 1720s were bad years for Danish–Norwegian agriculture and trade – competition was fierce and prices were falling. It was decided to allow the lottery to close at 20,000 tickets instead of 100,000, and it was then proposed to obtain the balance of the capital required by a 10 per cent tax on all wages. The *Cancelli* calculated that Denmark would be able to contribute 32,800 rdl. and Norway 19,900 rdl. A royal decree was issued accordingly. In the orders to the Bergen Company, it was stated that "if the money is not used for the continuation of the business and the propagation of the Gospel, the Company itself will be liable for the money". The lottery, after the draw, would give the Company 8,000 rdl. to which would be added the 52,700 rdl. raised by the "levy" noted above. Governor Undal, Bishop Müller, President Krog and Dean Tanche, all residents of Bergen, were appointed inspectors, to ensure that the public funds administered by the Bergen Company were used "solely to continue the work and the business. . . . and not for any other purpose. . . ."

Meanwhile the home-based directors of the Bergen Company prepared for the annual expedition. Two vessels were fitted out, under the command respectively of Hans Fæster and Jens Falck. They sailed early in April, but they had only been at sea a few days when they returned to Bergen. Meanwhile the royal decrees had arrived, so it was possible to send copies to Greenland. Hans Fæster was to sail direct to Haabets Øe thence to Nipisat, and then north with Jens Falck, to trade before returning to Haabets Øe and finally Bergen.[2] Falck was to sail direct to Nipisat and wait for Fæster, and after their journey together, return to Nipisat and thence to Bergen. With Fæster went the Chief Trader, Hartvig Jentoft, and Pôq, thus honouring the promise to take him back after a year. Jentoft was there only to accompany him and to assist with advice and practical help on Haabets Øe and Nipisat, but he was to return home with one of the vessels. The two ships both arrived at Haabets Øe at the end of May, and went north two days later. Hans Fæster, who must have left rather later for Nipisat, returned on 20 June with Claus Hartsen and the *Haabet* carrying the whole population of the Nipisat colony, who could not spend the winter there due to lack of provisions. The hard winter had prevented them from catching any whales, and they had consumed so much of their supplies that there was not enough to last out the winter. Hans Egede wrote in July that he could have let them have further supplies from the stocks on Haabets Øe if he had known of the shortages at Nipisat. So the first expansion of operations in Greenland was cut short for the time being.

All three ships reached Bergen safely with their respective cargoes of seal blubber, seal, fox and reindeer skins, and whalebones. Altogether, the blubber was refined into 188 barrels of whale oil, of which 135 were sold at auctions in September. Thirty-six barrels, 300 seal skins and 100 fox skins were sent to Hamburg, 1,480 seal skins, 664 fox skins, all the reindeer skins and all the 816 whalebones were sold in Bergen. The balance of items were held back. The receipts from the produce brought home were: from the balance of 1724 not sold straight away, 727 rdl., 5 mrk., 15 sk.; from the produce newly brought home, 1,914 rdl., 2 mrk., 9 sk. The Company's total revenue of 2,642 rdl. 2 mrk., 8 sk. was 672 rdl. less than the year before. At the auctions in Bergen the whale oil had fetched 7 rdl. per barrel, substantially less than in 1724. The general depression affected the Company's revenues for a long time.

These receipts did not nearly cover the cost of the year's preparations and other expenses. Insurance was indeed paid on the last ship, the *Printz Friderich*, but this amounted to only about 1,220 rdl. About 2,490 rdl. was received from the lottery fund and 955 rdl. from the "levy" from these and other sources the Company was able to enter 9,429 rdl., 6 sk. on the receipts side of the cash account. This strangely drawn-up statement of account, dated 22 February 1726, naturally balances at this figure. In both 1724 and 1725 the lottery fund was dipped into, and so was the "levy" in 1725. The debt incurred on borrowings amounted to 8,577 rdl. Thus the Bergen Company's finances were strained to the full at a time of falling prices and depressed markets.

In 1724, however, some progress had been made both in whaling and trading. The quantity of produce brought home had risen sharply, although this increase did little to compensate for the drop in receipts.

| | Seal and whale blubber (barrels) | Skins | | Whalebones |
		Seal	Fox	
1721	½			
1722	47	180		"a few"
1723	76	56	428	4
1724	266	510	811	1,310
1725	192	2,142	1,187	816

Skins were obviously easier to obtain than blubber, possibly because at that time and in the Godthåb area, the Greenlanders did not need the skins of all the seals they caught. On the other hand, most of the blubber was used or sold to the Dutch. The largest annual quantity of blubber received (in 1724) was accounted for by the single whale caught that year. So there was no expectation of obtaining any more blubber, except by going out and catching the seals and whales that provided it. On the other hand, the method of trading adapted itself easily to the purchase of skins.

Not until the 1724–5 season were trading expeditions undertaken on a greater scale with the pinnace, especially the "long boat", which was presumably shipped out in 1724. In previous years it had been the custom to buy from the Greenlanders who visited Haabets Øe, and this practice was continued at the same time as the expeditions were taking place. It was evidently not worthwhile making the expeditions in the autumn, and in the severest part of the winter, when the fjords were iced over, it was impossible to reach the Greenlanders' settlements. In the "Reports", trading expeditions are first mentioned in March 1725. The book-keeper then journeyed about 150 km. southwards along the coast with "the long boat" and returned with it loaded with blubber and pelts. A further two trading expeditions were reported in April and May, the destination of both being Pisugfik in the north, where quite good trading was done. Hans Egede wrote of the first of these two expeditions in his Reports: "The rogues were very reticent about trading, for they thought they could make a better profit thereby with other traders." Possibly Hans Egede was mistaken regarding the profit motive, and that the reason for the Greenlanders' reluctance to sell was that they were used to disposing of their produce to the Dutch. Neither before nor after was it ever observed that Greenlanders possessed any outstanding commercial talent.

That same spring Hans Egede was aboard a Dutch ship, and talked to the master. The Dutchman had lain in the anchorage for some days but done little trading. Business had declined: previously it had been possible to obtain a full cargo at little cost. Egede thought this was the Dutchmen's own fault, for by competing among themselves they had gradually undercut one another so that the price of Dutch barter merchandise had fallen considerably. The Greenlanders had thus been able to obtain enough of these goods, and so were not exerting themselves to produce commodities for barter. A similar complaint was made by Feykes Haan in his book. Dutch sailings to the Davis Strait had apparently not declined, so trading and whaling must still have been profitable. This was most probably a general commercial lament, inspired by Feykes Haan's book.

Hans Egede drew his own conclusions regarding "trade policy" from this conversation. He did not believe that the Greenlanders traded because of any special need for the goods they were able to obtain in this way; only a few items were real necessities for them. They traded "more from pleasure than from need". But this belief is displayed by the Greenlanders' long journeys to Sydbay in the spring, of which Egede himself repeatedly quoted examples. If life was to be breathed into the trade, colonies must be established at all the more populous points. Trading should cease for a few years, or prices should be raised. In this way the goods would once again be in demand and trade would once again get under way. Hans Egede here revealed his rather tough business instinct. He realized that the idea could probably not be put into effect until the foreign traders had been driven out of the country. More colonial settlements would help to this end, since they would discourage the foreigners from travelling so far for the sake of a small profit. The latter view was shared by the Bergen Company's directors.

Although Hans Egede and others wrote to Bergen of their immediate plans for establishing settlements, the news of the end of the Nipisat colony did not excite the directors at all. In accordance with his views on foreign trading and the Company's dealings with the Greenlanders, and as a corollary to the Company's idea that it was important to establish several colonies close to each other to afford the Greenlanders the best opportunity for trading, Hans Egede proposed in his letter of 9 June 1725 that five colonies be established south of Haabets Øe, three between Haabets Øe and Nipisat and two or three north of Nipisat going as far as Disko, twelve or thirteen in all. He was aware that this scheme would cost far more than the amount promised to date and therefore suggested that a tax should be imposed on the Greenlanders: each person (presumably each adult male) should contribute between half a barrel and one barrel of blubber or an appropriate quantity of skins. This plan must have taken the directors by surprise, as they had discussed far less comprehensive plans in the spring of 1725, after the ships had sailed and Refdahl had returned to Bergen.

The first priority however, was to put the Company's affairs in order. There were no rules governing the relationships of directors to each other or between shareholders and management; everything had been arranged on extremely informal lines. But with the advent of large blocks of capital which the Company had to administer, apart from that subscribed by shareholders, more permanent methods for running the business were needed; the link with the Government also required it. On Refdahl's return to Bergen, a meeting of the Company discussed draft articles for the future and certain staff matters. As usual, only a small number of shareholders attended. Warning signs of the Company's later collapse began to show themselves. One of the directors, Magnus Schiøtte, had begun to feel disquiet about Refdahl as a fellow-director; another director, Jens Fæster, fell ill at the beginning of June and died, leaving on the board only J. van der Lippe, Refdahl and Schiøtte. Van der Lippe seems to have done little in the

Company's service and, since Magnus Schiøtte was unhappy about Refdahl's work, the management was on the verge of breakdown. At a meeting in Bergen in May 1725, Refdahl made a plea for the issue and royal approval of a set of regulations for the Company. He also broached the question of the accounts; since the Company had now been promised the funds it required, the previous years operations must be brought to a conclusion. He stated, that he had, as acting book-keeper, closed the accounts and balanced the books for the preceding years, implying that they had been audited and found in order. Schiøtte could not agree with this, and indeed the accounts had not been audited; Refdahl had only kept a sort of cash book with no proper balance-sheet. He stated at the meeting that he had kept the books for 1721 and 1722 without remuneration, but had been persuaded to continue in 1723 and 1724 for an annual salary of 200 rdl. Now he no longer wished to continue, as it was necessary to employ several clerks in the Company's office. Business had grown considerably in the past years, and would do so still more in the coming years in view of the present plans.

Magnus Schiøtte would neither agree to the plans nor approve the accounts. As so few shareholders had been present on 23 May, an extract of the minutes was distributed to them on which they were to record their votes. On 25 May, Schiøtte issued his own statement of opinion: he refused to approve the accounts so long as it was impossible to ex-amine them – he demanded a "book in which the inventory of the Company's resources, by whatever name they were called, are shown according to their value", i.e. a ledger, on the basis of which it would be possible to strike a balance at any time. He wanted an expert book-keeper, and offered his own services to the Company, without remuneration, to discharge the ships arriving in 1725. He thought the regulations were too lengthy and could wait until things were in better order.

Magnus Schiøtte anticipated that Refdahl and van der Lippe would submit the draft regulations for royal approval, so he wrote to the Chief Secretary of the *Danske Cancelli* requesting that this "regulation" should be sent to the inspectors of the Company for their opinion. He wrote: "It is feared that there might possibly be some trouble if one did not soon find from the books, by finally closing them, the difference be-tween what has been transacted up to now and the capital and contri-butions which your Royal Majesty has most graciously presented to the Company." This was an unequivocal accusation against Refdahl of having maladministered the funds. A few days later Schiøtte submitted an equally strong complaint against his co-director to the inspectors of the Company.

In May the directors applied for permission to have the number of lottery tickets set at 25,000 instead of 20,000 as already approved. Indeed the 20,000 had been exceeded in the meantime. They received permission for this on 18 June, and instructions that the lottery was to be ready for drawing by 1 October the same year. (It was not.) This lottery was bedevilled by complications of all kinds. The royal edict to the inspectors had been issued on 16 March, but in June they still had not taken up their duties. This was too much for the active bishop-designate of Trondheim, Matthias Tanche, who appears to have been the driving force behind subsequent events. On 14 June he and the President in Bergen, Christian Krog, demanded that Undal, the governor, should summon the inspectors to a meeting, complaining that this ought to have been done long before. With this the "party grouping" between the inspectors was established – Tanche and Krog *versus* Undal and Bishop M. Müller. On 22 June, Tanche and Krog had not received a reply from Undal, so they themselves held a meeting at the Town Hall where they drafted a letter to the directors of the Bergen Company, strongly emphasizing that "this same most graciously given capital" should not be used for any purpose other than that to which the King had assented, namely the continuation of the mission and trading.

The governor's opinion was that they should not take up their duties until the moneys received were taken into use and there was further news from either the directors or the *Danske Cancelli*. But now Schiøtte's complaint, particularly about Refdahl, made it seem opportune to send the directors an enquiry about these circumstances. Undal stated in his letter that matters had apparently come to a head at the Company's office, where Schiøtte was now being prevented by Refdahl and Van der Lippe from reading the correspondence; when he had asked them whether they intended to exclude him from the board, Refdahl replied that they had grounds for doing so. Schiøtte had been appointed a director by the King, so this situation had to be clarified.

Soon afterwards Tanche and Krog wrote a caustic letter saying that although they would sign the governor's draft, they would simultaneously send their own much sharper letter. In general, Undal preferred not to put too many difficulties in the way of the Bergen Company, whereas Tanche (and with him the ageing President Krog) were obsessed with the idea that something was about to happen contrary to the royal edict, with the possible result that the funds received would not continue to be used for the benefit of the mission and the Trading Company. Tanche fought obstinately in the mission's cause. (Bishop Müller was not active in the dispute.)

This dispute reveals in a harsh light the conditions under which the

Bergen Company was forced to operate during its short life. Its dependence on state support was at once a help and an intolerable burden. Inevitably there would be clashes between those involved in the day-to-day operations and conversant with the difficulties – men with commercial experience who had to effect business transactions – and the administrators who were civil servants and officials with no commercial experience. In addition, there was the anxiety inseparable from being a subject in an autocracy; if the King's commands were commercially impossible to execute to the letter, then a clash was inevitable. In this connection, Christian Møinichen, now chief secretary to the *Danske Cancelli*, had been head of the commission which caused the abrupt departure of many government officials, one of them Frederik Rostgaard.

Not until August did Van der Lippe and Refdahl answer the inspector and reject Schiøtte's complaints. Tanche and Krog then sent the whole correspondence to the King with a memorandum. Thus began the process which led to the demise of the Bergen Company. The directors must have been unaware of the memorandum, otherwise they could scarcely have prevailed on Nils Bagge, the recorder, to become a director of the Bergen Company in September. It had been intended that the lottery should be drawn on 1 October, but even by late November this had not been done. In any case the directors had their hands full with the various auctions and with the uncertain task of preparing for the next year's expedition and expansion. A sketchy plan for 1726 survives which was evidently based on Hans Egede's letter of 9 June 1725. It mentions establishing one colony at latitude 60–61°N. and another between 68° and 69°N., at an estimated cost of 14–15,000 rdl. These colonies would have to be set up in order to establish intermediate stations in 1727 and send people out in the summer with tents to expand the trading. This plan did not materialize, but it is evidence of how the management tried continuously, in the light of their experience and their preconceptions, to find ways of expanding the organization in Greenland, despite the ever-present restriction of never knowing how much capital was available for investment.

The three directors Van der Lippe, Bagge and Refdahl learned that their draft regulations for the Company, which had been sent to the King for approval on 5 June, had been forwarded to the inspectors for their opinion, in accordance with Schiøtte's request to the Chief Secretary, Møinichen. The three asked the inspectors for the matter to be treated as urgent and made it clear that they could do nothing about the continuation of the *Dessein* until the regulations had been approved; they warned that none of the shareholders would touch the venture again should any more advances be required with the venture in such a perilous state, or unless the debt the Company had incurred for the continuation of the *Dessein* could first be paid out of the royal "bounty", as the "levy" was now called, according to the Company's petition.

In November 1725 Magnus Schiøtte resigned as a director with effect from the New Year. However at a Company meeting held in December, Schiøtte insisted that the ledger be produced, to which Refdahl had to state that none existed; so Schiøtte called for "proper accounts" to be drawn up. This demand was possibly based on talks with one of the Company's auditors – who had long ago been elected from among the shareholders. The chief auditor, Magister Caspar Rømer, a chaplain of Bergen Cathedral, had complained to the inspectors that it had so far proved impossible for him to collect any of his co-auditors together to examine the accounts. Interest among the shareholders was lacking, and it was obvious that people wanted as little to do with the venture as possible. Rømer continued by pointing out that the books and documents produced were only adequate as a *basis* for accounts, but did not constitute accounts themselves. The accounts eventually produced after much toil were little better, and it appears that Refdahl had undertaken a task beyond his capacity.

Bagge, the recorder, though disclaiming any personal responsibility for the transactions of previous years, nevertheless thought that their settlement should not prevent operations from being continued. As a shareholder he could only imagine that "the bounty" was intended to pay the debt, since the shareholders could not conceivably be liable for it; if the debt were not paid, neither he nor anyone else would have anything more to do with the Company. Not having "spent time in acquiring commercial knowledge", he wished to be released from his directorship and would carry on only provided he received an assurance that the directors would obtain royal permission to use the "bounty" to pay off the debts.

At a meeting of the directors, the inspectors and the shareholders on 8 December, the revenue and expenditure were stated by J. A. Refdahl, in answer to a direct question, to be the sums indicated in his memorandum to the King on 6 December 1724, in which he had calculated the revenues at 13,000 rdl., although in the accounts they only amounted to 12,440 rdl. He reckoned the expenditure at approximately 28,000 rdl., plus whatever was needed to equip the 1726 expedition.

Tanche asked Refdahl whether operations could be continued on the surplus from "the bounty" without further contributions from the shareholders, to which the reply was that the surplus would be so great that no new investment was required. This optimism was clearly unjustified in view of the estimated cost of establishing the two new colonies.

As regards the plans for 1726, Magnus Schiøtte suggested that three ships be sent out – one to take supplies to the colony on Haabets Øe, one to explore and trade with a view to establishing colonies later along the coast northwards from 60°N. and one with the same purpose northwards from latitude 70°N. If this was not approved, he would give up his investment as lost, abandon the Company completely and not concern himself any more with its affairs: he had spared no effort on the Company's activities, but he wanted to waste no more time on "extravagant projects".

Magnus Schiøtte's sober proposal was appropriate to the uncertainty of the situation. Refdahl and Van der Lippe – perhaps Bagge too – relied on the King agreeing to the settlement of the debts from "the bounty". If Schiøtte knew anything of Tanche's and Krog's memorandum, he cunningly concealed it. The royal decision was given on 11 January 1726, and caused consternation in Refdahl and Van der Lippe; Bagge too felt uneasy. Prompted by Tanche's and Krog's memorandum, the King called upon the inspectors to ensure that the preceding years' accounts were closed and that the funds donated by the King should not be mixed up with the previous years' expenses or used for any purpose other than the continuation of the trade and mission.

No doubt the Governor and the three directors acted in good faith when they construed the royal edict of 16 March 1724 as giving aid to the Company in its distressed situation, especially as the edict had the effect of a decision on the petitions of 1724, particularly Refdahl's report of 6 December, which vividly depicted the tribulations of the Company. If a stand had been taken in the edict on the use of the funds, beyond a vague statement of intention in connection with continuing the business and propagating religion, and it had been spelled out clearly that the funds must not be used to cover the Company's commitments, the Bergen Company would have gone into liquidation immediately. But this Company was part of "the venture", and must honour its commitments if "the business" was to continue. Vice-Bishop Matthias Tanche provided the literal interpretation of the edict; through Tanche's and Krog's memorandum of 28 June 1725 the *Cancelli* had become aware that there really was a problem of interpretation.

There is no question of the Bergen Company's directors in general, Refdahl in particular, having acted from motives of personal gain, and there is no evidence whatever of any corruption in the Company's financial affairs. Had the inclination existed, there was little chance of obtaining hidden profits from such sales outlets as existed for Greenland produce. Bagge, a lawyer who had been in practice many years, described the directors as men fitted to accept responsibility. The suspicion of corruption was, to some extent, Tanche's work, although

Schiøtte was the first to insinuate directly that "some extravagance" had taken place. This was later taken up and pursued by the *Danske Cancelli*, whose lack of commercial knowledge and understanding of business life led to the hopeless demand that the Bergen Company carry on with the new funds, without including past expenses with those the subsequent years. (Here we come back to Schiøtte's letter to Møinichen of 29 May (see p. 73) warning against mixing the past and future though without commenting on payment of the debts.)

The directors were not blameless in every respect. Their optimism and extravagant imaginings had caused them to over-extend the Company. Refdahl was mainly to blame for this, but the venture would have come to nothing, if the Dutch competition were not beaten off, and this could only be done by quick and effective expansion of the Greenland settlements. The Mission could not achieve anything without this expansion. His "extravagance" had lain in thinking it was possible to do this by allocating in advance the capital *expected* from the lottery and "bounty". The duty to continue the work – which had always fallen squarely on the directors, and which through the charter of 1723 was linked to the King, was the ultimate reason for all the distress. This duty was stressed by the directors in another petition to the King in September 1726 – part of the attempt to alter the edict of 11 January 1726. On receiving the edict, the Governor Undal and Bishop Müller hastened to close the accounts for the preceding years. The Governor reported at length to the King, trying once again to explain the situation. The debts had been incurred on the one hand through loans from private individuals and on the other through borrowing from the lottery fund – in both cases solely to continue the mission and the Company and in the certainty that the King would lend his promised assistance. The size of the total debt was now such that the directors could not pay it without facing ruin. Undal thus requested permission to pay the debts out of "the bounty" after a proper balance sheet had been drawn up. This very circumspect letter does not appear to have been dealt with by the *Cancelli*, let alone by the *Conseil*; the decision had been taken, and the course laid down was followed without reference to common sense.

The Bergen Company directors were in duty bound to make ready for the spring expedition. In the curtailed plan which they submitted to the inspectors, only two ships were to be sent out. At the beginning of April Captain Jens Falck was sent out with the *Egte Sophia*. It was intended that he should sail direct to Haabets Øe and, having made contact with land, proceed north and put in at Nordbay (the entrance to the present Nivâq bay, south-east of Egedesminde) where he was to find a site for establishing a colony in 1727. He was also to proceed

F

round Disko and go trading as far north as possible. However, he never reached Haabets Øe, for the ship disappeared with all hands, possibly in the adjoining waters. In early June various pieces of wreckage, including a Norwegian bucket, came ashore near the colony and on the surrounding islands. The *stor-is* was particularly abundant in those years and in both 1725 and 1726 large quantities drifted into the coast as far north as Haabets Øe. Greenlanders coming from the south reported that the sea was full of ice from Cape Farewell north to Haabets Øe. They had seen a ship stuck in it and had heard the people, up to their knees in water, calling for the pastor, but the ship had drifted out with the ice and not been seen again. It could have been the *Egte Sophia*.

The ice was packed so closely that Berent Hansen Wegner refused to sail for home in the middle of August. He had sailed the *Cron Printz Christian* from Bergen immediately with orders to make direct for Haabets Øe and, after unloading, south along the coast for trading. The Company had requested him to procure reindeer skins, for which there was a special demand at the auctions, rather than seal and fox skins. He had also been ordered to get close enough to "Kap Christian" (Cape Farewell) to explore the island with a view to ships calling to trade there. Wegner evidently by-passed the *stor-is* safely but had to wait to put into land, and was only able to berth the vessel 60–75 km. north of Haabets Øe. It was July and the ice still lay densely packed along the coast, so that he had to send a longboat through the skerries to the colony. He was thus unable to carry out the hazardous task he had been given.

Since the ships from Bergen had taken so long to arrive, the colonists were anxious: when no ship arrived by 11 June and the assistant who had been on a short trading expedition to the south reported that there were large quantities of pack-ice there, Hans Egede summoned the council. Provisions had almost run out and stocks of lead were depleted, which meant that they could not reckon on obtaining fresh meat by hunting, if they could not cast shot. It was thus decided to seek help from the Dutch at Sydbay. It was not that they were keen on the idea of seeking help from the Dutch. In September 1725 some Greenlanders coming from the north reported that three Dutch whalers had put in at Nipisat and burnt down the houses built there in 1724. In April 1726 Jacob Geelmuyden had travelled north to investigate, and a month later returned to confirm that the "dastardly deed" had in fact taken place. The local Greenlanders named the guilty captains, indicating that they were notorious among the Greenlanders for their untrustworthiness – they often stole the Greenlanders' catch. The same Greenlanders also explained to Geelmuyden that the Dutch had done this thing because they believed the settlement interfered with their livelihood. The burning of the houses was thus an unusually drastic expression of Dutch ill-will towards the Bergen Company's trade.

Otherwise Hans Egede had enjoyed good relations in his meetings with the Dutch and going aboard their ships. It was probably these encounters – aside from the dire need – which led him to seek their help, and indeed it turned out that his experiences had not deceived him. On the northward journey in June, he not only managed to buy a quantity of provisions for immediate relief, but the captain he spoke to also promised to call at Haabets Øe on his way home and let them have whatever else he could spare. The council also decided that Jacob Geelmuyden and nine of the men should accompany Hans Egede to Sydbay to join one of the Dutch ships there and travel to Bergen via Amsterdam or some other Dutch port. However, the Dutch ship had barely reached the open sea, when she met the *Cron Printz Christian*. So Geelmuyden boarded her, stayed with her until land was reached and returned to Haabets Øe on 15 July.

Hans Egede and the council in Greenland had taken a somewhat bitter view of the Colony's distressed situation. It had previously been thought necessary to lay in two years' stocks of provisions which would keep well, but it had now been demonstrated that things could go wrong – even if rescue came at the last moment. But the relief that came with Captain Wegner created fresh anxieties. The captain dared not risk his ship, crew and cargo by setting out on the homeward voyage – he had seen the ice extending 150 km. out to sea as far as 65°N. – so he decided to lay the vessel up for the winter. Thus thirty-seven persons had to get through the winter on the ship's provisions for the return journey and the supplies for the colony which it had brought out. Only in October was it possible to establish a system of rationing, because all though the autumn the men were away on expeditions and hunting trips. The diet sheet approved for the winter is shown below:

	Midday	*Evening*
Sunday	Pea soup and meat	Pea soup and meat
Monday	Barley porridge and salmon	Flour porridge
Tuesday	Barley porridge and stockfish	Flour porridge
Wednesday	Barley porridge and salmon	Flour porridge
Thursday	Pea soup and stockfish	Pea soup and stockfish
Friday	Barley porridge and salmon	Flour porridge
Saturday	Barley porridge and salmon	Flour porridge

Besides this bacon and cheese were served on holidays. In addition 4lb. of bread and the same amount of butter and three barrels of "small ale" for the men are mentioned, but "strong ale" was provided for the "council's table", and for the men at Christmas and New Year. Spirits could only be issued on Sundays and holidays, but some had to be kept in reserve for expeditions. Fresh food was obtained by hunting and fishing, but the salmon caught in the summer were salted.

No wonder the colonists were afflicted every year with scurvy. Scurvy-grass (*cocleare*) was gathered and medicated with spirits, although it was also eaten raw. Hans Egede seems to have been alone in escaping scurvy for many years. The large quantities of salted foods and the heavy diet of cereals were not beneficial to health. Otherwise this diet was not very different from the contemporary norm, being very similar to the diet of ordinary seamen in the Danish–Norwegian navy.

The people at Haabets Øe entered the 1726–7 season without knowing how the situation was developing for the Bergen Company. Through Berent Hansen Wegner various people had received copies of the letters sent with Jens Falck and thus something had been gleaned of the position. In their letter to Hans Egede the directors had clearly stated that they were waiting the King's final decision. There were some who had made no contribution to the venture who wanted to out-manoeuvre the shareholders, or at least the directors; these critics thought that the expenses incurred for "continuation of the work" so far should not be paid out of the "bounty". Hans Egede was little the wiser for that, but he did realize that the events of the summer and the power of the pack-ice had defeated all the plans made by the Company's directors, and that this year would bring them in no revenue.

In writing their letter the directors had been uncomfortably aware of Tanche and perhaps Schiøtte too; they still could not believe it was the King's intention that the new funds should be used solely for future capital investment and not for consolidating the Company. They accordingly repeated their petition to the King in March, writing to Møinichen, the Chief Secretary, at the same time. They emphasized that the final consequence would be "the total ruin of 'the *Dessein*' and ourselves" unless the King forestalled it.

Time passed and Tanche continued on his course with a proposal that gained a hearing with the Chief Secretary of the *Danske Cancelli*. It was therefore in vain that Bagge tried to plead the Company's case in August and expressed himself quite strongly regarding both Tanche and the Bergen Company's chairman.

At the beginning of September the directors Van der Lippe and Refdahl made another attempt in a petition both to clear themselves of various accusations and to clarify the situation. By that time a decision had already been taken on Tanche's proposal: on 9 September the King signed the edict to close down the Bergen Company. Only one colony was to be maintained. The money from the lottery was indeed to be used primarily for defraying the expenses for 1726, but thereafter the amount brought in by the "bounty" was to be transferred to the town council of Bergen, which was to invest the money in other ways so that it should stay intact; the income was to be used for continuation of the mission and for trading. As the balance was estimated at 42,000 rdl. and the rate of interest was normally 5 per cent, they thus expected to have more than 2,000 rdl. a year, plus the revenue from goods brought home (about 1,000 rdl. on the basis of previous experience). Here we have the *Cancelli*'s pinch-penny economy in a nutshell.

It is not to be wondered at that Van der Lippe and Refdahl were completely taken by surprise by this edict, which cut the ground from under their feet as well as the Company's. On 8 October they set out their views to the inspectors. They made it clear that they had known nothing previously of Tanche's and Krog's proposal to the King, and they once more outlined the Company's difficulties and pointed out that they had borrowed the fatal loans from private individuals and from the lottery fund solely to be able to continue the work. They were unable to prepare the accounts for the preceding years or plan further operations if simultaneously they had to find time to persuade the King to change his mind. They therefore resigned as directors for good, having discharged this task for six years with no reward but only difficulties and troubles. They requested the inspectors to make the necessary arrangements for continuing the work in good time, both as regards navigation and repatriation of Company and mission staff.

However, Tanche was still pursuing his own course. He attempted to stop Undal, the governor, from reporting Van der Lippe's and Refdahl's decision to resign, but without success. Tanche also complained to Møinichen, the Chief Secretary, about the directors' letter, at the same time hinting at malpractices in connection with "the King's money"; he had got hold of a letter written by Nils Bagge declaring to his co-directors that he did not feel himself liable for the debts previously incurred and stating that he could not agree to the "bounty" being used partly to defray these debts, although he would support an application that this should be done. This letter was dated the end of May, and Bagge kept his promise. He again tried to change the King's mind in an urgent letter written on 17 October.

Within and around the Bergen Company there was hectic activity during that month. On 18 October all shareholders attended a meeting, in person or by proxy, with the directors and inspectors, and stated that they regarded their investments as donations – many of them because they had given them up for lost. No one wanted anything more to do with "the work". Bärenfels, now promoted major, no longer wished to be involved. Tanche and Krog's proxy attempted to put to the shareholders a number of questions which were not inoffensive to the directors, but with one voice all declared their complete confidence in the probity of the directors, and refused to make any attempt to have new directors appointed, knowing full well that no one would take on the task "because they can see in advance what trouble, risk and disappointment the previous good men must have suffered for their six years of management without the slightest recompense". The shareholders put an end to all further negotiations by leaving it to the inspectors to discover some way of continuing the work with "the King's money". They had participated originally from honourable and Christian motives to the full extent of their resources, and had paid up their instalments until 1722, when they renounced any further financial obligations; they now wanted no more to do with the business.

Significantly the two parties in the inspectorate submitted their memoranda to the King on the same date (29 October). Undal and Bishop Müller appealed to the King to decide what more was to be done; Tanche and Krog's proxy did the same, but characteristically asked for money "to continue the abandoned work". The next day Bagge withdrew from any further part in the management. Although Tanche had requested money for the continuation of the work in 1727, he, like the other inspectors, dared not do anything until there was a royal decision on what was to be done and by whom. The King did not reply to this directly. Instead, Governor Undal and Bishop Müller received a royal order to call in the amount of "the bounty" which had not yet been paid from the Bergenhus district and town, and to stop all payments in connection with "the bounty" to the former directors, seeing that "we now, on account of the proven mismanagement by the directors, do not wish to remit any more money to them".

At the same time an order was sent to Ditlev Vibe, the Vicegerent of Norway, and Bishop Bartholomaeus Deichman in Christiania to form together a commission to investigate the Bergen Company, its directors and shareholders, and the inspectors; actions in relation to the lottery fund and "the bounty". The description in the order of the directors' management of the Company read more like a summary indictment than terms of reference. Because of the document's nature, it contained no plans for the immediate future, but the two commissioners were to give an opinion as to how the trade could be continued. It was incumbent on them to examine all witnesses within three months. So the year ended without the inspectors knowing the intentions of the King and the *Cancelli*. The offices of the Bergen Company still functioned, without directors but with a book-keeper and the men he employed – at his own expense. In February 1726 Peder Rafnsberg had been engaged, as Refdahl no longer wished to keep the Company's books, and was fully occupied bringing and keeping the accounts up to date (he was asked to close those for 1726 as soon as possible), controlling the assets at home and attending to and acting as custodian of the Company's correspondence. The inspectors corresponded with the former directors through him.

In January 1727 the Vicegerent of Norway served a summons on Refdahl and Van der Lippe; nevertheless, it was to these two men that the inspectors turned in their perplexity as to how to arrange for sailings and the despatch of supplies in 1727. At a shareholders' meeting in February, nobody volunteered to undertake the expedition, and it was left to the inspectors to find someone who would. Something had to be done so that "the pastors in Greenland and the Christian people living with them" should not starve to death. Refdahl and Van der Lippe agreed with this but declined to take part in any way.

At that point the King – and Møinichen – had already decided to approach Magnus Schiøtte. On 1 March 1727 Møinichen, the Chief Secretary, acting on behalf of the King, to whom the result of the shareholders' meeting had been reported, asked Magnus Schiøtte to lead the expedition for that year with two ships "at the lowest possible cost". He would be able to draw on the money being paid into "the bounty" from the town and diocese of Bergen. It would be his task to find a trustworthy person who could be sent to Greenland to obtain information on local conditions and whether it was worth continuing the venture. Thus, almost at the same moment as it decided to form a trust with the funds from "the bounty", the *Cancelli* allowed Schiøtte to draw on part of the capital amounting to more than a year's interest on the amount that could come in from the diocese and town of Bergen and with little hope that this withdrawal would be made good by the year's revenues from Greenland produce.

Schiøtte informed the inspectors of Møinichen's message on 22 March and requested a warrant for 1,000 rdl. immediately. With some difficulty on account of the late date and correspondingly higher freight rates, the vessels *De jonge Maria* (Captain Ebbe Mitzell) and the *Jomfru Maria* were despatched on 23 April and 15 May respectively. Aboard the first ship was the commissioner requested in Møinichen's letter. These two ships were to carry out the earlier plan of exploring to the north and south. With this expedition paid for by the King, the Bergen Company was finally phased out of the Greenland mission and trade. The clearing up that had to be done took a long time. Long outlasting the commission of inquiry and even as late as 1737, there were still repercussions both inside Bergen and between Bergen and the Government in Copenhagen.

Sailings were to continue for a few more years, some from Bergen, but these eventually stopped too. With wholly inadequate capital resources the Bergen Company had embarked on a completely new area of trade and shipping in the face of keen competition from the Dutch Davis Strait traders, who had ample capital backing and a knowledge of the market. Had there been sufficient capital – and sufficient interest in the undertaking in both kingdoms – the venture might have succeeded, but these elements were lacking. The Company was founded in a period of economic recession throughout Europe, when the prices of almost all commodities were falling. Furthermore, it was hindered by its dependence on the State. The ill-informed and vague decisions of the *Danske Cancelli*, culminating in the demand for "the bounty" to be put in trust, made it impossible for this undertaking, which had initially been created "with such honest and Christian intentions", to be continued on a commercial basis.

REFERENCES

1. Failure of the crops was rather frequent in Denmark, and the market prices steadily decreased up to 1730. Since 1718, when the Dutch put a duty on imports from Denmark, the cattle trade had just been kept going.
2. Referring to the octroi and the Royal order of 1691 the captain's instructions involved his acting as a sort of "sea police" and use the dubious orders as authority for seizing as prizes offenders against the monopoly. The instructions seem to have been copied from the former instructions, and so the Bergen Company wanted to maintain the King's sovereignty on a dubious basis. It savours of deliberate political trickery: the directors tried to push the government the way they wanted. It was a risky undertaking and may have had some influence on the government's uneasy feeling towards the Bergen directors. This policy of "pushing forward" pervades all the applications and letters from the directors, especially from Refdahl.

5

THE MISSION IN GREENLAND
1724–1727

The Bergen Company's dismal circumstances from 1722 to 1727 did not directly affect the operation in Greenland. Only when ships arrived was contact made for a short time. In Greenland the people of the Trading Company and the mission lived their lives of virtual isolation for the rest of the year and went about their business preoccupied with wind and weather and the acute problems arising from the shortage of merchandise and materials. Hans Egede was chiefly concerned with the often distressing situations he had to face; then he despaired of the whole enterprise and felt that he had taken on a task beyond his powers and had assumed a greater responsibility for others, including his own family, than he was capable of bearing. At the same time almost insuperable difficulties obstructed the work which was the *raison d'être* of the whole venture. These difficulties had to be surmounted and great privation had to be borne before he could entertain even a slender hope of seeing results from his own and the others' toil.

It did not take Egede long to discover that he had taken on the cultivation of a wilderness. Accordingly he restricted his activities, which must have been difficult for him to curb himself. Perhaps he reacted with instinctive wisdom, or perhaps he was compelled by circumstances to draw back – and to observe. With his very first "report" in 1722, he was able to send a *Short Description of Greenland and the nature of its inhabitants in so far as we are informed of them to date*. In twelve brief chapters he set out his observations, limited, of course, to the area immediately surrounding Haabets Øe. Besides this his description contained information which he could have obtained from his reading. In its short and concise form, it is generally similar to Feykes Haan's description of 1720, which it supplements. After the description had been sent home, copies of it were made, of which several have been preserved. The reports were read first by the directors of the Bergen Company, then by the delegates of the Missionskollegium and finally by the *Danske Cancelli*'s representatives.

It is apparent both from the reports and from this brief survey of Greenland and its inhabitants that Hans Egede must have been able, within a relatively short time, to understand what was said to him. The items of information which he collected and which he expressly states were obtained by him from Greenlanders may, of course, have been interpreted by Aron Augustinussen. However, there are examples of oral contact between Hans Egede and the Greenlanders when Aron could not have been present.

Hans Egede kept referring to the Greenland language as the greatest obstacle to his getting down to the mission's work. Time and again he resigned himself to the fact that through persistent study this barrier could eventually be removed. He could do this by living with the Greenlanders, as Aron did, but this was an extremely slow process and it also proved too great a strain on Egede's constitution; it cost him considerable effort to live in the Greenlanders' huts.[1]

However, such was the progress made by Hans Egede with his linguistic studies that he was able in his first report to draw up a glossary of 291 terms. Some words in the list are incomprehensible, and others appear to be misinterpreted, but many are correct. With these terms and with gestures he was able to make contact with the Greenlanders to the extent of understanding what they wanted and, for instance, asking them for a night's lodging; he could also explain several everyday matters to them. It is possible and even highly probable that the Greenlanders often said "Yes and amen" to his remarks without understanding him.

Gradually, as visits to the Greenlanders in the locality and the Greenlanders' stays on Haabets Øe became more frequent, the opportunities of learning the language increased. From October 1722 he arranged, together with his sons Poul and Niels, to spend a longer period among the Greenlanders – "as long as possible, since I can see no other way of gaining a proper command of their tongue except by continually and constantly associating with them."

During the second of these visits to the Greenlanders living nearby, a new method spontaneously presented itself. One Greenlander, Kojuch, wanted to come and live in the colony permanently. Hans Egede took him into the Company's service hoping thereby to learn the language.

Out of this arose the first minor clash between the two cultures. Hans Egede expected Kojuch (that is how Egede wrote his name) to stay in the colony all the time. He "took up his post" on 6 November. On 10 November Egede noted that he had returned home to mend his boat, and on the 15th he came back, only to go seal- and bird-hunting on the 23rd, returning on 1 December. "I perceive that he will be quite unreliable in his duties", wrote Egede, who plainly did not understand how it was possible to absent oneself at will having entered into a service commitment. Hans Egede therefore "contracted" with a second and later with a third Greenlander (called Kisack). He had to dismiss Kojuch because of his unreliability.

Hans Egede intended to make the Greenlandic language a positive element in the service of the faith. He had concluded that "these people are quite ignorant of the service of God" and therefore had no words or expressions in their language which Egede could use to illustrate and explain the most important elements of the Christian faith. Therefore, by means of pictures and signs linked with Danish words for the Christian concepts, he hoped to teach them these words, thus introducing them into the Greenlanders' language as loan-words. He wanted to go even further, however, and teach them to read with the object of training them as servants of the mission – i.e. catechists – though Egede does not yet use this word.

Here again Egede was faced with the claims of opposing cultures. The adult Greenlanders could see no purpose whatsoever in reading, maintaining that it was far more enjoyable to put to sea and catch seals and birds, which they could live on. Hans Egede had sufficient understanding to write in this connection that he did not wish to deprive them of their liberty provided he succeeded in achieving something worthwhile with them.

This linguistic method was obviously going to be fruitful. During his studies, religious elements cropped up which Hans Egede could make use of in his missionary work.

From the view generally held at that time that all people were descended from Adam and Eve (hence the Greenlanders too) it followed that all people must once have had some knowledge of God. There was nothing strange, therefore, in Egede seeking to find some knowledge of God among the Greenlanders, so it is perhaps surprising that he was not more shocked on finding that they had no religion. "One cannot but feel that the Greenlanders are absolutely atheistic and have virtually no knowledge of God", he wrote in his short description of Greenland, "but live like dumb cattle", that is to say like animals which cannot reason, for awareness of God for Hans Egede and his contemporaries was the main distinction between man and the animals. So low had these poor creatures sunk, through the works of the devil, that they lived like animals. How great must be the compassion for them and how important was it to work for their salvation and tear them from the devil's toils; Hans Egede did not dare conclude from the many signs of superstition which he saw that these stemmed from the devil and that "they must be engaged in some tricks of the devil", rather, by associating with the antithesis of God they must thus have some knowledge of God. He did not encounter any conceptions of the devil or anything which might resemble it.

Hans Egede reached this conclusion on the basis of his primitive picture and sign method. From his very first journey he had made rough sketches to illustrate simply the doctrine of the Bible "relating to the creation of Man, his Fall from grace and his redemption and salvation through Christ, the Son of God". It can be seen from his subsequent map-making that he was no mean artist; all the same it cannot have been easy to depict "Salvation through Christ" or to explain the drawing with his small vocabulary, or indeed for his listeners to grasp anything from the words and drawings.

Despite this, it is obvious from Hans Egede's reports that his Greenlandic audience derived pleasure from his efforts and listened "devoutly". He also dealt with the accounts of how Christ healed the sick and raised the dead just by touching them. The Greenlanders obviously understood the drawings and stories about this immediately and related them to the activities of their own *angákut*, and to Egede's clear-cut spiritual and material authority in the colony. They demanded – as mentioned before – that he should blow on them. Having done this once, he had to continue.

This caused Egede considerable distress and in some cases he tried refusing to blow on the sick and offered a prayer for the sick person at the bedside instead. With his faltering vocabulary he endeavoured at a death-bed to bring to the relatives present the comfort which, to his mind, could be afforded them by the Christian religion, explaining very literally about life after death. Although Hans Egede had to act as a healer and appear before the Greenlanders as an important *angákoq*, he could not in the long run be satisfied with this role. He was compared with the Greenlanders' own *angákut*, towards whom he adopted a condemnatory attitude as soon as he learned of their activities. It was not until he understood what activities the word embraced that he could take a stand against them; until then he thought the word meant "great", and so in his ignorance he called God *angákoq*.

Once again it was the language that had played this trick on Hans Egede, and he realized how poor was his mastery of the language and was extremely doubtful whether his Greenlandic had the desired meaning. "Meanwhile I must stammer my way along with them and endeavour by signs to leave some impression of God in their hearts; God alone, who knows the hidden effects of His words of grace, knows best whether these poor people can derive any profit therefrom for their better enlightenment". In other words, Egede believed in – or rather hoped for – a sort of "inner change", some mystical heavenly power in the words he "stammered with them" – in itself not fundamentally different from the Eskimo *inua* concept. For him it was a matter of course that God's word should have a special power – *inua* – and he did not doubt that the Greenlanders "with God's help and the power of His Word" would in time be able to understand the explanations given to them "besides which it must also be possible to keep them in good order and under some discipline, to which they would probably submit themselves, since they are quite flexible and amenable by nature".

His experiences with the Greenlanders who had come to work in the colony had given him some inkling of the obstacles that their wandering hunting expeditions represented for the mission; Egede was unaware of the need for these expeditions, or their significance, and regarded them simply as stupid wanderings for pleasure. Of course, he came from settled farming and urban societies, and from a parochial community in northern Norway, and did not know the way of life of a hunting culture under the conditions determined by nature, and so was bound to make far-reaching mistakes. He had always previously been in close contact with the idea of the authority of religion and the church, and the established moral code of which duty, obedience and order were the corner-stones, hence he could not but make demands which were irreconcilable with the equally ancient and well-established traditions and way of life of the Eskimo. Hans Egede had furthermore been brought up in an autocracy with its authoritarian structure, and had been subjected to discipline at home, at school and at the university. His office carried with it the obligation to intervene in people's morals and way of life, and to assert the laws of God and the King. Duty and order must always have appeared to him as an unavoidable necessity for himself and for others. In this stern attitude towards life there was no place for humour, hence in Hans Egede's reports or letters there are no situations or events which excite a smile, let alone laughter. A weighty and at times depressing seriousness pervades every word and every account, and suggests a mind carrying such heavy burdens that only God could lighten them. Hans Egede was earnest but also sensitive and compassionate. His every word and act bears witness to an unswerving obligation towards God and the King, and towards the people who depended on and trusted him, "the poor, ignorant people" whom it was his duty to convert and lead out of their blasphemous and bestial state. Their salvation was more important than their material lives. If they were unwilling to work for their own good, they must, by virtue of God's Word and law, be compelled to do so through correction, discipline and order. God's Word was being preached to them and it was blasphemy to oppose it, the devil was at work in a man when this happened and the devil must be opposed. In the society from which Hans Egede had come, action was followed by judgment and punishment, possibly even the death penalty. He was inextricably bound to the faith into which he had been born and in which he had grown up.

Therefore, when the Greenlanders with their concept of the right of use came into conflict with the foreigners' concept of the right of owner-ship, making use of objects in the colonists' possession simply because they needed them, Hans Egede and the other foreigners regarded this as stealing, which was the way the earlier Europeans had reacted. Hans Egede used such situations to conjure up the devil and all his works – in words that he could now string together – and preached eternal damnation with the wrath of the Old Testament. However, he did not always speak to them "harshly".

He could get nowhere, however, until he had a greater mastery of the language, and his progress was interminably slow. He received good help from the Greenlanders who lived in the colony. After he had dismissed Kojuch in December 1722, only two Greenlanders were left. By April 1723 they had made enough progress to be able to read a little, and Egede was hoping that something useful might come of all the pains taken by him and the two Greenlanders. He had ven-tured to compile a catechism in Danish and a sort of West Grèenlandic, according to which the two Greenlanders could answer questions. Not much was to be learned from that catechism, since the language was mostly incomprehensible; Egede himself admitted (just before writing down the catechism) that he was unable to compose any prayers in Greenlandic "in grammatical order and agreement". But sentences learnt by rote and meaningless repetition were, after all, regarded then as the acquisition of knowledge.

In this catechism Hans Egede made one mistake in particular which is easily understandable in view of his search for religious ideas and concepts in Greenlandic, with which he could link the Christian views of good and evil. He identified the devil with *Tôrnârssuk* (see I, p. 297) in the sense that this most powerful of all assistant spirits was the special helper of the *angákut* ("the witch-doctors") and thus the prin-ciple of evil in material form when the "witch-doctors" exercised their sorcery. Contrary to what was intended, the Greenlanders inevitably gathered from this that the devil was not quite as bad as the pastor claimed in his preaching, for *Tôrnârssuk* could very well be helpful, and in fact was neither absolutely evil nor absolutely good. For a long time this misconception of *Tôrnârssuk* was a hindrance to the mis-sion's activities, but it is possible that this same friendly spirit gradually came to smack of the devil in the minds of the Greenlanders too.

Besides this the catechism contained, in somewhat obstruse Danish, the very simplest of the elements of the Christian doctrine set out in twenty-three questions and answers. Hans Egede had striven for simplicity in the selection and wording of the elements, but he was again impeded by the complicated mode of expression then in vogue. He understood that simplicity was imperative, yet the catechism was and remained incomprehensible in the pseudo-Greenlandic in which it was written.

Hans Egede was not a man for deep theological speculation. He had a firm belief in his faith and was inspired by his sense of duty towards God, Church and King. He had been called to his office not by the King alone but also by a higher power. This call required action – in particular, preaching. Thus he became all the more concerned about the hours, days and years that were passing without his work achieving any demonstrable results. His earlier difficulties in setting up the mission were as nothing compared to the barriers that he had to overcome during his work in Greenland. He must have found it all the more encouraging to find that some of what he had said in his strange garbled Greenlandic had taken root in the Greenlanders' minds. On returning from a fishing trip, some of his people said that at the place where they had spent the night, a young son of the house in which they were staying had been drowned when his boat had capsized. The parents were inconsolable, weeping and wailing. Then one of the other Greenlanders told them not to weep and wail so much for he had heard *pelleste* [the pastor] tell of the resurrection of the dead on the Last Day, when they would all see each other again and enjoy eternal life. They would find their son again too. On being asked whether this was so, one of the men "who best understood what he [the pastor] was talking about" replied that it was. This seemed to comfort the bereaved people.

Besides Hans Egede there were others on Haabets Øe who took an interest in the language. It can be assumed that a man such as Hartvig Jentoft, the book-keeper and trader, did so; it was reported later that he was on good terms with the local Greenlanders, and he was able to speak with Pôq and Qiperoq.

As we have already seen, Hans Egede had apparently not been talking completely in vain, but this story of the bereaved parents must have confirmed his faith in the obvious inner power of "the Word"; in this case he had stumbled by chance upon what he had deliberately been striving for. Earlier, in his "Reports", he had given an account of the Greenlanders' burial customs, experience of which had given him an insight into their spiritual beliefs. He had gone into the Eskimo "spiritual beliefs" in detail and recorded that there was indeed a belief in the immortality of the soul. The Greenlanders must have this knowledge from God. Without expressing it in so many words, he had found here an element of faith which, in his opinion, must be derived from God, but strangely he did not draw any conclusions from it.

Language was still the main obstacle to a greater understanding of Greenlandic ideas and the enlightenment of "their darkened minds". He found that his sons learned the language with ease through being in the company of the Greenlandic boys who stayed in the colony for shorter or longer periods. Among the Greenlanders was one man with three sons who all proved more eager to learn than any who had stayed with Hans Egede before and whom he had taught. He had, of course, continued to teach them, but they were "unstable" and went off when it suited them, coming and going without any plan in their actions. Hans Egede regarded it as unjustifiable in relation to the one necessity. In the spring and summer, there was little point in teaching. On the other hand, teaching prevented Hans Egede from making expeditions, as it required his constant presence in the colony. Similarly, his pastoral duties in the colony, and the taking of services on Sundays and holy days, obliged him to stay at home or at least never to go far afield. Yet if he were to win the confidence of the Greenlanders and have any chance of teaching them, he also had to get out and about.

He tried to divide his energies; he relates that he did not neglect the surrounding Greenlanders, but went to them as often as he could to instruct them; when he returned to them to continue his teaching they had usually forgotten what they had learnt the last time. "I could very well continue to go among them", but since the most essential thing was to learn the language, "that will have to wait until either an assistant or a colleague is sent out to me, of whom I stand in great need both now and for the future". Alternatively, the Greenlanders whom he was teaching, together with his two sons, could eventually be taught enough to become assistants themselves – "which is, in fact, what I intend to do with them". Thus the idea of training Greenlanders as assistants (catechists) in the service of the mission gradually took shape in Hans Egede's plans for the future. He had already asked for an assistant and colleague in 1721, but not until 1723 was a suitable person found: Albert Top, who on 16 April 1723 received his letter of appointment as a missionary and was ordained a priest on board the vessel *Fridericus Quartus*. Henceforward, the two missionaries were able to stay with the Greenlanders in their homes and at the colony in turn, so that neither the instruction of the Greenlanders nor the morning and evening prayer meetings and the prescribed church services were neglected.

The number of days' travelling recorded increased considerably. While Hans Egede was away for seven days in 1721, twenty-two days in 1722 and twenty-eight days in the spring of 1723, Top's arrival enabled him to undertake the long journey south in August–September of 1723 as well as a journey north, in all another forty-seven days. During 1724 Hans Egede was away from the colony for sixty-nine days, while Top was away for only eleven. In October, however, he was transferred to the newly-established Nipisat colony, so that most of Hans Egede's travelling was done in the spring. Throughout the spring of 1725 Egede regularly visited homes in the neighbourhood, taking his son Poul with him; on these journeys he was only away for one or two days. He had to make one longer journey to Nipisat in April and May and was away altogether for twenty-three days. When Nipisat was abandoned, Top once more shared the rota on Haabets Øe, thus allowing Hans Egede to undertake longer journeys again; and so it continued.

These journeys had manifold objects; it was of prime importance to get to know the country in order to discover the best place to which the badly-sited first colony could be moved. It had always been intended that whaling should be carried on alongside trading, which meant that the most suitable whaling sites had to be found. Nipisat was established with this in mind. Besides, Hans Egede and the Bergen Company had to attend to the original objective of the whole venture: the discovery of the Norse settlements and their possible survivors. Thus the journeys did not just have one purpose, but were intended to achieve as much as possible. This included instruction of the Greenlanders, wherever they were found, and trading with them if possible. It was found during these journeys that stories about Hans Egede, and the settlement on Haabets Øe, had gone before him along the coast. Wherever he went, he was already known as the *pelleste*. He was well received everywhere and was often asked at the settlements to talk about "God and heavenly matters". It appeared that one of the Greenlanders, who had stayed in the colony and had received instruction for some time, had passed on his "learning" to the others whom he had visited on his hunting trips. On his long journey south in August 1723, Hans Egede and his party reached a settlement which was presumably situated on one of the large islands off the Sermilik fjord, half-way between Godthåb fjord and Fiskenæsset. The Greenlanders would not allow them to land and prepared to receive them with bows and arrows, but when they heard that it was the *pelleste* they changed their minds at once.

This fear of foreigners (*qavdlunât*) appears to have dominated the Greenlanders from the outset. In the following years when the men stayed with the Greenlanders quarrels occurred in which this fear of foreigners was obvious and took aggressive form. The neighbouring

G

Greenlanders soon realized that in his strange way Hans Egede wanted to help them, and had no objection to his staying.

Over the years some contact must have been established between the men and the Greenlanders, since, as we have mentioned, some of them learned enough Greenlandic to understand what was said. Yet the Greenlanders kept well away from the colony and its inhabitants. Individual families and larger groups sometimes came and settled there, but mostly stayed for a short time. The two Greenlanders whom Hans Egede took in to teach during the winter of 1722–3 were derided by their fellow-countrymen as *qavdlunât*. Hans Egede thought this was envy, because the two had an easy time at the colony, receiving food and clothes without much work in return. But had that been the case, it is likely that there would have been more people wanting to work in the colony; yet there was no question of that. Instead, something close to contempt was felt for the person who did not conform in his behaviour and who cut himself off from the community.

In place of these older Greenlanders, Hans Egede began to take in boys, usually orphans, to bring them up and teach them the Danish language and a trade. The first, who appears to have been taken in in February 1723, quickly proved to be teachable: that is to say he soon learned to recite the strangely phrased answers to the incomprehensible questions of the catechism.

The second one, whose name was Papa, came to the colony of his own accord. His parents were dead and he now wished, at the age of ten or twelve, to live with Hans Egede. A few months later Pôq came to Haabets Øe, having decided to accept Hans Egede's suggestion to accompany the ship to Copenhagen with another Greenlander. He was thus willing to spend the rest of the year in the colony until the ships arrived.

Each day Hans Egede held a class for Pôq and three Greenlandic boys, with the loyal help of Albert Top; at the same time Egede must have been teaching his own children. The four Greenlanders learned the alphabet, and could spell and put together words in Danish. On the other hand, Egede examined and instructed them in Christian knowledge in Greenlandic, in so far as the language he spoke could be so called. Their progress was not yet such that he was prepared to baptize them.

However, he did baptize a gravely ill child at the end of January 1724. Hans Egede felt qualms at having baptized the child, for if it survived and were not brought up in the Christian faith, the baptismal vows would be profaned. As the child soon died, Egede felt content; he had "baptized it, thereby offering it up to God as the first fruits of these heathen Greenlanders. . . ."

After this baptism, the others present wished to be baptized too, but Hans Egede refused; he was, as he said, unconvinced of their faith. They for their part maintained that they believed everything he told them. Egede was still reluctant, but once he saw that they were continuing to listen devoutly to the Word of God and were willing to learn God's Word and obey Him, he was prepared to baptize them.

Together with the instruction of the two young Greenlanders in the colony and of those living nearby when visiting their homes, this emphatic view conveys an essential feature of Hans Egede's outlook and method. He neither could nor would carry out any form of baptism until the adults at least had been instructed in the Christian religion, understood its most important elements, obligations and demands, and thus attained a soundly-based faith. Instruction was thus necessary, and they must learn to read. For Hans Egede, the Lutheran requirement of personal involvement was fundamental. It is doubtful whether he believed in revivalism as a stablizing factor: it was perhaps on this point that Hans Egede showed himself most clearly to be a follower of orthodox Lutheranism and far removed from the emotional revivalism emphasized by Pietism and its offshoots, which he regarded as shallow sentimentality and therefore harmful.

Instruction became a fundamental element in the activities of the Royal Mission. At first, the results seemed meagre and Hans Egede did not venture to carry out any baptisms. The Greenlanders who had spent the winter of 1723–4 in the colony and those living in the neighbourhood "know quite well . . . how to reply to all the points that we have been able to raise with them, but whether any true conversion and change has taken place in their hearts, I cannot be assured of since up to now I have noted nothing in them . . . but the usual coolness. Yet during prayers and the reading they have always behaved well and seemed willing to learn. Their unsettled way of life and wandering in the summer will be no small obstacle to their complete conversion, for which good and adequate measures, of which a suggestion is to be given to the authorities concerned, must necessarily make amends."

Hans Egede regarded this "wandering" or vagrancy, most of which occurred during the spring, summer and into the autumn, as a serious obstacle to the instruction which he endeavoured to carry out as regularly as he could. It hampered any real progress in the teaching of the Greenlanders whom he had taken in, when, apparently without reason, they disappeared to go hunting and fishing. He never understood that this moving from place to place during the summer half of the year was an economic necessity for the Eskimo *fanger* community; still he did not have the basis for understanding. He was among the very first to come face to face with such a social system at all, and on the basis of his own views he could not conceive of anyone failing to sacrifice everything for the sake of his own salvation, which was the most important – indeed the only – necessity.

The "measures" of which he said he would "make suggestions to the authorities concerned" were to some extent anticipated by the directors of the Bergen Company in their letter of 28 March 1724, expressing the hope that they would have enough capital to establish four colonies between Haabets Øe and Disko. When more colonies were established and manned with missionaries, "the savages" would "as it were, be surrounded by clergy so that whether they travelled south or north, a pastor would always be with them as a good example, whereby religion would be greatly advanced". That the Trading Company would also benefit in its fight against the Dutch was of secondary importance.

As mentioned before, Hans Egede was not immediately enthusiastic about the Company's plans and imaginings but wanted much more drastic action. In a *Perlustratio Grønlandiae* which he sent to the Company with Jens Falck on 2 August 1724, he set out his proposals. He suggested that "the inhabitants of this land be subject to tax as a whole, for I am certain that instead of applying in vain so often and laboriously to reluctant Christians for voluntary aid, one could with less trouble seek and obtain this from the heathens themselves". If three colonies were established and adequately manned, it would be possible to "hold these people down". Each summer an armed patrol would then be sent out to collect the tax, together with fines for offences. If the reasons for the fines and the tax were explained to the Greenlanders "they could probably be made to see reason and contribute with a good grace, provided that the tax were not too high in the first place". If this were not done, everything would be in vain, "for these poor people are quite unfitted to benefit from the word of God, so long as they live in their accustomed state of wildness and wilfulness".

In the vicinity of Haabets Øe, that is to say for about 8 km. into the Godthåb fjord system and as far south and immediately north of the colony, Hans Egede reckoned that about 200 familes were living. If they contributed one barrel of blubber or the equivalent of six rigsdaler each, they alone would be able to provide over 1,000 rigsdaler. Hans Egede was able to use his command of the language for a cunningly planned investigation of the Greenlanders' willingness to contribute. By saying that the King had sent him to Greenland and would send out more men to defend the Greenlanders against foreigners, and that it all cost a great deal, he persuaded them to agree to supply a sealskin or a fox skin each if the King would defend them. Hans Egede concluded from this that it would also be possible to get them to "pay tax".

No one could make out any social system whatsoever in the Eskimo society as it functioned in the surrounding area and in the areas where it was encountered on expeditions. Hans Egede and the others were to this extent right in thinking that, if the population were to be converted to Christianity, it was also necessary to introduce the culture in which the Christian faith had come into being and developed. Without recognizing it, Hans Egede had put his finger on the nub of the problem. The fact that he wrote of "holding down" and suggested the punitive levying of taxes can only mean, in the context of the autocratically governed Danish–Norwegian society, that he was bound to regard coercion and subjection to a governing authority as the best means of progress for both the individual and the community – the common good. It is not foreign to our modern way of thinking that a population should, in the form of taxes, pay the costs of measures for its own welfare. The Greenlanders' conversion was, in Hans Egede's view, for their own good, and thus it was not unreasonable that they should contribute a part of what it cost to make this conversion possible.

To give the people some idea of such an organized society and to learn Danish, he wanted to send selected Greenlanders on a visit to Denmark, but not for too long. The council in Greenland had passed a resolution in 1722 that some Greenlanders should be seized and sent to Denmark to instruct them in Christianity and to teach them Danish. In his short account of the Greenlanders' customs Egede discussed this scheme more fully, but toned down the somewhat strong wording. The directors of the Bergen Company were not enthusiastic, however, and took the opportunity of insisting that the Greenlanders should be well treated. Should it so happen, on the other hand, that one or other of them wanted to undertake such a journey of his own free will, they would not oppose it.

It is probably an indication of Hans Egede's own impatience that he put forward this proposal at all, since no further mention was made of it; on the contrary, he took the directors' hint. Finally in 1724, the journey of Pôq and Qiperoq was arranged, but with the tragic result that only Pôq returned the following year. Nevertheless, Pôq proved that he had gained a great deal from his visit.

Firstly, simply because he had made this journey, he acquired an undeserved celebrity among his fellows, which he did his best to maintain by making up a ballad which he often sang and probably "improved upon" all the time. Secondly, his own horizon was greatly extended by what he had seen. He had been amazed by the big houses in Copenhagen, Rundetårn (the Round Tower), soldiers, the many people he met, all of whom were friendly towards Qiperoq and himself, the firefighting equipment, land prices, the orphanage, lunatic asylums, the prison for vagrants, thieves and prostitutes, and the inns where they "drink the water that takes your senses away".[2] The cranes had filled him with wonder and so had the street lighting, which was by oil-lamps, the oil being made from blubber. Pôq was apparently fully aware of the importance of blubber. On being asked why the Danes did not come to Greenland where land was cheap, Pôq answered that no one would think of coming to Greenland if it were not for blubber.

However, he had most to tell concerning his visit to the King who had been extremely kind and given him five large chests full of gifts. This was an exaggeration, but he had been given European clothing, a complete set including a sword, and in Greenland he later appeared in this costume to the great astonishment of his fellow-countrymen. It is strange that, as far as we know, Pôq was never teased or scorned by his fellows on account of his journey. The stories he told of his travels made a great impression.

Pôq was full of admiration for the skills of Europeans, in particular the navigation on board the ships he travelled on. Since they were Danish–Norwegian ships and it was in Denmark that he had his most memorable experiences ashore, the Danes were the special objects of his admiration. This benefited relations between the Danish–Norwegian colony on Haabets Øe and the local Greenlanders, and later between Danes and Greenlanders generally. Admiration for what these foreigners could do was for long a characteristic feature of the Greenlanders' opinion of the Danes.

It is questionable how much direct use Pôq was to Hans Egede in the mission; it is significant that the latter did not baptize Pôq and his wife until 18 January 1728. After his homecoming Pôq's marriage plans had gone somewhat awry, but he succeeded in finding a wife, and the children born of the marriage were baptized immediately. Of the baptism of Pôq and his wife Hans Egede wrote rather dryly that it took place "after they had been instructed in Christian knowlege for some time" and that they themselves made their confession of faith and replied satisfactorily to all the questions concerning faith put to them. In August the same year, Pôq made another journey to Denmark with his wife and two children. In a letter to Frederik IV, Hans Egede wrote, as the reason for their journey, that "since they are only a source of expense and inconvenience to the colony here and cannot perform any service, and on account of the shortage of accommodation, which will be considerable this winter so that there will be no home for them, we are obliged most humbly to send them to you". From this understandable but rather strange reasoning, it is plain that Pôq had not afforded the mission much joy. The significance of his journey can be gleaned partly from what is recounted above and per-

haps from the contact with the Greenlandic language which Hans
Egede, his sons and Albert Top achieved through Pôq.

Indeed, a considerable advance in Hans Egede's linguistic ability
can be found in the catechism with which he ends his report for 1723–4.
Moreover, the Danish text is more straightforward and the wording
less cumbersome than in the previous version.

A source of much greater pride and profit for Hans Egede and Albert
Top was the relatively young Greenlander, Papa. He had accompanied
Top to Nipisat in 1724, partly to help the young missionary with the
language, and partly so that Top could instruct him further. This
became Top's chief task during that winter and he continued the
teaching after Papa, well prepared in advance and with an obvious
knowledge of "the main precepts of the Christian doctrine", was baptized at New Year in 1725. At this baptism he was named after King
Frederik IV and given the name Frederik Christian. Albert Top wrote a
highly enthusiastic letter to the directors of the Bergen Company about
the event and sent a sample of Frederik Christian's penmanship.
This man – the first Greenlander to be baptized of his own free will –
became a useful assistant in the mission until his early death in 1733.
In the daily study of the language he, like Poul and Niels Egede, was
indispensable.

There was still basic work to be done on the language. After Albert
Top's return in 1725, he and Hans Egede worked steadily at enlarging
their vocabulary and powers of composition, but it seemed to them
almost impossible that they would achieve anything like perfection.
What they found one day to be right proved wrong the next day.
Hans Egede says that, with the help of his children, he not only collected a number of equivalents but also arranged them in a system "according to certain rules and inflections"; they also started translating the
Sunday Gospel passages, which they then tried out on the Greenlanders. By 1724, with the help of his son Poul, Hans Egede was attempting to translate passages from the Bible. He was somewhat unsure of
his work and apologized for it in advance, because he was unable to
follow the Hebrew text exactly.

Through his progress in the language and his more frequent association with the Greenlanders, his knowledge of their religious ideas
also broadened continually. Wherever possible he opposed them.
When he was on an expedition up Godthåb fjord in March 1723,
he met a boy wearing an old piece of wood as an amulet round his neck.
Hans Egede managed to persuade the father to take the amulet off,
simply by explaining that it was of no use. The same thing happened
with an old woman with a raven's claw and a fox's jawbone as a guarantee of long life. When Hans Egede explained to her that if she believed

in God she would have eternal life and that the amulet was useless, she cut if off, satisfied with his promise. The women present who wore ornaments in their ears and round their necks asked whether they too should throw them away as displeasing to God, to which Hans Egede replied in the negative. These women must have appreciated clearly what was a trinket and what an amulet. No general conclusion can be drawn from this single example, but it may be that some mystical property was attributed to the trinkets, but of this there is no concrete proof.

This time Hans Egede used "the method of persuasion" which, together with patient instruction, was that which he most frequently used. Sometimes, however, his quick temper ran away with him, as when, on 17 December 1724, he was on the Kook islands[3] to instruct the Greenlanders there. One of those present had an amulet[4] round his neck. Hans Egede asked him to throw it away, but he refused "until I had to give him a few blows across the back (for nothing can make them see reason except beating and punishment, which I have to practise occasionally, having found that this worked)". This Greenlander then blamed the bad weather on Hans Egede's perpetual interference by means of reading and instruction. But Egede laid the blame on their impiety: God was punishing them by sending the bad weather. There is no doubt that he meant this seriously, for his own life was lived in the belief that the Lord's punishment struck here and now, as well as after death. Corporal chastisement was one of the few educational aids in those days, and Hans Egede too felt that he had benefited from it.

The previous month, in another case of a boy wearing an amulet, Hans Egede had first rebuked the bystanders verbally, and then seized the amulet from the boy's neck and thrown it out of the house. When the adults wanted to bring it in again, a real wrangle developed between one of the boy's uncles and Hans Egede, who lost his temper to such an extent that he threatened their lives if they were not obedient. He realized that he had gone too far and later excused himself by saying that his knowledge of the language did not allow him to explain his meaning clearly. So perhaps the bystanders did not understand his threat either, but only his anger, which was certainly of Old Testament proportions.

Apart from this there is no evidence in Hans Egede's reports of violence and abuse of power. Towards angákut, however, once he understood the nature of their activities he was inexorable. They, for their part, worked against him because they noticed that their influence was declining in proportion to his increasing authority. It was not until 1723–4 that he fully understood their activities and what angákoq meant. It sometimes seemed as though the ordinary Greenlanders were relieved when an *angákoq*'s power was destroyed. Hans Egede had threatened in all seriousness to kill these "witch-doctors" and this may have persuaded some of them to stop their activities. One *angákoq*, whom Hans Egede had admonished many times, was punished by the royal missionary with his own hand on 3 January 1725. But the Greenlanders as a whole were disinclined by nature to give up their old beliefs. For instance, they continued for a long time to observe the taboos which the *angákoq* had prescribed, especially in regard to diet. On a later occasion the trader, on a journey, reached a settlement situated so far to the south that it had not been visited before. This trader was Johan Georg Berenhart, who had travelled out as a surgeon with the *Haabet* in 1721 but had later taken over as book-keeper and trader after Hartvig Jentoft. When Berenhart attempted to land, the local *angákoq* tried to defend the settlement against the foreigners and began to conjure up spirits. Berenhart set about him and hit him "across the mouth". The *angákoq* then seized his bow and was about to shoot Berenhart, who meanwhile took hold of a musket which he aimed at the *angákoq*. The other Greenlanders persuaded the *angákoq* to flee – which was as well, since Berenhart's musket was not loaded. Possible murder due to mutual fear was thus avoided. On the European side, this fear was based on reports of attacks on shipwrecked sailors. Indeed, they had wanted to take soldiers with them to defend them against "the savages". On the Greenlanders' side, it was based on two facts: the tradition of the avengers who were coming, and on occasional experiences with Dutch whalers.

Hans Egede and the colony on Haabets Øe might otherwise have felt safe. He spoke of the Greenlanders' docile and gentle nature, and had previously reported how, to his amazement, five of his men had been a match for three hundred Greenlanders, precisely because they did not adopt an aggressive attitude. There was no hint of danger in all the years up to 1726, when some kind of conspiracy grew up which might have had disastrous consequences. Rumours reached Hans Egede that the Greenlanders living to the south were going to kill the trading assistant and his men when they went there to trade, and while the assistant was absent on his journey south, the Greenlanders of another settlement nearer Haabets Øe were to take advantage of the opportunity to kill those remaining at home. Hans Egede decided to forestall them. With Jacob Geelmuyden, at that time the trader on Haabets Øe, the operation was fixed for 5 April. Accompanied by seven or eight men, Egede descended on the settlement, taking away the headman, an *angákoq* called Elik, as a prisoner. There was no opposition, but all the inhabitants of the settlement who were present protested that they had nothing to do with the conspiracy. Elik was taken to

Haabets Øe and "had his legs put in irons and a beating which he accepted, being thankful that his life was spared". He was kept in irons for three days and then released "with the threat and reminder that if, in future, such roguery by him or anyone else was discovered they would die without mercy. . . ." Nothing more was heard of such conspiracies.

As we have already observed, the West Greenlanders' fear of foreigners stemmed partly from unpleasant experiences with the Dutch whalers and traders. It has already been said that the Dutch States-General were obliged to issue a decree on 18 November 1720, prohibiting attacks on and ill-treatment of the Greenland inhabitants. The Dutch whalers generally complied, or to be more exact they had no need of the decree's admonitions, but a few flouted it and continued to behave as they pleased. The Greenlanders knew these ones by name.

For instance, the ringleaders in the burning down of the houses in Nipisat in 1725 were old but mistrusted acquaintances of the Greenlanders. Six captains had been involved in the affair and four of them were known to the Greenlanders; of those, Hans Egede and Jacob Geelmuyden were able to identify two by their Dutch names. A few years before, one of them had shot two Greenlanders and it was perhaps he who had robbed the Greenlanders of two whales. Egede added in this connection, perhaps on his own account, that the Greenlanders often had to endure such injury from the foreign ships. Hans Egede reported as early as October 1721 that the neighbouring Greenlanders moved away, "for they do not yet trust us, they are seemingly very much afraid and jealous of their womenfolk and fear that we shall do them some harm". This fear for the women of the settlement may not have arisen solely from association with the Dutch, but may also be traceable to the memory of the three women kidnapped in 1654; it was said that relatives of the three women and people who had known them were still alive. The Danish–Norwegian Greenland navigators had not been blameless in this respect, but there were fewer incidents than with the Dutch. To the Greenlanders, however, there was no difference between Danish, Norwegian or Dutch.

But now the Danish–Norwegian Greenland navigators had drawn special attention to themselves by settling on the west coast of Greenland, which had not happened in Eskimo memory. The Dutch were there only during the spring and summer. Despite the risk involved in dealing with them, they were welcome, as they brought goods worth acquiring by barter. People travelled great distances to attend "the market" in Sydbay. In this way the Dutch Davis Strait traders had brought about a slight shift in the Eskimo economy, making it less self-sustaining than before. The "surplus production" had only been resorted to in a small degree, and for that reason there had been no significant break with the communal tradition. On the other hand, the journeys caused an upheaval in the hunting rotation, and the demand for fox and reindeer skins to some extent shifted the emphasis in hunting. Hence, some change in the material sector had already taken place in West Greenland's Eskimo culture, and this change implied a certain limited dependence on outside supplies.

The non-material side of the culture remained almost unaffected, except for some erosion of the *angákut*'s authority, due perhaps to their inability to protect the West Greenlanders from attack by foreigners. However, there is no concrete proof of changes in the spiritual culture caused by the seasonal commerce carried on by the Dutch.

From being of a seasonal nature for the Greenlanders, there were now signs of trading opportunities existing throughout the year, which had an immediate influence on the non-material culture. Remarkably quickly the powers of the *angákut* began to wane, the powers of the foreigners' *pelleste* apparently being greater. Furthermore, he spoke in almost incomprehensible words about things that were difficult to understand, and held mystical ceremonies with the other people in the group. On several occasions *angákut* had to yield to him. Even if what the *pelleste* said was sometimes incomprehensible, yet it sounded solemn, like the intonations of legend-tellers. The combined effect of these activities must have captured the Greenlanders' imagination early.

In his work, Hans Egede's patience was put to many severe tests. Besides the serious barrier of language, the Eskimo *fanger* culture also hindered his work. From the Eskimo point of view, his "perpetual reading and instruction" cut right across the Greenlanders' *fanger* activities, and this led to situations of acute conflict. The "indifference", described by Hans Egede and others as characteristic of the Greenlanders, was an outward sign of their resistance to the "reading and instruction". The concepts introduced by Hans Egede's words into the Eskimo world of the imagination were new and strange explanations of life and its mysteries. As Hans Egede's linguistic skill gradually improved, his stories assumed for the Greenlanders the stature of legends, even when concerned with the world beyond their sea. Pôq had the chance of seeing it, and his descriptions enabled the Greenlanders to understand the inconceivable. The way to that world apparently lay through the *pelleste*, but most of them had still to be content with accounts of it.

On the whole, despite chastisement, threats and angry speeches which inspired fear, Greenlanders were not directly wronged by Hans Egede or his companions. Once in a while, it did happen, but then an effort was made to discover who was guilty, and the injured party received compensation.

The original object of settling on the west coast of Greenland never left Hans Egede's mind. On his journeys into the fjords and southwards, he continually searched for traces of the Norsemen. So long as nobody succeeded in reaching the east coast, Egede and his contemporaries continued to believe that it would one day be possible to find the inhabitants of the Eastern Settlement alive and bring them "the light of the true gospel". Over the years, however, this hope must have worn thin, although the commitment to the goal remained alive. This commitment was transmitted by Hans Egede to the people he met on the west coast, whom, at least in 1723, he still regarded unhesitatingly as descendants of "the old Norsemen". They did not deny it when he said so to them.

Hans Egede's work was still in an embryonic stage when its financial basis collapsed during the winter of 1726–7.

REFERENCES

1. After describing the local population's mutual good relations, helpfulness and "affectionate sociability", and their friendliness towards himself and Aron, Hans Egede in his "Reports", MoG 54, p. 17, writes: "While it is gratifying to associate with them in such a way, it is insufferable because of the gross filthiness and stench of blubber and the like, which fills their huts to such an extent, that for one not accustomed to it living with them is rather hard."

2. Brandy was for a long time in north-west Greenlandic dialect called *silaerúnartoq*, i.e. "something which deprives you of your senses". In south-west Greenlandic there was another equally descriptive word, *kaujatdlak* i.e. "that by which you become unsteady or swinging". Now it is normally called by the Danish term *snaps* or *brændevin*, and sometimes *qaumassoq*, i.e. "that which shines white".

3. The Kook Islands are a group of skerries and smaller islands at the southern part of the mouth of Godthåb Fjord some hours' rowing from Haabets Øe.

4. As an example of how difficult it was just to perceive the pronunciation of the Greenlandic words, it can be mentioned here that Hans Egede heard the word for amulet, *ârnuaq*, as *angoach* (as he spells it, the *o* and the *a* pronounced separately, and the *ch* as in German), which according to "Otho Fabricius" vocabulary of 1804 is an interjection showing surprise and calling for attention.

6

1727 AUDIT AND COMMISSION

"The severe setbacks encountered by the *Dessein* during its second year, both by non-arrival of the ships and other adverse circumstances, undoubtedly caused the unexpected change which is seen to have taken place in the management of the venture during this year. . . . It is my heartfelt wish that Your Royal Majesty should take over the venture, as I feel that there is something wrong with the Company, which is due to their lack of agreement, half-heartedness and, at times, self-interest."

This harsh judgment was passed by Hans Egede on the directors, shareholders and activities of the Bergen Company. It was as though he caught an echo of the sounds which he had known all too well during 1719–21, and feared that his work in Greenland was about to end. He felt that he was still standing on the threshold – what a bitter blow if petty considerations of profit and the lack of financial resources were to cheat him of his goal. Hans Egede was therefore delighted and encouraged when ships were sent out on the King's orders and the Missionskollegium assured him in their letters that they were doing all they could with their feeble resources to further his work.

The opportunities open to the Missionskollegium were few and its influence was not great. It seems to have been consulted little in connection with the Greenland mission. The driving force lay in the *Danske Cancelli*, where Møinichen, the Chief Secretary, took up the matter much more energetically than his predecessor, Frederik Rostgaard. It is his name that appears at the foot of innumerable letters and memoranda in the next few years.

Since it was now the central administration in Copenhagen which, to an increasing extent, assumed the active management of Greenland affairs, other government offices gradually became involved. The *Danske Cancelli* naturally referred to them on special matters. This applied, of course, although not often, to the Missionskollegium and the *Rentekammer*, but when it came to the actual sailings, the General Commissariat of the Navy and the Admiralty (and later the General

Commissariat of the Army too) came into the picture, but at first all the threads were gathered together in the *Danske Cancelli*.

Out of this work grew a whole specialized organization to deal with the "Greenland *Dessein*", as the mission, the Trade and the sailings to Greenland gradually came to be called. This undertaking naturally called for an "inter-departmental" operation, the outcome of which was that, on 24 and 30 January 1729, the King directed a special commission to supervise the interests and business of the "Greenland *Dessein*".

When the central administration felt so strongly obliged to assume responsibility for the plan, the King became personally involved more actively than before, by virtue of the autocratic system. There was also a direct reason for this: the search for the Eastern Settlement was regarded as one of the main objects of the plan, and it was a cherished wish of those in power to bring the evangelical faith to the survivors, if any, in the Settlement. The King and the kingdoms were keenly conscious of a duty towards the Greenlanders, and so Hans Egede welcomed the Government's initiative, as can be seen from the passage in his letter quoted above. For him, as for Frederik IV, it was clearly the absolute monarch of Denmark–Norway who, in the tradition of the medieval Norwegian empire, had to take on the task – which appealed also to the Christian sense of duty of the King who, in these last years of his life, became extremely devout. There is no doubt that Hans Egede felt safe when he saw the King taking a direct part in the venture. He retained this confidence, although it wore thin.

When the King assumed responsibility for the various aspects of the undertaking, the planning for it had to be done close to him. In the first instance, however, it was important to attend to the most pressing matters, primarily the sailings and provisioning for 1727, and planning for the future had to be deferred. The Government showed its concern in several ways under the direction of Møinichen. First, a royal commissioner was to undertake an impartial investigation of the colony in Greenland, including possible further exploration. Secondly, local persons whose opinions could be taken seriously were asked to submit their views on the future organization and on the existing situation and experience so far gained. The commissioner's report and the statements of the local experts would be taken into account in future planning. Thirdly, the two-man commission was ordered on 10 January 1727, to investigate the circumstances of the Bergen Company, and submit proposals as to how the mission and trading were to be continued.

At the end of May *De jonge Maria*, carrying the commissioner, Christopher Jessen Pettersøn, reached Haabets Øe. In the harbour was Captain Berent Hansen Wegner who had spent the winter there with his ship the *Cron Printz Christian*. This vessel had already attempted to sail home in April, but because of the field-ice in the Davis Strait, the captain had had to return to Haabets Øe and wait until there was enough open water.

This had proved too much for Fridrich Henckell, one of the two barber-surgeons in the colony, who felt he was superfluous when necessity forced him to stay on when the new barber-surgeon arrived in 1726. He had wanted to return home at once "with the idea of acquainting the honorable directors with the present wretched state of ourselves and the work". The council felt that he must take full responsibility for doing so himself, but no one could see the point of his journey, for even if he reached Bergen that summer, no ships could be sent out. Henckell remained adamant and succeeded in getting on a hooker from Amsterdam.

This account shows how acute the situation was, but Hans Egede and the whole of the colony's "crew"[1] were spared the disgrace of a flight from Haabets Øe due to the arrival of *De jonge Maria*. It was a hectic time. Several meetings of the council were held, the stocks of provisions and merchandise had to be counted, and the various members of the council were to submit written statements in answer to the commissioner's questions. In a letter to Magnus Schiøtte dated 7 June 1727 the commissioner wrote: "There will be a great shortage of paper and sealing-wax in this country".

The commissioner did his work thoroughly; the many discussions throughout the whole of June and July were carefully minuted, and everything was scrupulously examined. We get, for example, a harrowing insight into the state of the buildings on Haabets Øe. Altogether there were seven buildings, some very inferior ones. The biggest was the dwelling-house erected in 1721. It had apparently not been altered over the years except inside, where "a small room in which the Rev. Albert Top resides had been partitioned off". The whole building still measured about 80 square metres, or 0·2 square metres per person. This did not leave much spare room. Hans Egede's study and the book-keeper's room were panelled with wood; the men's room was walled partly with brick and partly with rubble. The whole dwelling-house was covered outside by a wall of stone and turf. It was steep-roofed, with a loft above the rooms divided into three compartments. Half the roof was covered in with planks, the other half with laths and birch-bark.

The inventory of fixtures and fittings was Spartan in the extreme: five fixed bedsteads, three cupboards, a few fixed and a few loose benches, two small writing-desks, three tables, one of which belonged to Hans Egede. In the men's room there was a baking oven with "an open hearth before it". That was all. In addition, the occupants' personal possessions probably included no furniture apart from their chests in which they kept their personal belongings.

The floor was boarded throughout and there were fifteen "old windows". In a lean-to along the west side of the house a brewing copper had been walled in. At the north end there was a small store-room built of turf and stone.

In this house everyone had lived since 1721 and, according to the commissioner, it was in "such a condition that, though it may stand for a few more years, it is no longer serviceable". All the woodwork was rotten except for the loft and a few boards in the partitions. The house was built on a "bad boggy site . . . , so damp indeed that clothes hanging on the inside walls of the house rot. . . . This same house cannot be reckoned of any appreciable value. . . ."

The outhouses were in a somewhat better state. There was a ware-house built in 1722 to the same height as the dwelling-house (2·5 m), of brick and timber with a wooden lean-to along each of its long sides. Its wooden roof was weatherboarded. However, it was a very small warehouse of only some 66 cubic metres, so it could not hold the whole of the cargo from the *Haabet* which amounted to at least 100 reg. t. So in 1723 a larger warehouse was built, one long wall and one end wall being of brick and timber, the two other walls and both gables being wooden. Although this storeroom had a capacity of approxi-mately 115 cubic metres, even with the other it was still insufficient to take a whole ship's cargo, let alone store the produce due for trans-mission to Bergen.

Besides these there was a forge built of turf and stone, the amount of timber used being negligible so that the building was valueless. The cowshed was also built of turf and stone and a little wood: "just fit to shelter the cattle", the commissioner noted. The sixth building was described as "a small cabin" for general use, and later as a "privy"; it could not be assessed at any value. Seventh and last, there was "a little timber house that came here from Bergen in 1723", used perhaps as a workshop or store-room. It represented a value of 16 rigsdaler.

All these buildings were valued by the director, Jens Anderson Refdahl, at 400 rdl. in the general accounts on 22 February 1726. That was probably an over-estimation. Of the warehouses, one was "passable" and some of the materials could be re-used in the event of removal. The other was in good condition, and if that were moved too, most of the materials could be used again.

With the same thoroughness the commissioner set to work on the stocks of goods. It is remarkable that, with the extremely unfavourable storage conditions, Jacob Geelmuyden was able to report that only some 8 per cent of the stock of corn was "spoilt and quite inedible, and being used for the animals".

While this was happening on Haabets Øe, the assistant, Matthias Fersleff, and Captain Ebbe Mitzell had sailed northwards with *De jonge Maria* to explore. Within six days they reached Disko, landing at Skansen (so called by the Dutch), where they examined the coal deposit, and made an optimistic estimate of it. They also learned from the Greenlanders that there was more coal on the island's west coast, but did not investigate these deposits. They first travelled on to Rodebay, which Fersleff did not find suitable for settlement, and thence to Sandbay (south of the present-day Claushavn outpost), but found nowhere suitable for establishing a colony. They also travelled a little way north to the Jakobshavn ice-fjord, which impressed them as deeply as it has everyone who has seen at close quarters this glacier fjord, the biggest source of icebergs in Greenland. The last place they inspected was "Wiere Bay" where the colony of Christianshåb was later established. Fersleff gave a favourable description of the conditions there and, as regards the possibilities of access by sea, Mitzell was equally enthusiastic. Fersleff concluded his report by passing on what he had heard from the Greenlanders in the Bugt about the foreign whalers' treatment of its inhabitants. Both Fersleff's and Mitzell's reports were links in the series of expert opinions which the commissioner, Christopher Jessen Pettersøn, was collecting to lay before the two-man commission in Christiania and the *Danske Cancelli*.

All these experts judged the conditions in the same way, made more or less the same suggestions and presented a uniform, and equally brief, appraisal of the Greenlanders. Of course, Albert Top and Hans Egede were more concerned with the requirements of the mission and the possibilities of a thoroughgoing missionary effort than were Geelmuyden, Fersleff and (later) the barber-surgeon Fridrich Henckell. This uniformity of view is at least partly due to the endless discussions of conditions, requirements and possibilities that had taken place throughout the winter. Thus, the complaints of those concerned more or less consciously merged into a "higher unity", which each individual, through endless repetition, adopted as his own. Hans Egede's views set the tone, and his detailed answers to the commissioner's numerous questions were the most comprehensive. The other respondents then added individual contributions on matters of detail without departing from the general view.

Hans Egede admitted in his first statement that his previous proposal (June 1725) would not meet the case, but thought that there was hope of being able to maintain three colonies: the two southern ones (on latitude 60°–61° N. at Qaqortoq and on 64° N. near Haabets Øe

H

respectively) by trading alone, while the northern one (at Nipisat or at Rifkol on 67°–68° N.) could also be supported by whaling. He still estimated the expenses at about 2,000 rigsdaler per colony and believed that the two southern colonies would break even whilst the third would make a good profit.

He returned, however, to the idea he had formulated before in the almost stereotyped words: "If it were only a question of things temporal, establishment of the third colony would be enough. But since the main purpose in starting this whole venture was the glory of God and the enlightenment of these poor people, then it will be necessary to take steps to achieve this." He reverts to the method illustrated earlier – of subjecting the Greenlanders to "the yoke and discipline" and that they should be "governed by certain rules and laws". He still thought, moreover, that providing many places with pastors and catechists would enable the Greenlanders to be kept under proper surveillance, so that what they had learned would not be wasted. He outlined the plan which, to a large extent, was later adopted – "whereby each place at which there is a large gathering of the savages must have its catechist, for they live together here and there in large groups". The essence of his plan was to seek out the Greenlanders wherever they were, but its execution required manpower, not least catechists, who "must be taken from their own people . . . since they are best able to live among and deal with their own fellow-countrymen" under the missionaries' supervision. That is why he wanted seminaries established at each colony, where selected ten- to twelve-year-olds would be trained. As a transitional arrangement, he suggested that a few young Norwegians or Danes of poor parents be trained and sent out to work as catechists. This virtually decided the future operational policy of the royal mission. In addition, he suggested that chapels and small churches be built of local materials (stone and turf) and that the missionaries at the colonies should be provided with a serviceable boat and a crew. Over the years, Hans Egede had had ample experience of how dependence on the Trading Company's boats restricted his activities. They were always out on an expedition, collecting fuel or hunting, and their needs did not always coincide with his. This dependence on the Trading Company was later to bring the two institutions into conflict, heightened by the confined local conditions.

Putting Hans Egede's plans into effect would naturally involve expense, and he wrote that it was not certain that the trade which might result from the three colonies would cover it. As a further damper on over-elaborate planning, he continued by highlighting the fundamental problem in all trading activities: "They can do very well without the majority of our wares. . . ." Besides, the Greenlanders were "by both our own people and others being continually overwhelmed and supplied with many articles." Thus "they do not specially exert themselves to acquire anything except what they must have to sustain life". Hans Egede knew of no other way to obtain finance than the Greenlanders themselves "having to contribute some trifle for their own good". This could only be done by imposing some tax on them, and he was convinced the Greenlanders could afford to pay it. To achieve this, however, "these savages must be completely subjugated and made into slaves – and if not quite slaves" they must be subjected to correction and discipline.

Here again the expression used scarcely seems fitting for a missionary pastor, even allowing for the spirit of the age. In an autocratically governed society, submission to a ruling authority was the subject's duty. Hans Egede was, however, aware of the grim significance of the word "slave" and as the Greenlanders had not committed any direct crime, he toned down his statement soon afterwards.[2]

As for other practical arrangements for the future, the missionary Albert Top and the trader Jacob Geelmuyden both shared Hans Egede's enthusiasm for reviving the Nipisat experiment, as both thought that whaling could be carried on there profitably. Geelmuyden was also in favour of a colony being established to the south of Haabets Øe.

The assistant Matthias Fersleff, who had been on the expedition to explore the Disko Bugt, suggested that four colonies should be established. Besides the three already mentioned, one was also to be founded on latitude 68° or 69° N. It would thus be possible to cover the whole Bugt where the Dutch went whaling and trading. Since this decision resulted from his journey, it was obviously in his mind that the colony should be located in Wiere Bay. Only when the country was well covered with colonies would it be possible to levy the "tax" or contribution which he favoured. Fersleff's and Mitzell's report on their journey led Hans Egede to submit a supplementary opinion, to which Jacob Geelmuyden gave his written support. Both favoured a colony being established on the site suggested by Fersleff, thus increasing the number to four new settlements. Nipisat would have to be rebuilt and the colony on Haabets Øe moved.

During the preceding years Hans Egede had often expressed his wish that the colony should be transferred. Various places had been suggested and carefully examined, but attention was finally concentrated on the headland at the mouth of the big fjord system due east of Haaberts Øe. Everything there seemed suitable, as regards both hunting and fishing. It was also well situated for making visits to the Greenlanders who lived by the fjords. Yet the sole possible harbourage lay far from the best site for the colony's buildings, although a warehouse could probably be erected near the good harbour. According to Mitzell's report, there were a few "savages' houses" on the headland where they were thinking of building. Later this site became known as the worst imaginable place for hunting; however, a number of Greenlanders found it suitable.

On 2 August the commissioner, Christopher Jessen Pettersøn, closed his records, and the next day *De jonge Maria* put to sea. There were left on Haabets Øe "eleven men – apart from officers, of which there were nine, including the Reverend Hans Egede's family. In addition six Greenlanders also live with us in the house." Thus twenty-six persons were to spend yet another winter in the wretched house on the island, Egede and his family representing six of the nine "officers". The remaining three were Geelmuyden, the barber-surgeon Chr. Kieding and the assistant Jørgen Kopper. Matthias Fersleff and Albert Top had left.

Meanwhile Magnus Schiøtte had been active. Immediately after the arrival of the *Cron Printz Christian* he sent an account of the trade with Greenland to date to the Commission in Christiania and at the same time submitted a proposal backed by calculations of the potential earnings from whaling. His figures were not wholly convincing, and, perhaps to compensate for this, he assured them in conclusion: "If I had the means and resources, I would pursue this, my well-meant proposal, at my own risk."

The Commission in Christiania composed of Bishop Deichman and Vibe, the Vicegerent, arranged a series of hearings and received documents from persons who had been connected in any way with the Bergen Company. Because of this the proceedings were long drawn out and the Commission had to wait for the reports to come from Greenland. Magnus Schiøtte, who had been instructed to submit proposals for the continuation of the Trading Company, had to apply for an extension of time on the same grounds, for his calculations depended on the quantities of Greenland produce sent home and on these reports. However, Christopher Jessen Pettersøn seems to have been reluctant to make the reports available to him.

The Commission finally issued its comprehensive report on 22 November 1727. After many hearings and the perusal of accounts, reports, accusatory statements, counter-statements and amendments, the Commission reached the following decision:

Some of the directors of the Bergen Company had acknowledged that, by making various purchases during 1722 and the years immediately following, they had incurred a debt, which had been paid by drawing on the lottery fund without authority. The fact that the transactions had been among the directors themselves and between the management and individual shareholders was unflattering to them and bordered on improper administration. Refdahl had pointed out in vain that he and Van der Lippe had acted in good faith and that the purchases and expenditure involved had been necessary to keep "the work" going. But this was not accepted as grounds for a breach of the terms of the royal licence for the lottery, even though this did not stand out as clearly as in the letter of command concerning the "bounty", with which liberties had also been taken for the sake of "the work". Therefore the directors, shareholders and inspectors must be held liable for the sums drawn out irregularly, which, according to the audited accounts, amounted to 13,356 rdl. of the lottery fund (repayable within one year) and 10,917 rdl. of the "bounty" (repayable in three years). The latter sum was reduced to 3,662 rdl., since the Company's effects provided cover for the amount of the reduction. The Company's assets amounted to 36,589 rdl., which should have been more than adequate cover for the amounts which had to be repaid. But most of the assets were tied up in equipment and effects which, although having a "book value", were not realizable except at a loss. And if these effects were realized, there would be no means of continuing the Greenland trade and new things would have to be procured.

It therefore rested primarily with the directors and shareholders to repay the amounts indicated. If the shareholders could not do so, it would then devolve on Undal, the Governor, and Bishop Müller – Krog and Tanche having spoken out in time. Of the shareholders Hans Egede alone was exempted; as one of those who had invested most heavily in the Company, he would be liable for 1,420 rdl., but he had "been absent in Greenland in the service of the mission and the Company and, as he had not attended any of the directors' meetings, he could know little of and far less agree to what took place there or was decided by them and the other shareholders".

When they reduced the sum to be repaid, the Commission expressed its hope that the shareholders would set to and continue the work, for if they did not, the reduction would not be made. It quickly became apparent that none of the shareholders except Magnus Schiøtte wanted anything more to do with "the Greenland business", and he too did not want to be a partner.

Although the Commission's decision on the question of culpability was final, the matter was not thereby put right. During the next few years there were continual tugs-of-war over the accounts, expenditure and collection of debts – in particular settlement for the produce purchased in Greenland between 1725 and 1727, which belonged by right to the Bergen Company. Magnus Schiøtte was scrupulous that the transactions should be kept separate and that the Bergen Company received exactly its due, no more or less. Settlement of the affairs dragged on and was only completed in the mid-1740s, when Van der Lippe was the only director still alive. It had been impossible to pay out the lottery prizes because of lack of funds and because the list of winners had disappeared many years previously without trace. It was found by chance in 1744, when many of the winners were dead.

The Commission's second task as regards the basic material was far easier to tackle, although its evaluation and formulation of the final scheme for continuation of the work were difficult. It emerges clearly that both the Vicegerent and the bishop felt themselves incompetent to cope with the task at all. However, they were bound by their terms of reference to put forward such a scheme at the end of their report. Their scheme was, of course, founded partly on the experience gained from 1721 to 1727, partly on the reports sent from Greenland over the years and on Christopher Jessen Pettersøn's report; in addition, there was the plan put forward by the former barber-surgeon and trader, Berenhart, and finally the expert opinion of barber-surgeon Fridrich Henckell, submitted on his arrival in Bergen. The two members of the Commission viewed with scepticism these many reports and opinions from people who had been or were still in Greenland. They rejected Berenhart's proposal because he had a personal interest in the establishment of a colony in Disko Bay, since he would then have been in charge of trading in Greenland. However, he had since died.

Nor did they completely trust Hans Egede's proposal and opinion because he "by all kinds of persuasive arguments strives to see preserved and continued what he began . . .", yet they did not want to reject out of hand the proposals made by Hans Egede and the others, especially Albert Top, since he could be considered "completely disinterested . . . and all the more trustworthy since he relies on the evidence of his own eyes". Apart from Disko Bay and the regions north of Nipisat, it could not be denied that Hans Egede's local knowledge was good; nevertheless, greater importance was attached to Top's and Captain Ebbe Mitzell's reports.

The essence of the recommendations of Ermandinger and Schnell was that "the Mission and the Trading Company with God's help and blessing [can] certainly go on through sensible management, grow and increase daily if the work is continued with somewhat greater financial resources than has been the case over the last three years. . . ." It was quite clear to them what had hindered the Bergen Company and they stressed that nothing would come of the work if only one colony were to be maintained and the financing of both that and the Mission were based solely on the income from the "bounty". They suggested that Haabets Øe should become a station only because, as a colony, it had been in a district where hunting was poor. A new colony was to be set up at Nipisat on latitude 68° or 69° N.

When proposals brought to Bergen on *De jonge Maria* were read by Ermandinger and Schnell, the latter altered their own previous proposals in line with them, and now recommended that four colonies be established, including that transferred from Haabets Øe. In an estimate of the cost of establishing and operating these four colonies from 1728–31, they arrived at a sum of 60,632 rdl.

The Christiania Commission, introducing its final conclusions, examined the idea of moving the colony from Haabets Øe to Nûk, but expressed astonishment that the colony had been established on such an unsuitable site in the first place. The Commission was even more surprised that after so many years a better place had only now been found for siting the colony, only 11·5 km. from Haabets Øe, "which is sufficient evidence of the imprudence with which everything has been conducted to date and that the Rev. Hans Egede may well be a good pastor but is not a very provident householder. . . ." Deichman and Vibe here revealed their ignorance of conditions in Greenland and based their judgment of Hans Egede on a false assumption. As we have already seen, Hans Egede had stated unequivocally that the colony must be moved, and had gone exploring for a better place in the region. The Commission concluded, after these somewhat inaccurate remarks, that it would not pay to operate the colony on Haabets Øe any longer, but there would be neither time nor money in 1728 for anything other than the transfer of this colony.

The result of the Commission's distrust of the opinions received from Greenland was that they did not venture to suggest the immediate foundation of any more colonies. If the three new colonies were to be established at once, it would swallow up most of the capital (sums received through the "bounty"). The residue would not then be enough to pay for the operation of either the mission or the Trading Company. The Commission saw clearly that the cost of "the whole work" was increased by the interdependence of mission and the Trading Company which made the trade less profitable for the citizens of Bergen than, say, for the Dutch who had no trading and mission stations to maintain.

On the other hand, the Commission could not deny that the arguments put forward in the various opinions favouring the establishment of more colonies were weighty ones. It added a typical mercantilistic argument, that if the settlements were established and conducted successfully, "then God would gain many sons and Your Majesty's crown would acquire a future useful province and thus God's kingdom would have souls added to it and Your Majesty's kingdom subjects, to which the risk of one or two years of the expenses estimated cannot be compared, especially as the capital which has been given and allotted to this plan is there". It would, moreover, create "despondency" in the King's realms and territories, quite apart from "gratuitous judgments by other nations" if "a work begun both to the glory of God and the country's profit were to be either abandoned or carried on half-heartedly without attempting to see what more could be done in the matter". On the basis of the report of Ermandinger and Schnell, the Commission believed that the income from the 42,000 rdl. would be insufficient to pay the future expenses of the one colony, and that the capital would still have to be broken into.

The Commission thus favoured continuation and expansion on a trial basis, first by moving the colony on Haabets Øe in 1728 and then, in 1729–31, by rebuilding and extending Nipisat and also establishing another whaling station on latitude 69°. But it was not in favour of a fourth colony, partly because it would absorb too much capital, and partly for reasons of foreign policy. Development that was too vigorous would attract attention; other nations might awaken to the profitability of sailings to Greenland, and it was conceivable that the Dutch would strongly oppose the expansion "before the Company could stop them". They had already once burnt down the settlement at Nipisat.

At the same time an "active population policy" was suggested which, again for reasons of foreign policy, needed to be carried out slowly. The Commission dared not support the old desire for a ban on Dutch trading, and indeed they considered such a ban futile until "the Company was capable of preventing such things itself with armed vessels and manpower". If, on the other hand, arrangements were made for Norwegians to settle in Greenland "in some number", and if "some kind of fortification" were set up and the Company obtained at least a few armed sloops – and finally if the King were to set up an authority based in Greenland, only then would it be time to think of banning all foreign trading in and sailings to the country. The establishment of more colonies than the three would be quite beyond the Company's financial and administrative resources.

So Hans Egede's idea of setting up an authority in the country was in a way adopted, but on a quite different basis and at a different pace from what he had visualized. The Commission's motive for this appears to have been its concern about other countries – Denmark–Norway could not risk involvement in any external quarrel owing to a perilous financial situation at home. Also, when making its proposals, the Commission had always to regard the Royal Command of 16 March 1725 as being still valid, making only the revenues from the bounty available for future operations. This was also a reason why the Commission was actuated throughout by the belief that the Bergen Company would continue its activities in one way or another. This advice had already been given – for different reasons – by Ermandinger and Schnell in their report of September 1727.[3]

REFERENCES

1. The personnel of the colony on Haabets Øe was actually called "the crew" because the colony was organized as a ship; but instead of a captain and his officers, the "crew" was commanded by a missionary, a trader and their assistants, all of them called "officers", and this "group-title" was commonly used for the next 150 years. The members of the "crew" were called *matroser*, sailors, or *gemeene*, common men, which was in use until about 1800.
2. It is not likely that Hans Egede knew anything about the previous "Spanish discussion" – the so-called "Discussion of Valladolid" about the enslaving of the savages in Spanish America. Vídalín in his handwritten proposals about Greenland (1703) repudiated the Spanish methods and had something to say about the Valladolid discussion, which he partly misunderstood. As mentioned above, Hans Egede might have read his manuscript; he had never before this time used the words "slave", "enslaving" or "slavery". The conclusion from this and from his own "discussion" of the matter can only be that his concept of the "terms" was vague. From his treatment of the matter emerges an equally vague dislike of what it stood for.
3. They feared that the directors of the Bergen Company and the shareholders, if they were to repay from their private funds the illicitly drawn amount of 24,263 rdl. 2 sk., should feel themselves compelled to abandon the Company and sell equipment, ships and houses to cover the debt. They therefore proposed that a quite new board of directors be appointed and a more rational procedure in conducting the Company's affairs. What they feared perhaps really happened in 1728 when Refdahl and v. der Lippe managed to sell the Company's house in Bugården, in spite of that being among the Company's few assets.

7

THE ROYAL GREENLAND *DESSEIN*
1727–1728

The view formed by the Christiania Commission of the Bergen Company's position proved to be false. Perhaps it thought that a royal order to the Company's shareholders would ensure instant obedience and an undertaking to continue the "godly and Christian work". But the Government was unwilling to go that far. As the surviving directors of the Bergen Company and the shareholders living in Bergen had no intention of carrying on, the Commission's idea was foredoomed to failure. As for sailings in the coming year, there was only Magnus Schiøtte to turn to.

Vibe and Bishop Deichman must have appreciated the likelihood that the directors of the Bergen Company would be as reluctant to do anything about the 1728 sailings as they had been about those of 1727. In their capacity as Commission members, Vibe and Deichman asked Møinichen, the Chief Secretary, in October 1727 whether they should submit their report before the 1728 sailings had been arranged or whether these should be postponed until it could be seen from the Commission's report what was going to be done in this direction.

In mid-August 1727, Magnus Schiøtte had already pointed out to Vibe and Bishop Deichman that it was time to plan both the following year's expedition and the purchase and production of the merchandise to be "sold" in Greenland. The blades used for the women's knives (*ulos*) were made in Bergen. But, not satisfied with that, he also pressed for a decision concerning the future management of the Company. He had only received orders to superintend the sailings and shipment of supplies for 1727, and he therefore requested the Commission to obtain the necessary royal instructions and so "take care of the work abandoned by the directors and shareholders".

The enquiry made by the Christiania Commission was exactly one post too late. Magnus Schiøtte had kept up a correspondence with Møinichen, from whom he received a royal order, dated two days after the date of the Commission's enquiry, informing him that his "good and correct conduct in connection with the Bergen–Greenland Company's affairs hitherto" had met with approval at a high level. It was therefore decided that Schiøtte should be made a director of the Company and look for a co-director himself, the King reserving the right to choose the third director. Only three directors were wanted "to avoid all long-windedness and all kinds of arguments which always obstruct enterprises dependent on commerce and prompt despatch".

This letter, in fact, anticipated the proposal from Ermandinger and Schnell that the Bergen Company should be "reconstituted"; it was expected that the sailings and trading would be directed from Bergen by the Bergen Company. In practice, it no longer existed, as the directors had resigned from office and the shareholders had not appointed a new board, but it still had a legal status, which had to be maintained, as the circumstances of the Company were still being investigated by the Christiania Commission. In reality, the royal order to Schiøtte meant that he was being instructed from the highest level outside the Bergen Company to ensure continuation of trading and sailings in the coming years. However, the document did not specifically instruct him to arrange the sailings or allocate the capital necessary for this purpose. Therefore nothing was done about preparations for the following year's operations.

Because the Bergen Company still existed *de jure*, the inspectors were unable to give up their work. They reminded the Municipal authorities to account for the allocation of the "bounty" funds and explain why they could not be invested if funds were still available. There were apparently many who wanted to obtain shares in the form of cash loans. This was symptomatic of the scarcity of capital, and especially of liquid resources, in the commercial and industrial sector in Denmark–Norway early in the eighteenth century. The shortage of liquid assets was felt most strongly whenever it came to settling up with the ships and paying off the crews. Perhaps the Bergen Company and its immediate successors were particularly sensitive to this liquidity problem, probably due mainly to the stringent regime of the state-controlled economy. Also, such small quantities of Greenland produce had been brought back over the years that the revenue did not remotely cover expenditure. In this respect 1727 was no different from previous years.

Berent Hansen Wegner had brought back on the *Cron Printz Christian* 48 *cordeler*, 28 barrels of blubber, 5 barrels of spermaceti, 58 reindeer skins, 3 narwhal tusks, 64 whalebones, 852 seal skins and 508 fox skins – which fetched 1,693 rdl., 5 mrk., 2 sk. at auction. Most of this belonged to the Bergen Company, since it represented the shipment which should have arrived in 1726. The price received for the whale oil refined from the blubber was 8–9 rigsdaler per barrel. This price appeared higher than previously, but monetary devaluation had taken place in 1726–7.

Apart from the cargo of the *Cron Printz Christian*, which was the first to arrive, two other shipments were brought back which together amounted to 74 *cordeler*, 15 hogsheads and 13 barrels of blubber refined to produce oil, however, only 6 barrels of oil were sold at 8¼ rdl., the rest being held back because of insufficient bids. Neither were all the skins sold. There were a further 447 seal skins, 98 reindeer skins, 91 fox skins and 31 small white seal skins (probably of unborn seals) besides 20 whalebones and 1 narwhal tusk in one shipment. The total proceeds were 352 rdl., 1 mrk., 14 sk., many of the articles being withdrawn from the auction.

Once again it was the late arrival in Greenland that was responsible for the poor trade done. After Ebbe Mitzell and Matthias Fersleff had sailed round Disko Bugt trading, they had only procured 6 *cordeler* of blubber and very few whalebones, reindeer skins and seal skins. The rest of the shipment brought back by Mitzell was mostly purchased around Haabets Øe. With the small craft and methods in use, there was no chance of achieving big results.

Even by January 1728 the whale oil held back (about 160 barrels) was still not sold. It does not appear to have been disposed of until February–April, together with other Greenlandic produce and various types of provisions which could not be sent to Greenland because they had been in stock too long. The net proceeds of this sale were 1,641 rdl., 2 mark., 1½ sk. This involved and lengthy process seems to have been common: to obtain anything like a reasonable price, goods had to be held back until the demand rose, so limited was the market.

The question of sailings and provisioning for the next year was becoming urgent. At the close of 1727 neither the Christiania Commission nor Magnus Schiøtte had received orders to make the necessary arrangements; however, Schiøtte had made some preparations, which he communicated with some caution to Møinichen, the Chief Secretary, only in January 1728. On 16 January the Chief Secretary passed to Schiøtte the royal order concerning the 1728 sailings. The preamble to this letter gives some explanation as to why no instructions had been given earlier, and indeed, it conveys some dissatisfaction with the proposals put forward by the Christiania Commission. Obviously they had been waiting for the Commission's proposals before issuing instructions for the 1728 sailings, and when these did arrive – probably not until December – they were so far-reaching as to require careful consideration before an order-in-council could be expected. The need to act before having thought out how to do so may have accounted for Møinichen's invitation.

First of all the Government resolved on the inevitable; to issue orders for the despatch of supplies to the colony for the coming year 1728–9. However, presumably on the basis of concurring reports from those with direct experience of conditions in Greenland, they felt able to risk an experiment with whaling "on which many other nations make a handsome profit". Anything else would have to wait until it had been more carefully considered.[1] Schiøtte therefore received instructions to fit out two ships with provisions and merchandise for "the *colonies* in that country". Meanwhile, the two ships were also to be fitted out with whaling gear, which the crews had to be reasonably skilled in using. A voucher for the cash to pay the expenses would be given when Schiøtte's estimate of the revenue from the sale of produce brought back in 1727 was received.

In one of the letters from Møinichen, a new element was added to the preparations. Three or four horses were to be sent with the two vessels from Bergen to see whether they could survive. Besides, Schiøtte was supposed to find "a few stout-hearted persons ambitious for the King's glory who might be called foolhardy but are not". They were to undertake an exploratory expedition into the interior for some days. There was apparently some idea in the *Cancelli* of reaching the east coast by land, perhaps the first signs of the plan later carried out, but perhaps only further exploration of the west coast was envisaged with a view to establishing more colonies. The Christiania Commission had clearly indicated its lack of confidence in the abilities as explorers of those living in Greenland.

While he made preparations, Schiøtte asked the Bergen Company inspectors for money from the funds available; he claimed to have advanced some of his own, adding that he could not go on doing so. The inspectors, for their part, demanded the accounts for 1726–7, which they duly received but could not approve.

At about this time the designation "the Greenland *Dessein*" began to come into use, probably to distinguish the current sailings, trade and mission from the Bergen Company.[2]

Schiøtte had found it difficult to get hold of vessels that were also suited to whaling. The Bergen Company's *Fridericus Quartus* was declared unfit after a survey, since she would first have to undergo lengthy and costly repairs. It was impossible to charter other vessels – the ships he had selected were either chartered already or else the captains did not want to sail on charter to "the Greenland *Dessein*". The only vessel available was the *Cron Printz Christian*; Schiøtte had her refitted and loaded so quickly that she was able to sail on 12 March, and he finally succeeded in chartering the other ship required, which sailed at the end of April. Thus the idea of starting whaling, even modestly, had to be abandoned, at least for 1728.

In March Møinichen was able to give Schiøtte fresh orders partly based on a changed situation. He was authorized to assure Schiøtte that the transactions he had carried out were approved by the King. However, there were plans to send an armed vessel to Greenland to gain proper information about the nature of the country; it would be despatched from Copenhagen but would call at Bergen. Schiøtte must therefore arrange for two experienced mates and ten or twelve men "with sailing experience and a knowledge of these waters to man this vessel. . . .", and provisions amounting to one year's supplies for thirty to forty men were to be taken on, as the vessel was to spend the winter there so enabling the crew to explore the country. For this purpose two or three "of the type of boats used in Sundmøre" were to be purchased, their timbers being cut to shape and packed unassembled; assembly would take place in Greenland.

The pilot-galliot *West Vlieland* was to undertake this expedition. But the plans went further still. Almost as if to justify the Christiania Commission having advised against a ban on foreign trading, the report of Deichman and Vibe enumerated certain important prerequisites for such a ban to be issued. There was no properly appointed authority in Greenland and no "fortification", and it would be expedient to introduce some Norwegian settlers. It is inconceivable, however, that they intended these remarks to be acted upon immediately. However, the plans worked out in Copenhagen must have been inspired by the remarks, coupled with the impressions obtained from the statements or letters of Hans Egede, Geelmuyden and Albert Top. The desire to establish a governing authority emerged strongly from these documents.

The plan appears to have been concerned at first with the idea of settlement. The unfortunate idea, based on mercantilistic practice, was put forward of sending a number of convicts to Greenland.[3] It was therefore decided to send a further vessel, the royal merchantman *Morianen*, out from Copenhagen.

The General Commissariat of the Navy and the Admiralty had now been actively drawn into both the planning and execution of the plans. Møinichen and the two services suggested in April that the post of governor should be created in Greenland – to be occupied by an expert in naval matters. It was further suggested that a fort be built, in the form of a battery with the appropriate ordnance and ammunition, manpower, equipment and provisions, together with transport. Relative royal decrees were issued shortly afterwards. The fort was required to be "a sort of fortress surrounded by a moat", to be built in Greenland.

The King's preference for the governorship was given to a retired major, Claus En(e)vold Pårs, forty-five years of age, who, since leaving the army in 1722, had been living quietly in retirement on his large freehold farm in Vendsyssel. How this man was selected, or what his qualifications were, is a mystery. There was some sense in the Admiralty's suggestions of a governor being a naval expert, and a competent naval officer was available for nomination. The future was to show the unsuitability of Pårs for his post. As commandant of the proposed fort, the King appointed a twenty-nine-year-old first lieutenant, Jørgen Landorph, who was gazetted as captain of infantry. Twenty soldiers, all volunteers, were to man it. A military engineer and three sergeants, together with a master gunner and an assistant gunner were ordered out.

The idea of sending out convicts was also pursued further, though the number was reduced. Twelve military convicts detained in the *kastell* (castle) for both major and minor offences were to be released. Simultaneously the director of the Board of Guardians of the Poor was instructed to select ten women, "the youngest, healthiest and strongest", detained in the *Børnehuuset* (prison for vagrants, thieves and especially loose women) who, together with two others "already condemned to Greenland" were to be "mated" with the twelve freed convicts. The couples were to be formed by drawing lots. Poul Egede relates a touching story about this mass wedding which took place in the garrison church of Copenhagen. Two of those selected "who without drawing lots were intended for each other", found each other by the man drawing the slip with the name of his betrothed on it. Their crime was that the woman, having been given permission to visit her intended husband freely while he was imprisoned in Kronborg had once changed clothes with him; he then escaped, but was caught and put in the Kastell, she being detained in the *Børnehuuset*. "These two lived decently together and they alone of that rabble returned to Copenhagen."

It took three shiploads to transport all the people and their possessions, provisions, ammunition and building materials together with eleven horses. Pårs was presented with a mount by the King. The three or four horses which Schiøtte had been ordered to hold ready for shipment were thus abandoned in favour of the horses from Denmark. The latter were slung in girths, which chafed them badly during the sea-passage, and only six of the eleven reached their destination alive.

This motley convoy got under way during April and May, two of the vessels arriving in June. The *Morianen* with Pårs on board reached Haabets Øe on 1 July. The arrival of this vessel did not take Hans Egede and the other inhabitants of the colony by surprise, but he was surely impressed by this sudden royal intervention after the State's previous inaction. Writing to Magnus Schiøtte, he praised the initiative but at the same time expressed his concern: "May God in His grace show ways and means whereby the heavy expenses most graciously incurred might be recouped, which is not at all to be expected for the coming year, since all the arrangements made must be suspended for the winter where there is but little to be gained". He saw clearly that they must concentrate on moving the colony on Haabets Øe to the site singled out the year before. There were insufficient resources, men or building materials to re-establish the colony in the north and go whaling "which with the Lord's blessing might have profited the *Dessein*. . . . indeed, it is wholly to the advantage of the *Dessein* for the colony of Nepisene to be resumed and equipped with whaling gear and competent people, likewise Disko Bay in accordance with the suggestion I have most humbly made; if this is not done, then all other expenditure is futile and in vain".

In order not to waste the short summer, Hans Egede and the colony's council had already started building work on the north-facing coast of the headland, on the cape east of Haabets Øe. They had thus anticipated the decisions taken in Copenhagen. By 3 July the new council had met to discuss the transfer of the colony.

The composition of the new council was laid down in the instructions bearing the royal signature which Governor Pårs had received. The Governor was to preside over the council, and next below was the commandant of the proposed fort, Captain Jørgen Landorph. Third place was allotted to Hans Egede, which did not imply a down-grading, as he himself had wished to be freed of the administrative burden of dealing with practical problems not directly concerned with the mission.

The new council was bound to regard its most immediate task as that of viewing the new site for the colony. The journey of inspection took place on 4 and 5 July, when Captain Didrik Myhlenphort, commanding the *Morianen*, immediately observed that the harbour lay nearly 2 km. from where building had already been started. He could have wished for a better site, but as none had been found, it was preferable to carry on with the building. The place was not suitable for a fort but, on the other hand, a battery might be appropriate.

Nothing was to be gained by discussing this problem, so building proceeded. In addition to materials like stone and turf collected on the site, others had to be brought from elsewhere. Any serviceable timber from the former colony house had to be used, which meant pulling the house down over the heads of its occupants.

It was the wettest summer yet experienced anywhere in the region, and the rain was often driven through everything by a south-westerly gale. At first many of the people were quartered on the ships, but this was impractical for the builders, as the vessels were to be used for carrying building materials, and had to lie in the distant harbour, which was named "Danish Admiralty Harbour". By the beginning of August their tents were already so battered that new ones had to be improvised out of old sails from the *Cron Printz Christian*.

When the *Morianen* left for Copenhagen on 10 August, conditions worsened. The Governor himself had to take up residence in a Greenlander's abandoned hut which was roofed in for him, while most of his possessions had to stand out in the open. Provisions too were exposed to wind and weather and inevitably they were spoiled.

The materials, furthermore, proved inadequate, so that it was impossible to build accommodation for all the people who had to spend the winter there. It was therefore decided to keep the *Cron Printz Christian* to accommodate those for whom there was no room and partly for storage of property. Some goods were stored in one of the warehouses on Haabets Øe.

The bad weather continued. Brewing and baking had to be done and this led to a dispute. Pårs, as a soldier, wanted everything done in military fashion. Every so often he held an inspection, which irritated the paymaster and other "officers". Thus began the endless series of "trials" which Pårs launched.

Soldiers, convicts and the men of the former colony endured appalling conditions. Disease was added to the other hardships; at the beginning of August eight of them were sick. Once it rained for five days and nights on end and no bedding was left dry. Discontent spread, not least among the freed convicts. Only a fleeting warmth could be derived from the brandy ration. It was known that the house being built was intended for the "officers" only; a house for the men had not even been started. When work finally did start on it, there was no prospect of its being finished before the winter.

Under such conditions it seemed ironical to call the new colony Godthåb ("good hope"). On 29 August Hans Egede preached his first sermon at Nûk, the headland where the colony was situated, and his theme was the new name. For once, clear weather was reported with a wind from the south, veering south-east. After the service, dinner for the officers was served in the Governor's "house"; and after the dinner squalls and drizzle set in again.

In September sufficient progress had been made with the house for Pårs to move in. Now the old dwelling on Haabets Øe was demolished so that Hans Egede, his family and the others who were still living there had to move into the warehouse which was left standing.

I

Egede would not impose this on his family as a long-term measure, so he moved on 30 September into the still unfinished house at Godthåb where the walls had not had the chance to dry out properly due to the damp. There are no contemporary descriptions of this house, the outer walls of which still form the main components of "Godthåb's oldest house". Its foundations were of rough stone and clay; it was altered several times during the eighteenth century and the inside partition walls were removed. As it now stands, the house is presumably some-what larger than originally. The house was occupied first by Hans Egede and his family, which consisted of five now that Poul had gone to Denmark with the *Morianen* to study. Then there were Pårs and his housekeeper, Miss Titius, a young orphan girl he had taken in and who he later admitted was his mistress. Two young pastors, Ole Lange from Denmark and Henrik Miltzow from Norway, were given a room to share. Finally, the commandant, Jørgen Landorph, and the trader occupied the lower floor. In the loft a room was divided off for the other "officers", including the paymaster, Fleischer, the two barber-surgeons, von Helm and Chr. Kieding, and with the trader's assistant. Thus there were at least eighteen in all. We do not know whether the Green-landers kept by Hans Egede or the non-commissioned officers who came with the soldiers and convicts were accommodated in the "colony house" too.

As we have already noted, the colony's total labour force of twelve was accommodated in the *Cron Printz Christian* which was moored in the harbour. Here too was the pilot-cutter *West Vlieland* with her captain and crew – thirty in all. The volunteer soldiers with their sergeants, totalling twenty-three men together with the eleven released convicts and their wives, plus the five soldiers attached to Pårs and Landorph as servants and clerks – altogether some fifty persons – were lodged in a very long mud-hut, divided approximately across the middle into two rooms, the bigger one for the soldiers and the smaller for the married ex-convicts. The caboose was in the soldiers' room. The chimney from the hearth led up through the dividing wall where, on the side towards the second, smaller room, a couple of stove plates were built in. This was the sole source of heat in the room, just as the caboose was the only one in the soldiers' room, hence there was no heating except when food was being prepared. During the winter it became necessary to cut out the midday meal, so the fire was made up only twice a day. Not surprisingly, the occupants became ill. It was also not surprising that tensions among them came near to breaking-point. Hard work by day; guard duties, which Pårs conducted for as long as he could on the military lines customary in Denmark; cold, damp, filth and foul air in the only dwelling; shouting and bawling, drinking bouts and sexual acts in full view – all this swept them straight towards disaster. To this was added the fear of sickness and death which, from mid-October onwards, was thinning the ranks of these people all crammed together.

Before the end of 1728 nine had died and several more were ill: von Helm, the barber-surgeon, described the conditions in a report: ". . . there has been great weakness in this country from scurvy and consumption . . . the poor sleeping quarters and nursing which the people have received were the chief cause of death. They have lain in a stone and mud hut without any bedclothes brought with them from home, only the blankets which His Majesty most graciously contributed, so that they have been unable to keep warm". When they had to stay in bed, scurvy took hold of them. He continued: "When I visited my patients, I had to walk through water that covered my shoes inside the house . . .".

Women were giving birth in the midst of this confusion: but most of the infants died. Once even Pårs felt it his Christian duty to take a wife and husband "into his house", which probably meant they were installed in the loft of the officers' quarters. In his diary he wrote that it was "in order to preserve her from the bad lying-in conditions that exist in the men's house". He further enlarged on his good deeds: ". . . In the end the Governor had to go out and ask the pastor's wife to come and perform her Christian duty; the Governor almost suffered serious injury through running quickly over the slippery ground, but before the pastor's wife came, she was delivered of a daughter."

Pårs celebrated official holidays and royal birthdays with military honours, toasts and salutes for as long as possible. Thus the King's birthday was celebrated on 11 October: "the people" began celebrating the evening before and were all drunk before midnight (other people were dying in the house where their revelling took place). The following day a salute was fired from the improvised battery, the flag was hoisted and the celebration officially began. At dinner, toasts were drunk to all the royal household, followed by salutes of from five to nine shots. This dinner lasted until dark, when there was an extravagant firework display arranged by Bornholm, the master-gunner. Fleischer reported later how much gunpowder and ammunition had been used throughout the year for the many salutes fired. The festivities continued until morning with dancing and drinking. Singing was provided by the soldiers' wives. The Greenlanders present must surely have watched these happenings with amazement; they were so tired themselves that they lay down on the floor.

Internal disputes were continually flaring up between Pårs and almost all the other leaders. Each time "the Governor brought an action"

before the council, Hans Egede informed the council that he was unable to attend the meetings as often as before. "Just to sit for days on
end, wasting precious time to no purpose, listening to and being involved in paltry disputes, whereby nothing can be served, but which
vex everyone, is something I do not feel bound to do. Nor do I believe
that it is Your Royal Majesty's most gracious wish, for you would
much rather see the glory of God and the common good promoted
by all of us, without conflict and disagreements".

Pårs interfered even in trading matters, detecting swindles and embezzlement wherever he could, and perpetually demanding reports
and lists. After he had attacked the book-keeper and trader, Jørgen
Kopper, before the council in February 1728, Hans Egede intervened;
he "took up the dispute with the Governor and attacked him so hard
that the Governor was obliged to call witnesses, since the Rev. Hans
was unable to control his temper. Although the Governor asked him to
do so often, he would threaten himself and the Governor, which will be
explained more clearly in the minutes, since it is expected to result in
an action". This controversy was shelved, but the episode shows clearly
how Pårs fell out with everyone.

The men did not think much of him; indeed their only thought was
to get away from Greenland alive. Around Michaelmas 1728 Johan
Seckman, the pay-master, warned "the authorities" that rebellion
was brewing among the people, i.e. the soldiers and, especially, the
ex-convicts. According to Fleischer's statement in the council minutes
for 7 January, he had heard that "the Governor and the old pastor
(presumably Hans Egede) were to be the first to have their guts slit
open".

Two of the soldiers, one of them speaking Swedish, were supposed
on one occasion to have complained about the preparation of the food,
which was rationed due to the shortage of provisions, saying, "Devil
take me if I won't join in", to which the other replied: "Yes, brother,
anyone who doesn't join in will be fodder for the dogs". Later one
soldier allegedly said to another: "Never mind, brother, one day, devil
take me, we shall strike them all dead". The Swedish soldier Hageman, who was probably the one quoted above, is supposed to have
said: "The next time I go on an expedition with the Governor, damn
me if I don't send him to his rest".

Although there were no definite grounds for action, the Council
were shaken, and it was decided that all "officers" should keep watch
in turn. The sergeants could not be relied on since one of them, in an
argument with the barber-surgeon, had threatened his life – ". . . and
thus I for my part stood guard for four weeks until God smote the
wicked people with sickness; indeed, we were so afraid that none of

us dared go out of our quarters unless we were provided with arms". When the pastor went out to administer sacraments to the sick, he did not dare, even on this errand, to go without a weapon under his gown.

One soldier reported that Hageman had said to another soldier "that if things got too bad here, they would act together and soon put an end to it". The two were alleged to have said "The old pastor, may the devil take him . . . it is right that he should be struck dead for it is his fault that the twenty of us have to labour". Another had heard the same; the plan was that they would go off elsewhere and wait for the Dutch.

The idea of an uprising was already in circulation before the *Morianen* sailed in August. The people feared they would remain in Greenland for life: during the investigations one of the women gave evidence that a soldier had said that "if the people were not free after three years, they would find another way out." It was the soldier Hageman, one of the ex-convicts, who precipitated matters by running out of his quarters drunk to fetch and load a musket. He was arrested and put in irons. The whole rebel movement was engulfed by the sicknesses that thinned the ranks of those under suspicion. In February 1729 Hageman was released as his labour was valuable, but he became ill and died on 8 April.

When the danger had passed, it might have been expected that their common experience would have bound the leaders closer together, but this was not the case. Concurrently with the inquiry concerning "the rebels", relations between Pårs and the rest resumed their accustomed course. Captain Landorph assaulted Pårs while drunk. During the subsequent trial, Fleischer, a witness, could not refrain from holding Pårs up to ridicule: when he and Kopper, the book-keeper, had got Landorph out of the room, Pårs had immediately said: " 'Look, my nose is bleeding' . . . and a trickle of blood came out". Pårs put Landorph under arrest, but the latter had no intention of taking any notice of the order and told Pårs so, using an expression which the clerk hesitated to quote. To make Pårs look even more ridiculous, Miss Titius, his housekeeper and prospective mistress, became pregnant and named Captain Landorph as the father. (Her child died soon after birth.)

Hans Egede and the other two pastors managed to do little of their real work. Journeys were few because their usual oarsmen were sick, or engaged in other work and could not be spared from the colony. The increasing number of deaths caused a shortage of manpower.

In these circumstances Hans Egede's idea to train catechists was strengthened. This would make it possible, in the settlements where the population seemed more stable, for there always to be a teacher of Christianity, under the missionary's supervision. What troubled him was the problem of preventing the Greenlanders from backsliding; it was this that stopped him from baptizing small children, as he could not be certain that they would be brought up in the Christian faith even if the parents had consented to baptism. Hans Egede continued to insist that they must be fully aware of the implications of baptism before he would proceed with it.

On the other hand, these same infants troubled him greatly; he saw them die without baptism and felt this as a failure in his work. Gradually he assembled his thoughts on this problem sufficiently to be able to present a written plan to his two fellow-priests, Ole Lange and Henrik Miltzow. Essentially it was that the children of local parents who were known to lead decent lives should be baptized; even if they were not brought up in the Christian faith, it would be possible, when catechists had been trained, to have them instructed. The two agreed, and on this basis all three went into action. During the period that followed, forty-three children, aged from three months to five years, were baptized, all in families living on the Kook and Ravne islands and Haabets Øe, hence in the immediate neighbourhood of Godthåb. At that time, according to Hans Egede's statements, seventy-nine families, totalling about 350 people, were living in the three places. [4] Apart from this, Hans Egede and the two pastors were prisoners of circumstances able only to give spiritual comfort to the sick, hold weekly services for them and for the healthy, administer the sacrament to the dying and perform burials. The latter were a problem as the earth was not only scanty but frozen. [5]

If little was to be seen for the missionary work, there were also no great results to show from the trading. As the people in the colony could not be spared, the crew of the pilot-galliot was ordered out on one of the few expeditions that were made.

In between the council meetings to deal with Pårs' legal actions and the hearings of the various witnesses in the "rebellion case", there were discussions at individual meetings on the future. At an early stage, Hans Egede had submitted his proposal that the Greenlanders should contribute a form of tax, although in no circumstances was force to be used to obtain payment; it had to be pointed out that the King had sent so many people out to protect them against foreigners that it was only fair for them to contribute something to the King in return. The assistant was therefore to draw up a census list on the forthcoming expeditions and enter on it everyone's contribution. He was to tell them, moreover, that they had only to apply to the council if they suffered any wrong at the hands of foreigners or their own people, and the council would protect them on behalf of the King.

When the assistant came home from an expedition to the north in

October or November, he could only report that the Greenlanders there were not inclined to contribute anything; those living to the south were more willing. Yet conditions to the south were no more certain, for when the same assistant reached Kilengerme on a trading expedition in March and April, he came into conflict with the headman in the settlement. When he attempted to trade with the Greenlanders there, this headman intervened, saying that they could get better terms from the Dutch. They started arguing and the assistant threatened the headman with "a box on the ears", whereupon "the savage" attacked him and all the others joined in the fight. The assistant and his four travelling companions overpowered them, and then made a good bargain for eleven or twelve *cordeler* of blubber. This blubber was not regarded as tax, but the inhabitants promised to have collected that by the next visit.

On this occasion the assistant heard the Greenlanders speak of rumours that many people had died at Godthåb. They were, therefore, no longer afraid of foreigners but "would easily master us". Consequently it was decided by the council that in future guns should be taken on expeditions.

From this and similar reports we obtain some understanding of relations between the Greenlanders and the first colonists. The Greenlanders feared the foreigners, yet at the same time they were attracted by their goods. The relationship with Hans Egede seems to have been a special one. They were captivated by what he told them in his strange Greenlandic speech, and he was so good to them in various ways. It was true, he could loose his temper and be hard in anger, but Christian love and compassion completely eclipsed the other sides of his character. Put simply, they felt that he was concerned for their good.

The fear of Hans Egede and the others which was felt by the neighbouring Greenlanders appears to have been part of the missionaries' educational policy. Albert Top expressed this in his testimony to the Christiania Commission of 1727: "However many colonies there will be, I can assure you that it will also be possible eventually to make them obedient by a suitable method. For if, as is certainly the case, they now dread this one simple and wretched colony . . . occupied by a few people, and which has been and still is the terror of the whole country, then the Greenlanders will know far better how to fear and submit, once many better supported colonies are established among them. They will in truth scarcely dare to do anything of importance without permission."

Hans Egede recommended that, as a means of getting the Greenlanders to contribute a certain quantity of blubber as a form of tax, they should be deluded into thinking that foreigners would come to kill them, but that the King would take them under his protection if only they contributed to him one barrel of blubber per household in return – "since these poor creatures are very credible and fearful, they readily declare themselves willing to give and do what we require of them". His continual emphasis on the need to make the Greenlanders subject to "correction [or order] and discipline" suggests a fear of reprisals.

The fear of authority – from God and the King, through the administrative authorities right down to one's immediate superior – was an integral part of the European's way of life, even in private life where children feared their fathers and corporal punishment was an everyday occurence. If it was necessary in the colonists' society, then it was even more necessary in Greenland society. The Greenlanders had to be imbued with fear – of God and of temporal authority – so that it could act as an influence in the work of the mission and in social life. Paradoxically, this emphasis on fear was coupled with genuine sympathy for the hard life of the Greenlanders, and for the spiritual perdition to which, as heathens, they were foredoomed.

However, Eskimo society was by no means free from fear already – fear of life in general and its many inexplicable phenomena. There was the fear of breaking almost untenable taboos and of evil spirits and evil people who sought one's life. There was fear of other encampments. When Pårs was discussing in a report the question of establishing a colony to the south, right in the southern tip of Greenland, he stated that "according to information given us by the savages, the people around there [Cape Farewell] are hot-tempered and evil by nature"; some of the local Greenlanders had been down there three years earlier and had killed someone, so now dared not go there again.[6]

From this we can see that between the colonists and the Greenlanders' fear was mutual.

REFERENCES

1. The last two paragraphs do not take into account the Royal Order of 16 January 1728, but are rather an interpretation of it. At least there is, however, one quotation from it. It must be emphasized that the letter itself alone provides the basis for this interpretation. There is nothing else to support it, let alone the fact that preparations were made in a haphazard fashion and seem to have been dictated by each situation of crisis is as it arose.

2. "The Greenland *Dessein*" (The Danish also uses the French term), *Det grønlandske Dessein* was its actual name, *Dessein* having the somewhat special meaning of "project" or "enterprise".

3. It has not been possible to discover the person who originated this idea. The sources are silent except for a single letter from one of the admirals to Chief Secretary Møinichen. It tells that on 19 March 1728 in the evening they talked together. Møinichen confided to the admiral that the King had decided to send thirty or forty "male and female vagrants" to Greenland. The King usually "decides" on a proposal, which is then advanced (in this case) by the Chief Secretary of Danske Cancelli; this indicates that Møinichen had the idea.

4. On the Kook Islands thirty-four families, on Ravne Islands fifteen and on Haabets Øe thirty families (in five huts!), in all seventy-nine families. In 1728 Hans Egede counted on Kook Islands forty-eight families, consisting of 214 persons. That is an average of 4·5 persons per family. According to this average the seventy-nine families should total 356 persons.

5. Govenor Pårs reported on 4 August 1729: ". . . This winter has been at times rather hard. We had not enough healthy men to dig graves for the dead. The corpses therefore had to lie in a house eight, twelve or fourteen days before they could be buried."

6. In a letter to the Commission of 1729, dated 6 August 1730, Governor Pårs writes: ". . . When the Greenlanders who live in the South arrive in the North, or vice versa there is antipathy between them, with the result that they get into a battle among themselves, and shoot at each other with their arrows; sometimes four or five of them are shot to death, besides those who are wounded." (This is a translation made as near his style as possible. His letters were usually rather childish or "primitive" in form.) He lacked instructions on how, as Governor, he should act in such cases, but he proposed that the "criminals" should be deported to Svalbard, so this island(s) could be "populated". What he tells about the "war" between the two groups of Greenlanders may be taken *cum grano salis*. He had a lively imagination, and what he told was seldom well founded.

8

CONTINUATION OF THE *DESSEIN*
1729–1730

Necessity will usually bridge even supposedly unbridgeable chasms. A fair amount of communication and trade went on between the Greenlanders living in the south and those hunting farther north. Those living farthest to the south needed narwhal and walrus tusks, whalebone and even reindeer skin. The Greenlanders traded so extensively among themselves that Matthias Fersleff saw possibilities of exploiting it. He had noted prices, and reported that the southern Greenlanders gave one barrel of blubber for one reindeer skin. When this came to Magnus Schiøtte's knowledge, he calculated as follows: a shirt was worth 5 mrk. and was usually exchanged for 2 reindeer skins, but these fetched 16 mrk. when sold in Bergen; on the other hand, 2 barrels of blubber usually fetched 8–10 rdl. or more, hence, if reindeer skin was traded with shirts, i.e. for 2 mrk., 8sk. per skin and the reindeer skin resold to those living in the south for 1 barrel of blubber per skin, it should be possible to make a profit of 2 rdl., 4 mrk., 8 sk. "which is a striking difference". However, this form of trade with the extreme south did not come into being immediately.

The Greenlanders in the extreme south also traded by another route. In 1726, people had come from the east coast, by ways which have not been explained, bringing great whalebones which they exchanged for the goods they needed. The southern Greenlanders said that those living on the west coast occasionally undertook voyages along the east coast, where they presumably traded with the inhabitants.

Meanwhile, Scots as well as Dutchmen were venturing into these waters. While Matthias Fersleff was sailing along the north coast in 1728 and around Disko Bay, he was told that an "Englishman" Jan Andres (i.e. Ian Andrews, therefore presumably a Scot) had taken a whale from the Greenlanders who had just caught it. He had landed with his followers and taken what he found of blubber and skins without making any form of payment. A Dutchman, Cornelius Bunk, who had been involved in burning down the colony houses at Nipisat

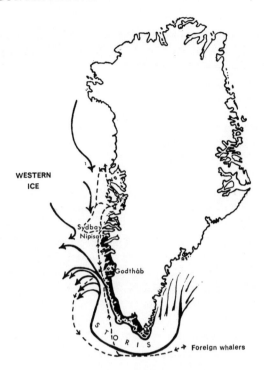

WESTERN
ICE

Sydbay
Nipisat

Godthåb

S T O R I S

→ Foreign whalers

Davis Strait navigation.

in 1725, had similarly taken a whale from the ice fjord in Jakobshavn, but had at least given them "bits and pieces" from his cargo. The same Greenlanders later slaughtered a whale in Disko Bay, but another Dutchman took most of it "for little or no payment". The Greenlanders complained loudly to Fersleff about these encroachments. He consoled them by saying that "such matters would be reported to the King, and the guilty would be punished". If the King would protect them, the Greenlanders replied, "all trade should be carried out with our ships to the King's advantage, and not with others".

The Greenlanders concerned, apparently on their own initiative, further suggested that some traders should live with them permanently. Blubber was easily obtainable in the bay, both in spring and autumn, but in winter the Greenlanders had to hunt from the ice and could not manage to drag home more than they needed. If traders were present, they could easily buy the large surplus left behind from them. For that matter, whaling could be carried on jointly in the spring – "even the priest could come, for they know nothing of what their fellow-countrymen in the south have learned from him".

On the one hand Dutch trading and whaling was in strong competition with Danish–Norwegian colonization and trade; on the other, the rough methods practised by individual Dutchmen made the Greenlanders in Disko Bay ask for a permanent colony to be founded. The Dutch whaling and trading was still, according to both Hans Egede and the traders, a restrictive factor; all reports, letters, replies and representations refer to this foreign activity. Contact was frequently made with the Dutch, nearly always on a friendly basis; most of the Dutch were ready to lend a helping hand in a difficult situation. However, Hans Egede and the traders wished more and more for a royal ban on their activities, which they thought would have an immediate effect. Egede had often discussed this with the Dutch whalers and traders, who had "intimated" that their principles would not permit them to sail to Greenland if the Danish–Norwegian King laid a ban on foreign trade there. For the present these requests bore no result. In general, the Danish–Norwegian Government followed the recommendations of the Christiania Commission.

Meanwhile the proposed fort needed some sort of purpose, as did the garrison sent out.[1] The whole year 1728–9 passed before the commandant took up his duties. It had been decided to build the fort at Nipisat when the colony was re-established, but its purpose was still not clear; it was presumably to protect this colony against attack by the Dutch, following the experience of 1725.

However, the transfer of the colony from Haabets Øe to Godthåb and the difficulties during the winter delayed the plan's execution. Pårs had to delay this and another project with which he had been entrusted – an expedition across country to the east coast. It was partly with this in mind that ten of the eleven horses had been sent out, the eleventh being for Pårs' personal (possibly ceremonial) use. Five of the horses died on the voyage, and the others did not survive the winter and spring.

By then Pårs had long since given up the original plan, which was to allow himself, with his party and baggage, to be transported overland to the east coast, deciding instead to go on foot. On 25 April, he set out accompanied by the commander of the pilot-galliot, Lieutenant Richart, the assistant, Jens Hjort who knew the Greenlandic language, and five "common men". They headed for Ameralik fjord (which became "Admiral fjord" in Pårs' writings). This was not the first time people had been inland, and it was known that the fjord valleys extended to the "ice-mountains". They took provisions for eight days – and by May 7 the expedition returned without having reached the east coast. The party had marched for two days up the fjord through rich terrain and on the third day reached the edge of the inland ice where "after advancing for a few hours in danger of our lives further progress became impossible". The numerous crevices from two to three fathoms wide in the marginal zone of the icecap halted them: "when we saw no further progress for ourselves we sat down on the ice, fired our rifles with nine Danish shots and drank the King's health with a glass of brandy. . . ." After "resting for an hour", they turned back again. Pårs' description makes the expedition seem more like a picnic than a serious expedition of discovery, even allowing for the contemporary style of writing. Nevertheless, this account contains the first description of the icecap. Pårs was amazed at the large boulders on its surface, and recounted his impression of the majestic sight: "for the iceberg is like looking at the wild sea where no land is to be seen, only the sky and glittering ice; underfoot the ice was sharp-edged like white sugar candy so that iron-soled boots were needed to make any progress, so bad was it for walking on".

On the way back, the little party passed through the present Austmannadal with its great river. Pårs observed the Norse home fields here, and thought he could see plough furrows; the vigorous growth in these valleys gave him the idea of establishing farms, and he suggested in his report to the King that one or more landowners or gentlemen farmers who had been sentenced for some serious offence should be "condemned to this country" for varying periods; they should be allocated a sufficient number of copyholders who had also been convicted. There was plenty of room in the valleys of the Ameralik fjord. However, this was a figment of Pårs' imagination; the Government was making plans for a settlement, but in a completely different more realistic direction.

Undoubtedly Pårs was not thinking only of the Ameralik fjord valleys for his project. In an earlier report he had discussed the possibilities of founding a colony farther south, where there might be fields to cultivate, and where he suggested building a fort as a protection against the inhabitants. Its garrison, of which he himself might be commandant, would be helpful to him as oarsmen and bodyguards, when he set out from there for the east coast. The idea of attempting to sail round Cape Farewell and up the east coast occurs here again. In 1723 Hans Egede had had the idea of penetrating the Frobisher Strait, which he sought but did not find. It did not, however, fall to Pårs' lot to undertake this voyage.

Pårs' and Landorph's next task was imminent. The master-gunner, Bornholm, sailed for Nipisat in a sloop at the end of April accompanied by five men. Pårs, Landorph and the rest of the crew were awaiting the arrival of a ship for a journey north: this ship, the *Fortuna*, arrived from Bergen at the end of May, and the remaining men with Landorph and Pårs, sailed to Nipisat, which now once more had a "crew". This "crew" had been partly supplemented from Bergen and Copenhagen, but not militarily. In Godthåb sickness and the poor food and living conditions had cost the lives of two of the seniors, one sergeant, ten volunteer soldiers, two servants, six ex-convicts, six of the latter's wives, and three children born of these marriages – some thirty people altogether. New recruits were essential.

Of the 100 people in Godthåb in 1728, including the pilot-galliot crew, forty-four or forty-five died. The dead included many craftsmen who were badly missed in the building work planned for Nipisat; no craftsmen had come out with the latest ships. Neither in Bergen nor in Copenhagen could anyone have any idea that conditions had turned out so badly. Slowness of communication was the greatest single restricting factor in the Greenland *Dessein*. The shortest time for a matter to be dealt with was at least a year. Even between Denmark and Norway it could be a month or longer. In many situations, therefore, those responsible for the shipments out and those in the colonies had to use their own judgement. A case in point was Hans Egede's decision on the practice of christening, where it so happened that the Missionskollegium applauded his action.

It was impossible, in 1728–9, to make clear in time to the authorities that what had been done hitherto, especially the sending out of numerous people who could not be got rid of immediately, had been mistaken. The authorities first got wind of this in 1729. Møinichen and the deputies of the Navy had a difficult task explaining to the King that the previous year's undertakings had been a failure. This was a delicate matter, and carried a certain risk for the King's advisers.

When the *Fortuna* arrived in Copenhagen in 1728, its cargo of Greenland products was valued and sold by auction at the end of August, realizing 1,105 rdl., 2 mrk., 12 sk. Presumably quite good prices were obtained for the goods. The reindeer skins yielded just what Magnus Schiøtte considered the current price, exactly 16 marks for two skins. The blubber which was valued at 11 rigsdaler per cordel or over 5 rdl. per barrel, realized, on average, 8 rdl. a barrel, a good price; Magnus Schiøtte had estimated the value at 4–5 rdl. per barrel.

The cargo of the *Morianen* fetched only 886 rdl., 5 mrk., 11 sk. The normal price bid for blubber was something over 7½ rdl. a barrel, higher than estimated by Magnus Schiøtte. But the prices received for seal and fox skins were low. The fox skins fetched barely 2 mrk. each at the first auction and 1½ mrk. at the second. Seal skins were not valued highly then, and brought less than 12 sk. each at the first auction and 10 sk. at the last. Official dissatisfaction was expressed at these prices. Efforts were made to hold back the goods, possibly to obtain a higher total return, but these tactics did not give the desired results; strangely, government officials considered the blubber prices too low and the cause of the poor profits. The reason given was that winter was a bad time to melt the blubber into oil, that the market had dropped off, and that the Iceland ships had arrived and had long since "filled the town with such goods", so satisfying the market.

The cargoes of 1728 were large compared with what had been brought home previously. On the other hand, the cargo brought home in 1729 was small, due to the building activity, and to sickness and deaths. Also, the cooper had died and there had been a shortage of barrels. The blubber had been left in the snow, where it had gradually shrunk, some completely melting away. The consignments that reached Bergen in 1727, 1728 and 1729 were sold by auction. When the accounts were drawn up eight years later, these auctions showed a total return of 21,467 rdl, 13 sk. against an expenditure of 21,721 rdl., 2 sk. in other words a loss of 253 rdl., 5 mrk., 5 sk. The oil sold in 1728 brought in 1,231 rdl. 7 sk., which, with the sale of commodities which arrived later, totalled 1,250 rdl, 1 mrk., 7 sk., but some oil was held back until 1735 when it was sold for 256 rdl., 5 mrk., 13 sk.

The total estimate of expenses for 1728, after payments in Copenhagen, came to 18,317 rdl., 75½ sk. which certain deductions reduced to 12,383 rdl., 69½ sk. As this was not covered by the auction's yield for that year, it was intended in Bergen to cover the deficit from the lottery and the "bounty". But it was still hoped to reduce this deficit. It was decided in 1728 to set up a management board for the *Dessein* in Bergen; Magnus Schiøtte complained of his difficulties in managing everything alone. Apparently Major-General J. F. Tuchsen, commandant of the Bergenhus, fort had been approached unofficially, and shortly afterwards, Tuchsen, Schiøtte and the Trade Secretary, Landberg, were appointed. Schiøtte was still short of cash: "Money is not to be had in these bad times", he writes in a letter of complaint. Later that year things went badly yet again. He could not "borrow money, because my credit on the Greenland business has diminished". The citizens of Bergen deeply mistrusted the Greenland trade. Or was there personal mistrust of Schiøtte? His correspondence gives the impression that he was at odds with most of Bergen: "It is unfortunate that the Greenland *Dessein* meets with so many snubs. Where the blame lies may some day come to light." The book-keeper had great trouble: "God knows who is the reason for all this, but it is only to be presumed that crooked people must have had a hand in obstructing the Greenland affair." Schiøtte was always at pains in his letters to emphasize how zealously he was managing matters on the King's behalf, perhaps "protesting too much".

But not everyone in Bergen was opposed to the Greenland *Dessein*. In October 1728 an old expert at Greenland navigation, Hans Mathias, offered his whaling vessel *St. Anna*, which had been whaling in Greenland in 1725, but nothing came of this.

On the other hand, the central administration felt that firmer leadership than Schiøtte's was needed for the *Dessein*, and so in 1729 a commission was appointed consisting of the Senior Secretary of the *Danske Cancelli*, Chr. Møinichen; the senior secretary to the Krigscancelli (War Office), Ditlev von Revenfeld, and the Deputy to the General Naval Commissariat, D. B. Weyse; Admiral A. Rosenpalm and Captain D. Myhlenphorth were later added by royal recommendation. The last-named had taken the *Morianen* to Greenland in 1728, and he had been considered originally by the Admiralty as governor and commandant of the fort. The terms of reference of the Commission were restricted to examining the reports sent from Greenland and giving its views on what could best be done with least expense to the King's Purse. The Commission, at its first meeting, decided to advise the King to send out only two ships, both from Copenhagen, to supply both colonies; it was believed that Nipisat was either already established, or would be by the time the ships arrived. Sending out a fully-equipped whaling ship was not recommended, but only five barges with whaling equipment and one whaling commander, five harpooners and twenty-five seamen. Building material and a master-builder should also be sent. They did not dare advise sending more.

The directors in Bergen were told to procure the building materials according to a detailed list, and were given little room for initiative. In addition, a ship was to be chartered to take out the supplies and the whaling personnel.

Once started, things moved quickly, but the lateness of the instructions (February 12) made everything more expensive. Only one ship, the *Cron Printz Christian*, which was laid up for the winter in Godthåb, belonged to the Company. The Bergen Company's previous directors had sold the other boats at the end of 1728. The *Haabet* had been broken up, but the *Fridericus Quartus* was lying near Bergen; when the Commission learned of this, it cancelled the sale, but the boat was not fit for a voyage.

As a result, very expensive charters had to be negotiated, and to obtain cash the Bergen directors drew on the holdings of earlier directors. The Bergen Town Council would not hand over any "bounty". The directors of the *Dessein* were continuously hounded by creditors. Finally they succeeded in chartering three boats and the whaling crew; the latter cost less than expected as a full complement could not be procured.

The Sukkertop mountains, Zuikerbrood, near Kangâmiut.

Stumps of whale ribs brought home by eighteenth-century whalers and used as a
rden fence in Ameland, Netherlands. (Photo Van der Meulen, Heemstede.)

3. The 'Greenland' warehouses in Keizersgracht, Amsterdam. (Photo Oorthuys, Amsterdam.)

. The sites on Haabets Øe in September 1967. Flagstaff and memorial erected in
921. (Photo Jørgen Benzon.)

5. Haabets Øe. View of the sites from the sound at low tide. (Photo Jørgen Benzon.)

6. Skerries and coast of Haabets Øe with the harbourage and sites to the right, centre. (Copyright Geodætisk Institut, A.242/67.)

8. Póq.

7. Qiperoq.

After paintings by B. Grodtschilling. (Arctic Institute, Gentofte, Denmark; MoG 129, I, figs. 29 and 28.)

9. Pôq and Qiperoq. Painting by B. Grodtschilling. (MoG 129, I, fig. 30.)

10. Pôq and Qiperoq. Painting by B. Grodtschilling. (National Museum, Copenhagen; photo Lennart Larsen.)

11. Hans Egede. Painted—probably at Bergen in 1718—by an unknown artist. Formerly in St. Knuds Church, Odense; presented to the newly-built Hans Egede Church in Godthåb in 1971. (Photo Wermundt Bendtsen, Odense.)

2. Giertrud Rasch, wife of Hans Egede. History as Plate 11. (Photo Wermundt ndtsen, Odense.)

13. 'True and accurate portrait of the godfearing and virtuous Greenland girl, Marie Epeyub's daughter . . .' Painting by M. Blumenthal, 1747. (National Museum, Copenhagen; photo Lennart Larsen.)

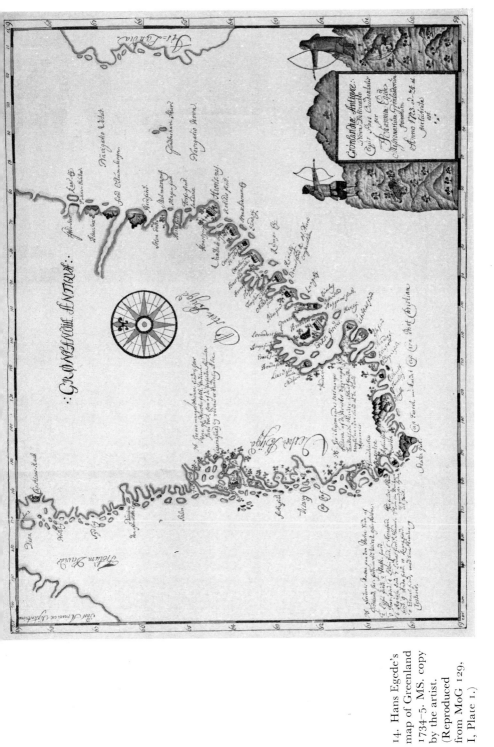

14. Hans Egede's map of Greenland 1734–5. MS. copy by the artist. (Reproduced from MoG 129, I, Plate 1.)

15. Oldest known photograph of Hans Egede's house in Godthåb. (Cf. Niels Egede's sketch plan, page 208;) Arctic Institute, Gentofte, Denmark.)

16. Governor Claus Enevold Pårs. (Miniature belonging to Vice-Admiral H. Vedel, Copenhagen; MoG 129, I, fig. 36.)

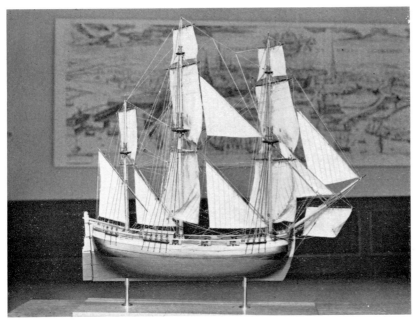

17. Model of three-masted fishing galliot *Fortuna*, built 1742. Possibly of the same type as the pilot galliot *West Vlieland*. (Original at the Commerce and Shipping Museum, Kronborg, Denmark; photo H. Hauch, Elsinore.)

18. Mass baptism at Ny Herrhut, from *L'Exposition de l'origine de l'unité des frères*. (Royal Library, Copenhagen.)

19. Hans Egede's note of 14 September 1733 to Just Vogel, an assistant, asking for
Frederik Christian's name to be taken off the supply roll.

20. Christian David. After a painting in the Brüder-Unität Archives, Herrnhut. (MoG 129, I, fig. 36.)

. Johann Beck. After a painting the Brüder–Unität Archives, errnhut. (MoG 129, I, fig. 38.)

22. Jacob Sewerin. After a painting traditionally attributed to C. G. Pilo (which is owned by Major-General P. Ramm, Copenhagen. Copy at the Ministry for Greenland. Photo Lennart Larsen.)

In the Commission it was decided not to establish any further colonies other than Nipisat, and that Jacob Geelmuyden and Matthias Fersleff should be re-engaged as book-keeper and trader at Nipisat and Godthåb respectively. Thus they began to get to the root of the problem. It was recommended that Pårs, Fleischer and Landorph, together with the soldiers and their wives, should be recalled; such a large number of people were involved that considerable savings could be made by not having to pay their wages and subsistence. But the King decided that Pårs and Fleischer should stay on indefinitely, while approving the re-engagement of Geelmuyden and Fersleff.

The Commission had been given the task of finding the cheapest way of operating both the sailings and the mission that year. In their search for economies, they again came up against the costly garrison and the Governor. This happened at a meeting in May, when it was too late for recall in 1729 to be possible. So the following year they again ventured to raise the question. They earnestly begged the King to consider the heavy and unproductive expenditure involved. The lack of enthusiasm for the whole enterprise is revealed by the King endorsing a resolution as late as May 21 that even for that year they "should see whether any advantages beyond those already found could be expected from this trade". Not a word about the recall, but there was an order that the ships should not unload their cargoes "if the inhabitants of the country . . . should have perished", but they should assure themselves before sailing for home that all were dead. This may seem a macabre answer to the question of saving by recalling superfluous people; however, it marked an advance towards a solution of the problem, although the authorities were not aware of this.

The Commission had also looked for other, more short-term possibilities of retrenchment. Geelmuyden and Fersleff were instructed that people in the Greenland colonies should buy any goods they needed at the "shop", i.e. from the trader's store. Such goods were to be sold at cost price without allowance for profit or expenses, but this buying could be done on account, so eliminating the need to send out wages, as there was no other use for ready cash – except gambling, which would now be avoided.

An inexpensive experiment to find out whether it was possible to cultivate in Greenland could also be permitted. Pårs' idea of agriculture in the Ameralik fjord and farther south had not yet reached the authorities, but in his own reports Hans Egede had repeatedly described his cultivation experiments farther inland. The old conceptions of Greenland's fertility still obviously played an important role. The Royal Chief Architect and Chief Keeper of the Royal Gardens, J. C. Krieger, requested in May 1729 that various types of seeds be sent to

K

Greenland; he also wanted a more detailed description of soil conditions there. He envisaged that the experiment would be followed up by reports, and the sending home of specimen plants and crops produced. Seeds and plants were sent out, and experiments made, but nothing came of it because of the difficulties of supervising the areas sown, and because there had not been time to reach the inland areas which were considered the most fertile.

Pårs' enthusiasm for the Ameralik fjord valley was shared by others. Hans Egede must have received a letter about J. C. Krieger's research plans, for he sent back a long account of conditions in Ujaragssuit, Ameralik, Pisigsarfik and Qôrqut.[2] The same was done from Nipisat, where a number of seeds and plants had also been sent. The following year it was reported that every experiment had failed.

These planting and sowing experiments may be seen in conjunction with certain plans for colonization, which included cattle-breeding and land-cultivation. The Christiania Commission had touched upon this idea but limited it to colonization by Norwegian farmers. Meanwhile, in 1729 the Governor of Iceland was called upon to examine the possibilites of having Icelandic families transferred to Greenland to develop its agricultural potential. No less than 166 people declared themselves willing to go to Greenland after the Governor's announcement.

It was not until New Year 1720 that the Commission again took up the matter. In regard to the recall of Pårs and the whole garrison, it was suggested instead that Icelandic families be sent; the Commission held firmly to the idea that the country should be occupied "by people able to support themselves". In May, the King decided that the Governor of Iceland should select twelve families from those who had declared themselves willing; six for the Godthåb area and six for the Nipisat area, but the following month it was decided to postpone the project until 1731, after which the whole thing came to nothing.

The question of settling permanently preoccupied certain people in Greenland. At Nipisat, the colony's cook and another man who acted as cooper, joiner and carpenter wished to settle and start a fishing industry, on condition that official support was received for three years. The council of Nipisat suggest that it should be considered, together with the idea that such families should be sent out to each colony. This proposal contains the germ of later ideas on Icelandic settlement.

The idea of settling down was not unfamiliar to those sent out, and must have been discussed many times. According to Pårs' journal, the paymaster Fleischer had said that he and some friends wanted to settle in the Ameralik fjord when the Governor and his men had gone. He would sow barley and oats experimentally, and then apply to the King for a piece of land, retire from the service, and farm. This announcement, perhaps made in a moment of irritation, came to nothing, like the later offers from the people in Nipisat.

The squabbles and disputes of the winter 1728–9 were set aside until Pårs, Landorph and their men left Godthåb for Nipisat to build the fort. The *Morianen* and the *Fortuna* had arrived with a new contingent in the middle of August. "No sooner had we arrived, than we had to listen reluctantly to the discord that had arisen amongst the few remaining people", Jacob Geelmuyden wrote to the 1729 Commission. Geelmuyden expected various troubles in the future and neither he nor Ole Lange, the missionary who was to serve at Nipisat, doubted the cause. Both attempted to protect themselves in advance from reports damaging to their reputations, that might possibly be sent to the authorities.

During 1729–30, it gradually became clear that Pårs was striving for a dictatorial position. Fleischer had already been aware of this in the summer of 1729. Although the disputes had been laid aside, disagreement among council members continued and important matters were seldom dealt with at the meetings. On the contrary, writs were issued and great arguments took place, mainly because the chairman claimed full powers and nothing could be said or done about it. The other members of the Council often made reasonable protests against such unfair actions and so became involved.

Pårs' behaviour caused the others to join forces against him, even though they did not hold very high opinions of each other. Everyone was relieved when the Governor departed for Godthåb at the end of August, and groaned when he returned at the end of April 1720. That same summer, in the Nipisat council, Pårs revealed his thoughts on the Governor's position in a debate on the sending home of two ex-convicts. Pårs wanted to keep them, but the other members unanimously wanted them sent home. "Therefore my opinion in this matter, as in so many others, counted for nothing." The other members always seemed to agree among themselves, from which Pårs concluded that they had previously made up their minds, always in opposition to him.

It was under these conditions that the building at Nipisat was begun. It was a large building with four wings containing living quarters, stables and storage space. However, a large quantity of goods had to be deposited in the open on a nearby island. The fort took the form of a battery erected a few steps from the main building.

The whaling which had been planned failed completely. They caught nothing, partly because one of the barges with all its equipment was wrecked, and partly because the cold was so intense that the crews could not work efficiently.[3] Finally, during the year, the blubber-cutter, a carpenter, a cooper and three seamen died, mostly from scurvy.

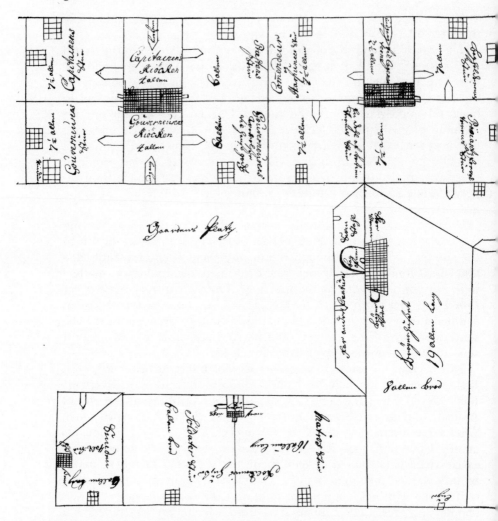

Sketch-plan of the building on the island of Nipisat, drawn by Jacob Geelmuyden. He describes the colony as being built round three sides of a square open to the west; in one of the east–west wings the men of the colony were lodged in the first instance. He states that the house measured 38 by $14\frac{1}{2}$ ells, inside the walls, but these measurements do not appear to tally with those on the sketch. The description is dated 29 June 1731, whereas the sketch seems to date from 1729–30, since the whalers' accommodation is indicated.

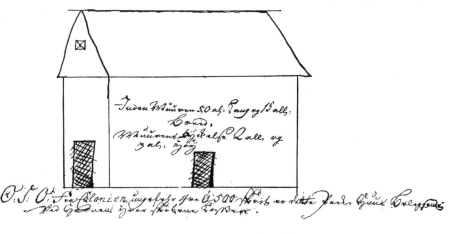

Sketch of the warehouse on the island of Nipisat, 1729-30.

The council in Nipisat wanted this fiasco brought to an end in 1720, and they succeeded by getting all the whaling people away on the *Cron Printz Christian*, which sailed on 9 August.

Meanwhile, the traders had not been idle. Expeditions north and south had brought them about 200 barrels of blubber, though not many skins; these were sent to Bergen, presumably on the *Cron Printz Christian*.

Nipisat was not a success. Even the missionary work had borne little fruit, and here again Pårs blamed the missionary Ole Lange, who had not mastered the language sufficiently. Although adequate experience had not yet been acquired, Pårs was right in thinking that the priests – apart from Hans Egede – knew too little of the language and stayed too short a time. Albert Top had been in Greenland for four years, but Ole Lange must have wished to leave, thus enabling Pårs to talk about the priests' short stay.

Therefore Pårs maintained, like others before him, that more colonies should be established, all with pastors who were linguistically qualified, and traders or assistants to look after the trade. He suggested establishing in all four colonies with small posts between them – starting in the south with a colony at Ûnartoq, then two outposts before Godthåb, followed by a further two before Nipisat, north of which only one outpost should be established before the Disko Bay, where the fourth colony would be set up on the site of the present Christianhåb. The plan was both well thought out and completely original. Thus Pårs showed a good understanding of what was needed; his criticisms were often correct, but this was constantly spoiled by boasting and malice. His self-importance reached laughable proportions, even for that time.

When two "English" (presumably Scots) whalers anchored at Nipisat, the ships saluted Pårs and each time he visited them the King's health was drunk. When the whalers returned the visit, Pårs wanted to greet them in the same way, but this time one of the soldiers was injured and had to be sent home, which resulted in a lengthy explanation of the enormous consumption of gunpowder.

Pårs longed to use the cannon which had arrived with the *Morianen* for other purposes besides firing salutes. He, in common with other Danish–Norwegian nationals in Greenland, wanted the Dutchmen and their trade banned from access to the coast. As soon as a Dutch trader dropped anchor in a harbour, immediately "hundreds of wild people" appeared. As long as the Dutch were close inshore or expected, no trade could be done. "The most displeasing thing is that it happens before our very eyes, here in the harbour." Pårs obviously did not want to limit himself to expostulations with the Dutch and threats that he would complain to the King, who would issue a ban on Dutch trade. He received the same answer as Hans Egede – that the Dutch traders would prefer not to sail to Greenland and would welcome such a ban.

Soon there was nowhere along the coast from Disko Bay down to the far south beyond Godthåb where Dutch traders had not been. It was often said that the Dutchmen gave better value, and had more goods to sell, than the traders of the Greenland *Dessein*. Pårs was angered by their form of trade. They gave one shirt for half a barrel of blubber, three knives for one fox skin, and even fish hooks and needles as well, whereas "we only give one knife for a fox skin". Thus the Dutchmen gave three times better value.

Hans Egede had previously maintained that the Greenlanders did not really need the goods offered to them, apart from a few items, thus importing which went beyond staple necessities must be considered a luxury trade. The assistant reported that once in the home of a Greenlander near Fiskefjord north of Godthåb, he noticed a dozen new copper-kettles of various types, several painted chests, wooden platters, tin dishes, brightly-coloured shirts, trousers, sweaters, hats, various carpenter's tools, tea-cups and other small articles in considerable quantity. They were hung all around the room "as decoration, like a little shop". Mass acquisition may have been considered a mark of status, but it is more probable that these "purchases" were of a different nature. In Disko Bay, Matthias Fersleff had witnessed the Dutch taking a whale from the Greenlanders who had caught it, and giving some of their cargo in exchange. The Greenlanders certainly did not want to buy these goods, but the Dutch trader simply took what he wanted of the whale, and gave a token payment in return out of common decency.

Governor Pårs himself played a singular role in the movement of goods. On the way from Godthåb to Nipisat, "by means of threats and the authority he held over the poor Greenlanders", he forced them to give him all kinds of skins and "things he saw that could be of use to him". On the same trip the Governor had allowed himself to be paid handsomely in kind by a Greenlander whom he had helped, while at the same time he accepted payment from this Greenlander's opponent.

Thus, it seems as if trading – if such a term can be used in this connection – was highly one-sided as far as demand was concerned. It was, and remained, the foreigners' "hunger for blubber" which determined the bargain. Any practical reason for the Greenlanders congregating when the ships laid anchor on the coast is thus hard to find. Once their frugal needs had been satisfied, all that remained was the excitement and festive atmosphere.

It is not clear whether or not alcohol played a role on these occasions. The older accounts agree on the Greenlanders' dislike for strong drinks. On the other hand, Pårs left an account of the festivities on Queen Anna Sophia's birthday in April 1729: the Greenlanders, having consumed good food and drink, were very happy. The Queen's name had to be repeated several times for them "and each time they took something in their glasses, the cheers were for Queen Anna Sophia", whereupon they waved their hands towards the window awaiting the proper salute which they had heard previously. On the King's birthday, in October 1728, Greenlanders were included, and after they had been given presents and ample food and drink they went home "drunk and happy". In other words European influences were beginning to make themselves felt.

Only inhabitants of the region nearest to Godthåb were exposed to this influence more or less constantly. The settlements farther to the north and south received only a few visits from the colony, but also sometimes from the Dutch.[4] Farther to the north and south, only rumours infiltrated. Now and again travellers or passing Greenlanders came and settled for a short period at Godthåb, also at Haabets Øe. Hans Egede preached or merely talked to them, and noticed that they were willing to listen.

It was Hans Egede's most important responsibility to teach the children who had been baptized in January and February at the nearest settlements. For this reason, he travelled for part of the time, when he could hire a boat, but sometimes he used "Papa", or Frederik Christian to use his baptismal name, as catechist. This experiment had apparently succeeded; even adult Greenlanders listened piously to Frederik Christian's addresses, and asked many questions, which he answered as best he could. "They [the adult Greenlanders] reminded him morning and night to read to the little ones", recounts Hans Egede, whose idea that it was necessary to train the Greenlanders as catechists seemed thus to have received strong support.

These autumn months saw growth at Godthåb; even trade was satisfactory. The calm atmosphere in the colony, where numbers were now greatly reduced, continued even after Pårs returned for the winter. Hans Egede had time and energy to travel round the settlements to preach and teach, but he was hindered by lack of boats and crew. Trading expeditions were a perpetual source of frustration, as there was no room on them for Egede or the missionary Miltzow. Frederik Christian could apparently manage a kayak and was therefore sent out several times; the same was true of Niels Egede, now nineteen years old and a complete master of the language. The difficulties of getting conveyance increased when one of the barges was wrecked by a sudden south-westerly wind off the colony. A dinghy from the shore rescued two of the crew of three, but the dinghy itself was smashed to pieces against the rocks – those on board managing to reach land unhurt. The long-boat at the colony was only saved at this time by the cargo of provisions which was being transported to the colony from Haabets Øe being thrown overboard.

Its technical equipment was one of the many weaknesses of the whole Greenland *Dessein*. Vessels were quickly worn out by the harsh treatment they received in all kinds of weather in the ice-packed waters, and by being bumped against rocks while moored. When Pårs was due to travel back to Nipisat in March 1720, the boat was in such a bad condition that water reached the gunwale; after the water had been baled out, it half filled up again during the night. Apart from this, there was just one "rickety and leaky boat" whose ability to keep out water was dependent on its being daubed with rancid butter the day before. Eventually, however, the Governor got away. By chance a Dutch skipper came into the settlement who he could not help, as he had neither nails nor tar to make the boat seaworthy, but Pårs bargained with him to take him on to Nipisat. Godthåb's assistant and crew returned with the boat as it was, loaded with four iron-banded blubber-filled casks: it cannot have been as dangerous as Pårs thought.

The four casks had been collected by the Greenlanders at Pisugfik, north of Godthåb, and put aside for collection as payment for that "tax" which Hans Egede and the Council had so often suggested. The Commission of 1729 had discussed Egede's suggestion and concluded that it was difficult to tax the Greenlanders. If a Greenlander would willingly give some blubber, then naturally this would not be prevented. Meanwhile the council might consider placing an empty barrel with each family. When it was filled it could be collected by the merchant, who would give "some small thing from his stock as compensation with the approval of the council. If they wanted to give more blubber it had to be duly paid for "in the best way that could be agreed". At first, the council at Nipisat decided to do nothing about this because they could not spare any barrels and had no contact with the people on the spot; the building work kept them too busy.

At Godthåb it was decided in mid-October to send the assistant on yet another trading expedition before Christmas, taking several empty barrels as suggested by the Commission "which must first be put into operation in the vicinity, before experimenting further afield". Accordingly, the assistant left one of these four iron-banded casks at Pisugfik in each of the four largest of its six houses. Two of the best men at each house were made responsible for the casks "and the wild men said that they would not deny the King tax, if they were assured of freedom from attack and injustice from strangers". The assistant gave them this assurance: they only heeded to turn to the Governor or Hans Egede for protection if they were in any way wronged.

Here was a clear, unambiguous establishment of the Council's authority – with either the Governor or Hans Egede in charge – with royal approval (even though such approval did not formally exist). It was a continuation of the practice advised by Hans Egede in 1727 and put into practice by Matthias Fersleff in that year at Disko Bay. By repeating this reassurance about the King's enforcement of the law and protection, an attempt was made to create a social order of the European type among the Greenlanders.

The "tax" from the inhabitants at Pisugfik was duly collected, and so the same procedure was repeated farther north, this time with eleven casks, each containing two barrels. This time they were left at several places and the Greenlanders promised to fill them with blubber. How many full casks resulted from this had not been recorded. Possibly the blubber received was included in the ordinary purchasing. It was one thing for the Greenlanders to say they were prepared to pay this levy, and another for them actually to do so, even if they were able to. It was dependent on there being as much blubber available farther south along the coast as there seemed to be in the Disko Bay area. There are signs that the catch was poor.

Strangely, there was little mention of famine among the Greenlanders in the various accounts. However, Pårs did write of such conditions in 1729. Here he recounted that there were often years when the Greenlanders starved, and had to eat the skins off their kayaks. Hans Egede told of Greenlanders often being found dead with lumps of kayak skin in their mouths. At such times, those living near the colony swarmed in. Twenty or thirty people might stay by the colony for several days, where naturally they could not be allowed to die publicly of hunger, but were given some of the scarce provisions. Such a situation could not continue indefinitely, and of course it meant considerable expense for the *Dessein.*

Pårs, by way of social assistance, provided free meals of dried cod fish, which was bought in Bergen, shipped to Greenland and distributed in times of hardship to the Greenlanders – an indication that the Greenland community, certainly along the coast south of Disko Bay, was not economically self-sufficient. It might be thought that the Greenlanders gave up too much of their blubber and other foods to both the Dutch and the colony's merchants, thus contributing to the famines, but the small amounts of blubber exported by the colonies cannot have impoverished them. However, whaling carried on by the Dutch on their own did not affect Greenland's economy.

Periods of hunger were known in earlier Eskimo communities and cannot on the whole be blamed on the trade; there are indeed instances of the Greenlanders refusing to give up their supplies.[5] Greenland's size and varied conditions makes no statement that is valid for one settlement or group of settlements valid for all. Famine around Godthåb could co-exist with relative plenty a dozen or so kilometres to the north or south.

In general, there was little mutual help between the Greenlanders' settlements. Each lived its own isolated life, while at the same time extensive trips and gatherings took place, often for hunting. Every year, a great number of Greenlanders met at Godthåb or in the Nipisat sound near Haabet's Øe at the end of April and beginning of May to catch lumpfish; one year Hans Egede counted a hundred families in tents there. Perhaps the seal migration through the many sounds also had a unifying effect. Certainly these numerous channels between the islands were the scene of an extensive seal-catching operation; the seal migration took place at the same time as the lumpfishing in Hans Egede's account.

REFERENCES

1. There is a small possibility that the Christiania Commission got the idea about the necessity of a fortress from Vídalín's proposals 1703. A copy of that MS. is still in the late Bishop Deichman's library, together with other MSS. concerning Greenland affairs (this library is more or less intact, and forms a substantial part of Oslo public library). Vídalín thought that a defence against the "savages" was inevitable, and therefore proposed an eventual colony organized behind the ramparts of a

fortress. In 1718 a "private" proposal to build a fortress in Greenland to protect a future European settlement was advanced to the King; but this does not seem to have been read by the Christiania Commission. It is most likely that the Christiania Commission's proposal is based upon purely traditional conceptions: a Royal project without a military "escort" was unimaginable.

2. These are all localities in the inner part of the Godthåb region. There had been medieval Norse settlements in all of them, as was already obvious to Hans Egede. In May Hans Egede had sown some barley at Qôrqut, a valley in a small fjord half way up one of the northern arms of Godthåb fjord. It grew well and was in the ear by the beginning of August. However the night frost came when it was ripening, hence it only yielded little; and during the winter the barley crops became mouldy. He therefore did not make further experiments. He thought, however, that vegetable seeds would succeed, and with this he would make some experiments. In Godthåb, at the colony itself, he had some success with his vegetables.

3. The barber-surgeon reported "that feet, fingers and faces were frostbitten, and more which I feel ashamed to mention".

4. Hans Egede in his *Relations* reports (7–14 April 1730) that a Dutch merchantman had anchored off Haabets Øe and bartered goods with the many Greenlanders passing by. The latter disappeared when the trader arrived from Godthåb, as they did not dare to do barter with the Dutch while he was present. At that time there was no clear official prohibition on trade between the Greenlanders and the Dutch, but perhaps the Greenlanders had sensed the antagonism that existed between the Danes and the Dutch, and either perceived that the trade was undesirable or were simply afraid of retaliatory measures from the permanent colonists. That was probably the only effect of the miserable soldiery in Godthåb and Nipisat. At any rate, this is the first indication we have that the Dutch trade felt the competition with the trade of the Danish colonies.

5. Hans Egede in his *Relations* reports, 14 October 1721: "There were landed about fifty seals, which they had caught, but the savages would by no means sell any of them to us, and pointed at their women and children, that they [the seals] were for them to eat and they had to subsist on them."

9

THE YEARS OF CRISIS
1730–1733

The scattered nature of the settlements impeded trade as well as the activities of the mission, thereby protecting and preserving Greenland culture. In the first ten years the colonies at Godthåb and Nipisat had made little impression on the Greenlanders beyond the immediate populations. Yet the source material leads us to believe that curiosity was aroused all along the coast, and that news of the Greenlanders' encounters with the settlers spread quickly by "*kamik* [moccasin] post".

However, it must have been something more than curiosity that made the Disko Bay Greenlanders want to have a pastor there, as Matthias Fersleff reported in 1727. It appears that their wish was sincere. In October 1730 Hans Egede was on the Kook islands off Godthåb, teaching the Greenlanders living there and baptizing their children. Among these was one who had come all the way from Disko Bay to request Hans Egede to visit them. "Say to the Speaker (for so they called me) that he is to come north to live with us". Then Hans Egede should have every privilege usually accorded to the foreign traders, who could speak only of blubber and of nothing that mattered.

With characteristic steadfastness Hans Egede continued his work, although his way was barred by every kind of hardship and difficulty. A few positive results and the rare victory of deep significance gave him encouragement. However, his conscience was troubled by the mass baptism of infants; he did what he could to have the baptized children instructed. He seems to have experienced some relief in being able to write in his "Report" on 28 November 1729 of the children on Haabets Øe: "Of those children baptized during the last winter six have already departed this life and as the first fruits entered God's Kingdom." Most of the children survived, however. Throughout the winter of 1729–30 Hans Egede continued to baptize the children, at the same time trying to continue the training of young Greenlanders as catechists. Frederik Christian was an example of what could be done, and showed that such training could benefit the mission. Egede sent him out and tried to persuade young Greenlanders to stay in the colony, permanently or for shorter periods, to receive instruction. The children and young people who stayed in the colony for long periods lived in the same way and on the same diet as the other colonists, and were entered on the colony's food allowance list and thus were to some extent weaned away from their old way of life. Efforts were made to obtain Greenlandic food for them, but this was seldom possible.

In July 1729 Hans Egede took two orphan boys under his wing. This was resented by their relatives, who took them away one night, but Egede got them back again in November. A little while afterwards Pårs also took in an orphan boy, and now wanted a girl as well. Egede easily obtained one, for "of this latter kind there were plenty to be had, but one could rarely and only with difficulty get hold of boys because however well they were seen to be treated by us, they were needed for work and as providers".

Hans Egede therefore tried a new approach, starting with a widow's son in 1731. He tried to persuade parents to allow their children to stay in the colony to be taught for a fairly short time at their own expense. But the Greenlanders did not like this idea, and hid the boys whenever Egede came to visit them. When he told them that he was unable to come more often and could not send anyone else, the parents in the settlement replied: "Then tell the King to send us more pastors." The Greenlanders in Godthåb obviously realized that one had to apply to the King in order to obtain what was needed. So frequently did Egede and the colonists speak of the King and his greatness, that the Greenlanders began to use this concept as an argument against those who said they came in the King's name. Not only had they heard of the King from Hans Egede and other Europeans, but they had Pôq's account also. Even so, the King must have seemed very remote, both as a person and as a power.

It was not, of course, simply to educate them that the colonists took young people into their homes. The wish expressed by Pårs for a lad and a girl probably arose from a desire for domestic help. Similarly, on 23 June 1730, Egede took into his service a young man called Inuk, whom he had met with a party of Greenlanders from the south, who had not travelled north for ten years. Inuk insisted on staying in Godthåb and Hans Egede indulged his wish because the colony was underpopulated and to see whether he could attend to odd jobs or be taught to do so. This was not a new idea. In 1727 Christopher Jessen Petterson asked the colonists: "Could not the Greenlanders be taken into service in the colonies and trained for any work that arises?" At that time Hans Egede had expressed strong doubts, but Jacob Geelmuyden had answered in the affirmative. Both felt that the

Greenlanders would need to be subjected to "coercion and discipline".[1] What happened to Inuk in 1730 is not known; but he was not mentioned again, and so was probably not a success.

Most of the Greenlanders living in the colonies were there to receive instruction for baptism and perhaps to act as catechists later. At Nipisat there were two baptized and two unbaptized Greenlanders, and at Godthåb Frederik Christian and Peder Wilding, who were both baptized, and perhaps three or four others. The numbers were not large, but there was little room, and food supplies were not likely to be increased until it could be decided whether the trade was to be run from Copenhagen or Bergen. Until then, the necessary capital could not be made available.

For the directors in Bergen, the situation in 1729 was desperate. The returning seamen and employees wanted their salaries and wages in cash, but there were neither funds to draw on, nor any hope of obtaining credit. They paid the most pressing expenses by drawing on the sums granted for the chartering of ships from Bergen; they could only do this when the ships had not yet returned. The revenue and expenditure of the Greenland *Dessein* had somehow become mixed up with those of the Bergen Company, probably through the current accounts and loans deposited with the Company's directors in 1728–9. Van Osten, the Governor of Bergen, again examined and attempted to unravel the accounts of the Bergen Company to try and disover the final sum owed by the directors. In a lengthy report, he set out his interpretation of "the Greenland undertaking and its finances . . . inasmuch as I have been able to elucidate such an involved and obscure business . . ."[2] But the matter dragged on for years, and was taken over by the *Rentekammer*.

Well into October, when the other ships had reached Bergen and settlement was due, no warrant for any money had been received. People living in Greenland wanted their accounts paid so that they could meet the debts they had incurred before emigrating. "So one trouble after another comes upon us, with our bare and empty hands to help us, since no goods are arriving here from Greenland and we have not been credited with any more than is shown in our account sent on 14 June."

The 1729 Commission appears to have been inactive throughout the autumn of that year after receiving news from Governor Furman concerning the settlement by Icelanders. The Commission apparently started to work out the funds spent so far in Bergen and Copenhagen, but then did nothing until early 1730. Not until then was the King informed of "the many and considerable expenses which this work, begun with such godly purpose for the conversion of the heathen, has already cost and will continue to cost" if sailings and shipments of supplies were to continue on the same scale as previously. Most of the lottery money and the "bounty" had been swallowed up, and the "Privy Purse" had advanced a considerable sum to the *Dessein*. So it was recommended that Pårs and the whole garrison should be recalled. Differences and disputes between the officers, and "the sinful and unchristian life" led by the common soldiers, formed a major part of reports from Greenland. The garrison was apparently unnecessary; the Greenlanders seemed friendly, even helpful.

The directors in Bergen were apparently ignorant of what was being planned in 1730. Magnus Schiøtte felt increasingly uneasy and uncertain throughout the year. When the *Cron Printz Christian* asked to put into Bergen because of a shortage of provisions the directors dared not allow her to do so. Schiøtte, who was then in Copenhagen, asked for instructions, not for himself but on behalf of Major-General Tuchsen "who, like myself, was most graciously appointed a director, but since the fitting out was arranged from Copenhagen, we are only directors in name"; in Schiøtte's absence, Tuchsen had to administer the affairs in Bergen. There was bitterness in Schiøtte's remark about the directors' authority, and at their inactivity throughout the year.

As we have seen, the Commission recognized that the garrison and Governor were serving no useful purpose and that the whaling was too costly. It could not then (April–May) have been known in Copenhagen that the whaling had been a complete failure. Because of the heavy expense, it was decided to abandon the more comprehensive programme and for the coming year, 1730–1, the two colonies were each to have one pastor, trader and assistant and only the essential men. Only one ship, the *Morianen*, was sent out to collect those who were to leave the country. The *Cron Printz Christian* was to return home with cargo. This was only decided at a very late stage, so the *Morianen* did not sail until mid-June.

Pårs and Landorph, and the council at Nipisat, were informed of the royal decision in an order. A few days later an order was despatched concerning the Icelandic settlement which was to take place in 1731. The idea of proceeding with the mission and colonization had not been abandoned; but with the proposed settlement, the whole *Dessein* was turned upside down. Until now it had been based on the principle that the mission was the main purpose and that the trader was there to support the mission. But imperceptibly the economic element had come to the forefront, although it was still emphasized that everything was being undertaken "for the godly purpose of conversion of the heathen". Now a settlement by Icelandic farmers was being added to the plan. The government appeared to be set on an increasingly active colonial policy in Greenland. But the tight economy which was still a feature of the Danish–Norwegian kingdoms meant that the whole undertaking was kept at such a low level economically that it could only be carried through and pay its way with great difficulty.

Another year was to pass before the costly complement of men could be removed from Greenland. The *Morianen* had sailed too late and dared not go direct to Nipisat, for which she was bound, but wintered in Godthåb. Nipisat did not receive news of the recall until October and then only because Ole Lange travelled from Nipisat to Godthåb by open boat, returning at the end of September.

In Copenhagen matters now became quieter. The death of Frederik IV on 12 October meant a further shelving of Greenland affairs. The accession of the new monarch also involved changes in the upper administration. The Commission of 24 January 1729 was automatically dissolved, because two of the members, including Møinichen, were obliged to resign their official posts in any case. The General Commissariat of the Navy was thus left to deal with Greenland affairs.

In this first year the general tendency of the new Conseil was towards big cuts in state expenditure, which did not accord with the plans for the army and navy of Poul Vendelbo Løvenørn, the new *gehejmeråd* and senior secretary for war. He probably saw the "Greenland *Dessein*" as an item on which he could economize without affecting his most important aim, which was to organize and equip the navy and army as well as possible. Presumably after verbal consultations with Christian VI, it was decided to recall everyone from Greenland, and a ship was chartered to collect them. All this took place before 17 April 1730 when the details of the recall were submitted for the King's approval. At the same time a decision was needed on what should happen if Hans Egede wished to remain there longer: what provisions would have to be left for him? Magnus Schiøtte had reported that there was a quantity of goods, especially barrels, in Greenland belonging to the "Bergen Greenland Company"; these could not now be collected. It was considered too expensive to send any ship for these items apart from the one that was being sent for the colonists and their provisions, ammunition, personal possessions and so on; the barrels and other goods mentioned would not even pay the expenses of a ship which might be chartered subsequently to fetch home Hans Egede and others who wanted to remain with him in Greenland. It seems that the General Commissariat of the Navy did not want Hans Egede to remain in Greenland, since fetching him the following year would cost too much.

On 23 April the King decided that "the pastor" and other employees could remain if they so wished, and could be spared whatever provisions and materials those returning home did not need for the voyage. But there was no promise to fetch them later or to send vessels the following year for any purpose. Christian VI approved the arrangements which makes clear the King's ignorance of Greenland affairs. Neither Iver Rosencrantz, who had replaced Møinichen, nor Poul Vendelbo Løvenørn was much interested in it. Plans for the settlement of Greenland by Icelanders were shelved. The main thing now was to be extricated from the whole business without further expense.

The Missionskollegium did not intervene; the matter was left entirely in the hands of the General Commissariat of the Navy. Why did the Kollegium not plead Hans Egede's case? Possibly this was due to the death in December 1730 of its first president, Johan Georg von Holstein, whose political influence, and with it that of the kollegium, had waned. It is only certain that in the spring of 1731 not one official voice was raised on behalf of the Greenland mission. Apparently anyone who could do so lay low when there was a change in government, for this was accompanied by purges and a general review of the past conduct of officials. In this way the hitherto powerful chief secretary, Møinichen, fell into disgrace with the King.

On receiving news of the position of the Greenland *Dessein*, Hans Egede wrote in his "Report": "These were extremely sad tidings for me and afflicted me more than anything else in the world, for it seemed that all the effort and pain endured in enlightening the poor ignorant people had been in vain. . . . My mind was thrown into the greatest confusion . . . for the poor Greenlanders, especially the little ones who were baptized [there were about 150], were as dear to my heart as any children could ever be to a fond mother." He realized that it would be impossible for him to stay without being guaranteed adequate provisions and assistance, and future support. Giertrud Rasch learned of the royal decision when the ship put into Godthåb, and suffered consequently from nervous strain; it is typical of the relationship between Hans Egede and his wife at that time that not until then did he seem to realize that Giertrud was as distressed as he at having to leave Greenland. He had not been aware of the extent to which she too had become involved both in the work with the Greenlanders and life in Greenland.

A crucial decision now had to be taken. These days in June–July 1731 marked the hour of destiny for the whole "Greenland undertaking" and for Hans Egede's life work. If they left Greenland now, it would be impossible – for them at any rate – to return and start their work again. If they took advantage of the permission to stay for a further period, there was always a faint possibility that the King's attitude could be changed. It was this possibility that was decisive.

L

On 12 July Hans Egede announced his decision to the council. Three days earlier the *Morianen* had arrived in Godthåb from Nipisat with some of the goods and most of the people; the *Caritas* had arrived the day before. The captains of both vessels were anxious to sail. Hans Egede had tried to persuade some of the people to remain with him and his family, but none wished to do so. The ships could not carry everything and what was left behind, as well as the buildings, had to be protected against theft and other damage. He therefore had to ask the council to "arrange for eight or ten persons to remain as well"; with these, and by assuming responsibility for the trade in addition to mission work, he would try by 1732 to pay the King for the assets in the form of the buildings, produce, merchandise for barter and fixtures that existed at Godthåb. He hoped that in the meantime someone would undertake to carry on with the *Dessein*, slender though this hope might be. If the King would not send ships out next year, he would himself make arrangements for some to be fitted out. As a final argument in favour of staying, he reminded the King that otherwise "the most holy sacrament of baptism of the many innocent little ones who have been baptized would be profaned, which I most surely believe your gracious Royal Majesty would not wish to hear and be aware of".

The council discussed Hans Egede's proposal but were unwilling to compel anyone to stay, chiefly because it was contrary to the royal command. However, against all expectations ten sailors were persuaded, although in the end it was not those ten who stayed, but four people from Bergen, the colony's two carpenters and four of the crew of the *Morianen*. Plenty of provisions and materials were left for those who stayed, including all the timber shipped out in 1730 for the proposed settlement by Icelanders. The quantities of merchandise left behind for Hans Egede were not large, but were probably enough to pay for what could be bought with the Godthåb colony as a base during the next year.

An unsuccessful attempt was made to get someone with a knowledge of the trade to stay, so Hans Egede suggested that this son Niels, then about twenty-one years old, should take over the trading. The council were willing to pay Niels a wage for taking on the duties of trader and book-keeper, and Hans was asked to name a sum. He replied that his son should be given remuneration "according to the competence and diligence shown". His father had previously employed Niels as a catechist, and this was his confirmation as a trader, and the beginning of his dual role which was to be a continuing feature of his career in Greenand.

Of the Greenlanders who had lived with Ole Lange, Matthias Fersleff, Miltzow, Landorph and Pårs, a boy who had been with Ole

Lange in the north ran away before the ship left. Six others went with the ships. The council had disagreed as to the advisability of taking these baptized Greenlanders to Denmark. Pôq and his family, and two young men and a girl, who were all baptized, had been sent with the 1728 ship to Copenhagen, and all had caught smallpox and died in April and May 1729. But people in Greenland were not aware that their deaths were caused by this disease, and attributed it to the change in climate. Ole Lange had misgivings about allowing Greenlanders to accompany the ships to Copenhagen again, but Pårs insisted that he wanted to take "his two Greenlanders" with him and so the others wanted to go as well. This proved a fateful step.

On board the ships leaving Greenland at the end of July were almost as many advocates for the continuation of "the work" as there were people on board. Also on board were many letters and reports, including Hans Egede's well-known letter, dated 20 July 1731, which seems to have brought about rapid changes. This letter reached Copenhagen with the *Morianen* on 2 September. Within days, Christian VI had changed his attitude towards both the Greenland mission and the Trading Company. There has been speculation as to the reasons for this *volte face* and who might have influenced the King. One theory is that the pious Count Nicolaus Ludwig von Zinzendorf won the King over. He was present at the King's coronation on 6 June, but there is no evidence that he played a decisive part in the King's change of attitude. Another theory is that the missionary Ole Lange made a strong plea to the King for the mission, and that this, with Hans Egede's letter, turned the scales. A letter he wrote to the King, making a number of requests and an earnest plea for the mission, does exist, and on it is a note in the King's hand.[3] Some days before, however, the King had already issued a printed proclamation referring to the mission's past activities and the trading and sailings. It seems that considerable results had been achieved, but it was hoped that a trading company would be more profitable. It was considered that the trade with Greenland "may be conducted and maintained more profitably and more providently, and be better managed by a company and partnership than by ourselves on our own account". The proclamation invited subjects to apply to become shareholders in a company to be set up, in which the King would also participate financially. The company would be granted a charter and reasonable privileges, and the General Commissariat of the Navy was to arrange for its establishment. The proclamation was to be published in Norway and Denmark. It stated, from the "latest information received", that over 200 Greenland families had been instructed in the Christian faith. This "information" was undoubtedly Hans Egede's letter of 20 July 1731, which also seems to have provided the basis for the invitation to the King's subjects to become shareholders: "Now I most humbly wish nothing rather than that your Royal Majesty should most graciously take it upon yourself to continue with the *Dessein,* but since it is acknowledged that merchants and private persons are able to conduct such undertakings with less expense and greater profit, I would think that many would be interested in participating in the trade."

However, the proclamation omits what undoubtedly made the greatest impression on the King. After the reference to "approximately 200 families", Egede had mentioned "over 100" children who had been baptized with their parents' consent; a list of these children's names was enclosed with the letter. Hans Egede wrote that he had decided to take advantage of the King's permission for him to stay because "I could not find it in my heart, if it is otherwise to rest with me, to leave these poor people who have advanced so far in the knowledge of God and to see the hallowed sacrament of baptism profaned for the infants who have been baptized."

Ole Lange's letter to the King also pleaded the case of the mission first and foremost, exhorting him "with true royal Christian zeal to carry on with the mission, considering the many infants who are baptized Christians, who would otherwise lack instruction in the knowledge of Christ as they grow up, whereby the means of hallowed redemption would be profaned in them, which God in His Grace forbid and avert such misfortune from Your Majesty. . . ." He reminded the King of Hans Egede's indefatigable zeal. [4]

The two men of God thus made a powerful appeal to the King as supreme guardian of the Church; his pious nature and deep sense of responsibility were touched. The King's *volte face* was as complete as it was rapid, and prompt action was ordered. Detailed negotiations were to start as quickly as possible with the Missionskollegium and sensible merchants to promote "Christianity, navigation and trade in and from Greenland". The first meeting to deal with the matter was held on 3 October. Fifteen people, including Pårs, Landorph, Schiøtte, Lange and Geelmuyden, had previously declared their willingness to continue the trade with Greenland, and eight prominent merchants were among the fifteen, including Frederik Holmsted, the wholesaler, and Jacob Sewerin. During October and the succeeding months many meetings were held, and this gathering gradually came to be regarded as a commission which was to arrive at a project for submission to the King.

That Jacob Sewerin took part in these meetings was perhaps due to Pårs, for while Pårs was in Greenland, Sewerin managed his personal finances. This remarkable businessman was familiar with the northern trade, for he had traded with Finnmark and Iceland, and had engaged in whaling off Svalbard. Although a member of Copenhagen City Council, he was alone in representing the city's merchants. Perhaps his earlier theological studies, although they did not result in his graduating in divinity, aroused his interest in the Greenland trade with its special task of subsidizing the mission. For whatever reason, he was an individualist on the 1731-2 Commission.

During October a number of people put forward their proposals. Magnus Schiøtte's were vague and were dropped from the discussions, but they are of interest in that he felt trade with Greenland should be conducted from both Bergen and Copenhagen; the sailings could best be made from Bergen, where men and goods were most easily obtainable. Wool was to be brought from Iceland, but harpooners (and presumably whaling masters) from the North Friesian Islands were most readily available in Copenhagen. He thought that the arrangements for 1732 should be made from Copenhagen.

Six "experts on Greenland" submitted a joint scheme. Among them were Captain Landorph, the missionary Ole Lange, and the traders Jacob Geelmuyden and Matthias Fersleff – their time in Greenland having evidently created a bond between them. They were joined by two of the naval officers assigned to the Greenland run. In general, their scheme was not followed, although Fersleff's idea of establishing a colony in Disko Bay was adopted for future use. Pårs did not agree, and submitted his own comments on their scheme, but these were not even acknowledged.

The naval authorities, who made enquiries in the duchies (Slesvig and Holstein) as to whether whaling-masters and crews were obtainable, received several suggestions, but it was considered too late to make any whaling plans for 1732. In this connection Geelmuyden's experiences at Nipisat are interesting: he had reported that between 28 January and 28 February an abundance of whales had been noted in the vicinity. It is remarkable that the Greenlanders reported whales to the colony and invited the men of the colony to come and help. But the collaboration that resulted was less successful than anticipated: evidently the very different methods of hunting and of processing the catch clashed. In any case, Geelmuyden could not be sure that there were so many whales in that locality and at that time every year.

Schiøtte's proposal was briefly discussed. He was pessimistic about business transactions being carried on in Bergen and wrote that the officials in Copenhagen should delegate a book-keeper to Bergen, if sailing arrangements were ever made from there. He clearly had little faith in his fellow-citizens. He favoured a total paid up capital of 100,000 rdl., divided into shares of 1,000 rdl. each; 5 per cent was to be paid up each year over five years. This corresponded to the annual expenditure incurred up to then – approximately 5,000 rdl. per annum – and so the difficulties regarding liquidity would have assumed an almost permanent character. This was probably why his proposal was ignored.

Jacob Sewerin submitted a proposal, based on a total expenditure of 16–17,000 rdl. This was countered by the second proposal of the Copenhagen merchants for a once and for all expenditure of 12–13,000 rdl. This proposal was drawn up by the wholesale merchant Holmsted and the Copenhagen brewer G. K. Kloumann, and supported by other merchants on the Commission and Captain Landorph.

The details of Sewerin's colonization proposals were very similar to Pårs' plan as set out in a report of 8 August 1729. The Commission rightly observed that his proposal for many small settlements accorded with Hans Egede's ideas for furthering the mission. Besides Godthåb and Nipisat in 1733, he suggested that a colony be established in the Disko Bay but none to the south of Godthåb. Otherwise no special consideration was paid to the repeated suggestions made by Hans Egede, whose detailed proposal of 30 April 1731 resembles both Sewerin's and Holmsted–Kloumann's proposals in many respects, has the laconic note in the margin: "No action." Holmsted and Kloumann wanted four colonies to be maintained – the two old ones plus one at Igaliko and one in the Christianshåb bay. The King was to support the mission completely, and the new company would take over all settlements and materials in Greenland free. It seems that everyone except Jacob Sewerin agreed to this latter plan. During the discussions, however, Sewerin received backing from two quarters. Pårs' support was dubious, since he naturally wanted to push his own proposal (which never materialized). Two of the officials of the central administration, however, wanted a compromise.

The autumn and winter of 1731–2 passed without any decisive move being made. Memoranda were submitted to the King in December and January, and were probably discussed by the *Conseil* on 7 March when the King approved its recommendation, which was accordingly incorporated in an order on 17 March to the General Commissariat of the Navy. The proposals contained in the memoranda to the King were regarded as inadequate, and it was felt that consideration should be given to the following points: "1, whether the mission is worth continuing with any great hopes of success in Greenland; 2, how the mission and the Trading Company might assist each other." The King wished to know, thirdly, the costs of the proposal for the first year, and finally whether any merchants were interested in the Trade. There was no question of a lottery or a special tax. A charter would be granted at the shareholders' request, and the company would be presented with the existing property in Greenland. The King would allocate to the mission annually "a certain sum, but would not consider any further costs, except insofar as we might be disposed, like other shareholders, to subscribe". By and large, the King had kept to the resolution of 19 September 1731; nevertheless, this order of 17 March 1732 signified a tightening up of the loose promises he had given in overmuch haste. He was obviously trying to protect the public purse against further unforeseen expenses.

After this communication, the Commission seems to have been somewhat subdued, for it was not until a month later that a meeting was arranged between the three merchants – Kloumann, Holmsted and Sewerin – and the Missionskollegium. Kloumann and Holmsted were cautious, for on 20 May they informed the General Commissariat of the Navy that no company could be established until the terms of the potential charter were known. They regarded the Bergen Company's old charter – which had obviously been under consideration – as inadequate. These views, and the King's statement that the charter was to be drawn up in accordance with the investors' wishes – hence not until the company had actually been formed and the cards were on the table – caused deadlock. The two merchants probably thought that the charter would at best be a compromise between their wishes and the Government's interests, and not, as had been stated, according to the wishes of investors. The Government, which had considered the Commission's proposals (in reality those of Kloumann and Holmsted) too vague, was just as imprecise in its offers. The merchants had seen the extent to which the liberal phrases of the resolution of 19 September had been toned down in the order of 17 March, and would thus presumably have no faith in royal promises that were so loosely worded.

Jacob Sewerin and the merchants Kloumann and Holmsted were originally to submit their opinions jointly. The merchants forwarded theirs to Sewerin on 20 May, but did not wait for his reply. Sewerin did not realize until later that there was going to be no discussion, and so his opinion was not made known until well into June. In general it was similar to that of the other two, though there were differences. He mentioned nothing about the charter. Sewerin did not doubt that the mission would and should be continued, and that it would be successful. He suggested that a number of students, ten or twelve, who might have the "gifts of grace" if not the requisite book learning, should serve the mission at the various settlements. By associating "meekly" with the Greenlanders they would be able to learn Greenlandic, and the Greenlanders would also be able to learn some Danish, so that they would "win each other over". If any of these students were acquainted with natural philosophy, mathematics, astronomy, mechanics or navigation, they would be useful to the Trading Company. Sewerin advocated Hans Egede's plan for setting up many smaller posts at intervals of about 100 km., which would be of advantage to both trade and mission and would enable smaller boats to be used for routine expeditions. Only two main colonies were to be maintained as collecting-points; hence, a central port system was being envisaged – an idea eventually put into practice only in 1943–5.

If the mission could serve the Trading Company in any other way, it would be on the moral plane, for once the Greenlanders had become attached to the missionaries, their moral obligation to trade solely with the Company's people and not with foreigners could be impressed upon them. Christian ethics would oblige the Greenlanders to supply unadulterated goods. Sewerin found it necessary to add that the Company's people must observe the same business ethics. Finally, he believed that the King must either accept responsibility for the expenses of setting up the colonies and of settling Icelanders or Norwegians, and the initial expenses incurred on other counts, or he must – apart from transferring the existing property and materials – also make available a sum of 12–16,000 rdl., apart from the mission expenses. The King had, after all, promised to bestow a certain annual sum on the mission. Sewerin had every confidence that people would eventually appear who were interested in the proposed company.

That, then, was all that happened in just under a year – things were no further forward. It had not been finally decided what was to be done, but only that the work was somehow to be continued. But the authorities could not allow Hans Egede to continue to live in Greenland without being informed of the situation, let alone without material help, and the Commission's negotiations in 1731–2 had shown how difficult it was to achieve an economic basis for carrying on. Arrangements were therefore made for a ship to be sent to Godthåb with supplies for the colony, and with instructions for Hans Egede should the Commission decide it would no longer be possible to support his ministry in Greenland. Egede's whole life's work hung by a thread. Throughout the winter of 1731–2 Hans, Giertrud and Niels worked with this uncertainty in their minds, and the news that came with the ship did not improve matters for them.

The handling of the 1732 sailing typifies the haphazard way in which the central administration dealt with the whole matter. On 12 April 1732 the King instructed the General Commissariat of the Navy that a ship was to be chartered. Provisions for one year were to be sent out, calculated on the basis of 12½ rations;[5] new men were also to go, including Jens Hjort who had been in Greenland for several years, working his way up to the position of assistant. He was to be a trader, along with the barber-surgeon, Chr. Kieding, who had also been in Greenland before. Hans Egede felt that a positive attitude was now being adopted. He was ordered to arrange passages home in a foreign ship for himself and all his companions, should no ship arrive from Denmark in 1733 at the right time of year (i.e. June). At the same time the King commanded that no more Greenlanders should be sent to Denmark without special permission. These instructions were not calculated to raise Hans Egede's hopes. It was still possible that the support agreed on in principle might be abandoned, so that it would not even be possible to send a ship.

The King further decided that one Matthias Jochimsen should be sent out with the ship to undertake exploration for minerals and to try and discover the Eastern Settlement. He would also look for sites where grain could be grown and cattle reared, with a view to settlement, so that others in Denmark, Norway or Iceland could follow.[6]

So Hans Egede and Giertrud Rasch fluctuated between hope and disappointment. Although he did not normally complain of his health, Hans wrote in June 1732 that he was "very much impaired in health and strength this year, more than heretofore, anxious thoughts over the ill-fate of poor Greenland being a chief cause". There had been more than enough to weigh on Hans Egede's mind in 1731–2. Trouble had started as soon as the ships left Godthåb. It was learned from Greenlanders passing through Godthåb on their way south that the Dutch had burnt down everything at Nipisat. Apparently several Dutch vessels had been anchored there, and more than ten pinnaces had put in to Nipisat; everything of value had been seized and the rest set on fire. A couple of Greenlanders' winter quarters nearby were also destroyed.

In the autumn and spring many Greenlanders visited Godthåb, going south in August–September and north in April. Some stayed for a time "to enjoy our company and hear God's word". Hans Egede's stories and preaching gradually took hold of certain individuals. One Greenlander who had listened to him for a short time in 1726, but had since lived in the south was reported to have known no peace of mind thinking of what had been said, especially concerning the "unpleasant and dreadful place of torment, whither he did not want to go". It had not escaped the Greenlanders' notice that the European population of Godthåb had been reduced, but possibly its reduction enabled those who stayed behind to come closer to the Greenlanders. Indeed Hans Egede wrote in his "Reports": " 'That you love us,' they said, 'we can easily understand, otherwise you too would have gone away from us in summer, like the others.' "

However, the Greenlanders were disillusioned about the King; he was powerful and had many people and ships and plenty of food, yet he could not send even one ship to Greenland or look after Hans Egede and the colonists. Hans Egede was unable to remove their bafflement on this score. But one thing they did now understand, and were always to keep in mind: there was a power far across the sea to the east which had to be reckoned with and which could intervene for good or for evil – as it did now in Hans Egede's case. Hans Egede continued to visit those living nearest, and to send out Frederik Christian to instruct the baptized children. The other baptized Greenlander who had been with Hans Egede for a long time – Peter Wilding – died on New Year's day 1732.

Niels Egede devoted his energies to trade, combining the material and the spiritual. Hans hoped that as much as possible would be bought, so as to make a good trading result in 1732. It was a disaster when both trading boats broke from their moorings in a gale during the night of 19 November. One boat was completely wrecked, and the other was not repaired till 24 April. Yet they succeeded in buying so much during the year that 135 barrels of blubber and a number of skins stood ready when the ship came. Busy as he was, Hans Egede did not forget the agricultural experiments, and in September 1731 Frederik Christian was sent to Qôrqut to fetch samples of what had been sown in the spring. The grain had developed only quite small kernels; the cabbages had grown to between 16 and 32 cm. "The turnips were best, for they were the size of a small teacup, the largest being as big as a small teapot. . . ." The crops grown on the old camp sites and those harvested in the garden at Godthåb were found to be average; the turnips at Godthåb were smaller, but the cabbages somewhat bigger. The beans and peas were ruined by bad weather in August. Hans Egede was as optimistic as ever: if only the weather were kind, there could yet be ample crops.

The Old Norse tradition, maintained by seventeenth-century writers, continued to have its influence. The Old Norse sites, of which Qôrqut was one of the smaller, afforded visible evidence of previous cultivation, but it was not known that in Norse times probably only hay for animal fodder was grown. It is strange that the experience of growing relatively good crops on the old camp sites and the complete loss of whatever was sown outside them did not suggest the idea of adding manure to the soil, an expedient that was known in those days. But Hans Egede merely noted that the soil outside the camp sites was dry and sandy.

The year from August 1731 to July 1732 was spent in all kinds of activity. That it was a busy one is reflected in the style of Hans Egede's journal: it is concise and to the point, far more so than the "Reports" sent home separately. He had good results to report. There seemed to be a greater understanding of the mission's work, and Frederik Christian, as a Greenlander, had a definite advantage when he preached, in that he had experienced what Hans or Niels Egede, as foreigners, could never experience. The frequency with which he was sent out to teach bears witness to Hans Egede's great trust in him.

Of the trading activities, Hans Egede wrote: "On the 14th [July] the ship left the colony with quite a good cargo of blubber, for it was the best year and the most that has ever been taken home from Greenland. Had we not been so unfortunate as to lose our trading craft, we would, with God's help, have had more, because the loss of the trading craft cost us three trading expeditions." This was not, in fact, the most that had ever been sent from Greenland, but the cargo was still among the biggest. From Godthåb alone 167 casks, equal to two barrels each, were shipped in 1731. The results were good even though the Dutch were active that year around Godthåb.

Hans Egede started 1732–3 with almost the same uncertainty about the future as in 1731. He had acquired more help and more people with a knowledge of the trade, and Niels Egede, although still giving his services to the trade, was able to concentrate more on the parallel mission activities. But in mid-August the longboat was completely wrecked during a hay-making expedition. The colony was left with only a yawl and a pinnace, which could take only five or six casks. The shortage of boats was a hindrance to Matthis Jochimsen, who was expected to discover the Eastern Settlement. The idea of crossing the inland ice had been abandoned, probably because of Pårs' experiences in 1729. So it was decided to try out Pårs' later plan to go south round Cape Farewell. The plan was discussed in Godthåb in April 1733, but crew members and boats were lacking and time was short since one more trading expedition to the north had to be made. However, it was decided to get a rather old pinnace made seaworthy, and on 20 April Matthis Jochimsen and Hjort the trader set out with eight men. They did not return until June, having been only as far as 61° N. – approximately the same point as Hans Egede had reached in 1723 – hence without accomplishing their mission. The expedition had been undertaken at the most unsuitable time, and ice had proved an obstacle.

In an attempt to improve the transport situation some men had been sent up to Nipisat where a boat had been left behind in 1731. But at the end of September they had to report that this too was gone, probably destroyed by the Dutch. Hans Egede was moved to exclaim, for the second time, that "from such unchristian action this envious nation's ill-will towards the Dessein is all too clear": the Dutch "have always mocked and derided" it, "and now, with the greatest pleasure, they have seen its ruin". Hans Egede's tone had changed from earlier reports. It seems all too probable that the Dutch traders regarded the Danish–Norwegian enterprise as a slightly comic affair.

If there was any question of inroads being made on the Greenland economy, it was the Dutch trading and whaling which were responsible. As we have seen, for the twelve years it had now operated, the Danish–Norwegian trade had been confined to a relatively short stretch of the west coast. Dutch trade in Disko Bay was far more widespread and had offshoots along the coast right down to the most southerly regions. Whalers from Scotland, England and Hamburg also appeared, but only for a limited period, and over a fairly confined area. The influence of these traders was also somewhat limited. Greenlanders on the west coast and, through further trading, those in neighbouring regions to the south and north, were able to obtain items such as "cutting and piercing" tools, or *ulos*, knives, hooks, needles, awls and tips for bird darts, and luxury articles such as beads and household utensils – kettles, cups, spoons, etc. – which they could have made from their own materials and had not needed hitherto. Clothes were also wanted: piece-goods of kersey and cotton, shirts, breeches. Wooden platters, or bowls, were sought after, and especially popular were wooden chests, that could be used in the home or for travelling. Shortage of narrow wooden boards was for a long time what gave Greenland "handicraft" its character.

This was the extent of the trade's material effect on everyday life. Otherwise culture was still based on the country's raw materials, which were processed by the individual. An example of apparently quite pointless "bulk buying" has already been mentioned. The trading was more a matter of "collecting" than proper trading, since the remuneration for the goods collected by the Dutch did not represent a reasonable price; there was no corresponding need on the part of the Greenlanders. Their requirements were soon met, and as was repeatedly stated by the Danish–Norwegian colonists: "the Greenlanders do not actually need our goods and can manage perfectly well without them."

In other sectors the Dutch trade and navigation along these coastal stretches may have had some influence. Sexual relations occurred between the Dutch and the Greenland women, and the lasting result of this contact was the mixed population of West Greenland. The health of the Greenlanders was also affected. It is probable that tuberculosis had already been brought to the country, by the Dutch and by the colonists who came from Copenhagen in 1728. Later in the century, tuberculosis certainly seemed to be an endemic ailment of long standing.

Spiritually, the Dutch had no effect, while the influence of the Danish–Norwegian mission went deep. It gradually broke down respect for the relatively few indigenous institutions of Greenland. Strangely, the most complex of these – the world of taboos – seems to have crumbled quickly. Taboos were self-contradictory and difficult to observe in practice, especially when they denied the elementary instincts of self-preservation. Judged by the "Reports", the activities of the angákut showed an increase in vitality. In the Godthåb district it seemed that, despite their rough treatment by Hans Egede and the other colonists, they kept their hold on the population. During the sickness and many deaths in the autumn and winter of 1728–9, Greenlanders from the northern area wanted to believe that it was an angákoq who wished them harm – indeed they were sure of it. The killing of ilisîtsut took place towards the end of the 1720s and again in 1732. Though Hans Egede forcibly pointed out the cruelty of killing these women, especially in the semi-ritual way in which it was done on the second occasion, the Greenlanders saw no wrong in it. After all, these victims were comparable to the criminals who they had heard were executed in Hans Egede's own country. They could not differentiate between the fancied actions of the witch and the proved misdeeds of the criminal. At the same time it was discovered, as Hans Egede wrote, that the angákut "were, to begin with, for ever casting spells on us that we might die and perish". It brought ignominy on the angákut, however, when nothing happened to Hans Egede, whom the Greenlanders thereby came to regard as stronger and wiser than their angákut. This undoubtedly contributed to the angákut's loss of prestige, but the Greenlanders still went in fear of them, for "we . . . cannot protect ourselves against their murderous tongues". "Religious" concepts were thus taking on a dual role. On the one hand, the Greenlanders expressed their belief in the God about whom Hans Egede told them and whose existence was manifested by Egede's invulnerability. On the other hand, they remained subservient to the traditional mystical powers of magic.

This duality was not strange to Hans Egede. The last witchcraft trial in Denmark had been in 1693, and in Germany in 1711. In the comedies of Holberg, the Danish playwright, witchcraft figured as an object of satire, and superstitious belief in magical mystical powers was by no means unknown to Egede and his contemporaries in northern Norway and other parts of the kingdom. This snatch of conversation, recorded by Hans Egede in January 1732, reveals a little of the struggle between the old and the new, but scarcely anything of its wider implications; we only know that the Greenlanders "listened devoutly to the spoken word", that "isolated terms connected with Christianity, sporadically remembered, exercised their minds", and were "thought over", and that "the Word" had "caught on". Individuals, travelling to places far from the Godthåb district, passed on what was being said there by Hans Egede and the other missionaries. It is a moot point whether such "news carriers" were themselves believers or whether they merely handed on good stories and new legends. The old legends and myths were still told and the other Eskimo institutions, like drum song contests, seemed to remain untouched by outside influences. Whatever the circumstances, it was certainly these "news carriers" who paved the way for the mission outside the Godthåb district. In the spiritual conversion of the Greenlanders, the religious-cultural influence was focused on Godthåb only for a short time and, to an even smaller degree on Nipisat. If the impact on West Greenland material culture was geographically limited, that on the spiritual culture was even more so.

At that time the Dutch presumably were not going north of Disko Bay or south of Fiskenaesset in any great numbers. Isolated traders ventured north through the Vajgat and in late summer when the ice had dispersed put into the coast as far down as the present-day Julianehåb district on their way home. If they appeared there at other times it was generally because they were castaways. In any case calls made outside the Disko Bay region and the safer part of the West Coast were rare. In the southern sector the Greenlanders lived their own lives, in which long journeys, especially from south to north and back again, created a tenuous link with happenings on that stretch of coast where the inhabitants were in contact with the outside world. Intercommunication with the southernmost parts of the east coast spread the few material goods obtained from foreigners by the West Greenlanders of the far south. Further north, the East Greenlanders kept up their old way of life; their form of Thule culture had gradually become distinctive. They hunted the mammals of the sea and ice; reindeer (decreasingly) and other large and small game of the interior were also important to them.

Now and then a whaler – Dutch, English, Scottish or even French – was wrecked in the ice off the east coast. A few survivors may have escaped ashore, only to die of hunger and cold or be killed. Few, if any, of the survivors were taken into Eskimo families. We can only guess at this for we know nothing and legend tells us nothing. The Blosseville coast, with its steep, grim gullies and dense polar ice, remained a desolate frontier region which for long periods barred the way to north-south traffic along the east coast.

Here and there, from Scoresby Sound to the complex of Franz Joseph Fjord, there were other settlements, but none of them was well populated. No thorough archaeological survey of the long coastal stretch from Cape York in the west to the creeks and islands of Franz Joseph Fjord in the east has ever been made. It appears, however, that eastward migrations round the north of Greenland still occurred through the long valleys to the west of Peary Land and out through Brønlunds Fjord, after which the migration route split into various branches southwards along the east coast. The groups involved were small but are the ancestors of most of the people still living on the stretch up to Scoresby Sound. It is likely that existence in the increasing cold became steadily harder, with the conditions for human life – and for reindeer – deteriorating all the time. Seals could still be caught, but the ice made this increasingly difficult. In the 1700s human existence depended mainly on these two animals, though some walruses too may have been caught.

In the north-west corner of Greenland the Eskimos continued to live a borderline existence as *fangers* on both sides of the sounds and between Greenland and Ellesmere Land. To what extent the connection was maintained southwards via Melville Bay to the present-day Upernavik region is not known either from archaeological finds or from written material. It seems unlikely, however, that in the eighteenth century there was any influence from the north on the material culture of Greenland's north-west coast; perhaps there was no basic change in the neo-Eskimo Thule culture. Nor is there any trace of southern influence to the north of Melville Bay. The kayak, as it had developed along the West Greenland coast over the centuries up to the eighteenth century, had not reached the Cape York region, which retained the heavier, broader type of kayak.

Yet isolation from the Eskimo world to the south did not prevent recollections of people living north of Melville Bay from surviving among the inhabitants of north-west Greenland. And in the Cape York region people had some idea of those who lived to the south. They "were accustomed to awaiting the departure of foreign sledges in order to attack them". This was apparently the same view as the Central Greenland Eskimos had of those living in the south of Greenland. The inhabitants of Upernavik were later notorious for their fierce reactions, especially towards foreigners, so there may have been some truth in the opinion of them held by the people of Cape York.

The relative isolation of the people of Cape York during the seventeenth and eighteenth centuries accounts for the wholly polar Eskimo nature of their culture. The numbers of the Polar Eskimos were continually augmented over the years by migrations from North America, but until the close of the nineteenth century they subsisted entirely on what they could catch by hunting and fishing on land, sea and ice. They were economically, socially and culturally independent, and remained uninfluenced by European civilization. The period during which the seas round these regions are navigable was normally too short for sailing ships to manage the outward and homeward voyages, and in any case there was no financial attraction in making journeys to these polar coasts, at least by comparison with the more southerly areas.

REFERENCES

1. In his answer to one of the items of the Royal Commissioners' questionnaire 1727 Hans Egede wrote: "Their [the Greenlanders'] laziness and sloth are so gross that they will not easily or willingly bring themselves to work, unless they are subjected and kept under control . . ." etc. Hans Egede's opinion of the Greenlanders' industry and working capacity reveals that he was rooted in the ethics of his time. To him hunting and fishing (when one had the opportunity to practise them) were not real work, but games or hobbies, especially when they involved what seemed to him senseless gadding about. According to his conceptions, work meant assiduity, supported by a deep sense of duty. He was therefore not able to regard the Greenlanders' activities, further hampered as they were by wind and weather, as work.

2. The burden of the task caused von Osten to write that he could have spent "a year and a day" making a thorough investigation of the accounts of the Bergen Company, "and finally run the risk of going out of my mind".

3. In his monograph *Hans Egede*, 1952, p. 130, Dr. Bobé cut out the legend about Graf Zinzendorf's influence (which he had reduced *ad absurdum* in the Danish edition of 1944), but elaborated the other legend (about Ole Lange) to the utmost. It has been my duty to prick that beautiful bubble, as it is mere conjecture, based upon an undated memorandum from Ole Lange. Bobé has dated it wrongly and misinterpreted it: he invents a private audience which Ole Lange was supposed to have with the King. It is nowhere mentioned in the source material, and no proof of it can be established. On the last page of the memorandum mentioned above the King by his own hand wrote an order to the General Commissariat of the Navy to speed up the negotiations, dated 19 September 1731. This order implies that the King's change of mind was already a fact. Ole Lange's memorandum was thus of no influence in the change of Greenland policy, and must be dated between 14 and 19 September.

4. In Ole Lange's undated letter or memorandum, as it is best to describe it (see note 3), only the first part deals with the continuation of the mission, as summarized in the text. In fact it consists of only a few lines. The second part deals with his personal affairs and aims, for which he begs the King's support.

5. This calculation of rations does not correspond to an equal number of persons; a child, for example, was usually calculated as entitled to a

half or three-quarters of a ration. The Greenlanders living in the colony houses and entered on the provisions list were allocated three rations per four men, because they were expected to do better from hunting and sealing than Europeans. There was thus a sort of discrimination.

6. This Matthis Jochimsen was a Norwegian (born about 1680, and reported to have died sometime after 1735). He had just been in Iceland to make investigations and had made a report which was highly praised. In 1732 he proposed to make similar investigations in Greenland and thought of crossing the Ice cap by skiing and using reindeer, partly for transport and partly for food; he imagined that he could milk the reindeer en route. The project for crossing the Icecap was not approved.

M

10

HANS EGEDE'S LAST YEARS
IN GREENLAND 1733–1736

The immediate future of the "Greenland *Dessein*" was still uncertain. It had "for two years now . . . lain *in extremis*", wrote Hans Egede in his "Reports" on 20 May 1733: he found it frustrating that it could take so long to reach a decision. After living for twelve years in the small, virtually closed community in Godthåb, he had naturally come to regard it as the centre of the world. But the continued existence of this centre depended on decisions reached in Copenhagen. Hans Egede was certainly not ignorant of the fact that any government decision took time; his personal experience in that direction had been all too great. But in 1732 he had, after all, been informed that the King was set on continuing with "the *Dessein*". It was simply a question of how this was to be done, and for Hans Egede it must have seemed that all initiative was crippled – *in extremis*.

The General Commissariat of the Navy left the Greenland plans in abeyance until October 1732. The 1731 Commission seemed to have been completely left out of it, but it may have been some letters from Matthias Fersleff and Jens Hjort, the trader, that spurred the General Commissariat into action. On 14 October 1732, a memorandum was presented to the King recommending that Hans Egede and those sent out to Godthåb be permitted to stay there for another year. This was equal to a postponement of the final decision – which was in fact necessary, for even if a decision on future organisation were reached during the winter, it would be difficult to complete the necessary preparations, especially that of the "company" which was to take over future trading; evidently there were still hopes of this company being formed.

On 10 March, the General Commissariat was able to inform Hans Egede that he had the King's permission to remain for another year, together with those sent out; however, Matthis Jochimsen was recalled. The General Commissariat would arrange for the necessary supplies to be sent out, but none of this brought a solution to the future of trading any nearer.

It is apparent from a memorandum that the matter came up for discussion, either in the *Conseil*, or possibly within an even smaller circle, after 31 March, as Carl Adolph von Plessen, Christian VI's Lord Chamberlain, who had strong connections with the Zinzendorf circles in Copenhagen, asked for the relevant documents. The discussions undoubtedly centred on the circumstances of the mission and, not least, on the question of permission for three Moravian brethren to go to Greenland. Perhaps the presence of these brethren in Copenhagen prompted Plessen's actions. Four days later (on 4 April 1733) at Frederiksborg castle, the King signed a promise to support Hans Egede and the Greenland mission with an annual grant of 2,000 rigsdaler and at the same time requested Egede's suggestions for the future organization of the mission within the financial limits specified. Egede was informed of the arrival of the three Moravian brethren who were to assist him in the work of the mission. This letter contained only empty words concerning the future of the trade, so there was no doubt it was the mission that preoccupied the King and the inner circle of his court: no solution had yet been found to the trading problem. Holmsted and Kloumann, the Copenhagen merchants, must have decided to shelve the matter completely; already, on 20 May 1732, they had half withdrawn from the negotiations. Now Jacob Sewerin stepped into the picture, but before entering into practical discussions, he wanted more detailed information on the conditions and possibilities in Greenland. It was not without significance that a knowledgeable person – his brother-in-law, Matthias Fersleff – obtained this information for him. At his own expense Jacob Sewerin despatched a vessel (a galliot), with Matthias Fersleff on board, to Disko Bay, in which he still cherished an interest, partly to trade and partly to investigate once more the chances of colonization there. To do this Sewerin must have obtained royal permission. After sailing northwards, his ship put in at Godthåb and then continued southwards along the coast: the *Dessein* included ideas for establishing colonies to the south of Godthåb. Everything looked promising, and good trade had been done in the Bay.

A royal ship sailed in accordance with the promise of 10 March, bringing Hans Egede necessary supplies and the message of 4 April. The promises for the future contained in the letter renewed his trust in the King and his belief in "the holy providence which, when all seems lost, only then shows the profuse abundance of [God's] power and glory and amid frailty and sore trials, miraculously accomplishes the work according to His will".

Activity in Godthåb also seems to have increased due to the news brought by the ship. There had long been a wish to build a warehouse near the harbour to facilitate the discharging of vessels. This was begun on 22 July and completed on 18 August. The Moravian Brethren who had come to Godthåb on board the royal vessel, of whom one was a carpenter, helped in this work. These three German-speaking Moravian brethren, Christian David, Matthaeus Stach and Christian Stach (the latter two were cousins), had been despatched from Copenhagen with an express recommendation to Hans Egede to make them welcome and use them as helpers at the mission – "for which they claim to be specially fitted". However, because of mutual misunderstandings, perhaps increased by language difficulties on both sides, the meeting between these emissaries of the Brethren's community at Herrnhut and Hans Egede was not quite as the King wished. For a missionary of the Danish–Norwegian state Church in Greenland it must have seemed surprising, to say the least, for the King to send laymen to help him – especially Moravian Brethren, who, if Hans Egede knew much about them at all, were bound to be regarded by him as non-followers of Luther.

During his stay in Copenhagen in 1731 Count Zinzendorf had been much interested in the missionary work in the Danish West Indies (the Virgin Islands) and also in Greenland, Finnmark and Trankebar. His interest, especially in the Tranquebar mission, dated from his young days; his concept of the Christian faith in conjunction with pietism was essentially linked to missionary work. The mission was bound to be the natural consequence of his overall concept. After coming into contact with the refugee brethren from Moravia, Zinzendorf had established Herrnhut on his estate, and so the organization of the brotherhood became a reality. It is said that he offered Frederik IV help with the mission in Greenland as early as 1727, but that nothing came of it.

He did not succeed either in 1731 in obtaining permission to send missionaries to Greenland. Nevertheless, it appears that he paved the way for execution of the Brethren's mission plans before leaving Copenhagen. On his return to Herrnhut his reports created such a stir that it was decided to seek permission to despatch missionaries to the Danish West Indies but there were difficulties in Copenhagen and they did not set out until October 1732.

The pietistic revival movement, which had been at work in Copenhagen ever since the mid 1720s, had through the influence of Zinzendorf and his associates acquired a "Herrnhut hue". There were many evangelical groups, each with its own shade of pietism, and those adopting the Moravian doctrine counted as one of these. Opposition to them was strong, and degenerated into disorderly scenes and clashes of various kinds. Similar differences were also evident among the clergy, the court clerics being deeply imbued with the Halle pietism and the orphanage chaplain, Enevold Ewald, being very close to the Moravians. The bishops and most of the Church's ministers were, however, opposed to the revival movements, which were almost separatist and in any case went against the dominant orthodoxy. The philosophers, writers, orators and administrators of the Age of Enlightenment, who so markedly based their concepts on reason rather than emotion and largely dissociated themselves from extremes, naturally turned against the somewhat hysterical revival movements. Since there was a strong lay element in these revival movements, and the Moravians – stressing the "understanding of the heart", not of the mind – laid great emphasis on "the lay priesthood", people with both feet planted in the age of reason obviously opposed revival movements in general and the Moravians in particular.

The threat from the revival movements to the established state church (the religious prop of the absolute monarchy) was bound to make the Government, and hence the King, apprehensive as to where they might lead. Christian VI, whose own religious outlook was influenced by pietism, and who took the events of the time very seriously, felt insecure in the apparently confused situation. Hence the attitudes he adopted were ill defined, and he became a victim of the changing influences.

The Lord Chamberlain, Carl Adolph von Plessen, who had not originally been very enthusiastic about Zinzendorf and his associates, came round to their views and eventually supported them strongly. Zinzendorf's report at Herrnhut in 1731 had captured the minds of two Moravians, Matthaeus Stach and Friedrich Böhnisch, both of whom wanted to go to Greenland. The latter, however, was not regarded as completely reliable, so Matthaeus received permission from the Brotherhood to take his cousin Christian Stach with him. One of the most influential of the Moravians, the carpenter Christian David, was to accompany them but was to stay only for a year until they had built a dwelling house. However, having wandered round Germany and the Baltic countries for many years, preaching the Moravians' concept of salvation, and because he had an almost mystical power over the Brotherhood, he became the *de facto* leader of the three – notably when they reached Copenhagen and were fêted in the highest circles after 4 April.

The three Moravians had arrived in Denmark virtually empty-handed. However, the generosity shown them there was all the greater on that account, and all their equipment, together with timber for house-building, was donated to them. They were enjoined by Zinzendorf to help Hans Egede in his ministry when they reached Greenland; but if he did not need them, they were to leave him in peace.

They were not to live with Hans Egede and the other colonists, but had to find a place of their own.[1] This situation already contained the germ of the acute differences that later arose between Hans Egede and "the Brethren", and in particular with Christian David. He was extolled for his deep religious convictions, his firm faith in the words of the Bible, his apostolic spirit and his happiness in poverty, character-istics that must have strongly influenced those with whom he came into contract. At the same time, however, he was criticized for being unwilling to listen to the Brethren, i.e. to submit himself to ecclesiasti-cal and domestic discipline. He was prone to cavilling, rather conceited, and indeed generally quarrelsome. A historian of Moravian missions belonging to a latter age described his discussion of the elements of the faith as being based on "somewhat confused lay dogmatism". There is also a reference to his misplaced zeal for obtaining conver-sions.

Hans Egede had somehow heard a good deal of gossip from Copen-hagen in advance of the Brethren's arrival, so that he was predisposed against them. The Moravians' resentment at the cool reception accord-ed them by Hans Egede laid the first stone in the wall that rose be-tween them and the royal missionaries. Without asking Hans Egede or the trader at Godthåb for advice and guidance, the three decided the day after their arrival to build their first house on a site at least a kilometre to the south of the colony's houses. There, at the bottom of a small cove, their future mission station was to be set up; the place was named Ny Herrnhut.

Although the Moravians' first actions had been such as to make communication between them and Hans Egede and the rest of the Godthåb colony difficult, nevertheless it seemed during the period immediately following that some intercourse would be achieved. Hans Egede realized that the gossip from Copenhagen was not to be trusted and set out to give these people material and intellectual help. The Moravians had no need of spiritual help; according to them, if any-thing, the reverse was true. It was precisely for this reason that anta-gonism flared up during the winter of 1733–4. In dealing with the difficult Greenlandic language, the Moravians found themselves for the first few years wholly dependent on Hans Egede. He tried to help them, using the method he then considered the best and quickest, but with their scanty book-learning and lack of training in abstract thinking, the three Moravians were not able by academic methods to learn a foreign language. Christian David was able to read, but could only write with difficulty. Hans Egede's method of language teaching was therefore distasteful to them and they made extremely little pro-gress.

Hans Egede, on his side, could not express himself well in German. He was well aware of this, as his conversations with the Moravians developed into profound discussions of the elements of faith and particularly the theological aspects of confession. Hans Egede preferred conducting the discussion in a correspondence, which has been preserved – and which became increasingly acrimonious. For this Christian David bore the sole responsibility. On the basis of his "rather confused lay dogmatism", he ventured into spheres beyond the capacity of his knowledge and intellect, actually overstepping the bounds of the Moravians' religious concept. In so doing he demonstrated, more sharply than was "politic", a confessional divergence between the evangelical Lutheran church and the Moravian revival movement. Zinzendorf and the subsequent Moravian missionaries in Greenland had to make desperate efforts to smooth out this divergence.

Without going too deeply into the exchange of opinions, it can be said briefly that Hans Egede advocated an orthodox Lutheran attitude towards justification by faith in God's grace. Christian David maintained, in line with Zinzendorf's views, that justification alone without the simultaneous sanctification led only to a passive faith, which did not manifest itself in the Christian way of life. A man not imbued with the love of Jesus, although both justified and sanctified by faith, was not truly converted. Outwardly such sanctification showed itself in bearing witness, pouring out one's heart, confessing one's sins and acting with charity. From his orthodox standpoint, Hans Egede was obliged to point out that this was at variance with the Augsburg confession, and that the Moravians could easily fall into the error of stressing salvation through good works and, in doing so, would be led into realms of "pure papism".

Thus the crucial question was: would the Moravians recognize the Augsburg Confession or would they reject it? Christian David evaded this ultimatum, and adopted no definite position on the subject; however, he hardened his tone towards Hans Egede, whom the Moravians regarded as an "unconverted priest". Zinzendorf had expressed himself quite clearly concerning such people: "an unconverted Lutheran is a loathsome thing". Christian David's view of the Augsburg Confession was to some extent dictated by the fact that he came from the old Moravian community, which was of pre-Reformation origin, dating right back to Jan Huss at the beginning of the fifteenth century.

If the Moravians would not accept the Augsburg Confession, Hans Egede had to regard them as opponents of the evangelical-Lutheran church, and thus would have nothing more to do with them; so the conflict prevailing in Denmark, and particularly in Copenhagen, was reflected in Greenland. It was partly through this that, in the years that followed, Christian VI dissociated himself from the Moravians, especially Zinzendorf, and the pietistic court circles with Moravian leanings lost their influence. The development of the dispute in Greenland was extremely distressing to Hans Egede on account of Christian David's self-righteous and argumentative character. He held himself in check for a long time, but at last his patience gave way and he ended the correspondence with a letter dated 24 February 1734, asking to be excused from receiving any further letters; if any more were received, they would go unanswered, and even unread, "because, thank Heaven, I know how to make better use of my time".

The cavilling correspondence and discussions on dogma were irritating and of little importance to Hans Egede beside the harsh realities of life. A month after the royal ship had sailed, all Hans Egede's previous work was virtually wiped out. The smallpox epidemic claimed its first victim on the 27 August 1733.

When the royal ship appeared on 20 May 1733, Hans Egede expressed his gratitude for the return of the two survivors of the six Greenlanders who went to Copenhagen in 1731. But one of them, a girl, had died on the voyage, so that only the boy, Carl, returned to Greenland, and he carried the infection with him. Moreover, the General Commissariat of the Navy informed Hans Egede of the King's command "that no Greenlander, male or female, must be allowed to come [to Denmark], even if they ask to do so themselves". The reasons for this were that those Greenlanders who had come to Denmark "have not been able to survive in this climate and on the diet customary in this country, but have got sick and died; apart from this they cannot be employed here advantageously to themselves. . . ." This command was later ignored.

The consequences of the infection were horrifying. Carl had visited several Greenlanders in the neighbourhood of Godhåb. For a time it seemed as though he himself was going to recover, but he fell ill again and died on 4 September. To begin with it was not realized that he was suffering from smallpox. Even after Carl's death, Hans Egede was not certain, but he wrote in his diary that Carl had infected the others "not only externally with a noxious and wasting scab and itching, but also internally. I think they must be infected with smallpox . . .". He wrote this on the death of the young Greenlander Frederick Christian, which came as a great blow to him. Both in his diary and in his "Reports" Hans Egede set down on that date, 14 September, the significance of Frederik Christian to the whole of his ministry. He had helped him not only with the language but with instruction. On a personal level, too, he had become very close to Hans Egede.

Behind the restrained wording of the diary entry, Hans Egede's sadness can be sensed: it was as though a weapon had been dashed from
his hand in the midst of the fight.[2]

After that one report followed the other to Godhåb about deaths in
various places, and by November the epidemic hit the settlements on
the islands around Godthåb. Greenlanders who had not yet noticed
the infection fled from their homes, but they carried it with them and
the disease broke out wherever they took refuge; thus it spread further
and further afield. The feeling of panic that gripped the Greenlanders
can be understood: in desperation one man killed his sister-in-law
believing she had sent his daughter and eldest son to their deaths by
witchcraft. Hand Egede was shocked by this manifestation of what he
regarded as the work of the devil among men.

Many of the panic-striken Greenlanders made their way to Godthåb for help. Individual members of decimated families came there
simply because they did not know where else to find shelter. Everything was done to house them, usually with the Greenlanders living
nearest. Some fled to the hinterland of the fjord, others to the south.
And everywhere the fugitives went the epidemic spread, and deaths
were noted almost daily in the diary and the "Reports". Many of those
who died belonged to groups of Greenlanders who had long been
receiving instruction from Hans Egede, with children whom, with an
uneasy mind, he had baptised as infants. Amid his grief over the many
deaths, Hans Egede was now able, in the light of his belief, to express
his consolation at having baptised them just the same.

Nevertheless the toll taken by the epidemic among these Greenlanders in particular must have brought Hans Egede to the edge of
despair. All, or at least the majority, of those to whom he had devoted
his energies over many years were now dead. Even if at many of the
deathbeds that he attended during this time, he saw evidence that his
words and teaching had led to what he thought a proper result, he
was nevertheless surprised that the Greenlanders were not more deeply
influenced in the religious sense by the catastrophe. Towards the New
Year this gave him cause for serious reflections, and self-reproach for
not having left the country in 1731.

It is not possible to know exactly how many died in the epidemic.
By November it was reported that all ten families living on the Ravne
islands had gone, though at that time some of them had not died, but
simply fled. The epidemic later caught up with those who had fled to
the south and with those among whom they took refuge. On 31 December Hans Egede wrote that nobody was left out of the forty families
who had lived on the Kook islands. The number of deaths mentioned
in the "Reports" before New Year 1733-4 is forty-five, to which must

be added the approximate figures from the Ravne and Kook islands – probably 200 altogether.

At the beginning of 1734 the epidemic spread still further, appearing to peter out only after the end of April. By then over seventy individual deaths had been mentioned in the "Reports". On 31 March, according to this source, all the Greenlanders 45–60 kilometres to the south of Godthåb – that is to say within the area extending to the islands a few kilometres south of Skinderhvalen – had succumbed. On 6 April Hans Egede noted that "of more than 200 families, which were wont to live within this area, namely two to three Danish miles (15–23 kilometres) south of the colony and up to three to four miles (23–30 kilometres) east and north of the colony, there are now scarcely thirty families left, so that this colony is now almost devoid of people. Apart from the said few remaining, nobody is to be found until you reach some ten miles (75 kilometres) south of the colony and some ten miles (75 kilometres) to the north. Here in the colony more than fifty people have died". If the average size family is reckoned to have been 4.5 persons at that time, the 170 or so families wiped out corresponds to approximately 850–900 persons.

Much later, on 7 November 1734, when Niels Egede was at Pisugfik in the north to buy what he could get under these circumstances, he found that, of the families which had occupied eight large houses there, only two were left. Here too some had fled, but the majority had died during the epidemic. He travelled thirty Danish miles (225 kilometres) northwards and met with no signs of life for the first fifteen Danish miles (113 kilometres). This is credible, since Jacob Sewerin reported to the King on 13 December 1734, presumably on the basis of information supplied by Hans Egede, that "of about 1,200 people, only eight souls are left. . . ." This tallies with the rough estimates set out above.

The many who made their way to Godthåb, some already sick, others becoming infected later, were cared for and nursed by Hans Egede and the colonists to the best of their ability. "The misery that we have seen these poor people endure all this time is beyond description", he exclaims, "as are the pains and inconvenience we have had with so many sick people." Most of those who were ill had to be accommodated in the room in the colonial house occupied by Hans Egede and his family who looked after them. With no hint of bitterness, but rather with great understanding, Hans Egede recorded that the people and the hands at the colony could not stand having the sick and the dying lodged in their quarters – where in any case, there was less room than in Hans Egede's house. "In brief, we had no peace throughout the winter by night or day because of them; indeed many times when they died during the night, so as not to be poisoned by evil odour and stench, I was obliged to rise from my bed and drag the corpse out of the room. . . ." At one point there were so many who came to Godthåb for help and shelter, that the Moravians had to be asked to look after some of them. The brethren do not appear to have given any other help during this time of tribulation. In the correspondence from the three that has been preserved, the epidemic is described with comparative brevity, and no mention is made of any part which they might have played; this silence must be regarded as evidence in itself.

On the other hand, their letters are full of criticisms of Hans Egede, his family and the colonists in general; they contain echoes of the correspondence between Hans Egede and Christian David. Against the background of the large number of lives claimed by the smallpox epidemic, it is remarkable to find Matthaeus Stach writing to a woman, a fellow Moravian, in Copenhagen that "Hans Egede has now been in the country for thirteen years and still not brought a single soul to Christ. . . ."

The smallpox epidemic and the correspondence with the Moravians had almost completely disheartened Hans Egede. His serious thoughts of abandoning everything and handing over to those with more freshness and energy are apparent from his entry in the "Report" for 15 March 1734. While giving other reasons, he wrote that "his mental and physical strength were already so much impaired" that he "could be of little more use to Greenland, nor endure it for much longer".

By his side Hans Egede had always had his stalwart wife, Giertrud Rasch. Throughout the winter she had devoted herself to the sick and dying to an even greater extent than he, if this were possible. At the same time, she had found the strength to support her husband through the mental crises which continually assailed him and the strains imposed by his relations with the Moravians. Hans Egede only mentions her contribution during this winter in a few words, but on 6 April 1734, he wrote in the "Report": "Not only I but my dear wife too suffered no little damage to our health and well-being through this, indeed from that day forward until God called her to Him she was not in good health".[3] The restraint and moderation of these words convey all the more strongly the excessive weight of the burdens borne by this sixty-year-old woman in the most straitened and cramped conditions imaginable. Despite her strength, this winter of grief proved too much for her.

The year passed in nursing and caring for the sick, sustaining them in their hour of death, burying the dead and comforting the survivors, who soon fell ill and died themselves. Hans Egede was amazed at "the great assurance and calmness of these people in their great suffering and misery". Time and again he had warned them against approaching the sick and spreading the infection, but they took no heed. He was also surprised that they did not behave as they were otherwise accustimed to, when there was a death in the family, and also that they did not seem to be aware of the danger threatening the survivors. Hans Egede did not attempt to explain this reaction of the Greenlanders, but he was nonetheless surprised at it.

The Greenlanders stricken by the epidemic probably reacted as they did, with panic, because epidemics seem to have been unknown in Greenland up till then. Periods of hunger, when settlements starved to death, were not comparable. The whole aspect of the disease with its external symptoms was quite foreign to them. The fact that they did not behave as usual when a death occurred reveals their perplexity when faced with an unaccustomed situation. None of the remedies in which they had hitherto had faith had any effect in their present predicament. Moreover, Hans Egede's teaching had shaken all the customary ideas. That too was probably why some fled to Godthåb; they were unconsciously seeking help from the man who had declared their previous customs and measures useless. Now they discovered his own helplessness too in the face of the epidemic. Their senses were numbed and they could not understand the danger of infection, despite Hans Egede's warnings.

As well as the sick, the women, children and old people who had entered Godthåb for refuge also had to be fed by the colony. The stock of provisions had to be stretched, and they had to use what they would otherwise have given to the animals or thrown away. "Some of them are so weak that they cannot find their own food," wrote Hans Egede to justify having to feed these Greenlanders.

The epidemic had a disastrous effect on the hunting and fishing carried on by the Greenlanders to support life on the one hand, and for sale to the colony on the other. As far as possible, trading expeditions to the various settlements were attempted, but usually the boats came home half-empty, bringing only tales of the raging epidemic. Nevertheless they tried to collect what they could, as well as what had been left behind by the fugitives and the dead, which was lying around for anyone to take. There was not much ready for shipment home, therefore, when the vessel arrived from Copenhagen with fresh supplies – and good news.

In the knowledge of the good commercial result shown by the voyage undertaken in 1733 on his behalf, Jacob Sewerin had declared himself willing to take over the Greenland Trading Company. Just how willing he really was is less certain. The negotiations in Copenhagen concerning the future of the Company appear to have got under

way sometime after New Year 1734. The General Commissariat of
the Navy announced on 31 March that no recommendation could be
given for Niels Egede "to enjoy any preferment for his services rendered [in Greenland] since it is still undecided whether support for the
mission and trade is to be continued"; but, when the decision was
to hand, they would do what they could for him. On 4 April 1733, the
royal decision was received but, as mentioned before, it dealt chiefly
with the mission. The ship that was sent out at state expense also
brought back, besides Matthis Jochimsen and others who were not to
stay in Godthåb any longer, the produce that had been obtained by
trading since July 1732.

In the late autumn of 1733 these goods were sold by auction, and the
cost of this expedition could then be calculated. The quantities brought
back were apparently of no great account, there being in all 163 barrels
of blubber, 126 fox skins, 100 seal skins, 18 reindeer skins and 15 baleen
plates. The prices obtained for these goods at auction were not very
high. The blubber (evidently unrefined) went for just over 6 rigsdaler
per barrel on average, i.e. a total of 990 rigsdaler; the other products
did not bring in large sums either. The proceeds of the auction amounted to 1,179 rigsdaler and 50 skilling. The expenditure on freight, food,
wages and cargo had been 3,196 rigsdaler and 85 skilling, leaving a
deficit of 2,017 rigsdaler and 35 skilling. Besides this there were the
wages for the men in the colony and for Hans Egede, both of which
were partly paid in kind. The cash wages were not charged to Navy
funds.

It is likely that Jacob Sewerin noted the prices fetched at auction
by the Greenland produce – which must have made him think twice
about the whole undertaking. On the other hand, he appears to have
fared better with the products brought back by his own vessel from
Disko Bay.

There was complete silence concerning plans for the continuation
of trading with Greenland, which may have been partly due to the
unhurried way the next year's plans had always been dealt with.
Dating back to the time of the Bergen Company, despite their unfortunate experiences, it had generally been after New Year before planning for the coming year had begun. Secondly, the silence may have
been due to the changes in the Government during the autumn and
winter of 1733–4, when the Lord Chamberlain, Carl Adolph von Plessen, resigned, and his brother, a deputy in the Finanskollegium, had
to vacate his office in favour of Johan Ludvig Holstein in 1734. That
same year the latter became President of the Missionskollegium. It
was J. L. Holstein's name that was at the top of the letter dated 6
March 1734, from the Finanskollegium and the Missionskollegium to

the King, recommending a charter for Jacob Sewerin. The union of the two "Colleges" under J. L. Holstein gives credence to his having been the driving force – by virtue of the Missionskollegium's obvious concern for the mission in Greenland – when it came to a decision concerning trade with, and sailings to, Greenland in the future. The mission was directly dependent on a more permanent arrangement being established.

Jacob Sewerin's introduction to his memorandum of 8 February 1734 to the King gives the impression of having been instigated by someone else, possibly Holstein. After first referring to his exploration of the country in 1733, he immediately went on to deal with the poor prospects for the growth of the mission and the profit to be obtained from trading. In this connection mention is made of the losses recorded by the General Commissariat of the Navy, "from which one would soon come to fear that this godly *Dessein* is in the long run bound to founder". Sewerin nevertheless reminded the King of his letter of 4 April 1733 to Hans Egede, in which the mission had been promised an annual payment of 2,000 rigsdaler from the King's purse. In the light of this promise he ventured to put forward a plan.

The worst obstacle which would continue to affect trading, he wrote, was the presence of foreign traders, especially if a colony were established in the Disko Bay. Such a colony would be the best means of depriving the foreign traders of any desire to continue their activities, but this required the King's financial backing. It appears that Jacob Sewerin envisaged squeezing the foreigners out by cutting the prices of the imported goods that were to be bartered for the Greenlanders' products, "and if they could first be ousted from the Disko Bay, their other trading in the south, which can scarcely be worth-while, would be bound to collapse automatically. . . ." He enumerated the points which, he considered, a charter ought to contain, and the privileges which should be granted along with it. Finally, he calculated the annual outlay over the first two years at 7,000 rigsdaler, on which he did not expect to see any return. "None the less, although a loss will be made here for the first two years, I hope to meet them [the expenses] in the third and fourth years and, please God, more than cover them in the fifth and sixth years, as after that it will depend on the most gracious wishes of Your Royal Majesty whether you yourself shall continue with the trade or transfer it to Your Majesty's subjects".

During February negotiations must have taken place between the officials of the Finanskollegium and the Missionskollegium, on the one hand, and Jacob Sewerin, on the other. So much is apparent from the recommendation which they submitted to the King jointly on 6 March 1734, accompanied by a draft charter. This draft agreed exactly with Jacob Sewerin's memorandum of 8 February, only formal amendments having been made to the wording of this in order to make it "clearer and to express the real meaning". On 15 March the charter was produced in its final form signed by the King, and Jacob Sewerin acknowledged it under his own hand and seal on 31 March. It was the deputies of the Finanskollegium, headed by J. L. Holstein, who countersigned the charter and the King's signature.

Under the charter, Jacob Sewerin undertook to establish a colony in the Disko Bay and to supply two missionaries there. It was explicitly mentioned that one of them was to be Poul Egede; it was Jacob Sewerin himself who, in his memorandum, had suggested the desirability of Hans Egede's eldest son being the first missionary in the Disko Bay. Sewerin was to maintain these missionaries in future, just as he was to take over maintenance of the mission in Godthåb. As regards the people then living in Godthåb, they were either to be taken into his service and paid by him in future, or they were to return to Denmark at his expense. All goods that had been brought back and were stored in Copenhagen were to be transferred to him free of charge, as were the goods and property, together with all buildings, existing in Godthåb. He was to return all fixtures, fittings, boats and tents without compensation upon expiry of the charter, and was to be credited for any merchandise, barrels and pinnaces at their estimated value. Up to the date of taking over, the State would pay for the food and wages for both the mission and trading people in Godthåb.

Jacob Sewerin was granted 3,000 rigsdaler per annum for the first three years, then 2,000 rigsdaler per annum for the next three years. Thus the charter was valid for six years, which was as Sewerin desired: he had expressed the wish that the people he engaged, in the service of both the mission and the trading company, should be guaranteed certain advantages after the termination of their service in Greenland. This meant clerical appointments in the case of the missionaries and "suitable employment" for the trading staff, and that the men should all be exempted from military service and be free to reside or carry on their trade anywhere in the country. All this was granted. All goods that were transported to or from Greenland or exported elsewhere from there were exempt from customs duty, consumption tax and town tolls, øresund dues and charges relating to other "royal waterways". In order to cover the cost of establishing further colonies, Jacob Sewerin could, if he thought fit, organize a lottery on the lines of that of 1724 (which had not been very successful).

For the period of the charter Jacob Sewerin was "unimpeded by all subjects, to benefit from the 'Stra Dawids' Greenland trade alone". The King therefore forbade "each and everyone, whether he be one of our own citizens or an alien and foreigner, to cause any hindrance, injury or encroachment to this trade and commerce in any way against the said Jacob Sewerin (and whomsoever he might hereafter take as an associate) and his heirs". Sewerin thus gained a monopoly of the trade with the colony of Godthåb and *any colonies he intended to establish* for the duration of the charter. The Government dared not go any further at that time in its attitude towards the "foreign traders", i.e. mainly the Dutch. The latter clause constituted a legitimate basis for the harder line taken against these foreign Davis Strait navigators.

Thus the charter granted Jacob Sewerin everything he had asked for in his memorandum, and met all his conditions. Meanwhile, between 15 and 31 March Sewerin had taken over before the charter was confirmed. From the General Commissariat of the Navy he received Hans Egede's requisitions dating from 1733, and from these he was able to appreciate the poor state of the colony, not least from the materials requisitioned for boat-building and other purposes. On the basis of this alone it was plain to Jacob Sewerin that, on account of the many disasters in 1732–3, it could be expected that much would be purchased during 1733–4. At the same time he called for a list of the existing equipment and materials at Godthåb, the granting of which the General Commissariat of the Navy recommended for royal approval. However, such approval was considered unnecessary, and a brief note was therefore pencilled on the recommendation to the effect that everything could be handed over to Sewerin against his receipt. Thus from this time until 1749 the name of Jacob Sewerin was inextricably bound up with the Greenland Trade and mission.

After signing the acknowledgment of the charter, the next task was to purchase the necessary goods and materials, and to load and despatch vessels. In all Sewerin sent out three vessels, two of them direct to Disko Bay. Aboard these ships were the new missionaries, Poul Egede and Andreas Bing, for the new colony; Martin Ohnsorg was on board the third ship, which was to call at Godthåb first and then meet the others in Disko Bay.

Jacob Sewerin's strong insistence on Poul Egede taking charge of the mission in Disko Bay must have been due to their having had earlier contact with each other. In 1733 Hans Egede had wanted his eldest son to join him as a helper, although he had still not graduated in divinity; Poul himself related how he received a message to this effect from the Missionskollegium a few days before the departure of the ship in 1733. He was reluctant to sail, and sought an audience with the King in order to be excused. He was not given an audience, but was informed that the King was satisfied provided he would travel out the next year after taking his final examination.

It is probable that from 1732 onwards Jacob Sewerin sought contact with those familiar with conditions in Greenland, and this would naturally have brought him into touch with Poul Egede. For Jacob Sewerin it was essential to have in Greenland people in whom he could have complete confidence, and Poul Egede was just such a person. The distance was great – for the Europeans of those days almost inconceivable. Hans Egede enjoyed such respect that his standing was beyond question. Matthias Fersleff, Sewerin's brother-in-law, and the resident trader in Godthåb, Jens Hjort, could also be relied upon.

To Hans Egede, who had looked forward to the day when his son Poul should start work as his helper in Godthåb, it was a disappointment that he was unable to welcome him immediately the ship called at Godthåb, and in fact had no opportunity of seeing his son again for some time. Hans Egede had specifically asked not to have Matthias Fersleff and Jens Hjort, and this wish was complied with. Both were engaged by Jacob Sewerin for the new colony, Matthias Fersleff being the first trader there. Niels Egede, on the other hand, was engaged as trader at Godthåb.

When the ship arrived on 15 June 1734, however, Hans Egede received the news that Jacob Sewerin had taken over the trade on his own under a royal charter without any great enthusiasm. He soberly noted that "the distinguished gentleman, Mr. Jacob Sewerin" was taking charge of the trade "for the praiseworthy purpose of propagating the glory of God", but it was only being done "on a trial basis" and "with most gracious royal assistance", "for a certain number of years". In his opinion it was too much for one man who also had other, complex affairs to attend to. He therefore entertained "little hope for the permanence and fruitful execution of the work". Once again pessimism crept into his mind: his outlook was still coloured by the winter's hardships and the gloomy picture presented by the critical situation in Godthåb.

The ship that had called in at Godthåb had already sailed on 21 June to Disko Bay, where the three vessels met on 14 July. After some reconnoitring in the bay which had, some time earlier, been chosen for establishing the new colony – the Wiere Bay of the Dutch – the building site was marked out. By the 25th, Poul Egede was able to preach his first sermon in the newly-erected house, and the same evening he left with the ship for Godthåb. The colony does not appear to have been given a name on that occasion. Not until Jacob Sewerin's report to the King on 13 December 1734 was the colony in Disko Bay called Christianshåb.

Immediately on arrival Poul Egede began his missionary work. In the bay off Christianshåb the ship was met by some Greenlanders in

N

kayaks; when Poul spoke to them in Greenlandic they were dumb-founded. His identity was soon established and then it turned out that he was already known; the Greenlanders of the Bay had already heard from travellers of the Pavia down there to the south. (Pavia was and is still the Greenlandic for Poul.) The same was true of their vague knowledge of the gospel; fragments garbled in the telling had reached the West Greenlanders of the Bay. Curiosity over something novel and strange had been aroused, and they apparently listened intently to what Poul Egede told them, as they had always listened to a good story-teller. With Poul Egede's sovereign command of the West Green-land language, it was, of course, possible for him to express himself in such a way that he could impress the new ideas upon his listeners. His knowledge of and fluency in Greenlandic were the most considerable of anyone at that time who was not an indigenous inhabitant. Even in Danish, his power of expression and his style were far superior to those of Hans Egede, both in the straightforward use of the language and in the clarity of presentation.

It was with ill-concealed dismay that the Greenlanders saw him leave again so soon, and they extracted from him a promise to come back as quickly as possible. Although Poul Egede wrote in his journal on arrival at Godthåb that he found all his family in good health, he was never-theless obliged to spend the winter there – on a provisional basis. Giertrud Rasch was ailing and Hans Egede was obviously tired, but both were carrying on with their work, and Poul Egede supported his father where he could. Thus the whole Egede family were together in one place, where they lived and breathed for the ministry to which they had all devoted their lives – in Poul Egede's case with perhaps a touch of sadness, thinking of the career as a naval officer to which he had been most strongly attracted.

The winter passed peacefully and the notes in the "Reports" are brief. Trading expeditions and missionary trips were made to the sur-rounding Greenlanders. Not all of them had died in the smallpox epidemic; some who had fled had returned, having been fortunate enough to escape infection, while others had miraculously recovered from attacks of the disease. This also applied to a few of the young people who lived in the colony and whom Hans Egede had baptized. Among them was the man later called Poul Grønlænder, who became an able catechist but who could not, in Hans Egede's eyes, measure up to Frederik Christian. The population, both on the islands and in the hinterland of the fjord, appears to have been increased to some extent by immigration, even though some Greenlanders complained at the end of November 1734 that time dragged for them with so many of their neighbours having died during the epidemic. It was still necessary to travel a long way to buy sufficient goods and to make contact with Greenlanders for teaching purposes. At intervals Greenlanders came to the colony on visits or on their travels, and Hans and Poul Egede took the opportunity, as usual, to talk with them about "their salvation". In many cases it was easier for them to make an impression than before, partly because they both had a better command of the language and partly because all these years had not passed without any effect on the Greenlanders, as the Moravians at Godthåb seemed to think.

During these days the "Reports" made no mention at all of the Moravians – or "the Germans", as they were often subsequently called. Neither Hans nor Poul Egede referred to them by so much as a single word. Another two Brethren arrived, Friedrich Böhnisch and Johann Beck, with the ship calling at Godthåb in 1734. Because of their luke-warm attitude towards the Augsburg Confession, Jacob Sewerin had been particularly dubious about allowing them to travel out. Now there were five missionaries of the Brethren living in their small house, Christian David having stayed even though it had been decided that he should return home in 1734.

There was apparently no improvement in their relations with Hans Egede, although, as the Moravian mission historians are unanimous in recording, the latter showed them the greatest goodwill, continued to help them by word and deed, and taught them the Greenlandic language. There could be no close understanding between them. Christian David appears to have remained in the background during the winter, since he was chiefly engaged in keeping house, and felt himself too old to learn languages and travel round, besides which he suffered from scurvy. He was five years younger than Hans Egede, and determined to return to Herrnhut in 1735, which he succeeded in doing.

Nor had Christian David been on the best terms with his immediate associates, as we have mentioned before; it was probably for this reason that he wanted to get away, as well as feeling himself unequal to this difficult missionary work, which did not yield the immediate results that he had been used to seeing at his many revival meetings elsewhere. None of the Moravian missionaries had managed to do any missionary work during the year 1733–4. The smallpox epidemic had removed almost all the people in the area among whom they could have carried on their ministry; Hans Egede and his family seemed unwilling to be "converted". Thus they would have preferred to pack their bags and move on to some other more populous part of Greenland and start on their own, but that was not practicable as in Greenland it was only possible to travel by sea and they had no boat.

Thus every circumstance forced them to stay put. Christian David seems to have felt obliged to remain in the background, which did not prevent differences on confessional matters still cropping up between them and Hans Egede. The main point in dispute was that Hans Egede demanded clear-cut allegiance to the Augsburg Confession, to which the Moravian missionaries would not subscribe. This matter and the whole correspondence were passed to Copenhagen and from there to Zinzendorf. The further course of the dispute can be dealt with briefly. Zinzendorf had to back down, and to shield Christian David as far as possible; he must have been aware that he had misjudged the situation in Copenhagen. After 1734 the King and the Government adopted a firmer attitude on ecclesiastical uniformity, which was bound to mean less freedom for revival movements. So Zinzendorf actually signed his letter of 13 May 1735, using the title "Der Gemeine zu Herrnhut und Mährischen Gemeine Augsburgischer Confession" ("the Herrnhut Community and the Moravian Community of the Augsburg Confession"), thus emphasizing its adherence to evangelical Lutheranism. At this time also, Christian VI began to tire of the Moravian count.

Thus the winter of 1734–5 was still clouded for Hans Egede by the disheartening relationship with the Moravians, which further deepened his depression. He made up his mind to leave Greenland, and tendered his resignation as a missionary in 1734. With the ship that arrived in 1735 he got permission to leave for Denmark and the King promised to look after his "sustenance".

During the spring the rounds of the inhabited settlements in the district were made as usual, as well as trips to those places where the Greenlanders usually camped during spring and summer, hunting and fishing. Everywhere he said his farewells. There are several restrained references in the "Reports" to the Greenlanders expressing their sorrow at his wanting to leave; to them he gave as his reason that he felt old and tired "and could no longer endure the vast amount of toil in that harsh country". One might be inclined to disregard these remarks by the Greenlanders because Hans Egede himself reported them, but the honesty and frankness of the "Reports" as a whole make it impossible to doubt their truth. Even though he was tired out by the work, it was still typical of the man that he should have given a further reason for his departure, and one that he believed would have an edifying effect: "In part the cause is their indifference and the fact that they do not reflect on and take to heart with proper devotion the Word of God that I teach them; therefore I have now grown weary of teaching them any more, seeing that it avails little or nothing." The Greenlanders to whom he addressed this reproach naturally protested, to which Hans

Egede replied that even though he was leaving, his son Poul and others were staying.

But Hans Egede did not get away in 1735, and so Poul Egede remained in Godthåb with him. On 8 August Hans Egede wrote in his diary that his wife was often obliged to stay in bed through weakness. Day by day, it grew plainer that her life was nearing its end and, in these circumstances, Hans Egede dared not expose her to the hardships of a sea voyage. Poul, for his part, dared not leave his father to carry on the mission work at Godthåb alone. Although a colleague had come with the ship in 1734, and the missionary for Christianshåb in 1735 had been obliged to stay at Godthåb for lack of provisions, Hans Egede would have been overburdened; the new arrivals did not know the language well and had to be regularly instructed in it.

From the beginning of September Giertrud Rasch's condition grew worse. When Hans Egede came home from a mission trip on 25 November, he found her "mortally weak and frail, with no hope of recovery". Barely a month later, on 21 December, she died. Without high-flown phrases but with a pulsating undertone of profound grief beneath his simple words, Hans Egede interpreted the personal relationship that had existed between husband and wife within the work for the mission's cause in Greenland. He knew what she had sacrificed for his idea and how completely she had collaborated with him in working towards the common aim, and how it was she who inspired him with the courage to carry on when adversity or the all too slow progress disheartened him. He knew what support was now being taken from him.

"On top of all the other trials and tribulations assailing me in Greenland", wrote Hans Egede on 21 December, "comes this death". The scant progress with his missionary work was still causing him anxiety. While many of those baptized had died during the smallpox epidemic, few new candidates for baptism had presented themselves. One feels that the Moravians had let Hans Egede know their own view of his ministry; it must have looked to him as though his efforts had been in vain. These last years in Greenland were an intensely depressive period for him; in March 1736 he was on the verge of breakdown. He suffered isolated attacks in the period that followed, but these were less severe. It is reported that for the first time in the fifteen years he had been in Greenland he suffered from scurvy as well. By the middle of May he had regained his previous good health to the extent of being able to take a boat and row over to the Nipisat sound and preach to the Greenlanders who were, as usual, there for the fishing; but it was not till Whit Sunday, 20 May, that he ventured to preach in the colony.

And so, day by day, his departure drew nearer. On 29 July he preached his farewell sermon. "Moved to do so by the sorry outcome of my purpose dedicated to God", he had chosen as his text the words of the prophet Isaiah: "Then I said, I have laboured in vain, I have spent my strength for nought, and in vain: yet surely my judgment is with the Lord, and my reward with my God." (Is. 49:4.) Hans Egede could not have expressed more clearly his deep disappointment over the little which, to his mind, he had accomplished and how far he was from the goal that he had set himself. He was unable to achieve any more in Greenland, but he hoped "on reaching home safely, to be able to contribute more to the furtherance of the *Dessein.* . . . For as I did not come to Greenland for the sake of earthly gain and benefit, so neither have I departed thence for the sake of earthly gain and benefit, but the glory of God alone and the enlightenment of these poor ignorant people have been, are, and shall be my sole aim and the unremitting desire of my heart until I die".

It was only his own presence in Greenland that he considered pointless, so he was not quite without hope for the future of the ministry there. And, as he said in his farewell sermon, he continued to work for the goal he had set himself during his youth in Denmark. On 9 August, Hans Egede left Greenland, never to revisit the scene of his work. On 24 September the ship dropped anchor in Copenhagen. Shortly after the vessel's arrival Giertrud Rasch was buried in the churchyard of the Nicolajkirke.[4]

REFERENCES

1. There has been some discussion of Count Zinzendorf's instructions concerning the three Moravians' attitude to Hans Egede. There seems no doubt that Zinzendorf's real meaning was that they should offer their help to Hans Egede, but not force it upon him. As for their settling down separated from the others in Godthåb, it must be remembered that they could only maintain their communal and domestic discipline by living as a separated "unity" ("the Unity of Brethren" was just one of their names). This was the material and spiritual assurance of the individual member of the "unity" and the only guarantee to the "mother-unity" in Herrnhut. Hans Egede was quite unaware of their customs, and was therefore bound to interpret their immediate separation as an indication of antagonism.

2. A simple piece of paper happened to be found in a bunch of prosaic vouchers concerning the accounts of the colony for the year 1733. This piece of paper shows the feelings which affected Hans Egede on that very day, 14 September. (Its facsimile appears in plate 19.) It was his duty to maintain the provisions list, getting the names of the persons under his

command entered or struck off as the case might be. This applied also to the Greenlanders, some of whom lived at Hans Egede's for education, others like Frederik Christian as assistants. On the very day when Frederik Christian died Hans Egede had to notify the trader's assistant that the former's name should be struck off the provisions list. As he wrote, a tear dropped from his eyes down to the paper, and he brushed it away with his hand. The smudged lines tell as much.

3. This indicates that, at any rate, these words are written later than 6 April, because Giertrud Rasch died a year and a half later, on 21 December 1735. This want of "precision" in the "Reports" is due to the fact that the quotation is from Hans Egede's edition, drafted by himself, and printed with the title *Circumstantial and Detailed Relation* in 1738. The original "Reports", dating from 1725 until 1736, exists only in part.

4. This churchyard was in the heart of the city of Copenhagen. In the big fire of 1795 the churchyard was damaged, and later it was abandoned. No one knew then where Hans Egede and Giertrud Rasch had their graves, nor did anyone care. A sandstone "epitaphium" has been placed in the wall of Nikolaj church, which is now no longer used as a place of worship.

II

DUTCH ACTIVITY
1734–1750

In Copenhagen a meeting undoubtedly took place between Hans
Egede, now tired and marked by his years in Greenland, and Jacob
Sewerin, the one-time student of divinity. Believing in its possibilities,
Sewerin had taken over the Greenland trade, had Christianshåb
established and arranged for sailings to the two colonies that now
existed. Plans for the future occupied his mind. The very restrained
optimism expressed by Hans Egede in the winter of 1734–5 and on his
departure in 1736 was surely difficult to conceal from Jacob Sewerin
and was not calculated to raise the latter's hopes or to dispel the
anxieties created by the first years.

Although Jacob Sewerin had allowed for losses during these years,
that made in 1734 must have struck him as even larger than he had
feared. He was alarmed, and in December that year unburdened
himself to the King, illustrating his position with, among other things,
a somewhat hastily estimated loss of over 5,000 rdl. He asked for a
further grant of 1,000 rdl. for each of the first two years and applied
at the same time for a preferential loan on his estate of 8,000 or 4,000 rdl.
He obtained neither; indeed, the Government did not wish to "hear
of further costs" over and above the grant that had been fixed at
3,000 rdl. per annum for the first three years.

The 53 *cordeler* (nearly 146 barrels) of blubber, plus some skins and
baleen, which were all that was brought back in 1734, had an immediately discouraging effect. If we disregard the year 1726, when the
only ship sent out had to winter in Greenland with the result that
nothing was brought home, and the unfortunate year 1728–9, we have
to go back to the first years of colonization to find smaller amounts.
However, the reason that so little was sent home in 1733–4 was the
smallpox epidemic, which had not only hindered hunting and fishing
but also restricted expeditions. Besides, blubber prices were apparently
falling. According to Sewerin's own figures from September 1738, the
146 barrels fetched 636 rdl. in all, or $4\frac{1}{2}$ rdl. per barrel. In 1728, prices

of from $7\frac{1}{2}$ to 8 rdl. per barrel had been realized; yet Magnus Schiøtte had at that time estimated just over 5 rdl. per barrel. The low price and the small returns were discouraging.

In another sense, the variety of cargo sent home gave support to the wish to establish more colonies. The risk of the trade's revenues being a matter of chance at a single colony, and the consequent advantage of spreading the risk, became self-evident. The establishment of more colonies was a question of capital, which was hard to find when the proceeds from trading were so small. For the time being they had to be satisfied with Christianshåb as a new colony.

This colony had been deliberately established in the Bay in a central position, in order not only to exploit the possibilities to the full but also to be where the Dutch carried on most of their trading. Right from the days of the Bergen Company it had been repeatedly stressed how important it was to wrest from the Dutch their trade along the west coast of Greenland; no trade would pay until they had been ousted; but to bring this about in those days of mercantilism, help from the State authorities was needed.

There is no doubt that the Dutch whalers and merchants – traders, as the colonists called them – immediately interpreted the establishment of Christianshåb as an intensification of the competition that already existed. This, among other things, is apparent from the first report received by Jacob Sewerin from the new colony, in 1735. The report was almost solely concerned with Dutch trading. Matthias Fersleff, the trader, and Jens Hjort, the assistant, felt that there would be no hope of progress for Christianshåb, even if it were "the best and most profitable place in Greenland", so long as the Dutch were able to trade freely, as they were then doing. The local Greenlanders had come to the colony with complaints of encroachments by the Dutch. Although they maintained that a Dutch whaler and trader had robbed them of a whale a few kilometres south of the colony, Hjort was powerless to do anything when he got there, since the trader insisted that he had given goods in exchange for the whale. ". . . So we had to let things take their course and hold our peace, which made the Greenlanders feel quite cool towards us, as they had hoped we would stand up for them."

It caused even greater annoyance, and a direct loss, when the trader let the Greenlanders have goods on credit and a Dutch trader subsequently stole the blubber, which the Greenlanders concerned had collected to pay for the goods. That happened on a number of occasions, and Hjort had himself seen it occur in Sandbay immediately to the north of the colony. In this instance, too, Hjort had attempted to intervene, referring to the Dutch States-General proclamation of 1720;

the Dutch captain replied that they now felt obliged to seize the blubber they wanted. They were not, in fact, prepared to see the colonies' traders purchasing all the blubber from the Greenlanders. Furthermore, the Dutch traders intended to get the States-General to support them, and then they would "come with such force that they would fear neither us nor the Greenlanders, so that there would be both murder and bloodshed".

It was not only the Dutch who were competing with Sewerin: a vessel from Altona was also reported, sailing under charter to Denmark, but also trying to damage the colony's trade and "set the Greenlanders against us". The report provided heaven-sent support for an application to the King for Government help in stopping all foreign trading – which did, indeed, infringe the charter granted by the Government to Jacob Sewerin.

Any action at all on the part of the Government in relation to the Dutch would undeniably have diplomatic repercussions, and the Government was therefore forced to proceed with caution. But that did not mean that nothing was done. The Government realized at one and the same time that the situation called for its help, but equally that it was necessary to tread warily: it sent several ships to cruise in the waters between the south-west coast of Norway and Scotland during 1735. It was presumably the task of the admiralty to investigate, as far as it could, the extent of the Davis Strait traffic so as to obtain some basis on which to judge the arguments of Sewerin and others. (He had not been the first to emphasize the ruinous effect of Dutch competition.)

It is apparent from some of the reports preserved from two of these warships that quite a number of Dutch and Hamburg vessels were sailing to Greenland. But in particular it was the ships from Hamburg that they were after. Accordingly, one of the warships reported that a ship on the Greenland run named *Die Stadt Hamburg* was not even flying a Hamburg flag or carrying a Hamburg sea-pass but came from the Netherlands. This gave the impression that the Dutch were trying to hide behind a foreign flag. However, this appears to be an isolated case; elsewhere the various ships mentioned have good Dutch-sounding names. In that particular instance, it is also quite possible that it was a Hamburg ship on charter to a Dutch merchant; furthermore, many Danish and Norwegian vessels bore Dutch names.

These reports may have had a positive influence on the attitude adopted by the Government, following Jacob Sewerin's memorandum of 11 November 1735, which was couched in more optimistic terms than his plaint of the previous year. A number of Greenlanders had moved to Godthåb, giving rise to hopes of future productivity. The new colony of Christianshåb was also shaping well. During that year, 316 barrels of blubber plus skins and baleen, worth over 351 rdl. on the market, had been collected; the year in fact showed a loss, but only about one-third as large as that of the previous year. The total losses for the first two years amounted to nearly 50 per cent of the revenues: this was a considerable handicap to the sailings.

Although the Government was clearly unwilling to give further financial help, it had to keep its promise of a monopoly which was contained in the charter. Using the report from Christianshåb as a basis, Jacob Sewerin therefore requested the King to make representations to the Dutch Government to enforce the ban on the Dutch Greenland navigators against trading with Greenlanders "who live within 10 Danish miles [75 km.] of the colonies already established, or which may be established anywhere hereafter, and [that the Dutch navigators should] allow the Greenlanders everywhere to keep peacefully whatever they may acquire, afloat or ashore, through their industry and labour, and not to deprive them of it or forcibly extort anything from them . . .". This is surely the first time that territorial limits for the established colonies are mentioned – and called for – in terms of specific distances (about 75 kilometres).

At the same time Sewerin wanted the Government to enforce the trading ban on the King's own subjects, through the Customs, especially in Altona, Bergen and Ribe. The latter step was the easiest to carry out since it did not involve relations with foreign countries. Two months after Sewerin's memorandum, the desired order was issued to the various Customs houses, but the territorial limits of the individual colonies were not fixed at 10 Danish miles, as Jacob Sewerin had wished, only the vague expression "within some miles of the colonies in Greenland" being used in relation to trading.

Jacob Sewerin's first wish, which he would have liked to see fulfilled as soon as possible was the enforcement of a ban on foreign countries trading with Greenland; but this could not be carried out promptly by the Government, which possibly felt that its sovereignty must be unequivocally asserted before proceeding with formal measures against the States-General. The cruising of the warships in the waters between the south-west coast of Norway and Scotland in 1735 could be interpreted as an opening gambit, an assertion of the *dominium maris septentrionalis* (rule over the northern sea) by Denmark–Norway in the sixteenth and seventeenth centuries.[1]

In 1736, the Government felt able to go further and send a frigate to the Davis Strait, primarily to cruise in the Disko Bay, thus to show the flag at sea and assert sovereignty. The frigate *Blaa Heire*'s appearance in mid-May in the waters west of Greenland came as a surprise to the Dutch. Out in the Davis Strait they took to their heels on discovering that she was a man-of-war. The same thing happened in the Disko Bay. Up to the beginning of August the *Blaa Heire* hailed a number of Dutch vessels; they were boarded and informed of the trading ban, with the threat of confiscation of ship and cargo in case of infringement. (The territorial limit of 10 Danish miles around the colonies does not appear to have been asserted). Not all the Dutch vessels reacted by taking flight. Poul Egede related that the master of one of Jacob Sewerin's ships at Sandbay to the north of Christianshåb boarded two Dutch vessels, informed the masters of the ban and advised them that a royal frigate was keeping the Bugt clear. To this, one of the masters replied that this would not frighten their principals; if it came to that, they had the capital to send out armed merchantment. Thus they had to assume that the Dutch traders with their lightly armed vessels had only fled at the sight of the warship but that the presence of the latter in Greenland waters might have consequences at Government level.

It annoyed Jacob Sewerin that the frigate had arrived so late in 1736 and was therefore of not the slightest benefit to the Trading Company. In his report to the Missionskollegium in January, in reply to the latter's question, he answered that payment of the mission's expenses by the Trading Company depended, among other things, on whether the King took the necessary measures to have the unauthorized foreign trading stopped. This was a weighty argument, and some effective action had to be taken.

It was obviously at the instance of Hans Egede that, during the first few months of 1737, the Government evinced more concentrated activity all round in connection with both the Trading Company and the Mission. One of the results of this was that by February an attempt was made to deal with Jacob Sewerin's complaint about the delay in sending out the frigate. The Admiralty instructed commander Wodroff to fit out the *Blaa Heire* for a long voyage, and exactly one month later he sailed for Greenland, arriving there in nineteen days.

During the same period the department of foreign affairs of the *Tyske Cancelli* seems to have been working, a memorandum having been sent to the Danish minister in the Hague dealing with the Dutch traders' conduct in Greenland in general, and in the Disko Bay in particular, towards both the Greenlanders and His Majesty's colonies. In view of the damage suffered in Greenland, the Government sent a frigate to patrol Greenland waters, especially in the Disko Bay, in order to protect the colonies and drive away any ships that came within four Danish miles (30 km) of the coast, approached "our settlements" or landed within thirty Danish miles on either side of the colonies. Finally, the minister was to bear in mind that measures were being taken against vessels sailing in these waters without permission and behaving like pirates. There was no question of preventing Dutch whalers from whaling in the Davis Strait. The Government emphasized that the minister should be discreet, not mentioning the matter to any state official, but waiting for others to mention it first.

This document was notable in that it embodied Jacob Sewerin's wish that the King should at least assert the monopoly and ban trading for foreigners within a limit of fifteen Danish miles on either side of the colonies already established and those to be established in the future, even though he did not at this time wish to apply the trading ban to the whole of the coastal stretch. At sea he only wanted a two-mile limit, whereas the Government seemed to want to abide by the practice that had grown up of fixing the limit for territorial waters at four Danish miles.

The government was inconsistent and imprecise in issuing its orders: the instructions to lieutenant-commander Wodroff of the *Blaa Heire* stated that the territorial limit north and south of Christianshåb was ten to fifteen Danish miles, and further designated the whole of the so-called south-east Bugt with all adjacent islands and "harbours", together with the coast as far as Manîtsoq island north of present-day Egedesminde, and to the north of Christianshåb as far as the bay on Arveprinsens Ejland where Ritenbenk was later established, called by the Dutch Zwarte Vogel Bay. The outer islands in the Bugt were outside the limit, while Nordbay and Nivâq Bugt were within it.

From the time the frigate *Blaa Heire* reached this area in mid-May until the beginning of June, she hailed twenty-four whalers, and presumably traders, and gave them formal warnings, with the result that in the whole of the inner sector of the Disko Bay not a single Dutchman was to be seen after that time. Of the twenty-four vessels hailed, however, six were encountered on their way through the Davis Strait, including one French and two Spanish ships (all three of them Basque) and one from Altona; later she met two from Bremen as well. Thus she had succeeded in warning eighteen Dutch vessels. Another Dutch ship was crushed in the ice and a French one was wrecked on a skerry at Rifkol (Ũmánaq beyond Agto, Egedesminde). Several Dutchmen had eluded the frigate either by going off to whale in the western ice or – as some of them stated later – by sailing north of Disko to catch whales and to trade with the Greenlanders living there. Yet that in itself was an acknowledgement of the ban on trading near Christianshåb.

Thus the patrolling done by the *Blaa Heire* had its effect. The trader in Christianshåb was offered more blubber than he was able to collect by the local Greenlanders, some of whom expressed annoyance at not being able to dispose of the blubber they had on their hands. All this proved that it was possible to secure the trade in the colonies, but that the sanctions must be given force. A frigate, however, was not the right vessel for the job. She certainly travelled faster than the relatively small broad-beamed whalers, but the slim lines of the frigate's hull made the vessel unsuitable in the ice, which always had to be expected in the Bay.

Those Greenlanders who had not been able to dispose of their surplus catch because the Dutch traders had fled and Christianshåb could not take it all had some cause to regret the foreigners' absence. Poul Egede, who returned to Christianshåb in the summer of 1736, had his work cut out to pacify them. Thus the Greenlanders continued to be both repelled and attracted by the Dutch. When, in May 1737, Poul Egede visited some Greenlanders on an island near the colony of Christianshåb, they were singing and dancing to celebrate the approach of four Dutch whalers, though the ships could not get through the ice, nor could the Greenlanders approach the ships across the ice; however, they were looking forward to doing good business. However, Poul Egede had plenty of merchandise in his vessel, and so set himself up as a trader on the spot, and within two days he had bought up everything they had to sell, so that there was nothing left for the Dutchmen when they were eventually able to get through the ice. Hence, if the trader and his assistant were out early enough, it was possible to forestall the Dutch. On a later occasion the Greenlanders described the Dutch traders as having "no other conversation but blubber, blubber, tubs full, etc." The attitude of the Greenlanders in the Bay went from one extreme to the other, due partly to their not having the necessary ability and experience to adopt consistent attitudes; also the Greenlanders were in the middle between the two opposing parties and might equally be interested or uninterested in either party. It was frequently asserted that the Dutch gave better value, but just as often they took the Greenlanders' products from them by force, without giving adequate "barter goods" in exchange. On the other hand, though the colonies were not always able to satisfy the obvious needs of the Greenlanders, there was no mention of brutal methods, let alone of robbery. The Greenlanders told Poul Egede in 1737 that he was better to trade with, for he brought them things that they had not heard of before and asked for other things than merely filling the blubber tub.

The clashes between the Dutch and Jacob Sewerin's monopoly in the Disko Bay emerged at Government level in 1738. The Dutch envoy in Copenhagen presented a protest to the *Conseil* of the Danish–Norwegian King under instructions from the States-General. He complained of Wodroff's action in 1737 and of his and subsequently Matthias Fersleff's obstruction of the Dutch traders in the business which they had now been carrying on for over fifty years. The shipowners had complained to their governments (in the individual states), and the envoy had been instructed to request the King of Denmark–Norway to give his officers orders not to obstruct Dutch trading in those areas where it had previously been their custom to trade.

On 20 February, this complaint was dealt with by the *Conseil*, and it was decided to reply in accordance with the document sent to the Danish ambassador in the Hague the previous year. As far as the affair itself was concerned, the reply was word for word the same as the memorandum to the minister; it was despatched two days later, and a note was sent to the ambassador at the same time. This turned out a wise move, just as it was to have informed him of the *Blaa Heire*'s patrolling and the Government's attitude. Thus when the Grand Pensionary (the expert legal secretary of the Dutch States-General) approached the Danish minister in The Hague and referred to the Dutch traders' grievances, the minister was able to reply in accordance with the memorandum and note, as he reported on 12 April.

In the meantime the Dutch envoy in Copenhagen had reacted immediately to the *Tyske Cancelli*'s reply of 22 February. On the 23rd he informed the *Conseil* that the gravamen of his complaint had not been answered. He also made it clear that he had no desire to excuse ships without legal ship's papers, or any other infringements, which were severely punished in the Netherlands. The document sounded like a sort of withdrawal, since the envoy admitted to being unfamiliar with the geography of Greenland so that he did not understand the territorial limits that had been laid down. He thus contented himself with asking the King to declare that he did not want to obstruct the Dutch in their fishing or trading in those areas where they had previously fished or traded. To this he received no reply, the only possible interpretation being that the Government regarded the envoy's letter of 23 February as a sign that the Dutch Government preferred to withdraw from the matter and, at any rate, did not wish to apply any pressure to the Danish Government.

The latter, however, was still bent on enforcing the trading ban, but after Wodroff's critical remarks about the frigate, was not keen to send another warship to these waters. It would be best if the same result could be achieved at less expense. The matter must have been discussed between the Government (whoever the negotiator or negotiators were) and Jacob Sewerin, and at these negotiations it was suggested that Sewerin's ships be equipped as armed merchantmen, and a grant of 2,000 rdl. was made towards providing the necessary armament and ammunition. The result of this new measure was to intensify the clashes between the Dutch traders and Sewerin's people.

According to the royal instructions sent to Sewerin on 21 February

1738, the three ships to be sent out that year were primarily to watch "how the foreign traders make their round of the Disko Bay". If it was found or could be proved that, after being warned or contrary to promises given either during the frigate's two expeditions or in 1738, foreign traders had nevertheless ventured to trade, Sewerin's ships were entitled to seize the traders' ships and cargoes as prizes. This was to apply in the Disko Bay within the limits previously laid down. A new clause was then added to the effect that the same rights (and obligations) obtained for Sewerin's people, if foreigners stole from the Greenlanders or "otherwise treated them badly" outside the limits in the Disko Bay.

At the beginning of June a Dutch trader ventured ashore on Jacobsholmen just north-west of Christianshåb. Matthias Fersleff went out with armed pinnaces, caught the trader red-handed and seized the ship as a prize without the Dutch daring to put up any resistance. The master was proved to have been one of those who had pledged himself to respect the ban. At the Jakobshavn ice-fjord, a Dutch trader was also reported to have done business, although the Christianshåb trader had been nearby, but unable to prevent him. The Dutch were also said to have threatened the strongest of reprisals, if any Dutchman was taken. But one of the armed merchantmen fired warning shots with live ammunition, and the result was that the Dutch ships in the Bugt preferred to flee.

As the seizure of the vessel at Christianshåb might have had diplomatic consequences, Jacob Sewerin reported everything that had happened to the Government. The latter "approved" of what had been done, and promised Sewerin their support over the seizure. In support of his people's actions in Greenland, Sewerin had asked for an official Government statement (called a proclamation) to be issued, and had submitted a draft wording for it. This was naturally linked with the extension of his charter. It is apparent from the *Cancelli*'s handling of the matter of extending the charter – without any mention of the proclamation at all – that the Government obviously did not want to commit themselves to a statement without closer consideration. At the end of February 1739, however, the Government took steps to draw up the desired statement.

In 1739 Sewerin once again made use of individual armed merchantmen. As in the previous year, he received a grant towards fitting them out.[2] The threats uttered by the Dutch induced the Government to lend Sewerin ten cannon for the defence of the colonies. Thus they were ready for anything.

These preparations appear to have been justified, as the situation in the Disko Bay was more tense that summer than ever before. The newly-arrived Dutch traders were, if that was possible, more truculent than ever. In the vicinity of the Christianshåb colony there was shooting every day, with and without targets. Shots were fired at the ice from the Dutch vessels, presumably in order to get through it more quickly, but it appeared significant as they had not done this before. The Greenlanders on the islands panicked and left their settlements, and when four Dutch ships appeared off Christianshåb, they took headlong flight. However, Poul Egede went on board, and on one of them was an inspector from the Netherlands on his way to see the Moravian brethren at Godthåb – which, in itself, was peaceful enough.

The Dutch masters of the vessels were nevertheless disposed to offer resistance, in incidents like that of the previous year when a ship was seized as a prize. They later sailed northwards and hove to in Makelijk Oud, the harbour of what was later Jakobshavn. Three of Jacob Sewerin's ships arrived there, and as the harbour was situated within the colony's limits, the Dutch were trespassing. Fersleff, who, as the trader at Christianshåb, was aboard one of Jacob Sewerin's vessels, had the royal flag hoisted on one of the armed merchantmen, and requested the Dutch to comply with the order they had been given to leave the harbour. But instead they hoisted the "Prince and States Flag", and refused to come aboard the armed merchantman. Together with the three masters, Fersleff then decided to fire warning shots, which had no effect. After the three Danish vessels had dropped anchor, closing the harbour entrance, a live shot was fired first as a warning and then, when that did not induce the Dutch to come on board, although they did strike their flag, the Danish vessels opened fire, and continued for an hour and a quarter. The Dutch suffered damage to sails and rigging, one receiving two shots in the side and one in the middle of the main-mast. The Dutch surrendered without returning the Danes' fire, although they had armed themselves to the teeth beforehand and their cannons were at the ready. They had been unable to use their cannon because the Danish ships were out of range. All four Dutch vessels were seized as prizes and taken to Christianshåb. That is the story of the "famous naval battle off Makelijk Oud".

The vessels seized were held at Christianshåb for the time being; two of them were not in good condition, but the other two were taken to Denmark in July with a partly Dutch crew. By an irony of fate one of Sewerin's ships got into difficulties off the Dutch coast and was taken over by the very Amsterdam shipowners whose vessels had been seized in the "naval battle". Thus both the shipowners and the Dutch government held a trump card. During the rest of that year and into the next, there was an animated correspondence over the affair, involving the Dutch Government, the Dutch envoy in Copenhagen and

o

the Danish minister in the Hague. A further complication was that the cargo of one of the vessels seized included a considerable quantity of goods for the brethren in Godthåb. The inspector who was on the ship complained to the King, who decided that the brethren's goods should be duly handed over to them. The final outcome regarding the ships seized was in Sewerin's favour. The two ships that remained behind in Christianshåb are believed to have been used for house-building at the colony.

The skirmish at Makelijk Oud had meanwhile given plenty of support to Jacob Sewerin's wish for the publication of a forthright declaration banning foreign trading within his trading areas in Greenland. As always, this desire was tied up with the extension of his charter. Protracted consideration and negotiations took place before agreement was reached for its extension, but it was reached eventually. At least a month after the charter was renewed, the royal proclamation of 9 April 1740 was published – just before sailings to the Greenland colonies started for that year. By virtue of the renewed charter, and on the grounds that the King of Denmark–Norway was "the absolute hereditary monarch and lord of the said Greenland with its adjacent islands", Jacob Sewerin received permission to seize and capture anyone, subject or foreigner, trading contrary to the charter granted "with the colonies in our said land of Greenland, either already established or to be established hereafter . . . and also within the limits fixed for them", who stole from the Greenlanders or used force against them "in any place in Greenland wheresoever, at sea or ashore". The boundaries of the colonies were in general fixed at 10–15 Danish miles on each side. There was an element of vagueness about this, since no limit was laid down for the territorial waters. This vagueness was possibly intentional because during the preceding negotiations and representations to the King the limits at sea had been discussed. The so-called "Greenland Commission" of 1738 had recommended in a report the observance of a limit of 4 Danish miles at sea, as was enforced in the waters around Iceland and the Faroes, but the Commission expressly mentioned that Jacob Sewerin wanted a limit of 15 to 20 Danish miles on all sides of the colonies. The definition of the boundaries in the proclamation must thus be regarded as a sort of compromise, the limits set being smaller than Jacob Sewerin wanted, yet saying nothing explicitly in writing about the territorial waters. Hence the definition of boundaries in the proclamation must be interpreted as applying to the seaward side as well.

However, the most significant aspect of the proclamation of 9 April 1740 was that it was clearly founded on sovereignty, the most clear-cut and far-reaching declaration of sovereignty in the series so far. That

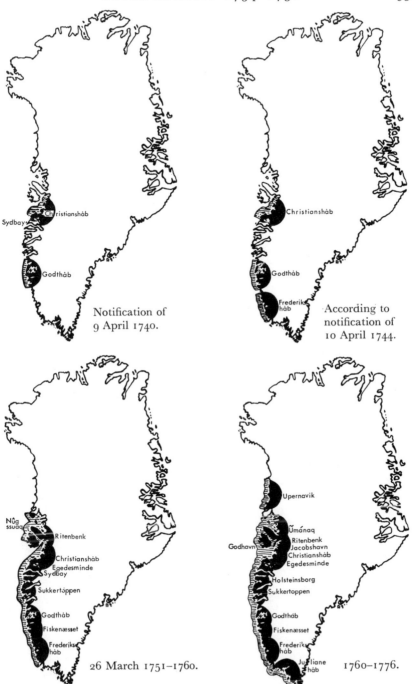

Notification of
9 April 1740.

According to
notification of
10 April 1744.

26 March 1751–1760.

1760–1776.

Eighteenth-century Greenland. By a decree of 18 March 1776, the hitherto open
stretch between Ŭmánaq and Upernavik was formally closed. Horizontal hatching
indicates closed territorial waters.

the Danes were now prepared to go so far was presumably due to their having an obviously greater knowledge of the country's geography than any other government, although they were not aware of the full extent of Greenland. Also, the Dutch envoy in Copenhagen had openly, though probably unwisely, confessed his ignorance. A strong contributory factor, too, was probably the unwillingness of the Netherlands to create acute antagonism over what, for the States-General, was the relatively unimportant problem of Dutch trading on the Greenland coasts. Whaling, which was the principal enterprise, could perfectly well be carried on in the Davis Strait and show an adequate profit without any conflict with the colonies on the coast. The Dutch shipowners who had an interest in trading on the coast occupied a politically weak position in their own country, as the traders sent out had obviously acted contrary to the States-General's proclamation of 18 November 1720, which expressly barred violence and robbery.

It was precisely against violence and robbery that the closing paragraph of the proclamation of 9 April 1740 was directed. By virtue of the Danish–Norwegian King's sovereignty over the whole of Greenland with its adjacent islands, the obligation inherent in such sovereignty to protect the country's inhabitants by law applied to all Greenlanders regardless of whether they lived within or outside the colonial regions. The King delegated this obligation to provide legal protection to Jacob Sewerin, who was bound and entitled to uphold the rights and obligations of such sovereignty as long as his charter lasted. The extent to which he was able to do so was a different matter.

Jacob Sewerin anticipated the summer of 1740 somewhat uneasily in relation to Dutch activity. He alleged, on the basis of reports from the Netherlands, that one ship was being equipped there with fourteen cannon and one with eight, and there was yet another of whose armament he had no details. At the same time he referred to Dutch ships sailing to the southernmost part of the west coast. Jacob Sewerin would "with God's help" do whatever he could, but should the foreigners undertake anything "desperate" either against the colony, i.e. Christianshåb, or his vessels, "far too much would be lost by the Greenlanders in regard of both their faith in and affection for us".

In other words it was essential to assert the King's power to protect the Greenlanders – not only for the sake of trade, so that the Dutch could be kept out, but for the mission's sake too, in order to promote its ministry. To these factors regard for the King's prestige was now added. Hans Egede's remarks and Matthias Fersleff's reference to the King's protection had now became transformed into a binding obligation. Simultaneously this obligation came to form an important thread in the pattern of ideas that increasingly dominated the policy adopted towards Greenland.

In the Disko Bay itself the Greenlanders reacted to the events in widely differing ways. When the vessel was seized in 1738, some mocked the arrested Dutchmen, others thought of the seizure as theft, making the colonists no better than the Dutch who stole the Greenlanders' catch, while yet others accepted it as a matter of course as though it were a joint catch, and demanded their share of the ship and cargo as *fangers*. Later, some Greenlanders, in their anxiety, goaded the others into believing that they in their turn were now being robbed and made preparations to resist. But Poul Egede pacified them, referring to the King's renewed statement that it was his will that they should not be wronged. According to Poul Egede's account, some had said in a tone of respect mingled with fear after the skirmish at Makelijk Oud: "Your master must be a truly great master, since the Dutchmen were so afraid of his servants. Suppose he had come himself!" The reports of succeeding years imply, however, that the respect did not remain quite so high, though the fear of the Dutch did not change.

Neither then nor for some time after did the proclamation of 9 April 1740 have any special effect on the Dutch. The masters were presented with the proclamation as occasion arose, and put their signature to it with a promise of compliance, but others continued to navigate the forbidden areas undeterred. Niels Egede, who was the trader at Christianshåb from 1740–3, reported violence and robbery, rape and kidnapping. However, there was an appreciable difference in the Greenlanders' reaction towards the Dutch compared with previous years. First, they turned more often to the people of the colony for help, just as they diligently reported the movements and conduct of the Dutch in the Bugt. Secondly, in some cases they adopted a less frightened attitude towards the foreigners after the two Dutch "defeats" in 1738 and 1739. This attitude was evidently transmitted also to the Greenlanders who lived outside the "closed" part of the Bay.

Relations with the Dutch could take a more hostile turn. Thus in 1742 Niels Egede reported mass killings of Dutchmen. It happened on Disko – the locality was not more closely identified – when a Dutch skipper thought that a Greenlander had not filled the tub with enough blubber, whereupon he went to help himself, despite the Greenlander's protests. In his anger the Greenlander then fetched his bow and arrows and mortally wounded the skipper from behind. When the latter called for help, his companions fled. This acted as a signal to the other Greenlanders present and they pursued the Dutch down to the coast and out to sea. Only one Dutchman survived, and he reached his ship wounded. It seems that the situation was seldom so serious. At Rodebay on one occasion the Greenlanders played a trick on the Dutch. Some of the crew from a ship went ashore to trade. It was within the boundaries, hence illegal, and the skipper therefore put one of his men on watch. One of the local Greenlanders, with the knowledge of the others, donned European clothing and, musket in hand, he took up his position some way off behind a rock. The Greenlanders pointed to him and said to the Dutch that it was Niels Egede and his men coming. The Dutch immediately took to their heels, fled to the ship and put to sea, leaving all their merchandise behind them, to the great delight of the Greenlanders.

One element in this account merits special attention. The Greenlander who acted the part of Niels Egede had a "flint-lock" musket. This is surely the first time that a Greenlander is reported as being in possession of such a weapon. Guns, gunpowder and lead for shot were not at first sold in the colonies. The muskets came from the Dutch, who must have supplied ammunition too. So this was a completely new article which the Dutch introduced in these years, and they did a good trade, the Greenlanders being avid buyers. However, there were some fatal consequences, as several Dutch traders and sailors were killed in arguments by shots from the guns which they had themselves sold to the Greenlanders.

With such a popular article in circulation and with continual infringements of the ban imposed by the proclamation, the trade suffered heavy losses. Although the trader N. C. Geelmuyden, in his 1749 report, did not put Dutch competition as the greatest hindrance he had to suffer first, he nevertheless regarded it as considerable. It was therefore important to establish more colonies and smaller trading stations and to site the export harbours for the ships of the Greenland trade in such a way that, unhindered by ice at home, they could set out early enough to forestall the Dutch. And then some means or other had to be found to prevent the Dutch selling firearms and ammunition, for these weapons diverted the Greenlanders away from sealing to reindeer hunting, which caused tremendous harm both to the Greenlanders' livelihood and to the Trading Company.

The presence of the flintlock from the mid-1740s onwards undoubtedly made serious inroads into West Greenland Eskimo civilization. It disturbed the whole of the hunting and fishing cycle, and from it there stemmed changes in the Greenlanders' occupations and in the whole social economy, with an increased dependence on supplies from outside.

REFERENCES

1. At that time, in the dawn of international law, single events were creating norms. The normative regulations were not yet fixed, but they may have the necessary precautionary effect. The reason why the Danish–Norwegian Government did not want to declare explicit limits of territory was presumably because such limits should be maintained effectively by force, and that was impossible; such maintenance implied the possibility of acute situations which might develop into diplomatic entanglements. Better to keep the limits vague and let future activity vindicate the rights and keep the possibility of calming down any tense contingencies.

2. This way of enlarging the Danish–Norwegian Navy had been used several times during the seventeenth and eighteenth centuries, and had been beneficial both in strengthening the Navy and in raising a merchant marine, in Denmark as well as in Norway. The ships were built as was usual for merchantships, but with subsidies from the state, especially with regard to the armament. These ships were compelled in case of war to sail under the command of the Admiralty. In peacetime they could sail wherever their owners wanted, but had to be kept in order because of their possible use in war. They had the right to hoist the flag of the Danish Royal Navy when acting as men-of-war and when in domestic waters, of being saluted by other ships as if they were Royal Navy ships.

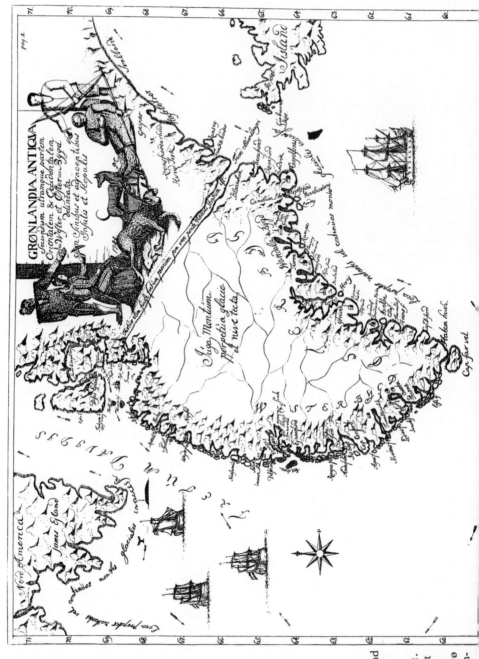

Map of Greenland from *Det gamle Grønlands nye Perlustration*, 1741. (From loose sheet in Bülow Collection; No. 35, Sorø Academy, Copen-

12

JACOB SEWERIN'S TRADING COMPANY
1734–1745

The first few years of Jacob Sewerin's Greenland Trading Company must be regarded as a "trial period", which is probably how he himself regarded them. It took time for him to adjust, as he had to do, to such a specialized undertaking, which involved extraneous obligations. He received grants on account of the special obligations, and it was a matter of finding out by experience whether these had been adequately estimated. By 1734 the annual grant proved to have been fixed too low, but there appeared to be no hope of altering it as long as the charter was in force.

It was not surprising, therefore, that during this trial period Jacob Sewerin's attention was directed especially towards the circumstances – such as Dutch competition – which constituted a direct threat to the progress anticipated. By establishing Christianshåb, Jacob Sewerin was hoping to procure whatever business Godthåb could not handle on its own, and at the same time put the Dutch out of business. However, neither of these objects could be achieved in the short term.

The purchase – i.e. the Greenland products that were collected at the colonies for processing and resale in Copenhagen or other European markets – apparently rose during the year 1735-7 from 434 to 797 barrels of blubber. This was an average of over 200 barrels per annum more than that for the period 1725–33. The quantities of skins and baleen showed wider fluctuations. From 1735–8, receipts rose, whereas expenses fluctuated. Yet each year was marked by a heavy loss, although this varied considerably, the smallest being 1,223 rdl., the greatest nearly 3,681 rdl. In 1738 Sewerin calculated that his receipts had risen by 33 per cent, while expenditure had risen by nearly 53 per cent. The advance on the state subsidy that he had been granted for 1739 was included in these receipts. The marked rise in expenditure was partly due to "arming" – in defence against possible attack by the Dutch, even though a grant had been given towards fitting out the ships. Presumably this aid towards fitting out was swallowed up by the costs relating to a chartered ship, whereas Sewerin himself had to pay for the fitting out of his own vessels. In the same year he estimated his total loss at 16,780 rdl., including in his calculation annual interest of 6 per cent, increased office expenses and a very modest annual personal "salary". According to this statement, therefore, he had still not progressed at the end of four years of the six-year charter beyond the first stage – the years of loss – which at one time he had reckoned would last for only two years. This situation was not such as to make him optimistic, the less so as it must have had repercussions on his personal fortune.

It caused surprise therefore when, in 1736, he bought an estate in Northern Jutland – Dronninglund, Dronninggård and Hals Ladegård with appurtenant farms, churches, tithes, etc. – for the considerable sum of 60,000 rdl. He did so on credit, however, at 4 per cent, in the same way that, throughout his life, he had lived on bills of exchange and other forms of credit. Thus the purchase of property was by no means a cash investment but was rather intended to facilitate his shipping business and trading. Much of the estate was covered by oak and beech forests which could provide timber for shipbuilding and repairs. On the Bølden farm, to the west of Hals, near the eastern branch of the Limfjord, Sewerin established a harbour and a shipbuilding yard, together with a whale oil distillery. His hopes were reflected in the name he gave the place – *Grønlands Lykke* (Greenland's Fortune). From there the annual sailings could take place as early as possible, to forestall the Dutch, unhindered by the ice that occurred in the more southerly Danish waters. As the son of the recorder of Saeby, he knew the district, and may have given him satisfaction to be the owner of Dronninglund. Claus Enevold Pårs, for whom he had acted as a trustee, had his freehold farm in Serridslev, not far from Dronninglund.

The heavy costs involved in the sailings to the colonies and in supplying them obliged Sewerin to be niggardly in carrying anything more than the essential people and goods. The Moravian brethren, who were apparently going to continue to operate their mission at Godthåb, caused him considerable expense in terms of freight and supplies, without Sewerin receiving any remuneration for it. The maintenance of this group of people had not been taken into account in the authorities' grant.

The needs of the Moravian brethren had usually been supplied from the Netherlands, which meant Dutch ships putting in at the colony or in its vicinity – Sewerin naturally regarded this as an encroachment on his rights under the charter, although he was under no obligation whatsoever towards the brethren at Ny Herrnhut. He complained of the strain on the economy of Godthåb caused by the presence of this community, through their consumption of Greenland products and through their hunting, fishing and collection of fuel. He was in favour of "such carriage of aliens, either by nationality or religion" provided they paid the extra costs involved and reported in good time. The King conceded him the latter, having a clear appreciation of the trouble caused by the Moravians, yet being unwilling to condemn them altogether.

This situation represented not only the experience Sewerin had harvested over the first four years of the charter period, but part of the work of preparing for the extension of the charter after 1740. This preliminary work began as early as 1737. The relative discussions concerned the future form of the mission and the trading company, among other things, because the charter of 1734 obliged Sewerin to pay and supply the missionaries – for which purpose he received the annual grant. Both Hans Egede and Sewerin submitted many suggestions and proposed amendments during the succeeding years and an extensive correspondence was generated.

In December 1737 it is apparent that Sewerin was already bent on increasing the number of colonies with a settlement to the south. At the same time both he and Hans Egede felt that the number of missionaries must be increased, and that in addition catechists' posts should be created. The other things suggested by Hans Egede around that time for the furtherance of the mission did not directly affect the renewal of Sewerin's charter.

It was clear that both the trading company and the mission ought to be extended from a purely geographical viewpoint. But Sewerin did not feel that he could extend the scope of his activities as long as he received the same grant. If there were to be more missionaries, an appropriate increase in the grant had to be made. Consequently the idea was mooted during the Conseil's discussions in the middle of February 1738 that the mission and trading company should be run separately. The Missionskollegium, through its chairman J. L. Holstein, who was also senior secretary in the *Danske Cancelli*, hinted at a quite unfounded distrust of Jacob Sewerin's probity over supplying the missionaries. The separation did not take place, but the fact that it was raised revealed the growing antagonism between the two institutions in Greenland.

On the same occasion the Conseil discussed how and with whom Jacob Sewerin should eventually discuss the terms of the renewed charter. As a result, four men of high rank were appointed as negotiators on 31 February 1738. They were Otto Thott, the head of the Commercekollegium established in 1735, Andreas Hojer the former royal historian (secretary of the Missionskollegium and lately also a member of the kollegium of the *Danske Cancelli*), Frederik Holmsted, the Copenhagen wholesaler who had previously taken an interest in the Greenland trade, and Marcus Wøldike, a professor of theology and a member of the Missionskollegium. This four-member board was thereafter known as "the Greenland Commission".

Hans Egede's scepticism regarding the capability of one individual to cope with the Greenland trade had to some extent begun to affect Sewerin, reinforced by the losses he had incurred. He looked forward to the time when a well-organized company would be able to take over the trade with the colonies; this was especially relevant to the whaling potentialities, which would always far exceed the financial resources he had available to exploit them. This hope did not prevent him from putting forward proposals for expanding the activities then under his management; he had every intention of carrying on but with a renewed charter.

During the 1738 discussions the old idea of true colonization was brought up, and Sewerin's proposal for settlement by Icelanders and people from Finnmark arose from the idea of a colony being established in the southernmost part of Greenland's west coast. In March, he suggested that the local authorities in those two regions be approached to gauge the interest and determine the state subsidy for emigration and for the initial living expenses. At a meeting of the *Conseil* it was decided that the commission should enter into correspondence with the local authorities – from whom, during the year, it received replies. In Iceland, one joiner alone could entertain the idea of emigrating but he required too big a security; no one else was interested there or in Finnmark, so the plan was shelved.

In 1738 the commission had had some further correspondence with Sewerin, in which he reiterated his wish for an extension of six, eight or ten years but specified that on being given one year's notice, he would withdraw in favour of a more permanent arrangement. Sewerin thought that to separate the Trading Company and the mission would be of little advantage to the latter, as he estimated the costs for Godthåb and Christianshåb alone at 7,000 rdl. per annum. Moreover, the Commission had asked him whether he could contemplate a lower annual grant than the 5,000 rdl. which he wanted on renewal of the charter, in answer to which Sewerin referred them to his statement showing losses of over 16,000 rdl. and his application for a fourth preferential loan of 5–6,000 rdl. Indeed, he had used the 1739 subsidy the previous year, and been granted 2,000 rdl. for defence purposes in 1739.

At the end of January 1739 the draft charter came before the *Conseil*.

In its covering letter the commission stated rather dishearteningly that "no one else would be likely to want to become involved in the Greenland affair at present after the clashes that have recently occurred with the Dutch". It was recommended that Sewerin be given the charter, mainly on the desired terms, with a subsidy of 5,000 rigsdaler per annum for a period of ten years. "But in general we can only humbly admit that we do not understand how it is still possible through this charter to have any hope of profit and permanence in this difficult trade". The draft charter was approved and Sewerin was informed accordingly.

After all these troubles and long drawn-out negotiations it would seem natural for Sewerin to have lost the last remnants of his inclination to continue with the undertaking, but he reacted in the very opposite way. Even according to his own statements, he had only made repeated losses, so did he have anything like an accurate knowledge of his own financial position? Virtually no accounts are extant and those that do exist imply that his private and business finances were all combined. Sewerin certainly had some idea of the situation, but his optimism made him believe that it would work out; and this optimism was coupled with his sense of obligation towards the work which had been begun with high Christian intentions, and which he had undertaken to support financially. A rather bad beginning had been made, and the work was far from being completed. He was also under an obligation to the King to continue, and he had to agree to carry on with the trading company as a basis for work towards the higher aims of God and King. We must assume that this was also the basis of his arguments at the time of the last renewal of the charter – in 1743-4 when his optimism seemed to be a shade more well-founded.

In 1739, Sewerin had expressed a wish to see the charter in draft, yet even towards the end of the year the matter had not advanced. Yet he complained to the King of the slowness and officiousness of the commission, and asked for someone to be appointed to act as a "patron and senior director of Greenland affairs", to whom he could refer in acute situations requiring prompt action, "the lack of which may otherwise often cause inconvenience". This letter caused Christian VI to write anxiously to Count J. L. Holstein, revealing considerable understanding not only of the problems of the officials in the central administration, but also of Sewerin's need for someone to provide effective administrative action. However, it was decided that the commission should continue to deal with Greenlandic affairs, presumably because no one in the central administration could cover the differing interests of both the mission and the trading company while questions of foreign politics had to be considered at the same time.

Although Jacob Sewerin had made it plain that he had little use for the commission, he had to swallow his pride and negotiate with them. He appears to have stayed at Dronninglund for most of the year, but was in Copenhagen on 11 January, when his exasperation flared up suddenly during the negotiations. According to the minutes, he intimated that "in the present circumstances he no longer felt able to continue with this Greenland trade". The commission members tried to calm him, but Sewerin picked up the draft charter and walked out of the meeting. Three days later he put forward a new draft, stating that he would now only enter into a contract for three to four years provided he got back his ship, which was being held in the Netherlands with her master and cargo, plus an advance of 5,000 rdl. in addition to the subsidy for the first year. To offset this advance he would mortgage Dronninglund. The commission was not enthusiastic about these conditions – it wanted a better and safer method – but it saw no alternative to humouring him. On the other hand, there were several points on which his wishes had to be rejected and others, including the return of the captured vessel, in respect of which the commission undertook to do what it could.

Final execution of the charter was becoming urgent. When January and most of February passed, still with nothing apparently being done, Sewerin gradually reached explosion point. On 24 February he gave the commission a formal ultimatum that unless he received definite news within fourteen days, and instructions were issued to the exchequer to pay out the subsidy, "I shall be obliged most humbly to inform His Royal Majesty of my inability to proceed, through no fault of mine". However, the charter was already on its way, and on 4 March it received the King's signature. The instructions to the *Rentekammer* – the Finanskollegium, as it was now called – were not issued until 1 April, and even then he still did not receive all the money at once. A mortgage deed had to be drawn up first for payment of the advance for 1743 and the Finanskollegium therefore wished to investigate through the Governor at Ålborg whether he had felled an excessive number of trees in his forests, thus reducing the security.

Payment of the grants was important to Sewerin, since his credit possibilities were, on his own admission, limited. But still more important were the ratification of the charter and the proclamation against trading by foreigners. When the charter was at last issued, Sewerin was bound by it to support for the next four years four missionaries plus two or more Greenlanders at each colony as catechists, as and when they were trained. He was to supply their wages and physical needs. For the two schools in the colonies, he undertook to provide premises and pay for equipment. He was to supply the children, twenty to twenty-four of them at each place, with a certain amount of food, clothing, bedding and kayaks. The teachers and other persons in charge of the children, as well as the missionaries, were each to be paid at least 10 rdl. per annum by him, and he was to provide them with food, clothing, light and heating. These obligations were more far-reaching than under the terms of the previous charter. Then there was an additional onerous stipulation founded on untoward experiences in the past: he was obliged to keep the colonies stocked with a whole year's supply of various essential provisions so that one colony could help another whose supply ship had failed to arrive.

Against these obligations were enumerated the rights which Sewerin was to enjoy in return. First was the grant, fixed at 5,000 rdl. per annum, of which 2,000 rdl. was to be used for defence purposes and the remaining 3,000 for the mission. Against a mortgage on Dronninglund, he was to be paid the grant for the fourth year during the first year. The mortgage was to serve as a guarantee that the sailings would actually be undertaken.

All the officials of the mission and the trading company with good conduct were to be eligible for a suitable post, on their return home after four to six years' service. Likewise, all the "men", in other words the hands and labourers, were to be exempt from military service wherever they settled in the country.

All goods destined for Greenland or imported for the oil distillery at Hals or into Copenhagen were exempted from customs duty, consumption tax, town tolls or other dues in Øresund, the Belts or any other of "the King's waterways". In addition, there was the right to a royal sea-pass (which might be useful in encounters with armed vessels of foreign nations), the right to auction the goods brought home, and the benefit of all buildings and effects in Greenland, together with the appropriate ships and boats, to be handed back without remuneration on expiry of the charter if it was not renewed. For the four years during which the charter was valid, Jacob Sewerin and his partners would "without let or hindrance, whether from our own subjects or foreigners, alone enjoy the trade with those colonies already established or to be established hereafter in Greenland, so that he alone, and no other, shall be permitted to trade within a predetermined distance of each of these same colonies", in other words, he was given a trading monopoly.

During the negotiations, Sewerin had spoken of the difficulty he had in finding anyone willing to invest in the Trading Company, because of its substantial loss in the very first year. He was on his own, as he had been during the discussions before 1733. However, the

Commission had little confidence in his financial and commercial ability; they would rather see the Trading Company "on a firmer footing", and so Sewerin was bound by the charter to look for investors and even if he could not procure any, he was "to take one or more persons into the business with him", who were to be kept currently informed of everything concerning the trading company, even if not participating in it financially. This was a safety measure to prevent the whole undertaking coming to a standstill if Sewerin were to die suddenly. If he did die, it would be possible to terminate the charter, giving one year's notice to his heirs and any investors. However, he never found a single person to take an interest, let alone a partner.[1]

Even before the first charter was executed in 1734, Jacob Sewerin had wanted a "permanent lottery" by means of which, as he calculated, he could have sufficient to cover his losses during the first few years. The 1734 charter allowed him to arrange one whenever he wanted, but this permission was now withdrawn. He wanted the promise made in 1734 fulfilled, but this concession was not thought possible, as the previous Greenland lottery had not been a success, and one unsuccessful lottery would prejudice future ones. Referring to his heavy losses and failing credit, he wrote to the King asking for help – even if his letter did not specify the form of such help, he must have been thinking of having the earlier refusal of the lottery set aside; still, his wishes were not met. After all, the prizes for the previous lottery held to promote the Greenland mission and trading company were still unpaid. Sewerin had to manage for the time being without a lottery.

One provision of the charter is particularly noteworthy, namely the promise, made to missionaries and others employed by the mission and the Trading Company, of suitable employment after a number of years' service in Greenland. Sewerin had insisted on this partly in the hope of thus getting good people into his service, but also out of human concern. The same applied to the "men": by getting them exempted from conscription, he might be able to induce farmers from Dronninglund and men from northern Norway to enter the Greenland service.

That his people, especially the "men", should be of good character was essential. There had been unpleasant experiences not only with the artisans, labourers and hands sent out to the colonies, but also with ships' crews, Danish as well as foreign. In another connection Poul Egede wrote: "It is just as rare to find a considerate Greenlander as a God-fearing sailor from the [Danish] navy. Of the former I have seen very few but of the latter none." "The men" in particular were inclined to get drunk, particularly during holidays and other festive occasions. There was no way of influencing foreign seamen, the only thing was to get rid of them. The Danes could be selected and, if necessary, sent home and replaced. Up to now no fault had been found with the missionaries, although the Missionskollegium had doubts about the Trading Company's employees, and were extremely mistrustful of the "men" sent out. "We hope", wrote the Missionskollegium to Sewerin in 1729, "that Mr. Sewerin will earnestly impress on his employees in the country and recommend them to avoid and to punish seriously anything which might offend or provoke the local inhabitants and defeat the main purpose of the costly venture".

Sewerin therefore started to replace the "men" with farm labourers from Dronninglund, who were willing enough because they had the prospect of escaping from both "adscription"[2] and compulsory military service. This replacement process was welcomed in Greenland. Furthermore, it was intended that the catechists sent out by the Missionskollegium should assist with the local trade, and accordingly two were posted to each of the existing colonies in 1739. The pastors were ordered to instruct them in the Greenlandic language, and that they should "assist Mr. Sewerin's people in all possible ways to transact the business of the Trading Company so that they may in time become fit for service as catechists and in the work of the Trading Company in that country, just as these institutions are presumably already able, and will be more so in the future, to assist each other", especially if "decent, Christian-minded persons . . ., who can induce the poor Greenlanders to seek both our trade and our instruction with some confidence", were employed. On the other hand, Sewerin was asked to impress on his employees the need to invite the Greenlanders with whom they came into contact to seek such instruction. There was obviously a feeling, however vague, that since a mission had been started in the country, an educational and a moral religious commitment towards the population was involved. This commitment was the responsibility of both the mission's representatives in Greenland and the employees of the trading company and its "men". A trading enterprise that also transmitted culture was considered to be a complete unit. It seems that Niels Egede's personality and work were in people's minds; he had shown that one man could simultaneously operate as a trader and be a missionary.

Niels Egede returned to Greenland in 1739 and was now the Godthåb trader in Sewerin's service. Poul Egede was then in his third year as the missionary at Christianshåb, but he was obliged to return to Denmark in the following year on account of "weakness of the eyes", whereupon Niels Egede was transferred to Christianshåb, and he continued to work there for the Trading Company and the mission until 1743, when he too felt that he had to leave Greenland. Thus the Egede family were still influencing the work being done.

P

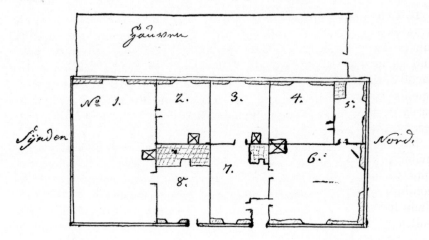

Niels Egede's plan and description of the dwelling-house in Godthåb in 1740, recorded in July 1865. (Central Record Office, Copenhagen. Inward letters concerning the Greenland Mission; file 1765, as enclosure to No. 12a.)

It is clear from an examination of staff records that the interest in working in Greenland was disseminated among relatives and acquaintances. The eighteenth century saw several generations of the Egedes and their relatives working in Greenland, to be followed later by Jacob Sewerin's family. While this was not unnatural, it illustrates how remote Greenland seemed to the ordinary Dane. People could not easily be got to go there to work. The charter's promise of future preferment might perhaps help in the future.

But even then there were already references to the theme that was a major preoccupation in the following decades, and again in recent times: those sent out did not stay in the country long enough. The conditions in Greenland were not tempting, and the hard, strenuous daily life, to which people from milder climates were unaccustomed, called both for calories and for outstanding strength and energy, both physical and mental. As we know, people were unaware of the need for vitamins, but they suffered more from their lack in Greenland than at home. Scurvy was therefore a common cause of lost working-days, and indeed almost every year it cost lives. Deaths among the workforce meant more work for the survivors, for no replacement could be sent out until the news had been brought by sea to the trading company or mission in Denmark, who could then only make the necessary arrangements in conjunction with sailings scheduled for the next year.

In the late 1720s and early 1740s there were no major events in Greenland apart from the perpetual skirmishes with the Dutch in the Bugt. There are only scattered hints in the sources regarding trading conditions. No accounts have been found for these years, and much correspondence has disappeared, so that it is impossible to discern the development of the Trading Company at all clearly.

There is no new evidence of how the West Greenlander lived in places outside the two colonial districts. Both there and north of Melville Bay, and at the "back of the land" in East Greenland,[3] life was probably much as it had been earlier in the century with varying success in hunting and fishing, abundance alternating with death and starvation. Greenlanders entered the two colonial districts on their travels from the north and south. Occasionally they stayed for a year or more, only to move off again. Both north of the Bugt and south of Godthåb. the West Greenlanders came into contact with the Dutch, particularly northwards from Ũmanaq. The field ice mostly prevented foreigners from visiting the southernmost part. Just as infrequent was contact with the colonies. However, those Greenlanders who settled in the colonies were continuously affected and influenced by both trading company and mission.

The trader or his assistant and some of the others went out into the district from time to time to purchase the local Greenland products in return for their merchandise, of which they took a suitable assortment with them. Sometimes the missionary or the catechist accompanied these trading expeditions, and at other times missionary journeys were made when no trading was done. The system of Poul and Niels Egede, who practised as missionaries and traders simultaneously, was not adopted by others, whether missionaries or traders.

Trading was done according to a pattern which seemed to have developed spontaneously in the course of colonization. Its form was determined by the scattered nature of the settlements, the local climate, the hunting and fishing conditions and the prey of the *fangers*. Apart from differences determined by locality, the trading methods resembled each other to some extent. Expeditions out into the district were undertaken late in the winter season, seldom before March, but they continued until late in the autumn, and in Godthåb sometimes nearly until Christmas. They were made in open boats – large pinnaces, propelled partly by oars and partly by sail. Only relatively small quantities of local products or merchandise could therefore be transported in and out of the colony on each expedition. Christianshåb becoming ice-bound put an end to the expeditions, which could not be resumed until late in the spring. No trading by sledge was possible. At both colonies it was frequently necessary during the expeditions to deposit the produce purchased for collection later. The storage depots were well-concealed in the Bugt, not to prevent the Greenlanders from making free with the products – this never happened as far as we know – but to secure them from the Dutch.

When people were not engaged on the expeditions, there were plenty of other jobs to be done in the colonies. There was the weekly weighing, measuring and distribution of foodstuffs and merchandise, and the sale of necessities which the colonists required partly to enable them to barter for fresh food from the local *fanger*, and partly for their own hunting trips, when it was the intention to provide fresh game. One older practice was for the trader at the colony to supply the more skilled hunters among the colonists with muskets, powder and shot to obtain food for the colony and so relieve the monotony of their diet. Besides this, fuel had to be collected – either driftwood, or heather and juniper. In summer, turves were cut. All in all, the labour of the individual was essential to the colony's welfare.

One of the toughest and dirtiest jobs done by the "men" in the colonies was stowing away the blubber purchased in barrels or casks. If the blubber was frozen, the work was relatively easy, although frost-bite on hands and faces was common. When the blubber was not frozen it had to be put into barrels quickly so as not to waste the oil.

The quantity and quality of Greenland products were, of course, dependent on wind and weather. If the blubber lay for long in the open, exposed to sun and wind, some of the oil would seep away, thus it was best to get it into casks at once, especially during warm spells. It is uncertain whether the practice, attempted previously, of lodging a number of barrels with certain settlements for filling was continued. At the colonies any blubber not casked immediately was stored in "blubber bins" (large partly sunken chests) to be put into casks as the cooper produced them. At that time and right up to the 1930s the cooper was an extremely important craftsman in the colony. Trading activities were severely restricted if the artisans skilled in cooperage either became ill and unfit for work, or died – leaving aside the human misery that could result.

When blubber and other Greenland products were being purchased, the Greenlanders' own requirements appear to have been deliberately taken into account. At Godthåb the "blubber position" at the beginning of the 1740s was apparently not favourable either for the Greenlanders or the trading company. In 1737, Godthåb is said to have been able to supply a record quantity of 135 casks of blubber, that is approximately 370 barrels, constituting about two-thirds of the total sent home that year; this was the largest quantity contributed by Godthåb in many years. Niels Egede reported in 1739 –40 that the boats were coming back from the expeditions fully loaded, but he did not mention the quantities he had collected, nor that there had been periods of famine. In 1740, however, his successor at Godthåb, N. C. Geelmuyden, reported in his journal right from January onwards that there was famine, that hunting and fishing had failed, and that lamps were extinguished in houses both north and south of Godthåb and on the plateaux at the head of the fjords. The winter had apparently been unusually severe, which was the supposed cause of the seals having moved away. At Pisugfik to the north of Godthåb the situation from late autumn onwards was said to have been so bad that the lamps had had to be put out. Hence many had travelled northwards to look for better hunting grounds or to buy blubber. When Geelmuyden went on a northward trading expedition up the coast at the end of May 1741, there was still no blubber at Pisugfik and the coast seemed deserted from Napassoq north to Hamburger sound, where the crew of an *umiak* told him that the reason for flight had been a rumour that the missionaries were going to take away their young children. (Such a rumour could scarcely have had any force north of Pisugfik, where the missionaries were never seen at that time.)

Geelmuyden's journal entries show that during these periods of famine the Greenlanders tried to buy their blubber requirements from each other. Several times lengthy journeys to buy blubber for the lamps are mentioned. During that winter such journeys were often fruitless, as the shortage was general. Not until June did the situation ease somewhat to the south. A number of southern Greenlanders were at Godthåb on their way to the Disko Bugt; so the journeys over long distances were still being made. At Christianshåb trading was apparently not satisfactory either. In one place the *fangers* intimated that hunting and fishing as a whole were no longer as good as they had once been. They dared not sell any of their stocks before spring, "as it often happens that they suffer want in the winter. I therefore begged them not to sell until they knew that they were provided for."

Only a short time after the establishment of Christianshåb it was realized that one of the best hunting areas in the district was to the north of present-day Jakobshavn's Isfjord. There was located the heavily populated settlement of Sermermiut, which had been continuously inhabited since the thirteenth century and where archaeologists have proved human habitation around 1400 BC. It seems that as early as 1735 trading expeditions came as far as that point, and it was one of the goals of Poul Egede's journey in the district immediately after his arrival in 1736. On 17 July he was in Makelijk Oud "where there was a whole host of tents". The place was used as a summer settlement by some of the Sermermiut people. Many times in the following years, both in winter by sledge and in summer, either on board ship or in the Trading Company's pinnaces, Poul Egede made his way north to Sermermiut and Makelijk Oud.

The opportunities for buying at this place must have been considerable from very early times. In the short interval between the ice breaking up and the arrival of the ships, the craft stationed at Christianshåb could not carry down all that was bought at these northern stations, so it was arranged that one of the ships should collect the goods direct from there. Casks therefore had to be ready on the spot to store them, but whether they were empty or full, these casks could not be left lying exposed to wind and weather. It was therefore decided in 1738 to build a blubber warehouse at Makelijk Oud: this was the beginning of the Jakobshavn trading post.

The number of settlements in the Bugt were not increased simply to afford an opportunity for increasing the Trading Company's purchases; it was also done in order to extend the boundaries of the district, which was in conformity with the charter and the royal proclamation of 1740. This expansion was in fact an automatic consequence of the establishment of new settlements, and can be regarded as part of the attempt to

drive the Dutch out of business. Jacob Sewerin seems also to have worked on plans for a whale fishery in the Bugt, as he had previously intimated. Such an expansion of his activities would call for new settlements. (Previously he had considered it more than he could take on
financially.)

During the negotiations concerning the extension of the charter,
Sewerin had envisaged expanding his trading activities on the more
southerly part of the west coast. Further plans for the formal colonization by people from Iceland and the Nordland regions in Norway
had to be abandoned at that time, but they continued to command
attention. In the negotiations, the colonization plans had become linked
with Hans Egede's proposal to look for the Eastern Settlement, and to
find any descendants of the Norse population that might still survive.

At the beginning of January 1737, six months after his return, Hans
Egede submitted a comprehensive proposal (now lost) for exploring
the south and beyond, round Cape Farewell, in order to find the Eastern
Settlement. He offered his services in undertaking the expedition,
the goal of which – i.e. the discovery of the Norse population – had
been the starting-point of the whole of his "Greenland *Dessein*". Such
an undertaking naturally needed capital, and it was referred to the
Missionskollegium, which for the sake of expediency postponed it
until the charter negotiations were completed. Although Hans Egede
may have been promised the chance of discussing the plan verbally,
once he had submitted a detailed written report, the matter was
left in abeyance until 1740. Hans Egede reminded the Missionskollegium of it in that year, and in September decided to ask Jacob Sewerin
whether he would consider carrying out the plan in return for "encouragement", i.e. financial support without any precise sum being
fixed.

Despite the fact that Sewerin's finances were not – to judge by his
own complaint to the King in April 1740 – in a sound state, they
must have improved during the year to the point where he could feel
optimistic enough to make fresh plans, which incorporated Hans
Egede's idea of looking for the Eastern Settlement. Perhaps the word
"encouragement" lent wings to his imagination. In January 1741 he
sent the King a lengthy proposal concerning the establishment of
two new colonies, one between Godthåb and Cape Farewell and the
other between Godthåb and Christianshåb.

It was important that there should not be more than one missionary
at each of these new settlements, whereas there were two at each of
the existing colonies. Thus with the help of trained Greenlanders, the
existing missionary personnel could cope with four colonial settlements. Such a distribution of forces also meant that the whole stretch

of coast from the Bugt to a point some distance south of Godthåb would be covered. This would also make it easier to keep the foreigners out, and would promote the conversion of the heathen. The financial advantages both for Sewerin and for the kingdom were mentioned last in the plan. Sewerin suggested that a house should be built for the use of the missionary or his deputy north of Christianshåb (by which Make-lijk Oud was obviously meant). He was afraid that Christianshåb would have to be moved from the site that had been found for it be-cause "the soil is being eroded year by year", and furthermore God-thåb, in his opinion, had been established too far into the fjord where the harbour facilities were poor, and should be moved to the coast where the Greenlanders did most of their business. Taking everything into account, he estimated the cost at about 7,000 rdl. once and for all. Because he could use the ships for other purposes, a considerable proportion of the costs of the operation could be used to finance other transactions. It emerges from later negotiations that he needed approxi-mately 4,000 rdl. He did not wish to be paid until the houses had been built on the two new colony sites. The transfer of Christianshåb and Godthåb to better sites slipped out of the negotiations, and never again became of real interest, although the idea was ventilated several times subsequently.

It goes without saying that the Government were only too pleased, as Christian VI put it, that a way had been found to control the coast over a length of "150 Danish miles" (Danish miles, i.e. over 1,100 km.), that trade was being carried on there, that Christianity was being preached, that plans were being made for the exploration of the East coast and that it was possible for all this to be done at relatively little expense – a point which appears to have appealed particularly to the King. A royal decree sent to both the Missionskollegium and Sewerin approved the building of the house at Makelijk Oud and the establish-ment of the two new colonies. Sewerin was to receive half his payment when the house and one colony were reported ready and the other half when the second colony had been established. Sewerin was to continue receiving 5,000 rdl. annual subsidy, and the advance for 1743 which had been paid to him was to be written off if he would agree to extend his obligations until 1750. As he had promised to do so in advance – provided the notice of termination affecting his heirs, if any, were can-celled before expiry of the charter – he did agree, and the offending termination clause was deleted by this same decree.

Sewerin must have expected the proposal regarding the house at Makelijk Oud to be approved. In April he shipped the timber to Christianshåb, and at the end of June the house had been built – "wholly of timber". At the instance of Alsbach, the missionary at

Christianshåb, Sewerin suggested that the place should receive a name incorporating his own: hence, "Jacobshavn" was approved by the King. To begin with, at any rate, this house was to be used only to accommodate the missionary during his mission work in the summer, but it soon became customary for merchandise and provisions to be stored behind its solid woodwork.

At the end of November 1741 Sewerin was able to report that he had arranged for the trader in Godthåb, N. C. Geelmuyden, to reconnoitre to the south with a view to establishing a new colonial settlement. Two sites were selected as suitable: one on 62°, probably Pâmiut, and the other 60 km. further south, possibly in the fjord which cuts inland to the north of the Tindingen mountain (Kingigtoq). Sewerin planned to populate the southern colony with people from the Nordland districts. In 1738 the Commission failed to persuade the Nordland people to fall in with this idea, whereupon Sewerin then took the matter into his own hands and arranged for one of his assistants, Niels Rasch, who had been in Christianshåb, to travel to Nordland. During the winter of 1739–40 Rasch managed to persuade six "able Nordland fellows" to undertake the journey to Greenland with the object of establishing the southern colony and, if they wished, settling in the country permanently. Perhaps this would encourage other Nordland people to follow their example.

At the same time two Lapps promised to stay in Greenland to domesticate reindeer, but they were dissuaded from the idea by their own people, and so the plan had to be abandoned this time. However, Jacob Sewerin was not prepared to shelve the idea, and so he requested support in the form of a royal command to the local authorities in the Nordland districts or Finnmark to give their assistance. Any families that wanted to settle would need financial aid during a transitional period, so he asked for that too. In 1742, both requests were granted; however, the financial assistance was confined to 200 rdl. per annum for two years for distribution to the families. In the meantime, it proved impossible to persuade the Lapps to pull up their roots. Only the six "Nordland fellows" went to Greenland, and among them at least two were of significance in its later development.

When he granted the requests, the King decided that the southern colony should be named Frederikshåb – thus incorporating the name of the Crown Prince. Possibly Christian VI wanted to forestall any commoner who might wish to give it his own name. The royal naming brought no luck, at least to begin with. N. C. Geelmuyden, the trader, sailed with his people from Godthåb inside the field ice down to Pâmiut, which was finally chosen for the settlement, but the second ship, with a quantity of building materials on board, had to turn back and winter in Norway, leaving the house-building half finished. The first ship foundered on the way home.

In the years that followed, the *stor-is* presented a constant obstacle to the prosperity of this newly-established colony. During these years it happened to be particularly widespread far up into the Davis Strait. In 1743 the supply ship failed to arrive, and provisions had to be ordered from Godthåb, and in the following year the ship bound for Frederikshåb struck an iceberg and sank. Geelmuyden, who had moved to Godthåb, left the colony and Greenland but his assistant, Lars Dalager, who was Jacob Sewerin's brother-in-law and who had come to Frederikshåb in 1742, stayed on. However, he was to see the colony's ship fail to arrive again in 1745. Not till the following year did the ship, whose first port of call was Frederikshåb, force a way through the *stor-is*, but she became so hemmed in by the ice there that she did not reach her other destinations. Three ships had been lost, one been obliged to winter there, and in the sixth year the colony's ship had to cruise off-shore in vain only to turn back in the end.

Jacob Sewerin would have preferred to abandon this colony which was costing him so dear. He had suggested that it should be served from Godthåb by means of a boat stationed there, but both the Godthåb trader and Lars Dalager declared it impracticable to deliver supplies in this way. This "pained" Sewerin "since Friderichs-Haabs colony . . . could remain the best trading post of them all". He suggested that it be maintained only as a mission station, which could be kept supplied by small boats from Godthåb. Even though Frederikshåb had proved to be a good trading area in itself, he regarded it as being far too heavily handicapped by navigational difficulties for trading to be maintained there. It was not completely abandoned, however, although Dalager left there in 1748 and Sewerin recommended its dissolution.

The second colony north of Godthåb on the route to Christianshåb did not come into being in Sewerin's time. Nevertheless, he applied in 1745 for payment of the second half of the state subsidy which had been promised him in 1742. The first half had been paid after the house at Jakobshavn and the Frederikshåb colony had been built, but in 1745 the *Rentekammer* was disinclined to pay him more until he proved that the colonies were established and submitted a list of the houses on the sites. So the 2,000 rdl. he needed to relieve the strain on his finances were not forthcoming.

In fact we have only Sewerin's word for it that his Greenland business was financially unsound. The accounts, apart from a few random general statements, have not been preserved, and little can be gleaned from the scattered journal entries. From Godthåb there were reports of one trading expedition to the south in November 1743 when purchases were so large that the trader was obliged to set up a special depot for the blubber he had bought; it could not be collected until March the following year. On his outward journey he had often given the Greenlanders goods on credit, and on his return he had received for every single item its value again in the form of blubber. In January and February the weather had been stormy, preventing hunting and fishing and expeditions, and resulting in want on the plateau of the inner Godthåb fjord. Many people had been forced to move out towards the sea coast where among other things there was plenty of birdhunting.

Hunting and fishing conditions were still a compelling reason for the nomadic life of the Greenlanders. For instance, those from Godthåb Fjord had had to leave their winter houses as early as the end of February and go to live in tents near the Kangeq settlement at the mouth of the fjord system. Nearby was the Nipisat sound, where there were big migrations of seals in the autumn which usually afforded the hope of a reasonable catch. Greenlanders were also continually settling in the colony of Godthåb itself, though some only for a few years. At Ny Herrnhut also the Brethren were attracting some Greenlanders.

The mission was still worried by the Greenlanders moving around so much and so often and living in scattered groups. It would have liked to see them gathered together in the colonies in order to promote daily instruction and observe religious services with morning and evening prayers. Here was a case of conflict with the Trading Company's interests. The scattered settlements were a serious drain on the Trading Company, and it was seldom possible at Godthåb, for instance, to make a sufficient number of expeditions into the fjord system itself, the scattered settlement was nevertheless preferable since it afforded the best coverage of the hunting and fishing opportunities, and thus opened up the best prospects for trading. It was best to go out and meet the inhabitants on their own ground, and one way of doing it was to establish more colonies. One missionary with this idea suggested that trading posts should be established along the coast, where most Greenlanders either came or lived, thus making it possible to keep up contact with them at all times.

If several trading posts were set up, it might also ease the strenuous trading rounds, provided that trading staff were allocated to the posts, or at least catechists, who could attend to the trading at the same time. Any reduction in the trading done in the actual colonies was welcome, but such dispersal would place an extra burden on the trader, whose responsibility still remained the same.

REFERENCES

1. "Most of the merchants here have for many years (and not without justice) regarded my enterprises as far too haphazard, and unprofitable," wrote Jacob Sewerin to the Greenland Commission on 24 February 1740.

2. The Adscription is printed as a proper name because it is meant as an approximate translation of the Danish term *Stavnsbåndet*. In 1733 by Royal decree every farmer who was not a freeholder was bound, with the male members of his family, to live on the estate in which he was born (*adscripti glebae*), from the fourteenth to the thirty-sixth year of age, later from the fourth to the fortieth, without being serf or villeins. They were furthermore bound to obtain the copyhold of a farm on the estate. They could, however, buy their freedom. The conscription for the Army was connected with this Adscription, only sons of copyholders being conscripted. In 1788 the Stavnsbånd was repealed.

3. In West Greenland Eskimo dialect East Greenland is called (*Nunap*) *Tunua*, which means "the back of the land". Of course, the East Greenlanders call the West coast *Nunap Tunua*.

13

JACOB SEWERIN RETIRES
1745–1749

For many reasons trading activities based on the Greenland colonies were hard to conduct. The main financial risk was borne squarely by Jacob Sewerin, who could not disclaim his responsibility towards the traders in Greenland or towards the masters of ships in those distant harbours or en route if losses or accidents occurred; yet he could not supervise them closely from Copenhagen or Dronninglund. Traders and ship's masters thus enjoyed an agreeable freedom, but for trade and sailings to run smoothly and yield a good profit – or indeed break even – it was essential that this freedom should not be abused. The probity of individuals was under severe strain. No major fraud or embezzlement occurred, but there were petty swindles and some who lined their own pockets at the expense of Jacob Sewerin and of the Greenland population. Outright losses on trade with the Greenlanders are not mentioned; there was no serious risk attached to giving credit – so it was reported in relation to the 1743 expeditions from Godthåb.

The trader in Greenland occupied a halfway position. On the one hand, the welfare of all the colonists and eventually of some Greenlanders depended on the trader's management of his affairs and requisitioning of supplies, and how he wielded his local power. On the other hand, the co-operation, goodwill and industry of each individual colonist was essential to the success of the whole enterprise. The individual played a far greater part in Greenland than he did in his native land; the result might be beneficial or it could take the form of slackness. Personal antagonisms were always making themselves felt, fostered by the intimate living conditions in the colony houses.

Trade was done and affairs were managed on the responsibility of the trader who was accountable to "the patron" (Jacob Sewerin). If he was not careful, irregularities might occur, yet it was difficult for the trader to pin down such irregularities even if he was aware of the culprit's identity. Niels Rasch, who had been assistant and then trader at Christianshåb and for a year at Godthåb, gave a good example of such irregularities in his long 1747 memorandum: "I often experienced the misfortune which attended the smith, when I was last in Greenland, where iron was stolen and wrought by night, so that it could be bartered with the Greenlanders for fox, reindeer and seal skins and even blubber for himself and his comrades. These, in turn, were sold to the masters of ships for spirits when they put in to land, and they also had other goods to be procured for trading when they came back, so that a trader ashore has often experienced considerable trouble and annoyance with his drunken and unruly workpeople at those times when ships lay off the colony or in some harbour nearby." This had happened in Godthåb in 1742 or 1743, when Rasch had been trader there.

There was no question of irregularities as such when the barber–surgeon von Osten reported in 1743 that "both Dutchmen and colonists carry on a mighty trade in that country, selling to the Greenlanders – who are avid for them – both flint-locks and powder". Thus it was not just the Dutch who supplied the Greenlanders with those items. There was great fear of the consequences of supplying the Greenlanders with fire-arms: cases were known of Dutchmen being murdered, but "acts of retaliation" against the people usually came to nothing; the colonists had no reason to feel unsafe on account of the Greenland population. Relations between them were generally free of animosity, probably because the people sent out by Jacob Sewerin were of relatively good character. The Greenlanders also enjoyed a relationship with him, albeit a distant one. Several of them who had gone to Denmark during his time (despite the earlier royal ban) had noticed his kindliness. In Greenland he was known as *nâlagarput* (our lord) "since they know it is he who arranges for the Trading Company's goods to be brought to them". Otherwise he was generally called "Greenland's patron".

The Vendsyssel peasants from Dronninglund and the surrounding district whom Jacob Sewerin had persuaded to enter his service in Greenland were respectable but apparently not as tough as might have been wished. When provisions had to be rationed in 1742 because of the ship's late arrival, "the greedy farmers from Jutland became . . . very impatient because they could not fill their bellies to bursting-point" and were prepared to seek a homeward passage with the Dutch. However, Niels Egede persuaded them to stay. "Now the Jutland farmers are quite disheartened and do not venture out because of the biting cold", he related in February 1743. Nevertheless, some among them genuinely wanted to stay, and therefore sought permission to marry Greenlandic women. One such was the outstanding Johannes Pedersen Dorf, who obtained permission to marry and was a credit to both mission and Trading Company until his death at a great age. This was the start of the series of mixed marriages. Although this helped to bring about closer contact between the Greenlandic population and the colonists, the same end was also achieved in other ways. Economic interdependence slowly grew. The very existence of the mission and the Trading Company in Greenland was bound to depend on the size of the catch and hence the greatest possible volume of purchases. Conversely, the Greenlandic population's need for the goods provided by the traders was slowly increasing.

This interdependence could of course, develop into actual collaboration between Greenlanders and colonists. That such collaboration should develop satisfactorily depended, in turn, on the personality of the leading colonist: here Niels Egede stood out. For example, near Jacobsholmen, an island off Christianhåb, the Greenlanders caught a whale, and the great crowd that gathered held up the flensing. Niels Egede appeared and so arranged matters that all had a share of the whale. A few days later the Greenlanders caught another whale, but could not tow it to a suitable place for flensing, and asked Niels Egede for help; he thereupon instructed the supply ship that had arrived to take the whale in tow to a nearby bay, and the Greenlanders asked him again to organize the flensing. In this case the Trading Company gained by the collaboration since a considerable part of the blubber and baleen went to it as payment for the tow, and part was sold to the colony.

It was just this collaboration over whaling which made Niels Egede and others call many times for organized whaling based on the coast. Indeed, this motivated the establishment of Nipisat in 1724 and 1729, although the idea was never allowed to develop. It was also impossible to put such whaling into practice in the 1740s, since it called for equipment which Jacob Sewerin could not afford.

The statements of stocks for 1745 to 1748 indicate the part that could be played by whaling. In 1745 687½ barrels of blubber were brought home, and sales amounted to 55 barrels of brown oil (i.e. inferior oil produced from the "finks" after the first rendering) and 476 barrels of clear oil (this could have originated from either seals or whales). The price of whale oil in 1745 varied between 13 and 14 rdl. per barrel, and in 1748 between 11 and 15 rdl. The sale receipts for these years are unknown, but at an average price of 13 rdl. per barrel, the 476 barrels of clear oil in 1745 alone would have yielded 6,188 rdl.

Baleen originated only from whaling. In 1745, 1,540 pieces – 728 "standard" and 813 "substandard" – were brought home. The standard fetched 3 marks per pound, the substandard 24 skillinger. This was apparently the highest total to date. Fashion called increasingly for "bones" as stiffeners in petticoats, stays, etc., and a tailor was among Sewerin's customers. With such an abundant supply, the trade in baleen was a paying proposition. With an average weight for standard baleen of 6 pounds, and for substandard of 1·8 pounds, the 728 standards pieces of baleen brought home in 1745 would have weighed 4,368 pounds, and so fetched some 2,184 rdl. Similarly the 812 substandard pieces of ballen, weighing 1,461·6 pounds would, at 24 skillinger per pound, have yielded 365 rdl. Throughout 1734 Sewerin had recorded and calculated an income from all classes of Greenland products rising from 979 rdl. to 3,985 rdl. When this latter figure is compared with the conservative estimate of income from oil and baleen alone of 8,737 rdl. in 1745, Jacob Sewerin's revenues from the Greenland trade can be seen to have at least doubled.

It is more difficult to estimate expenditure. Sewerin's private records contain a statement relating to the fitting out of a ship in 1747: supplying it with provisions, materials and merchandise for a single colony, including supplies for the crew and repair materials, cost approximately 1,350 rdl. As three ships were sent out in 1745, the total expense could have been approximately 4,050 rdl., plus the pay of the officers and crew, wages for the mission and Trading Company officials and "men" in Greenland, and insurance, making about 7,350 rdl. in all. Sewerin estimated his expenses in connection with the "Grønlands Lykke" establishment and his other administrative outgoings in 1738 at approximately 1,000 rdl.; later they probably rose. It sounds thus reasonable to estimate his total expenditure at around 9,000 rdl.

To the revenues of 8,737 rdl. calculated above must be added the subsidies of 5,000 rdl. per annum, which thus contributed, almost exactly, his profit. However, over the years Sewerin had to carry the initial losses, and he suffered capital losses through the loss of ships. Interest payments, depreciation, replacements and servicing of current debts would have left little if he was to fulfil all his commitments. In absolute terms the calculation presented for 1745, fraught with uncertainty as it is, gives some substance to the claim of several of his contemporaries that in the long run it would be possible for the Greenland trade to cover the costs of the mission, especially if the whale fishery were expanded and operated from the coast in conjunction with the Greenlanders of the Bugt.

On the basis of Jacob Sewerin's statements of stocks for 1745–8, his Greenland trading activities can be followed more closely. The quantities of blubber brought home appeared as follows:

The annual average of 916 barrels is nearly double that for 1734–7. In 1745–8, which were roughly Jacob Sewerin's last four years, he seems to have sold everything: 3,174⅖ barrels of oil were sold, which is the approximate equivalent of the quantity of blubber. Although the period involved is a short one, it is nevertheless striking that the figures fluctuated so much more than during the earlier period when they rose steadily. Hence the Greenland trade was risky, and called for solid financial backing from the operator. Corresponding fluctuations were apparent in other Greenlandic goods shipped home.

	Origin	Barrels	Barrels
1745	All colonies		687½
1746	All colonies		1,033½
1747	The Bugt	409½	
	Godthåb	281	
	Frederikshåb	116	
			806½
1748	The Bugt	958	
	Godthåb	180	
			1,138
	Total		3,665½

Sewerin's stock-lists afford further insight into his business. The quantities of baleen and skins brought home in 1745–8 are shown in the table below. It is immediately apparent how small were the quantities involved, and that fluctuations were also present. In the case of baleen this was presumably due to whaling being done on a casual basis. The same applied to purchases of by-products; no part of the whales, large or small, caught by the Greenlanders was handed over to the Trading Company. The "specialities" of the various colonies affected results. Thus comparatively few skins came from the Bugt, which supplied most of the whaling products and blubber; as we see below, Frederikshåb's "speciality" was fox skins. Fluctuations in the quantities of skins brought home are probably due to variations in the amount of cargo space available each year; in 1745 and 1746 there were only three ships; in 1747 and 1748 four made the voyage.

Few seal skins were shipped, as there was little demand for them on the Danish–Norwegian market, which could be supplied from home production, and the consumption of skins, especially seal skins, was high in Greenland itself. Reindeer skins sold badly, as the demand for them was met by Finnmark traders. However, there was a ready market for fox skins.

Jacob Sewerin invariably succeeded in doing well, selling out each year. The oil, baleen and skins were disposed of chiefly around Dronninglund and in Copenhagen, but in some years he was obliged to send quantities to the Netherlands. By 1748 Sewerin was tired of piecemeal trading, and virtually the whole stock of baleen and skins went to the Netherlands with one of his own skippers.

Q

	BROUGHT HOME				SOLD			
Colony of origin	Baleen	Rein-deer skins	Fox skins	Seal skins	Baleen	Rein-deer skins	Fox skins	Seal skins
1745								
Christianshåb and Jakobshavn	1,540	8	15		1,550			
Godthåb		24	400	40			412	
Total	1,540	32	415	40	1,550		412	
1746								
Christianshåb and Jakobshavn	295		12		720			
Godthåb and Frederikshåb		58	970	50		85	985	90
Total	295	58	982	50	720	85	985	90
1747 Unspecified								
Total	244	59	1,470	36	244	64	1,470	33
1748								
Christianshåb	154	40	100	178				
Jakobshavn	196	10	33	120	350	90	743	328
Godthåb		57	210	30				
Frederikshåb			400					
Total	350	107	743	328	350	90	743	328
In stock						17		
						107		

The growth of Jacob Sewerin's business during the 1740s was too slow. At the same time he was aware of the large capital gains of the Dutch through whaling. Although he received a grant for maintaining the mission and a subsidy for setting up Jakobshavn and Frederikshåb, trading and sailing continued to show a loss; losing ships increased his burdens and he was always faced with Dutch competition. In 1744 the proclamation of 9 April 1740 became due for renewal, and Sewerin wanted it amended so that it would be valid for six years – the term of his charter – and moreover he wanted trading and navigation banned between 61° and 69°N. The 1738 commission opposed his suggestion, and when the proclamation was renewed in April, 1744, the only substantial amendment was that it should be valid "hereafter until we give notice to the contrary". By means of this purely technical amendment, which brought the proclamation into line with Danish tradition, future amendments and renewals in case of an expansion of the colonial settlements were obviated.

This, however, was the façade, which only became significant later. Finance was the immediate problem. In 1745 Sewerin tried to obtain payment of the second half of the grants for establishing the new colonies, but the *Rentekammer* would not agree. He applied at the same time to have the advance for 1743 remitted and for a further 10,000 rdl. in return for waiving the right to hold a lottery – also in vain. At the end of February 1746 he aired his troubles again, this time to the Missionskollegium, in particular about his loss over the mission, which he reckoned at 40,000 rdl. The Missionskollegium replied that if he wanted help he must apply to the King. Sewerin seems not to have approached the King again on this subject although he complained to the King on two counts: first, the conduct of the Greenlanders towards the mission and the *angákut*, and secondly, the sale by the Dutch of guns, powder and shot, which infringed the trading ban and, more important, attracted the Greenlanders away from sealing to reindeer-hunting, which damaged both the reindeer herds and the Greenlanders' standard of living. In reply the King enjoined Sewerin to inform the Greenlanders in his name that they must stay away from the *angákut* and see that their children received instruction, and tell them that the use of guns for reindeer-hunting was forbidden. Instead, they were to go sealing and refrain from buying guns and ammunition from the Dutch in return fror baleen. Jacob Sewerin would supply them with "sufficient". The King's order also contains the draft of an open letter to "the inhabitants of Greenland", phrased so as to be a model for translation. However, its tone is threatening and might have had a different effect from that intended; there is no sign that it was ever published.

In the autumn Christian VI died, and the politically tense situation that accompanied a change of monarch under an autocratic form of government meant that a sector of activity like the Greenland Trading Company and mission could receive little attention. Apart from this, Sewerin's own tiredness was beginning to show, especially in his relations with his supposed colleagues. His relationship with Hans Egede appears to have been friendly, but Egede was far from satisfied with Sewerin's officious interventions in the conduct of the mission. This applied to the situation at Frederikshåb and to the proposal to move the Trading Company away from Godthåb, besides which at one point he suggested handing over the mission there to the Moravians. Hans Egede thought it unreasonable for Sewerin to request a higher subsidy to carry on with the sailings and the mission and to cover his losses. "He considers it invidious that Sewerin has always concealed his proposals and applications from him" – which suggests little if any intimacy between them. Hans Egede complained that the buildings at Godthåb were being allowed to fall into disrepair although materials necessary for repair has been requisitioned.

This and Sewerin's continuous complaints over his losses confirmed the misgivings that Hans Egede had expressed in 1734 over any individual assuming responsibility for the Greenland *Dessein*. Earlier in the year in a letter, the Missionskollegium had earnestly admonished Sewerin not to let the missions fall into decay but to keep them properly supplied and to help the missionaries rather than complain about them. As regards the lottery and compensation for his losses, he must apply to the King. At a meeting on 23 December 1746 it was decided to collect opinions "concerning a better way to organize the work of both the Trading Company and mission in Greenland when the charter now granted to Sewerin terminates next year"; these opinions were to be obtained from Hans Egede, Niels Rasch and Matthias Fersleff. Rasch was now the royal bailiff in the Lofoten Islands and Fersleff was mayor of Helsingør.

By February 1747 Fersleff's not very imaginative opinion was to hand; no proposal from Hans Egede is to be found. Neils Rasch's opinion suggested possible methods of production which were tried out subsequently, while he recommended above all that both the Trading Company and the mission should be taken over and administered by the State. Rasch's judgment was based on the view that the State would have to come into the picture sooner or later; he doubted whether any individual would undertake the Trading Company venture in future. A company might possibly be set up, but when it came to questions such as settlement by colonists, the establishment of new colonies or a search for the Eastern Settlement, such a company would not undertake these tasks unless the State made a financial contribution. A company's need to negotiate with the central administration would lead to delays in sending out ships each year. His main suggestion, therefore, was that the King, through his absolute power, should "assume all responsibility for poor Greenland in order to determine properly once and for all whether it is worth the trouble or not". The enterprise was to be administered by a single director responsible for the transactions in every detail, who would submit accounts to the

King's privy purse each year. The servants of the Trading Company in Greenland were to receive their remuneration in cash and kind, plus percentages of the value of purchases at any given time.

Rasch itemized the possible savings, but his opinion was that the sales of oil had fetched such good prices that the revenues would easily cover the mission's expenses, given the suggested economies. These economies related to barrelled goods, the unnecessary engagement of artisans and labourers and the purchase and manufacture of goods that were used for barter. These goods could just as well be obtained from Norway and Denmark and there was no need to buy them at far greater cost in the Netherlands and the Baltic countries. Rasch also wanted to increase the variety of goods, including wood for *umiaks* and back posts for sledges. "The advantages of this would be that the more things the Greenlanders saw, the more they would want and consequently the more diligent and industrious they would become; thus it would be possible for the money that previously went to foreigners for barter goods to remain in the country". Such mercantilistic thinking must have sounded sweetly in the ears of the trade experts.

Rasch's ideas on the successful conduct and needs of the mission are illuminating in another connection. In this case, however, he was especially critical of the quality of the staff sent out not only for the mission itself, but also for the Trading Company, particularly "the ungodliness of the hands, which has often been appalling". The discord among those sent out, clerics and laymen alike, was a source of vexation to both heathen and Christians. There ought to be one person with supreme authority in the country. One criticism he made of the whole colonization plan was that the colonies were so far apart from one another, and he therefore suggested establishing one at Nipisat (again) or a little further north at Sydbay (Ukîvik), and another 200 kilometres south of Frederikshåb, i.e. where Julianehåb was later situated.

After much interesting information about conditions in the southernmost part of West Greenland and on the East coast and on the occurrence of ice around Cape Farewell, Rasch suggested that the search for the Eastern Settlement, which was assumed to be sited on the East coast, could be made from Ûnartoq if a colony were established in the south – or, alternatively, from the West coast of Iceland. He envisaged not *umiaks* but small ships being used, in pairs. He nevertheless came back to the establishment of a colony in the far south and thought this would have a further use – viz. in "peopling the country".

In southernmost Greenland it would finally be possible with patience and repeated experimentation to grow barley and keep cattle. At least ten families must be found who would undertake this work and settle there. As an inducement they should be given the right to take all the land they needed, and be exempt from taxes for twenty years. Naturally enough, it was again Nordland families or Lapps whom he thought best suited to such colonization. He estimated that the enterprise would cost c. 3,000 rigsdaler to put into operation; but it would stand or fall on whether the desired number of families could be persuaded to emigrate.

The final point in Rasch's long memorandum dealt with the whaling (he could only speak of the West coast since nobody knew anything of conditions on the East coast). In Disko Bay and as far as the area around Nipisat he thought that it would profit Greenlanders to carry on whaling in collaboration with Europeans, the main task of the latter being to assist in towing catch to a suitable place for flensing. This plan may or may not have been inspired by Niels Egede's experience, but it was the first detailed and rational exposition. Rasch advocated organized whaling based on the Schleswig island of Sild and on the Norwegian Andenaes in Spitsbergen, Jan Mayen Land and Bjørne Øen to the north-west of Norway.

The interest of the Rasch memorandum is its reference back to previous experience and to unrealized plans – some later put into practice. Among other things, it was the intention in sending the Nordland men to Greenland in 1742 that they should settle on the plateaux in the heart of the fjords and raise cattle, in conjunction with hunting and fishing – thus effectively colonizing Greenland. Rasch also envisaged these settlers being able to carry on trade locally, thus acting as middlemen between the colony and the local Greenlanders. But this settlement did not take place because the men from Nordland found permanent employment in the colonies.

Peter Olsen Walløe, the Trading Company's assistant at Christianhåb, found that the promotion promised him by Jacob Sewerin on his second journey to Greenland did not materialize. He had gone to Christianshåb to stay for an unspecified number of years, in the hope that the promise, stated in the charter, to employees with long service would eventually be honoured. In 1748, Walløe applied for and received royal permission to settle as an independent trader anywhere in Greenland that he wished provided it was not too near any of the colonies, or to the detriment of the Trading Company. He could settle near Godthåb or "wherever he may find it most convenient to obtain a livelihood by shooting and fishing, together with whatever other occupation he might pursue for his own account for his livelihood and support". Jacob Sewerin found Walløe's plan both "commendable" and "pious" and, wishing him every success, suggested Ameralik fjord, where there was good hunting. He promised that the colony's trader would buy the skins of any reindeer he shot, and hoped to be able to send cows and sheep to the area in order to start cattle-rearing. He wished that more of the people he had sent to Greenland would follow Walløe's example.

Yet this pioneer undertaking came to nothing. Difficulties and obstacles of every kind arose so that when he finally reached Godthåb with a companion in an *umiak* he just managed to buy a few skins during the winter and the following spring. There was no question of settling at Ameralik; on the contrary he travelled to the southernmost point in Greenland and there spent the winter. On his way back in 1750, he bought a quantity of fox skins to the chagrin of the trader at Frederikshåb. There was a sad ending to his activity as an independent trader, as Sewerin's successors refused to recognize his "royal letter of independence", although he was employed on other tasks.

It is difficult to grasp Sewerin's true intention at this stage. At the end of 1748 he sent a lengthy report to the Missionskollegium with his ideas for future arrangements. The report, including a complaint about his losses over the years, was laid before the King, and on 7 March he received a royal letter granting remission of the 5,000 rdl. he had received in advance and the promise of a further 5,000 for 1749. At the same time he was awarded the same sum from the lottery in aid of the Pauper Administration (Board of Guardians) in Copenhagen. As the charter expired on 15 March 1750 Sewerin was to arrange sailings and supplies to the colonies until the end of July 1750, as he had offered to do.

Meanwhile complaints had been received in 1748 about Sewerin's supplying of Christianshåb, Jakobshavn and other places. This caused the Missionskollegium to send him a caustic letter, but he repudiated its charges and admonitions to make proper use of the royal subsidy; he pointed out that he had taken over an almost deserted colony and that there were now four (obviously counting Jakobshavn) and that both the mission and trading were expanding. All this had been done in fifteen years at little expense to the State but "irreparable loss to me and mine". If his plan of December 1748 were adopted, there would in fifteen years be more Christians than heathens. He concluded his letter (presumably written after receiving the King's rescript of 7 March): "On the same basis [the proposal and report of December 1748] for a few more years, please God, either in a company or without one, I offer my most humble services for the good of the Greenland *Dessein*".

Although negotiations had apparently been in progress for some time with the General Trading Company, neither it nor the Government had reached a decisive conclusion. During 1749 the directors of the General Trading Company tried to inform themselves of what was to be taken over from Sewerin before they would promise to carry on trading and supplying the mission. In April, the Missionskollegium received instructions from the King to give the company the necessary information about the mission's affairs and Sewerin received similar instructions. The report which Sewerin drew up showed a startling lack of information which could help the company in its deliberations on taking over the trade. From the verbose and general description of his achievements in Greenland over the last sixteen years it emerged that he had stayed in Copenhagen during the autumn and winter partly with the object of looking for a company through which he could carry on with the trade; this would give the General Trading Company a whole year in which to consider its position. A Copenhagen merchant, Fr. Holmsted, had been on the 1738 commission and a director of the Trading Company, and during the discussions of 1733-4 had appeared to treat Sewerin with scant respect. He and G. K. Kloumann, the brewer, had alienated Sewerin by submitting their proposal behind his back; the latter, always the individualist, cannot in 1749 have relished the idea of his business falling into this merchant's hands, or of having to give information to Holmsted and others.

Sewerin depicted the Greenland trade in the darkest colours, blaming its plight on the Dutch bartering of firearms and ammunition for skins and baleen: "Now it is not so much the Dutch traders that he is up against – he reckons he has driven them out of the areas covered by his monopoly. On the contrary, it is the whalers, to whom the Greenlanders travel outside the colonial districts, with whom he is unable to compete." Once again he mentioned the consequences of this trade: "The Greenlanders go reindeer-hunting and neglect their summer hunting so that most of the blubber bought is winter blubber." The size of the purchases that reached Dronninglund and the prices obtained for the oil in the years up to 1748 give little substance to Sewerin's excuses for not managing to break even as he put it. There is a sad touch in the concluding words of his letter. He offered the Company his good offices, should the Government transfer the Greenland sailing to the Trading Company; he would be in a position to "procure reliable and commodious ships at reasonable prices together with a number of seamen and landsmen and also endeavour to obtain some shares in the Company in order, God willing, to continue making use of my dear-bought knowledge of Greenland . . . as far as possible. At least I can advise and say what should not be done. . . ."

However, the Trading Company did not find this letter useful, and approached two former traders in Greenland, N. C. Geelmuyden and Sewerin's brother-in-law, Matthias Fersleff, now mayor of Helsingør, for more information, even though Fersleff had left Greenland in 1739 and Geelmuyden in 1744. Of the reports submitted by the two men, Geelmuyden's was the more profitable, and he was even invited to give his opinion on various points in Fersleff's memorandum. Geelmuyden gave a brief account of the settlements in Greenland, the number of employees, and a rough estimate of the products from each individual colony, with the average annual output. As the latter figures tended rather towards the upper limit, the information was somewhat misleading for the Trading Company directors. Geelmuyden's report was mainly concerned with proposals for the future regarding new settlements, fishing (especially to meet domestic requirements), cattle-rearing and whaling; there was also an account of the harm done by the sale of sporting weapons. It was vital to get the Greenlanders back to their former sealing, not only to provide for themselves but also so that the Trading Company could acquire their surplus production. Blubber was the product best able to sustain the Trading Company.

Geelmuyden's experience derived from his service with Sewerin in Godthåb and Frederikshåb. He had no first-hand knowledge of conditions in the Bugt; thus his pronouncements on a possible whale-fishery would have been based on the knowledge and ideas of someone else, presumably Niels Egede, whose advice, strangely enough, was not sought; since 1745 he had been employed in the weights and measures office at Alborg. Hans and Poul Egede were also not consulted; perhaps they were assumed to be too wrapped up in "the work" to be relied on for realistic information. Yet the voices of the Egedes were heard through the submissions of Geelmuyden and Fersleff. It was their plans, their endlessly repeated proposals for new settlements and their ideas which were now being presented with roughly similar arguments. The resignation of Hans Egede as adviser to the Mission-skollegium in 1747 could not have been an obstacle to his advice being sought on this fundamental matter; moreover, Poul Egede had been appointed as his successor. However, Sewerin also apparently noticed a chill wind blowing, and at the end of November he felt obliged to inform the King of the accumulated difficulties in connection with the possible transfer of trading to the General Trading Company. A meeting with the directors had been mentioned to him, but nothing had so far come of it. Because of illness and the time of year he had to leave Copenhagen for Dronninglund. He would have liked to make over his ships to the Trading Company and to have seen his experienced skippers and seamen engaged for further sailings; he did not see how it could operate without experienced men and suitable ships.

Besides this, there were many problems in Greenland. Christianhåb might have to be moved; the Dutch, after a short interval, had resumed their sailings (they had participated in the Austrian War of Succession);

Frederikshåb was yielding nothing at all; a big deficit had arisen on sailings to Godthåb, and so on. To rectify all these matters and to allow both the Missionskollegium and the Trading Company adequate time to consider their future plans, Sewerin offered to arrange sailings and supplies to Greenland for one more year. In the light of both the royal instructions earlier in the year, and the current situation as depicted in his letter, his offer must have been due either to idealism in relation to the "*Dessein*", or to a belief that he could remedy the shortcomings in the colonies by the time the transfer took place in accordance with the terms of the charter. It is probable that he felt an obligation towards the mission, the Trading Company, the Government, those working for the mission and not least the Greenlanders who were now largely dependent on – or rather accustomed to – supplies from outside.

Sewerin's opinion was forwarded for consideration to the Trading Company, who flatly denied having agreed on anything with him, but rather complained of the inadequacy of his information. In any case, the directors of the Trading Company considered themselves capable of coping with the 1750 sailings. However, they required the King to instruct Sewerin to "come forward with the requisite information concerning the present state of trading, the mission society and colonies in Greenland", for the reason that "sailing to Greenland and the charge of the mission have now been most graciously transferred to the Company on certain terms".

It is possible that this view and the report submitted by the directors of the Trading Company on 5 December speeded up consideration of the matter in the *Conseil*, for the directors approached the King on 13 December concerning the transfer, and six days later Frederik V issued an order concerning the transfer of the Greenland trade sailing and the mission for a consideration of 5,000 rdl. per annum for two to three years. At the same time Jacob Sewerin was instructed to submit all necessary particulars quickly as requested in an order of 11 April, and to hand over the requisite papers.

All that now remained for Jacob Sewerin to do was to wind up his Greenland affairs; this was not achieved without friction between him and the directors of the Trading Company, although they bought three of his ships. The differences between him and the Company reached government level where they were dealt with summarily, his charter being extended in March 1750 until the end of June. He apparently sent out only one ship to collect purchased goods which, under the charter, belonged to him, and it brought to Grønlands Lykke at Hals 244¼ barrels of blubber for Jacob Sewerin, together with 16 "bilge-casks" of blubber and 1,073 assorted pieces of baleen.

Disputes between the directors of the Trading Company and Jacob Sewerin went on into the 1750s. These concerned the state of the colonies in regard to buildings and equipment. Also isolated minor accounts were outstanding between Sewerin and the trading staff in Greenland. One such involved a pair of rifles which had been promised to Greenlanders at Jakobshavn, having already been paid for in baleen. Sewerin strongly disapproved of the sale of firearms, but the company insisted on the two Greenlanders receiving their rifles.

On 23 March 1753, little more than a fortnight after the death of his third wife, Jacob Sewerin died, and the grief in Dronninglund over these two deaths is said to have been great. It inspired the bishop of Ålborg, Broder Brorson, to write a lengthy verse elegy, of which the following is a summary of the description of Sewerin's personal traits: Gentle, well-bred, of sober mind, and enjoying much repute for learning amongst the learned throughout Denmark. His word was ever his bond. Though always circumspect and prudent, he was not always successful. He was a good and honest friend. Another man's want or distress touched him deeply. In adversity he never lost his steadfast and noble character, standing firm when others fell by the wayside. Despite his own wisdom, he never played the sage. Experience taught him his trade, though fate was not kind to him. He governed his estate by example and charity, not by harsh comments. That was his outstanding trait.

Behind the rhetoric of the bishop's lines, we discern the features of a man full of concern for his fellow-men; he was remembered thus by the farmers at Dronninglund. He amassed no fortune through commerce and his estate was proved at only 9,000 rigsdaler. Right to the end, his trading with Greenland and Finnmark showed a deficit.

It is a wonder that he steadfastly carried on with such unprofitable business enterprises. As a business man he went his own way from beginning to end: "Seeing that I trained to become a minister before becoming a merchant (wherein I was undoubtedly chosen as a humble instrument in the hands of God to assist in the conversion of the heathen in Greenland) I duly undertook this enterprise – as important as it was unknown – with no other object, and certainly not to make a profit, but solely in the hope of being able to break even"; the good of the mission had been his "only care . . . and yet notwithstanding all my trouble and expense on account of divers calamities and inconveniences. I almost lost all hope for this Greenland mission which is of paramount concern in the whole business; indeed for a long time I went in fear that I might be the last quack doctor in Greenland!'- It was no ordinary merchant who could carry on his business under' takings from such motives, and reduce his own fortune and contribu-

tion, at the same time stating clearly his commitment to a higher obligation and his fear that this would not be fulfilled if he were forced to
give up.

We can repeat the judgment of a later age on Jacob Sewerin:
"In Sewerin's attitude towards Greenland there was a good measure
of idealism, spiritual concern and compassion for his fellow-men."

14

THE MISSION:
ITS BACKGROUND AND PRINCIPLES
1733–1750

"It is as clear as day that here is the greatest hope for the best and noblest thing in all this, which is the glory of God and the enlightenment of the ignorant." These words, written by Jacob Sewerin in 1732, might equally have come from Hans Egede. In almost all Sewerin's surviving letters, documents, proposals and memoranda, he always gave the mission pride of place in "the Greenland *Dessein*". The Trading Company came second, since its sole object was to give the mission material and financial support. Thus the principle was still the same as when the Greenland mission and Trading Company had first started. On that point Hans Egede and Sewerin were entirely at one.

It was, therefore, quite natural for the Missionskollegium to ask Sewerin's opinion of the suggestions which Hans Egede made shortly after his arrival in Copenhagen in September 1736. Egede was soon fully occupied with the fulfilment of the promise he had made during his farewell sermon in Godthåb. His audience with the serious-minded Christian VI at Fredensborg may have given him renewed courage, for the King listened to his account of his Greenland ministry with great interest. There is no doubt that for the King, this meeting was a moving experience. Both men were conscious of their respective vocations. In appearance Hans Egede seemed to lack physical strength, but he was surrounded by an aura of spiritual power which emanated from the steady open gaze of the blue eyes which dominated his long narrow face.

In October 1736, Egede presented a long memorandum to the King and the Missionskollegium, containing a clear, concise review of the development of the mission since 1721. However, his object was not to look back, but to set out what should be done to promote the mission in future. In his view, the work had to be reorganized since the Greenlanders were "not absolutely unwilling to receive his holy truth provided the arrangements were otherwise adequate to carry out such an important task". The two missionaries at each colony could not visit the Greenlanders in their winter quarters from the end of September to April more often than once a month in the case of those living nearest and twice a year for those living farthest away, and then only with the Trading Company's boats when the latter made expeditions. Hence missionary teaching was not very effective, and it was further hindered by the missionaries' lack of proficiency in the Greenlandic language; their teaching was confined to reading from the printed or handwritten material they carried with them. Egede had no suggestion to make regarding these visits. However, he thought that the missionaries should be given the opportunity of learning the language before being sent out to Greenland. This applied not only to the graduates in divinity who wanted to be missionaries, of whom there should continue to be two at each of the two colonies, but also to the ten catechists at each colony, whom Hans Egede also considered necessary. The missionaries should still have an academic background, but he suggested that the catechists be selected from among suitable boys at the Vajsenhus (orphanage, set up in 1727), about the functioning of which he really knew nothing.

Hans Egede undertook to teach Greenlandic to both the students and the orphanage boys, but he was obliged to ask that his own livelihood be assured. He did not mention the costs relating to the students but he estimated that each catechist would cost 50 rigsdaler annually in wages, an additional outgoing that would total 1,000 rdl. In January 1737, Sewerin confirmed Egede's opinion that two missionaries and ten catechists were required at each colony. He reckoned, however, that each of them would cost over 66 rdl. excluding their provisions and their transport to and within Greenland. He thought that an undue financial burden on the mission could be avoided if over a period Greenlanders were trained as catechists. Furthermore, he thought that the earliest by which this could be put into practice was 1739.

The Missionskollegium acted with remarkable speed. On 15 January 1737 an address to the King was signed setting out the whole plan in concrete form on the basis of Egede's and Sewerin's almost identical recommendations. However, the Missionskollegium was bound to draw attention to the fact that the Greenland mission did not come within their province since it had nothing to do with the selection, instruction, sending out or remuneration of the missionaries. Everything had been done on Hans Egede's initiative, and the missionaries were at present in Sewerin's service. If the Greenland mission were to be under the authority of the Missionskollegium in future, which was perhaps the view of the King, they were bound to ask for a royal command to this effect.

They also recommended the establishment of an "academy or an obligatory seminary", through which the missionaries could be given, in advance, some proficiency in the language and knowledge of the people's customs and principal failings, and thus of the right way to win them over. For the students this should be arranged at the Regensen (Royal College), and the University of Copenhagen should be asked about the possibility of their being awarded scholarships. As for the orphanage boys, the Missionskollegium was sceptical, because it would be difficult to teach them the language so quickly, and because there were so few of a suitable age at the time; it would, never at any time be possible to procure as many as twenty suitable boys. Meanwhile it would be two or three years before the missionaries and catechists, if any, could be adequately trained. By then Sewerin's charter would have expired and it was uncertain whether he would carry on. If he did not, all the preparatory work would be wasted *"unless Your Royal Majesty would most graciously take the Greenland work upon yourself"*. This clause is one of many pointers towards the eventual taking over of the whole of "the Greenland *Dessein*" by the State.

Hans Egede had envisaged the financial support for the catechists' and students' needs coming from "pious Christians" apart from the Regensen, the Vajsenhus and scholarships. The Missionskollegium, however, put little faith in that idea considering the poor result of the Greenland lottery of 1724 and the resentment caused by the Greenland tax. Nor was it possible to provide for the remuneration of Hans Egede on that basis. Further subsidies would be needed for the future payment of missionaries and catechists, seeing that Sewerin was apparently unwilling to maintain any more people in the mission's service than those he had so far sent out.

On the basis of its memorandum Christian VI ordered, on 8 February 1737, first that the Missionskollegium should assume responsibility for the Greenland mission, which was thus established as a government concern, contributed by the central administration, although it was still administratively bound by Sewerin's charter until that finally expired. (This dual administration must surely have driven a wedge between the Trading Company and the mission – we have already seen the unpleasantnesses to which Sewerin was subjected by the Missionskollegium.) Secondly, the King said that he had arranged for the University of Copenhagen to be approached to establish a seminary for instructing students in the Greenlanders' language and customs. Thirdly, he wished that a number of the orphanage boys should be allowed to stay in the Vajsenhus beyond the usual age limit until they had been adequately trained for their work as catechists.

Fourthly, as the Missionskollegium had suggested, the King should

take on "this work and hence the mission . . . , to be maintained
at our expense, but meantime everything is to be prepared to this end".
Fifthly, the King made an immediate grant of 500 rdl., partly to re-
munerate Hans Egede and partly for expenses in connection with
the future Greenland seminarists and trainee catechists, to be followed
by 1,000 rdl. when the latter were taken into service. The number of
missionaries and catechists was to be fixed by the Missionskollegium.

Thus was founded the Seminarium Groenlandicum which from then
onwards was responsible for training the prospective Greenland missionaries and pastors. Sewerin suggested that Hans Egede should be
appointed chaplain to the Vajsenhus when the office fell vacant, and
that this office should in future be linked with a *Lingvae Grønlandicae*
professorship. However, it proved impracticable to give Egede a post
at the Vajsenhus; nor could he be given accommodation there, as he
wanted. This was decided at a meeting in the Missionskollegium on
4 April, when it was also fixed that the number of seminarists who were
to be awarded scholarships to attend the Regensen should provi-
sionally be fixed at four. The university had left this matter to the King
to decide.

It was difficult to interest the orphanage boys in a future in Greenland. It had been the wish of both Sewerin and the Missionskollegium
that their training should fit them for service to the mission and the
Trading Company. Some of the boys selected immediately asked to be
released, but . . . "if they cannot be persuaded, they must not be forced"
was the laconic reply of the Missionskollegium. The twenty boys called
were not to be found; only five were suitable and they followed the
course of instruction steadfastly.

Hans Egede's idea that "pious Christians" would undoubtedly be
willing to support the mission financially was not completely rejected;
in April 1737 he reiterated his proposal, and the Missionskollegium
decided to distribute a report and a notice of the founding of the new
institution, with a recommendation of the work "to good Christians".
Out of this came the little pamphlet *Short account of the nature of the Greenland mission,* which was issued in May of that year. It did not have the
desired effect, and the Missionskollegium was thus satisfied that its
only course was to rely on a State subsidy.

This little pamphlet formed the prelude to Hans Egede's work as a
writer in the following years. As a continuation or expansion of the
little tract, the *Detailed and comprehensive report concerning the beginning and
continuation of the Greenland mission,* followed in 1738. This too was envisaged as a tract, heralded by the *Short account.* It was a very much
abridged version of his journal notes for 1721 to 1736. In 1740 a German translation was published.

During these years, he was working on his best-known book, *Det gamle Grønlands nye Perlustration* (New description of old Greenland), published in 1741. It was probably not the first but it was the longest and most comprehensive description of Greenland up to that time, and was based on direct personal experience and observations. At the same time it contained Egede's assessment of the West Greenland Eskimo civilization as a whole. His judgments, which appear somewhat dogmatic and at times censorious in the "Reports" and letters and memoranda, were here considerably toned down, The *Perlustration* contains a much better view of life on the rough coast, as seen by one who had experience of it and who was interested in ethnography. It also contains the first description and systematic outline of the West Greenland language, or indeed of any Eskimo language. This description was built up according to the system familiar to Hans Egede – the Latin division into parts of speech – but he ran into difficulties as soon as he came to the morphology and was obliged to introduce terms hitherto unknown or little used in regard to grammar to formulate new concepts. Notwithstanding, everything was forced to follow the Latin system. His remarks on syntax were brief, and here too serious difficulties must have arisen in adapting the language to an established pattern which was and is essentially foreign to the Eskimo tongue.

There exists in manuscript at least one longer grammatical work with Hans Egede's name on the title page, which was never published. The account of the language in the *Perlustration* is surely condensed from such a source. The manuscript is entitled *Grammatica Groenlandica per Johannem Egede concepta* and was copied possibly by the secretary of the Missionskollegium, from one of the manuscript grammars which Hans Egede used when teaching in the newly founded Seminarium Groenlandicum. Although Hans Egede's name is on the title page, all his accounts of the West Greenland language are also based on the observations and current knowledge of Poul Egede, Niels Egede and Frederik Christian, apart from his own studies. This joint effort was field-work in more than one sense – linguistically, new ground was being broken, while it was only possible in practice to study the language in the field. However, their research had a definite purpose, since their aim was to make it possible to teach the language, primarily to the people of the mission. Thus both the grammar and usable texts were necessary. As mentioned above, a written language was created, but when translations were made, a number of new terms and combinations of words were introduced into the language covering concepts which had previously been unknown in West Greenland, or indeed in any Eskimo language.

The main object of the translations was to give the missionaries a

R

textual basis for everyday conversation with the local population
and for their instruction, also to provide those Greenlanders who could
read with texts in their own language, and finally to have textual appar-
atus for actually teaching Greenlandic. Poul Egede probably made the
greatest contribution to this translation work. It was he who knew the
language best and who had the strongest feeling for the right Greenlandic expressions for the many facts and ideas contained in the texts.
None of this was put into print for the time being, however, and people
had to make do with manuscript copies. This was presumably due to
both Hans and Poul Egede refusing to regard the translations that were
made as final but rather the subject of constant revision. The printing
costs, moreover, would have been considerable, and it was impossible
to anticipate any adequate return. It was the Vajsenhus which had the
Egedes' writings printed, just as it printed (against payment) other
documents for the Missionskollegium.

At the same time as teaching the students and orphanage boys,
Hans Egede acted as adviser to the Missionskollegium. Some memoranda and documents from his pen are still preserved, mostly recorded
in the minute-book of the Missionskollegium. He held the title of dean
to the Greenland mission until 1740. On 4 February 1740 in a memorandum on the future of the mission, he applied to be appointed by the
King "with the name and rank of superintendent of this mission" to
select, nominate for acceptance and teach the potential seminarists,
to issue instructions to missionaries and catechists travelling out, and
"to supervise them so as to see whether they perform their duties with
appropriate diligence and loyalty, and to receive information and
figures from them as to the progress made each year by the Greenlanders, especially in Christian knowledge and conduct, and anything
else that might be considered necessary· for the furtherance of the
Greenlanders' conversion" – in short a royal confirmation of the office
which he had already been carrying out for several years. The title
"superintendent" or bishop might seem somewhat inflated, as the
Greenland mission did not correspond to a diocese in scope, but the
duties were essentially those of a bishop. The Missionskollegium followed up his petition with an almost identical recommendation,
further emphasizing Hans Egede's pioneer work. The Missionskollegium undoubtedly thought up the title of superintendent–bishop
as an honour rather than as an official appointment. As for Hans Egede
himself, ambition for honours was foreign to his nature, and his
application must be seen partly as a safeguard against being pushed
aside now that the Missionskollegium had taken over the mission, and
partly to find a place for the mission within the organization of the
Danish state church and its official hierarchy; hitherto it had not be-

longed to any diocese. The King approved the recommendation of
the Missionskollegium on 18 March.

Until 1747, Hans Egede zealously fulfilled this half-advisory, half-
administrative and supervisory post, assisted increasingly by Poul
Egede after his homecoming. He and his son worked at improving the
linguistic aids and translations of the religious writings used for teaching in Copenhagen and Greenland. Poul Egede continued the translations of the testaments which he had begun in Christianshåb while a
missionary there, and he probably let his father revise these translations, for "to differentiate between Hans Egede and his son in regard
to authorship is virtually impossible" (Bobé). This applies to the
Perlustration as well as the grammatical works. Direct evidence of this
intermixing is afforded by Poul Egede's remarks in 1736 on his adapta-
tion of the little catechism and the prayers and hymns Hans Egede
had translated for services and prayer meetings. He considered himself
obliged to undertake this revision, feeling that he was more proficient
in the language.

The Bible translations, however, were largely the work of Poul
Egede, although Hans had previously translated isolated texts to use
in religious services and teaching. In any case it would have been difficult for Hans to change the translations of the testaments very much
for they were the result of considerable reflection and had been extensively recast with the close collaboration of intelligent Greenlanders.

The task of translating the Bible was begun by Poul Egede in January 1737, although he foresaw that he would be hampered in this work
both because the Greenlandic language lacked many fitting words
and expressions, and because of the many visits of Greenlanders who
had come from far to see him. At the end of June he finished translating
the second book of Moses. In many places the absence of Greenlandic
terms had obliged him to use Danish words, which he expected to
become naturalized in time and which were probably already understood. Hans Egede had already used this method, but his son's mastery
of the language was now such that he realized the need to employ
special words to a far greater extent for those ideas that were not covered at all by Greenlandic. Thus began the process of evolution in the
West Greenlandic language which, starting with the "church language"
gradually came to include the lay language as well. Because of the
flexibility and the possibilities of combination in Eskimo languages,
new Greenlandic words went on being created. The loan-words took
on a Greenlandicized form, and were used and pronounced along with
the everyday language, regardless of dialect. This in itself helped to
bring the two cultures together. Poul Egede's task was to make the
Bible available to the Greenlanders, and it was therefore essential to

find the expressions and word-forms most compatible with colloquial Greenlandic; and continual recasting and critical revision of what had already been translated was necessary to keep pace with his ever greater familiarity with the Greenlandic language.

Nevertheless, the changes upset Arnarsâq, the Greenlandic woman whom Poul Egede used as a catechumen shortly after his return to Christianshåb, and who, after her baptism, was a tireless and thoughtful helper with an independent mind. She asked whether it was permissible to change God's words so often, and whether He might not be angered by it. "I do not doubt," she said, "that the Word is true, but those who are not well versed in it might think it is not the truth, since it varies so much and is treated like a sick person who is always having to be dosed." She still thought that "what has been written before is understandable and sufficiently correct".

This last sentence shows that a new spiritual tradition was growing up side by side with the new vocabulary linked to it. The Word of God could not be tampered with and changed at will. The spiritual upheaval was so great that people clung to linguistic forms which enabled the new ideas to be formulated both outwardly and within their own minds. This bond between the new spiritual tradition and its linguistic expression was made even stronger by the catechism, which was made up of set questions and answers, often elaborately formulated, and containing quotations from the Bible. It became common practice in Denmark–Norway, as well as in Greenland, for these answers to be reproduced word for word, at the catechising sessions which were held almost daily. Knowledge at that time was often encapsulated in passages of text, slavishly repeated. This kind of wordbound knowledge had already reached the Bugt before Poul Egede arrived there. The Greenlanders who came from the south and stayed there for a time brought the scattered "beliefs" with them as good story-telling material. Thus the ground could be found to have been prepared, but the formal method of catechizing was not calculated to develop reflection by the individual. In his mission work Poul Egede was on the look-out for "reflective Greenlanders", but he found very few. The "indifference" with which Hans Egede so often charged the Greenlanders among whom he worked and which was also noted by Poul, probably stemmed from this mechanical learning of passages only partly understood. The educational environment played a considerable part, of course. The children and young people educated at the mission were naturally the most ready to identify themselves with Christian teaching. Because of the "requirements as to knowledge" that were enforced, it was not possible to convey sufficient "baptismal knowledge" to Greenlanders who did not live in the immediate neighbourhood of the colony. Of the Greenlanders who were influenced by the Christian missionaries, Frederik Christian was a shining hope for Hans Egede, but he died all too soon. Others, not quite so promising, took his place. Among the survivors of the smallpox epidemic at Godthåb was the man later known as Poul Grønlaender, who worked there as a catechist until his death in a shooting accident in 1765. Among the brighter children in Godthåb in the years preceding 1736 was the boy Púngujôq, whom Poul Egede took with him to Christianshåb to continue his instruction as a catechumen and to give his teacher linguistic help. In that year Poul Egede baptized him with the name Hans.[1]

The value of Hans Púngujôq to Poul Egede and his successors at the mission in the Bugt became very great. He made sound criticisms of the translating work, but Poul Egede had to manage without him in 1738–9 while he was visiting Denmark: although it was forbidden to send Greenlanders to Copenhagen, a "dispensation" was granted in this case, presumably because Hans Púngujôq had survived the smallpox epidemic of 1733–4. Poul Egede hoped he would return "with a mass of new information for his fellow-countrymen who had urged him to make this journey". In Copenhagen he was undoubtedly taught by Hans Egede, who suggested in February 1739 that he should be sent out as a catechist together with "some orphan boys". It is not known to what extent his visit benefited his work; he was something of an introvert, and there is silence concerning his later life, which must surely have been one of steady dedication to his work as a catechist.

The woman Arnarsâq caused far more excitement. She was "more talkative and bolder, so that she often brings up instances and questions of which she wants to be sure, whether or not their discussion is normally tolerated". She had come to Christianshåb with some of her family in November 1736 and wanted to stay there to receive instruction. Only a month later Poul Egede expressed amazement at her "reflectiveness": she did not keep "the little she herself has learnt" to herself but discussed it with her companions. In her he found the most compelling contradiction of his statement concerning the Greenlanders' lack of reflection. Both she and Hans Púngujôq expressed misgivings over the Old Testament accounts of original sin, guile, treachery and polygamy. They would have preferred an expurgated version of the Mosaic books. Perhaps this factor was partly the cause of Poul Egede laying aside the translation of the Old Testament after he had completed the first three Mosaic books, and switching to the Gospels. The direct cause, however, was an invitation to do so from Professor Marcus Wøldike, of which Hans Egede wrote to his son in a letter carried by the 1739 ship.[2] By the end of that year St. Matthew's Gospel was ready but the work was hampered by his growing "weakness of the eyes", probably resulting from snow-blindness. St. Mark's Gospel was completed in March 1740. Poul Egede then turned to Erik Pontoppidan's catechism "as being a book which, for the present, may be more useful to the Greenlanders than the Bible". This catechism was "adapted to this people's mode of thought, speech and life".[3] By the end of May he had completed this work and evaluated the drafting himself as follows: "Morals in Greenland are different from those of Europe, and I found it necessary for these people, who did not know God, to make Him known to them first before attempting to teach them His Will – first the Lawgiver, then His Law. Thus the second part became the first in my abbreviated version which I later wrote for beginners."

Poul Egede sought to ensure that the catechism consistently followed the principle he had applied less rigorously to the Bible translations. To a modern Dane it is difficult to imagine Pontoppidan's catechism being used in Greenland but it was rather a completely recast and adapted version, which should more accurately be called Poul Egede's catechism. In 1741 Hans Egede submitted a catechism in manuscript to the Missionskollegium entitled *Elementa Fidei Christianae*, of which the Greenlandic text comprised the order of salvation, Luther's catechism (or rather the "shorter" catechism), a few prayers and hymns, and baptismal formulae for adults and children; Poul Egede, after his return to Copenhagen, possibly lent a hand with it. *Elementa Fidei Christianae* was printed during the spring and sent out with the ships in 1742. There were thus no funds available for printing Poul's Pontoppidan version, and this was not done until 1756, but probably manuscript copies were in use in the meantime. Poul Egede's achievement is noteworthy: this catechism was drawn up (and continually revised) taking Greenlandic conditions into account at every point, hence in the hands of successive missionaries it was a vital aid to their daily ministry and in transmitting European cultural elements to the Greenlandic population.

Most Greenlanders who attended baptismal instruction, as adults or as young people, acquired their knowledge by word of mouth. But with the children and a few young people, reading and writing played a greater part in their daily instruction. Of the seventeen baptized adults at Christianshåb in 1743, only three could read and write (Hans Púngujôq was one of them), four could spell to some extent, and eight were apparently illiterate. We do not know whether Arnarsâq could read and write and the same goes for a ten-year-old boy whose knowledge was highly praised in other respects; nothing is extant from their hands.

Hans Egede had been teaching both children and young people on

Haabets Øe and at Godthåb, but this "school" was started on his own initiative and was to some extent supported by him. Poul Egede built up his "school" on the same casual basis. The children had either been handed over to the mission for a period by their parents, or were orphans taken in by the missionary. There were very few parents resident at the colony who allowed their children to go to school.

This "taking in" of children caused great difficulties for Hans Egede, and it aroused the fear that the missionaries intended to rob parents of their children. Parents did not always take their children back, however. In fact, Poul Egede tells of a boy, Tullimaq, who came to him in April 1740, sent by his mother with a request to look after him until the summer, but when the mother came to fetch her son at the beginning of June, it was obvious that Tullimaq preferred to stay. So the mother asked for payment for him and Poul Egede virtually "bought" him for two rigsdalers' worth of merchandise; the mother was more eager for the latter than for her son. Such a case must have been extremely rare.

Poul Egede also took in adults at the mission. When taking two young girls "who also board with us", he put his trust in "good Mr. Sewerin's spirit of tolerance, as I hope he is more intent on gaining the souls of these poor people than their blubber"; it would have been easier for Jacob Sewerin to accept such an arrangement if trading had been in a flourishing state.

The financial basis and "legal authority" for these schools were established at one and the same time. The charter, as extended in 1740, made it incumbent on Sewerin to maintain a school at each of the two colonies. These were plainly to be boarding schools since he was to provide the children with their board (either Greenlandic food supplemented by bread, butter and stockfish or half a man's ration from the trader at the colony), wearing apparel and bedding and, for the boys, kayaks as well. Two "orphanage boys", one to each colony, were to be sent out from Denmark as their preceptors. In 1743, the school facilities at Christianshåb were already being utilized to the full; the same was probably also true of Godthåb. This situation had developed gradually. Nowhere was there any question of schooling for all children; the pupils had to be selected from among those willing to learn.

This more regular school-teaching was occupying an excessive amount of the missionaries' time; indeed, the very idea of founding the Seminarium Groenlandicum was that catechists should be trained as teachers. In 1739 its first five "graduates" – all orphanage boys – were sent out, two to Godthåb, three to Christianshåb, on the understanding that two of the three catechists for Christianshåb were to be "shared" with the Trading Company. One of these returned home in 1741, and the other entered the Trading Company as an assistant in 1742. To offset this, one of Sewerin's Vendsyssel farmhands, Johannes Pedersen Dorf, who married a Greenland woman in 1747, was engaged as a catechist in 1741. In Godthåb only one of the two catechists – Berthel Laersen, subsequently the missionary at Sukkertoppen for many years – carried on with the work, the other being sent home in 1740 as unfit for the job.

When the charter was extended in 1740 it was urged, presumably at the request of Sewerin, that out of the young people receiving instruction at the colonies, those should be selected at each place who were considered most suitable to assist the missionaries in teaching the children; one of the two *"praeceptores"* in charge of "the boarding pupils" was to be a native of Greenland. Sewerin had expressed the hope that in time it would be possible for Greenlanders to be trained as catechists, thus making it unnecessary to employ Danes; this wish was dictated by financial as well as linguistic reasons. This consideration caused Hans Púngujôq to be engaged as a catechist in 1739. In Godthåb, Poul Grønlaender appears to have first acted as interpreter for the missionary – that was in 1738, when there was no guarantee that Sewerin would pay the catechists' wages; he cannot have been officially appointed as a catechist before Hans Púngujôq.

Hans Egede felt that the education which had been available so far to young Greenlanders at the missions in Greenland was inadequate for them to qualify as catechists and hence as teachers for other Greenlanders. His suggestion of 1739, influenced probably by discussions concerning the charter extension, was therefore to establish *"seminaria* of young Greenlanders in Greenland itself"*. Once again he thought that the necessary financial backing could be obtained through private contributions. The Missionskollegium postponed discussion of the proposal, however, until "there are a larger number of teachers and Danish catechists in the country with a knowledge of Greenlandic and thus able to examine young Greenlanders". The idea of a seminary or catechist training in Greenland was not taken up until much later and after Hans Egede's resignation as adviser to the Missionskollegium.

Nevertheless the Missionskollegium continued to be concerned with the training of missionaries and catechists. In 1744, when it contemplated sending four orphanage boys to Greenland to learn the language and at the same time undertake studies leading to graduation in divinity, enquiries were first made from Hans Egede. He considered that it would take up too much of the missionary's time, unless the foreign language part of the academic training were waived, in which case an intelligent Greenlander might just as well, and at less expense, "be so promoted, which would greatly encourage the others". In response to a simultaneous enquiry, Hans Egede replied that he could well envisage young Greenlanders being brought to Copenhagen to be educated – presumably in divinity – if this were not inadvisable on health grounds. This scheme must have been followed up, for the following year a missionary in Christianshåb replied that he feared it would be difficult to educate the Greenlanders up to the level required for academic studies, partly because of "the great ignorance of the Greenlandic language still existing", which meant that no one could give them the necessary instruction, and that he considered it impossible to teach them in Danish. If it were merely a question of teaching the young people divinity "in their own mother tongue", that could be done as easily in Greenland as anywhere else. This was the first time that the idea of educating Greenlanders in Denmark was discussed, but it seems that the whole matter was now shelved.

Thus sufficient progress was made at the missions in Greenland to ensure that a selected group of children should receive instruction in "book learning". For the great majority of children and adults, however, the information considered necessary for baptism had to be memorized. This was crammed into their minds with endless verbal repetition by the missionary or catechist in his strange Greenlandic with its foreign terms.

REFERENCES

1. *Púngujôq* means something like "the almost quite bent". Otho Fabricius' vocabulary 1804 has "*Pungiók*: 1. a creeping hunter; 2. a bogeyman, who bends himself to scare the children". It is probably in the first sense that it is used as a name.
2. Marcus Wøldike (1699–1750) was a professor of theology at the University of Copenhagen and a member of the Missionskollegium. He was greatly attached to the Egedes, especially to Poul Egede.
3. Erik Pontoppidan (1698–1764) was a bishop, professor of theology and author of several historical and topographical books as well as homiletic works, among them his cathechism. He showed significant traces of hallensic pietism, and from 1735 he was a chaplain to the Royal Court. He was also a member of the Missionskollegium.

15

THE MISSION IN GREENLAND
1733–1750

The notions of God as creator of the world, animals and men, which appear to have reached the Bugt with the Greenlanders from the south, were mainly fragmentary and half-understood. To judge from his "Reports", Poul Egede seems to have concentrated on Old Testament stories, which he was translating at the time. Although not explicitly stated, it can be gathered from the notes and questions put to him by the Greenlanders that the Lutheran concepts of sin and grace were his principal concerns, these being difficult fare for the Greenlanders, who were little accustomed to abstract ideas. Judgment and judgment-day, with their sinister concomitants of punishment and the devil, came to assume considerable importance in their minds.

When the storms during the winter of 1740–1 lasted for a long time, the Greenlanders thought that judgment-day was at hand. "They were so devout", related Niels Egede, "that they prayed and read wherever they went; many strangers who knew nothing else repeated the Lord's Prayer continually and asked me to give them some instruction and comfort". The Lord's Prayer seems to have been used as a sort of ritual incantation, just as in Old Norse times, or as with traditional Eskimo magic incantations.

When instruction in the catechism was given, even verbally, God was bound to appear as the lawgiver. The Ten Commandments were learnt even though "they are difficult things which GOD has commanded, for not all of us [Greenlanders] are equal to abiding by what you have just said". This frankness was typical of the materialistic attitude of the West Greenland Eskimos, which spilled over into their religious concepts.

The constant fear of the supernatural powers, on the part of the Bugt Greenlanders almost made Poul Egede despair: "The Greenlanders talk only of seals; for they do not so much ask advice about being saved as about how to catch seals. And when they are told of the glory of eternal life, they immediately ask: Are there plenty of seals

there too?" Some regarded the church service and the religious ceremonies as a kind of popular entertainment on a par with song contests
and spiritualistic seances.[1] At a baptism ceremony held in 1740 in conjunction with a service, many unbaptized outsiders were present.
They listened attentively to what Poul Egede and the three boys
being baptized had to say, but they did not pursue the matter further.

The religious services were clearly not going to kindle men's souls;
the will to believe was awakened by quite other means. The Greenlanders whom Poul Egede instructed were so moved by his teaching
that they spontaneously passed their knowledge on to others, who then
came to Poul to hear and learn more. This encouraged him to feel that
ministry was not in vain, and to cherish hopes for the future. The Greenlanders in the district themselves thought the solution lay in their
simply being able to receive more regular instruction at the different
settlements.

The desire for more places where instruction could be given dove-
tailed into Hans Egede's wish that catechists be sent out or that Greenlanders be trained for the work. He realized that it was not beneficial
to have the Greenlanders gathered together at the colony sites because
of their reliance on hunting and fishing; they must be sought out –
the activity must be disseminated. Greenlanders living further away,
who encountered the mission on a trip to Christianshåb, called for a
colony to be established – "they lived so far away and could not have
the same knowledge as the others". Gradually the mission's teaching
spread around Disko Bay. Poul Egede and his successors were untiring
on their journeys round the Bugt, using all the local means of transport
and going on foot when necessary. Jakobshavn – after the house had
been built in 1738 – was often their goal, but the settlements in between
and immediately around Christianshåb were also frequently visited.
At the more distant places the missionaries often had no house in which
to stay. They therefore began to build houses in the Eskimo style –
which was how Claushavn came to be established in 1741.

Wherever Poul Egede and his successors journeyed, they came across
the activities of the *angákut*. In Disko Bay, said Poul Egede, "the Devil
holds his Greenlandic academy where there are plenty of *angekut*".
Numerous *angákut* séances are mentioned in his "Reports". Time and
again Poul Egede entered into discussions with *angákut*, and tried, by
inviting them to practise their arts, to expose their "fraud". This gambit
usually succeeded: the *angákoq* would give a variety of excuses not to
perform. Whenever he found taboos being imposed, he tried to make
the people understand that they were pointless. He often succeeded in
making the *angákut* appear ineffective and even absurd in their eyes.

Poul asked to be told the *angákut*'s stories – the mythical explanations of different natural phenomena – and would then substitute the scientific explanations of his own time, ridiculing the *angákut*'s myths, but he also made himself appear as a "wizard" and soothsayer, for instance by forecasting the sun's return after the winter darkness almost to the day. In order to understand his adversary aright he tried to learn his methods, including his special vocabulary. Then, for example, he could undermine their power simply by pointing out that they used words in the opposite sense to their normal meaning. But he can never have completely mastered their jargon. One *angákoq* who taught Poul Egede a number of his terms thought that it was a good thing for him to know them, as then he would be able to understand what their mutterings meant as they practised sorcery – "you ought to know it since you too are a great *angekok*".

Possibly the *angákut* were shrewd enough to realize that Poul Egede was trying to get an inside view of their activities. Several of them pretended to adopt his cause with the idea of gaining advantage over him. They spread the judgment-day story but said that they had been to heaven and learned there that the pillars of heaven were crumbling. But they were not believed, and lost ground. Just once an *angákoq* admitted with dignity: "We know nothing of it, our forefathers spoke thus before us. We do not go outside our own country, therefore we know nothing, but you [Europeans] travel right across the sea and reach many places, that is why you are so wise." A typical example of an *angákoq* wanting to hold his own towards him was related by Poul Egede himself, although he did not understand the true meaning of the man's action. Three Greenlanders came to the colony one day and gave Poul a "written message" from one of their fellows. This consisted of a piece of wood on which a sign like a large upturned "V" had been inked with lamp-black and train oil. "We have heard that you are a wise man, can you understand this? If you can, you must be even wiser." The sign was incomprehensible to Poul Egede who wanted to know what their companion, an *angákoq*, meant by it. The three then explained that the *angákoq* had said that they were to tell Poul Egede, if he did not understand the "message", that he wanted to buy a pair of blue breeches. It is possible that this *angákoq* wanted to impress his own people by being able to send "written messages" in the same way as letters were sent from the south to the Bugt with kayakers and other travelling Greenlanders.

The effect of exposing *angákut* was that, over the years, they went "rather out of fashion", as Poul Egede was able to write in 1740. Nevertheless the loss of their ministrations must have been felt, because eighteen months later Niels Egede reported that Greenlanders from a settlement near Christianshåb had asked for a way to procure plenty of seals and beluga since, as they said, the *angákut* were now defeated and their powers had deserted them. He also agreed that their activity was declining in the Christianshåb district, but at the same time people said that they were missing a social function which had hitherto been an "effective guarantee" of their livelihood. Thus a belief persisted that the *angákut* had been effective in his time. Now the stronger powers coming from outside would have to provide a valid system of "insurance" to replace the one which had been lost.

Poul Egede gradually acquired a deep knowledge of the *angákut's* activities. Many myths were told to him. Indeed, much of the material related to him, events he had experienced and situations he had studied, were included in the *Perlustration* and demonstrate his role in its composition (which Hans Egede acknowledged). The Greenlanders soon began to doubt these tales. "They are probably telling lies about this too as usual", declared a Greenlander in the Bugt in 1737 after relating a mythical tale.[2]

Although they continued to be told, fables and myths lost much of their value for the Greenlandic population and the *angákut*, while they long continued to practise, lost more and more ground. On the whole, the popular religious tradition that had prevailed up till that time collapsed quickly, at least at a superficial level. The collapse was symbolized by the *angákoq's* wish "in writing" for a pair of blue breeches – a wish that incidentally affords a glimpse of the material needs that were imposing themselves only two years after the establishment of Christianshåb.

The situation of culture-contact which arose in the Bugt within a few years had a strange outcome on one particular occasion. Every attempt was made by those living further away, always led by the *angákut*, to thwart the growth of the mission. This caused antagonism between the pagans and the baptized and catechumens in the colony. In February 1743 twenty-four sledges came from settlements to the south of Christianshåb to arrange a song contest against the Greenlanders of the colony; to the Greenlanders this was a test of strength. In songs and satirical ditties they mocked the colony Greenlanders for learning the missionaries' ways, but they were given "song for song", and beaten and humiliated by the colony Greenlanders and had to depart in shame. Although the visitors outnumbered the colony Greenlanders, they were pursued "far out over the ice". This clear outcome must have had a significant effect on the minds of the Eskimo people. It was a strange situation for missionaries, catechists and Trading Company staff (including Niels Egede) to see such an essentially Eskimo weapon being used by the local Greenlanders for the mission's benefit. There is no indication that the mission disapproved of this means of defence; on the contrary, Niels Egede's account contains a note of triumph. It is tempting to conclude that the song contest did not follow the traditional pattern. It must, of course, have been difficult for recent converts to compose satirical ditties with sufficient bite in them: it is conceivable that they responded by singing the hymns they had learned. Indeed, one major aspect of the events described which did not accord with tradition was that *all* the colony Greenlanders sang; it was not a song contest between individuals. This and the unaccustomed hymns could have confused the outsiders and destroyed their confidence, so that they lost the contest.

This event was also significant in that it helped to make the traditional legal remedy in personal disputes impracticable, and thus marked a further stage in the collapse of West Greenland Eskimo culture, which in this case was aided and abetted by the Greenlanders themselves. This breakdown of the Eskimo spiritual culture in the south-eastern part of Disko Bay must be seen in conjunction with the material and economic influences that were having a powerful effect on everyday life at the same time. Certainly the economic factor accelerated progress: for some time it had been exerting its influence through the Dutch, but this was now intensified through the establishment of colonies by Jacob Sewerin and the permanent presence of the Trading Company.

Why was the number of Greenlanders in the Bay not large enough to keep the cultural tradition alive? One probable reason is that the Greenlanders of the Bay had been exposed to outside influences for longer than the population of Central Greenland with the Dutch, and from 1734 onwards the permanent mission and Trading Company operating there more intensively than elsewhere in Greenland, due to the south-eastern part of the Bay being more densely populated than other coastal areas. The population there also seems to have been more "stable"; they did not go on so many or such long journeys as those living further south. We have no statistics to support our assumption that the population around Disko Bay was larger than that in the south; however, Godthåb had been exposed to the catastrophic effects of the smallpox epidemic, and the toll had still not been made good even in the 1740s. The Greenlanders of the Bay had not yet been exposed to such an epidemic.

The Bay Greenlanders were not free from diseases, either those with fatal consequences or epidemics. Dysentery occurred almost every year and seems to have been especially prevalent in the Bay during the years we are considering, at times assuming epidemic proportions. The infection was probably carried south by those who journeyed there and back, as it also occurred in Godthåb and district and much farther south. Tuberculosis also occurred both in Godthåb and the Bay, but there are indications that it had existed in both places for a long time.

It had become the practice to send out an assortment of common medicaments to either the missionary or the trader, but Hans Egede did not consider this enough and wanted the colonies provided "with an able surgeon and physician together with the necessary medicaments so that the poor people in the country may not either perish or be obliged to quit their posts prematurely". Thus Hans Egede seems to have felt that a surgeon or barber-surgeon, such as had been in Greenland previously, was not acceptable but that a proper physician was wanted. The surgeons sent out had also acted as physicians and were put in charge of the medicine-chests; they did not confine their practice to the colonists and soldiers but also looked after sick Greenlanders when necessary, as during the smallpox epidemic.

From 1734 onwards, however, there had been no surgeon in Greenland. Hans Egede's suggestion that someone who was both a surgeon and a doctor should be sent out was forwarded by the Missionskollegium to Jacob Sewerin to induce him to pay the expenses. Sewerin was asked only about a surgeon and replied that he considered "such people unnecessary in that country". Hans Egede, in raising the matter, had had in mind the medical graduate Johan Andreas van Osten, then twenty-eight years old, and Sewerin replied that he would be willing to provide this young man with board and accommodation, but the Missionskollegium would have to find some other source for paying his salary. As the Missionskollegium was always hard pressed financially, it only granted van Osten an annual wage of 50 rdl., i.e. one-third of that received by a missionary, but as promised, Jacob Sewerin contributed board and accommodation, as well as lighting and heating. For two years from 1742, van Osten was in Godthåb as physician to Greenlanders and colonists, the first doctor in Greenland. As a sideline he had plans to explore the district, and he also conceived a fantastic scheme to melt the ice by means of large concave mirrors. The Missionskollegium either could not or would not support him in executing any of these plans, which was presumably one reason why he returned to Copenhagen after so short a stay. He had no immediate successors.

After the departure of Poul Egede and shortly after Hans Egede left Godthåb, the mission there was handed over to two Danish missionaries who were quite new to the country and had nothing like the Egedes' linguistic knowledge. One of them left Greenland in 1739, the year that Niels Egede returned to Godthåb. The mission gained no ground during that period, as the two relatively young missionaries could scarcely have assumed the Egedes' mantle; possibly this is one reason why Niels Egede was sent to Godthåb, accompanied by the missionary Christen Lauritsen Drachardt. The latter had shown pietistic tendencies in his student days, and this tendency was to affect the mission at Godthåb, where he soon made contact with the Moravians.

At Ny Herrnhut near Godthåb, the missionaries of the Brethren had made great efforts to create a following among the Greenlanders. The lay missionaries had only a poor knowledge of the language, which prevented them from making closer contact with the population and the migrants, although they were visited by a few people. A group of Greenlanders are alleged to have claimed that the Moravians did not understand them, but the same group also said that teaching was now different from what it had been formerly.

This statement was made in February 1740. It was quite true that a change had occurred at that time in the Moravians' missionary methods. In March 1735, a good eighteen months after their arrival, the three Brethren formally agreed that their ministry should concentrate on central themes bearing witness to Christ's death on the cross and the accompanying salvation, which were to bring unbelievers "to obedience in the faith". In view of the Brethren's superficial knowledge of Greenlandic at this time, this decision cannot have been based on experience gained in their missionary work, but simply a common commitment to the beliefs that were the foundation of their teaching everywhere: salvation "through the blood of the Lamb". They must also have recognized that, in terms of language and education, they were not yet capable of imparting to the Greenlanders sufficient knowledge for them to be seized by the truth of the faith. So they fell back on the central evangelistic and revivalist theme of their movement at home. Revival – *die Rührung des Herzens* – was and must continue to be their main hope in Greenland too, and was to be attained through "simple stories about the incarnation, a life of righteousness, and the passion and death of Jesus". The years immediately after 1735 apparently justified their view.

In June 1738 a group of Greenlanders from the south who were passing through the Godthåb district visited the Brethren at Ny Herrnhut. One of the Brethren there, Johann Beck, was engaged at the time in copying out translated passages from the Gospels, and at their request he read some of the translation aloud – the story of Jesus in the garden of Gethsemane. One of the travellers, Qajarnaq, asked to hear this story again, "for I should also like to be saved"; this referred to the remarks on eternal life with which Johann Beck had prefaced the reading. Then followed a typical Moravian scene: Beck was so "moved" by Qajarnaq's words that, with tears in his eyes, he related the whole story of Jesus' passion "and God's counsel for our salvation". Of the

Greenlanders present, one group then left Ny Herrnhut, while the other remained in the grip of the revivalists.

During the ensuing period, Qajarnaq visited them again and again, eventually settling down and remaining there for the rest of his life. Johann Beck wrote of him that he was quick to grasp what he heard, and often he was moved to tears. Great importance was attached to this weeping as an expression of commitment and strong inner emotions. Qajarnaq had "a hook fast in his heart which he will probably never be rid of".

This event, which a later missionary of the Brethren, Carl Julius Spindler, immortalized in an epic poem in Greenlandic (1891) introduced a new epoch for the Brethren's mission in Greenland. With their growing proficiency in the language, and by deliberately simplifying the gospel story, they succeeded in expanding the revival, particularly among Greenlanders coming from the south, but gradually spreading to the surrounding district, in particular the Kangeq settlement in the mouth of the fjord opposite Godthåb. From 1738 onwards they made a point of telling simple stories so that the hearers were aroused emotionally. When, after a short period of instruction, they expressed the wish to be baptized, this was done. Afterwards the catechism was learned in order to broaden the commitment and to enable a more profound confession of faith. This was the very opposite to the practice of the royal mission ever since Hans Egede's early days. For adults or young people it had insisted on catechism and then confession of faith before baptism; only infants had been baptized shortly after birth, and infants whose parents were baptized were baptized themselves as a matter of course.

Baptism was the principal stumbling-block between the royal mission at Godthåb and the Moravians. It appears that the Moravians baptized Qajarnaq and his immediate family, with others, in March 1739, and in doing so were breaking the law. Drachardt, who felt a growing attachment for the Brethren, must have connived at this; he took part in their baptism ceremonies, and later allowed the Brethren to participate in the mission's services. He also went out increasingly with the Brethren in their boats. This led to resentment among the Greenlanders who were visited neither by the Moravians nor, in consequence, by Drachardt, who at the same time was on bad terms with both his fellow-missionary Sylow, who had come to Godthåb in 1740, and the Trading Company. Sylow was transferred to Frederikshåb when it was established in 1742 and no other missionary replaced him in Godthåb, but conditions did not improve.

Drachardt and Berthel Laersen, the catechist who had come to Godthåb at the same time as he had, were in sole charge of the mission.

s

This was connected with the fact that the handing over of the Godthåb mission completely to the Moravians had been seriously considered. The idea was abandoned, however, and Sewerin countered
by suggesting that the Moravians should move from Godthåb to various places in the heart of the fjord, and use the land there for horticulture and cattle rearing. But he had no more confidence in this idea
being carried out than in the suggestion he made at the same time that
the Moravians, if they were not willing to move out of the Godthåb
district, should at least enter the service of the Trading Company as the
craftsmen they were, and that they should assist the missionary as catechists. The Missionskollegium would not back up these schemes;
although Christian VI had largely dissociated himself from Zinzendorf and the pietistic separatist movements, the position of the
Brethren still called for delicate handling.

As far as religious ceremonies were concerned, a ban could be enforced against the Moravians restricting their activities, but it could
not be denied that they were there by royal permission, and there they
stayed. Sewerin's involvement in the matter arose from his fear of infringements of his trading and navigation monopoly, and from disputes in connection with supplies for the Moravians in Godthåb
when their ship from the Netherlands was among those captured in
the "naval skirmish at Makelijk Oud". Sewerin was ordered to hand
over the goods that were intended for them, although the rest of the
ship's cargo, the ship and her captain were subject to a separate court
ruling. The years that followed saw continuous trouble between Sewerin
and the Brethren.

In 1742, it was announced that one of the Brethren's missionaries in
Greenland, Matthaeus Stach, had been ordained to the ministry while
on a visit to Germany. The Missionskollegium was accordingly obliged
to recommend to the King that Stach be recognized as the pastor of
the Moravian Brethren at Ny Herrnhut. With this the Brethren were
released from even formal dependence on the royal mission at Godthåb, just as they had in practice dissociated themselves from it almost
from the beginning. Now, as the number of Greenlandic members
of the congregation gradually increased, they were free to organize
their religious community. As long as Drachardt represented the royal
mission at Godthåb no difficulties were anticipated.

Mission historians have disagreed in assessing the Moravians'
activities in Greenland. They were much criticized in their own time.
Arnarsâq, who returned to Greenland in 1741 and stayed in Godthåb
for a few years, tried to make Drachardt more rigid over church doctrine, but without success. She could not bear to see the consequences
of his preaching and missionary work. Head-hanging, begging and

hypocrisy are the expressions attributed to her by Niels Egede, who also mentioned that an old woman from Godthåb said that Drachardt had recommended the Greenlanders to kneel down on a bare rock, put their faces against the stone surface and call upon the spirit of God, whereupon the rock would answer what they must do. The Moravians had also taught them to do this.

There was naturally a split between the Greenlanders too, as Hans Egede had always feared. In Christianshåb it led to "fights between those who had come from Godthåb and our own people". The royal missionaries, apart from Drachardt, only taught people to pray, but the Moravians and Drachardt taught them "how to know God's will". Niels Egede reported the two stories quoted above with great tolerance; however great his astonishment, he defended the Moravians and Drachardt by saying that because they could not speak Greenlandic well, people must have misunderstood their meaning.

Although the Moravians' knowledge of the language must have increased over the years, their command of the spoken language was poor, and they had great difficulty in translating doctrinal points. Some insight into the Moravians' language problems is afforded by Niels Egede's story of two young girls from the south who "spoke . . . simple debased Greenlandic to me. . . . I asked them to speak proper Greenlandic as I understood it better; they answered that they had got into such a habit through talking incorrectly to the Brethren, since at Godthåb they could not speak otherwise". They could scarcely understand the Moravians when they were reading aloud although they could understand them in normal speech. Berthel Laersen, the catechist, was the most proficient at Greenlandic; he had benefited from Hans Egede's instruction before leaving home.

The following year (1742) Niels Egede wanted to "examine" a few Greenlanders who had stayed in the south, in Godthåb, for a whole winter. They replied in "some gibberish, preceding each word with *tava teina*", the equivalent of *tauva táuna* in modern Greenlandic, meaning "then this" – or, in other words, a phrase for a speaker at a loss for precise words. When Arnarsâq came to Christianshåb in 1743, she brought with her many New Testament texts which she had been taught at Godthåb. Niels Egede explained them as best he could, "but it seemed to me that they [the Moravians] would do far better to go on teaching what has been translated by those who know the language". For his part, he would not undertake to translate texts from the Bible, although his knowledge of colloquial Greenlandic was as good as anyone's. Both the Moravians and Drachardt attempted to carry out translations.

After the baptism of Qajarnaq who was given the name of Samuel, visits to Ny Herrnhut increased. In August 1740 the Brethren had begun to translate the four Gospels, hoping for Samuel's assistance, but he died soon afterward in February 1741. The words of commemorating his death which were entered in the diary revealed the dubious method of translating that had been adopted: often, working on the translation, they were completely baffled, but at such times they had only to recite to Samuel a few verses consisting of "half-words", and he was at once able to put them together. By "half-words" they presumably meant root-words or "substantives" without prefixes and suffixes; as the meaning is almost always conveyed by these, the dangers can be appreciated.

As far as we know these translations no longer exist; they were written down, and it may have been fragments of them that Arnarsâq took with her to Christianshåb in 1743. They also probably reached Hans Egede, for in January 1744 he requested the Missionskollegium to obtain Drachardt's "translated biblical texts and commentaries for inspection together with the religious songs composed by the Moravians . . .'. Drachardt had begun to use them at prayer meetings and services instead of the hymns that were already translated – by the Egedes and others; but at the same time the missionary was to be reminded to base his instruction on Luther's catechism.

Drachardt appreciated that he was under observation. However, both before and after going to Greenland, he enjoyed the patronage of Bishop Erik Pontoppidan, a member of the Missionskollegium, to whom he sent a lengthy written reply to all the spiritual and temporal charges against him. In April 1745 Hans Egede submitted a written criticism of the written works and translations of Drachardt and the Moravians. In it he doubted whether Drachardt could enlighten the Greenlanders at all with "such Greenlandic scribblings of his own". He felt Drachardt should be enjoined to make use of the translations already available "as neither he nor the others [i.e. the Moravians] are capable of doing it better". However, the Missionskollegium was unwilling to pursue the matter further, which perhaps reflected Pontoppidan's influence as well as the characteristic delicacy with which "Moravian affairs" were still handled. Moreover, Drachardt had already promised to make more diligent use of Hans Egede's translations and, in accordance with the Missionskollegium's recommendation, to use Luther's catechism in instructing the Greenlanders.

Pontoppidan's protection of Drachardt and the "delicacy" shown by the Missionskollegium are apparent in the lack of reaction when Drachardt was accepted into the Brethren at Ny Herrnhut in 1745 after marrying one of their women. Attention was paid not so much to what had happened, as to the fact that he conducted himself cautiously, in accordance with the royal order and with the ritual which had to be observed "as far as possible". The Missionskollegium assured him of promotion in due course, provided he gave continued proof of his diligence. It was not considered necessary to send out another missionary to Godthåb. Drachardt's actions would be of less intrinsic importance had they not at the same time revealed the patterns of behaviour of the Missionskollegium, Hans Egede and the Godthåb mission and, finally, the effect on the local population and their reactions to it.

In 1745 Hans Egede expressed to the Missionskollegium his fear of an inadmissible mixing of the two congregations at Godthåb. He also made known his anxiety that Drachardt was proceeding too quickly with the administration of baptism. He had baptized eighteen persons in 1744/5, including old people who, it was well known, found the necessary knowledge difficult to assimilate within a short period. Egede was obviously worried that Drachardt was baptizing them on a Moravian "revivalist basis"; he expressly stated that "the Greenlanders are inclined to sham and to try to please when they find it to their advantage", an experience which missions in all times and places have had to face. On the other hand, in a situation where revival and a short period of preparation appeared to take the place of a moderate amount of basic knowledge adapted to the individual (Hans Egede's practice) there was danger that the person who shammed and looked for his own advantage would be the one who easily got what he wanted. Head-hanging as Arnarsâq had described, was part and parcel of begging: "Whenever . . . they needed something they went to Mr. Drachardt and hung their heads, rolled their eyes upwards and sighed, then he believed them and gave them what they wanted and said that that is how God's children should be". But Arnarsâq, seeing the discord among them and "falsity towards God and their teachers", showed them up to Drachardt and the Moravians; they did not believe her and listened to others who knew how "to act with guile". However it is hardly surprising that the Greenlanders, for whom a materialistic society was essential, looked for the easiest way into the new society that was emerging at a time when their own was on the point of collapse, especially when this method of entry was so easy.

During 1746 Hans Egede, who received the foregoing information from his son Niels who returned to Denmark in 1743, received further information from the Greenlandic catechist Poul Grønlaender, among others. Faithful to Hans Egede, who had instructed and baptized him, and following his practice, Poul Grønlaender steadfastly continued his ministry, and it was probably due to his efforts that the entire Godthåb congregation, small as it was, had not been swallowed up by the Moravian congregation. Even though the stationed catechist, Berthel Laersen, leaned strongly towards *nordlît*, as the Moravians were called by the Greenlanders, he did not go as far as Drachardt. This too would have kept deserters in check; Laersen was respected by the Greenlanders on account of his ever-increasing linguistic skills.

At the end of the year Hans Egede laid the new material before the Missionskollegium. The differences between the congregation at God-thåb and the followers of the Brethren had further degenerated. It was said by the latter that the people of Godthåb had only "a literal know-ledge", learned from men; after Drachardt finally joined the Brethren, he denounced "all instruction in the Word of God and the Lutheran catechism" as "unprofitable", and on the contrary, refers them "solely to their own experience and feelings. . . ." Hans Egede now regarded Drachardt as not merely "useless but harmful as well". Typically, the Missionskollegium took no decision on this matter, and this may have induced Hans Egede to submit a memorandum to the King in January 1747 on his own initiative, by-passing the Missionskolle-gium, and complaining about the dissension in Godthåb and the Mora-vians' denunciation of the teachers of the royal mission. He asked for Drachardt to be dismissed. With a barely concealed reproof for having submitted this memorandum without reference to the Kollegium, the memorandum was sent back to Hans Egede for further elucidation, which was apparently the end of the matter.

Yet it had another indirect consequence. Hans Egede realized that he was getting nowhere in his campaign against the Moravians and Drachardt, and he was particularly distressed by the dissension in God-thåb. His own experience with the early Moravians told him to expect events to repeat themselves; it must have seemed to him impossible to bring about a union between the two missions operating in the Godthåb district, and to bring the Moravians under the state church. It seemed a defeat for his ministry among the Greenlanders to abandon the Godthåb mission which would also constitute a clear betrayal of those Greenlanders who had allied themselves with the mission. He must have suffered profound disillusionment and a feeling that his strength and influence were waning or had left him altogether. In 1747 he retired as adviser to the Missionskollegium, and was never again to deal officially with Greenland affairs. From now on Poul Egede acted as adviser in his father's stead, and on his behalf continued teaching at the Seminarium Groenlandicum. He had taken part in this teaching immediately on his arrival in Copenhagen in 1740. In April 1741 he became the pastor of Vartov, a not very onerous living, so that he was able to fulfil his Greenlandic commitments. In 1735 he had made a start on his *Dictionarium Gronlando-Danicum*, which he completed during the 1740s. The Danish text was then trans-lated into Latin, and in 1750 his *Dictionarium groenlandico-latinum* was published, the first dictionary of an Eskimo language ever to appear.

He also continued his translation of the New Testament so that the four Gospels could be printed: these were published in 1744. The 1740s were a seminal decade for Greenlandic books. Even though the books that were printed in Greenlandic were not intended for general sale, each of these publications was in its own way of paramount importance to future missionaries, alongside the handwritten grammars. It was thus possible to acquaint them with the mysteries of the West Greenlandic language to a far greater extent than their predecessors, so that they went out to their ministry better equipped. For the people of the Trading Company in Greenland too these books were a great help, especially the dictionary, although they learnt most of their Greenlandic by direct contrast.

From 1740 onwards Poul Egede had not only to teach the divinity students and selected orphanage boys but also visiting Greenlanders. He had brought Arnarsâq and a Greenlandic lad to Denmark with him but they returned to Greenland the following year. When Sylow, the missionary, came back from Frederikshåb in 1746, he brought with him five Greenlanders – a young girl and four boys. The girl was the self-assured "choleric" (which can perhaps best be interpreted as "cheeky") Maria who, like Arnarsâq, showed a remarkable critical and reflective capacity. She was a great help to Poul Egede with his translations, but only for a year, as she followed Sylow to Norway and died there in 1748. Two of the boys who had come over in 1746 also accompanied Sylow to Norway, and later returned home to Greenland. The other two, Andreas and Jørgen, remained in Copenhagen to be trained as catechists, but we do not know what became of them afterwards, as there is no mention of their returning to Greenland.

After this period, no indication is given for a long while of any Greenlanders being accepted for training in Copenhagen; this was perhaps avoided deliberately, or may have been due to the small number of "suitable" Greenlanders. Hence this form of training was bound to be occasional and regarded as somewhat experimental. It had come to be tried because of a realistic preoccupation with the problem of training people with adequate linguistic skills efficiently and quickly for the service of the mission. One factor which restricted further expansion of the scheme, apart from the small number of suitable candidates, was the fear of disease, especially smallpox. Lack of financial resources was a further obstacle, and was one reason why Hans Egede put forward his idea for a catechist seminary in Greenland itself.

From the Brethren's growing flock at Ny Herrnhut, individual Greenlanders were also selected to cross the Atlantic. In 1747 Matthaeus

Stach once again travelled to Germany, taking with him five baptized Greenlanders. They visited the Netherlands, England and America, besides Herrnhut and other places in Germany. Two of them died in Germany before they could go on to England and America; the other three returned to Ny Herrnhut in 1749. They were taken to Germany to experience life among the Brethren in the mother communities, and to have their faith strengthened. In fact, it also resulted in one of them, a young girl, who had been baptized in 1742, asking permission to organize and run a sister-house.

After Qajarnaq's baptism in 1738 more and more Greenlanders came to Ny Herrnhut every year. The consequent linguistic contact between the mission Brethren and the visiting Greenlanders led to the missionaries' proficiency in Greenlandic increasing, and thus their spoken words and revivalist prayer meetings became more effective. As more people were baptized and joined the congregation, they settled at Ny Herrnhut and naturally the missionaries' linguistic proficiency increased still further. Equally, the missionaries' influence on the Greenlanders was strengthened.

The baptismal ceremonies at Ny Herrnhut followed each other so closely that it is possible to follow the tremendous growth in the congregation through them. In 1739, as mentioned, Qajarnaq was baptized and with him his wife and two children. In the next two years there seem to have been no baptisms, then in 1742 there were five, and in 1743 there were eleven, and the first wedding took place between a Greenland couple who were believers. In 1744, nine Greenlanders came to Ny Herrnhut and were baptized the same year – by comparison, several years were spent in preparation for baptism at the royal mission. At the end of 1745, the congregation at Ny Herrnhut numbered fifty-three. Among the baptized Greenlanders, however, were some living at Kangeq, the settlement in the mouth of the Godthåb fjord. In the same year the first baptism of an infant whose parents were baptized was carried out by the Brethren.

The Brethren continued to grow. In 1746 twenty-six were baptized, including one from Kangeq; in 1747 the congregation consisted of 134, of whom fifty-two were baptized in that year, although in all 180 Greenlanders lived at Ny Herrnhut. By comparison, only about 100 people lived at Godthåb. Of the large number at Ny Herrnhut some forty-five must have been catechumens, for in 1748 fifty-three were baptized, some of whom had presumably moved there during the year, or lived at Kangeq. Annual figures for baptisms and deaths are reported by Cranz, and it can be roughly estimated that by the end of 1750 the Brethren's congregation numbered 250 members. Thus it is little wonder that there was not enough room in the timber house built in 1733–4. A successful appeal was made to the mother communities, and in 1747 a new meeting-house was shipped out from the Netherlands in a specially charted vessel. On board this ship was the former missionary Christian David, now aged fifty-six, who wanted to be present at the building of this new house, a worthy symbol of the growth in the Brethren's mission. No such large or commodious house had ever been seen by the Greenlanders before, and it undoubtedly helped to boost the membership, especially when compared with the cramped and barely adequate buildings of the Godthåb mission: it was in the years following its erection that the large numbers of baptisms were recorded.

Keeping pace with the growth of the congregation, members were increasingly organized along the lines of the Moravian communities in Germany and the Netherlands. This organization was bound up with the strict church discipline which linked the separate groups and individuals together in a kind of "cell" system. Besides this there were the daily morning and evening devotions apart from meetings (services) on Sundays and holy-days, prayer-hours, conversation hours, choir-meetings and catechizing. Once a man and his family had joined the congregation, the latter exerted a tight hold on him. The elders of the congregation were in a position of authority hitherto unknown in Greenland society. The missionaries were worried about the danger to the individual when he went hunting and fishing, but they could do nothing about this; on the other hand, they were able to keep the "flock" together when it set off for the head of the fjord in the spring to catch *angmagssat* (capelin). These expeditions had developed a strange blend of fishing and devotions. On occasions a reindeer-hunter would break away from the gathering and go off on his own over the moors. There was nothing to be done about that, although there might be reproaches; it was impossible to "organize" that kind of hunting.

This conflict between a very rigid communal life and individuality was a phenomenon long known in West Greenland Eskimo society. Perhaps the individual West Greenlander felt more at home with the Brethren than with the royal mission and its colony where there was greater emphasis on demands on the individual without a social community being established, the latter being almost impossible for the royal mission, whose baptized Greenlanders and catechumens lived scattered among the settlements in the region.

Here was the fundamental difference between the royal mission and that of the Brethren; the latter virtually chained their proselytes to particular places. The only exception to begin with was Kangeq, but even that was not far from Ny Herrnhut. As long as the congregation did not become too big for the hunting and fishing facilities at

Godthåb, it was possible for this concentration of the population to take place without danger to the economy; yet such an "agglomeration" was and remained essentially alien to the Eskimo economy and would only work for a time.

At Ny Herrnhut the Greenlanders' winter-houses were sited near the new meeting-house, as was the sister-house erected in the autumn of 1749. The young girls would continue to carry out their duties in the families to which they belonged, but would otherwise live in the sister-house and sleep there "so that they do not, as previously, have occasion to see and hear various things which might give rise to unnecessary and harmful thoughts on their part"; whether it was such ideas that prompted the young Greenlandic girl to suggest the building of a sister-house is not specifically related. If these were indeed her thoughts, she was the first to show that the ethical concept of the West Greenland Eskimo family and household community with its communal life were on the point of dissolution. In the long run, the Brethren's organization was the greatest encroachment on this Eskimo tradition, although the Moravians had no desire to disrupt the family as an institution.

Moravian customs gradually crept into everyday life, fostered by the increasingly close ties of daily fellowship. The children – both the missionaries' own and those of the Greenlanders – came under its influence early. Although not too much importance was attached to schooling, a reading class was set up for the children, a separate teacher being appointed in 1749, for the boys only; girls and boys were, of course, taught separately. To begin with they were taught to read and write in Greenlandic and German, but German was discontinued as "serving no purpose". German Moravian hymns, translated into Greenlandic and sung to German tunes, were learnt, as were translated Danish hymns. Music and singing played a much greater part among the Brethren than at the royal mission, whose prayer-meetings and services were far less festive. However, music and singing were still in their infancy at Ny Herrnhut due to lack of resources and means of giving proper instruction.

When the baptized members of the brethren's congregation were sufficient to form a flock and when relations with the royal mission were cordial on account of the missionary Drachardt, the Christmas Eve procession was started, and this custom continued to be observed in Greenland right up to the 1940s although it was in decline all the time and in the end was only kept up by children. The members of the Brethren's congregation walked together over the frozen, snow-covered moss to Godthåb on 24 December 1744 halting before each house and singing a carol. The baptized from Ny Herrnhut assembled with the baptized from Godthåb for a joint prayer-meeting in the little church at Godthåb; afterwards the trader gave them all a meal. On the way back a few verses were again sung in front of each house. Thus European culture penetrated daily life in Greenland in many ways, and was helped by the fact that the foreigners could scarcely be regarded any longer as "coming from outside". The Moravians in particular seemed to belong there because they mostly stayed for a long time, some even for life. Their children were born there and grew up with the children of those who moved in. As time passed, the influence and authority of the permanent residents grew accordingly.

The foreigners gradually came to organize the year. Formerly the Eskimo had been quite content with the changing of the seasons and the known migratory habits of the animals he hunted. Wind and weather might upset everything, but on the whole there was a predictable series of changes in a relatively rigid sequence, which applied also to the rising and setting of the sun, its height over the horizon, the period of darkness, the midnight sun in the north and finally the phases of the moon and the tide. Besides that there was a rough system for reckoning longer periods of time, but this was more an individual measure, in relation to important events in one's own life or the life of the settlement. Yet these events were not remembered for very long. Perhaps a relic of this persisted in what Poul Egede heard in the Bay, namely that time was calculated from "*pellesingvoak*: the coming of little pastor [Hans Egede] to the country"; that was not likely to fade from the memory. The individual and his immediate family had their private calendar based on landmarks in the growing-up of their children, especially the boys. As for the ages of individuals, only vague ideas were retained; under foreign influence birthdays and dates of baptism became increasingly important.

The division of the year into weeks and months complicated the whole system of reckoning time. Under the new system, it was essential to remember holidays – both religious and civil – first and foremost Sunday, *sapât(e)*; after all, the third commandment had to be observed. In this matter people were obliged to rely on the missionary's authority, while some followed the children in Christianshåb in making their own "weekly calendar", consisting simply of a piece of wood with seven holes in it, into which the children fitted a little wooden peg for each day of the week "so that they shall not mistake Sunday".[3] However, this observance of the sabbath gave rise to various kinds of conflicts. Was it permissible, for instance, to go hunting on a Sunday when the weather was set fair after several days of gales or if there were tempting reports of seals on the move? Was this to desecrate the sabbath and profane God's law? Even the missionaries were in doubt.

It was, as they said at Christianshåb, difficult to practise the observance of God's law in accordance with the words of the catechism. Although the Moravians in their teaching did not attach great importance to knowledge, Luther's small catechism played its part. They were bound by it in the same way as they were bound by the Augsburg Confession, and Zinzendorf had been obliged to affirm their absolute recognition of this article of faith of the Danish–Norwegian state church, upon which the continued presence of the Moravians in Greenland was conditional. From an administrative point of view also, conformity was the main principle of autocracy.

The recognition by the Moravians of this article of faith of the evangelical Lutheran state church came into Jacob Sewerin's repeated suggestions that the Moravians be allowed to take over the mission at Godthåb. However, he over-estimated their numbers when he wrote that there were more than three hundred souls, but then he added that they were "far more sensibly brought up as regards both their way of life and their skill in gaining a livelihood than our mission's young people". The missionary appointed to Frederikshåb, a meek individual, would be well suited to handle this transition. This would provide a solution to the dilemma concerning Drachardt, who had gone over to the Moravians completely. The Missionskollegium do not appear to have discussed this proposal at all; for them it was doubtless an extreme solution to a delicate problem.

Sewerin linked this suggestion with his other proposal to abandon Frederikshåb completely. The mission at this most southerly of the colonies, which because of the navigational difficulties and its small population could scarcely be called a colony at all, was proving more successful than had been anticipated. Sylow, the missionary there, had at least managed to make some contact with the local Greenlanders, despite his somewhat fiery nature. Because of his quick temper and Drachardt's naïvete, the two missionaries had immediately fallen out in Godthåb and the strife only ended when Sylow went to Frederikshåb in 1742. There he was soon at odds with the Greenlanders. He described them as "barbaric and wild, thievish and adulterous", and when he "spoke to them about their singing, drum-playing, superstition, whoring and gluttony, they became so furious that their limbs shook with rage and they used hard words against him too". His life was in danger because he had attempted "with misplaced zeal" to put a stop to their "games and merriment". As superintendent of the mission, Hans Egede did not care for this form of missionary activity and thought that it caused more harm than good. Nevertheless, Sylow had managed to instruct and baptize fifty-three people by the time he left Frederikshåb in 1746. After that the colony was without a missionary for a year, partly because Sewerin was trying to get the place abandoned. A successor was sent out to the mission in 1747, and with him was a catechist who had previously done two years' good service at Frederikshåb. The missionary (a somewhat milder man than Sylow) and the catechist won the confidence of the local population, and the mission made progress despite difficult conditions.

Sylow had described "the Southerners" as more barbaric and wild than the Greenlanders who lived further north. It was said that retaliatory murders and the killing of witches occurred there more frequently than in the north. Neither the Godthåb district nor the Bay region was free from these gruesome manifestations of superstition and immemorial tradition. One retaliatory killing in Godthåb was that of a supposed *ilisîtsoq*, who was alleged to have killed the avenger's son by witchcraft. This supposed *ilisîtsoq* was the brother-in-law of Qajarnaq, so the Moravians were dragged into the affair, a complaint being lodged at the colony. There the missionaries and the Trading Company staff took up the matter and, together with the Moravians, succeeded in catching some of the killers who, after publicly admitting their complicity in killing this *ilisîtsoq*, were bound and beaten. According to the Moravian account, however, only those accomplices who had received instruction in Christianity were beaten, while the only one who had no knowlege of it was given a lesson in the Ten Commandments and released. This happened in 1739. The following year Niels Egede came to Godthåb and the sequence of events was recounted to him by the still aggrieved killers and their companions. They considered their punishment unjust because they had previously been told that sorcerers ought to die. Niels Egede sought to defend the conduct of the missionaries, traders and Moravians and pointed out that the punishment had been inflicted so as to protect other Greenlanders from a similar fate. It was right that people who, merely on the word of an *angákoq*, declared another to be an *ilisîtsoq* and killed him should suffer death themselves. In Denmark it was only the authorities who could try people for crimes and inflict penalties, whereas in this case the pastors had acted as the authorities. His hearers reacted to Niels Egede's discourse by saying "that they had just as much right to be executioners as we did".

Here was an important clash of views. One consequence was that for long afterwards the local inhabitants were reluctant to have anything to do with the mission. The clash also revealed the incompatibility of the Greenlandic and European concepts of justice. The Greenlanders felt themselves deeply wronged: they had been degraded by the flogging although, according to their own way of thinking and their traditional view of punishment, they had acted rightly and had openly admitted to killing an *ilisîtsoq*. Perhaps they thought too that their confession had disposed of the matter, as was the custom in the Eskimo world on both sides of the Davis Strait. The Europeans had on their side a tradition of submission to a judicial and punitive authority. They could not understand the Greenlanders' legal tradition. They were bound to protect their congregations and any people who allied themselves with them, and so fell back on preconceived and familiar notions. In this situation they must have felt keenly the absence of a higher temporal authority. The problem was insoluble and the conflict between the two cultures was intensified.

Poul Egede was exposed to similar though not quite such dangerous situations in Disko Bay, where, in 1739, the Greenlanders wanted him to arrange for a woman to be put to death because she had murdered her husband in order to marry another man. Poul Egede admitted that she ought to die, but he explained to those present that this could not be done without laws and a sentence ordered by the King, and he tried to explain the difficult principle that the accused·was to be regarded as innocent until found guilty beyond all doubt, and could only then be sentenced – "which they too had to admit was fair". Poul Egede had always disapproved of killing because of an *angákoq*'s denunciation of an *ilisîtsoq*. The killing of witches continued to take place both in the Bay and elsewhere along the coast of West Greenland.

What was and was not to be regarded as theft raised further problems. Once a young man broke into the house at Jakobshavn and took some bread. He did not think of this as theft because he was hungry; besides, the bread was just lying there not being used and was capable of "doing its duty" in regard to him. These differing views of what constituted a criminal act could only reach fusion after much time and conveyance over a far wider cultural area. This conveyance was only at a very early stage. The first European colonists completely lacked the experience that would enable them to act "rightly" in specific situations and they had to take action on the basis of their own traditions.

Outside the criminal sphere there was also confrontation between the Greenlandic and Danish legal traditions. A case in point was the law on marriage and above all the matter of monogamy versus polygamy. Poul Egede had once been obliged to intervene when a husband, to his wife's great displeasure, had taken a second wife. He told the Greenlanders present how a Danish–Norwegian wife would normally react if her husband took a mistress into the home. The viewpoint of the male Greenlander was stated clearly: "Then the womenfolk in your country must be foolish, since they want their men to themselves and want to make themselves masters over them. We speak ill of those of our women who are jealous – they are despicable and wicked".

The husband in question had given his first wife a black eye. Because of his Christian concept of morals, Poul Egede was bound to censure the men but "the women began to prick up their ears at that". The men reproached Poul Egede, saying "You are spoiling our women with your talk". When Poul Egede was leaving, the wife in question came up and gave him a piece of *beluga-mátak*.

Poul Egede, without being aware of it, was driving a wedge between the Greenlandic man and woman in the name of the European view of marriage, although his motive was purely humanitarian. The position of the Greenlandic woman in society was extremely insecure. The lucky one who bore sons and kept her "powers of attraction" for a long time sat firmly in the saddle as a wife, and as a widow she could act as an authoritative *itoq* (master of the house). Otherwise Poul Egede drew a depressing picture of the West Greenland woman's position. "The women get the worst of it. If a girl marries young, then she must put up with being called man-mad. If she waits too long, she is scarcely given house-room on account of her *angiak* (illegitimate child).[4] If she marries, she gets beaten if she is not obedient and mild and if she does not bear her husband children. If she becomes a widow, she must be the others' servant, rather their slave. Finally, if she reaches a great age, she is pronounced a witch, which is usually followed by stones and slaughter. Even after death she is destined to be tortured and tormented by ravens in the next world." Women could almost be said to be without rights, and subject to man's authority and the will of the settlement and of any *angákoq* that came along.

At a church wedding in Christianshåb a Greenlander expressed his point of view on hearing the formula of the sanctity of marriage. This brought to light a minor "conflict" between the two cultural traditions. According to ritual, the bride was supposed to say "yes" clearly in answer to the question whether she would take the bridegroom to be her husband. But the "yes" was only muttered softly "since it casts great shame on a virgin if she says "yes" when she is asked that". "Then they must have no modesty" was the verdict of those present on Danish brides when they were told that this "yes" was customary. This bashfulness has continued to be true of weddings right up to the present day. When the formula concerning indissolubility was pronounced, the visiting (i.e. unbaptized) Greenlanders thought that this would please the Greenlandic women, for then they could disobey their husbands without running the risk of being thrown out. So to the Greenlandic man this formula was an assault on the husband's authority and a threat to the stability of society.

As time went by, however, Greenlandic women were taken as their lawful wedded wives by colonists, and this had a good influence.

Before 1750 this had only happened in isolated cases like those of the catechists Johannes Pedersen Dorf and Jens Pedersen Mørk, both in Christianshåb in 1747. In practice the difference in legal status between the Greenlandic woman and her Danish contemporary was only slight.

The paradox was that in Greenland, as in other places, it was the women, especially the older ones, who, notwithstanding their low legal status, maintained tradition and resisted the introduction of new, unknown forces. In its early stages, colonization also caused a breach between the generations. The young people came to Godthåb to receive instruction in Christianity, whereas the old ones came "to come by some food and clothing". The young were happy to listen to the missionary and the old kept their countenance for a time, but when the missionary had gone, the old people laughed at the young. The older men defended themselves, "putting the blame on the old crones who always try to lead them astray . . .". However, this kind of conflict between the generations was not common.

The mission – and with it the influence of religious and intellectual culture – had a somewhat fitful career in the years 1721–50. A start had to be made in those sectors where contact could be established, allowing for the scattered population, members of which visited the colony for varying periods. It is impossible to draw a graph for the growth of the colonies and the royal mission – there were so many movements about the district or to the north or south. The Moravians alone could keep some statistics, as they deliberately gathered together the members of the congregation and the catechumens at Ny Herrnhut. Moreover, many Greenlanders moved to Ny Herrnhut from the south, Qajarnaq and his family coming from the most southernly part of Greenland.

The attraction of the colonies for the Greenlanders was the "social" arrangements that followed in the wake of the mission. People in distress and need turned to the colony; orphans were adopted. There was also, before 1750, a move away from the Greenlandic economy, with individual Greenlanders entering the service of the colonists as labourers or domestic servants. It was one thing to perform an occasional service (and there are many examples of these being performed by Greenlanders on their own initiative) but quite another to enter into permanent service for board and perhaps lodging with a corresponding wage in the form of merchandise. A man who entered into another's service was despised, and a Greenland labourer was thus a social outcast in the eyes of his fellow-countrymen.

Moreover, the independent *fanger* looked down on the European who tended the colony's cattle; it was even more undignified to be "the cattle's servant". Animals had to be treated with courtesy, but not waited on – this was the tradition of the Eskimo *fanger*. When hunting and fishing failed there were all kinds of explanations for the animals' absence, but all assumed that they had been "offended" in one way or another. An *angákoq* at Jakobshavn ice-fjord had visited an *arnaquagssáq* and eaten halibut with her, learning that the weather was so stormy that the seals had left the land because "the Jutes in Jutland were alleged to have played monkey-tricks with the blubber that came from Greenland the previous year"; the seals had been "offended". The idea that game animals should be treated with respect is common to all Eskimos. When Niels Egede, who relates this story, asked whether they really believed in it, they replied that everybody believed in it. He does not say how far "everybody" meant *inuit* (i.e. Eskimos) only, thus implying a repudiation of European ideas, or whether they meant people in general. The inhabitants of the Bugt and Central Greenland were once and for all placed between two cultures.

The thread of events which led to their occupying this position during the relatively short period from about 1710 to 1750 can only be glimpsed now and again; hence we can only speculate upon the reasons for it. Is it not possible that the wise "reflective" Greenlander indicated an important reason, or a complex of reasons, when in 1737 he compared the restricted nature of the small, isolated communities of West Greenland with the *qavdlunât's* world outside? Whether these *qavdlunât* were Danish–Norwegian, Dutch, English, Scots or Biscayan, to the Bay Greenlanders they must have presented a similar face which typified the world outside the realm of thought of the West Greenlanders. They were typified by the Danish–Norwegians especially, as they were always present and they had brought the mission.

All that was "new", both of a material and an intellectual-religious nature, flooded in on the coastal population. These foreigners acted in a way incomprehensible to the Eskimos of West Greenland. It was enough to note that these foreigners were "strange and odd-thinking,"[5] without trying to understand them, and so by virtue of the trait in Eskimo thinking that allows two or more contradictory elements to run parallel, it was possible not to bother to understand but merely to note. It is possible that this attitude accounted for what Hans and Poul Egede and many succeeding colonial officials in Greenland took for indifference. It is also possibly the reason why everything passed off with such relative lack of conflict. Perhaps too it explains why the Christian religion was able to co-exist among the baptized Greenlanders alongside all kinds of traditional "pagan" customs and views.

Added to the mission's repeated attacks on the weak Eskimo religious tradition was the pressure of outside economic factors: the ability to resist was reduced in step with increasing economic dependence.

T

REFERENCES

1. Poul Egede once blamed a woman, who prided herself on her faith, for cheerfully attending an *angákoq*'s séance, but caring less about attending a service. She answered: "This [the séance] is pleasant too!" (Poul Egede's *Continuation of the Relations*, MoG 120, p. 103, 22/4 1740.

2. This is quoted from his *Continuation of the Relations*, printed in 1741. In his *Efterretninger om Grønland* (Information about Greenland), 1788, he tells the story somewhat differently. Here the Greenlander says: "This is probably a lie as usual, isn't it?" Poul Egede affirming this, the Greenlander said: "I thought so!"

3. Niels Egede told this in his *Third Continuation of the Relations*, MoG 120, p. 162, written on 13 August, 1741, only seven years after the foundation of Christianshåb! Perhaps the children got the idea from Poul Egede who later (1788) narrated that he himself by means of such a "calendar stick" had been able in 1737 to "predict" the return of the sun on 9 January.

4. *Angiak* = *ángiaq* means, in modern West Greenlandic, "a child born clandestinely". In the Eskimo tradition such an "undue child" was bewitched and might cause failures in hunting and fishing. Very often all the inhabitants of an Eskimo settlement would endeavour to trace and find the corpse or abortive fœtus of such a child after a supposed clandestine birth.

5. This is a (translated) quotation from Poul Egede's above-mentioned (note 2) *Efterretninger* 1788, p. 133. In West Greenlandic a person said: "*Sillan okoa, ingmikut Isumaglit.*" This Poul Egede translated as "Those strange people, with their special way of thinking." *Sillan* sounds like a sort of exclamation, equivalent, say, to "Good gracious". The "correct" translation may then be: "Good gracious, strange beings with strange opinions!"

16

THE TRADING COMPANY:
EXPANSION AND ENDEAVOUR
1750–1774

Jacob Sewerin did not have the capital himself, and did not receive the financial backing, which would have enabled him to expand the business in Greenland. The inadequate capital contribution by the authorities was probably due in part to the Government's reluctance to become involved in this remote, risky and in every way extraordinary undertaking. From the start the Government had had to be dragged into the venture, despite all the historical, constitutional and political motives and Christian obligations which were present, but the crown was forced, step by step into an ever-increasing involvement.

Expansion of trade in Greenland was essential if the venture were ever to be profitable. For Sewerin this choice was difficult, both personally and economically – personally, because he felt committed to the Government, the mission and the Greenlanders too and probably towards the Egedes as well, and financially since he had a record of losses behind him, and had little hope of future success. Economic resources of a quite different order were needed and the Government thought it could find these in the Royal Chartered General Trading Company.

As we have seen, this Company was established in 1747 as the result of a number of considerations, one being the desire to centralize the trade, to some extent in defiance of Copenhagen's merchants, who appear to have been more liberally inclined. However, only centralization of foreign trade had been envisaged so that when the Trading Company was formed, it dealt with sectors of this export and import business.

The capital was fixed at 500,000 rdl. divided into 1,000 shares. The amount of each share was to be subscribed by instalments as called for, thus following the principle adapted for the Bergen Company, in which Magnus Schiøtte had proposed in 1731. However, it was difficult to get this to function smoothly. Between 1747 and 1749

273

only about 300,000 rdl. had actually been subscribed. The Company did not dare to call in the last two instalments; instead, an attempt was made to survive by means of loans, preferably from the shareholders or some other form of credit. They did not venture to call in the fourth instalment until 1757, but the result of this was that the shareholders began to sell off their shares at low prices. The Trading Company bought up these shares but this did not increase its capital. It could not be self-financing, since the profits were too low.

When, therefore, the Iceland and Finnmark trade was transferred to it in 1763, a further injection of capital was required, first 200 rdl. and then a further 100 rdl per share. The subscriptions were slow in coming in, and in the meantime everything had to be borrowed. In 1773 the Kurantbank, which was being hard pressed from other directions, demanded payment of the 270,000 rdl. due to it.

This quick review of the Trading Company's financial position illustrates the difficulty of obtaining adequate capital in eighteenth-century Denmark although, apart from a fairly short period, economic conditions for trade and shipping were favourable during the time the Trading Company was in existence. Although it had extensive commitments outside Greenland, east, west and south, its capital resources and potential were much greater than those of Jacob Sewerin. In 1749/50, when the Greenland trade was transferred to it, it was even a company in which there were confident expectations.

Neither the management nor the shareholders as a whole had any special qualifications for entering the Greenland trade. As mentioned previously, only one of the directors, Holmsted, had been in any way connected with the problems of trading with Greenland, but he had already retired from the management of the Trading Company in 1752. The shareholders, big or small, were Copenhagen merchants – wholesalers, a few land-owners, some military men and well-to-do clergymen, and some senior and junior civil servants. Only a few high-ranking civil servants in the central administration had any official experience of Greenland affairs. There is every sign that the Company took over the Greenland trade, not from any burning wish to do so but because of Government pressure. Three members of the royal family were among the shareholders, owning some 8 per cent of the shares. They exerted no direct influence, but the royal presence made itself felt indirectly, the Danske *Cancelli*'s inquiry about the taking over of the Greenland *Dessein* reflected the Government's and hence the King's wishes. Thus, when the Trading Company decided to take over the Greenland trade, this may have been a return for the many advantages derived by the Company from its close contact with the authorities.

During the negotiations in 1749, leading up to this new commitment, the Trading Company directors stipulated that they should receive the same annual State subsidy of 5,000 rdl. as Sewerin had done after the last extension of the charter, and on the same conditions. With this transfer to the Trading Company of the trade, sailings and supplying of the mission, there was no longer any hint of a crisis – trading, sailing and the mission were in no danger of being abandoned. Such progress had been made by 1750 that their continuance was beyond dispute. In 1752 an extension was granted for six years and approval was given for the continued payment of the 5,000 rdl. for 1752/3. In 1758, a licence valid until the June 1768 was obtained, after which extensions were apparently granted almost automatically until the Trading Company's activities came to an end.

The Trading Company obtained an increase of the subsidy in October 1756, amounting to 2,000 rdl. a year, of which a quarter was to go to the mission. This increase took account of the fact that several stations had been established and their operation had increased spending on the mission as well as on trading and sailings; rising prices over the years also warranted a bigger subsidy. From 1750 to 1773, the last year in which the Trading Company undertook sailings to Greenland, the State paid a total of 169,891 rdl. to the Company. The colonies established earlier had been taken over without their capital value being assessed but with the obligation to maintain them.

Time after time it had been urged that more colonies should be established along the West coast so as to form an unbroken chain from north to south, mainly so that the mission could achieve closer contact with the Greenlanders and so achieve its aims; at the same time it could check their "roaming". Stations further south would also prepare the way for a southward movement around Cape Farewell with a view to reaching the imagined Eastern Settlement. More colonies could increase the volume of the trade; purchase from the Greenlanders would increase, and products otherwise wasted or sold to the Dutch would be made profitable. Finally, a close-knit chain of colonies would help to crowd out the Dutch following on the royal proclamations of April 1740 and April 1744.

The establishment of new settlements, whether colonies or so-called stations, occurred during the life of the Trading Company more or less in three periods of activity – 1752–6, 1758–63 and 1771–4. During the first period there was the Claushavn station north of Christianshåb (1752), then the Fiskenæsset station halfway between Godthåb and Frederikshåb (1754). In order to capture the trade in the Bay, Ritenbenk was established on the Nûgssuaq peninsula (1755) where the station of Sarqaq now stands. At the same time a thrust was made against what had hitherto been the Dutch headquarters at Sydbay, by

first rather cautiously approaching it from the south with the establishment of Sukkertoppen near the present station of Kangâmiut (1755).
After that they took the bull by the horns and established a whaling
station at Sydbay itself (1756). The next settlement period began with
the Company venturing further out through the Vajgat and establishing the Nûgssuaq station. This barren site existed as a station only
from 1758 to 1761, when it was moved to Umánaq. Meanwhile on
the coast between the Bay and Sydbay, the colony Egedesminde was
established in 1759 in Eqalugssuit Bay, 35 km. north of Nordre Strøm-
fjord. South of Sydbay another whaling station, Amerdloq, was set
up in 1759. A little further to the west, Holsteinborg was established
in 1764. The third period included Upernavik (1771), Godhavn (1773)
and, last of all, the plan for the establishment of Julianehåb (1774).
The last two were set up when the Trading Company was virtually
on its last legs, and Julianehåb was not finally recognized until 1776.

From this brief catalogue of the new settlements, the policy adopted
by the Trading Company, emerges. In the first period this was mainly
to secure the Bay, fill the empty space between this and Godthåb,
and finally set up a station on the way south to the Frederikshåb colony
which was difficult to reach by ship. In the second period the policy
was continued of first filling the area between Kangâmiut and the Bay,
and of venturing right into the heart of the competitors' territory. As
the Dutch had already begun as early as the 1740s to sail to the coast
north of Nûgssuaq, this was followed up by the establishment of the
northern settlements. Last of all came the most northerly and the most
southerly ventures of the century. Here there was not so much risk of
competition from the Dutch.

The struggle against foreign trading – contraband, as it was called –
was almost fruitless. This was because the relationship between the
Dutch and the Greenlanders always had this strange dual quality of
attraction and repulsion. The same applied to the Trading Company's
relationship with the colonists. It seems that even its own people sometimes disobeyed the strict ban on any form of association with foreign
ships except in emergencies, which was implicit in the charters and
was extended to apply to the takeover by the Trading Company, as
well as being expressly set out in both the royal proclamation of 9 April
1740, and its renewal in 1744. But it was almost impossible for the directors to prevent the colonists from trading with the foreigners. They
were nevertheless made responsible for seeing that the Greenlanders
were not in collusion with them. The missionaries felt obliged to report
home about this – no doubt as a sort of defence against their being
occasionally accused of underhand trading with the local Greenlanders "to the Company's detriment". The problem of illicit trading,

moreover, also became a source of increased friction between the missionaries and the Trading Company officials.

The directors could do no more than impose a few ineffectual measures against illicit trading by foreigners. The best remedy against competition was to send out the best possible goods, reasonably priced, and see that as much as possible was sold to and collected from the districts, so that there was nothing to sell to the foreigners, and the trade would thus dwindle away of its own accord. The latter course was specially recommended to the trader in Egedesminde after this colony had been moved northwards in 1763; foreign traders had arrived at Gammel (Old) Egedesminde. Apart from keeping a watchful eye on any foreign traders who might approach the colonial districts, the Company traders were admonished to "deal well and kindly with both Greenlanders and the people of the colony, we regard as being the best means of keeping the Greenlanders both from wandering and trading with foreigners".

When N. C. Geelmuyden went out in 1750 to investigate the state of the colonies, he reported "the extremely harmful trade carried on in this country by the Dutch to the great detriment of the illustrious Company". Not only the traders but also the whalers were competitors since the latter brought with them big chests full of "flints, also gunpowder and shot in abundance which they sell to the Greenlanders at a low and miserable profit". It was thought, however, that this trade was carried on not so much at the behest of the shipowners but more on the captains' own initiative. Nevertheless, this caused the Greenlanders to frequent the places where the Dutch came, and there to sell their goods, for which the Dutch paid more than had hitherto been possible for the Danish traders. "This causes the Greenlanders to detest and have contempt for us, to the extreme detriment both of the traders and the mission. . . . It is absolutely essential for the Dutch to be reminded once more not to carry on trade in this land". He even cautiously suggests forcible means like Sewerin's armed merchantmen in the late 1730s. This caution was due to the circumspection necessary in relations with the Dutch. A rider to the proclamation of 9 April 1740/4, which was still in force, expressly excepted "His Majesty's colonies in Greenland", together with the other northern possessions of the Danish–Norwegian King, for the first time. This was contained in a commercial treaty with France dated 23 August 1742. This exception clause is seen again in the "Friendship, Trade and Shipping Treaty" with Genoa signed in Paris on 13 March, 1756, in which all the most northerly land regions were barred even to the most friendly and most favoured nations.[1] However, this practice does not seem to have been continued in commercial treaties later in the century.

Although it was now not really necessary, the Government felt obliged in 1751 to define more precisely the boundaries of its colonies and stations present or future. The boundary was to extend 112·5 km. on either side of each colony; in addition, all islands in Disko Bay were expressly named from the outlying Vester Ejlande and including Kronprinsens Ejland, Hvalfiske Ejlande, as they were then called, as far to the north-east as Zwarte Vogel Bay, a long inlet in the middle of the west coast of Arveprinsens Ejland. Hence almost the whole of the Bay was barred with the exception of the waters round Disko and the passage through the Vajgat.

The decree of 1751 apparently did not restrict the foreign traders' activities: the Government did not even know of their existence and, if it did, took no notice. With peaceful intentions and to escape the ice, six Dutch ships put in at Godthåb in 1752 while nine vessels of the same fleet were locked in the ice. The crews of the ships which had put in behaved well, but the Greenlanders both from the Herrnhutter congregation and from Godthåb went aboard. There was sickness on the ships and a disastrous epidemic followed, in which many died.

When N. C. Geelmuyden, this time as chief trader, went out in 1753 to inspect the Bay colonies, he was given orders to look out for "contraband traders", with authority to capture ships engaged in illicit trading and take them as prizes to Copenhagen. In 1754 the captains of the Trading Company's vessels received similar orders. One of these captains was about to establish the colony of Ritenbenk at Sarqaq on Nûgssuaq. His ship was well armed and to give his actions royal confirmation he took the proclamation with him.

Talk still circulated on the subject of kidnappings. It was reported from two sources that the father of a family living in Frederikshåb had been kidnapped near Godthåb by a Dutch whaler, and in the report the trader described the Dutch trading as being more and more intolerable. He also reported English "contraband traders", one of whom had sailed up and down the coast throughout the spring and "plundered from the Greenlanders at various places".

Lars Dalager, the trader in Godthåb, thought that it was also English whalers (and "contraband traders") who in 1756 had "snatched away" all the whaling products just inside the northern colony boundary. In that year the Dutch made off with blubber and whalebone from five whales in the region around Sydbay and a foreigner again attempted to kidnap a Greenlander from Godthåb. This foreigner was an "American", i.e. a whaler from the British colonies in North America. That undertaking failed, whereas the captain's "contraband trading", which was described as "piracy", had apparently succeeded.

This vigilance against the foreign traders was crowned with success in 1756 when a Dutch whaler and "contraband trader" was captured. The vessel was taken to Copenhagen and declared a prize, as it had been engaged exclusively in prohibited trading. The Trading Company urged the foreign department of the *Tyske Cancelli*, of which the director was Johan H. E. Bernstorff, to act, but without any immediate result. In March 1758 the Trading Company took the matter up with the King. This was done especially because it was intended to establish a colony on the extremity of Nûgssuaq, the northern boundary of which would extend almost to 73°N.; the decree of 1751 should therefore be tightened up to apply to "all harbours and places in general without exception, whether on the land together with the surrounding islands, or beyond for a certain distance from the land". The territorial waters are fixed at four miles (30 km). The ban imposed by all previous proclamations and decrees on unauthorized trading and the use of force against the population was repeated and reinforced in the proclamation of 22 April 1758, while its scope was extended as the Directors had requested. The proclamation was published in 1759, which led to protests from the Dutch. After three years of diplomatic activity the matter ended in the settlement of 1762. The ban on trading could stand but whaling would not be prevented. There must be no coastal navigation and no putting into port except in an emergency or to take on fresh water. The Danish–Norwegian position as set out in the proclamation of 1758 was thus affirmed, and this through Anglo–French mediation, hence these two countries also indirectly recognized the closure of the coast. In pace with the establishment of colonies, the West coast was gradually closed by right. The Danish–Norwegian Government considered it was entitled to grant a trading and navigation monopoly to a single commercial undertaking within the dual monarchy – Greenland continued to be constitutionally a dependency under the Norwegian crown. As in previous proclamations and decrees, protection of the inhabitants' lives and property was to be guaranteed. The protective monopoly continued to grow throughout the eighteenth century.

Proclamations, agreements and constitutional instruments are one thing, but what occurs in practice is another. The directors of the Trading Company had only a slender hope that the proclamation would have the desired effect even if all the servants of the Company did their duty; but reports were received from the Missionskollegium accusing the trading officials of illicit trading with the foreigners. Publication of the proclamation abroad seems to have had an immediate favourable effect. No Dutch coastal navigation was reported at Sukkertoppen in 1761 and the directors of the Trading Company expressed the hope, in consequence, that the Greenlanders would

wander less without the incentive of Dutch trading. But both the hopes
and the agreement came to naught. However, as early as 1765, and in
the following years, the directors had to face the fact that the foreign
traffic on the coast was continuing as before. Both the missionaries and
the traders continually reported the presence of foreign illicit traders –
Dutch, English and French.[2] In order to close the Bay completely, the
directors decided in 1773 to establish a station on Disko, as the local
trade officials had urged for some time.

Thus the monopoly of the Trading Company expired without having
achieved more than a negligible restraint on the foreign trading and
navigation activities. Indeed, the problems become more complicated
and difficult because the English and French "illicit traders" were
becoming more aggressive. There were also difficulties with the Trading Company's own people. Although their cheating was only on a
small scale, the directors were for ever on the look-out. Any loop-holes
in the monopoly had to be closed and therefore they attacked Peder
Olsen Walløe's free trade activities. Under the licence given him by
Jacob Sewerin he had continued his itinerant trading as though there
had been no change in the operation of the monopoly. But his business
did not now give him the expected return. When he undertook a private expedition north from Godthåb in 1749 he acquired a quantity
of baleen and fox and seal skins. In exchange most Greenlanders
wanted firearms and ammunition. He had himself preached against
the sale of firearms, but he overcame his scruples. The same skins that
he had acquired were a bitter thorn in the flesh of the Trading Company
directors, because Sewerin's agreement with Walløe obliged the trader
to pay him more for the skins than the normal market price.

In 1749–50 Walløe made a long journey south through the Frederikshåb district. All those living in the south were now being supplied
by him, and the skins which these southerners would otherwise have
brought to Frederikshåb or further north were acquired by Walløe,
and the trade then had to buy them afterwards from him at a higher
price. There was a chance that this free trading activity might spread.
N. C. Geelmuyden reported that some of the "common men" from
home stationed in the colony, who had married Greenlandic women,
were thinking of going into business with Walløe. To stop this the Trading Company took Walløe into its service – to make a reconnaissance of
southernmost West Greenland. This journey was bound up with the
Trading Company's settlement programme, in which the new settlements intended for the area south of Frederikshåb were only lightly
touched on. A closer investigation there was necessary before detailed
planning or decisions were possible. Hans Egede had recommended
that the Trading Company should delegate the reconnaissance work to

Walløe, who could at the same time try to round "Hukken" and proceed up the east coast to the Eastern Settlement. Hans Egede's inextinguishable hope of seeing his original object brought to fruition had driven him to abandon his otherwise withdrawn existence.

In the summer of 1751 Walløe set out on the hazardous journey by *umiak*. He wintered where the town of Julianehåb now stands, rounded Cape Farewell the following summer and reached an island north of Lindenovs Fjord on the East coast despite ice difficulties. But here the pack-ice stopped him, and he turned back. In June 1753 he was again on the West coast at Frederikshåb, but this time he returned to Denmark, never to come again to Greenland.

At the Trading Company offices dust gathered on Walløe's reports. The directors had shelved the whole matter for the time being. When Anders Olsen, the trader from Sukkertoppen, came back in 1759 to the idea of a colonial settlement in the far south, the directors replied that it had been decided not to proceed with the matter "on account of the . . . virtual impossibility of sailing to this station annually". Reference was made to information already to hand, including Walløe's diaries. However, the captains who sailed these waters each year would be required to investigate the ice conditions. When the plan was reverted to in 1764, it was still felt that insufficient information was available, and the traders at Sukkertoppen, Godthåb and Frederikshåb were requested to collect further details, particularly about the ice. The next year Lars Dalager in Godthåb was again told that not enough information had been collected. They dared not pass a resolution yet to put the plan into effect. Walløe went to live on Bornholm and was completely forgotten for some twenty years or so.

In their relations with the free-traders the Trading Company directors were not always consistent. Two of Sewerin's "Nordland fellows", the brothers Anders and Hans Olsen, had expressed a desire to settle somewhere and carry on private trading. This time the directors did not object and promised to support them if they settled at Kangâmiut-Sukkertoppen – Hans Olsen was even promised higher prices for skins. In the winter of 1752–3 the two brothers had stayed there, finding greater opportunities for buying because they had enough goods to give in exchange. Now they returned to Godthåb, where Anders Olsen once again worked for the trader. Hans on the other hand, wanted to manage on his own by trading further north in 1754. Both intended to resume their free trading sooner or later. The Trading Company, too, had thought that, with the Olsens' help, a trading post could be established at Kangâmiut–Sukkertoppen on the cheap, but on a free trader basis this failed.

The Trading Company gave Anders Olsen another problem to solve.

In 1754 Lars Dalager was back in their service, this time as trader in Godthåb. That same year, under his supervision, Anders Olsen as senior assistant established the Fiskenæsset station. The two of them also had the job of considering where the colony north of Godthåb should be located. Thus the following year Anders Olsen was appointed trader in order to establish the Sukkertoppen colony on the very site where he had lived with his brother in 1752–3: Kangâmiut. This time the Trading Company had to bear the expenses and arrange for the necessary materials for house-building to be sent out.

Like the settlements in Disko Bay, the establishment of Sukkertoppen was a link partly in "covering" the coast and partly in the attempts to procure a profitable share of the Greenlanders' whaling catch. The settlement at Sydbay in 1756, on the other hand, was a further link in the Trading Company's own more comprehensive whaling activity. In mercantile circles whaling was looked on as a source of financial profit. If it could be carried on "internally" it would contribute to a favourable balance of trade, since it called for small imports but – so it was hoped – yielded high export values. Behind the formation of the Trading Company there probably also lay the idea that it would carry on the whaling *and* take over of the Greenland Trade.

In 1749 the Trading Company had already started active whaling around Svalbard and off the West Greenland coast. Four ships were bought for this purpose. The yield fluctuated and towards 1756 the general feeling among the participants and the directors was that this side of the business should be given up. With a State subsidy an attempt was made to carry on but the yield was no better on that account and in 1758 this form of whaling was given up completely.

It was by then a long time since Niels Egede had put forward his suggestion that whaling be carried on together with the Greenlanders at Christianshåb. From 1745 he was employed as weigher, measurer and sorter at Ålborg and as such was not directly concerned with Greenland and its problems, but he could not keep away from what had occupied him for so many years, and may have heard of the Trading Company's difficulties over whaling. He did not, however, wish to go to Christianshåb himself, but wanted simply to pass on information as to his methods. He sent his suggestion, improbably, to the Missions-kollegium, who asked for further details and also whether he would be willing to make the first journey himself. Niels Egede immediately gave a detailed account of his idea; he was thinking of several *umiaks*, working together, each manned by six to eight persons, including one armed with a harpoon to which a large bladder was fastened. When the whale had been killed it would be towed to the nearby flensing vessel, and not to the land, for the whale might thereby sink, and ashore many people might want – and take – their share of it, so that none would be left for the trade. This could not be stopped as it was the custom. As for himself, he could envisage taking up his duties again, but only on the first voyage and with a guarantee of being able to return to his post in Ålborg. Thereupon the Missionskollegium decided that they could not adopt the suggestion on account of the difficulties involved "especially since [the Trading] Company was involved". It might be possible to return to the matter later.

Niels Egede assured the Company that his proposal was not to be interpreted as an encroachment on the Trading Company's rights, his sole purpose being "the advancement of the country and relieving His Majesty of the high costs which are incurred each year". He now had "an intense desire to see my most humble proposal crowned with success". He then offered, with some support from the King, to charter a ship himself and, without interfering with the Trading Company's rights, test his proposal in practice. The Missionskollegium apparently dared not join in this venture, for the last letter from Niels Egede does not seem to have even been discussed at any meeting. The matter therefore died out – on this occasion.

The directors of the Trading Company were presumably unaware of this correspondence, of which no trace has been found in the Company's papers. However, the directors had the same idea when Sydbay was established. The senior assistant was sent a pinnace with the necessary whaling implements "in order, with the help of the Greenlanders (during the coming winter, to carry out a trial)". On arrival at Sydbay the senior assistant, who had now been appointed trader, took it as a good omen for the success of the whaling that all the Greenlanders' winter houses there were provided with rafters of whalebone instead of driftwood fences. To be sure, twenty or thirty dwellings had been abandoned because a number of the inhabitants had died of an epidemic which had spread there from the north a few years before, and others had fled for the same reason.

The following year the trader had another pinnace sent out with whaling implements, together with two labourers who were certainly not skilled whalers. The directors had hoped to be able to find such persons, but had not had any success. In other words, there was no question of collaboration between the Greenlanders and the whalers as suggested by Niels Egede, nor was there in succeeding years even after the establishment of Amerdloq in 1759 in the fjord east of the present Holsteinsborg. The following year the director insisted on the trader at Sydbay – who was noted for being tough with his subordinates as well as with the Greenland inhabitants – proceeding with caution, should the post's whalers get hold of a whale which had already been harpooned by Greenland catchers. In this case the trader must try to get the matter settled as best he could, either by buying that part of the whale to which "the inhabitants" might rightly and fairly be entitled, or by dividing it in a way which did not give rise to antagonism between the trading people and "them". "For the Company's interests must be considered, but without wronging the inhabitants as this might have harmful consequences for the future. . . ." By the very fact of expressly writing "the inhabitants" and "them", and not the Greenland catchers who had first struck the whale, the directors made it clear that they wanted full consideration to be given to the local catch-sharing customs. This bears witness to the fact that, on the one hand, the men at the top showed some understanding of the Greenlanders' etiquette and customs and, on the other hand, desired that due consideration be given to the Greenlanders, hence also to protect them economically. Perhaps "the understanding" was tinged with the profit motive, for it had been known for a whole whale to slip through the trade's hands.

Meanwhile Niels Egede had returned to service in Greenland. Tired of his straitened financial circumstances in Alborg, he had applied to return there. In 1759, with the honorary rank of captain in the infantry, he travelled to the northern part of the West coast to establish a new colony between Sydbay and Disko Bay. In August he was able to report home that it had been set up in a good place – a better one, he believed, than the directors had specified. They for their part were not so enthusiastic, but had to put up with it. They also agreed to the name suggested by him for the new colony – Egedesminde – just as, with some hesitation, the name Holsteinsborg was approved for Sydbay, although in both cases it was the mission people, Hans Egede and J. L. Holstein, who were being commemorated. The chairman of the Trading Company, Count C. A. von Berckentin, had his name perpetuated anagramatically in the colony at Sarqaq, Ritenben(c)k.

At Egedesminde there was no question of whaling based on Niels Egede's proposal of 1754; the Trading Company was apparently unaware of his ideas or did not want to put them into effect. Whatever the circumstances, the new colony was not a success and in 1761 he was transferred as trader to Sydbay–Holsteinsborg, where he found himself in the thick of the whaling. This seemed most successful off the more southerly Amerdloq, to which Sydbay was moved in 1764, and set up at Ulkebugt west of the Amerdloq station. With a short interval (1764–7) Niels Egede and his family lived here until he went home in 1782. In 1776 his son Jørgen took over as trader.

Although Niels Egede was certainly zealous in managing the Holsteinsborg whaling, it did not meet with the success anticipated. It is true that a number of Greenlanders moved to the station, but the catch was poor at times and so few seals were caught that there was a shortage of skins for clothes and boats. There was occasional collaboration with the local Greenland *fangers* and *umiaks* were used for whaling. Hence to some extent Niels Egede's ideas were put into practice, but the result was not brilliant.

In 1762 the whaling was a failure but in 1763 six whales were caught. In 1765 the trader had to turn over to the Greenlanders the only whale caught to relieve their total lack of food and heating. In 1766 and 1767 the catch failed completely. In 1768, on the other hand, one whale was caught and three dead ones were obtained which yielded 150 barrels of blubber and 900 of baleen after the Greenlanders had received their share. There is no detailed information until 1772 when four large whales and one small one were obtained.

Niels Egede's deep interest in the promotion of whaling found expression in his improvement of the harpoon then in use. The directors of the Trading Company had this harpoon made in Copenhagen and sent it to Greenland in 1763. It is thought that his idea was a harpoon with several barbs. This made it heavier than its predecessor, so that the directors doubted whether it could be implanted in the whale manually. Often the Greenland whalers hit a whale but it would then disappear with harpoon, line and bladder. The directors thought the bladders must therefore be too small. They could not afford the considerable loss of tackle, so they urged Niels Egede to try and prevail on the whalers to use not only the largest obtainable bladders but two of them at once; in return, the Greenlanders could be sure of a good supply of tackle and strong lines. This however, was not easy since the Greenlanders believed that one bladder was "just as good as twenty-four", as the missionary H. C. Glahn wrote when a Greenlander implanted the second harpoon with bladder into a whale in the spring of 1768. This is typical of the way they came up against the West Greenland catching traditions when trying to introduce what, to European eyes, were more rational methods. Tradition in such an activity was the more difficult to change because of its religious associations.

The fluctuating success of the whaling and the sparse opportunities for making catches led to instability in the population of the settlement. It was essential for the continuation of whaling that there should be enough crew members available. An attempt had been made in 1762 to persuade those who had moved away to return; and in 1765–6, when the catch was poor and the need great – apart from the short period when people had made the most of a single whale – all who had moved in went away again. In 1767–8 there only remained those Greenlanders who had been baptized, the catechumens and four of the "heathens", who were willing to take part in the whaling. All the others left Holsteinsborg. At this station it was important to keep the Greenland population together on account of the whaling, which moreover, was of benefit to the mission.

Thus the Trading Company never made any reasonably large or stable profit from whaling in and off Greenland. In 1764 C. C. Dalager, the trader at Ritenbenk, suggested that this colony should be moved from Sarqaq to Klokkerhuk, the south-west tip of the large island in Disko Bay which later received the name of Arveprinsens Ejland (its Greenlandic name is unknown, if it ever existed). Klokkerhuk is clearly a Dutch name. Whaling would be attempted here. The directors did not agree to this immediately, no doubt because of the uncertainty of whaling at Holsteinsborg, but also presumably because they did not feel in a position to cope with any more financial burdens associated with whaling. In 1767, after years when whaling at Holsteinsborg had apparently failed, the directors ordered C. C. Dalager – without moving Ritenbenk – to try to catch whales off Klokkerhuk. They also sent men from Holsteinsborg to the colony of Egedesminde, which had been moved northwards in 1763, to try out, there too, the possibilities of whaling "from land". If possible the crew and the pinnaces from Egedesminde were to go whaling off Klokkerhuk. These whaling attempts were unsuccessful.

The reasons for the whaling failures can only be guessed at. Probably the crewmen were too few and had insufficient experience, and too little had been invested in boats and whaling tackle. The losses and the fiasco with the whaling ships in 1750–8 had shown that the coastal resources of the Trading company which were large by Danish–Norwegian standards, were not sufficient to finance such an operation. The big catches made by foreign whalers were due to a much greater investment with more and bigger ships, better and more plentiful equipment, more skilled men on board and a greater number of ordinary seamen. Once again the Danish–Norwegian lack of capital barred the way to a natural development of productive activities.

Efforts were made by the Trading Company to discover on that coastline which was specially allocated to it other commercial opportunities requiring less capital. When the plans were being made to establish the whaling colony at Sydbay, the trader was asked to investigate the potentialities of salmon and cod fishing. N. C. Geelmuyden supplied the information; he differentiated between fishing that could only be of advantage to the country's inhabitants and that on which the trade might make a profit. Fishing for "sea-trout and, to some extent, small salmon" (presumably meaning salmon and char) was worthwhile if done rationally with line or net. He described the

3. Dwelling-house at Christianshåb, photographed in 1941.

4. 'Soldier'. Painted wood carving, believed to have been executed by Poul Egede. The plaque is fixed over the door of the dwelling-house above.

I. N. J.

ELEMENTA
FIDEI CHRISTIANÆ,

in qvibus
In Grônlandorum Vernacula propo-
nuntur :

1. Ordo Salutis.

2. Catechismus Lutheri.

3. Precatiunculæ qvædam &Pſalmi.

item:

4. Formula Baptitzandi adultos &
Infantes.

In uſum Chriſtianæ Grônlandicæ Ju-
ventutis.

Collecta per

H. E.

———————————————————

Hafniæ 1742,

Evangelium

Okaufek tuffarnerfok

ʒub Niarnanik Innungortomik,
okaufianiglo, Ufornartuleniglo, tokomel-
lo umarmello, Killaliarmello, Innuin
annauniartlugit, aggerromartomiglo,
tokorfut tomafa umartitfar-
tortlugit.

Karalit okaufiet attuartlugo

aglekpaka

Paul Egede.

Kongib Iglorperkfoarne, Kiöbenhavnme,
1744.

26. Title page of Poul Egede's translation of the Gospels, 1744. (Royal Library, Copenhagen.)

. Eight of the Ten Commandments in
oul Egede's Catechism and ABC, 1757.
Royal Library, Copenhagen.)

Kol-lit Gub o-kau-fit mal-lig-
ek-fa-vut.
Si-ur-lek o-kau-fek ta-mei-pok:
Al-la-mik Gud kai-feng-i-la-tit, u-
ang-a kis-fi-ma Gud-i-o-vung-a.
O-kau-fi-et ai-pa.
Gub ak-ka tei-ner-ly-feng-i-let; Gub
ping-i-fu-i-feng-i-la ak-ka-nik mit-tar-
tok.
O-kau-fek ping-a-ju-et.
Sab-bat (ul-lut ar-bang-et ai-pet)
er-ka-vi-uk.
O-kau-fek fis-fa-mat.
Ang-u-til-lo arng-nel-lo nal-leis-fo-
a:kit, a-jor-feng-e-kul-lu-tit, nu-na-
mil-lo in-u-to-kang-o-kul-lu-tit.
O-kau-fek tel-li-mat.
In-nung-nut to-kot-fi-fa-rau-nek.
O-kau-fi-a ar-bang-et.
Arng-nau-na-ka-ri-a-rau-nek, ang-
un-nun-er-te-ka-ri-a-rau-neg-lo.
Ar-bang-et ai-pet o-kau-fi-a.
Tig-lis-fa-rau-nek.
Ar-bang-et ping-a-ju-et.
In-mu-ka-tit feg-lu-tig-is-fa-rau-
na-go.

XX 2   2·

CATECHISMUS LUTHERI.

Pars Ima.

Decalogus ɔ: Inneitſiſit Kollit.

Qv. I. Iſumavtivnik piſſaugut?
Rſ. Nagga, Gud Pingortiſirſavut, Attata-
vut, Nallegarput Inneitſiſeinik kollenik py-
atigut. Okauſit tauko kollit malligekſavut
v: malligomarpavut.

Qv.2.Siurlek okauſek ɔ: Inneitſit,kannoepa?

Rſ. Imeipok: Allamik Gud kaiſeng-
ilatit, uanga kiſſima Gudigogama.

Qv. 3. Sumik Gud pekorſengila Inneitſimi-
ne Siurlerme?

Rſ. Gudipillunik pekorſengilak ɔ: Gudi-
ungitſut nallekkongilei aſſakonnagillo tet-
tigakonnagillo.

Qv.4. Sumigme pekorſya?

Rſ. Ingminut kiſſiet neglekovok eikſig-
ekullunilo nallekkullunilo tettigekovok.

Qv.5. Okauſien aipa kanno epa?

Rſ. Imeipok: Nullekauet Gudivin
akka teinerlyſſengilet,Nallekab ping-
itſuiſengimago akkanik teinerluktok
ɔ: mittartok.

Qv.6.Su-

---

28 and 29 (opposite). Page from the *Elementa Fidei Christianae*, showing the Ten Commandments; questions and answers concerning the Second and Third Commandments. (Royal Library, Copenhagen.)

15

Qv. 6. Sumik Gud pekorſengila Inneitſiſin
aipane?

Rſ. Atterminik teinerlukorſengileik ɔ:
mittekkorſengilak. Immennalo: Serrakong-
ilatigut tornakonnatalo ſeglokorſengilak.

Qv. 7. Tameiliortut ɔ: Serrarſullo kannok
piſſoagit?

Rſ. Pingitſuiſengilei-og, akſorſoarle pit-
 jaromarpei.

Qv. 8. Kanngme pekkoatigut?

Rſ. Ajorſoranguta Gud kennubigiſoar-
put, uſorallugo kytkiuvigallugolo.

Qv. 9. Okauſek pingajuet kannœpa?

Rſ. Imeipok: Sabath ɔ: kaſſuerſarbium
ullua (v: ullut arbanget aipa) erkagiuk
helliggllugo.

Qv. 10. Suna pekoau?

Rſ. Sabath kaſſuerſarbium ullua (teima
attekarpok Gub ullok tauna Sorarmet Sil-
larſoak tamat ſennegarniuk ullun arbeneg-
lit) erkakullugo helligekullugolo, immen-
na: ullok naulugo Gum okauſe tuſſaromi-
neiſavut nalleklugit atlello ajokarſorlugit.

Qv. 11. Suname pekongilau?

Rſ. Sennakongilatigut ullok arbanget aipane, okauſelo aſſiginneiſengilavut.

Qv. 12.

Perfpectivifche Zeichnung von Neu-Herrnhuth in Grönland.

Perfpectivifche Zeichnung von Lichtenfels in Grönland.

Andreas Söfer sculpsit.

30. Views of Ny Herrnhut and Lichtenfels—certainly much embellished. After Cranz, *History of Greenland*. (Royal Library, Copenhagen.)

31. Matthæus Stach, by Karl Muller: 'Der Weg des M. Stach', Berlin, 1926. (MoG 129, I, fig. 37.)

32. Holsteinborg's first church.   (Photo J. Møller, *c.* 1910; Arctic Institute, Gentofte, Denmark.)

33. Jakobshavn church on its original site. (Photo *c.* 1912; Arctic Institute, Gentofte, Denmark.)

34. Niels Egede, probably his only existing portrait, a privately-owned pastel. (MoG 120, p. 123.)

35. Poul Egede. According to the signature, this is J. F. Clemens' original drawing for the etching by P. E. Efterr. Dr. Bobé suggests in MoG 120, I, p. 330, as does H. Ostermann, in D. biogr. L. VI, p. 228, that the portrait is part of a painting by Jens Juel, but no such portrait has been found. (Royal Collection of Etchings, Copenhagen.)

6. Poul Egede. Painting by unknown artist. (Privately owned; photo Royal
Library, Copenhagen.)

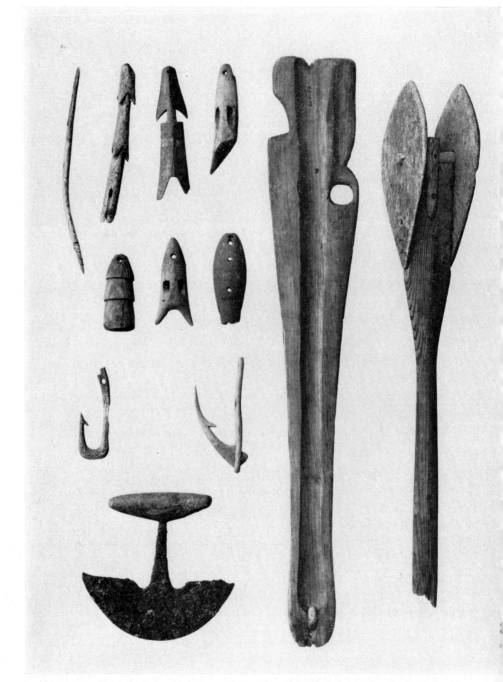

37. Eskimo hunting tools, 1650–1800. Left: arrow head, bird spear head, two harpoons, wound plug, harpoon head, line and sinker, hooks, *ulo* with imported blade. Right: throwing stick and winged tail of harpoon. (National Museum, Copenhagen.)

8. Imported articles and Danish ceramics. From top left: shot-making tongs, lead ball shot, iron nail, knife handles (top, Greenland copy; bottom, European), complete knives with handles carved in Greenland. Porcelain and china jars, clay pipes and glass beads. (National Museum, Copenhagen.)

39. Upper part of the gravestone of a Dutch whaling master. Whaling scene shown in relief. Ameland, Netherlands. (Photo Van der Meulen, Heemstede.)

10. Model of fishing
hooker *Rødefjord*, 1778.
Similar to the hookers
built for whaling and
sealing.

11. Model of snow brig
Umenack, built for the
Royal Greenland Trade
in 1778. (Both models
in the Trade and
Shipping Museum,
Kronborg, Denmark.
Photos H. Hauch,
Helsingør.)

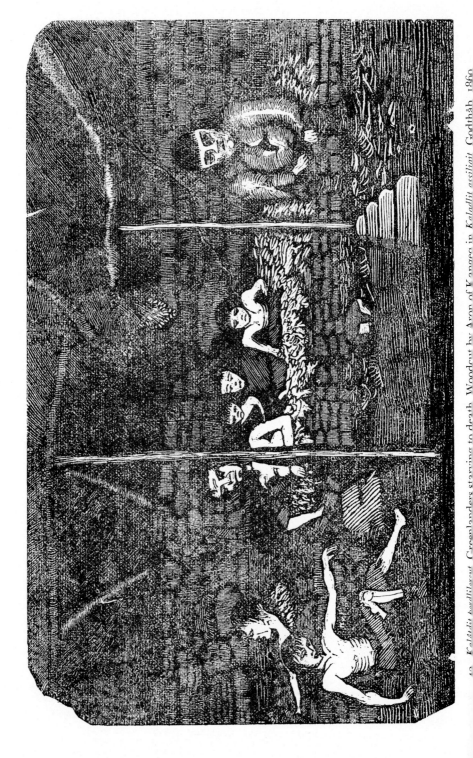

Kalâdlit toqrdl'illoqut. Greenlanders starving to death. Woodcut by Aron of Kangeq in Kaladlit assilialiait Godthåb, 1860

Greenlanders' fishing technique, sometimes with a harpoon, sometimes with "a stone fence", but thought the yield too small. Such fish could be consumed locally or sent to places in Greenland where they were not available. He specified the kind of fish – fjord cod, red-fish, halibut and capelin – which could only be used domestically. The fishing which could be of benefit to the trade, according to Geelmuyden, was Greenland shark and seal catching, He referred to fishing off the coast of Northern Norway for Greenland shark which was not common off Greenland. He referred to the liver which was rich in oil. Seal-catching was the most important item of all.

Therefore, according to Geelmuyden, there was not much benefit to be gained by the Company from fishing. Nevertheless the directors wanted tests made. In 1757, following Geelmuyden's remarks on the correct fishing tackle, a large net, a set-net together with a bow-net and fishing lines, were despatched, partly for salmon and partly for halibut.[3] Salted and smoked samples of these were requested. The halibut samples sent were not promising, whereas larger consignments of salted cod and salmon were welcomed, and these fish became a barter product.

In this report of 1749, Geelmuyden specially emphasized that the region south of Godthåb abounded in fish, and here the Fiskenæsset station was established in 1754.[4] It continued to be the task of the senior assistant at this station to carry out fishing trials, relating to fjord and sea cod and salmon – the small and medium-sized cod were to be dried during the winter. If the reports and estimates relating to the fishing were favourable, more tackle and, if necessary, more men would be sent out. However, neither fishing trials nor any subsequent fishing was to interfere with the Greenlanders' seal-catching; the fishing must be done by the colony's own men. In the following years it must have declined, for in both 1757 and 1758 "they can seldom get a meal of it" and "have scarcely been able to obtain 1 quarter of fish". The directors expressed disappointment but nevertheless wished the trials off Fiskenæsset to continue. Ten years later there were better results. The senior assistant at that time had sent home split and salted cod. The directors did not hesitate to declare freshly caught cod an article of barter, for each barrel of which there was to be exchanged "½ roll or 4 pounds of tobacco or 8 iron arrowheads or 8 ordinary knives or 200 fish-hooks, and the Greenlanders can choose whichever they want". Only a few years later matters reverted to the trial stage. Throughout the fishing industry various methods of processing were tried – salting and drying of cod, production of clippfish, par and *raekling*, and salting of halibut[5] – but the result in every case was negative. Paradoxically, dried coalfish had to be sent for distribution in the colonies in emergencies.

U

Seal-catching was the most important "fishing industry" at all the colonies and stations along the coast. Geelmuyden had dealt with this in his report, suggesting that net-catching be tried. The Eskimo technique was to place small nets under the ice – ice-net catching. Geelmuyden was thinking of seals caught in open water nets, stretched out in narrow channels through which the seals passed. In 1758 Lars Dalager at Godthåb suggested that this should be tried, for it was a possible way of employing Greenlanders who did not own kayaks. It appears that nets were sent out for seal-catching around Sukkertoppen before 1761, but the directors informed Dalager that no information had been received as to how they had worked, and nets could therefore not be despatched to Godthåb. It was later reported that the Sukkertoppen nets were too weak. In the north, on the other hand, nets were used for ice-net catching with larger Danish-made nets. In the Trading Company's time this net catching only took place at Ũmánaq. There it seems to have yielded a big return.

The surplus from the seal catch was bartered for blubber and skins. The blubber was refined from the 1750s onwards at the Trading Company's own refinery near Trangraven on Christianshavn. In the process of refining, seal and whale oil were apparently mixed together because after 1758–9 the whaling yielded such a small quantity. Only in one year, 1755, was a relatively large quantity of oil produced from both whale and seal blubber – 3,538 barrels. Otherwise the production figures for 1752–73 range from 806 barrels (1752) to 2,755 barrels (1772–3). From 1752 to 1773 there was nothing like a steady increase from year to year. The production figures did not keep pace with the increase in the establishment of colonies, as might have been expected. Production nevertheless amounted on average to more than double. Jacob Sewerin's whale oil sales for 1745–8. Sewerin had sold an average of 916 barrels of whale oil over four years whereas the Trading Company had sold an average of 1,937 barrels. Meanwhile, however, the number of settlements had more than doubled.

Unforeseeable factors often effected production. Epidemics might unfit the population for work, or ice conditions could hamper or even completely stop expeditions at a vital time. The weather throughout a whole spring could be intolerable. Or the catch might fail one year in one place, and another year in one or more other places for no explicable reason, or the seals might change their routes. Much blame for the sparse amount bartered was also laid on purchases by the Dutch and on the sale of flintlocks and ammunition. In 1749 N. C. Geelmuyden blamed the Dutch flintlock trade for the fact that the Greenlanders in Disko Bay travelled south and stayed by the fjords hunting reindeer for most of the spring and summer, neglecting the sealing, which meant that in the winter they were short of both skins and blubber and consequently could not part with any of their small seal catch to the traders. Lars Dalager in his memorandum of 1752 held the same view regarding the Godthåb district; the continual multiplication of flintlocks and powder caused sealing to be neglected, and the Greenlanders became so impoverished that those previously able to sell one to two barrels of blubber could now scarcely obtain that they needed for their lamps. This trade in firearms had to be stopped by banning Dutch commerce.

However, the Trading Company's policy on this fundamental subject was quite different. Even in Sewerin's time firearms and ammunition had apparently been supplied to the Greenlanders. Geelmuyden thought in 1750 that, in making their purchases from the Greenlanders, the missionaries should not only offer those articles that most attracted the Greenlanders, such as flintlocks, powder and shot. In 1757 the directors arranged for rifles to be sent out that were thicker in the barrel and had deeper rifling in order to satisfy the Greenlanders so that they should not be given any reason to engage in prohibited trade. Thus, the directors intended to rival the foreign traders with better goods, even if the sale of those goods was prejudicial to the blubber production.

Having seen the want and distress at Godthåb in 1758 caused by the growth of reindeer hunting, which was resulting in only middling quality skins being bartered and the reindeer stock dwindling, Lars Dalager saw no alternative to relieving them of their flintlocks, and he succeeded during the winter in buying up about fifty of them for which he paid with "3 rolls of tobacco and 300 ells of linen cloth". He destroyed all the flintlocks he bought, and himself bore the cost of the tobacco, worth at least 5 rdl. The linen cloth, however, was shown in the stock-list, and he covered it by lending the Company's rifles out for an annual charge. The reindeer skins he received in payment for hire of the guns were sold for blubber. It is probable that reindeer hunting declined as the number of wild reindeer dwindled.

It was not possible to turn back the clock. Now that weapons with ball and shot had been introduced into West Greenland, the only expedient was that of Lars Dalager, to provide the Greenlanders with good, durable and reliable weapons. These weapons and accessories, together with powder and shot, became the barter goods from then on. This introduced a completely new factor into Greenland society, namely maintenance of the weapons. This problem did not make itself felt immediately but quickly grew. The Greenlanders also did not know how to handle weapons or how to take safety precautions. So for the first time we hear of accidental shootings. The catechist Poul Grønlænder was killed in an accident in 1765, caused by one of the Trading Company's people. Although firearms were a common commodity, the Trading Company always tried to restrict their sale to the minimum. Flints for the flintlocks could be given as a bonus, but were limited to one only per person and if more were wanted they had to be paid for.

The Trading Company could, of course, have refrained from buying skins at all. Whether fox, seal, reindeer or bear, only low prices could be obtained for them in Europe. Fox skins were the most profitable, so the directors kept a watchful eye on the Company's exclusive right to buy them. In many cases the foxes were shot by the colonists or by Greenlanders hired by them for this task. But the majority were still caught in the traditional stone traps. The reindeer skins sent to Copenhagen were not worth much. For bearskins the most that could be given was the value of "$1\frac{1}{2}$ to 2 shirts", i.e. no more than 1 rigsdaler. The types of skin used as waterproofing for kayaks and *umiaks* were not barter commodities. Nevertheless some trade was carried on in such skins, usually direct between "producer" and consumer and without reference to the colony's trader.

The various ivory products – narwhal and walrus tusks – could be bought for resale informally on the West coast. During the Trading Company's time, a new barter commodity emerged – eiderdown. In 1770 it was declared a monopoly article and was bartered along the whole coast wherever it could be collected.

Greenland's possible "mineral riches", from gold to salt, had always occupied the imagination of Europeans. The Trading Company directors were no different from others in this respect, but their plans suffered from lack of capital and energy. Already in 1722, Hans Egede knew of the coal deposits on Disko, but he did not mention them in the *Perlustration* of 1741, nor did Poul and Niels Egede or Geelmuyden in their reports. The Dutch were already aware of the deposits. In 1728 Magnus Schiøtte was considering how to exploit them and Hans Egede thought that they could be exploited by establishing a colony in the Disko region. Nothing came of it, however.

In the meantime the coal seams on Disko aroused no special interest. The Missionskollegium was dragged into the more practical arrangements; in February 1749 the secretary, Finckenhagen, briefly described the position, quantity and quality of the coal (burned well but somewhat evil-smelling) and the poor harbour facilities. In the same document the Greenlanders' remarkable "worship" of this island was reported. When Greenlanders strange to the island first set foot there they threw themselves "flat on the ground in order to kiss it and to show towards this land something resembling divine worship". If this report is correct, the religious veneration is bound up with the legend that in the distant past Disko was towed to its present position from the south. Poul Egede was advised to kiss the ground when landing on the island for the first time.

But none of this led to exploitation of the coal deposits either at Skansen, where they had been noted by Matthias Fersleff and Capt. Ebbe Mitzell in 1727, or along the west coast of Disko where it was known that there was also coal. The Trading Company probably could not find the minimum amount of capital needed for preliminary investigations. It was cheaper to send the fuel required from Europe.

The Trading Company was not inclined to finance any form of mining operation. They knew, for example, of Greenland marble but did not think of exploiting it. To create other opportunities of employment for Greenlanders in Godthåb district, where the traditional Greenland occupation had not caught on, Lars Dalager thought of inducing them to make domestic articles out of the soft soapstone, steatite. If this type of stone could be obtained in fairly large blocks and in sufficient quantity, the directors would have been interested, but misunderstood or channelled into a direction which led nowhere, this affair also came to nothing.

REFERENCES

1. The Genoa Treaty of 1756, Article 2, has: "... *bien entendu que des sudits Royaumes, Etats, Havres, Ports et Rivières de la Domination Danoise seront exceptées entièrement les contrées éloignées du Nord, comme l'Islande, Ferroe, les colonies de sa Majesté dans la Groenlande, le Nordland et le Finmark, tous pays défendus même aux nations les plus amies et les plus favorisées"*. This paragraph of exception is not included in the Convention between Great Britain and Denmark–Norway 1780, nor in the *Convention maritime* between Russia and Denmark–Norway 1780, nor in the Danish–Russian Commercial Treaty, 1782. The wording (and the spelling) of the Genoa Treaty 1756 is taken from *Danske Tractater 1725–1800*, Copenhagen 1882, p. 55. The other treaties here mentioned are printed in the same edition, respectively pp. 379, 380 and 391.

2. The French whalers (and thus illicit traders too) were called by the Greenlanders of Egedesminde "*Pauktut*, i.e. blackened – because they usually are blackened from the smoke, which pours out from the fire when they burn their train oil they are used to burning on board their ships, and from other filthiness", reports the missionary H. C. Glahn, 5 August, 1766, in a letter to the Missionskollegium (unprinted and here translated from the original). The term *brænde tran* means literally "burn train oil", that is to produce train oil by burning, melting blubber.

3. *Hellefisk* is *Rheinhardus hipposoides*, and *helleflynder* is *hippoglossus vulgaris*.

Only the latter has an English name; it is often called *Greenland halibut* or simply *halibut*. The Danish Greenland Marinebiological Investigations have often been in want of an English name for *hellefisk*, because the Latin name is inconvenient in some contexts. They suggested to introduce the name *black halibut*, as in German *Schwarzscholle* and Norwegian *blåkveite*. In the following text the term *black halibut* will be used.

4. The name Fiskenæsset means "the headland from which one may fish".

5. *Rav* is dried, salted or smoked fins of halibut. *Rækling* is dried strips of meat from the belly of the halibut or the black halibut.

17

TRADE IN GREENLAND
1750–1774

The prosperity of the Trading Company depended first and foremost, as Geelmuyden wrote in 1749, on the "greatest vigilance and industry" on the part of the local trade officials. The technical equipment, in the form of boats and barrel goods, should have been plentiful, but it seldom was. If the trading posts were established relatively close together, this would make the exporting of produce easier. It would also prevent the Greenlanders' surplus blubber being left to lie in the open, and going to waste. These may have been the reasons why the trade did not get hold of as much blubber as might have been anticipated.

Buying and selling in the colonies and stations of West Greenland, private trading between the colonists and local Greenlanders, any form of payment for services rendered, and indeed economic exchange transactions of every kind were carried out on a barter basis, and because of the small quantities involved, this was particularly inconvenient. The accounting system of the traders and assistants was full of unavoidable sources of error. It was almost impossible to maintain uniform prices either for buying or selling. It gradually became the custom to send out a price-list annually to each trader, with prices of the articles for sale to the colonists and the goods which could be used as barter with the Greenland population. There was no sharp distinction between the two categories. The colonists often used the goods they were able to buy for bartering with the Greenlanders, so that the latter came by articles not intended for them – for example, firearms, gunpowder and lead shot – which was why the traders went over to selling them direct to the Greenlanders.

The barter trade itself prevented observance of the price-lists, because it was not always possible to give exact value for value. The prices therefore varied from one trading post to another. Later price-lists gave quotations in cash so that the trader himself had to estimate the equivalent in trading commodities. Alteration of prices for barter trading involved great difficulties. However, as the following random samples from the price-lists show, no great changes took place between 1730 and 1772.

BLUBBER IN BARRELS

	1730	1731	1755–6	1756–7	1757–8	1758–9	1770–1	1771–2
White shirts	I	I	I	I	I	I	I	
Kersey breeches	$\frac{1}{2}$	$\frac{1}{2}$	$\frac{1}{2}$*	$\frac{2}{3}$	$\frac{2}{3}$	†		
Kersey, per *alen* ($\frac{2}{3}$ cm.)						*$\frac{1}{3}$	$\frac{1}{3}$	$\frac{2}{5}$
Painted chests	$\frac{1}{2}$	$\frac{1}{2}$		good $\frac{1}{2}$	good $\frac{1}{2}$	$\frac{1}{3}$	I	good $\frac{1}{2}$
Knives with ivory handles	$\frac{1}{4}$	$\frac{1}{4}$		$\frac{1}{4}$	$\frac{1}{4}$	$\frac{1}{4}$		$\frac{1}{3}$
Small sword-blades	$\frac{1}{4}$	$\frac{1}{4}$		$\frac{2}{3}$	$\frac{1}{2}$	$\frac{1}{2}$		

* Equivalent of 2 reindeer skins.   † From 1758 onwards breeches do not appear in the accounts.

The following were both common barter articles throughout the century and had equivalent values.

	1730	1731	1755–6	1756–7	1757–8	1758–9	1770–1	1771–2
			Scrapers					
Blubber in barrels	$\frac{1}{4}$	$\frac{1}{4}$	$\frac{9}{20}$	$\frac{1}{2}$	$\frac{1}{2}$	$\frac{2}{5}$–$\frac{1}{2}$	$\frac{1}{2}$	
Whalebones	I	I	I	I	I	I	I	
Reindeer skins	I	I	I	I	I	I	I	
Fox skins	I	2	2	2	2	2	2	
Seal skins	2	3–4	3	3	3	3	3	

	1730	1731	1755–6	1756–7	1757–8	1758–9	1770–1	1771–2
			Iron arrowheads					
Blubber in barrels	$\frac{1}{4}$	$\frac{1}{4}$	–	$\frac{1}{6}$* $\frac{1}{5}$ $\frac{1}{3}$	$\frac{1}{4}$ $\frac{1}{3}$	$\frac{1}{6}$ $\frac{1}{4}$ $\frac{1}{3}$	–	–
Fox skins	I	I	–	–	–	–	I	I
Seal skins	2	2–3	–	–	–	–	2	2

* From 1756 onwards two types were sold, one with barbs, the other smooth. The latter is shown in succeeding years as the cheapest.

Thus prices remained more or less constant. Changes in price of the relevant articles in Copenhagen did not have any appreciable effect on buying and selling in Greenland. Although the amount of trade done was not great, considerable difficulty was found in accounting for sales.

When checked in Copenhagen it was found time after time on converting into cash that in the aggregate either too much or too little had been given per barrel of blubber or else too little; seldom was the fixed price of 1 rigsdaler per barrel actually achieved.

The fixed price schedule, which was taken over from "the Royal Trade" in 1727–33 and which perhaps had existed long before that time, established the society of West Greenland in a permanent economic vacuum which, however, made possible later a socially balanced price policy. The main impression, however, is that up to 1782 the traditional prices and equivalents were maintained in the barter trade because annual changes would cause accounting and trading chaos. Thus a price tradition was created and the Greenland consumer became used to relatively stable prices.

The vacuum was broken by foreign traders with their goods and their barter trade, but this had no effect on prices in the colonies' barter trade. It was said that the Greenlanders would rather buy the various articles of hardware at the colonies at a higher price than the goods they could get for less blubber and whalebone from the Dutch. Thus it seems that the Greenlanders were quality-conscious in their purchases, and that the poor quality of the Dutch goods was responsible for the gradual falling off in their trade noticeable towards 1774.

"You must see that the wares for the Greenlanders are disposed of in such a way that 1 barrel of blubber is taken in exchange for 2 rigsdalers' worth of hardware and skins and whalebone in proportion", wrote the directors in 1766 to C. C. Dalager, the trader at Ritenbenk, adopting the principle that the most important, most easily divisible product should be used as the basis of calculation. But the real difficulty was to find the right equivalent in each individual case. So, like his brother Lars, C. C. Dalager asked for a price-list which the traders could use as a rough guide, but the directors were reluctant "because the trade was not to become too constrained". Responsibility was thus being transferred to the traders, although the directors were still ready with written reprimands when the variations were too obvious, especially "to the Company's disadvantage". There were certain colonial districts in Greenland where "luxury is enthroned". In the letter to C. C. Dalager the directors contradicted themselves, for in 1763 a price-list had been sent to Petersen, the trader in Frederikshåb which laid down prices in barrels or parts of barrels of blubber for certain goods (see list below).

The inexactness of all this price-fixing when variations in quality were taken into account is apparent from the directors' letter to the Frederikshåb trader in 1764: "How these are to be taken in payment for or with blubber, cannot be determined by any fixed tariff but must depend on the trader's own judgment, to the extent that he finds them of good quality and in the Company's best interest. For there has been from the outset in the colony an accepted current price of 5 to 6 prime and good quality grey fox skins in exchange for a barrel of blubber and always 2 white against 1 grey; likewise 6 saddle-back sealskins or skins of common seal "with large spots", 8 with small spots and 10 small ordinary with small spots have been reckoned against 1 barrel of blubber; you must try to adhere to these prices as far as possible."[1]

PRICE RATES

	*Cask blubber**
1 Company chest	$\frac{1}{3}$
1 rifle with accessories at the very least	5
other weapons pro rata accordingly	
1 Icelandic jerkin	$\frac{1}{2}$
1 Company lath, according to thickness	$\frac{1}{8}$, $\frac{1}{6}$ to $\frac{1}{4}$
1 Company board, ditto	$\frac{1}{4}$ to $\frac{1}{2}$
1 ell coloured kersey	$\frac{1}{6}$
1 copper or brass kettle per pound	$\frac{1}{6}$
1 copper or brass ladle	$\frac{1}{3}$
1 pound fine gunpowder	$\frac{1}{2}$
2 pounds shot	$\frac{1}{6}$
1 pound lead	$\frac{1}{12}$
1 pound Dutch tobacco	$\frac{1}{6}$

In a letter to Fiskenæsset there is added to the list:

1 comb	$\frac{1}{12}$
1 fine-toothed comb	$\frac{1}{24}$
1 pair ordinary scissors	$\frac{1}{12}$
1 pound of ordinary large and small beads	$\frac{1}{3}$

* 1 cask = 2 barrels

Further complications arose when differences developed in the trade between the northern and southern colonies. From Holsteinsborg northwards whale and seal blubber was bought in casks, barrels or fractions thereof. This was possible because of the large quantities available for barter. It is doubtful where the same applied in the Sukkertoppen and Godthåb districts. Possibly in the Sukkertoppen district they measured in barrels for buying purposes alongside another barter measure; perhaps this applies to Godthåb too, at Fiskenæsset and Frederikshåb and, towards the end of the period, in the very south, it had, at any rate, become the practice to buy whole seals or parts thereof. Whale blubber was relatively seldom supplied; when it was, the quantity of blubber was probably measured in barrels. This circumstance was, however, concealed from the directors, since the shipments home and the accounts related to "casks of blubber". Not until about 1782, when gauged blubber measures were introduced, did this

southern buying practice come to light. Naturally in the southern
colonies this provided another source of error which could cause discrepancies between the selling and buying accounts. This implied a
further excuse for the traders' "adjustment" of the accounts and was
yet another reason for approximation and lack of uniformity in bartering, that is, in the prices used in the individual exchanges. Also differences in trading customs evolved between the northern colonial
districts and the southern. Perhaps this helped to lay the foundation for
the subsequent administrative separation of the two "regions".

To even out price differences between individual purchases and sales,
it was the custom from the 1720s onwards to give a make-weight. For
this the smaller types of goods were used – needles, beads, combs,
fish-hooks, toys, thimbles and the like. Flints for the muskets might also
be thrown in. They could only be sold for blubber in large quantities
and were therefore suitable for rounding off a transaction. But because
they were a make-weight, these goods ceased to be considered as actual
payment in the Greenlanders' eyes.

When new articles came on the scene, a price, usually in the form
of a money value, had to be fixed. Then the trader could work out for
himself to which, and in what quantity of the various trading commodities he should apply this price. Hence a new custom arose. The
relative stability of prices in the colonies grew during the eighteenth
century into a firm and unchangeable tradition.

The correspondence between traders and directors is full of exchanges
of opinion concerning the prices obtained in that or in previous years.
The traders often tried to explain away prices that were too high or
too low. In 1761 Lars Dalager gave a scarcely credible explanation of
why his prices seemed to depart from "the standards". His revenue
from trading had decreased because everyone else in the colony was
trading as well; "it has even gone so far that when doing a deal it has
been necessary to adjust prices to the so-called current market price."
The directors found it hard to believe that this was the reason for his
selling barter goods at lower prices than previously in the colony, and
lower than the prices maintained in other colonies. Lars Dalager must
have wanted it to appear that the trader in his transactions had to
take into account the prices offered by the colonists and the mission
employees at Godthåb and Ny Herrnhut for their private and institutional purchases. But such purchases could never be a decisive factor
in "price-fixing" when the local trader was by far the biggest buyer,
and did his buying outside the colonial settlement. The directors said
they did not understand what trading could be involved, "especially as
it is known that no trading may be carried on other than by the
Company". But if trading was taking place outside the monopoly none

the less, it was up to the trader to see that it was stopped and that those involved were punished. Lars Dalager's explanation, not convincing otherwise, could have been connected with his growing antipathy to the Royal mission.

The traders, deeply involved in the barter trade, could not adhere to the principle of exchange according to a fixed value, however much they might be expected to do so. Inexpert as book-keepers, they were forced by their dependence on the Trading Company, to resort to excuses. Nobody then realized that an unavoidable clash was taking place between the unsystematic subsistence economy and the relatively well-organized monetary economy. Nobody could have realized it, and this gave birth to the formula so widely used later: "the special Greenland conditions".

The widely varying prices did not only vex the directors and the traders, but gave rise to complaints from the Greenlanders as well. The directors feared that the price differences would lead to mass migration, and that the Greenlanders would move to those settlements where they got the best bargains. However, we know too little about population movements in West Greenland at that time to say whether this fear was justified.

After the establishment of Frederikshåb and Fiskenæsset the usual northward journeys of the Greenlanders living farthest to the south fell off. There is only one clear example of Greenlanders going to a colony away from their own district – supposedly because the trader of the original district failed to visit their settlement so enabling them to dispose of their blubber and satisfy their material needs.

Any differences in value given for Greenlandic products between the various trading posts could be spread from one place to another by "mocassin post", but in Disko Bay, where the colonial districts were near to each other, these could be readily picked up direct by the trading Greenlanders. The latter, however, probably did not understand the equalizing factor which lay hidden from them in the make-weight, and were only concerned with the measure of blubber which they had to pay. Who could decide for each individual whether he had received too much or too little? The blubber measures used were inaccurate and certainly were not checked. Everything was characteristically vague and approximate, hence the traders were in a cleft stick between what was practically possible in a barter economy and the directors' continual demands for stability and accuracy. The conflict between means and aims in Greenland policy is thus clearly visible, but was not clearly expressed, because it was not appreciated that the trade had exactly the same objective as the mission. However, the directors, under pressure from the Company's poor financial situation, went back more and more to the principle that the Greenland trade must yield a surplus or at least break even. This policy was bound to breed a growing antagonism between trade and mission.

It was for fear of other sources of "disorder" that the directors were reluctant to send out new goods. They did not want the colonists or the Greenlanders to become used to obtaining new or more expensive goods through the trade, and the goods must not be sold more cheaply than formerly. Already in 1758 there was a substantial argument for proper commercial principles being adopted. Regarding imported foodstuffs, Niels Egede was reprimanded for having entered $\frac{1}{2}$ barrel of barley meal, 116 pounds hard tack and 16 pounds *rottskiaer* (split dried cod) as well as one "skippund" (159 kilos) of coalfish as having been supplied to Greenlanders. The coalfish was permissible, since it was sent out for the Greenlanders in times of need, but as for the rest, he was told that this must not occur again, as the Greenlanders were on no account to become accustomed to European victuals, other than coalfish. This attitude was taken solely because shipment of provisions to the colonies took up excessive space in the vessels and was unprofitable. It was also thought, with some justification, that the Greenlandic population would resort to begging or credit buying which would not be covered by the products of their hunting. But with Niels Egede, the immediate shortage of food was his compelling reason for supplying provisions.

The directors were obliged, however, to send out some new goods – for example, firearms and ammunition. Brandy and other spirits came under the regulations concerning "European provisions". Brandy was only to be given to the Greenlanders for medicinal purposes. On the other hand, demand for tobacco gradually increased. The Greenlanders first used tobacco at Godthåb in the 1750s. Lars Dalager writes: "It is strange how the Greenlanders who live closest to us have in such a short time become so strongly addicted to tobacco; very few use it for smoking, but all of them take it as snuff, and the first and last thing they say is 'give me a little tobacco or a pinch of snuff'." The consumption of tobacco would within a few years become the best business, "for I have already seen them take the clothes off their backs to pay for tobacco". He himself had never made it an article of sale, except in payment for a bird or fish. "Otherwise they would have made such demands on my snuff box that in these past few years I could not have managed with less than fifty pounds of tobacco each year." Lars Dalager said that some wanted to see this trade banned, but that he personally did not mind. This imaginative man revealed his modern outlook towards the creation and commercial exploitation of need as an incentive to productivity when he wrote: "Instead of a Greenlander buying shirts, stockings, caps or pewter and copper utensils, which are all goods he can well do without, he can buy tobacco, snuff-boxes and handkerchiefs and he is thus always obliged to be more industrious if he cannot do without the latter and yet wants some of the former."

In 1758 matters had developed so far that even the Greenlanders at Ny Herrnhut sold their skins for tobacco, "to which the whole community is addicted". The quantity of tobacco sold in Godthåb rose from 63 pounds in 1755/6 to 362 pounds in 1770/1. The management apparently hesitated to send tobacco out to other colonies as a general article of trade – except for the colonists. In 1766 a sample of Norwegian snuff tobacco was sent out "as it is understood the Greenlanders are desirous of tobacco". Tobacco was not smoked but taken as snuff or chewed: only twice does the sale of pipes appear in the accounts from Godthåb. The growing need for tobacco was never linked with the Dutch, who would naturally have introduced this luxury, then relatively cheap. But there is every indication that the colonists' small-scale trading and payment for services rendered awoke and fed the craving for tobacco.

The range of goods otherwise offered for sale in exchange for blubber or its equivalents was not substantially different from those which appeared in the lists from 1730 and 1731. The accounts from Sukkertoppen and Godthåb suggest the goods most in demand in the colonies. As already mentioned, useful odds and ends such as sewing needles, hooks and flints were used as make-weights. These could mount up to large quantities: thus in 1756–9 Anders Olsen at Sukkertoppen gave away 9,400 "ordinary sewing needles" and 500 hooks. Polished sewing needles were generally sold, yet in 1758–9 Olsen used 200 as make-weights.

A comparison of sales to the Greenlanders at Sukkertoppen and Godthåb in 1756–9 shows that Sukkertoppen consumed a wider variety of purchases over the whole range of "small wares". The list enumerates sixty-one articles and varieties, whereas in the Godthåb accounts only twenty-nine articles and varieties appear. Among the latter are to be found what was most in demand both in Sukkertoppen and in Godthåb – striped shirts, striped or checked linen and kersey by the *alen* (55 cm.), knives with handles of *lignum vitae*, "childrens' knives", files and rasps, iron arrow-heads and scrapers, to which were added firearms, gunpowder, lead shot and spare parts. Other manufactured goods sold to the Greenlanders were calico, woollen caps and stockings for children and adults, white shirts and Silesian linen by the *alen*. There were various iron tools and fish-hooks. Domestic articles included knives and forks with more refined handles, spoons, copper and tinplate kettles, copper and brass ladles, dishes, bowls, pewter mugs, horn and bone combs, thimbles, mirrors, scissors, wooden boxes, sewing shields, finger rings, beads and also the apparently indispensable chests. Timber in such forms as boards, spruce poles and laths was only purchased by the Greenlanders to a small extent in this period; in the southern colonies driftwood was plentiful.

Much of the merchandise shipped out – and most of the provisions, which constituted part of their remuneration – went to the colonists and the mission employees. Any other necessaries could be ordered, as so-called commission goods, but these were restricted to the minimum. It was regarded as vital to keep wages as low as possible, both in cash and kind, which explains why skilled men could not be obtained for whaling. No one could make his fortune working for the Trading Company in Greenland. Of the host of widely differing types of men who travelled to Greenland in the Trading Company's service during the eighteenth century, the great majority stayed permanently. Some were recalled early because of misconduct or illness, but most remained. The catechists sent out to the mission generally settled for good, which however was not true of the pastors.

Not all those sent to Greenland in the Company service were angels. The harsh living conditions were not likely to refine their often coarse natures. They lived crowded together in colony houses which were far too small. A sharp distinction prevailed between officers and men. They had different food allowances and each group ate on its own. This communal eating in groups came to an end of its own accord soon after 1750, partly because the men split up into different households – European and half-Greenlander – through marriage, and partly because of disagreement amongst themselves.

The trader enjoyed a position of considerable power in the colony. On him depended the atmosphere prevailing there. His power was based, first and foremost, on his responsibility for distribution of the provisions, i.e. the portion of the wages which was measured in kind, the provisions that were communally prepared, and the dry goods to which everyone was entitled. He automatically arranged for all handicraft work carried out in the colonial settlement and the mission. Because he was in charge of all crafts, so he controlled all traffic, at least in the southern colonies. In districts where dog-sledges could be driven, his freedom was greater.

The trader was the local representative of the Trading Company and he had to ensure that its interests were being looked after. Thus, he had to run the business with zeal and, without squeezing the Greenlanders for every last item of their produce, he was to see that they stuck to their whale catching. At the same time a watchful eye had to be kept over the work of the men. He was to show piety himself and to exhort the staff to do the same; his own behaviour must be an example, and at all costs conduce to harmony and not discord. If he caught the "men" behaving badly towards other fellow-colonists or towards Greenlanders, he was to report and punish them and, if necessary, send the offenders home. He could impose fines to be paid into the poor-fund, in short act as policeman and magistrate in one, referring doubtful cases to the pastor or catechist, chief clerk, carpenter and cooper. This was all that remained of "the council" of Hans Egede's time. He was to wield the same powers over the Greenlanders if they committed offences. This combination of trading, administration and magisterial authority was typical of the colonial monopolies established by Europeans at that time, except that mostly the trader exercised no authority over the local population, except for his Company's employees. The trader in the West Greenland colonies could bring the local Greenlanders under his jurisdiction because there was nothing recognizable, in European terms, as a judicial institution, and a total lack of normal "law and order".

On the other hand it was also the trader's task to protect the Greenlanders' interests against encroachment – a degree of responsibility often quite beyond his powers both as regards knowledge, experience and moral fibre. Some were weak and inconsistent; others became petty local despots. Only a few could maintain a balance; and Niels Egede was pre-eminent among these because of his long experience and personal integrity.

The traders, as the appointed authority, needed backing in the form of rules which, with their total ignorance of law, they could follow, but the company failed to provide it. In serious cases the directors advised that "the council" be convened and that the offender be punished as it saw fit. They avoided adopting a definite attitude, for instance, by stating that the penalty should be fixed according to how "bad, persistent and refractory" the guilty persons were, "which can be judged far better by those who are present than by those who are absent. Capital offenders should be sent home in custody by the first ship." Cases in which the sentence might be for life imprisonment were, in Danish monopoly undertakings, always to be brought before a royal court. In a case against one of the "men", a deckhand at Ritenbenk, the directors were obliged to lay down more detailed rules for fines. "These were fixed at 2, 4, 6 to 8 rdl., to be imposed according the degree of insubordination he had shown or swearing and other unseemly things he had indulged in. When an offence is committed against officers or Greenlanders the fines must always be higher than when one 'common man' commits an offence against another. . . ." Otherwise, they left the trader to fix the fines.

Punishment of "the men" could extend to flogging according to Company instructions, but no such case was recorded. Lars Dalager entered in the Godthåb inventory for 1759: "Outside the church door, 1 new pillory with requisite irons." Whether it was ever used is not known. The most severe penalty which the trader or "council" could impose was repatriation. This might not seem like a punishment, and indeed was a relief for many. However, the person sent home got no pay, let alone help in obtaining employment on his return home. But it could greatly relieve the atmosphere in a neighbourhood when "persons who in their dealings with others had done objectionable things both among the Europeans and among the Greenlanders" were repatriated.

Thus while great caution was exercised in punishing any offences committed by Greenlanders, various penalties were meted out to the colonists. In Umánaq a Greenlandic catechumen murdered a baptized Greenlander. The missionary did not know what to do, but banished the murderer and laid the matter before the Missionskollegium. In this case the trade was not involved. The missionary concluded: "Should any punishment be imposed on him, regarded by both baptized and unbaptized as just, it is necessary for the Company's officers to ask for assistance from those concerned, without which this cannot be carried out." "Those concerned" might be the Trading Company since there were no rules for such crimes committed by Greenlanders. The directors were regarded as the highest temporal authority below the King, to whom the case could also have been referred. The matter was not pursued but the killer stayed well away from the colony thereafter. The lack of a proper court and a penal law in Greenland was all too evident from the cases in which a course of action could not be decided, or where the traditional West Greenland methods were no longer effective.

In cases of simple larceny or burglary committed by Greenlanders nothing was done, often because these crimes were carried out in collusion or because the merchant could corner the culprit in some other way. It was usually easy to discover a thief. Informers were common, though not in the European sense. Generally "the informer" had no idea that a "theft" had been committed, but merely reported that he had seen so-and-so in possession of whatever was missing. This happened in 1749 to Peder Olsen Walløe at Julianehåb (as it later became). "The thief" himself came and returned what had been stolen, but Walløe nevertheless gave him "a few thumps on the back". He later added that the Greenlanders did not consider it wrong to steal from Europeans, although they seldom took anything unlawfully from their fellow-countrymen; however, very few actual thefts committed by Greenlanders are recorded.

X

Clashes could easily occur between the people sent out and the local population, but they did not result in punishment. There was a tendency to penalize the European with a reprimand or a fine, but not the Greenlander in the case, although the latter might have started the dispute. Once a Greenland catechumen in a settlement assaulted the stationed catechist, and the catechumen, an advanced man, was reprimanded in the presence of Niels Egede, the senior assistant, the missionary and all the local population. In this way things became more peaceful.

The Greenlanders' reaction to the behaviour of the rougher men stationed in their country was generally one of unconcealed surprise that the Europeans "who are said to be believers, for they know God's word, cannot agree or love each other better". The Greenlanders regarded with contempt one seaman who had to put up with beatings and blows from his trader which they themselves would only have given to dogs – so wrote Poul Egede. The Trading Company's directors could only urge the trader to try to maintain order and keep "the men" disciplined and occupied. If the Greenlanders avoided the colonists on account of their bad behaviour, it would affect the Company's revenues.

The desire for "law and order", which became more and more insistent, was expressed in connection with revenge killing after one death which was said to have been caused by an *ilisîtsoq*. Jæger, the missionary at Holsteinsborg, called on this occasion for a "lenient" penal law to be established in the colonies. The penalty for killing should be "a few blows on the body and also a period of banishment from one district to another, if this is possible, or something of the sort, adjusted to meet the circumstances. . . ." But his desire for a generally applicable rule was side-stepped. Lars Dalager had already asked in the 1750s for "a few rules of justice, by which offences and disorder should be considered . . ." Danish law could not apply in Greenland as the circumstances of the country and the nature of the people were so different. He thought that Poul Egede, "who undeniably has the most thorough experience of Greenland and who would be willing to collaborate", should draw up these rules, which should be translated into Greenlandic for the information of honest people; "now . . . they go around as if in a fog". These ideas, however, were never carried out. Clearly it was impossible to introduce Danish law; nevertheless certain Danish regulations then in force did creep in, as for example in the Church regarding admission to communion. If a person stayed away, the pastor could refuse him communion if he suddenly wanted it. The missionary Thorhallesen wanted to enforce this rule on both the stationed people and the Greenlanders. Danish law made itself felt in other ways, as when decisions were referred to the trader or missionary.

Lars Dalager once had to umpire a dispute between two Greenlanders over the ownership of a shot reindeer; his decision was final.
In this way the trader was gradually pushed by the Greenlanders
themselves into a position of temporal authority to which even the missionary and catechist had to defer. Lars Dalager and many others
mentioned another problem closely allied to the desire for "law and
order". Precisely because of the absence of rules to follow, decisions on
similar cases varied from place to place and according to changes in
personnel. In Dalager's opinion, the Greenland population was well
aware that a higher authority existed in Denmark. Apart from the
inconsistency of decisions by officials in the individual Greenland
colonies, "they reason, as many of us do, according to the inaccurate
proverb, 'like master, like man' " – hence the Greenlanders inevitably
regarded the authorities in Denmark as arbitrary. Even those living in
remote parts had intimated this. In itself this revealed the flashpoint
between the West Greenlandic tradition and the tradition which the
people sent out from Denmark brought with them.

Lars Dalager indicated other areas where differences in the concept
of law arose. When a fox-trap had been abandoned by its builder but
was used by someone else to make a catch, by Greenland tradition the
catch belonged to the user, whereas the right to the trap could be
reasserted by the man who had built it. This tradition conflicted with
the Danish–Norwegian concept of ownership of the trap and any catch
made with it. Here we have the Greenlanders' sharp distinction between
right of use and right of possession, compared with the European
concept which combined the two elements more closely in ownership
(cf. I, p. 305 et seq.,). If a borrowed article was damaged while in use,
it was, according to the Greenland tradition, the owner's loss and the
owner was not entitled to compensation from the borrower. When a
Greenland hunter bought an iron arrowhead on credit and lost it
before he had paid his debt, he refused to pay; if he was compelled to
acknowledge the debt, he only paid part. However, this only applied
to boats, arrowheads, fishing-lines and the like. If he borrowed a
domestic utensil and this was broken while in use, he recognized the
borrower's duty to replace it – a point of agreement with the Danish
concept.

It was for this reason that the Greenlanders largely bought on credit.
If an article so purchased did not satisfy, "the purchaser" returned it,
even if he had used it. He thus regarded the transaction as a loan.
A kind of hire-purchase system developed fairly naturally when a
hunter wanted to buy bigger articles such as a boat or a firearm; part
of the payment was made immediately and credit was obtained for the
balance. If the buyer died before the balance was paid, the trader

could not claim the amount outstanding from his surviving relatives; although Dalager does not say so, it can be added that the trader could not take back the article concerned. "This is a prejudicial rule for the colonies' traders who are increasingly obliged to give credit, from which I have this year suffered especially, for many of my debtors have died and have thereby caused me much confusion."

Credit was a serious problem for the traders, especially when a change in the management of a colony or outpost was imminent. At such times the casual trading methods were revealed. Anders Olsen, for example, usually left relatively large amounts owing to him at each of his posts when he moved on. When a senior assistant at Jakobshavn was being transferred to Ritenbenk, he was ordered to submit a list of the amounts due both from Greenlanders and colonists to the trader in Christianshåb. These credit lists later appeared as a common accounting feature in the colonies. Possibly they originated in the credit system already in use in Sewerin's time.

The giving of credit was necessary on account of the seasonal nature of whale hunting. In poor hunting seasons, many Greenlanders who lived near to colonies or outposts came into the trading post in winter to trade and borrow from the trade officials. It was often necessary "to give them a helping hand" in times of need, to establish something in the nature of social security, an element which was properly the mission's concern. The Company as such could have had a direct interest in giving credit, because – at any rate according to the European view – this more or less obliged Greenland production to be bartered right from the outset. The Greenlanders might thus be encouraged to "show greater diligence in trapping", as it was frequently expressed. For such a reason, possibly, the directors did not make greater efforts to stamp out the credit system. On the other hand, the Greenlanders became used to living on credit, and regarding the goods "bought" as a loan, in accordance with Dalager's view.

An ingenious form of exploiting the credit system is supposed to have occurred in Disko Bay in the 1750s: the Greenland hunters took goods on credit from the trader at the colony and then sold the blubber, which they really owed to the Company trader, to the Dutch traders for cheaper goods, especially firearms and ammunition. It was a missionary at Claushavn–Christianshåb who reported this, and he noted that it was mainly the unbaptized who carried on this commerce. To a European such actions were reprehensible – although Europeans were not above doing the same thing. The credit system made it easier for the Greenlanders to buy imported consumer articles. Hence these articles became a more and more common feature of everyday life, and brought about changes in its quality. Dependence on this import trade consequently increased, although the population was not equally dependent in all settlements. The last colonies and outposts to be established trailed behind in the race, but caught up quickly. No one in West Greenland any longer laboriously made his wife's *ulos* (scrapers) or his own knives. The new needs created by the credit system opened the way for changes in the material culture. The district around Godthåb was the first to be "modernized". Those who travelled to this area or passed through it also obtained their provisions there and so the needs became more widespread.

The material aspect of everyday life in Godthåb and other localities in 1750–74 is depicted by Lars Dalager in his diaries. Concerning clothes, he says that the men began to use neckerchiefs, buckles on shoes and decorative garters; the breeches which the women sewed for the men were provided with pockets, in which there was room for snuff-boxes and handkerchiefs. The women wore a cambric or linen modesty-piece, or a garment covering their shoulders and breasts, fitted with a collar and embroidered with bows and wide silk ribbons. They did not, however, take to wearing skirts but still wore breeches. Lars Dalager writes: "It is said that a new cut has been discovered for their breeches, which is most advantageous, but in what it actually consists I cannot say." The colours preferred at first were shades of red, but in the 1750s dark blue and white became favourites. "Thus a blue coat and white hose with a knitted cap on his head are the height of finery for a Greenlander." In the north blue was popular, in the south red. The relatively large sales of kerseys and linen indicate that imported cloths were in everyday use, except for hunting. In the north, clothing made from skins remained an absolute necessity. Perhaps in the south the *tingmiaq* (the close-fitting fur from birdskins) was covered over with fabric. Calico and patterned cotton fabrics appeared in the Godthåb sales accounts for 1770–2, but only in small quantities.

Behind this outward show the traditional ways survived. Dalager had "many times seen, when they reached the shore, that they dashed their harpoons and arrows with such force against stones, that they are picked up in splinters". When the arrows did not function – i.e. strike and kill – it was the arrows that were at fault. New ones of a different shape had to be devised. Thus the man also had to change his methods. This was not easy, so he reverted to the kinds of implements used previously and sought advice from the *angákoq*, for he could get no help with such matters from the trader and missionary. People resorted to the traditional authority.

The traditional trading customs among Greenlanders were maintained. If they had something to sell but the potential buyer had not inspected it, they were careful not to describe the article too favourably;

rather they made it seem of less worth then it was. Lars Dalager relates that "on the other hand when dealing with us, they lie monstrously, for when a Greenlander says that he has enough wares to pay for a shirt, one can be sure that the value is scarcely that of a knife or an iron arrowhead". However, because of Dalager's personal authority, no attempt was made to fool him.

This subjection to authority, both traditional and foreign, showed itself in a great variety of ways. Very often the post was carried between Frederikshåb and Godthåb by kayak and this distance was covered in an incredibly short time. The kayakers considered this task a great honour, and did not stop when they came to a settlement in mid-journey, although this was customary. The "postillion" said self-consciously: "My time is short since I am carrying the word of the masters through the land." In their capacity as "postmen", the Greenland kayakers performed services for the Trading Company and mission, for which they were paid in kind – in summer by one shirt and one stockfish "for consumption" and in winter double. In accordance with European tradition and custom, such payment was made in return for other services. "You have an errand somewhere or other. If there is no Danish craft to be had, you have to use a Greenland one and Greenland oarswomen. For this too you use goods. It is the Company's belief that no one trades to his own disadvantage – the Greenlanders are of the same belief. Without payment they will not work." The payment was always made in kind. This was a new element in the picture of West Greenland material culture, but it was quickly taken as normal.

The employment of Greenland staff became more and more general. As a rule they worked for their keep and for gifts. As for occasional labour, it is mentioned several times that Greenland "marksmen" were hired to go bird-shooting in return for guns and ammunition and a share of the bag. Greenland labour was also hired for the ice-net catch.

More permanent employment with the Trading Company only occurred in a few isolated instances. There was still a lack of confidence in the stability of the Greenland labour force. In 1756 Lars Dalager had taken on a married man, Qivioq, who could feed himself, his wife and his children in no other way. Dalager wanted to "apply" him to the service of the Trading Company. But if he wished Qivioq to accompany him on a trading expedition, he had to starve him for a few days beforehand, because if the man was well fed and provisioned he failed to appear. However, the Trading Company were less pessimistic than Dalager for they were willing for Greenlanders to be trained in their service – by this means they could save on sending out men from Denmark, who were difficult to find. They were willing to pay Greenlanders wages in accordance with their ability and industry.

From other settlements the Trading Company had better experience. In 1755 or 1756 the senior assistants at Jakobshavn had taken on a Greenlander, Aron, who proved "honest and diligent". He was "granted" an annual wage of "one half of a man's victuals of the scheduled sorts of provisions, namely bread, butter, fish, peas and groats together with 4 or 5 rigsdalers' worth of the Company's goods – and we desire nothing more than to see more young Greenlanders of this kind fitted for the Company's service in time." The reason was the same: to be free of the need to send out labourers from home. The directors contradicted their own policy by granting Aron a food ration, since they preferred Greenlanders not to become used to imported foodstuffs. On the other hand, they could not expect him to maintain himself completely as a hunter while being employed in the colony. His wages were raised to 6 rigsdaler per annum in 1759. When in 1763 he wished to travel to Denmark, the Company felt obliged to refuse him permission for fear of infection. In 1765 he married a Greenland woman, and the missionary Jørgen Sverdrup reported that he could not keep a wife and children on the wages and food he received: "He is himself a poor hunter, because he broke a leg as a child and did not learn to row a kayak". He was therefore partially disabled. Employment by the Company or the mission was the salvation of such people; they were thus afforded a livelihood which Eskimo society could not give them.

From Sverdrup's statement about Aron's wages and food ration it is clear that, in fixing the wage, allowance was made for his being able to hunt and fish for his own domestic requirements, as much if not more than the other men employed. This was difficult to manage if he was to do his work properly. By fixing the food ration at a half portion it was shown that not more than half a man's contribution was expected, though at the same time the directors put pressure on the trader by requiring that Aron be kept hard at work. A labourer sent out received 30 rigsdaler a year as a starting wage together with full "ordinary victuals" valued at 20–30 rigsdaler. The term "Greenlandic wages" was thus introduced into West Greenland society.

Aron's pay set the standard not only for others employed by the Trading Company but also for the native catechists in the mission's service. In 1763 the senior assistant at Jakobshavn was permitted to employ another Greenland workman if he merited the same wages as Aron. At Frederikshåb, the trader had thought of paying half a man's victuals plus an annual value of 80 pounds of Dutch tobacco, equivalent to 10 rigsdaler, but the directors would not agree. The Greenlanders were quite content with 7 to 9 rigsdaler in wages, the directors felt;

those already employed received only 5 to 6 rigsdaler, but their wages could always be increased if they proved competent. However, this was not done for some time. The replies to Christoffer Jessen Pettersøn's questionnaires of 1727 and later had shown the universal opinion to be of the stability of Greenlanders working for the company to be negative. This preconceived distrust was bound to dictate caution in employing native labour.

The concept of "native" was meanwhile losing its clear definition. Due to the gradually rising number of marriages between Greenland women and the men stationed in the country, there arose the problem of the children's upbringing. It was not always suitable for the boys to be trained as hunters, although this was sometimes successful. These "half breeds", as they were summarily named, were regarded as Greenlanders by the authorities, simply because they were born in the country and not from any racial standpoint. More and more of these "half breeds" were born out of wedlock. If the mother could be married to a Greenland hunter it was possible for the boys to be brought up as hunters and so to fit into Greenland life. Although this could apply to some boys born of mixed marriages, others found themselves in a sort of no man's land where they had no opportunities of fitting into the Greenland way of life, while they did not grow up as Europeans.

However, these problems were only at an embryonic stage. Meanwhile, the directors were willing for sons of mixed marriages to be trained for service with the Company in some craft which was needed in the colonies, or alternatively for service with the mission. No mention is made of girls' education. That was the mother's responsibility, and followed the traditional Greenland pattern. The marital problems, by long-established tradition, came within the province of the Church, and hence, in the Greenland setting, of the mission.

The Company's interest in the development of Greenland labour was, as already mentioned, conditioned by the difficulty in obtaining sufficient workers. Nevertheless, there was a steady growth in the number of men stationed, first on account of the new settlements and secondly in connection with whaling. As this lasted only a few years and the men were sent home again, the figure for 1765 gives the most comprehensive picture of the position. In the nine colonies, with the outposts attached to them, 102 men were employed in all, made up of 20 "officers", 26 subordinates or artisans, and 56 "sailors" or "common men", i.e. boatmen and labourers. This did not include the handful of Greenlanders employed. When the Company took over the Greenland trade, Jacob Sewerin had a workforce of 35. The nearly threefold rise in the number of stationed men up to 1765 was also partly accounted for by a larger number being stationed at the individual colonies. A comparison between the numbers stationed by the Company in 1749 and 1765 respectively at the four colonies existing in the former year shows this growth:

		Traders and assistants	Craftsmen (coopers, carpenters, etc.)	Labourers	Total
Jakobshavn	1749	2	2	2	6
	1765	2	4	4	10
Christianshåb	1749	2	2	5	9
	1765	2	4	11	17
Godthåb	1749	2	2	8	12
	1750	3	6	9	18
Frederikshåb	1749	2	2	4	8
	1750	2	1	4	7

Although Godthåb was not where the greatest amount of bartering was done, it was nevertheless where there were most Company employees, closely followed by the other "old" colony Christianshåb. The big increase in Godthåb and Christianshåb was due to both colonies having large districts, which involved difficult and lengthy expeditions. If one adds to the total figure for the nine colonies the missionaries, stationed priests and Moravian missionaries, the number of Europeans was around 150, apart from their children and wives, who brought the total up to about 300. No labourers were married to European women.

Although the total of Europeans was small compared to the number of Greenlanders in West Greenland, the latter can be assumed to have declined within the colonial districts in the first part of the period 1750–74. In 1757, Lars Dalager could "testify for a fact that over the distance of sixty Danish miles (450 kilometres) of coast known to me for fifteen years, two-thirds of the inhabitants have vanished". He repeats this assertion in 1767. In 1752, epidemics, like the dysentery mentioned earlier, appear to have greatly depleted the population in the Disko Bay area as well as to the South. In the 1750s sickness was reported from both Holsteinsborg and Godthåb. Lars Dalager wrote in 1759: "May God preserve the few remaining Greenlanders from such a general and sudden mortality as occurred a few years ago, otherwise the colonies themselves will receive extreme unction." This "mortality" occurred in 1754, and in 1758 he reckoned that, apart from the Greenlanders who lived near Ny Herrnhut and a score of families within the Godthåb fjord compound, there were only twenty-six *fangers* left in the whole district. Dalager's information must be regarded with some suspicion, as it had at least one ulterior motive: to show how wretched was the Royal mission's administration at Godthåb and how excellent was the Moravian mission in every respect.

The Moravians enjoyed steady growth over the whole period, with a considerable number moving to Ny Herrnhut from the south. Arrivals and departures occurred annually at the various colonies, so that a proper census under the administrative conditions then existing was impossible from the outset. Along the whole coast there were continuous movements of varying numbers over varying distances.

The Godthåb "census rolls" for 1771 and 1772 show a decline from the first year to the next:

	Married		Single, children, widows and widowers		
	M	F	M	F	Total
1771	81	80	148	237	546
1772	71	71	139	214	495
				Reduction	51

These figures include the colony and all the settlements from Pisugfik in the north to the Qilángait islands in the south, baptized and unbaptized. In the same two years at Ny Herrnhut there were 529 and 535 respectively, so that the combined total for the district was 1,075 in 1771 and 1,030 in 1772, an overall reduction of 45. There was an increase in the number of baptized persons at Godthåb from 122 in 1752 to 283 in 1771, and again to 296 in 1772.

As to the proportion of married men to the rest in the whole district, there were 157 in 1771, and 153 in 1772. This figure represents about 15 per cent of the total of Greenlanders in each year: they were the element who carried on the local hunting operations, together with an undefined number of single men. Since in the past there had usually been a large number of children under the age of fourteen, it can probably be reckoned that of the single men, boys and widowers registered, the great majority were children under the age of fourteen. The percentage of wage-earners in the population as whole should therefore be reckoned at about 25 per cent of the total. On this quarter depended the general maintenance of life in Godthåb district as well as the revenues of the Trading Company in the area. This percentage corresponds more or less to that obtained with greater certainty from nineteenth- and twentieth-century statistics.

These random figures do not help us to calculate the size of the whole population in the eighteenth century, which one can only assume from correspondence and reports to have been declining. One can only guess at the causes of this. The fluctuation in trapping conditions and unusually long and severe periods of famine may have resulted in deaths at particular places. The trapping opportunities relative to the number of inhabitants in any particular place could affect the standard of living and the food situation. If there were too many people relative to what could be caught, it was, if not a disaster, still a source of impoverishment. Epidemics, of course, were a frequent threat.

Distribution of population was therefore a substantial problem which differed from one colonial district to the next. This complicated conditions for the two institutions, Trading Company and the mission, which were becoming ever more firmly established. Their interests virtually compelled them to adopt some kind of settlement and population policy, in which the Company's main idea was economic and mercantilistic, whereas the mission's was moral and religious education. This caused conflicts, which were intensified locally by the particular interests and desire for gain of individuals.

In the Trading Company the old idea of populating Godthåbs fjord with Icelanders raised its head again, true to the spirit of traditional mercantilism. To make a reconnaissance with a view to sending out Icelandic families, the Icelandic-born pastor Egill Thorhallesen was sent out in 1765 by the Company in consultation with the Missionskollegium. He stayed at Godthåb for two years and made summer explorations of the fjord settlements to the north and south of the colony, after which he joined the Godthåb mission. Having done so he was in no doubt that Icelandic families could make a livelihood for themselves in these fjords, but the cost, especially at the outset, would be heavy, particularly since the Icelanders were in wretched circumstances. He emphasized in his reports that if the plan was carried out, the settlements must be dispersed as the Greenlanders of the fjord were considerably interested in settling near these families.

Nothing in fact transpired from Thorhallesen's exploration except his brilliant description of the region.

REFERENCES

1. The names of the different types of seal are sometimes difficult to interpret. The spotted seal has large spots, so here it must be the *phoca vitulina*. The meaning of "those with small spots" is more doubtful. Probably it is the ringed or fjord seal, *pusa hispida* (el. *phoca foetida*). The small ordinary skins may be from the grey seal (*halichoeris grypus*).

2. To illustrate the sales of the goods most in demand, there follows a statement of the sales for certain years:

		1756/7	1757/8	1758/9	1769/70	1770/1	1771/2
Striped shirts, each	Ghb.	20	13	25	0	0	0
	Sktp.	25	39	47			
Blue striped or check	Ghb.	229·5	220·5	158	228	357	277
linen, by the *alen*	Sktp.	11	90	86			
Kersey by the *alen*	Ghb.	83·75	91	178·75	270·5	186	187
	Sktp.	84	79	135·5			
Common knives	Ghb.	26	9	32	6	16	18
	Sktp.	12	40	40			
"Childrens knives"	Ghb.	47	46	66	13	15	15
	Sktp.	40	85	34			
Files and rasps	Ghb.	27	13	24	0	0	2
	Sktp.	37	10	30			
Arrowblades, serrated	Ghb.	65	44	106	16	69	23
and sharpened, each	Sktp.	110	36	86			
Ulos (Womens knives)	Ghb.	29	29	46	4	40	0
each	Sktp.	40	27	64			
Rifles and shot-guns,	Ghb.	3	6	8	1	2	4
each	Sktp.	4	3	4			
Powder, fine and	Ghb.	32	28	32	31	10·5	10·5
coarse, per lb.	Sktp.	43	28	58			
Lead, per lb.	Ghb.	16	50	79·5	50	32	40
	Sktp.	64	54	48			
Shot, per lb.	Ghb.	32	0	0	0	0	0
	Sktp.	22	22	24			

(The *alen* expressed above is the Danish measure of length, approx. 2 feet or 63 cm. The "pound" is the Danish pound of 500 grammes, not the English pound of 453·6 grammes.)

No further analysis has been drawn from this. It is interesting to see, for example, how the sale of *ulos* in Sukkertoppen rose in the year after the establishment of the colony, whereas in Godthåb it was more stable. In Godthåb overall sales declined a great deal during the last years of the period. As a whole it was not large quantities being sold. Estimating four *alen* of kersey to a pair of trousers, about seventy Greenlanders may have got new trousers in 1771–2. The figures derive from the accounts mentioned earlier.

18

THE MISSION
1750–1782

Egill Thorhallesen was one of several gifted, idealistic, yet tolerant missionaries who were sent to Greenland by the Missionskollegium in the years from 1750 to 1782. Among them were still men connected by some family tie with the Egedes, such as Laurits Alsbach, Peter Egede, Niels Brønlund Bloch, Henric Christopher Glahn and Hans Egede Saabye. This connection acted as both a stimulus and a limitation since the tradition handed down from the Egedes worked against as well as for them. Many of the understandable yet mistaken views of both Hans Egede and his son Poul were acquired by their successors. The charisma of the spiritual pioneers made it difficult for new and perhaps more accurate points of view to be accepted. Through the Seminarium Groenlandicum the tradition was also injected into the growing number of students who "mortgaged" themselves (as it was known among the theological students when they applied for and were given a place at the seminary), and thus into the staff and the community.

Here Poul Egede set his mark on the rising generation of missionaries after Hans Egede retired in 1747. When the old bishop went to live outside Copenhagen, Poul was obliged to take over most of his official duties, although Hans continued to receive the missionaries' reports and summarized them for the Missionskollegium. In 1758, the year of Hans Egede's death, Poul became Dean and Inspector of the Greenland mission. As a result of his studies of the Greenlandic language and his publications during these years, he was appointed professor in 1761; thus Jacob Sewerin's wish for a chair of *Lingvæ Grønlandicæ* was finally realized, even although Poul Egede was not connected with Copenhagen University and his professorship was therefore only honorary. As Dean, he was adviser to the Missionskollegium on Greenland matters, but was not actually appointed to the Kollegium until 1774 when he became director of the Vajsenhus orphanage. In 1779 he was given the title of bishop, but it was not thought feasible to appoint him a real bishop like his father.

The dictionary that Poul Egede had worked on for so many years was published in 1750 with the title *Dictionarium groenlandico-latinum*. This book filled a great need, being the first dictionary in the world of an Eskimo language. Anyone needing to penetrate the mysteries of West Greenlandic could, after 1760, also refer to Poul Egede's grammar. This work was the first comprehensive attempt to analyse the Greenlandic language, in regard both to its morphology and its syntax. It is true that his system was based on that of Latin, which can be said to differ fundamentally from West Greenlandic. It was not until much later that a grammatical analysis on the basis of the language itself was achieved. After 1760 the student was spared the tedium of transcription.

Concurrently with these two indispensable aids, Poul Egede continued his translating. In 1758 he submitted his translation of *The Acts of the Apostles* which was immediately printed along with that of the Gospels completed the same year. At the same time he had been struggling with translations of the Epistles, to which he devoted even greater effort. Thus, both to finish his work on the dictionary and to enable him to continue translating the Bible, he expressed a wish to collaborate with those missionaries working in Greenland who were specially proficient in the language. But it was a long way across the Atlantic, and he therefore asked for authority to obtain the still active missionaries' remarks and corrections. For this reason he was appointed Dean and Inspector.

Among the missionaries sent out in the 1750s was Rasmus Bruun, one of the most notable linguistic scholars of his time. In Godthåb he translated a large number of hymns, and the year after he returned home (1760) he published the first Greenland hymn-book. In his spare time as a missionary he had also busied himself with translations from the New Testament. In 1761 Poul Egede announced that he and Bruun were working together on translating the Epistle to the Romans, but they had reached no further than the end of the third chapter in a month. Nevertheless, their translation of the whole New Testament was completed and printed in 1766 – it had been no small undertaking to find names for objects, expressions and circumstances still completely foreign to the Greenland people.

In 1755, Bruun described his difficulties in translation, this time of Luther's catechism. He had been obliged to borrow a few Danish words, which he still "tried to adapt to the Greenland pronunciation". Most of them are ill-sounding in their Greenlandic forms. His catechist, Berthel Laersen, dissociated himself vehemently from Bruun's translations the following year because of this too liberal introduction of foreign words: "I have also taken pains not to introduce Danish words, as far as possible, since the Greenlanders can neither understand them nor pronounce them". He also thought Bruun's translations too full of unnatural expressions. Laersen by contrast made use of Greenlandic words which "are able to some extent to convey the meaning of the Danish and which are immediately intelligible and understandable to a Greenlander as soon as he heard them". But he too, though married to a Greenland woman and living in close contact with Greenland society, was worried about his translations and never satisfied with them. Despite his gradually deepening knowledge of the language, he was always critical of his own works and cautious in judging those of others.

Translations were also undertaken by the increasing number of Moravian missionaries with a knowledge of Greenlandic. These were more concerned with the daily routine, more with speech than with writing, although the translators, like the royal mission, used transcripts at first and second hand. A remark of Rasmus Bruun gives a brief insight into their methods. It appears that a missionary named Johann Beck used an "explanatory" translation of the word "publican". This is presumably the source of the practice, later a characteristic one, of giving in Greenlandic, where no precise word exists or can be formed from the language's own resources, a brief description – which however, does not always cover the shade of meaning of the "translated" word.[1] This typifies the sisyphean struggle then – and indeed still – being waged by translators. The dislike of introducing foreign words into West Greenlandic stems from this practice. But these "explanatory translations" were in themselves clumsy. The possibility of forming words with the suffixes – *ussaq* ("that which resembles") or *-ut* ("means of . . ."), inherent in the West Greenlandic language, was not exploited by the translators to the same extent as by the Greenlanders themselves. In the linguistic sphere, cultural influences were at their peak, and the areas of conflict were many, with the people of the mission standing half-way between the two languages. The position of a Greenland-born catechist could invite ridicule. A church gradually came to be known as *oqalugfik*, viz. "the place where someone speaks". Hans Egede himself says that he was called "the Speaker" – in West Greenlandic *oqalugtoq* – and that his spoken Greenlandic did not sound very good to the Greenlanders at that time.

It was not the best Greenlandic that resounded from the existing "natural" pulpits in the areas along the coast. The great majority of missionaries never gained sufficient command of the language in the relatively short time they were active in the country. One individual came out in such haste that he had to use an interpreter not only for conducting the service but also when he gave his sermon. The interpreter was one of the stationed catechists, most of whom stayed in Greenland for a long time, some for the rest of their lives. Only one or two of the stationed mission officials achieved as great a command of Greenlandic as H. C. Glahn, who thought in the language when he wrote.

Preaching and the mission work involved not only various language difficulties but also the even more difficult task of explaining ideas. This limitation was encountered as regards both language and context when the catechisms were taught. The catechisms (*Elementa Fidei Christianiæ*) sent from Denmark were not much of a help. Hence Rasmus Bruun attempted a new translation. As he worked on it he found himself confronted with a strange complexity of problems. He suggested that the missionaries' talks on the catechisms should be collected and completely revised, giving them "a Greenlandic interpretation which would be comprehensible to the Greenlanders and more edifying than if one had to explain the sins of the *Kablunakks*, which received most punishment in the other explanations of the catechisms". His reason was that "they should be different from the explanations in regard to many truths which were acceptable in Denmark but which must be heeded more often there than in Greenland; for instance dancing, gaming, drinking, sexual passion, enticement and profiteering among others are not customary among the Greenlanders". There is something comic about the difficulties experienced by the mission in explaining and indicating the penalties for European sins, which were not normally committed in West Greenland society. Attention was thus being freshly drawn to the existence of such sins. Bruun's way of thinking and scientific method in basing the mission's work, in its form and content, on the society in which it was operating, were sound. But like so many "right" ideas, Bruun's were in advance of their time and so came to nothing.

God's word was a different matter: it was unchangeable. For the formal thinker it was dangerous and presumptuous to change or rewrite God's word in the literal sense, and if anything it was even more dangerous to rewrite Luther's explanations, to which the Danes were committed to the letter. There were already plenty of dogmatic problems, and to get round them it was necessary to compromise – like Hans Egede who had originally translated "Give us this day our daily bread" in the Lord's Prayer by "Give us this day that which tastes good" (since he thought that *mamaq* meant "food") and later by "Give us this day the seal-meat we need".

Nevertheless work on language training continued. The editions of books printed for the Missionskollegium were not very big, and those that were sent out fared badly. The baptized Greenlanders who could read wore out an unbound book within a year "because they have little opportunity for keeping and preserving such things". As a consequence of the small editions, the lack of teaching aids was felt fairly quickly, particularly as instruction in reading became more and more widespread. Hence copying was done and, in short, people made their own textbooks in each place. Henric Christopher Glahn, for instance, left three notebooks containing a history of the Bible, as well as notes and observations on the language, which long figured in the inventory of the Holsteinsborg mission.

Otho Fabricius, the missionary at Frederikshåb, regarded the shortage of suitable literature as a big obstacle to all aspects of the mission's activities. Nevertheless he resorted to "home manufacture" himself when in 1774 he proposed an "Order of Salvation", which he had used among his congregation and now suggested should be printed. It was "adapted to the simple Greenlanders' ideas". The older books were both inadequate and incorrectly translated; the latter defect, however, could now be remedied, thanks to a "better acquaintance with the richness of the language", so each missionary produced his own textbooks, which spread confusion among those of the baptized who moved around from place to place. At the same time he submitted manuscripts of a new catechism, mentioning a bigger manuscript for a new amended dictionary. He submitted the latter for approval somewhat later, and it was only published in 1804 after much revision.

This translating activity and continual copying, and the great need for more printed books and pamphlets, are a major feature of the mission's work. Written material was essential for maintaining and renewing Christian knowledge. Teaching the children to spell and read, and some to write, was therefore a prime duty of the mission. In Hans Egede's *ABC* of 1739 certain parts of the catechism were included simply as spelling and reading exercises, and thus instruction in reading and Christianity were combined. However there must have been those who thought it unnecessary for the Greenlanders to be able "to read books", as it was called, since Glahn felt obliged to argue for its usefulness in 1768.

Glahn had gone to Greenland in 1763 and was stationed at Holsteinsborg (Amerdloq) until he left the country in 1769. His interests were wide, and he showed a lively concern for the practical side of his work. As regards teaching, he had already remarked early on that the psychological Greenland phenomenon *igtôrneq* (I, p. 248) was a stumbling block. It was particularly difficult for the Greenland-born catechists to overcome this *igtôrneq*; but it was also difficult for the children and young people to answer questions put to them when a number of them were gathered together. So he had the idea of encouraging the

Y

young to teach their nearest relatives, and always subsequently used the form of mutual instruction. He got the children who could spell to help those who were learning while they themselves progressed with reading.

The older people found great difficulty in acquiring the knowledge required in order for them to be put forward for baptism. Glahn reported an example from Holsteinsborg of the determination of older people when they were determined to be baptized. Two elderly women had attended Bible classes for six years, "and for most of the time proved very diligent". Before he left Holsteinsborg he baptized them, since he realized that there was no hope of their learning any more, however long they studied. According to the missionary at Frederikshåb, it was extremely difficult "in the course of one winter" to teach adults "who come from among the heathens" to read. It was much easier with those who had lived among the baptized since childhood or for some years. The same applied to understanding and adoption of the Christian faith. Among the baptized these matters were discussed, and a spiritual environment was created. Despite its relatively heavy demands in the wider practical fields of knowledge, the mission had succeeded in making its message penetrate people's minds.

A steady growth was clearly taking place at that time with individual local differences. It was natural that everywhere, as at Holsteinsborg, the younger age-groups found it much easier to absorb knowledge than did their elders. When Bruun, the missionary, came to Godthåb in 1752 everyone who had been baptized by the Royal mission was assembled there. He examined them there and then, with Berthel Laersen as interpreter, in the "Order of Salvation" and Luther's Catechism, and all were able to give good answers, "the old ones only according to the sense but the young according to the tenor of the words". Here we see how formal repetition was valued above an answer which expressed the meaning other than in the approved words.

No doubt Berthel Laersen's report was dictated by the wish to show his own work in the most flattering light. Bruun apparently had a rather different view from Laersen of the state of knowledge of the baptized people in Godthåb. After the missionary Drachardt returned to Denmark in 1751, Laersen had to run the mission together with Poul Grønlænder. Although not so markedly as Drachardt, he too leaned towards the Moravian view. Bruun thought that the Greenlanders in the congregation did not know much about Luther's Catechism or the Order of Salvation. They were "captivated by Moravian principles, and do not know for certain the doctrine of the Holy Trinity, but they call Jesus the Father and the Creator, etc., all according to the known Moravian method of teaching". Moravian songs were used instead of the translated hymns. The prayers that had been translated were also not used. "They claimed that they must pray from the heart, yet they are still not capable of doing so for want of sufficient knowledge". The congregation under the Godthåb mission was "confused and in a poor way". According to Hans Egede, the presence of an ever-growing number of brethren at Ny Herrnhut caused confusion. The missionaries at Godthåb were forced to operate on two fronts, conducting their own missionary activity and simultaneously opposing the Moravians, which was as wearing for both parties as it was confusing for the Greenlanders.

This animosity at Godthåb between the representatives of the Royal Mission and the Brethren on the spiritual level developed into equally intense material competition. It was inevitable that the Greenlanders connected with the two missions should join in this competition, in which the tactics employed were not always edifying. The conflict was not just between the theologically better trained Danish missionaries and the "unlearned" Brethren. Bruun, probably the most "academic" of the eighteenth-century missionaries, was extremely aloof towards the Brethren from his arrival in 1752 until he went home in 1760, but had contact with one of them, Johann Beck, through whom he believed he could "in time persuade them to adopt a uniform doctrine" – in which he was certainly not successful. On the other hand, he pointed out that the economic situation, which gave the Moravians an advantage in regard to both the Greenlanders and the Trading Company, was the reason for the Godthåb mission being in such a wretched state.

In the years that followed, the conflict became even more bitter. The Godthåb mission had grown in Bruun's time from 96 in 1752 to 163 two years later, despite an epidemic in which some had died. Apparently this growth continued, but parallel with it the flocks of the Brethren increased too, in itself a potent reason for increased competition.[2]

In 1754 Lars Dalager came to Godthåb as trader, and even before that time he had criticized the work by the missionaries sent out by the Missionskollegium. He may also possibly have heard from Rasmus Bruun and his successors the judgment-day sermons that he criticized so strongly in his journal. He protested against the abuse from the pulpit which was directed at himself and the Trading Company employees. In any case it seems that the disputes only flared up in earnest after his arrival in Godthåb, not during Bruun's missionary period, and again even more fiercely after 1760. However, not all the blame can be laid at Lars Dalager's door. Other more fundamental elements played their part. First was the question of the basis of faith, or more precisely of conversion and baptism. Time and again the Brethren were enjoined to bind themselves to Luther's catechism. Thus, whenever the Royal missionary in Godthåb found that the Brethren's teachers, even if not actually denying them, still neglected to instruct the catechumens in those elements of faith which royal missionaries have unflaggingly to impress on them, this was regarded as a breach of duty, almost bordering on treason.

This was strictly no concern of the Godthåb missionary. However, the competitive factor introduced into the situation right from the start made it impossible for the matter to remain one for the individual parties directly involved. Comparisons between the two congregations were inevitable. They passed judgment on each other's sermons and forms of prayer, and the Godthåb catechumens were derided by those newly baptized by the Moravians because they had to wait so long for baptism. The whole affair seems to have developed into the formation of local groups with all imaginable characterstics of group feeling and conflicts. The Godthåb people, who belonged to the weaker congregation both materially and financially, viewed the Moravians' fine meeting-house with ill-concealed envy. Bruun drew the attention of the Missionskollegium to the outward differences, and later on Thorhallesen tried unsuccessfully to get surplices sent out in order to make the service in Godthåb more colourful: the ordained teachers of the Brethren wore white robes when giving communion. The desire for a better chapel at Godthåb was partly competitive in spirit.

For the censorious mutual appraisal between the two congregations, the Brethren's own teachers were partly to blame. They regarded both the missionaries and the baptized Greenlanders at Godthåb as "unconverted". Of Arnarsâq and another baptized North Greenlander, the Brethren wrote in 1741 that "they certainly had some knowledge but had not yet had any experience of the Holy Ghost. May Jesus have mercy on their souls!" The lay members at Ny Herrnhut were the worst offenders. In connection with the request for surplices, Thorhallesen remarked that the native members of the Brethren were beginning to see visions which they spoke of to the members of the Godthåb congregation: in a dream one man at Ny Herrnhut had seen tôrnârssuk (in the vernacular of that time, equivalent to Satan) clothed in a long black robe. There was no doubt that he had in mind the Godthåb missionary's cassock. False rumours circulated concerning the practice of forbidden arts. This Lilliputian society showed its worst aspects in gossip and spite.

When the economic conflict began to be felt, an absurd situation developed. Lars Dalager was probably responsible for this becoming a personal feud. He was for ever calling attention to the flourishing

condition of the Moravian community and the excellent institutions by
which they could maintain the zeal of their members, as well as providing them with a livelihood. Against this he drew a picture of the
miserable circumstances of the Godthåb community, completely for-
getting that this difference was to be explained by different conditions,
including those that the very growth in the Brethren's congregation
had brought about. The growth came from outside the district.
The majority came from the south and some all the way from what
later became the Julianehåb area. It was realized in Ny Herrnhut
that they might gradually become over-populated, the chances of
making a living thus being jeopardized. But this influx of Greenlanders
from the south was undoubtedly regarded by the people of Godthåb
as an invasion of the hunting fields over which they had the right of
use. An intense feud arose subsequently between the Greenlanders of
the Brethren's community and the people of Godthåb – for instance
at Pisugfik where the inhabitants in 1777 described the Moravian hunters as *ardluit* (blubber-grabbers). The year before, Niels Egede had
complained that the *fangers* from Ny Herrnhut penetrated into the
Holsteinsborg district and hindered the trapping of the local inhabitants.

It is true that these two examples had nothing to do with the acute
conflict in Godthåb in the 1760s, but it seems that the competition due
to over-population had already become evident to the Godthåb
section of the community. Further, the Godthåb congregation did not
live only in the colony but also in various places around the fjords to
the north and north-east and out along the coast. To the south there
was only one place, the Qilángait islands, where for a short time the
number of settlers was fairly large, but it was later abandoned.[3] This
settlement actually belonged to the Godthåb parish but there were
difficulties involved in serving it. It was not successfully served until
1771 when Thorhallesen installed a catechist who had been sent out
from Denmark on one of the islands. But by then the inhabitants
were about to divide themselves between the Moravians and the
mission at Godthåb, and move away.

Lars Dalager apparently allowed himself to be dazzled by the outward form of the Brethren. He extolled their services and prayers.
Time and again he defended the Moravians strongly both to the
Missionskollegium and to the Board of the Trading Company. In doing this he never feared for his own security; indeed he seems to have
enjoyed turning against the authorities and telling them the "truth".
With a fairly short experience behind him he put his finger on the
sorest point for the mission – the short time that the missionaries
stayed there. Changing personnel, changing methods and always a

period of transition during which "the newly arrived successor . . . has to feel his way forward in everything" were the bane of the mission. On the other hand, as we have already mentioned, he praised the Moravians' institutions and the spirit of waiting on providence which reigned among the Brethren. He described the royal mission at Godthåb as "a powerless limb under the Trading Company" – to the very face of the Secretary of the Missionskollegium. He dared not express to the Kollegium his views on matters of faith, although he did so to the less theologically informed Trading Company directors: "It has been an all too costly and, for the colony, an all too oppressive mission that has been run here for some years. God knows to what purpose". As to the "general complaint" regarding the difference in doctrine between the Brethren and the Mission, he wrote that it was obvious since it revealed itself in deeds. "It was to be desired that this matter might one day be given proper consideration when it would be clearly shown whose deeds were best founded on the precepts of the revealed word and common sense". Two years earlier he had been considering whether to join the Brethren so as to spend his "old age" under their protection.

During the time of Rasmus Bruun's successor Dalager's contempt for the Godthåb mission crystallized into an extremely unpleasant correspondence in which the Brethren also participated. It reached its peak, however, in the time of the next missionary against whom Dalager set the labourers and the other Trading Company employees; in every conceivable way this unfortunate man was ridiculed, his services were interrupted and he was cheated over his provisions. The sailors too showed open scorn for the missionary and the catechists. In 1765 one of the colonists accidentally shot the catechist Poul Grønlænder, a disaster which further clouded the atmosphere at Godthåb. At this time Thorhallesen arrived in Godthåb and witnessed his colleague, the missionary Bjørn – the personification of gentleness – being knocked down by Lars Dalager with his bare fists. This brutal act had its consequences for Dalager: in 1767 he was ordered to leave Godthåb.

This long conflict widened the breach between the Mission and the Trading Company, because Dalager, who was undoubtedly a reliable trader, had given the impression that the Brethren were extremely useful in the country from an economic point of view. He considered only the visible results at Ny Herrnhut without considering that they were largely due to the Brethren obtaining most of their supplies without the Trading Company. Their economy depended to a considerable degree on well-wishers in Denmark and the Netherlands. On the other hand, the Greenlanders' surplus catch went to the colony for barter, so that the trader there suffered no "inconvenience" from the Brethren. But against this he had to supply the Royal Mission, which was certainly onerous, as the Mission's initially small number of *fangers* were unable to contribute as much as those of the Brethren's community. Furthermore, when it came to comparing the "spiritual results" among the Godthåb congregation with those at Ny Herrnhut, he overlooked the demoralizing effect of his own and the colonists' behaviour over the years on the people of Godthåb. The Brethren were spared the brutality and fighting, the drunkenness and rowdiness, and the general lawlessness witnessed by the Godthåbers although they lived only a short distance overland from Godthåb. Immorality and exploitation of the local Greenlanders were common in the colony, whereas at Ny Herrnhut, although the church discipline and compulsion became more and more rigid in the Brethren's congregation, a spirit of collaboration reigned.

The Trading Company directors were gradually drawn over to the Moravians' side, first because of Dalager and later on account of the general ill-will towards the Royal Mission, but mostly because the directors saw ways of reducing their costs through the Brethren's community – an understandable reaction since their policy was restricted by lack of capital and meagre trading profits. This became clear in 1754 when Fiskenæsset was established as a trading station but not as a mission; it was impossible for the Trading Company and for the Missionskollegium to appoint a missionary to the station because there were funds neither for a colony house big enough to accommodate him, nor for his annual salary.

Dalager had already suggested to the Missionskollegium the same year that they should "think of transferring the mission to the Moravian Brethren". Anders Olsen, who was appointed to establish the station and who had Moravian leanings, had offered to teach the catechism to the local Greenlanders with the help of his Greenland-born wife. The following year he repeated this proposal, but no move was made by the Missionskollegium.

In 1754 Matthæus Stach and another of the Brethren chanced to be at Fiskenæsset on their way back to Europe and took the opportunity of surveying the ground. The following year it was suggested to the chairman of the Trading Company, Count Berckentin, that the Brethren should set up a mission station there, but no decision was taken. Dalager then apparently acted on his own initiative and made a direct request to the Brethren to set up the station. Still nothing was done, but in Herrnhut itself Johann Beck, the pastor that winter, suggested that Matthæus Stach should undertake its establishment and this was agreed. Finally in 1758 Stach travelled to Fiskenæsset and set up the Lichtenfels station.

Dalager reported the *fait accompli* to the directors of the Trading

Company, who did not object to the Moravians' establishing themselves at Fiskenæsset, "so long as they do not take upon themselves more than is permitted by the royal ordinances granted to them". His quite arbitrary interpretation of this ordinance was that the establishment of the Moravians at Fiskenæsset did not go "against the will of His Majesty whose most gracious charters to them go much further". Not till 1760 did the Missionskollegium complain that the directors had not consulted them first on this matter, the Moravians' new establishment being absolutely contrary to the permit they had originally been given. This interpretation was Dalager's and not the correct one.[4] The Trading Company passed the matter to the Missionskollegium, which ordered the Moravians to move out of Fiskenæsset. However, the Kollegium quickly changed its ground; it decided that, "since they are there, they must be allowed to remain". But there was to be no recurrence, as the kollegium wrote to the directors. This message was a very mild enforcement of the ordinance of 13 February 1750, which made no reference to their possible establishment anywhere other than at Ny Herrnhut, and only forbade them from making many journeys, receiving supplies from private ships and taking Greenlanders with them to Europe or elsewhere.

This accentuated the conflict between the Company's interests and the competence of the Missionskollegium. In correspondence with both Godthåb and Fiskenæsset in the following years, the Company expressed continuing satisfaction with the presence of the Moravians at Fiskenæsset, because they made "every effort to see that the roaming Greenlanders were persuaded to settle down near the station and in the surrounding district". The Company and the mission went their separate ways.

The Brethren continued their work of extending and improving conditions at Ny Herrnhut. Gradually they organized the community in the same way as they had done elsewhere. The personal freedom of the individual was subjected to the will of God; one way this was expressed was that the community decided all important issues by ballot. To organize themselves and enforce church discipline, it was essential that the members should be closely linked with the place. The promise to live near Ny Herrnhut was, if not actually part of the baptismal vow, either a prerequisite for receiving baptism or a consequence of it.

The physical division of the community which began in 1749 with the construction of the first "sister house" was continued. The congregation was divided into "choirs" consisting respectively of the married, the widowed, young single men and young single women, the latter two categories being separated. The choirs held "choir meetings" where people sang, prayed and gave witness, often weeping freely. The same thing happened at special prayer hours. Many of the customs and ceremonies used, such as the love-feast (often at night), the washing of feet, and the kiss of peace were quite foreign to the Danish mission. Exclusion from participation in the ceremonies was one method of maintaining religious discipline, for it also meant exclusion from the community. Just how significant that was to the Greenlanders in the community and to those aspiring to join is clear from Cranz's story of a widow who left the Moravians because they did not baptize her quickly enough; it was too humiliating to be among those who had to leave the church when it was announced after the sermon that it was time for the unbaptized to go home.

An air of gaiety was inseparable from the Brethren's meetings. Dalager described this vividly. He is astonished at how the Brethren "now, after the passage of a few years, have built a fine little church or meeting-house, how on Sundays at the sound of trumpets more than three hundred Greenlanders stream in, one of whom takes a wind instrument, another a violin, the third a zither and so on, to which the choir intones songs of praise and thanksgiving". Cranz reports that the Moravians' instrumental music consisted of a combination of two or three violins and a couple of flutes, and sometimes a couple of zithers – just such as a small village might produce. A few Greenlanders had learnt to handle these instruments, while others were able to play the French horn and trumpet. Both instrumental and vocal duets were played – there was serious musical ability among these Greenlanders. Singing was an essential feature of the Brethren's meetings: "The congregation is accustomed to singing in a slow, lingering and slurred way", which in the twentieth century is still characteristic of church singing everywhere in Greenland. The Moravians brought European music and song culture to Greenland. At the royal mission's services and prayer meetings hymns were also sung, but without instrumental accompaniment.

This important cultural element lasted longer than others which the Moravians of that time introduced into the everyday life of Greenland. Their various institutions, such as the "sister house", came to an end in the 1760s, although the widow-house continued and took over the name of "sister house"; the organization crumbled. However, the church discipline and order that had prevailed around Ny Herrnhut, and which was also maintained at places where the Brethren established missions later were preserved. In 1765, Thorhallesen described their establishments as "superb". It was mainly the wives and daughters of the married brethren who maintained the characteristic tidiness and outward order of their establishments, such as their fine gardens. What was done by the Moravian women in humility and without complaint certainly had far-reaching significance; peace permeated the Moravians' mission establishments.

Such peace was not in evidence at other places in Greenland where the Trading Company and mission were supposed to be collaborating. There were exceptions, such as Holsteinsborg, Egedesminde and to some extent Sukkertoppen, but elsewhere there were frequent changes of missionary, fights between the employees of the two institutions, and shortage of funds to extend the mission and provide the necessary equipment. Even so, intensive work was done towards the fundamental goal – the conversion of Greenland to Christianity.

It accorded with the rationalistic spirit of the age (then beginning to show itself in Denmark) that most of the missionaries working in West Greenland in 1750–82 were as interested in material conditions and development as in the non-material. The reports, letters and journals that have been preserved speak as much about trapping and employment, social conditions and personal difficulties as about the missionary work and teaching. Conversely, the Missionskollegium did surprisingly little during the same period to support and aid its missionaries and stationed catechists. In some places, the missionary and native priest led an isolated existence, being forced to keep apart from their fellow-countrymen because of the conflict with the Company's local staff. Contact with the local population was difficult, especially owing to the language problem. Nor was the lack of funds which plagued the mission's activities calculated to make the local hardships and dependence on the local trader easier to bear.

The limited subsidy which was granted to the mission barred it from providing the new settlements with suitable missionaries. This in itself helped to divert the work in Greenland from its real purpose; the Trading Company and the mission were running side by side, but the Company now tended to emerge as the superior partner. It was the Company which established the new settlements, simply from the viewpoint that trading ought to be extended in order to make the Company pay, and in order to drive out the Dutch. The mission thus had to accomplish its task in the settlement as best it could. This attitude may well be regarded as reflecting the Company's own economic difficulties, not emotional antagonism towards the mission as such. That the directors' decisions in individual cases gave this impression is another matter.

When Fiskenæsset was set up, it was clearly demonstrated that the permission given by the Missionskollegium to the establishment of the Brethren's community at Lichtenfels after the event was probably solely due to there being no one available who could be appointed and to the trade not having allowed for a missionary's accommodation. When

Ritenbenk was established in 1755, the place had to be served by the catechist Dorf from Christianshåb, which thus had to do without him for a while. At Claushavn and Jakobshavn it was eventually arranged that missionaries could work there throughout the year and not just on summer visits. These two places being more populous were more important than Christianshåb.

At the beginning of the 1750s the mission in Disko Bay developed a revivalist nature. Without lapsing into tearful sentimentality, or dogmatic or ceremonial eccentricities, the two missionaries who worked there during these years were marked with Moravian piety. They therefore attached more importance to the individual's spiritual awakening than to the hard work of teaching. But a revival usually depends on the personality behind it. As missionaries in Disko Bay were always changing from the mid-1750s onwards, the revival died out and a sort of reaction set in. The "dissolute sailors" had an unfortunate effect on the situation. One missionary (in Christianshåb), unable to cope with the opposition he encountered and the difficulties put in his path, broke down and committed suicide.

Hence, the prosperity of the mission in the Bay came to depend largely on the catechists who were sent out by the Missionskollegium. Three of them were to play an important part in this way, one being Johannes Pedersen Dorf, who, as had been done in the past, acted as both catechist and assistant trader, in both of which capacities he came to Ritenbenk. On his return two years later, he was appointed to Jakobshavn where he continued to fulfil the same dual function. When Egedesminde was established in 1759 he was moved there the following year, and like the trader there, Niels Egede, he was both missionary and employee of the Trading Company.

The second of the three catechists was Jens Pedersen Mørk, who like Dorf was married to a Greenland woman. Both continued in the tradition of Poul Egede, under whose influence they had come. Mørk achieved fame by working from 1757 until his death in 1780 as priest at Claushavn. Working with a succession of missionaries, and at times carrying on the work alone for several years, he personified continuity in the school and mission work at Claushavn, and progress there was marked by unusual calm and harmony. He was proficient in the Greenlandic language and made translations of sermons.

The last of the catechists in Disko Bay referred to by name was Jacob Poulsen Møller, who had come to Christianshåb in 1751 and soon became a valuable helper for the ever-changing missionaries. He too married a daughter of the people. Like the other catechists he was employed in various places. During the vacancy at Jakobshavn in 1763–4 he was the sole mission official there, which perhaps went to his head: the next year, when the missionary Jørgen Sverdrup arrived, he began to act as a prophet with polygamy as his main theme. He was sent to Denmark, but partly because of his Greenland family and partly because of the Missionskollegium staff shortage, he was sent out again.

Through their marriages to Greenlanders all three of these catechists came closer to the Greenland population than other employees of the mission. As a result, the gap between the population and the mission narrowed, and through their permanent ties with the country, the mission acquired the kind of continuity which characterized the work of the Brethren; it created a feeling of trust between mission and population, without which the mission could make no progress.

This feeling of trust was also probably behind the fact that people streamed to Egedesminde when Niels Egede established this new colony in 1759. It was deliberate and with due regard for financial considerations that it was Niels Egede who established Egedesminde thus saving a missionary. But he said immediately that he could not do everything at the new colony. For this reason the directors of the Trading Company the following year appointed Dorf as catechist and assistant at the new colony and it was he who moved it to its new site in 1763, now fully employed by the Company as trader. However, he still carried on as priest; Gammel (Old) Egedesminde and Ny (New) Egedesminde were both served in the summer by the Holsteinsborg missionary and in the winter by one of the missionaries in Disko Bay. The colony did not get its own missionary until 1769. Few people lived at Egedesminde itself, although there were a number to the south of it.

This missionary began to take an interest in the population of the islands west of the Bay and on the south coast of Disko. There were many people living there and the fishing was always good. In 1773, an assistant came from Holsteinsborg with fourteen baptized Holsteinsborgers to settle on Disko; one of them wanted to be the other's "teacher". The missionary himself hoped to be able to settle in Disko the following year for the rest of his time in Greenland, but he was unable to do so: and Godhavn (the new whaling station) did not have its own missionary until 1783.

North of Disko conditions were, if possible, even more difficult for the mission. The new colony Nûgssuaq had no mission at all during the three years of its existence; nor, when the colony was moved to Umánaq in 1761, was it possible to have a missionary sent out from home. Not until four years later did Umánaq have its first missionary. During those years no form of missionary work was carried on among the local population. Either rumours from the south gave forbidding descriptions of the missionaries, or the Trading Company people used the missionary as a threat. After the missionary came to the colony, almost all the local Greenlanders came to visit him, "but when I explained to them who I was and why I had been sent to the country, they made a concerted rush for the door without giving a reason". Probably, he went on to say, "most of them are *angakoks* and incredibly depraved", and they could have heard how certain missionaries treated such persons. But the atmosphere soon changed and later he had little peace from their visits. Eight years later, the missionary then in office was able to report that the congregation consisted of ninety-one baptized persons.

The most northerly colony, Upernavik, was established in 1771, as we have already seen, but there were good reasons for doubting whether it would be possible to get a missionary to take up the work so far north and in such an inhospitable place. The Trading Company therefore put off building a dwelling-house for the missionary for as long as it possibly could, and the Royal Greenland Trading Company, once it was established, did the same. The missionary finally sent out in 1779 never had even tolerable living conditions. Upernavik was then a source of great difficulties to both the Trading Company and the mission.

Life was not nearly so hard in the more southerly settlements established in this period, although there were difficulties enough. Some of the problems however, were the same – for instance, the bad relations between the mission and traders, between missionary and catechists and between trade employees and the "sailors". Despite or perhaps because of these difficulties, the mission worked steadily towards its goal.

Holsteinsborg was given its first permanent site in 1764. When Sydbay was established in 1756, it was decided to send a missionary there, but few Greenlanders lived there for long, and the mission was thus partly superfluous. So the station was moved in 1759 to Amerdloq, where many more people were living, and the mission maintained itself there until 1767 when everything was transferred to the nearby colony. The first trader at Sydbay, a rough type of man, was soon recalled home, and replaced first by Niels Egede and, when the colony was set up on its present site, by the trader C. F. A. Wulff. This honest and hardworking man was one of four orphanage boys sent out in 1751 to Christianshåb. He was soon so proficient in Greenlandic that he was able to win his spurs, especially at Claushavn during the revival. He entered the service of the Trading Company, working part-time at Sydbay, and went over to full-time service in 1764 although, like Niels Egede, he continued to serve the mission. Three years later Niels Egede came back to Holsteinsborg and Wulff went to Copenhagen and worked for the Trading Company there.

It was not due solely to these two fine traders that the mission for a long time made such good progress at Holsteinsborg. Throughout this period missionaries who were capable, tolerant and intelligent held office there, foremost among them being Henric Christopher Glahn. Arnarsâq stayed with him for a year in 1763–4, after which she went to join Sverdrup, the missionary in Jakobshavn; in both places she served the mission. The peace of the place was to some extent broken when whaling was resumed in the 1770s. There had been some doubts about moving the colony from Sydbay to Holsteinsborg. This brought it much closer to the colony of Sukkertoppen, established in 1755 at Kangâmiut, a bare 130 km. from Holsteinsborg. This did not have the effect that had been feared, particularly as in 1783 Sukkertoppen was finally moved some 50 km. to the south. From the start in 1755 there was heated discussion about the mission at this new colony. Anders Olsen, who had founded Fiskenæsset the previous year, was to establish it. Olsen had leanings towards the Brethren and so suggested that they should set up a station at Sukkertoppen just as they had thought of doing at Fiskenæsset; he seems to have been unaware of the conflicts between the mission and the Brethren which were not, however, as heated then as they were a few years later. Anyway after much correspondence, it was decided that the Godthåb catechist, Berthel Laersen, should move to the new colony. This finally took place in 1757. Laersen and Olsen were already friends, which promised well for relations between mission and trade. Both were honest, Laersen probably having greater talents.

Under Laersen's calm but resolute influence the number baptized grew steadily over the years. Yet he felt dissatisfied because the ordained missionary at Godthåb did not always manage to come to Sukkertoppen to celebrate communion and carry out baptisms and marriages. The Missionskollegium then offered to ordain Laersen although he was not a graduate in divinity. After two years' reflection he accepted, and was ordained a missionary in 1764, remaining in that capacity there until his death in 1782. He was the first catechist to be ordained in Greenland. The Missionskollegium's offer to Laersen was once again primarily an outcome of its financial distress. The house was too small to accommodate an ordained missionary as well; the Trading Company's enforced parsimony had seen to that. It was necessary to use the fund granted to keep missionaries in those places where they were already. To Frederikshåb, which was always difficult to reach by sea, the Missionskollegium did not always succeed in sending a missionary. One of Jacob Sewerin's relatives, Jochum Grønbech, who from 1746 had been an assistant at various places in the service of the Company and an acting trader at Frederikshåb during its early difficult period, went over after some hesitation to the service of the mission. From 1751 to 1767, with the help of his Greenland wife, Grønbech maintained the continuity in the mission there. He was a gentle person and well liked by the population, with whom he had strong ties because of his marriage and his fluency in Greenlandic.

Of the successive missionaries at Frederikshåb Otho Fabricius was the most gifted. His tireless observations of nature did not relate directly to his mission duties, but his scientific methods led him to alter his professional approach by taking as his starting-point the actual conditions at the settlement and in the district. (The new procedure was also due to difficulties in getting good catechists.) The scattered population had to be instructed; if the unbaptized could not come to him because of the trapping, he must follow them. He therefore learned to row a kayak with astonishing speed so that he could be with his catechumens.

Fabricius stayed in Greenland only for five years. In 1772, the year before he came home, he told the Missionskollegium that physical disabilities and "poor eyesight" unfitted him to continue his duties, but "internal" anxieties and "a very disadvantageous situation in which these have placed me in the last few years *vis-à-vis* the Greenlanders" were the main reasons for his applying for home leave. At the beginning he had not thought he would give up this work so soon, "but then I had quite different notions of a mission in this country, which grievous experience has taught me is far too limited and beset with obstacles to be able to make any great and satisfactory progress". He had previously drawn the attention of the Missionskollegium to "a number of these obstacles . . . and as long as these cannot be abolished or better regulated, one gradually grows tired under the burden". Perhaps he could be more useful elsewhere "and have the opportunity of extending [my] studies, which must here lie almost dormant". It was as a disappointed man that he left Greenland – disappointed over the conditions under which the mission was forced to operate and the poor support it received from home. This was the result of shortage of the necessary funds. Yet Fabricius left behind many baptized people at Frederikshåb and under his successors the number of baptized in the district further increased. However, many of the pagans who received instruction were from the south, which was one of the reasons why the mission wished to increase its activities there.

Thus the old desire to reach the Eastern Settlements, the Company's wish to cover the coast as far as Cape Farewell and, finally, the mission's need to ease the burden on Godthåb and Frederikshåb coincided with both the material and spiritual needs of the population in the extreme south. At this point the Moravians come into the picture again.

On the basis of a Godthåb missionary's long report on the Moravians' circumstances at Godthåb in 1765 and the far-reaching proposals of Egill Thorhallesen and another missionary for improving the mission there, the Missionskollegium had called upon the leaders of the Brethren to produce their charters and authority to carry on their work in Greenland. The Brethren were unable to produce anything other than the royal permit of March 1742, relating to the permission given to Matthæus Stach to minister. In 1769 the Missionskollegium recorded that the Moravians had no true royal charter, and it was not prepared to obtain one for them now. On the other hand, it would have been manifestly unjust to ask them to give up their mission and leave Greenland. The secretary of the Missionskollegium therefore put forward the resolution that "the kollegium . . . in order to free itself from all responsibility and possible future appeals, requires the usual oath of allegiance and submission to the spiritual and temporal authorities in general and the Missionskollegium as authority in particular". The only effect of this was that through Fr. Quist, the royal confessor, a royal proclamation was signed in December 1771 exempting the Moravian Brethren from any inspecting authority as regards their teaching, church or mission other than their own bishop, and they were given a specially worded oath of allegiance. This proclamation was the only instance where Struensee's cabinet[5] concerned itself with Greenland.

The Moravians must have been uncertain during these years whether they would continue in Greenland. Nevertheless Matthæus Stach undertook a long journey to the south in 1765-8 as far as Igaliko, or Julianehåb, fjord. It seems that the Brethren were hesitant about establishing a station so far south. In Copenhagen it was discussed between the Missionskollegium and the *Danske Cancelli* whether it was expedient to set limits to how far the Brethren should spread. The *Cancelli* would not agree to this (1771) for fear that the Moravians might become dissatisfied and leave the country. The only thing that could be agreed upon was the desirability of indicating to the Brethren's teachers that they should refrain from unfair competition; the same admonition would be given to the royal missionaries.

In 1772 Anders Olsen told the Trading Company's directors that he wished to resign as trader at Sukkertoppen, and suggested that a colony be established in the south, or at least that a journey of exploration should be made there. Both ideas were accepted. The following year he reached the place where Peder Olsen Walløe had spent the winter: Olsen considered it suitable for a colony, and after some discussion one was established there. With royal approval it was named in 1776 after the Queen Dowager Juliane Marie – Julianae Haab, Julianes-Haab, Julianehåb.

Simultaneously with Olsen's arrival at Julianehåb, the Brethren established their station even further south, calling it Lichtenau. The directors of the Trading Company immediately stated that they could neither give permission to the Moravians to establish a settlement south of Frederikshåb, nor forbid them from doing so. They were obviously trying to avoid being caught between the Missionskollegium and Guldberg's government.[6] However, the Missionskollegium, which had already made representations to the *Danske Cancelli* concerning the Brethren's arbitrary conduct, wished "this dangerous sect" to be forbidden to extend its activities under penalty of banishment. The much-quoted benefits to the country which the Brethren's presence was supposed to provide were repudiated; their handicrafts were unusable and they did neither trapping nor fishing themselves, while they preached false doctrines and notoriously confused the population.

This led to a series of declarations during 1776 and 1777, culminating with the *Cancelli*, in agreement with the Missionskollegium, ordering the Trading Company through its employees in Julianehåb and all colonies and stations along the coast to see that the Moravians did not spread without prior permission. The Royal Greenland Trading Company subsequently did not dare to ship supplies to the newly-established Moravian station, where the physical conditions, especially regarding accommodation now became stringent. Thorhallesen thought this had prevented them from "getting their choir meetings, the mainstay of their religion, properly going", and they had made little progress in the district. The outcome was that the Brethren stayed at Lichtenau and developed it into an attractive settlement, partly through successful horticulture.

Thorhallesen was mistaken in claiming that these southern Brethren had had their wings clipped from the start. By 1780, with the usual speed of baptism, they already numbered over 200 members. The royal mission at Julianehåb on the other hand was dogged by bad luck. The missionary sent from Denmark died when his ship was lost. In the meantime a stationed catechist looked after the mission and did the best he could. Not until 1779 was it possible for a missionary to be installed there. The population of the district was scattered, so the missionary adopted the practice developed at Godthåb of establishing subsidiary missions run by a catechist, either one from Denmark or a Greenlander. The number of catchists sent out had grown throughout the period, but towards the end the number of native catechists was rising too – young men of Greenland birth who were trained by the local missionary if they were thought "fit and proper" for the trying task of being the sole champion of the spirit in a small station. In the schools women were often used as teachers, especially for the smaller children; they were also seen to carry on a sort of indoor mission within their own family circles. Arnarsâq's example in both respects inspired others.

The isolation of the work was felt not only by the catechists but by the missionaries who, in certain places, had exhausting disputes with the Trading Company's employees. The inconsistency in the mission's activities, especially between the spirited teachings of the ever-changing missionaries and their *ad hoc* advice and decisions in individual cases of doubt and conflict were plain to see and often discussed. It was not just the difference between the Moravian and royal missions that was noticed. Otho Fabricius wrote in 1768 of his distress at hearing the Greenlanders talking of the differences between one colony and another. The mission ought to be consistent both in "church routine and customs" (presumably ritual and religious discipline) and in "method of instruction . . . so that at least the Moravians cannot, as is usual, have this to reproach us with, as I have already unfortunately had to experience".

The resignation of Glahn the same year and Fabricius' letter of 1768 causes the Missionskollegium to ask Glahn to inspect several places along the coast on his journey home – a task from which Glahn humbly but resolutely begged to be excused, pointing out that Jørgen Sverdrup at Jakobshavn and Egill Thorhallesen at Godthåb were better placed to carry out useful inspections, provided each carried it out *in his own* province, (there was a difference between north and south in particular because the Brethren played an important role in the south and none in the north).

The Missionskollegium took a long time in coming to a decision. When Glahn arrived in Copenhagen in 1769 the matter was naturally discussed again. In 1770 Poul Egede put forward Glahn's suggestion of two vice-deans, who would be better able to give effect to the Missionskollegium's ideas. The Moravian congregations prided themselves on having "episcopate, co-episcopate, presbyteries, diaconate, etc., etc.", so the royal mission might "be made equally impressive" if it had two vice-deans. Hierarchy of authorities and titles was on its way to becoming a factor in West Greenland society.

The royal appointment in 1773 of Sverdrup and Thorhallesen as vice-deans and inspectors for the most northerly and most southerly missions respectively was made effective. These two vice-deans, each in his own area, were meant both to test the Christian knowledge of the baptized and catechumens and to inquire into their conduct; apart from this spiritual task, they were also to interest themselves in the nutritional and living conditions of these Greenlanders, and report on these as on all other matters to the Missionskollegium. The church registers were to be put in order and unified. The teaching in individual schools was to be supervised, and they were to take charge of the training and induction of the native priests; as regards the instruction, they were to see that the standards required and the knowledge imparted were of a piece. They were also to study the wild life, especially anything that might improve the country's economy. The two vice-deans were periodically to meet and confer at some point on the coast and were to mediate in disputes between the mission and the local representatives of the Trading Company.

The work of Thorhallesen and Sverdrup is thought to have resulted in greater uniformity and better order in the Royal Mission. Thorhallesen's work was short-lived, since he left Greenland in 1775, yet he succeeded in travelling over the whole of his region, but he did not meet Sverdrup at Holsteinsborg. He was not replaced as vice-dean so that the southern diaconate was quickly left to its own devices again. Sverdrup, on the other hand, worked untiringly in his dual role as missionary at Jakobshavn and as vice-dean until he returned to Denmark on leave in 1788.

REFERENCES

1. It may be sufficient to refer to the "translation" of, for example, "world history", which retranslated says: "the world's [or the world inhabitants'] about their progress [in time and space] narratives" (*silamiut ingerdlausiánik oqalugtuat*); or of "the economic life in society": "the most proper way in which one can purchase anything in society" (*inuiaqatigîgne iluanârutigssatigut pigssarsiorneq*).

2. It is difficult to be objective in describing this long drawn-out and discreditable affair. David Cranz, the historiographer of the Brethren, stayed at Ny Herrnhut in Greenland in 1761–2. In his *Historie von Grönland*, 1765, he does not mention the discrepancies which existed in the years before and after the time of his residence. Our description must therefore rely on sources from other camps, especially on the surviving letters and diaries, most of which are in the archives of the Missionskollegium. These sources nourished the Mission historian Hother Ostermann's very subjective, sometimes rancorous narratives. From his one-sided source material he too has given a one-sided treatment, although here and there he represents the Brethren according to their deserts. Ostermann's narrative was of course deplored by the Brethren (Karl Müller, *200 Jahre Brüdermission I–II*, Herrnhut, 1931 *et seq.*). In the text to which this note is an introduction, a more critical treatment of the source material is attempted; however it is given importance according to what is muted by the influence of the affair.

3. Another far smaller settlement was situated in the bay of Qarajat, about 25 km. due south of Godthåb. This settlement had sixteen inhabitants in 1771. A year later this number was reduced to ten, all of them apparently members of one family.

4. It is an open question which ordinance Dalager interpreted in the letter to the Directors. In fact no Royal privilege to the Moravians exists according them permission to settle down in Greenland. We only have the letter of introduction to Hans Egede of 4 April 1733, and later the different letters and orders concerning their transport and provisions, the latest being the ordinance of 2 February 1750. It is possibly the notifications of 20 November 1744 and 29 January 1745, (about persons staying with or on journeys to the Moravians), which are deliberately interpreted by Lars Dalager, and it seems that it was just those which the Missionskollegium had in mind. When the Brethren were later asked for documentation of their privileges in Greenland it was naturally very difficult for them to find any, because it did not exist. The Missionskollegium claimed in 1760 that the Moravians' settlement at Fiskenæsset was in defiance of the notifications of 9 April 1740, 10 April 1744 and 26 March 1751 concerning prohibition of navigation and trade on the colony districts, including settlement on the coasts without Royal permission. This claim was clearly justified, as the Moravians had infringed these notifications.

5. Struensee's period of "cabinet government" lasted from September 1770 to January 1772. This German-born former physician obtained full power, the King's mental incapacity growing more and more pronounced. His period of government saw a flow of reforms in the spirit of enlightened despotism, but his ideas did not embrace Greenland affairs. There is a comprehensive literature on Struensee, including English works.

6. Guldberg is Ove Høegh-Guldberg (1731–1808) who, as the teacher of the Hereditary Prince Frederik (half-brother to the King) co-operated in the fall of Struensee in 1772, and was the actual leader of the government until 1784. He played (as will be told later) a leading part also in the development of Greenland affairs.

19

THE MISSION
AND CULTURAL CHANGES
1750–1782

"It is almost indescribable what close attention the Greenlanders pay to our words, acts and gestures, and how easily they can be hurt over a little thing", wrote Lars Dalager in the 1750s.[1] He had reported earlier that the Greenlanders, when alone together, generally talked of "the *Kablunakks* [*gavdlunât*] – namely ourselves – and the trade with us and do not forget to repeat everything that they find ridiculous in us." Niels Egede had observed how the way the Moravians and the missionary Drachardt talked and behaved generally had rubbed off on their Greenlander converts. The Moravians' jargon was picked up quickly by the community.

The influence of the Greenlanders on each other and their discussions among themselves apparently had a significant effect. Both proceeded at a more even level, what was difficult to understand being passed over and what was being talked about better grasped. The difficult part was perhaps discussed with the Greenlandic-speaking catechist, whether stationed or native-born; the missionary himself was sometimes quite an exalted authority although this cannot be said of missionaries such as Glahn, Saabye, Thorhallesen, Fabricius and, least of all, about Jørgen Sverdrup. Even such an authority might have his rival in the same neighbourhood. It was, as already mentioned, the older generation who opposed the change in the young people. An old widow, who must clearly have had a powerful *itoq* authority, prevented her eldest married son and his wife, children, brothers and sisters from staying at Holsteinsborg for instruction. Once she was dead, the son promised they would all come.

The sense of community played an important role, as was shown by the growth of the Moravians' congregation. The example of the individual or his household influenced the mass, and vice versa. This may partly explain why the mission grew in spurts, while influences hostile to it from any group could cause regression for a time, as in Disko Bay

339

in the 1750s. The revival which took place in Godthåb and its immediate vicinity at the end of the 1760s happened suddenly, with consequences felt along the whole coast. It spread like wildfire from place to
place, the result being that the missions grew, the number of baptized
increased and more and more wanted instruction for baptism. In July
1777 the catechist Thorkild Magnusson, a nephew of Thorhallesen, was
able to inform the Missionskollegium that he hoped to be able to "do
something in regard to the only remaining unbaptized family here in
the northern fjord" – this about fifty-six years after Hans Egede made
the first laborious start.

The revival had started at Godthåb itself, but had then spread
southwards when families from the Qilángait Islands and Qarajat Bay
came to Godthåb in 1768 and demanded instruction. Simultaneously
the spark flew north to Pisugfik, which had been the target of Hans
Egede's early mission tours. Influenced by a great *angákoq* there, all the
inhabitants had decided to move to Godthåb to receive instruction.
There had "come over" this *angákoq*, "who has hitherto been an oracle
among them, . . . a strange terror and emotion", and in the winter of
1768 the missionary was sent for. Thorhallesen could not go himself,
and sent an enlightened Greenlander in his place to comply with their
wishes. This was for Thorhallesen the most gratifying experience he had
ever known, but it became for him "a wretched and laborious bargain".
The Moravians intervened, not with the intention of settling at Pisugfik,
but because they wanted to take the inhabitants away to Ny Herrnhut,
including the *angákoq*. Thorhallesen had to oppose this forcibly and
gave the Moravians' leaders a warning. Pisugfik had long been the
Royal Mission's domain and any revival there was primarily the
mission's responsibility to support, and Thorhallesen realized the
economic hazards involved in gathering together too many people in
one place. By attracting only some of the Pisugfikers to them, the
Moravians would be recklessly bringing about an increase which might
have adverse consequences.

On this problem of settlement, the interests of the mission and the
Trading Company were inextricably interwoven. What would have
appeared the essential object – to promote or at least maintain the
population's means of livelihood and food – often cut across the line of
development which the mission and Trading Company pursued –
sometimes ignoring their lack of economic resources. Right from the
beginning of both the mission and the Trading Company, the
"roaming" had been denounced. This embraced not only movements
due to the hunting cycle but also more lengthy journeys along the coast.
Resulting from the mission's wish to keep the population in one place,
or in a small number of places within easy reach of each other, for the

purposes of teaching the children and adults, a sort of conurbation arose. The Trading Company, for its part, wanted the *fangers* to concentrate on the animals that afforded the best barter and therefore to remain where the hunting was best. But they also wanted expeditions restricted as much as possible, so as to facilitate bartering, and the products put in store as quickly as possible ready for dispatch. However, the colonies were established where access was easiest by sea and harbour facilities existed, less account being taken of the possibilities of making a livelihood. Hence, when a new colony was established, the Trading Company wished the Greenlanders with their families to settle near to it so that it would become well populated and yield a better profit. Right into the 1760s the management were still urging the traders at Sukkertoppen to ensure that the Greenlanders' "roaming" should eventually stop.

The Trading Company could already see that there was possibly an optimum size for a colonial settlement, even though the directors did not seem to realize it fully. At Jakobshavn, the chief assistant was praised for having attracted more people to his station than his predecessors had done. At the same time, it could be observed that the trading profit was no larger than it had been ten years before. As soon as a colony was established, it acted like a magnet. This happened at Egedesminde when Niels Egede established the southern settlement, as well as later when it was moved northwards. The trader Dorf, who also acted as a catechist, informed the Missionskollegium that he had persuaded the population to continue to live where they normally did because there was still no missionary at Egedesminde, but he had no doubt "that there would still be enough people drawn there".

The mission's views in the 1750s were to some extent represented by the Christianshåb missionary Bloch, who said that he had never regarded the checking of the Greenlanders' "roaming" tendencies as absolutely essential. He was of the opinion that, for instance, at Claushavn there were such abundant hunting facilities (in 1753) that they "can by God's blessing obtain their essential needs without having to seek elsewhere . . . ." He therefore preferred to settle at Claushavn where many Greenlanders lived and hunting conditions were good at that time, rather than at Christianshåb. This represented a quite different line of thought, namely to establish the mission where most Greenlanders already lived – a far more sensible idea. But when a colony had once been established and most of the essential buildings were erected, it was not so easy to move. This was proved whenever, during the first sixty years of the century, attempts were made to move Godthåb. As regards Claushavn, the approach of Bloch appears to have been right. Even in 1775 the missionary Hans Egede Saabye thought it inadvisable to try to move the local baptized Greenlanders, from the point of view of either the trade or the mission. But he emphasized that to draw conclusions on all the colonies from the experience of one was a mistake.

This influx naturally did not yet have a serious effect on the colonies and outposts which were the last to be established in the period up to 1782. On the other hand, it did do so at Sukkertoppen. When this colony was established, virtually no Greenlanders lived there, but the missionary Berthel Laersen anticipated that some would move in. He proved correct, and ten years later he reported that two settlements far to the south in the district had been practically abandoned. In 1770 he had over sixty catechumens – probably a result of the revivalist wave from Godthåb – and the congregation had increased to about 300.

At Holsteinsborg special conditions prevailed. Not many people lived at the mission, nor had they when the colony was first moved there in 1764. Four years later Niels Egede wanted the few who did live in the colony to move away. There were several settlements under the Holsteinsborg mission, staffed by catechists of whom only one had been sent out from Denmark, the others being the so-called native catechists. Subsequently, the number of Greenlanders residing at the colonial settlement grew.

Niels Egede gave his opinion in rather acrimonious terms about this "concentration", as the influxes were called. He had heard from Godthåb and Sukkertoppen that all the Greenlanders in those regions were "now prepared to live at the colonies . . . for they see that the Moravians have received so many of them . . . the trade is impaired, the colonists lose, the Greenlanders become layabouts and beggars, and the unfortunate marriages with the Danes also contribute to both poverty and contempt." The Greenlanders should look after themselves and live where it best suited them from the point of view of their livelihood, and native catechists should be appointed to instruct them, all under the missionary's supervision. However, he was no more confident that the Greenlanders would "look after themselves" than earlier, when he said that it must be strictly forbidden either to force them or entice them with gifts to move to the colonies. Niels Egede's words are difficult to interpret with certainty. His damning assessment of the Greenlanders, which he pronounced in 1769, seems out of keeping with the fact that he continually returned to the country and ended by living there almost permanently. There is no concrete evidence of any missionary or trader making any payment or gifts to persuade the Greenlanders to move to the colony or attach themselves to the Brethren. Moreover, there is no mention of compulsion ever being applied to any Greenlanders. That it might have been advantageous for them to stay in the colony is another matter – in times of need they could get help there. There is ample confirmation of the impoverishment caused by the influx into the colonial settlements, "the concentration" of people in places where work was not plentiful. However, as in the case of Claushavn, this was not true everywhere.

At Frederikshåb, both the missionaries and the traders gradually realized that the people were averse to leaving their trapping grounds. It is true that a few moved to the Frederikshåb colony first as catechumens, subsequently forming a growing congregation. However, most of the population in the district preferred to remain in the places they knew. Furthermore, Frederikshåb was a poor trapping ground. As usual, the colony had been established with harbouring, building and fresh water facilities in mind. The majority of those baptized as the years went by lived at the Natdla settlement on one of the islands off the colony itself. As at Holsteinsborg later, a stationed catechist lived there permanently.

At Frederikshåb, as in many other places, it was the widows, usually with dependent children, who made their way to the colony. The life of such widows and their children in the small settlements, even if they had near relatives, was certainly not attractive, and it was understandable for them to go to the mission where help might be available when needed, and to the colony where there were opportunities of work. This was why the stationed catechist Jochum Grønbech, one-time trader at Frederikshåb, and the missionary Myhlenphort, who took up his duties in 1761, both showed interest in the economy of the colonial population; both worked hard to improve it from the scanty funds available. In 1768, the year Otho Fabricius took up his duties, the revival movement reached the Frederikshåb district, and the number of converts at the colony began to grow at a perilous rate. Grønbech had died the year before and no new catechist had replaced him. Some at least of the Greenlanders must have sensed the danger in this increase of population on the relatively poor trapping ground; they informed Fabricius of their intention to leave, and asked him to go with them; they did not want to lose the spiritual help of the mission. In the winter of 1770–1 a number of them moved to Iluilârssuk, about 25 km. south of the colony. Too often at Frederikshåb, there were days when the *fangers* could not put out in their kayaks, whereas at Iluilârssuk there were better possibilities for expeditions, and trapping was more plentiful.

This exodus proved beneficial. Another evacuation arranged by the Frederikshåb trader in 1769 (to Kungmiut, 65 km. south of the colony) was less successful. Some of those who moved returned, while others travelled further north. The few who remained later wanted to move away because the missionary was unable to visit them often enough

during the winter. Otho Fabricius had to comply with their wishes in
1771. This disclosed an insoluble conflict between spiritual and material
necessities. It could only be overcome by appointing catechists and
building dwellings and school-houses for them in the various places,
and it seems that both the Missionskollegium and the Trading Company
shrank from the expense.

This desire for the appointment of several catechists was strong at
Godthåb, even before the Pisugfik revival. Because of the intolerable
situation at the colony between the mission on one side, and Dalager
and the other Trading Company employees on the other, the missionaries Thorhallesen and Bjørn wanted the mission moved away from
Godthåb, to avoid the economic and moral corruption exerted by the
traders on the mission and the Greenlanders. The catechists would be
the so-called native catechists who would be appointed to the places
usually lived in by Greenlanders who had not attached themselves to
the mission. This suggestion was not acted upon, but when the Pisugfik
revival came, Thorhallesen had to take new measures to prevent the
population of this northern area from moving to Godthåb. Some people
had moved to Godthåb as early as 1768 from the other places to which
the revival had spread, but they had had no success with their trapping.
Those who had remained behind in their settlements did not want to
move away, but were eager to receive instruction in order to be
baptized. Thorhallesen was therefore obliged to request the Missionskollegium for funds to build two or three small houses which he and the
catechist could take it in turns to occupy on visits. On his own initiative,
but in collaboration with Hans R. Storm, Godthåb's new and far more
kindly-disposed trader, he had already had a modest hut erected at
Pisugfik, where the need was greatest.

Thus Thorhallesen started to expand the Godthåb mission by means
of what he called "lay missions", i.e. annexes erected in the smaller
settlements where the population was familiar with the trapping
conditions. Such annexes had as their spiritual mentor either a stationed
catechist or a native one. This led to a continuous growth in the number
of baptized, which continued over the years until few pagans were left.
This arrangement also benefited the Trading Company. The Pisugfikers
certainly began to notice the competition from the Moravians' Greenlanders, but their bartering improved and so did their own living
standards. It was the catechists who came off worst. The grants needed
for their houses were hard to obtain, as were the necessary building
materials which had to be sent from Denmark. Here, and at many other
places along the coast, and in many different ways, Otho Fabricius'
remarks about the mission being hampered at every term were confirmed.

Between 1765–75, however, most colonies continued to experience a growth in the number of inhabitants. This assertion cannot be proved but is based on remarks in correspondence and the need in the colonies for more spacious meeting rooms and classrooms. For the Trading Company this growth was noticeable in the barter transacted. The mission was blamed for this continued "concentration", which was apparent to the Trading Company directors from reports they received, and the directors therefore requested the Missionskollegium in 1775 to urge the missionaries "to take care that the Greenlanders do not become perverted or change the nation's ancient and original economy and mode of life, which might be damaging, not only to the mission itself, but especially to the Trading Company, and a burden and an expense." By this approach the solution to the problem was shirked, and the rift between the Company and the mission deepened. The Company was representing itself as the party most seriously harmed by a situation which it had in fact greatly helped to bring about.

The Missionskollegium was not an institution which asserted itself, and in this instance it must have known that the strong man of the Government – the King's Secretary, Ove Høegh-Guldberg – was backing the Trading Company. Orders were therefore immediately sent out to the missionaries to make the necessary arrangements, in agreement with the local traders, for the evacuation of the baptized so that "they are distributed and directed to places known by experience to be the most productive of food". The directors allowed the traders to think that it was the Missionskollegium's actions which they were being ordered to support.

The order took no account of the differing conditions that prevailed at the various colonies and mission posts. It prompted the missionary at Frederikshåb to report that only a very few Greenlanders spent the winter in that colony, and thus evacuation was inappropriate. The Greenlanders at Iluilârssuk were thinking of moving to a better place. The settlement even further to the south at Kûngmiut, which had previously been abandoned, was now populated again, but the population would only stay there if the trader would let them have rifles on credit. The missionary had to admit that these rifles were necessary at Kûngmiut if the inhabitants were to take advantage of the spotted seal migrations in March. The Greenlanders were learning how to fish in troubled waters, and take advantage of the situation.

There was no reason to do anything further at Godthåb than had already been initiated at the beginning of the 1770s, except in the case of the cramped Moravian congregation. This had grown to 535 members in 1772 and was still growing – partly due to the establishment of Lichtenfels and partly to the growing mission at Frederikshåb, which in turn caused the influx of Greenlanders from the far south into Godthåb to fall off. In 1768–70 the Brethren thought they did not want any more adherents because it was difficult to exercise the control they considered necessary over so many, and as already mentioned there was a limit to how many the place could support. This was a reason for the establishment of Lichtenfels; the establishment of Lichtenau in 1774 did not "relieve" the congregation at Ny Herrnhut to any great extent.

However, an exodus from Ny Herrnhut would have compromised the whole discipline of the congregation, which the Brethren wished to maintain; if an evacuation were carried out within the Godthåb district itself, those evacuated would come up against the Greenlanders evacuated by the royal mission. The number of good trapping grounds in the Godthåb district was limited. So the Brethren went underground to avoid the order relating to splitting up, although there is no indication of how it could have been carried out in their case. It probably happened because the good-natured trader Hans R. Storm took them under his wing to avoid trouble. The silence regarding the Moravians' existence during these years indicates that the cover was effective.

At Sukkertoppen evacuation was carried out in accordance with all the rules. Through the trader's zeal and Berthel Laersen's complacency, it was so quick and effective that Laersen had to inform the Missionskollegium in 1777 that, if the trader ordered all Greenlanders away from the colony, his presence would be superfluous. At Holsteinsborg, because of the resumption of whaling, the very opposite of an evacuation occurred. In Disko Bay area Claushavn and Jakobshavn were certainly the best trapping grounds, so that an evacuation from these would have been absurd. At Ûmánaq the population carried on as usual. In the end the Egedesminde missionary concluded that it would still be beneficial if the population continued to live scattered but that it was necessary to have catechists appointed as teachers. Thus one came back to the crux of the whole mission work – limited funds. All in all, the evacuation orders of the Missionskollegium and of the Trading Company were an empty demonstration. Perhaps it was that the mission had to be shown its proper place in relation to the trade – the predominance of the Trading Company in the following years might suggest this – or perhaps the whole operation was due to the directors' ignorance of life in the Greenland colonial districts where situations developed according to climate and trapping opportunities. These were decisive factors, but the mission, Trading Company and whaling stations attracted the Greenlanders, so that the colonial populations continued to grow. The outcome of this was a desire in certain places for larger meeting houses, which was aroused by the Moravians' church hall; also the growth of the congregation made it impossible to continue using the so-called church room, which was in the stone house built in 1728 (marked 6 in Niels Egede's sketch of its ground plan – see page 208). Before 1754 work had started on a larger church building which Lars Dalager received orders to complete, but it must have been sited too close to the river which flows past the stone building, because in 1756 this building is mentioned as having been destroyed by the river during the thaw "more than a year ago". The building was reconstructed in 1756–7, when it is described in greater detail in the inventory as a timber frame building 15 metres long and 7 metres wide, with brick infill between the timbers. The church hall occupied 10 metres of the length of the building and its full width. The rest was taken up on the south side by a narrow "porch", which was a lobby and at the same time a store-room for church furniture. At the other end the hall was partitioned off from the school-room. The loft was used for storing the baptized Green-landers' dried *angmagssat* (capelin). This church building at Godthåb cannot have been very solidly constructed, as only ten years later it needed radical repairs. After Thorhallesen was sent out there were always two missionaries in the settlement, and the school-room then had to be taken over to provide rooms for one of the missionaries and a stationed catechist. Presumably the school was then held in the catechist's room or in a hut. Finally, in 1770, a grant was made to repair the building from the foundations upwards. At the same time its width was increased by two metres. This only enlarged the living accommodation slightly. The size of the chapel remained the same, this was as far as the available capital would stretch.

No doubt it was the knowledge of this shortage of capital which caused people in other colonies to take matters into their own hands. This happened first in Holsteinsborg and in a way which especially pleased the mission. The revival had spread from Godthåb and had had the same effect at Holsteinsborg as elsewhere: the number of baptized increased. After a successful whaling catch in the spring of 1771 the baptized Greenlanders offered a number of casks of blubber and delivered them straightway expressly as a contribution to the construc-tion of a church or meeting-house, which the congregation desperately needed. The missionary wrote that it had come as a complete surprise to him and that it was done entirely on the initiative of baptized people who even offered to contribute more later if the whaling was successful. The proceeds of the blubber so collected were to be used in Denmark to purchase the necessary building materials. Over the next two years these materials reached Holsteinsborg and on 6 January 1775 the small but solidly-built church was consecrated – the first towards which the Greenland congregation had itself made the main contribution.

The desire for a church or meeting-house was cherished by the baptized Greenlanders in many other places too. At Frederikshåb a different procedure was followed from that at Holsteinsborg. Here the people overcame their wishful thinking and contented themselves with a building of turf and stone with a turf-covered wooden roof. With great difficulty Otho Fabricius succeeded in getting the necessary materials sent out during 1772 and 1773 but the building that resulted was a miserable one. On one plot, however, the baptized Greenlanders had not abandoned their dreams. They wanted a bell "like the one at Godthåb, but the trader cannot be persuaded to order one, and the mission's funds apparently will not stand such an expense". Whether their wish was fulfilled is not revealed. Although unfinished, the church was in use from August 1772.

The revival at Godthåb also reached Disko Bay, where the number of baptized increased everywhere. At Jakobshavn, where Jørgen Sverdrup was missionary from 1765 until 1788, so many were baptized in the early 1770s that the missionary's room could no longer accommodate the congregation. The Holsteinsborg experience was copied, and after a whaling trip in 1777 the local Greenlanders collected 27 casks of blubber and 12 standard pieces of baleen, which raised over 500 rigsdaler when sold. Sverdrup reported the congregation's wishes to the Missionskollegium, and attached his own rough plan of the church. At the same time the Greenland congregation sent a separate petition to the Kollegium. The many new settlements that were to be established in the Bay in those years delayed the despatch of material for the church at Jakobshavn, which would in any case cost more than the sums collected. The congregation had bound itself to make further deliveries of negotiable goods, and it paid in all 85 per cent of the total building cost, the Missionskollegium and the Trading Company meeting the remainder. In 1782 the fine building was ready. With its heavy timber construction it could certainly vie with the Moravians' church hall, which Godthåb's church was far from being able to do. However, all further church building then came temporarily to an end.

In most places where there were trained teachers (pastors and either Danish or native catechists), it was still necessary to hold school in the catechist's room, in the hut where he had his living quarters, or in some family hut or other where there was enough space. Churches, where they existed, were too expensive to heat every day. Education, as we have already seen, had developed from being for the few who were taken on at the colony as boarders, into something for every child living in a settlement; hence a schoolroom was imperative. At Jakobshavn Jørgen Sverdrup himself paid for the building and maintenance of a turf hut for this purpose.

These were the conditions under which the missionaries and catechists were supposed to work. The Missionskollegium was only able to provide them with basic funds for promoting spiritual life. The shortage of money also affected salaries: the missionary was usually paid 150 rigsdaler a year, as well as rations, equivalent in the 1740s to about 50 rigsdaler. The food ration received by missionaries, traders and assistants was the so-called officers' ration (half as much again as a private soldier's) besides which a quantity of wine and so-called spices were provided. Ordinary brandy was part of the private soldier's subsistence allowance, whereas the officers received "French brandy" or cognac. The provisions supplied were seldom appetizing, let alone conducive to good health. It gradually became the custom for the colony to hold two years' supplies of the most essential European stores. This could not be adhered to in some years when for any reason the colony's supply ship failed to turn up. The traders had standing orders that the oldest supplies should be distributed before new ones were broken into, which meant that fresh food, save what could be obtained through trapping, fishing and hunting, was almost never eaten. If one could not spare the time to obtain fresh food by one's own efforts then one had to try and obtain it by barter. Thus, the missionaries, the stationed catechists and probably the Company's own people too, could appropriate imported goods up to a limited amount and use them to barter for meat, game and fish from local *fangers* and fishermen. Anything else that the stationed Danes wanted in the way of special goods had to be ordered from Copenhagen. It was the ordering of so-called commission goods which gave rise to all kinds of delaying tactics and prying by the Trading Company. Both provisions and commission goods took up a lot of space in the small vessels, and the Company therefore levied a high freight charge on commission goods (15 per cent) to reduce orders to the minimum.

Because of the requirement that two years' stock of provisions should be kept, there were often clearance sales of perishable commodities at the store. Bacon and butter became rancid, the salt meat became slimy, and bread, biscuits and hard tack went mouldy. The biscuits often had to have the dust and cobwebs brushed off them. "It is quite odd to sit with the bread on one side of the plate and a brush on the other", noted H. C. Glahn. But even these biscuits were better than the stone-hard dry hard tack. The stationed catechists also received provisions as part of their remuneration, but this consisted only of one private soldiers' ration and a smaller quantity of goods for barter. Their cash wages varied between 10 and 15 rigsdaler a year to start with, but after about ten years' service they might rise for the deserving to 50 rigsdaler – at which time they might also aspire to an officer's ration. Overall, it was substantially less than the salary reached by the Trading Company's assistants, who also had officers' rations. It was also generally less than what was paid to the labourers in the colonies.

The mission employees were scorned for their low pay. Traders, assistants and even the humble labourers showed their contempt at every opportunity. In many cases this feeling communicated itself to the local Greenlanders so that they too felt entitled to look down on the catechists. Only the presence of truly outstanding men in the mission's employ induced respect for their work, and where a stationed catechist lived on his own, he had authority. Many stationed catechists married baptized Greenlandic women, but some of these left the service of the mission and joined the Trading Company, although one returned to the mission after a period as trader. This occurred because in Jacob Sewerin's time the catechists had been sent out to serve both the mission and the Trading Company. As evidence of the "division of labour" in Greenland, which developed more and more, those sent out were later allowed to work for only one of the two institutions. It was often necessary to exhort both sides to be mutually tolerant and sociable. Collaboration between them was a rarity. The general opinion held of the catechists was expressed as follows by the trader and former priest, Johannes Pedersen Dorf, to his son in 1772: "If Poul Egede should offer you [a position] as catechist, decline it, for I am spending a lot of money for you to learn something, not just to become their errand-boy." The son was being educated in Denmark.

The need for catechists to be sent out from Denmark was great, but to satisfy it was impossible due to the Missionskollegium's shortage of financial resources. Thorhallesen begged for suitable candidates to be sent out, but he emphasized at the same time that conditions for them must be bearable from the outset "so that they will not be too great a burden on the missionary or be regarded by the other Europeans here with scorn". He did not dare to rely on native catechists. After a visit to the settlement in Qarajat Bay south of Godthåb, Thorhallesen said he was reasonably content with the inhabitants' knowledge, but . . . "weakness and confusion of ideas must always be expected so long as their instruction must be left mostly to the native catechists, in whom a misplaced consideration for their fellow-countrymen often breeds an equally misplaced indulgence over God's affairs." The *igtôrneq* which the various missionaries had noted with regret in the Greenland catechists was recognized by Thorhallesen as a serious obstacle in their work. The native catechists were indeed torn between their home environment and the demands made on them as moral and religious counsellors.

Lars Dalager clearly found the native catechists incompetent and nothing but a source of expense to the mission, but little weight can be given to his opinions concerning the teaching and work of the royal mission, coloured as they are by his incomprehensible contempt for the mission in general and its branch at Godthåb in particular. In 1758 the Godthåb missionary had six young Greenlanders whom he intended to train for the mission's service. At the same time the old and worthy stationed catechist at Claushavn, Jens Pedersen, expressed his doubts about employing native priests because he feared that they would leave when they felt the inclination. This tendency to leave a job which had been held over a fairly long period gradually became a recognized phenomenon both within the trade and in private employment.

It is unknown exactly how many native catechists were employed in Greenland. Few are heard of over any length of time, but there is no mention anywhere of native catechists running away from their duties. However, Lars Dalager had taken the Greenlander Qivioq into service as a labourer in 1756; and this man stayed in the colony's employment right up to 1799, but his attendance could never be relied upon. It was in connection with Qivioq that Lars Dalager opposed Greenlanders being employed in the service either of the Company or the mission. Such a Greenlander would be removed from his natural sources of livelihood and become unproductive. As he had to rely on the Trading Company and would thus eat some imported food, he would be drawn further way from his natural living conditions.

The remuneration of the native catechists was fraught with this dilemma. Time and again missionaries' letters show that the Greenland-born catechists could not survive on the small additional food ration, which they had only won with difficulty. To subsist at all, they had to go hunting in addition to their work as catechists. Thus Jørgen Sverdrup reported of the native catechist Nicolaj that he received 12 rigsdaler in wages and half a portion of all the coarse foods. This could not have sufficed for his family, had not Sverdrup helped him from his own rations. Between September and May the catechist's official work prevented him from going ice-fishing or hunting – while an illness had made him unfit to paddle a kayak, so that he could not procure anything in the short summer either. The following year the missionary Hans Egede Saabye at Claushavn tried to explain the problem to the Missionskollegium. If a native catechist worked steadily and faithfully at his job, he urged, it should be taken for granted that he could thereby earn his daily bread. The 10 rigsdaler he received in cash was not enough. He had to teach while others went trapping and, if he wanted to buy any of the catch, he had to pay with provisions or other goods. All the talk about the Greenlanders being enticed away from their "national" diet was ill-founded. The native catechist's half-ration of

AA

imported provisions had to be divided many times – first, he and his family had to consume some of it to live on, and then it had to be used as barter to obtain fresh food. From this it can be seen how little enticement entered into it.

All the sons of the missionary Berthel Laersen worked as catechists, serving in the settlements far from the Sukkertoppen colony. One in particular – Frederik – was a clever *fanger*, but could not use his skill because of his work as a catechist. The food ration was a necessity for his sons for a special reason: since childhood they had been accustomed to both European and Greenlandic food. Here we have our first insight into such a mixed Danish–Greenlandic household. Laersen did not succeed in getting the food ration settled – whereupon he informed the Missionskollegium that his sons' duties as catechists must henceforward take second place, when they had to obtain their daily food through trapping alone. The matter ended with their eventually being granted the food ration. In many instances the missionary on the spot, on his own initiative and counting on subsequent approval, engaged native catechists. However, the Trading Company directors' recommendation to the Missionskollegium not to encourage the population to become accustomed to "foreign" foodstuffs had its effect.

Whatever the reasons for it, this wages policy towards those born in Greenland created a gap between the Greenlanders and those sent out from Denmark. Precedent set the norm in all administration, and one had been established. Unexplained concepts about not enticing isolated individuals away from their "native" way of life probably had their roots in equally unexplained concepts with regard to the productivity of the Greenland population as a whole. This mercantilistic population and employment policy was cut across by the mission's need for workers with a knowledge of Greenlandic in greater numbers than it could afford. It is possible that on the basis of its economic attitude towards the employment of Greenlanders generally, the Trading Company did not recruit more of them into its service in order not to take them away from the only productive livelihood available to most of them, namely trapping. Lars Dalager, indeed, poked fun at the way the mission took good *fangers* away from their livelihood and turned them to missionary work – in his opinion a mediocre occupation. A split between the reputation and power of the Company and the aims and means of the mission became more and more evident, and this gradually weakened the position of the mission, while the Missionskollegium, overshadowed by the *Danske Cancelli*, could not make its own decisions.

The missionaries realized right from Hans Egede's time that the young Greenlanders would have to be educated and trained if they were to act as catechists, which was natural, seeing that Europeans had also to be trained for that work. In addition to the training, however, the environmental factor in education played its part. The Greenlanders – rather, the few who were employed in the colonies – had grown up in an environment where labouring was regarded as a task unworthy of a human being. On the other hand, most of those engaged as native catechists had had the opposite experience – they were used to such work being respected: Frederik Christian had already noted this respect among his fellow-countrymen.

It was probably this very factor which led Jørgen Sverdrup to regard children of mixed marriages as well suited for training as catechists. He pointed this out to the Missionskollegium in 1769. These children, among other things, knew the language perfectly and had known their settlement companions since childhood. Deservedly or not, their origin gave them a certain social *cachet*, which could be useful for them. Even though Sverdrup probably did not know Berthel Laersen's sons personally, he must have heard about them, and they were indeed an outstanding example of the truth of his thesis.

REFERENCES

1. Dalager wrote in his diary: "The most efficacious measure by which the Greenlanders may be won, is a rational association with them, because they are more likely to follow examples than to obey the most profound admonitory sermon."

20

MARRIAGE, INHERITANCE
AND WELFARE
1750–1782

As time went by a number of the Danish and Norwegians traders
and mission staff in the colonies contracted marriages with Greenland
women. The children of such marriages were given the somewhat
"colonial" name of "half-breeds". As with other marriages, some of
these mixed marriages were good and some not so good, and there
were of course half-breeds born out of wedlock as well. The latter was
less of a social or moral calamity then it might have been in European
society. In many cases it was the responsibility of the community to
look after such children, and indeed both mother and child. If the
child's paternity was established (through the mother's declaration and
an admission by the father), it became the practice in time for the
father, if he could not or would not marry the girl, to pay an annual
maintenance allowance of 5 rdl. Payment was to be made until the
child was fourteen years old. However, it was not always so easy to
collect this allowance: in most cases it was stopped from his wages,
but if the man had left his job and returned to Denmark, there was no
way of enforcing payment. There were also those who evaded their
obligations, sometimes after they had been making payments for a time.
Whether or not mother and child received help in such cases depended
on the mother's relations or as a secondary resource on the scanty
poor fund of the mission. The Trading Company assumed no responsibilities in this respect.

Cases of adultery were dealt with severely. Fines had to be paid
both to the authorities and to the Trading Company. These fines
amounted to 6¾ *lod* (half-ounces = 111.38 g.) of silver or 3 rdl.,
2 mrk., 4 sk. to the authorities and 6 rigsdaler to the Trading Company.
If the "guilty parties" did not marry, a maintenance allowance of
36 *lod* of silver (594 g.) or 18 rdl. to the authorities and 12 rdl. to the
Company was imposed, as well as 5 rdl. for a child. If they married
each other, the maintenance allowance was waived. The fines were

imposed "according to the law", Danish law in this sector being applicable in Greenland. It is strange, however, that no fines were fixed for the woman. In accordance with Christian V's *Danske Lov* of 1683 (the Danish Civic Law and Criminal Code) the woman was liable to a fine of 12 *lod* of silver (198 g.) and the man to one of 24 *lod* (396 g.) for extra-marital sexual relations. In Greenland the woman went scot-free. Hence it was established *de facto* that the responsibility lay with the man alone.

Casual relationships were one thing but the problems of "mixed" marriages were another. So long as these marriages were contracted with "good men" – honourable, industrious and reliable men who had been sent out from Denmark – everything went tolerably well. But it was impossible to prevent less desirable individuals among those sent out from marrying baptized Greenland women. Jacob Sewerin's attitude towards "Greenland marriages", as they were called, was at first adopted by the Trading Company. But the missionaries Bloch and Peter Egede spoke out as early as 1752 against the growing demand for marriage licences. Bloch regarded them as "not only directly contrary to the mission, the glory of God and the spreading of Christ's Kingdom among the heathen, but also extremely harmful". As soon as the baptized girls who were undergoing education in the colonies took it into their heads that they wanted to marry a Dane they rejected their former way of life, disdaining suitors among the young Greenlanders who were baptized or seeking baptism; the latter retaliated by threatening to find themselves wives in heathen fashion among the unbaptized. They reproached the missionaries, on the one hand, for the generally poor behaviour of the man sent out and, on the other, expressed the contempt felt by the ordinary West Greenlander for foreigners who could not support their familes in accordance with Greenland customs. Bloch and Peter Egede also considered that these marriages would result in the families becoming a burden on the Trading Company when the husbands became too old for work.

The remarks of Bloch and Peter Egede were occasioned by some "hands" expressing the wish to enter into marriages with baptized Greenlandic women; one of them had been caught in the act of making love with a girl. The Company had not given its permission for the marriages. It appears, however, that two of the men had in fact obtained permission from both the Missionskollegium and the Trading Company to get married. The incident caused the Trading Company to draw up a list of eleven conditions for permission to be granted, and the commitments which those concerned undertook. Throughout the following years (until the Instructions of 1782), this list of 31 March 1753 became a kind of marriage contract. To qualify for permission it was necessary for the persons concerned to be of blameless life, healthy, and of proved diligence in the service of the Company; for both parties to wish to marry, and for the woman to have the consent of her parents or her relatives, or of the missionary (the last-named as guardian). The Trading Company employee concerned undertook to remain in the country permanently, to live a decent life and to bring up the children of the marriage "so that they may in due time be able and fitted to serve the country both in the mission and in the Company". He undertook further to remain in the Company's service and to be loyal and honest. In consideration for a reduction in wages, the Company allowed the man two whole rations for his wife and children, in addition to his own ration. Finally, the Company promised that preference would be given to the man in question when appointing "traders and collectors in remote trading posts which cannot be visited by the colony's own people", provided, of course, that he was found suitable and had shown himself loyal and able. The man had to sign these conditions and undertakings and confirm on oath that he would abide by them. Always provided that the requirements were scrupulously observed, the Company would then support the family permanently.

In one of the points in the contract the Company gave permission for the husband to purchase goods in the colony on credit at cost if he and his Greenland family were unable to manage on the three rations. This quickly proved to have been a rash promise for it was not long before the directors found that more goods were being bought on credit than the person concerned could pay for out of his wages. The trader had to be careful to see that the man did not get into debt with the Company so that nothing would be left for the family if he died.

After these regulations were introduced, the number of marriages between men sent out from Denmark and baptized Greenland women increased. Traders, assistants and deserving craftsmen in the colonies were given permission to marry. A number of families whose members later played leading roles in Greenland originated from these mixed marriages in the latter half of the eighteenth century.

The contracting of such marriages was subject to a lengthy procedure. The man first had to apply to the local missionary who had to investigate his circumstances. The application then had to be submitted both to the Missionskollegium and the Trading Company directors (the latter only if the applicant was employed by the Company). After that he had to wait a year for the licence to be granted – if it was granted – before the wedding ceremony could take place. If the idea of marriage should only occur to the man in the summer just after the ship for that year had sailed, it might take all of two years before the licence was to hand; it required exceptional moral fibre to wait for so long. Hence the missionary sometimes preferred to marry a couple without waiting for permission, which was preferable from both a humane and a social point of view.

With the rising number of Greenland marriages, however, the number of individual problems increased. In 1763 the directors of the Trading Company were already having misgivings and regarded those who wanted to marry Greenland women as fated, "for we now realize all too clearly the harmful consequences of such marriages for the future".

Niels Egede inveighed against mixed marriages: "Instead of a good clean housewife, they have got a sow, turning any useful children they may have into useless ones. They are fit for neither one thing nor the other, nor can they support themselves like an ordinary Greenlander but everything they need must be bought from other Greenlanders, so that our people have fallen into disrepute through being unable to support themselves and are likened to useless old codgers". He had tried to get the husbands to educate their wives, but this was to no avail; the wives had their own way. Yet twelve years later he changed his opinion, possibly due to the mellowness of old age, but he emphasized that "now [in 1781] the Greenland women are more enlightened, so that they are not inferior to any Danish women". He also thought that in every case the children of the mixed marriages had turned out better than expected; hence marriages of this type should be permitted.

It is plain that the attitude adopted towards Greenland marriages by the directors of the Company, the Missionskollegium, traders, missionaries and others, contained no element of what we now call "discrimination" – in this case against the Greenland women. Indeed, rather the reverse, in that the authorities had little confidence in the Danish emigrants' moral conduct as Christians or in their stability as husbands. Niels Egede's use of this word "sow" was based on his general experience of the standard of hygiene and tidiness common in West Greenland. But the changed views which he later expressed and his attempt to get the husbands to educate their Greenland wives indicate that he believed it was only a question of education and development. In 1781 he emphasized the highly beneficial effect already, and in the future, of good marriages. The opposition to such marriages by the Trading Company, and later by the Royal Greenland Trading Company, was due mainly to the fear that the population would be drawn away step by step from the way of life which they believed to be the only possible and productive one in Greenland. There was, moreover, anxiety about the economic risk they were running with the maintenance obligations which might devolve on the Trading Company. The immediate consequence of a marriage contracted between a Greenland woman and a "hand", a craftsman, an assistant or a trader, indeed even with a missionary or an emigrant catechist, was an accommodation problem. The shared room and communal housekeeping of the "hands" could not accommodate a family, which was bound to increase year by year, and neither the trader, the assistant, the missionary nor the emigrant catechist had rooms that were large enough for a family. When Jørgen Sverdrup married, he was compelled to install his Greenland family in a turf house in Jakobshavn while he himself used his room as a study. And it was impossible for a "hand" who married a Greenland woman to go and live in his wife's family's home: he could not become a member of the community in the house, since he simply would not be regarded as an equal provider. Hence for every one of these marriages a house had to be built – usually a turf hut built in the Greenland fashion. Whatever the husband might bring home from his hunting and fishing could not provide enough in the way of food and clothing, let alone heating and fuel, for the household. Most of these things had to be obtained from the colony or bought from the Greenland *fangers*, and the Company was obliged to face the fact that some increase in the supply of provisions to the colonies was necessary.

Both the mission and the Trading Company directors were concerned about the fate of the children of the mixed marriages. As early as 1753 the catechist Dorf, who later became the trader at Egedesminde, raised the question of his children's upbringing and education: he wanted them to learn Danish because, being with their own age-group all the time, they only spoke Greenlandic. It has already been mentioned that the Trading Company were in favour of the children of mixed marriages being trained, if suitable, as craftsmen or for the service of the mission or Trading Company, and the directors of the Royal Greenland Trading Company also accepted this view. In a circular letter to all the colonies in 1777 they laid down what amounted almost to a professional code (they referred only to boys): "The future policy will be to see that from boyhood he shall be brought up in such a way that he may in due course be useful in the service of the Trading Company, in particular the children of traders and assistants, those of craftsmen in their fathers' trades and those of labourers on expeditions and whaling and other fishing, when under certain circumstaces . . . some help will be given towards such education." This policy apparently won no support, as it was not included in the 1782 Instructions. However, the directors let it be clearly understood that their objection permitting Greenland marriages was to save on the expensive European food supplies. An attempt was made to abolish the food ration but, to offset this, wages were increased, one boy being granted 10 rigsdaler a year for helping his father as a sort of apprentice cooper.

In law the children of mixed marriages were considered as Greenlanders. For this reason Poul Egede thought that, having Greenland forbears on their mother's side, they did not need permission to marry. However, it was laid down that the usual marriage contract should be signed, i.e. in accordance with the regulations of 1753. It can thus be seen that a well-defined social and utilitarian purpose lay behind these stipulations. The autocracy's mercantilistic view of the population problem was always decisive.

There were, nonetheless, many other problems arising from the mixed marriages. The directors of the Trading Company felt obliged to lay down certain procedures for the Missionskollegium in respect of the widows of emigrant employees. Hitherto it had been found from experience (short though this was in the Company case) that the widows had been left sufficiently endowed with both money and private possessions to enable them to get married again – to one of their fellow-countrymen. Thus they suffered no hardship. The directors nevertheless wanted the traders to be aware of such circumstances; the missionaries were to intervene. Still, this view of the Trading Company directors must have been based on inadequate experience, for the very next year the Missionskollegium reported on a widow left in straitened circumstances. (The mission looked after her.) Such factors may have helped the directors of the Trading Company to change their attitude towards mixed marriages.

When a death occurred, the estate of the deceased had to be formally settled and administered. In these cases the lack of legal experience or of general legal procedures in West Greenland became starkly clear. Moreover, it sometimes led to clashes with the "right of inheritance" – rather the lack of it – in Eskimo society. It had gradually become the custom for the nearest adult male simply to take over the possessions of a deceased *fanger*. "Grave-goods" were no longer placed with the corpse. This had been a cruel practice; if the dead man had left growing children, especially boys, they might later have made use of the father's gear. One plausible explanation for the later custom would be that these belongings had to be looked after – particularly kayaks, *umiaks* and tents, which had to be maintained with the proper skins; this was something that a widow with young children could not do. In 1765 a case was reported which illustrated this custom. A thirteen-year-old boy, whose father had died just at the time the lad acquired his own kayak but before he was strong enough to go sealing on his own, saw his kayak fall into disrepair and his stepmother and her relatives take possession of everything that he should have inherited from his father, so that he had to live on their charity. Based on the European view of law and justice, the missionaries could have intervened, but had they done so they would have acted against custom and usage, and they would not have helped those involved. Maintenance, after all, was the main problem, if rapid deterioration of the dead man's effects was to be avoided. This was successfully achieved in 1770 at Holsteinsborg where a dead man's belongings had been scattered far and wide but were reassembled through the missionary's intervention. The widow and children were thus able to keep their dignity, and their salvation was complete when a capable provider moved in with them and married the widow's only daughter, taking over the gear and looking after it.

There were also problems connected with the settlement of the estates of deceased Danish emigrants who had contracted Greenland marriages, for here there might be some conflict with the Greenland practice. When the catechist J. Grønbech died at Frederikshåb in the autumn of 1767, a number of articles which he left were put up for auction on behalf of the estate, as was usual in the colonies. In this case, the rules according to Christian V's Norwegian or Danish Law had to be complied with as far as possible, and the transfer put into effect. As a result of the auction the widow would receive funds, so that it was then possible to make the proper distribution. At the auction the other Europeans in the colony had purchased various effects from the estate, which the Greenlanders living there presumably interpreted as taking what properly belonged to the widow and her relatives. Otho Fabricius, the missionary there at the time, therefore wanted the widow to receive as quickly as possible tangible assets for the amount entered to her credit in the trader's accounts. Not until 1770 was Grønbech's estate finally cleared up, with the widow receiving some goods against her credit.

Special problems arose when an emigrant who had married a Greenland woman died leaving outstanding credits with the Trading Company. In regard to inheritance the Greenland natural economy and Danish practice were incompatible and this created acute difficulties. The money could not be paid out because money was not used in Greenland, but it had somehow to be administered. The Overformynderie (public trustee's office) in Copenhagen which usually dealt with such matters was not competent to administer the money which, under Danish law, ought to go to the children of the first marriage. It devolved on the Royal Greenland Trading Company to act as guardian for the widow as well as for the children. The money was then invested in the Royal *Extra-Skatte-Casse* under the Overskattedirektion (supreme tax authority) in Copenhagen at 3 per cent interest, which was thereafter made available to the widow and children each year in kind.

In these cases relating to succession and the settlement of estates we see how the legal and economic sectors gradually became merged and how this process changed people's living conditions as well as their attitude towards society. The old West Greenland customs were broken down, perhaps because they were neither exact nor firmly established. An attempt was made to substitute something for what was being taken away, and this, of course, was Danish law and practice. The fact that the cases were concrete and clear-cut made people want established rules to follow.

Other matrimonial problems occurred, both in mixed marriages and in those between Greenlanders. As happens wherever marriage is hedged about with rules to maintain its integrity and stability, breaches of the rules occurred. Infidelity and repudiation, which had no effect on marriage in West Greenland Eskimo society, nearly wrecked church marriages contracted between baptized people. Such deviations had a far more destructive effect in those small communities where the mission still represented the church militant. Divorce was a serious matter, which in Denmark at that time required a judgment or royal assent after passing through the ecclesiastical courts. The first recorded granting of a divorce where the woman was a Greenlander occurred in 1756. A trading assistant in Christianshåb had left his wife and under-age children in 1752 and disappeared without trace; royal consent to a divorce was subsequently given. Such behaviour in a husband was likely to heighten respect neither for the emigrants, the Church as an institution nor for the legal validity of the marriage ceremony.

Jørgen Sverdrup, the missionary, took up the problem of the dissolution of baptized Greenlanders' marriages. It quite often happened, he wrote, "that a married couple leave each other over a trifling matter in the fashion of heathens and seek new spouses". This was in 1767, when the catechist Jacob Poulsen Møller made his debut as a prophet with polygamy as his main theme. Sverdrup gave several examples; in one case he tried to set up a court dealing with matrimonial offences, which in this case would have pronounced the man innocent in the *de facto* divorce so that he could legally marry again. Punishment of the party responsible for the breakdown of the marriage was impossible, partly because in most cases both parties were guilty and partly because it was the pastor who would have to impose and enforce the penalty; this would not have helped his pastoral work or the activities of the mission. He had already been nicknamed *isumalugtoq* (the bad-tempered one) simply because he disapproved of their "irregularities". The only punishment he could imagine being effective was excommunication. This would be publicised in all the colonies so that the trading offices would not thereafter accept blubber or other goods offered for sale by the excommunicated person. He doubted, however, whether it would be possible to get the Trading Company to cooperate – "it generally happens that the more disobediently a Greenlander acts towards the missionaries, the more acceptable and more pleasing he becomes to others". Once again the need for public order and more prompt settlement of urgent cases was evident, with the central authorities and courts of law so far away. Co-operation between mission and Trading Company was lacking. The Trading Company directors and employees could adopt whatever moral code it chose but the church was bound to assert its own attitude.

Another divorce led Sverdrup to define his views on marriage law. In this case he did not dare proceed with the marriage of a man and his newly-chosen bride until the Missionskollegium had pronounced on the matter. He was well aware that a divorce arranged privately, as in this case, was not valid according to Danish law and that remarriage to another was incompatible with that law. "But I doubt whether the laws of the Fatherland can in this case, as in many others, be applied to the inhabitants of this country, especially where these laws are not made known to them and no authority is appointed to see that the laws are obeyed". Other missions were also continually voicing the need for authority, order and legal support. In Holsteinsborg the reaction of some of the baptized people was to wish that some form or other of church discipline should be introduced since they felt that "such a course would also have a good effect on the sinners among them". Perhaps Moravian influence can be detected here.

The clash between traditional Eskimo polygamy (a man usually did not have more than two wives) and the church requirement of monogamy led to conflict whenever those concerned were seeking baptismal instruction. In this connection all the missionaries experienced difficulty throughout the century. Which of the wives was to relinquish her position? Could polygamists be accepted for baptismal instruction at all? If the husband agreed to keep one wife and repudiate the other or others, who was going to look after the cast-off wives and their children? Lars Dalager tells of a man who would not attend instruction because his second wife had borne him sons and he was therefore unwilling to repudiate her and so lose his paternal authority over the boys. As late as 1771 the missionary at Holsteinsborg asked the Missionskollegium for its ruling where a polygamist wanted to be baptized; the Kollegium was uncertain. Other similar cases were referred back for consideration and in certain cases permission was given for the man to keep both his wives. No final ruling had been given by the time the problem solved itself, with polygamy coming to an end.

It is difficult on the basis of surviving documents to attempt an analysis of the changes in thought and mental conflicts of a population of individualists. When a Greenlander told Niels Egede that his people "believed everyone", Egede's pessimistic appraisal of the vacuum in the ordinary Greenlanders' religion, as he described it in 1769, was confirmed. "What then are we to think of such people, who answer 'Yes' to every foolish thing you say to them and are not steadfast in anything . . . ?" The pastors demanded that the people should believe them even if what they said was incomprehensible and impossible to express in material terms; the *angákut* required their belief too, for they demonstrated their ability by means of miracles and skills. To either party, their hearers would say "Yes, we believe!" This attitude, however, is entirely typical of people in the process of cultural change.

Lars Dalager reported that the *angákut* were losing ground, often because they were not always successful in saving "the soul" or "healing" it. Nothing was more common, he said, than to see young people holding the *angákoq* up to ridicule. During a spiritual seance, two brothers jumped to their feet and took hold of the *angákoq* who claimed that he was flying. They threw him out of the house, shouting "Now fly, you liar, and take your devil with you to Hell". Dalager also pointed out that there were almost as many Greenland pagan beliefs as there were *angákut*. Regarding amulets, he could see no principle behind them "for they differ so much from each other that old folk are often heard to express their astonishment at some strange newly-adopted meaning".

Lars Dalager's descriptions of changing religious ideas date from the 1750s, but they applied only to the central regions of the west coast. The missions kept pace with the development of the colonies, and missionaries were always coming into contact with new groups of people among whom the old religious tradition lived on. They waged a constant struggle preaching against the *angákut* and their mysterious hold over the Greenlanders, and against *ilisîtsui*, amulets or any other superstitions; their success was made easier and quicker because the breakdown of the old traditions spread steadily outward from the mid-Greenland centres.

Other traditions in the Eskimo world of the imagination, not specifically religious, were crumbling at the same time. The Moravians, who supervised "their" Greenlanders for almost every minute of the day, issued categorical bans on all "heathen" pleasures. It is true that the Greenlanders found a substitute in the semi-ecstasy of the Moravian meetings and in hymn singing, almost no leisure was left to them in which to keep alive their own tradition of song and story-telling. Eventually many hymns were translated by both the Moravians and the royal mission; the missionary Bruun's hymnal, which contained 288 hymns, was used for most of that period.

As regards the Eskimo song tradition, the Moravians and the royal mission regarded all Eskimo traditions as heathen and hence unacceptable, and so everything was banned, even including the most innocent of nursery songs and lullabies. Here again it was in the central region of the West Coast that the destruction of tradition was greatest. However, in the Holsteinsborg district Henric Christopher Glahn was able to study those Eskimo songs that still survived. He concluded – surely to the surprise of his contemporaries – that a grave mistake was being made in not differentiating between the various kinds of songs, and he expressed this in his comments on David Cranz's history of Greenland and in a separate treatise.

Glahn made a sharp distinction between songs that were permissible and those that were not. In the latter category belonged all magic songs, spells that could be sung and songs used at *angákoq* seances. Among those that were permissible he listed first and foremost the satirical songs which were composed for and sung at song-contests. These, as he rightly believed, were elements in a sort of trial. "For someone who has any sense of honour, this [public derision for his misdeeds] is surely the severest punishment that can be imagined and, among a free people, something like the most intelligent. . . . To take these away is to take away everything that serves to maintain right and justice under the existing constitution." Glahn defined a second class of permissible songs, which included repetitions of satirical songs, those celebrating outstanding feats – especially in trapping, those used purely for entertainment (these were somewhat coarse, and at times even obscene) – private songs with a refrain which "it is no more depraved to sing than it is to hum the melody of a hymn or ballad", and finally cradle-songs or nursery rhymes. These last were composed and crooned for each individual child, a practice which has continued right to the present day. Lastly Glahn mentions the more personal satirical songs, which were used for private "trials".

Whatever impression Glahn's view may have made, the proportion of old ballads and songs rescued from the general disintegration was small, and only the tradition of children's songs, known as "fondling-songs", remained intact. Glahn tells of an elderly widow who remembered some magic verses or spells from her youth but she would not say what they were and pretended that she had forgotten them. "Both she and her son assert that they contain words that are abominable for any enlightened person to hear, which is quite credible." No doubt such spells or magic-songs (*serratit*) were included among Glahn's "impermissible" songs. These parts of the Eskimo cultural tradition were deliberately suppressed, and thus vanished into oblivion. Other customs suffered the same fate. Amulets, which were usually worn on a so-called amulet-belt, had been condemned by all missionaries. Glahn once found that a man attending baptismal instruction wore an amulet-belt, but he learned also that this man wore it only because he liked it and not from superstition. Because he had met a baptized person using the amulet-belt to measure the girth of his waist, Glahn was satisfied with this explanation.

Some more or less mystical ideas were still preserved, which had fairly close parallels in Scandinavian superstition. This applied to the giving of names. Right up to the present day the Eskimo custom of calling children after someone has been preserved, at least to some extent, because they are convinced that this is efficacious. Dalager relates that the Greenlanders considered they underwent a change of name at baptism, after which they used only the new name and no other. Behind this custom there still lay the idea of a connection between the individual's soul and his name. Moreover, names from both the Old and New Testaments gradually appeared alongside the most common Danish–Norwegian names – Jørgen, Niels, Peter, Jens, Hans, etc. In everyday speech these soon became Greenlandicized, but the forms were recognizable.

As in any society, belief and superstition were interwoven. For many people belief in the evangelical-Lutheran type of Christianity must have become deeply rooted. This would be especially true of congregations who gave up part of their catch to build themselves a church, and of the woman who arrived with her companions at Holsteinsborg in May 1777 from a place about 75 km. south of the colony. She had brought her new-born baby with her to be baptized, but she was also sick, and together with other women, sought the help of the Holsteinsborg barber-surgeon. Medical aid from barber-surgeons was only available where whaling-stations had been set up after 1774, but the barber-surgeons sent out to look after the whaling crews would naturally attend to sickness among the local population. Away from the stations people had to manage with the range of common medicines that were still being sent out. The missionaries were usually in charge of these medicine-chests, inexpertly making shift with old household remedies. Rasch, the missionary at Frederikshåb, confessed in 1757 to having given up prescribing medicine because the Greenlanders did not want it and would not take it. Brandy was his panacea, for both internal and external use. When he had persuaded the Greenlanders to take a dose of the true medicine, "either to induce sweating or as a purge", he still had to give them a dram of brandy; they had faith in that, but not in the medicine. "To induce sweating I have sometimes given them brandy and gunpowder, sometimes brandy and pepper; as a purge they have had a dose of rhubarb and jalap-root mixed with brandy.

I have used camphor mixed with brandy for almost all external applications, the same being a sovereign eye-salve, . . . for dry swellings I
have used spice bags filled with camomile flowers, elder flowers and
dry camphor."

Not much is known of the diseases prevalent in Greenland at that
time. It appears that xerophthalmia was still prevalent. Niels Egede
in several places mentions the annual spring cough and "weakness of
the chest". One barber-surgeon mentions "inflammatory fevers and
spasmodic coughing" and "malignant abscesses", the latter being a
particular scourge among the Greenlanders. At Holsteinsborg there
was an outbreak of dysentery in 1776. Epidemics still went unchecked.
When medicines were sent out, the largest quantities were for "side-
stitches, scurvy and eye troubles" (1775). According to Niels Egede,
the woman who came to Holsteinsborg in 1777 with her baby was
"vomiting blood". All probably suffered from tuberculosis.

The widely fluctuating and often poor state of nutrition among
the Greenlanders was frequently the cause of illness, and reduced their
resistance to epidemics. In 1775 the missionary Hans Egede Saabye
wrote that "there has not, according to the oldest folk, been a winter
like the past one in Greenland for the last thirty to forty years; at
Christmas or early in January famine began here. The Greenlanders
had little in reserve, as the catch was especially poor last autumn, so
it was not caused through improvidence – hence they were all the more
to be pitied. The ice set in and remained without any openings throughout the winter so that nothing could be caught. The Greenlanders
chewed up a quantity of skins and other foul things, but that would
scarcely have enabled them to exist until July. Some of them, particularly those living some distance away from the Danes, were grey with
hunger and so feeble that when at last there was open water, they were
scarcely able to row their boats out. No end was seen to the affliction,
which grew worse with every day". Help did come, and they were
"more or less fit by the beginning of June when the ice went away and
they started to go catching, whereupon they fell ill again, partly due to
undernourishment, partly because the weather turned cold and damp,
and remained so well into July".

Year after year, in different places, but sometimes in the same region
for several years running, there were famines, usually in late winter and
spring. These periods of starvation with little or no opportunities for
catching were not all caused by the Greenlanders disposing of their
excess catch to the Trading Company; as we have seen, the catch could
fail during the autumn, making it impossible to build up stocks. The
lack of catching opportunities was always emphasized as the cause of
famine. The trader was to ensure that no more was bought off the

Greenlanders than their own supplies of food would allow, and there are records of traders refraining from purchasing the catcher's products because an emergency situation was likely or had already begun. Sometimes the catch of a whale saved the people for a time.

An individual Greenlander in one of the colonies might find himself in want simply by being within easy reach of the trading station. Glahn considered that the young people went short of skins because their providers traded those from the catch for scraps of tobacco and useless objects, so that there were no skins either for the children's clothes or – just as vital – for covering the kayaks and *umiaks*. So the youngsters who should have become catchers had to stay at home without being taught to row a kayak. "I shall say nothing of many adolescents being allowed to act as kitchen scavengers so that a pastor often has to drive them away whip in hand". This form of want was one thing but, as Glahn himself stressed, real famines were quite another. If more is heard about them after 1750 than before, this can be ascribed first to the increase in the number of colonial settlements and secondly to the unfortunate development whereby more and more people turned to the mission and the Trading Company when they were in need.

The trader N. C. Geelmuyden noted in his journal for 1750 that the Missionskollegium had instructed that merchandise to the value of 16 to 24 rigsdaler be bought each year from the local trader and used to buy Greenlandic food for distribution among the most needy baptized people and schoolchildren (presumably children accepted in the missionary's school as boarders). The distribution was only to take place in winter. He felt it was necessary "for the mission's sake", by which he must have meant that the mission could not refuse to help the needy. However by 1752 this sum was already proving inadequate, and the Christianshåb missionaries were obliged to exceed it by 37.5 per cent. The provisions they bought were hard tack (ship's biscuits), barley groats, peas, coalfish and *rotskær* (split, wind-dried stockfish). That was indeed spoiling the Greenlanders with European victuals, but over the years up to 1782 this principle frequently had to go by the board in times of want and hunger.

In 1754 Rasmus Bruun, the Godthåb missionary, promised that he would no longer give the Greenland children "any European food but strive to obtain their own". It had been necessary, however, to buy a quantity of stockfish for widows and children. The custom gradually arose of the Trading Company dispatching one skippund (160 kilos) of coalfish in the form of *rotskær* for distribution in emergencies, but it was repeatedly laid down that under no circumstances must bread or other types of provisions be distributed. Without reference to the needs of the individual colonies, the extent of aid was fixed uniformly all along the west coast, which meant, of course, that in some places it was insufficient. Thus Anders Olsen at Sukkertoppen and Niels Egede were both forced to distribute provisions, especially to widows and orphans.

However, at the whaling stations established after 1774, where the Greenlanders stayed in order to take part in the whaling, the Royal Greenland Trading Company had to act against its own principle concerning imported provisions. Throughout the whaling season, stockfish, ship's biscuit and split peas were to be supplied, but apparently only to the families whose breadwinners were participating in the whaling; the provisions sent out were not intended for "idle lads, girls or the repudiated wives of unbaptized Greenlanders who might make their way to the colony". In other words, the provisions were not intended as an emergency or charitable arrangement but as a food ration for Greenlanders taking part in the whaling.

The Trading Company tried to indemnify itself for the provisions that were given out despite the ban; in times of want they were generally distributed on the initiative of the traders concerned, in a desperate situation. To maintain some control, the traders were required to keep lists of those to whom provisions were given, which had to be certified by the missionary and an assistant. This did not prevent the directors from reprimanding traders who offended against the ban on distributing provisions, although it was considered unfair to hold them accountable. Sometimes smaller trading stations could find themselves suddenly in dire want, as at Fiskenæsset in the winter of 1780 when three *fangers* were accidentally drowned in their kayaks. This made the assistant in charge of the post hold back a barrel of blubber and seventy-two seal skins from those traded in to keep the needy orphaned children of the men in reasonable health. The same assistant purchased blubber and skins from the *fangers* who were determined to sell these products during the good times, but he kept them and distributed some of them later when times were hard.

Individual hardship could arise through breaking with Eskimo tradition; missionary Transe of Frederikshåb related how such a situation could develop. When, for example, a baptized breadwinner died or became too old to work, the whole family made its way to the mission, perhaps leaving behind relatives who could have helped them. Also *fangers* would come to live near the mission after baptism and their families were bound to rely on the mission's help if they lost their breadwinner, because unbaptized relatives could not or would not help them. The mission's other Greenlanders could not provide for them, having enough to do looking after their own. "If the trader, as the authorized representative of the directors of the Trading Company, is willing either to provide help too sparingly or to provide nothing at all, and the mission fund cannot help, there is no question as to whether the missionary will do so or not – he is all the more strongly obliged to". It was a matter of Christian charity. Transe revealed that the trader discriminated between heathen and baptized; he could look after the former and provide for them whereas the baptized must stick to the missionary.

In 1777 the Christianshåb missionary asked if part of the stockfish which had been sent to Greenland could be allocated to him for charitable use. When Greenlanders came to the colony, they went to see him, and something had to be given to them – a little tobacco or a slice of bread and butter. "If not, he goes away saying: 'Pellese tauna erliktokau' [palase táuna erdligtûqaoq: this pastor is a horrible miser]". If that happened he seldom came back to the missionary, whereas he might go and see the trader several times without getting a morsel from him. All this "charity" was making a large hole in the missionary's allocations of provisions. The Christianshåb missionary's account tallies with Glahn's mention of "kitchen scavengers" and the reference to Drachardt's weakness towards Greenlanders who came begging. On the other hand, the missionary may have misunderstood the traditional form of visiting in Greenland, where it was good manners for the visitor to be given something to eat and there was no question of begging.

The problem of how to treat widows and orphans was constant and of increasing urgency. Orphaned children had been of concern early in the colonization era, and Hans Egede had channelled them into a sort of boarding school education. This was feasible only so long as the number was limited, but gradually more colonies were set up, and the problems worsened. It has already been mentioned that small groups of this kind moved into the colonies to seek a better life. It was often reported by the missionaries that most of the people at any given place were poor widows and orphans; when Holsteinsborg was founded, there had been only one fatherless family in the locality. For a group of widows and children, who had moved with him from the north the missionary had to provide every kind of clothing, accommodation, tents, cooking vessels, kayaks for the boys to practise in, fuel, skins to sleep on – in fact everything. He therefore suggested that the Missionskollegium should set up a permanent stock of tents and kayaks to loan out – a sound scheme of occupational assistance. However the Missionskollegium obtained an opinion from Poul Egede, who stated flatly that it was pernicious. The missionary at Jakobshavn had attacked the problem in a more practical way. He acquired some merchandise in order to buy or have made a pair of kayaks which could be lent out to young men, who could then operate as *fangers* and earn enough to acquire kayaks of their own. This fell through when the missionary died the following year. Niels Rasch, the missionary, in Frederikshåb also wanted to lend out kayaks with the appropriate tackle to young boys who were poor, but this too came to nothing. However, missionary Myhlenphort put his own plans into execution more or less independently. He fixed up not just one or two but many impoverished young newcomers with kayaks or kayak equipment. Widows, who would otherwise have been a continual burden were put to work making soapstone lamps and kettles, and carrying on their own salmon-fishery with nets. With the proceeds from the sale of soapstone articlés one widow was able to buy a kayak for her son and keep her tent and *umiak* in good order.

But it seemed impossible for this example to be followed elsewhere. It is true that in 1776 the directors of the Royal Greenland Trading Company authorized not only help by the mission in cases of hardship, but intended to send out, as well as the usual quantities of dried fish, nets for catching *angmagssat*. This evoked a strong response from the missionary Hans Egede Saabye. "Catching implements have, to be sure, been sent to the Greenlanders, but they consist of two herring scoops, implements which the old Greenland women make from very common things and which therefore are not in short supply. May things never come to such a pass that the Greenlanders need this sort of help." Two scoops were of little help for fifty or sixty breadwinners.

In other places, more intelligent assistance was given. The Godthåb trader helped seven poor youths at Qilángait by giving them wood, skins and oars for kayaks, and he had helped the orphan boys of the Brethren's congregation in the same way on the Company's behalf. That similar aid towards self-help was fairly widespread seems clear from a letter of the Royal Greenland Trading Company directors in 1777 to Hans Raun, the senior assistant at Fiskenaesset, saying it had been agreed that the Trading Company should take charge of all abandoned Greenlandic children and provide them with the where-withal to support themselves "according to the fashion of the country". He was asked to look for boys "to give essential help, to clothe and feed them in the Greenland manner and to see that from their youth they were trained as *fangers* and hunters to live on the food the Greenlanders were used to, which is available in the district". They were also to be instructed in Christianity by the missionary. Some sort of policy can be discerned in this plan: the letter continued with directives concerning the education and training of children of mixed marriages. In general it meant insisting on the Greenland population and those born in the country observing as far as possible the Greenland way of life or taking up work that would benefit the country.

This simple form of active welfare work with arrangements to promote employment was born in Greenland out of confrontation with extraordinarily harsh living conditions, where it was unquestionable that the individual's distressed situation was not his own fault. The only possible way of giving help was in the form of commodities, and the step from this idea to providing help in the form of equipment to produce commodities essential to life was a short one. The idea manifested itself in different forms as far apart as Holsteinsborg, Jakobshavn and Frederikshåb – most effectively under the hand of missionary Myhlenphort at Frederikshåb in the 1760s. At last it was officially accepted in part – for adolescent males only. The concept was fundamentally different from poor relief systems current at that time.

In the field of social welfare, as in all other areas of the Greenland enterprises, the temporal authorities were slow to accept the need for taking action. Once a decision had been made it was upheld and changes were resisted. The central administration was of course reluctant to alter established practice and anxious to maintain uniformity, but, most important, it was out of contact with the prevailing local conditions. The Trading Company was also governed by the principle of keeping the Greenlanders to their way of life "as determined by nature" almost at any cost: in this principle lay a contradiction between aim and practice which ran parallel to the friction between uniformity and personal development of the individual in Greenland. Contemporaries were unaware of this, but it found expression in, among other things, quarrels between the Trading Company and the mission. The Company felt obliged to enforce uniformity, even though in practice there always had to be compromises; the mission, with its evangelical-Lutheran principles, gave prominence to the individual.

However, the mission itself was in conflict. Its work for the development and education of the individual was often at variance with its strong desire for stability and order – which itself was a prerequisite for calm and peaceful attention to the individual. Interest in fostering the development of isolated individuals led to some missionaries taking Greenlanders home with them when they left the country to continue their education in Denmark. However, it was definitely forbidden for Greenlanders to be sent to Denmark for education. The Brethren had received strict instructions, which they obeyed, in an ordinance in February 1750 forbidding Greenlanders to accompany them on their journeys outside Greenland. Missionary Gregersen from Godthåb took the Greenlander Barnabas with him to train as a catechist, but he was a poor pupil and so the venture was unsuccessful. He did not return home and stayed with Gregersen until his death in 1777. Apart from this case, few instances are known, and these were of little *tamanna nuannekau tipeitsunignartlunilo, Gub kittornarangatigut, allello Kajumigillarangautigit pilluakattigekkulluta. ajokarforniaromaralloarpakka nuannaromaublunga illifimagauko tamanna Gub tamauta ikioromarpatigut, Illipse amerlenartluse. Uangale ikinartlunga. Nunable penik pigaufinga, Nallegarfoit, Kijeisfaunga nunakatirtut, asfakangaufinga, illurkut Kijavonga annoarfennik nekfiekfaunik pigaufinga aualajallerfonga Nunang voamnut. Kemeisfoaufe Guble nejoromarpase illegellungalo uanga Gudmut tukfiartuinnartuk-fak pilluarkullufe Killable. nunablo puenik tammanik*

Eunikke

*Kiöbenharnme Ullok 3 April 17**.*

Last page of a letter written by the Greenland woman, Eunike, to the Missionskollegium, dated 3 April 1770. (Central Record Office, Copenhagen.)

significance in the further development of Greenland. A young Greenland girl by the name of Eunike was in Copenhagen in 1769–70, helping Poul Egede who was then revising his translation of the New Testament. After her return to Greenland in 1770 she had difficulty in settling down in her native environment. In 1779 Poul Egede reported that a young Greenland woman had come to Copenhagen the previous year. She was poor and had travelled to Copenhagen in the hope of returning home a rich woman. It is unknown how she reached Denmark, but she had to be given a free passage home to Úmánaq, as she was penniless. This case reflects the notions oruinary Greenlanders must have entertained of conditions and opportunities in Denmark: it was the rich country where the King lived and the rich emigrants in Greenland came from.

In time the children of emigrants also raised problems which, sooner or later, had to be solved. Senior officials who had married Greenland women wanted their children educated in Denmark from the age of eleven or twelve. A trader at Christianshåb sent two of his children to Copenhagen on his own initiative, asking for them to be maintained. The outcome is unknown, but it is likely that sooner or later they were sent back, since the Missionskollegium was bound, like the directors of the Trading Company, to consider the children of mixed marriages as Greenlanders, regardless of their fathers' position, and as Greenlanders they were to remain in Greenland. However, some exceptions were allowed, as when Jørgen Sverdrup, who had married a Greenlander, left Jakobshavn for good he took his adopted daughter with him, although she was of pure Greenland extraction. The question of education was never tackled: only once during the period 1750–82 was there any question of even partial education in Denmark of a person born in Greenland; this was the case of trader Dorf's son around 1772.

Internal development in West Greenland within the colonial districts during the period from 1750 to 1782 presents a kaleidoscopic picture. Trends are scarcely discernible. It is as though the whole enterprise were split up into individual cases with decisions being arrived at at *ad hoc*. Objectives were vague and over-general in scope. Yet this impression is of a piece with the composition of the small communities in West Greenland, each with its individual character. Here we may find the explanation of why the colonization effort had to be split up, and why it had a destructive effect on Eskimo cultural tradition. All the same, the desire for greater unity and order in the small communities and in the country as a whole grew stronger all the time, and in consequence appeals to government were pressed home with more determination.

21

THE ROYAL GREENLAND TRADE
AND FISHERY 1774–1781

It was in the nature of the autocratic system to control everything from the centre; but inevitably people everywhere became accustomed to not being able to do anything of importance without the assent of the central authority. Its mercantilist policy led the autocracy to intervene in the economy to subsidize or regulate it. The state therefore came to take a more or less direct part in various ventures. In the Greenland venture, lack of capital made itself felt time after time during the period from 1721 to 1774. For this reason, no doubt, the Trading Company dealt *ad hoc* with each case as it arose, and expansion occurred by fits and starts, owing much to chance. The capital dribbled in, but with each new settlement it proved inadequate. The official subsidies were laid down in the charter, and were once or twice increased when the charter was renewed, but it was not possible between renewals to request a higher grant for each stage of expansion. The charter represented a commitment for a specific number of years, and thus restricted development. The request for an increase in the grants to the mission was one of the causes of the conflict between the Missionskollegium and the Trading Company.

Around 1774 the Trading Company's finances began to deteriorate alarmingly. Over the years the Company had incurred heavy losses on whaling, not only around Greenland but, probably to an even greater extent, in other parts of the North Atlantic. In addition, the market was continuing to worsen for the grain trade, an important side of the Company's business. The directors pursued a rash credit policy, and by 1755 had to recognize quite large sums as doubtful debts. Through energetic debt-collecting, they succeeded in halving this onerous item, but the Company was obliged to borrow in order to survive. This was presumably due to too much investment in fixed assets, so that the Company's liquidity was under constant strain. The years 1761–4 were apparently profitable, and advantage was immediately taken of this improved situation to give the shareholders an annual dividend of 6⅔ per cent. It was clearly a common procedure at that time for excess cash in hand to be distributed at the year's end without any thought being given to the need to replace capital or depreciations or to pay interest on capital invested.

With the same working capital as before, the Iceland and Finnmark trade were taken over in 1763, which resulted in good results – on paper – for the years immediately following. In 1766, however, a shareholder made a crushing criticism of the Company's management, particularly the large bank loans which it had taken up; he demanded the winding up of the unprofitable sides of the business, and as a consequence it was finally decided to limit operations to the Greenland, Finnmark and Iceland trades. In the years that followed, only the Greenland trade appears to have been profitable; however, the profits from this were not enough to compensate for the ever-increasing deficit from the operations of the Company as a whole. The Iceland trade was mainly to blame. The directors and shareholders intended nevertheless to carry on, as they were obliged to under the charter. The total value of the assets in all the Company's ventures in Iceland, Finnmark, the West Indies and Greenland, together with its premises and oil refinery in Copenhagen, its ships, etc., was established at 701,942 rdl. Against this were liabilities amounting to 415,678 rdl. This was no mean capital, but the assets consisted mainly of "book values", and most of them were unrealizable – certainly at the figures shown – so that it would have been impossible to borrow anything like a corresponding amount on them. It is tragi-comic that the Company's liquid assets amounted to only 763 rdl. If operations were to be continued, the first necessity was to raise a loan.

Of the liabilities, 261,270 rdl. represented the Company's debts, including 237,500 rdl. solely to the Kurantbank, which had been taken over by the State in 1773. If a new loan was to be raised, it would have to be negotiated with this bank, which was itself under strain at that time. This was possibly a reason for the Government's refusal to allow the continuation of the Trading Company which, both under its charters and because of its debt to the Kurantbank, was dependent on the State. After Struensee's fall in 1772, the new Government set up several commissions, including an Extraordinary Finance Commission. Its members were Otto Thott, Baron Heinrich Carl Schimmelmann, the financier, and Joachim Otto Schack-Rathlou, a former ambassador to Sweden. Behind this commission, like all the others, stood the real leader of the Government, Crown Prince Frederik's private secretary, Ove Høegh-Guldberg. He interfered in the work of the finance commission in a way that became usual in all areas of public administration, namely by means of orders-in-council.

By an order-in-council written in Guldberg's own hand, it was abruptly decreed that the Royal Chartered General Trading Company should cease to exist. The State took over the shares at a rate of 300 rdl. per share (they were worth 286 rdl. according to the accounts). The end came in May 1774. It must have pained the old mercantilist Otto Thott to see the Company disappear; he had been there at its foundation in 1747, although he had not completely approved of its policy over the years.

The main feature of general trade policy in the so-called Guldberg period of Danish history (1772–84) was the concentration of trade and industry by means of massive State participation. The other character-istic feature of contemporary politics was that greater emphasis than before was laid on the State as a whole, i.e. all the King's realms and territories. It was in just such a climate that H. C. Schimmelmann could flourish. This merchant, originally from Pomerania, had had an almost legendary career in Denmark and had acquired a reputation as a financial genius. His contacts with shipowners and financial circles in Hamburg placed him in a strong position. A wide-ranging whaling industry was operated from Hamburg, with a coresponding trade in whale oil. Opportunities therefore existed for a market for whaling products. The Holstein towns of Glückstadt and Altona competed in whaling on a modest scale. Whaling-masters and crew were all recruited from Rømø, Sild, Amrum and Føhr, as well as some crew from the Slesvig and Holstein towns. These places were all within the King's dominions.

Centralization of whaling might thus fit in well with the aims of the Government's trade policy. To this extent the winding up of the Trading Company suited the Government, and orders were immediately given for it to be taken over by the State. The Greenland trade, along with the whaling, now came to mean more to the Government than it might otherwise have done. Concentration went even further. By royal decrees issued in April and May 1774, the Iceland, Finnmark and Greenland trade was taken over by the State and combined with the Faroes trade which had been carried on at the royal expense since 1709. The former directors of the Trading Company continued in office, though under the control of the Overskattedirektion, through 1774 and into 1775; then on 13 April 1775 it was decided that the Iceland, Finnmark and Faroe Islands Trading Company should have its own board of directors and be separated from the Royal Greenland Trade, both financially and administratively – with effect from 1 January 1776. The previous boards were therefore to continue in office until then.

By the same decree, the Royal Greenland Trade was to take over all the Trading Company's buildings and other property in Greenland

and its ships and craft which were suitable for whaling and *robbeslag* (seal catching, usually on the ice). The Trading Company was also to cede the oil refinery and enough land to allow for its expansion.

The Government intended, through the administrative partition, to concentrate the whaling industry and, through heavy investment in both plant and ships, to compete with the Dutch. But whaling, and all other kinds of fishing, were to be carried on from bases in Finnmark, Iceland and the Faroes. As each of the two sectors had its own individual character, it was best for each to be managed by its own board of directors, a view expressed in an Overskattedirektion memorandum to the King of 10 April 1775. The memorandum stated that it was impossible to estimate the cost of the large capital items, "but in any case royal permission is requested to pay the requisite sums out of the tax fund"; this was approved by royal order. Such a position of privilege no private institution could ever have attained.

The Iceland, Finnmark and Faroe Islands Trade was to be provided with fifty large hookers, each of 34–36 commercial cargoes, i.e. about 70 registered tons. The fishery was to be operated by fifty sloops, each of 12–14 commercial cargoes each, and for the Greenland whaling and sealing, fifty vessels were to be built each of 100–200 commercial cargoes. Not all of these 150 vessels were to be built at once, but so that operations would be started at the right time in 1776, work on several large vessels for whaling and sealing, five hookers and five sloops, was to be put in hand. Apart from these vessels, the directors had three others which the King had presented to the venture, a large frigate (*Kongens Gave*), a smaller frigate (*Holsteinborg*) and a bombardier galliot (*Den Gloende*). The *Holsteinborg* was to sail to the colony of Holsteinsborg as quickly as possible with crew and pinnaces to winter there and test the "fishing" (presumably whaling) in the spring of 1776.

It had been ordered that whalers should be stationed at Holsteinsborg and on Disko, and they were to attempt to carry on whaling from land in January, February and March before the Dutch reached the Davis Strait. So pinnaces, tackle, provisions and the requisite housing materials were to be sent out. Although the directors had received reports on the whaling possibilities from Christian Wulff, a warehouse clerk who had been a trader at Holsteinsborg between 1764 and 1767, their plans seem not to have been adequately thought out. Wulff had suggested various possible whaling bases further away in the Bay, but admitted that they were not suitable places for Europeans to spend the winter. He was sceptical about whaling at Holsteinsborg, but recommended fishing for Greenland shark.

In Holsteinsborg, Niels Egede received the whaling crew sent out without enthusiasm; however, he felt compelled to give his assurance that he would carry out the King's wishes diligently. At the same time, he advised caution. The way he had practised whaling with the Greenlanders for several years was the best, but perhaps it could be improved on. It was best, he maintained, to start at Egedesminde and on Disko, but here too he warned them to be cautious, beginning on a small scale and seeing whether the prospects were good. The directors on their side regarded the Holsteinsborg arrangements as experimental, in this respect agreeing with Niels Egede. The difference was that Niels Egede wanted whaling carried on in collaboration with the local Greenlanders and mistrusted the people sent out. According to the plan, the latter were to whale on their own, and the local Greenlanders were only to be given a minor role.

It was dangerous to criticize, because the plans had received the supreme blessing of Guldberg. It had been decided in April 1775, during discussions on the whole new regime, that the secretary of the Gehejmekabinet should attend meetings of the joint boards, since Guldberg showed "commendable zeal as regards the fisheries". His sole interest in this connection was in the great project which the Government had initiated. In line with mercantilistic tradition, the reason of state was given prominence, although decisions concerning the arrangements were given the appearance of being taken for the common good. Greenland society and its welfare entered little into Guldberg's considerations.

The Holsteinsborg experiment did not take the course that Niels Egede feared, but it was disastrous in a different way. The whaling master who had arrived in 1775 returned home with his mission unaccomplished; the men fell sick, so some accompanied him on the homeward voyage; the expedition to Disko in the spring was abandoned. The experiment had obviously been set up in such haste that men of insufficient experience were engaged, and the necessary equipment had not been provided, although a couple of pinnaces and some whaling tackle had been sent out. Niels Egede blamed the failure on the lack of pinnaces and tackle. But he also agreed with the local Greenlanders that the European whalers in their heavy pinnaces made too much noise – with their oars and through the boats grating against the ice. They scared the whales away long before they had come within range of them. If they were determined to use European boats, the light English boats with a crew of seven were better than pinnaces. But he once again urged that the attempt should not be made on too large a scale. If the directors still intended to experiment with whaling from pinnaces, the men must be stationed at the fjord entrance where there was seldom ice, and they would have to be provided with everything there – housing, fuel, provisions and whatever else they needed.

Niels Egede's reports both for 1775 and 1776 were treated with respect due to his experience. But the danger of crossing the path of the Royal Trading Company directors was learned by missionary Jaeger in Holsteinsborg, who had tried to prevent the local Greenlanders from associating too closely with the whalers sent out from Denmark, who, he felt, would not have a good influence on them. Consequently he had put obstacles in the way of the Greenlanders giving help to the whalers. This resulted in a caustic letter from the directors to the Missions-kollegium requesting that the missionaries be instructed not to work against participation of the Greenlanders in whaling but rather to foster it – not only in the Greenlanders' interests, but also that they might become more skilled at it. The Missionskollegium, in a dignified reply, pointed out that the directors had been misinformed; nevertheless, it agreed that the missionaries should be given rules for their conduct in regard to whaling.

The great enterprise got off to a rather halting start, far from the expectations with which the new directors had taken up office at the beginning of 1776. The senior director was Joachim Godske, Count Moltke, who had long been a senior official in the finance and customs department. Then the Icelandic jurist Jon Erichsen was appointed a director; he too was a senior finance and customs official. In addition Peter Borré was made a director, having been a member of the board of the General Trading Company since 1759. These three were also directors of the Iceland, Finnmark and Faroe Islands Trade. Thus the separation at this level was not complete, as it was in the administration of the four trading sectors. Johan F. Arensburg, a former officer of dragoons and later Army Paymaster and general administrator of the official lottery, was appointed managing director of the Royal Greenland Trade, Whaling and Sealing; why he was selected for this post is unexplained. The remaining seats on the board were filled by the Bavarian-born Copenhagen merchant Johann Ludwig Zinn, and the North Friesian, Peter Matthiesen, formerly burgomaster of Copenhagen. The latter was an important figure on the board, having been made director of the Trade and Fisheries Institute in Altona in that year. He was in touch with the whalers of his native island of Föhr, and as a corresponding member of the board he was instrumental in maintaining contact with the whaling captains and shipbuilders in Holstein and Slesvig, and was also in close touch with the market for whaling products in Hamburg. He was also in constant touch with the financier H. C. Schimmelmann, who was often in Hamburg, and who was a member of the Overskattedirektion, which controlled both boards of directors of the northern trading companies. The very composition of the board of directors was an indication of which of its activities was to be considered the most important: namely, whaling first, followed by fishery. The Greenland trade proper came last in order of importance, as emerged plainly from a memorandum from the Overskattedirektion to the King in April 1775 and which formed a basis for the whole set-up that came into force on 1 January 1776.

When the whaling was planned and implemented, it was fully realized that the venture would meet with fierce competition from both the Dutch and the English off the West coast of Greenland, and the directors received reports of poaching by foreign whalers. From Godhavn the trader, Svend Sandgreen, gave a detailed account of a clash between an English whaler and Godhavn's colonists and Green-landers in May 1774. About 25 km. due east of the colony the local people had harpooned a whale and managed to kill it. With difficulty they succeeded in towing it to a point only two furlongs from their destination. Then the drift-ice cast their boat and the whale ashore, just as the tide was going out. The men made the whale fast to a stranded ice hummock and marked it with buoys, and then went home for a brief rest. They had scarcely reached home before the alarm was given. An English whaler, which had had her boats out in the vicinity for some time but had caught nothing, had laid to beside the whale and started to move it away. Sandgreen, the whalers and the Greenlanders went there post-haste and loaded firearms were brandished, but the shots fired went wide. At last a pair of Dutch whalers made their appearance, and the English retired.

It was probably opposition to the English as their whaling competi-tors that caused the Dutch to give some demonstration of support in this instance. At the same time there were reports of the Dutch buying up Greenland produce in the neighbourhood of Ũmánaq. Four Dutch whalers stated that they too were going to trade, although they knew of the ban and had previously complied with it, but if no penalty was imposed for infringing it, they could not afford not to trade. The Dutch in the Davis Strait seem to have been regarded as falling into two groups, one consisting of the whalers and the other of those whom trader Dorf called "*Smoserne*".[1] The latter traded openly on their own account, so that they sailed for lower wages than the whaling men who did not trade. The Dutch whaling masters who did not go in for trading felt themselves subject to wage pressure, and tried to compensate for their lower wages by trading. Hence it was to be expected that foreign trading with the Greenlanders in these parts would increase.

Johan Hammond, the trader at Ũmánaq, confirmed Dorf's state-ments in his report. It would probably not be possible to keep the foreigners away, unless a well-manned and well-armed frigate were posted in the area. It must arrive in May in order to cruise in the channel to catch the Dutchmen, "for I cannot stave them off with four men in a boat", yet he might be molested by the Greenlanders if he forbade them to trade with the foreigners. The master of the vessel that sailed to Ûmánaq confirmed Hammond's and Dorf's statements. He emphasized the need for a royal order applicable throughout the King's reign, because the foreigners were perfectly well acquainted with the previous proclamations, but it was clear they no longer had any effect.

The directors of the General Trading Company had made representations at the highest level concerning the foreigners' "interference with the Greenlanders' livelihood in respect of whaling" and hoped to obtain "some useful measure." However, the dissolution of the Company led to nothing being done about this plea. The new interim board of directors wrote to C. C. Dalager, the Jakobshavn trader, in May 1774, asking him to keep a look-out for "illicit traders from North America"; "some measures against them" had been sought "which we shall press to have applied."

These reports were enclosed with a memorandum submitted by the directors to the Overskattedirektion in November 1774 requesting a revised proclamation against trading and forcible trespass by foreigners, and demanding either that a frigate be sent to Icelandic waters or that ships sent to both Iceland and Greenland be fitted out as armed merchantment, as formerly, and here the matter seems to have reached a temporary standstill. Foreign policy was involved, and careful consideration was necessary. The Foreign Minister, A. P. Bernstorff, also a member of the Overskattedirektion, was friendly towards the English, and this problem had to be dealt with in a way that would not affect English interests adversely.

Bernstorff must have known that in 1775 the directors had sent four cannon to Godhavn to arm the trader against any possible attack. That could have been explained as a standard defence measure, but the trader in Godhavn was dismayed, because with his few colonists he would not have been able to operate all four cannon should the occasion arise, and in any case no one had been trained to use them. The directors had envisaged the local Greenlanders helping in an emergency, but they undertook to send out a skilled gunner. It never became necessary to use the cannon, which was fortunate since, as far as is known, no gunner was ever sent to Greenland.

On 18 March 1776 the Trading Company directors' fresh application finally bore fruit when the King issued a new decree, much more detailed than any previous proclamation. With the earlier proclamations this decree forms part of the constitutional basis for Danish sovereignty over Greenland. Referring to the proclamations of 1751 and 1758 and to "Warnings and Notices" as well as complaints of encroachments which had taken place over the years, the King found himself, "as rightful and absolute hereditary monarch and lord", obliged to repeat and renew all warnings and bans issued previously and to add some detailed explanatory provisions. These were as follows:

1. The present Greenland Trade, Whaling and Fishery had a monopoly of navigation and trading "to and with the colonies and trading posts that are already established or that may hereafter be established in Greenland and the adjacent islands in the Davis Strait and Disko Bay, as well as all other harbours or settlements located there". It was forbidden both to foreigners and to "our own subjects, whoever they may be" to sail to or trade in the places mentioned, which "at the present time extend from latitude 60° N. to latitude 73° N., as well as any others that may be established in future in that country". New settlements would be duly made known.

2. No foreigner or [Danish] national, except the authorized trading company, was allowed to trade in the open sea with the Greenlanders or the colonists. Those vessels which were hailed either by His Majesty's or the Trade's cruisers would be bound to submit themselves to searching. Furthermore it was forbidden, either ashore or at sea, to steal from the Greenlanders, to kidnap them or to use force against them or "the Danish colonies and trading posts and their men" or their property.

3. Any ship whose crew broke these regulations was liable to be searched, attacked, captured and arrested with a view to seizure of the vessels and goods by the authorities. The prizes were to be taken to Copenhagen. After investigation and a verdict being given by the Admiralty, the prize would revert to the chartered Trade.

4. In the event of shipwreck or lack of fresh water, it would be permitted to put into the coast but not to stay there any longer than necessary or to infringe the bans in other respects upon pain of the same penalty.

Notwithstanding the previous proclamations and bans, it was this decree which became the main legal basis for the monopoly and the closure of the country. It was later referred to in all relevant cases, and has formed the basis for subsequent regulations up to the present time. The decree was actually applied in 1776, and it did not come too soon. From Godhavn in 1775 trader Sandgreen reported illegal trading and the forcible encroachment by foreigners on "the Greenlanders' livelihood". A Dutchman had forcibly stolen from the Greenlanders a whale that they had harpooned. As they pursued it, the Dutch crossed their course and even tried to run down the *umiaks*. The Trader's old ship the *Lovisenborg*, cruising in the Davis Strait to keep an eye on foreign vessels, sent discouraging reports of foreign interference with trade in Ũmánaq Bay and Disko Bay. The local Greenlanders went on board the foreign vessels, sold everything they had and neglected their fishing at the most favourable time. Limits would have to be fixed at sea and two well-armed ships should patrol the area.

That same summer one English and two Dutch ships were captured by the Trading Company's vessels and taken to Copenhagen, where, on the basis of the decree, they were convicted of breaking the trading ban. However, the Overskattedirektion referred the matter to the foreign affairs department of the *Tyske Cancelli* before sentence was executed. Here A. P. Bernstorff's influence came into play: he did not want awkward repercussions. The British and Dutch ambassadors both intervened, pleading extenuating circumstances, and the upshot was that the King resolved that the vessels should be released as soon as the costs of taking them as prizes had been reimbursed. Although in general the political situation was tense, the American War of Independence having just started, and both the British and Dutch had many other more pressing concerns, there was no desire in Denmark to risk diplomatic complications with those countries, even though the King's action ran counter to the decisions and regulations of the Admiralty and the Greenland Trading Company and, through the latter, the Overskattedirektion.

This was, in any case, one of the last instances of Dutch vessels infringing the regulations. Dutch activity in the Davis Strait dwindled abruptly from 1777, which was probably the most disastrous year in the history of the international Greenland navigation. Storms and drift-ice off the East coast of Greenland caused the total loss of twenty-eight Dutch and Hamburg whalers. Reports were still coming in from the West coast the following year of how groups of sailors managed to reach safety: using pinnaces and drifting on ice-floes, they rounded Cape Farewell and reached the West coast. Some landed in the far south, while others drifted further north. From Godthåb, the missionary Thomas Wiborg related the story of one company of sailors: on 1 November 1777, a pinnace holding twenty-four men reached Godthåb from the south. They came from six different Dutch and Hamburg whaling vessels, which had been operating in the waters near Spitsbergen, and had been driven by a north-easterly gale into the belt of ice off Gael Hamke bay at latitude 72° N. There three of the vessels sank, but most of the crew saved themselves by climbing on to the ice floes. Fifteen of them stayed there while the remainder made their way across the ice to a fourth vessel, on which there were now altogether 286 men. They then drifted rather than sailed southwards, but at least 110 km. to the east of Cape Farewell this ship too was wrecked. Six captains and 230 men left the ice floe upon which they had climbed to

CC

safety, while the rest of those who had been saved stayed on it. Those remaining behind were fortunate enough to get hold of a pinnace and drifted round Cape Farewell. On 19 October all but three of them got into the pinnace and rowed and drifted along the coast, reaching Qilángait Bay ten days later. From there they continued to Godthåb, where they were given help. The ship had been wrecked on 20 August, and it had taken them more than two months to travel a distance of nearly 3,000 km.[2]

Thomas Wiborg reported that at the end of March 1778, six men were discovered on a little island some 25 km. from Pisugfik (north of Godthåb). They had wintered there from 24 November 1777, having drifted there on different ice floes from somewhere east of Cape Farewell where their ship had been wrecked. They had had two pinnaces and some provisions, but one pinnace was dashed to pieces in a gale when they were trying to gain shelter on an island. With the other they reached the island where they were found and from which they did not dare to move, a distance of about 1,000 km. Some of the ship-wrecked men reached as far as Holsteinsborg in their journey across the ice. Eleven had stayed with the whalers since November 1777. Nineteen had come from the south in April–May 1778, but had been taken on to Egedesminde; still more were expected, probably those picked up along the coast to the south. The loss of so many vessels resulted in a great reduction in the Dutch trade in the years following, to which the American War of Independence also contributed. Whaling and Davis Strait sailings from Hamburg were also restricted. This was partly due to the competition to get whaling masters from the North Friesian Islands, where the Danish whalers, with support from their government, could apparently offer more tempting conditions.

The whaling project started in 1775 was to be worked out in even greater detail the following year, and to this end full details of harbours and whaling conditions were requested from the traders in all colonies from Godthåb northwards. It was stated to them in a circular that it was the directors' intention, on orders from the King, to establish settlements ashore and arrange for some whalers to winter there, not only to forestall foreign whalers but also to take advantage of any opportunities for whaling that might occur during the winter. A long questionnaire was sent with the circular dealing first with whaling possibilities, harbour conditions and ice-free localities, then asking information on the possibilities of catching seals with nets, fishing for Greenland shark and the existence of fishing banks. Then there was a request for suggestions as to how to protect the eider-duck during its nesting period and finally for observations concerning minerals, including deposits of coal, graphite and clay.

It was not as if the Davis Strait whaling had made such a big profit for the eight vessels sent out in 1776; only four had brought back any catch, in all fourteen whales. The thirty-nine ships belonging to the Dutch which were in the Davis Strait that year brought back a quantity per vessel that was twice as large. The Danish whalers off Spitsbergen had fared somewhat better: the eight ships that sailed to those waters had brought home in all twenty-three whales. If the whaling had had to rely on its own resources, it would have shown a loss, and there was no good reason to view the future optimistically, although the first year's whaling season had been experimental. H. C. Schimmelmann had studied the news from Greenland during the summer of 1776. Replies to the circular and questionnaire had not come in, hence he must have based his opinions solely on the reports from Niels Egede and the whaling master (Holsteinsborg), Dorf (Egedesminde) and Sandgreen (Godhavn). He believed in the possibilities of land-based whaling in winter, but noted that this was probably not feasible without help from the Greenlanders, which he supported enthusiastically. He also advocated the use of *umiaks*, and the directors were to see that enough of these craft were available at Egedesminde and Holsteinsborg. If participation by Greenland *fangers* was to be achieved, all other considerations must be subordinated to the interests of whaling.

The drafting of plans for whaling in Greenland presented no obstacles to the development of the wider programme. In January 1776 it was decided that eight new vessels should be built for whaling and be ready for fitting out in 1777 and efforts were made to sign on the best possible whaling masters. Even 1777, a year of disaster for Dutch and Hamburg whaling, only saw a slight setback for Danish whaling and navigation in Greenland. The outward-bound vessels were unable to complete their voyages and had to return, some of them to Norway; those that had wintered in Greenland reached home safely but without significant catch. However, one whaler who had wintered at Holsteinsborg brought home the products from three whales – equivalent to the average annual catch of a Dutch whaler. Besides that, the Greenland-based whaling at Holsteinsborg yielded that colony 146 casks (292 barrels) of blubber. As a whole, the whaling had made a loss, but some proof had nevertheless been afforded that land-based whaling was possible.

The necessary arrangements therefore had to be made quickly. In 1777 there were only three places from which whaling could be carried out: Godhavn, Egedesminde and Holsteinsborg. This is not to say that there was no whaling elsewhere. Around the settlements in the Bay there was whaling from *umiaks* and, when the opportunity offered, by means of a whale-lock (*savssat*, or as it became known in Greenland

Forestilling af en Dansk Grönlands=Fahrer, ved Hvalfiske=Fangsten under Spitzbergen.

A Danish Greenland ship whaling off Svalbard. Engraving from Carl Pontoppidan's *Hval- og Robbefangsten, etc.*
(Whaling and sealing, etc.), 1785. (Royal Library, Copenhagen.)

'*sovs*).[3] The latter method was regarded as uneconomic. Land-based whaling would have to be organized quite differently. In 1776 the manager of one of the Trade's warehouses, who had certainly never been in Greenland, suggested that Ritenbenk be transferred from its existing site on the Nûgssuaq peninsula to Zwarte Vogel Bay on the west side of the large island, which was to be given the name of Arveprinsens Ejland. The same year the ship's captain who sailed to Ritenbenk and the trader in the colony both investigated conditions at the proposed site, and both found it suitable. There were opportunities both for catching in winter on the ice and for whaling in open water when the ice had gone; the winter catch would be from sealing and trapping beluga. By whaling from there it would be possible to obtain a share in the many whales from which foreigners were now profiting. Illicit trading by foreigners could thereby be checked. However, the transfer did not take place immediately. It was two years before a ship could put in at Ritenbenk, and then everyone on board was in such a poor state that it was impossible to think of moving the colony: this only occurred in 1781.

The story of this venture illustrates the way the whole Greenland project stretched human endurance to the limit, and it is clear from the pressure they exerted on the ships' crews and the colonists that those in charge of the Overskattedirektion and the Trading Company minimized these difficulties. Corruption and attempts by outsiders to hamper the development were exposed, which created an atmosphere that was not conducive to collaboration between colonists on one side and whalers and the crews of the Trading Company's other ships on the other, and between all of these and the mission people. Yet collaboration between the whalers and the Greenlanders was apparently a matter of moment to the Government. Guldberg wrote to Schimmelmann on the subject in June 1777: it was important to obtain accurate information on all aspects, including the Greenlanders catching methods and the extent of their association with the Danes stationed there. Year by year greater skill in whaling would be attained, provided that the same people were sent out every year. From Niels Egede's journal Guldberg knew "what effect an association between us and the Greenlanders can have", and the whaling master had given several examples. (Thus Guldberg read the journal sent back from Greenland and had spoken with people who had come home.) He expressed the Government's desire for urgency in expanding the whale fishery.

In 1776 a small whaling station was established outside Egedesminde, and on Hvalfiske Ejland (subsequently named Kronprinsens Ejland) there was a temporary station; about half-way between these two settlements lay Hunde Ejland, "well situated for winter whaling from land", where a station could be suitably sited the following year. This settlement was a link in the plans for the great advance that was to take place in 1778 with the establishment of several stations. It was as if a whaling craze had seized the entire coast. Even in Godthåb it was thought that there might be possibilities for whaling beyond the islands west of Pisugfik. Sixteen of the vessels which were out whaling in the spring of 1778 were to be sent out again as quickly as possible after their return to take up their winter stations, two vessels each to Holsteinsborg (with Nipisat), Godhavn, Fortune Bay (west of Godhavn), Hvalfiske (Kronprinsens) Ejland, Hunde Ejland, and Zwarte Vogel Bay, and one each to Jakobshavn, Rodebay, Klokkerhuk and Isefjorden, a harbour close to Claushavn. The traders in Christianshåb and Jakobshavn must agree between themselves where they were to be stationed. Then a further eight ships were to be sent into the Strait for whaling, taking with them building materials for eleven houses for the crews, which were to be erected at the settlements in addition to the storehouses already sent out and a house built in Greenland fashion for each ship. Furthermore an *umiak* was to be procured for each vessel. Each ship would have a surgeon aboard, who would attend to the whalers and the Greenlanders and stationed men living in the district. Two sloops were to be sent to carry coal from Ũmánaq and so provide the whaling stations with fuel. Four larger vessels were also to be built which would be able to take up their stations in Greenland in August–September 1779 for winter whaling. The Overskattedirektion ordered the directors of the Trade and Fishery to see that all this was arranged in accordance with the royal decree.

One of the orders – to procure an *umiak* for each vessel – was difficult to carry out. It was almost impossible to obtain skins for *umiaks* at Holsteinsborg, while at Egedesminde, according to Dorf, the Greenlanders now preferred to use pinnaces and the Trading Company's lines for their catch. Trying this out in the winter of 1776–7, they had caught six large whales and a smaller one in conjunction with the whaler. The desired collaboration between Greenlanders and whalers had thus met with success here. On the other hand, the situation in 1778 was less good for six of the vessels sent out in the spring. The ice was packed solid in the Bay, even west of Disko, and it would be impossible for them to put into the places where they were supposed to call before 1 June. So, after unloading their casks and pinnaces on Kronprinsens Ejland, as trader Dorf advised, they sailed for home. They had also caught no whales. This strengthened misgivings which Guldberg had expressed previously. Early in 1777, on the basis of journals and reports from the traders, he had told the directors of his disapproval of the way previous plans had been executed in Greenland. In their reply the directors adroitly cleared themselves, but when the ships returned later in 1777 without any significant catch, an investigation was made into their conduct while whaling; however, no grounds for reproaching the whaling masters could be found. It was therefore distressing that again in 1778 six whalers should return home with their mission only partly accomplished.

At the same time difficulties were experienced in signing on whaling masters and crew for the whalers which were to go in the autumn to take up their winter stations. The directors accordingly asked the Admiralitetskollegium for help with compulsory enlistment of the crews still lacking. The Admiralty referred them to the North Friesian charters of 1735 and 1741 and advised against using force which would "give rise to unrest among these not so very peaceable folk". With few exceptions the whaling crews refused to sign on for winter whaling; possibly the events of 1777 had killed their enthusiasm. However, the necessary crews were somehow obtained by the masters, and coercion was avoided. It seems that whaling during 1778/9 was more successful than in previous years.

All this time the expenses were gradually mounting up into considerable sums. The cost of equipping the whalers for "the Royal Greenland Trade and Fishery" were as follows:

	Rdl.	Mrk.	Sk.
1777	16,089	0	15
1778	72,690	5	6
1779	47,400	2	4

Revenue consisted chiefly of the grants from State funds. Nevertheless, apart from the first year when it was 6,038 rdl. the deficit grew:

		Rdl.	Mrk.	Sk.
1777	deficit	2,666	2	7
1778	,,	3,547	0	7
1779	,,	3,979	5	12

The whaling settlements in Greenland also cost money:

	Rdl.	Mrk.	Sk.
1776–7	25,491	3	9
1777–8	20,955	3	8
1779	7,079	1	9

The receipts in this account were minimal and so the sum transferred to the balance sheet each year grew from 24,619 rdl., 2 mrk., 13 sk. to 51,565 rdl., 5 mrk., 1 sk. However, since the (very moderate) receipts from whaling were entered in other accounts, it is not clear to what extent whaling and the whaling stations paid. Neither was it clear at the time: it was only known what large sums were being expended and how little return there was in the way of whales caught.

Even in 1774 it had been possible to obtain 20 rdl. for a barrel of whale oil, but in the next few years it proved impossible to get this price at auction; in 1776 a price of 14 rdl. had to be fixed per barrel of whale oil and a half-rigsdaler less for seal oil, provided the buyer took five barrels, otherwise the price was 1 rigsdaler more per barrel. The next year it was thought possible to fix the prices at $14\frac{1}{2}$, 16 and 17 rdl. per barrel of whale oil, and between 16 and almost 18 rdl. per barrel of seal oil. A special blended oil was produced, consisting of whale, seal and fish-liver oil, which sold at approximately the same price. The blend was supposed to be of superior quality. In 1778 and 1779, prices were roughly the same.

Contact was maintained with the market in Bergen, where the prices of whale and seal oil as well as fish-liver oil were somewhat lower than in Copenhagen, and where a number of foreign buyers of whale oil obtained slight price reductions. From this time onwards, prices were fairly stable, but still lower than before 1776. The war, the 1777 disaster and the decline in Dutch and Hamburg whaling should have combined to raise whale oil prices, but with the oil being sold at auction in Copenhagen and Bergen, the home buyers tended to establish the price. Neither Copenhagen nor Bergen was well known abroad as a centre for whale oil, and their markets continued to be restricted; hence nothing was gained in this sector from the market conditions which were so favourable elsewhere.

The position of the whaling in and based on Greenland worried Guldberg and the Overskattedirektion. By an order-in-council of 26 March 1779, signed by the King but drafted by Guldberg, two "competent persons", Johan Friderich Schwabe and Bendt Olrik, were to sail to Godhavn in September, observe the winter whaling and visit the northern colonies in the spring, Schwabe spending the rest of the time in Godhavn and Olrik in Jakobshavn. Both were lawyers, and Schwabe had been a district judge in Norway. These officials were to enquire into conditions in Greenland on behalf of the State. It is characteristic of Guldberg that only in the northern colonies were the conditions to be investigated, as they were the base for whaling operations, which were Guldberg's chief concern. It was intended, however, that when the two lawyers had returned home after being in the country for two years, they should be appointed as royal representatives in Greenland, directing the trade and supervising those in charge of the colonies.

The plans for 1779 embraced not only whaling but all aspects of the Greenland trade. Julianehåb, the new colony, and Frederikshåb were each to be visited by one vessel; Ūmánaq and Upernavik were to share one. Sukkertoppen, Holsteinsborg, Egedesminde, Christianshåb, Jakobshavn, Ritenbenk and Godhavn were to be supplied separately by the whalers allotted to them. The ship sailing to Sukkertoppen would go to Nipisat afterwards and be stationed there. Godthåb and Fiskenæsset were to receive their supplies aboard two hookers, which would then be sent out to fish for cod.

In 1775 the warehouse clerk Wulff had proposed fishing for Greenland shark, the sub-arctic shark which has a large liver rich in oil. He suggested that it be carried on at Holsteinsborg. The General Trading company had in its time initiated several fishing tests, not only for Greenland shark but for other fish too, on the basis of which, together with Wulff's memorandum, the directors decided in 1776 to arrange proper fishing tests at Holsteinsborg to cover Greenland shark, halibut and cod. For this purpose two foremen and four men were sent out. Instructions were went at the same time to the trader Jørgen Egede, Niels Egede's son, as to how the fish was to be treated and preserved for despatch. No profit was expected on halibut, which was to be caught and eaten in Greenland. Two large iron cauldrons were sent out in which the Greenland shark and cod livers were to be melted out and the oil sent home in barrels.

Niels Egede had been involved in the abandonment of previous fishing tests at Holsteinsborg, and commented on this new experiment: "Forgive me now if I ask about one thing. Who was it who wanted to involve the exalted directors in fresh expenditure, by keeping people here fishing for cod and other kinds of fish? I have absolutely no knowledge of any cod-fishery. As regards catching whales and sharks, tests can probably be made in time by the colonists to see whether anything is to be gained thereby before seriously engaging in expense." At about the same time Dorf in Egedesminde had received orders to investigate the possibilities of fishing for Greenland shark in the sea near Egedesminde and in the Sydostbugt (the south-east part of Disko Bay).

The directors' expectations from fishing were confirmed. From Godthåb came a detailed report on the sea-cod fishery in May and from the middle of June until September off Kangeq. There was always halibut in plenty, but it was possible for cod to disappear completely for a period of up to four years. Most years the fish frequented the shoals that lay far out. Dorf and one of the old Greenland shipmasters both gave similar accounts of the sea-cod on the banks. At the directors' request, more information about the fishing possibilities was sent again the next year, which made them even more sure that the fishery could pay its way. It was therefore decided that a hooker should be sent to investigate the fishery and actually fish; in particular the harbours and fishing grounds from Holsteinsborg north to Egedesminde were to be surveyed and charted. The next year the captain was to carry on charting Disko Bay as far as the Vajgat; however, the scheme had to be left in abeyance until 1779 as the captain could not be persuaded to sail out on the terms offered.

The Trade gained little from the experiments. After 1777 it appears that all sales of such fishery products as shark-liver oil, for which sales figures are recorded, ceased. One lasting result was that the authorities were now aware of the existence and approximate position of the three banks off the central west coast of Greenland – Fyllas Banke off Godthåb, Lille Hellefiske Banke off Sukkertoppen, and Store Hellefiske Banke from Holsteinsborg to a point slightly south-east of Egedesminde; Dorf at Egedesminde expressly wrote that he had often seen Green-landers making good catches on the Store Hellefiske Banke. In 1778 reports on the fishing along the more southerly coastal stretches were numerous, and all of them indicated that fishing for halibut and to some extent for sharks was the most profitable; the cod-fishery, apart from catching the small fjord cod for domestic consumption, was extremely uncertain. As the yield from fishing in the more northerly reaches was inadequate, it was decided in the plans for 1779 to abandon the fishery at Holsteinsborg and arrange for the hookers to go from there to Godthåb and fish for halibut on the bank. This met with no success: fishing was and remained an all too uncertain source of revenue for the Trade.

The directors of the Trade were on the look-out for new production opportunities in Greenland, and were anxious at the same time to preserve the monopoly rights over the products which were traditionally sold to them. Their interest in eiderdown was simply a by-product of their struggle against the illicit trading that went on within the colonial districts of Greenland. Once again it was C. F. A. Wulff, the former catechist and trader at Holsteinsborg, now the trade's warehouse manager in Copenhagen, who was to the fore. In March 1776 he drew the directors' attention to the illicit trading being carried on by "private persons" in Greenland. Merchandise was "obtained on credit" for the Greenlanders, who had to pay for it with eiderdown. The nests had been plundered by people using their own and hired boats and men, thereby driving the eider-duck away from places where it had bred in large numbers. People had also been buying up all the down they could on the pretext of wanting to use it for bedding "and thereby made a great profit to the detriment of the Trade". Wulff suggested that the down should be collected for the Trade, but with due care that the birds should not be driven away from their breeding grounds; "the closest watch must also be kept on the Greenlanders, as far as possible, to see that they do not deal with the bird and its young as cruelly as hitherto, trying as best one can to show them their own considerable loss thereby. . . ." On the other hand, they might stand to gain by the rational collection of down without ransacking the breeding grounds, since they would obtain payment for it from the Trade. Wulff's memorandum led to the inclusion of a question on the eider-duck in the circular of April–May 1776 mentioned above, which did not, however, mention the possibility of illicit trading. However, the traders knew well enough what was behind the question. Answers came from both Egedesminde and Holsteinsborg the very same year. Dorf in Egedesminde reported on the systematic collection of eggs and down on the islands, not only by the people of the district but also by *umiak*-loads of men from Jakobshavn and Christianshåb. Dutchmen and Englishmen visited the outlying islands and made a clean sweep of the eggs and down. "When the eider-duck and the black guillemot are destroyed, Egedesminde will lose all the fresh food it should have." The steadily growing exclusiveness of the colonial districts finds expression here: fishing and poaching by outriders was an intolerable encroachment. The claim to a trapping-ground, which was traditional among the Eskimos of West Greenland, had been inflated by the traders to take in the whole district. During the latter half of the eighteenth century the colonies cut themselves off from each other to an increasing extent.

The same argument was used in Niels Egede's reply. He complained that the Moravians from Godthåb, by collecting eggs and down, interfered not only with the livelihood of Holsteinborg's Greenlanders but with his own, and he was aware of the illicit trading, since he reported that one of the colony's own hands had smuggled out "several lispund" of down (1 lispund = c. 8 kg.). Jørgen Egede felt that it was impossible to cope with these depredations: the Greenlanders thought of themselves as a free people, and the eggs and down were collected on islands far too remote for any control to be maintained. At any attempt to forbid them to take eggs and young and destroy the eider-duck "they simply laugh and say that this is their country, and consequently everything it offers is theirs to do with as it suits them and as they like".

Nevertheless the directors proceeded further as they had begun. They were not inclined, as Jørgen Egede had expected, to issue a ban. On the other hand, by fixing a price for the down traded in they tried to canalize "production". Presumably in order to discourage the collection of down, the price was fixed at 6 sk. per lb. It was soon made known from Sukkertoppen that this would have to be increased to 20 sk. per lb. if the arrangements were to produce any result. At this price the down would be cleaned; for uncleaned down only 8 skillinger would be given. The aim of the directors was always – but now explicitly – to concentrate all trade in the hands of the traders in order to combat any form of illicit trading. In this way the Trade, for the time being, disposed of the eiderdown problem.

Of far greater interest to the directors, the Statsbalancedirektion (formerly Overskattedirektion) and Guldberg, and much more important for rationalizing the whaling and the general operation of the Greenland settlements, was the possibility of exploiting the local coal deposits. The coal-basins on Disko were well enough known but were not exploited. Now, however, coal deposits were reported near Úmánaq. In 1776 a ship's captain took samples from there and from one of the remoter camps on Disko home with him to Denmark. These samples were examined and found good enough at least for burning in a stove. It was then decided to send an "inspector of mines", who had been employed at the colliery on Bornholm, to carry out an investigation – the outcome of which was that the Disko coal was indeed usable, but the distance from Godhavn and the local harbourage conditions made it almost impossible to collect. The directors of the Trade had more faith in coal-mining at Úmánaq; an investigation in 1778 showed that exploitation would be worthwhile. However, in 1781 it became apparent that the possibilities had been judged too optimistically: the seam from which coal could be extracted was only about two feet deep and lay below 6–9 m. of rock which would have to be cleared away before it could be worked. There would then be no more than a month's supply for the colony.

So nothing came of these plans, nor of attempts to mine graphite which was also to be found near Úmánaq. In 1776 the directors believed that large veins of rock-salt existed in the Greenlandic mountains, but these were old rumours and reports that had become exaggerated with time. No one in Greenland now could say anything definite about these "good and pure" salt deposits.

The order to collect minerals and describe the deposits that was circulated in 1776 may not appear important in itself, yet it marked the first step towards a systematic geological survey of Greenland, with a view to exploiting its mineral deposits.

REFERENCES

1. It is dubious what this *Smoserne* means. It is obviously a peculiar phonetical spelling for *Smovserne* which may mean "the gluttons", but more likely is a slangy pejorative term directed at illicit trade and usury: *Yid*, German *Schmaus*, typical for the traditional mild anti-semitism of those times.

2. This is also mentioned in the report from the missionary Wiborg dated 28 August 1778. He further reported that one of the sailors, Marcus Voss from Hamburg (in fact von Travemünde), had kept a regular and careful diary, on the basis of which a narrative was drafted and printed as a leaflet in Lübeck, reprinted in Brinner, *Die Deutsche Grönlandsfahrt*, Berlin 1913, p. 534 *et seq.*

3. A whale-lock occurs when the different whales gather in a relatively narrow open ice-hole for breath; they are "locked up" by the ice-field and unable to reach the open sea. Sometimes a great crowd of whales struggle for breath and the surface waters of the ice-hole seem to boil, as the struggling animals crowd into the narrow hole. *Savssat* in West Greenlandic derives from the verb *sapivâ*, which means "bar his way".

22

THE ROYAL TRADE IN GREENLAND
1774–1781

The coal-mining failures revealed how ill-informed were those stationed in Greenland, the managers of the Trade at home and even high-ranking Government officials. Through the constantly repeated instructions to the traders to report on anything of note that was observed, and by the diligent perusal of journals, reports and letters, it was sought to obtain the necessary knowledge. The need for an expert description of Greenland was pressing.

The missionary Otho Fabricius was fully aware of this. When he returned from Greenland in 1774 he began working out his idea of a topographical description of the country, to replace Hans Egede's *Perlustration* and give far more factual and accurate information than the Moravian, David Cranz, had been able to contribute. Fabricius must have begun work while still in Greenland, for in October 1774 he had already submitted a plan of the work, part of which was ready for making a fair copy, the rest could be written out if he received the necessary facilities. Before Fabricius went off to his Norwegian benefice, however, two tasks were officially entrusted to him – one the description of Greenland, following his own suggestion, the other a new dictionary. However, this great work never emerged. Until 1783, Fabricius' duties took him to parishes far from the centres of knowledge where the sources he needed could be found, and the requisite descriptions of districts in Greenland which he did not know personally eluded him. The demand made of the missionaries that they should describe their districts could not be met with the means of transport available to them, and without several years of continuous travel, and their missionary work would have suffered. Several missionaries declined outright to comply with his requests. This is most likely why in 1780 he printed the part of the work that he had already started. This was his famous *Fauna Grœnlandica*, the first systematic description of its kind, which showed to the world the richness and variety of the sub-arctic fauna, although based mainly on his own observations over a short period and on a limited stretch of coast. Of the comprehensive description of Greenland, only fragmentary drawings and some drafts still exist.

All the schemes planned and started in the 1770s were either plagued by misfortune or met insurmountable difficulties. Perhaps the plans were laid on too frail a basis. Difficulties were usually due to natural conditions and the climate, but sometimes also because before and during the planning stage those concerned were misinformed, if not deceived. Both the directors and the Government wanted to see positive results at an earlier stage than would have been possible even under the most favourable conditions, and when the results failed to appear, plans were cancelled in order to start on something new or go about matters differently. The directors of the Trading Company felt a need to obtain results, and thus demonstrate their efficiency to the Government, from whom considerable capital sums were flowing into the Royal Greenland Trade and Fishery. However, purchases of Greenland products in all the colonies provided a handsome annual income between 1776 and April 1781 when the directors were changed.

Revenue from all goods received 1776–81

	Rdl.	Mrk.	Sk.
1776	27,570	1	11
1777	31,875	3	10
1778	12,291	2	13
1779	44,531	5	0
1780	74,014	5	12

The low figure for 1778 was due to navigation difficulties. The overall rise would have given grounds for optimism, but for the deficit which was accumulating at the same time.

Deficits extracted from the ledger account for all the colonies 1776–81

	Rdl.	Mrk.	Sk.
1776	6,628	5	2
1777	11,685	5	3
1778	40,980	0	3
1779	26,434	2	6
1780	[14,488 surplus]		
1781 up to 30.4.81	12,500	1	0

This meant a total deficit of 83,741 rdl., 1 mrk., 14 sk. which occurred despite an annual subsidy from the Finanskollegium of 7,000 rdl., for operating expenses, and other revenues. Costs rose steeply up to 1779, though somewhat less in 1780; these included the running of

the colonies and maintenance of their stocks, wages, supplies of provisions and merchandise, and new capital expenditure on buildings
and boats. These items cannot be extracted from the accounts, which
therefore give a rather distorted picture, the more so at that time,
since the colonies' accounts were debited from the outset with the estimated valuation of the thirteen colonies which were taken over on
1 January 1776 from the Trade's interim board of directors. When the
balance was duly transferred from the credit side of one year to the debit
side of the next, the deficit in the colonies' accounts grew to 168,263
rigsdaler net as at 30 April 1781, more than double the total "operating
deficit" as shown above, which is probably nearer the truth. Capital
assets were not then generally shown in the accounts except before being taken over by another company; on the other hand, fresh capital
expenditure figured among the actual outgoings. The relatively large
and generally rising revenue from goods sold on credit shows, by comparison with the previous companies' revenue in this area, some growth
in production for barter in Greenland. Over twenty years the Trading
Company had produced and sold an annual average of 1937 barrels
of mixed seal and whale oil. In 1776 this had already been equalled by
the Royal Greenland Trade, and was exceeded in the following years.

Just as the Royal Greenland Trade took over the colonies already
founded, it was also obliged to pursue the Trading Company's partly
executed plans for new settlements, and the Government's own settlement plans which it intended to have carried out by the Trading
Company. The settlements on which a start had been made were
Upernavik and Godhavn, and a subsidy of 7,753 rdl. towards their
completion was paid in 1776 – which included a contribution towards
the establishment of Julianehåb following Anders Olsen's report in
1774 of his exploration of the region. The southern tip of the peninsula
separating the Tunugdliarfik fjord and the Igaliko fjord was considered
the most suitable site for the Julianehåb colony, and building materials,
supplies and some merchandise were sent out to him in 1775. The
difficulties that had been experienced with sailings to Frederikshåb
recurred on the very first sailing to the future colony. The hooker
sent out left Copenhagen in mid-April, and sighted Cape Farewell
in early June. At the same time the *stor-is* came into view: enormous
icebergs and huge unbroken floes. For nearly a fortnight the hooker
cruised before the belt of ice without finding the smallest crack in it;
then it headed north. Off Frederikshåb the captain tried unsuccessfully
to get through the ice-belt, and on'y when he reached Fiskenæsset,
managed to bring the hooker into harbour. This was about 14 June.
From there kayak-men were sent out to investigate the ice conditions
and whether there was a chance of steering a southward course between

the ice and the coast. There was, and the hooker reached Frederikshåb safely. The captain now proceeded south with two Greenlanders as pilots (known in Greenland as *kendtmænd*). The newly-fledged assistant reported that he would not have thought them "so sound in their knowledge as they were, for long before we came to the place, they were able to recognize where they were and report whether there were skerries or not, but they did not know the nearest haven for the ship should ice bar the way or a southerly wind drive the ice inshore". It was the first time that the captain had sailed this stretch. Such conditions were met with by many Greenland captains. The dangers were great, but the Greenland *kendtmænd* knew the waters through which they so often paddled their kayaks.

It is nevertheless surprising that after thirty years of sailings to Frederikshåb, with pack-ice obstructing them almost every year, it was still not known when it was best to call at this colony and with it the new colony where the pack-ice was bound to be even more of an obstacle. However, it had become a firm tradition over the years, for the Greenland ships to leave as early in the spring as possible since it was vital to reach the places where houses were to be built before frost and snow made building work impossible. Anders Olsen in his report expressed his relief that the ship had arrived safely, and so early that it was possible before its departure to get one of the dwellings sufficiently advanced for people to move in; the walls of the outhouses were also built and the rafters were ready for fixing. From the summer of 1775 the colony was a reality.

Meanwhile purchases had been few, so there was no significant return cargo for the ship. The reason for this reveals much concerning the Greenlanders' attitude to trading as a whole. Olsen had expected to be able to purchase blubber and skins from the local Greenlanders on a sort of credit system, against the supply of equivalents in merchandise when supplies came in later. This, he maintained, was the way it was done in the other colonies, but presumably only when the colony had run out of merchandise with which to pay for products traded in. Otherwise, the impression is rather that in most colonies the giving of credit worked the other way round, but in the newly founded colony Olsen was unable to obtain any blubber or skins against deferred payment: when the local Greenlanders found he had no merchandise with which to pay them, they would not part with their produce. This section of the coastal population, who had grown accustomed to seeing ships arriving with merchandise almost every year, had developed some commercial sophistication. But in the Julianehåb region the Greenlanders were presumably more used to "cash" exchange transactions, which Olsen attributed not only to their trading

DD!

trips northwards into the Dutch "market", but also to the calls made in the district formerly by the Dutch and now by North Americans. Olsen had tried to obtain some merchandise from Frederikshåb, but the trader there had been unfriendly and refused to help which incidentally resulted in his being recalled and dismissed. When the ship finally arrived, Olsen was able to purchase some blubber but no skins.

Towards the Americans, whom they were accustomed to seeing off-shore at various times of the year and harbouring in the outer islands, the Greenlanders of the region had hitherto acted with reserve. However, in the spring of 1775 an American vessel had put into a harbour at Nunarssuit, the peninsula forming the northern boundary of the Julianehåb bay – Frobisher's Cape Desolation. The local Green-landers had gone on board the vessel "where they were well and correctly received". In itself this call was not an instance of illicit trading, since the Julianehåb colony had not yet been duly "promulgated" and Nunarssuit lay outside the Frederikshåb region; nonetheless, Olsen's report on the matter probably contributed to the passing of the Royal Decree of 18 March 1776. It is striking that Olsen expressly mentioned the reserve shown by the Greenlanders of the district towards these foreigners. Perhaps it was due to the tradition of the avenger who was to come and bring retribution for the killing of the Norse population. It was in this very area of the coast that the legends concerning the hostilities between the Norse population and the immigrant Eskimos lived on; indeed, it was from here that Niels Egede had been told the legend of the foreigners' massacre of the Norsemen. Niels Egede believed that these foreigners were "raiders who belonged to the English privateers", i.e. New Englanders, Newfoundlanders or Canadians.

The old idea of reaching the Eastern Settlement and any survivors of the Norse population lay behind the plans for founding Julianehåb. Certainly the main object was to bring this section of the West coast into the Trade's – and the mission's – sphere of influence, in order to benefit from the production of the Greenlanders living there, to make contact with the East-Greenlanders, who regularly came and went through the region near Cape Farewell, and to get the Greenlanders living in the south to settle in the region as *fangers* and not make the long journeys north. The idea of reaching the Eastern Settlement had certainly faded into the background, but Hans Egede's original idea had not been abandoned, even by the Government. Anders Olsen was keenly interested in the Norse ruins. He travelled around in the region, although elderly and sometimes ill, and in 1776 or 1777 he must have undertaken a fairly extensive journey "18 miles southwards and 6 miles along the south-east or eastern side of Cape Farewell". If Julianehåb was the point of departure, 18 Danish miles or 135 km. extends to a little further south than the present-day Frederiksdal.

As early as 1770 the so-called Icelandic Land Commission had been instructed to consider the possibility of sending any ships which had wintered in Iceland on voyages to the west to survey the east coast of Greenland in the hope of discovering the Eastern Settlement. Commission concluded that no expedition to the east coast of Greenland could be undertaken with the vessels that normally called at Iceland. Two vessels would have to make the journey because of the dangers, and both should be especially built to negotiate ice. The finding of this commission was referred to by Jon Erichsen, a deputy in the Rentekammer, and as such a director of the Royal Greenland Trade and Fishery, in a statement to the chief director in February 1777. He assumed that the Eastern Settlement had existed or perhaps still did exist on the east coast of Greenland, and believed that sailings to it could therefore best be undertaken from the west coast of Iceland; he acknowledged that for a century attempts to reach the supposed Eastern Settlement had been determined instead by rector Arngrim Vídalín's idea (1703) of reaching the east coast by ship from the west coast of Greenland. Erichsen could not know that his own opinion was based on fundamental misunderstandings and that his premise, especially regarding movements of the ice, was erroneous.

Erichsen's statement did not immediately have the desired result, as Løvenørn's expedition to the east coast did not take place until 1786. But in 1777 the statement may have given impetus to the exploration of the Julianehåb district. It was essential to obtain better and more detailed information than Anders Olsen had been able to obtain. No one thought of Peder Olsen Walløe's journals. It was therefore decided to send the former Upernavik trader, Andreas Bruun, on an expedition to explore the many fjords of the Julianehåb district where cattle-raising might be possible. At Guldberg's request, the trader-assistant Aron Arctander was to accompany Bruun. Arctander's journal is significant because he was more interested in the Norse ruins than Bruun. In surveying the stretch from Nunarssuit to Cape Farewell Bruun was to concern himself with the economic possibilities and Arctander with the ruins. The expedition lasted from 1777 to 1779, and they succeeded in exploring the coastal margin and some distance into some of the fjords. Arctander took special interest in the fjords around Julianehåb. His sketches and surveys of the ruins formed the basis of H.P. von Eggers' location of the Norse place-names of the Eastern Settlement in the Julianehåb district; he had previously arrived at the same view theoretically. (Eggers' treatise on this subject was only published in 1792.)

Bruun investigated the possibilities of cattle-raising and other traditional Greenlandic pursuits as thoroughly as possible. He was not
much impressed by the fishing and trapping possibilities, but everywhere he went he examined the layers of soil and the grassy plains
and estimated the possibilities of cultivation and grazing. Nowhere
did he calculate the animal husbandry potential at more than forty
sheep, two cows and one or two horses. The directors wanted to see
whether the result of the surveys would hold out the hope that a few
Icelandic families might be able to settle in this southern region of
Greenland. The expectations were modest but Bruun's report did nothing to enhance them, and once again nothing came of the plan for an
Icelandic settlement.

As here were still difficulties in sailing to the new colony, it was
decided that in 1780 the largest available colonial supplyship should
sail to Frederikshåb, taking supplies for Julianehåb and Frederikshåb
to the latter colony, from which the other would have to fetch them by
boat – this was only to happen if ice was present in as big a quantity
as in previous years. That year Julianehåb sent home 278½ casks
of blubber, 6,230 seal skins, 509 fox skins and 3 whole bear skins.
This was a substantial amount, and it was impossible to collect the
produce of both Frederikshåb and Julianehåb purchased each year
in one ship.

Despite some long outstanding debts on his account at Sukkertoppen and his own admitted deficiencies in writing and arithmetic,
Anders Olsen continued as trader at Julianehåb until he retired in
1780 and went to live at Igaliko, the old episcopal seat of Garðar.
There he realized the plan for cattle-raising which the directors had
considered, and he and his descendants carried on a type of farming,
based on the raising of cattle and sheep, which is still in existence.

From the time when Hans Egede had some cattle and sheep sent out
in 1723, cattle, sheep, goats, pigs and all kinds of poultry had been kept
in the various colonies. With the cramped conditions, this was often
unpleasant for those living in the house, as for instance at Frederikshåb where the trader built his pigsty right up against the outer wall
of the missionary's room, so that the latter had no peace by night or
day because of the grunting and rooting. Apart from the forms of animal
life which were strange to the Greenlanders, there was nothing intrinsically alien to their minds in keeping domestic animals. After all they
kept dogs, partly for pulling sledges and partly for their skins, but these
animals were only given the minimum of attention. Now the Greenlanders saw the colonists' animals being attended to and fed daily.
The language affords evidence of their gradually becoming accustomed
to seeing such domestic animals, which were soon given special

West Greenlandic names. For instance, the cow was called *ugsik*, clearly a loan word (*okse* = ox). According to Otho Fabricius, however, it was called *umingmák*, the Eskimo name for the musk-ox; as this did not exist in West Greenland, its name could safely be transferred to an animal that resembled it. Nowadays in West Greenlandic a cow is often called *nerssússuaq*, meaning "the big land animal"; in the eighteenth century, according to Fabricius' dictionary, the horse was regarded as the big land animal. The hen was called *tukingarsolik*, i.e. "that which is supplied with something running lengthwise". Fabricius' explanation for this was that a hen's tail characteristically follows the longitudinal axis of the body whereas the tails of other birds are set transversely. Very early, the common name for a sheep became *saua* (or in Fabricius *sàua*), which is undoubtedly the Norwegian word *sau*. The presence of these domestic animals, with which many Greenlanders became familiar in time, had a significance other than the obvious one in that they served to help Greenlanders to a better understanding of the Bible stories and parables.

Anders Olsen was the first to attempt cattle-rearing proper as a primary occupation and to succeed at it, but the idea of establishing some form of animal husbandry was focused on sheep. From the first time the question of Icelandic settlement was discussed, sheep-rearing was included as an essential element in the plans. It had already been practised by the Moravians, traders and missionaries at Godthåb, but on a very small scale and only for domestic use, especially with regard to wool. When the directors requested information about possible sheep-rearing in 1774, Storm, the Godthåb trader, said he saw no point in making tests on the coastal margin, in reply to which the directors suggested he should investigate the possibilities in the fjord regions; he was also asked to find out whether anyone living there would experiment with sheep. This can only have meant getting Greenlanders to keep sheep, as the directors were well aware that no Europeans, not even Moravians, lived inland along the fjords. Storm made it clear that to get the Greenlandic *fangers* and hunter to experiment with sheep-rearing was impracticable, but did suggest that, as a start, one or two European families might settle in the fjord regions behind the colony. The matter was then shelved for further consideration, presumably in connection with the possibility of Icelandic settlement, and so the scheme fell through. Thus people were on the look-out for ways of expanding production in Greenland, though uncertainty of the commercial outcome and capital shortage acted as a continual brake.

During development of the shore-based whaling industry, it became clear that it had three distinct sectors: (1) that done by the whalers in outstations; (2) that in which both Greenlanders and whalers sent out took part, and (3) the traditional Greenland style of whaling. The colonists might occasionally participate in the second and third. The traditional Greenland whaling using *umiaks* had continued over the years, and as always happened, a number of the whales they harpooned were lost, and a settlement further away might then benefit from a carcass being washed up; the Trade directors were understandably incensed when they heard of such losses. The Greenland whaling within the Bay during the 1770s became a considerable source of income for the local Greenlanders; it was now more rationally operated, because the Jakobshavn trader C. C. Dalager, and especially his sons, looked after it. It developed particularly after the change-over was made from *umiaks* to light pinnaces, as suggested by Niels Egede in Holsteinsborg. "European" whaling tackle, both harpoons and lines, came into use at the same time – C. C. Dalager felt that two skilled men should be available to maintain it.

When the whaling at Godhavn started in 1773, it was done, as already mentioned, with a number of whaling men who had been sent out to Holsteinsborg, and whom trader Sandgreen took with him to the new settlement, but there were too few men to be effective. Thus the directors of the General Trading Company were pleased the following year when Disko was found to have more inhabitants than had previously been supposed. A few Greenlanders soon moved to the site. The missionary in Ũmánaq complained, however, that the number of baptized there had decreased, since about forty people had moved to Disko in order to wait for the whaling and "enjoy Danish victuals which rumour has it are being distributed there in abundance". Yet the other whaling stations appear to have attracted only a few of their own local inhabitants. In reports and letters these population movements are only casually referred to.

During the lengthy process of transferring Ritenbenk from Nûgssuaq, trader Dorf's son Carl, who usually lived in Egedesminde, spent a winter in Zwarte Vogel Bay, where a few Greenland families from Egedesminde went with him and experimented with whaling from there. The whalers that sailed to Disko Bay at the end of August 1780 carried a letter from the Company informing the trader of Egedesminde that these families, preferably with a few more, were to be given the chance of moving with Carl Dorf to Zwarte Vogel Bay and settling there permanently; they would receive help with the building of houses and there would be a permanent agreement in respect of whaling. The families were willing to move in 1781, but the whaler bearing the directors' letter only reached Egedesminde when it was too late to start building winter houses on a completely new site. How many of the Greenland families actually settled in Ritenbenk we do not know, but the colony was eventually moved in the summer of 1781 by the senior assistant in charge. If any people did move from Egedesminde, this was the first State-subsidized removal of a population group in Greenland – and on a voluntary basis.

The most distinctive and completely localized form of whaling was the use of a whale-lock (*savssat* or *søvs*). Dorf tells how in 1750 the *savssat* saved the population at Egedesminde from the usual famine. There was an exceptionally large catch of over 1,000 belugas and twenty-one whales. Some were lost and the blubber and baleen went to the Dutch, but the event was still memorable. Even for a small *savssat* firearms were necessary. In the incredible melée at the open hole in the ice, where the wretched animals fight for air with every ounce of strength, harpooning is impossible. So Dorf asked for proper rifles to sell to the *fangers*, as those who had good guns were able to supply ever-increasing quantities for trading, besides keeping themselves well supplied.

Dependent on the winter ice-layer as this form of whale-catching was, *savssat* was carried on outside the Bay too, owing everything to chance as regards both time and place. An opportunity for *savssat* could not be relied on every year. If a *savssat* was rumoured to be in operation somewhere, a crowd of people would swarm to it in a surprisingly short time from widely scattered places around. The Ũmánaq trader reported in 1781 that the Greenlanders living about 50 km. north of the colony were talking of a whale-lock situated about 100 km. away this *savssat* gave them a good catch, but the trader could not reach it with pinnaces because of the ice; consequently much of the blubber from the animals killed was left lying on the ice, where it either melted away or disappeared, unless foreign whalers got hold of it – this was a familiar situation throughout the century.

Where the whaling was operated mainly by the Greenland *fangers* there were no problems regarding blubber, baleen or meat; the catch belonged to the Greenlanders and the Trade only received what was bartered at the colony. The whaling tradition that existed at each place tended to be respected by the Greenlanders; in many places it appears to have been that everyone was entitled to as much as he could get for himself and as a result the flensing was often done at a dangerous speed. Where different forms of whaling were carried on from the same place or were combined, some form of organization was necessary.

During 1777–8 it became more and more common for the local Greenlanders to borrow pinnaces, harpoons and lines. The practice had begun at Godhavn and Egedesminde and spread from there – it was caused partly by the difficulty of obtaining skins to cover the *umiaks* – but the directors were opposed to it, as they were afraid of expensive equipment being lost or damaged. C. C. Dalager also considered it essential that trained harpooners should look after boats and equipment. Nevertheless the directors had to acquiesce.

In 1779 certain rules for sharing the catch were laid down. In principle the catch made by the whaling vessels was to be kept quite separate from any other catch; everything caught by the colony's men with or without the help of Greenlanders belonged to the colony. Any Greenlanders who helped would naturally receive payment in the form of merchandise, according to the agreements they concluded with the whaling-masters when helping them on board their vessels. At Godhavn, a precedent was established for the size of the payment: it was agreed with the Greenlanders who might have helped in catching and flensing at sea that a part would be paid in kind, equivalent to 1 rigsdaler for every two barrels of blubber. This was a kind of group piece-work agreement, with the payment divided among the individuals in the group that had taken part. They received nothing of the actual catch beyond the *kræng*, i.e. the meat on the inner side of the blubber. Blubber and baleen were taken by the whaler. If the colony's men and the local Greenlanders made a catch jointly, using the colony's craft and whaling tackle, the catch was to be divided up as fairly as possible according to the effort contributed. This proportion was to be fixed each year in advance by agreement between the trader and the local people. It was always explicit that anything the local Greenlanders caught with their own tackle and craft would belong to them, to be bartered if they wished.

These rules, imperfect and vague as they were, meant that a step had been taken away from Greenland tradition, which lacked rules in this respect, towards the long-cherished desire for more clearly defined rules to govern society. A break had also been made with the rule that the person or crew who first implanted a harpoon in a whale enjoyed some prior right to the whale; this rule, which resembled Greenland custom or usage relating to the capture of other animals, only applied to situations where the whaling vessel or the colony's men had assisted in the whaling. Now it was laid down that the one who had contributed most to killing and securing the whale should be suitably rewarded. Obviously such a break with established tradition generated conflicts, which was why it had been laid down that an agreement on payment should be reached in advance with the local Greenlanders each year. At Claushavn the local Greenlanders would not agree in 1781 to the former method of payment as they had played the chief part in catching the whales. In the case of two catches they had received half the baleen but none of the blubber, yet they were no longer willing to participate on those terms. The trader at Christianshåb, which also covered Claushavn, thought it only fair for them to have half the blubber as well as the baleen; otherwise they would receive nothing of value for the time and energy they spent on whaling, while neglecting their other hunting. The Greenlanders of Claushavn therefore sought the directors' permission to borrow pinnaces and equipment in order to go whaling on their own without outside help, in exchange for half the blubber and baleen as payment for the hire of the craft and tackle. The directors agreed, although with some reluctance. But the trader's proposal was altered so that the Greenland partners were to have half the blubber, but all the baleen was to go to the Trading Company in payment for the hire of craft and tackle. The trader's proposal had in fact related to whaling done independently by the Greenlanders and not to joint whaling, but the directors decided as they did simply because there were no hands on the whaler sent out.

The directors' confused attitudes were done partly to varying circumstances. At the settlements in the inner part of the Bay the local Greenlanders carried on their normal livelihood as *fangers* in addition to whaling, whereas those in places like Godhavn were largely dependent on whaling. At Godhavn people were lent both pinnaces and tackle for whaling without any deduction for hire when they traded in their catch. Sandgreen, the trader, presumably did this because whaling was the chief means of livelihood for the local Greenlanders. In 1782 he asked the directors what attitude he should adopt. The Godhavn Greenlanders had been warned by other Greenlanders in the Bay to beware of what they considered the unfair payment being claimed elsewhere for tackle lent for whaling, which might be lost. Sandgreen maintained that the Trading Company had always supported the Greenlanders by lending them such things, without any deduction at bartering time. The directors replied by insisting on the payment that was fixed elsewhere for the hire: half the blubber and all the baleen.

This affair reveals not only the isolation of the individual colonies in relation to each other, causing intrinsically similar problems to develop very differently, but also how the Greenlanders' reaction to unfair treatment took a relatively long time to be expressed. The old, surprisingly swift "bush telegraph" – "the *kamik* post" – had not declined in speed and efficiency, but it seemed to be restricted to the native Greenland population more than ever before. In the case in point the directors felt obliged to uphold the rules laid down.

It was not always possible for the directors to enforce the rules and principles that they and their predecessors had established. The men on the ships stationed for the winter in Greenland often could not be persuaded to sign on at the whaling stations, and the result was frequently an acute shortage of labour. Although in general it was considered undesirable to take the Greenland sealers away from their hunting, the employment of Greenlanders nevertheless became essential for the running of the whaling stations. Where this was done, a Greenland whaling "hand" was to have one man's ration of bread, butter, groats, peas and fish plus 5 rdl. per month in wages like the other hands. This was a departure from the strongly asserted principle of not "spoiling" the Greenland population with "Danish victuals".

Collaboration between the men sent out and the local Greenland whalers was hampered in various ways. Jaeger, the missionary at Holsteinsborg, complained of the Greenlanders' unwillingness to go whaling with these men. "The free availability of everything they acquire among themselves, to which they are accustomed, gives rise to a natural fear of the discipline and order which would be imposed by entering into partnership in such fishing, using Greenland and European methods together." However, he wrote in the same letter that the whalers stationed there in the winter of 1776–7 had caught three whales, partly with the Greenlanders' help, all of which had to be flensed by the Greenlanders. Enough whaling-men were never sent out, especially the "blubber-strippers", who were skilled in flensing.

Dorf, the trader in Egedesminde, mentions an isolated instance of the Greenlanders' superstition being the cause of their not wanting to go on a joint whaling expedition. The Greenland sealers would not accompany the whaling assistant Adam Thorning on a trip, because he would talk of how he would implant the harpoon in the whale, give it the death-blow and then do the flensing – all in a particular way. The whale, they said, had heard this and would therefore smash boat after boat to bits and kill the occupants. Dorf could not dissuade them from this belief.

The difficulty of procuring Greenlanders as hands for the whalers stationed there through the winter was a recurring argument of the whaling-masters for higher pay when they were about to set sail for Greenland. They also used the familiar argument that Greenland labour could not be relied on. Yet another whaling-master's journal was full of his praise for the skill and reliability of the Greenlanders in keeping a look-out for whales. Occasionally the payment issue degenerated to the point where the Greenlander partners simply took possession of the part of the whale which they considered their due after it was caught, even though contrary to the agreement. Such incidents compromised any form of arrangement, especially when the directors would refrain from prosecuting the Greenland *fangers* for a *fait accompli*.

The day-to-day association between Greenlanders and the whaling-men stationed in the country for the winter was a thorn in the missionaries, flesh since these crews undoubtedly exerted a bad influence. In 1779 the crews were forbidden to have "any illicit associations with the Greenlanders or to do any trade whatsoever with them". Their clothing made of skins was to be sewn or repaired by older Greenland women, by arrangement with the whaling assistant. There was to be no fraternization either in the men's own dwellings or in the Greenlanders' houses, but of course this ban was not observed. At Godhavn, breaches of it developed into disorderly scenes, when the strictly forbidden brandy played a leading part. The matter ended with the men being ordered to pay fines into the Trade's poor fund. Trader Sandgreen reported of this occasion that the men were "as usual" visiting the Greenlanders' houses, and he had therefore been obliged by his instructions to intervene, whereupon the disorder had spread.

The Bay missionaries also complained that Greenlanders from the "outer islands" – Vester Kronprinsens and Hunde – went aboard foreign whalers which came there in the spring. "Here even more than elsewhere, looseness and drunkenness are rife". Greenlanders who went aboard these ships were idle more than vicious "for a number of them, both women and men . . . stay with them sometimes for whole months on their northward voyages and do not come ashore again until the return journey". In the meantime they neglected their own trapping, "but they are not losers thereby, since they live the good life on European victuals for as long as they are aboard, and the services they render – sometimes innocent but often extremely depraved – are so well paid by the foreigners that they not only obtain what they need by barter from others but even have something left over, which is detrimental to the Trade". At the same time there were complaints about the abuse of spirits. "The vice of drunkenness has unfortunately become rife among many of those living in or near the colonies." It might be desirable for the mission and the colonies to be kept entirely separate as regards settlement. The contrast between the spiritual aims of the mission and the behaviour of the secular Danes in the colony generated a sense of division which increasingly dominated the work of colonization. The cases reported, the obvious lack of order, the disappointing return and the intermittent operation of the whole whale-fishery induced the Government to arrange for a thorough investigation of the whole undertaking.

The conduct of the whaling was the main object of the proposed investigation, but the trading side could be investigated at the same time. Among other things, there were signs of "internal illicit trading" – i.e. bartering and sending home of Greenland products for private profit, in contravention of the Royal Greenland Trade's monopoly.

When the General Trading Company was on its last legs the directors eventually unmasked an actual instance. For several years they had suspected unauthorized transactions, and issued warning notices to all traders to be on the look out for them. Then in 1774 the directors discovered that Dorf, the former catechist and later trader at Egedesminde, had sold, through Wulff, the warehouse manager and his former colleague and childhood friend, a quantity of baleen. Because of Dorf's past services and probably also because the directors were about to retire, no proceedings were taken, but he was sharply reminded to keep to the straight and narrow path. This incident throws a curious light on the zeal with which the same warehouse manager, Wulff, drew the directors' attention two years later to a supposed illicit trade in fox skins. However, this traffic had to be prevented somehow, since it involved the objectionable practice of a colonist or missionary lending a gun and ammunition to a Greenlander working for him especially for shooting foxes – which the lender then sold in Greenland. This was a kind of exploitation of Greenland labour of which neither the Trade nor the mission could approve in the long term.

In 1779 the customs authorities in Copenhagen managed to expose two ship's captains, one of whom had brought four barrels of blubber from Greenland illegally while the other had taken them to be sold in Jutland. The Statsbalancedirektion, which became involved in the case, wanted a severe penalty to be imposed as a warning to others, particularly because such offences were unlikely to be discovered very often.

The directors continued to be obsessed with the fear of illicit trading, and felt compelled to send a reminder to the Missionskollegium, since in the next case to be investigated where the amounts involved were found to be trivial, it was the missionaries in Upernavik and Ūmánaq who were the culprits. This incident increased the directors' mistrust of the mission's people.

At the same time as he drew the directors' attention to the illicit trade in fox skins, Wulff mentioned the desirability of restricting the lending and sale of firearms and ammunition. Niels Egede had touched on this subject in 1775 although he realized it was impossible to abolish the use of firearms all at once. In any case, firearms sent out had to be of reasonable quality; both Niels Egede and Dorf, the trader in Egedesminde, had complained of inferior ones being sent out. Dorf even got the missionary and his own assistant, Adam Thorning, to testify how the Trading Company were the direct losers through sending out such poor firearms which misfired even when they were new. Thus at Egedesminde, at least, guns had become essential for the Greenland *fangers*, and with their increasing use the problem of maintenance increased. Unserviceable weapons had to be sent to Copenhagen for repair. The Greenland *fangers* once left the firearms exposed to damp so that they rusted. There was no established tradition of maintenance and it took years for one to develop.

The complaints that the merchandise sent out was inferior were well founded. In 1775 the Overskattedirektion intervened in the arrangements made by the directors regarding the Iceland and Finnmark trade. In this case the suppliers who, in their tenders, had undertaken to supply specific goods of a given quality, found they could not obtain them and supplied inferior goods. Without suggesting any attempt to defraud, the Overskattedirektion requested the directors of the Trade to obtain good quality merchandise privately and to stop buying through tenders. The following year complaints about higher prices and poorer quality poured in. The directors could only point to the price increases that had occurred on the European markets due to the war. Meanwhile, supplies of merchandise for the Iceland, Finnmark and Greenland trade were all being incorporated into the Danish–Norwegian State's imports as a whole. In true mercantilistic fashion, the Overskattedirektion wanted to know what goods were being imported for this purpose the Government sought to avoid foreign purchases as much as possible, and to buy at home. The Greenland Trade showed that, apart from linens, minor quantities of other merchandise for barter in Greenland, and materials for building ships and keeping the whalers and colonies supplied with barrels, nothing else was imported. Of the total spent on purchases in 1777, 3,400 rdl. accounted for merchandise for barter in Greenland, and 61,090 rdl. went on shipbuilding and equipment; the latter expenses would only continue as long as the tonnage was being expanded.

The price rises in Europe were bound to affect the barter prices in Greenland. For instance, in 1778 the prices of the three kinds of tobacco sent out almost doubled, which set off strong reactions among both the Greenlanders and the people sent out. It was reported from Julianehåb, the newly founded colony, that the junior employees could not manage on the 14 rdl. in kind which they were allowed to draw each year, if the consumption of tobacco for bartering was to be covered. The Greenlanders thought that the price was lower elsewhere in Greenland, and at Fiskenæsset they expressed the same opinion. There the use of tobacco had become so well established that competent and incompetent breadwinners alike bought excessive quantities at the increased price, and thus came to lack real necessities. The price had to be reduced, and the loss recouped by keener buying – this was the view of the senior assistant on the spot. At Upernavik, however, after the trader had instructed his assistant to inform the surrounding Greenlanders of the tobacco increases on his autumn expedition, "they became almost desperate and surrounded him". The assistant told the Greenlanders that the price increase was a royal order and that both they and the Danes were going to pay the same higher price. To this the Greenlanders stated as one man "that if they did not get as much tobacco for their skin wares now as formerly, they would not let the great master [the King] have one skin", whereupon not one skin was traded during the whole of that year. In the end the trader had to give in and buy, using tobacco as an article of barter at the old rate. He reckoned later that, had he been able to use the new tobacco price, he could have bought 300 more skins than he was now able to send home. This earned the trader a strong reprimand from the directors, who nevertheless took no further action. These same people at Upernavik showed themselves extremely quality-conscious regarding other kinds of merchandise. It was impossible to sell them red kersey, whereas the blue was very much in demand. Large-bore firearms were also greatly sought after. The trader sent home twenty-nine tin kettles that had rusted after being used for catching dripping rain in the warehouse "so I am unable to dispose of them to the Greenlanders as they are very particular about damaged goods".

Not only the Greenlanders reacted to the tobacco price increase, but also those employed in the colony and mission. In 1776 an attempt had been made to limit the consumption of both tobacco and gunpowder by restricting the quantity of each commodity to what any one person could use. There was an immediate reaction from the missionaries at Sukkertoppen and Frederikshåb respectively. If they were not allowed to get freely what they required and were prepared to pay for, they would not, as Berthel Laersen wrote from Sukkertoppen, be able to obtain fresh food, skins for clothing, tents and *umiaks*, let alone pay the oarsmen for the missionaries' visits to the outlying settlements. It would be impossible to rely on any help without payment in the form of tobacco and sometimes powder or shot.

In most places there was considerable demand for the merchandise that was available for sale, so that a system of credit or deferred payment was still a necessity, when winter shortages and famines occurred. Then the Greenland *fangers* had nothing to give in exchange, but had to buy on credit. It might take a long time for the outstanding debts to be collected. We have seen how Anders Olsen had substantial amounts owing by the Sukkertoppen Greenlanders when he moved from there and these took years to collect. Niels Egede wrote in 1781 that the people of Holsteinsborg had promised to pay off a little of their debts each year, but when times were bad they were naturally unable to catch anything beyond what was needed to subsist and for further purchases. So, for good or ill, the credit economy took its place in West Greenland society. Yet without the credit system the whaling at Holsteinsborg, for example, could have ceased because the Greenlanders were short of tackle. Or the people of Upernavik would not have caught as many belugas through *savssat*, if they had had to harpoon them, being unable to shoot them without the ammunition they could only obtain on credit.

The trader in each colony was in a dilemma, since he was there to buy as much as possible, in his own interest and that of the Trade, yet at the same time he had to be responsible for the stock of merchandise he used for bartering and for the price in royal currency, fixed according to the price list sent to him. The directors insisted that the price list for purchasing should be observed. Auditing the colonies' accounts often resulted in the calculation of the actual cost per barrel of the blubber bought. In 1776 an assistant who had been in charge at Christianshåb for a whole year in the trader's absence was severely reprimanded for having "allowed himself to be satisfied" with half the blubber for the merchandise, so that a cask of blubber had cost the Trade a little more than 3 rdl. (almost double the approved rate); the assistant should have given credit.

The produce bought might have been expected to fetch a higher price when sold in Copenhagen, thus justifying a higher rate for its purchase, but this was not the case. Hence the traditional barter ratio could not be maintained. The Greenlanders were used to fixed prices and simply refused to accept the possibility of their products changing in value; after all, there was no change in their nature, nor was the Trade less eager to buy them. The traders too were naturally unhappy with the price changes, to which they reacted in different ways. Some omitted to alter prices, but compensated by using an inaccurate measuring barrel, even one without a bottom, placing it over a measured hole in the ground, which had to be filled up before the measuring proper began. Others failed to alter the buying prices. Others again obeyed their instructions. Hence a lack of uniformity arose among the buying prices in the various colonies and the news spread rapidly via the "*kamik* post". The directors continued to insist that the price list be observed and that trading should be in accordance with good business practice; in other words, it was a question of "bargaining" and not just of collecting. These two requirements could not be reconciled, and the resulting lack of uniformity made the population discontented and the Trade's employees feel insecure. When to this was added the constant pressure on the traders to buy in as much as possible, conditions understandably became increasingly chaotic. In some places there was even a sliding scale of prices in order to stimulate trade; for instance, the trader at Frederikshåb paid above the rate allowed for produce exchanged.

Buying still went on in accordance with previously established custom. There were expeditions in spring and summer in the southern colonies, and in summer and late autumn in the northern colonies. The old idea of locating barrels in the trapping areas was taken up again at the end of the 1770s. This was successful at Fiskenæsset and Godthåb, although in that district the Greenlander families were scattered over many different trapping areas during the summer and often only stayed in one place for a relatively short time. It was also tried out with success at Ritenbenk. To increase production and hence the amount of seal blubber exchanged, the directors sought to extend the use of nets for catching. This method proved unsuccessful in the south, i.e. in the Sukkertoppen, Godthåb, Fiskenæsset and Frederikshåb districts. At Julianehab there had been no experience of it so far, but at Holsteinsborg, on the other hand, there had been successful experiments with the netting of saddleback seals. At Egedesminde it was agreed to experiment with the netting of both saddlebacks and belugas. Netting was continued on an experimental basis throughout 1782.

So as to stimulate the Greenlanders' sealing and "guide them to a better economy", Det Kongelige Landhusholdningsselskab (the Royal Agronomic Society) offered a number of prizes to Greenlanders in Disko Bay "to encourage them in their whaling and sealing, the blubber from which is to be delivered to the Trade, together with the catching of capelin for winter food". The directors, in fact, had just decided to award prizes to the *fangers* who supplied most blubber (with a minimum of six casks) and the sealer who supplied the most saddleback seal skins (minimum of fifty). The prizes were one rigsdaler's worth of merchandise for blubber, and two rigsdalers' worth for skins. As far as the directors were concerned, the Agronomic Society could award the proposed prize for sealing, the preserving of *angmagssat* and the production of dried meat and halibut. In the end prizes were only awarded for sealing, and only Egedesminde truly benefited. The list of winners was submitted in 1779, but no prizes were sent out in 1780. When they finally arrived in 1781, one of the major winners had died. In Egedesminde one winner received goods to the value of 4 rigsdaler and so must have delivered twenty-four barrels of seal blubber. The Trade's prize list, however, appears to have had a cooler reception, and only left its mark on whaling.

Egedesminde was not always a good hunting place. Dorf forecast ruin for both the Trade and the mission if they remained there. This however, only applied to the colony itself; the real hunting-grounds lay about ten miles away. The *fangers* who moved into the colony could not support themselves and their dependants. Dorf's judgment was partly correct, but was influenced by a winter of famine and sickness (1774-5). This situation was not peculiar to Egedesminde, but applied to all the Bay colonies, where conditions did not improve until the ice disappeared. Dorf had starving people begging at his door till early May.

In 1776 another discouraging account was given of conditions in the Bugt, this time by a ship's captain who had been to various places where everyone was ill with "consumption, spitting of blood and retching". In the tents near Zwarte Vogel Bay "there was not one of them who could fetch enough water for another to quench his thirst". Claushavn and Jakobshavn seem to have been the only places where conditions were more or less tolerable, although there too diseases and epidemics caused deaths.

It has already been mentioned that the trapping cycles (resulting in a more nomadic existence) were not a prominent feature of life in the Bay. In the Ūmánaq region to the north, conditions were rather different. There the order to evacuate the colony's Greenlanders was singularly misjudged, and only created confusion and distrust among the management. In general most Greenlanders moved out in the summer, each to his own site, returning to the colony in winter. Nowhere in the whole region was considered a suitable space for living in all the year round. The order, if carried out, would not be in the Greenlanders' best interests and they doubted whether the management meant it for their good at all. Here was a direct conflict between the Trade's wishes and tradition. As had so often happened before, it proved impossible to carryout the instructions and thus, as at Ūmánaq, they were ignored.

At Upernavik during these years beluga trapping gave a big catch to the Greenland population, but not to the Trading Company. As the catching was largely by *savssat*, and the Greenland sealers were unable to bring all the blubber ashore, a large part of the catch was frequently left lying on the ice. It was therefore decided to build a house nearby so that the assistant could be ready to barter and help in transporting the blubber with his men. High expectations concerning the future of this colony were held both by the directors and by those on the spot.

Around 1781 conditions to the south were precarious. In Holsteinsborg the winter of 1780-1 was a failure for the sealers, resulting in want and starvation. At times there was not a scrap of blubber, and the lamps were put out. The Greenlanders who were to go on the look-out for whales had to dry their wet furs by the stove in trader Jørgen

EE

Egede's room. Life in Sukkertoppen from 1775 onwards was affected by the growing possibility of moving the colony south. The trader there had referred to the prospects of whaling off some small islands, Sātungmiut, due east of Manîtsoq island, to which Sukkertoppen was finally transferred. The trader had wintered there in 1777–8 and found good whaling opportunities. The outcome, however, was that he did not catch a single whale that winter, nor the next. Nonetheless, in 1778 he finally submitted a proposal for moving the colony, which was carried out in 1781. It was not the whaling possibilities in themselves which determined the move, but rather the settlement by most of the district's population in that part of the region after moving away from Old Sukkertoppen or Kangâmiut.

Hence, this transfer of a colony did not mean any expansion of the Trade's operations, although it brought about over the years a more intensive exploitation of the whaling and sealing potential of the district. In the far south, on the other hand, the establishment of Juliane-håb meant an initial increase in bartering. The trader Andreas Bruun, on the reconnaissance trip he made in 1777–8, had left Poul Egede's sister's son, Caspar Alsbach, at Nanortalik. He was to have been stationed in Upernavik, but was unable to reach there from the south, so he was a supernumerary in Julianehåb and therefore of use in buying blubber and skins in this most southerly region. There arose the curious situation of the people of Nanortalik taking back the blubber that they had sold to Alsbach. It just lay there without being used and apparently no one else fetched it. This trader thought that the whole southern district could be covered by expeditions from Juliane-håb, and this opinion later proved sound.

Most reports and letters from traders in the colonies complained of bad conditions. How was it possible to exist in such circumstances? The answer must be that the reports emphasized the bad conditions that needed to be remedied or alleviated, and there was necessarily a difference in living standards between the colonists, who were used to better things, and the Greenlanders. Despite endemic and epidemic diseases, and periods of famine when the catch failed, the Greenlanders survived. The Danish farmer, who was reputed to be well fed, in fact knew all about hunger; but deficiency diseases and epidemics sapped the vigour of ordinary people from Denmark, Norway, Iceland and the Faroe Islands.

It is impossible to estimate the size of the Greenland population around 1782. In 1776 the directors had ordered a "general census of all inhabitants" to be made each year, but the order was not carried out at all the colonies. Registers of the congregations sent by the missionaries to the Missionskollegium, together with their journals, were lost in a fire. It seems that only the Godthåb trader complied with the order, but his census was haphazard, since it had to be carried out during his various spring expeditions. Subject to every reservation, a comparison can nevertheless be made with earlier population figures from Godthåb. According to reports of 1771 and 1772 there were respectively 1,075 and 1,030 persons in the Godthåb district. In 1777 the trader stated that the colony (the whole district including Ny Herrnhut) contained 961 "souls", which he later classified as 462 at the Royal Mission, 493 at Ny Herrnhut and six unbaptized. A comparison with the 1771 and 1772 figures showed a decline both in the Royal Mission and the Brethren's congregation. The drop in the latter from 535 in 1772 to 493 in 1777 can be explained by the fact that a number of people went south with the Brethren to found Lichtenau in 1774. But in May 1780 the number at Ny Herrnhut, including a few settlements in the district, was 510. At the same time the trader estimated the number at the Royal Mission at just over 450 making a total above 960 persons. Thus the population figure for the Godthåb district showed a continuing decline, most noticeable at the Royal Mission. It is impossible to ascertain the reason. Migration may account for the Royal Mission figures, as the chances of moving to other districts were less restricted for the Greenlanders there than in the Brethren's congregation. Considering that the figures for Godthåb represent a decade, we can detect a downward trend in the numbers of Greenlanders, which the many reports of starvation and disease support.

Population movements from one district to another cannot be ascertained, nor, therefore, whether the movements were greater or less than formerly. From Ũmánaq it was reported that the whaling at Godhavn attracted population but this was only an isolated report. At a few places people had come a considerable distance to settle at a colony, but these were very few. Niels Egede remarked in 1781, concerning the distance between Frederikshåb and Holsteinsborg, that "it is too far between them, and it is seldom now that anyone journeys between them." This suggests that communication through chance travellers along the coast was becoming a thing of the past, and with it long-distance migrations. This was presumably a consequence of the demarcation of colonial districts and the tendency of the Trade to force the Greenlanders living in a district always to trade at the appropriate colony. The traders were watchful to the point of jealousy that "their" Greenlanders did not trade at other colonies – a result of each colony being a self-contained commercial entity usually served by a particular ship. The fact that the Greenlanders obtained credit from the trader naturally strengthened the latter's dislike of seeing them sell their produce to other traders from whom they had not received credit. Finally, every since 1721 both the Trade and the mission, for their own reasons, had combated the Greenlanders' excessive tendency to wander.

Gradually over the century a process of differentiation took place which was heightened by the whaling projects. Each colonial district had acquired its own special character, either because of the sealing and whaling, the animals or fish caught, navigational conditions and hence provisioning, the local employment situation or, finally because of special mission institutions. This process of differentiation contributed, without contemporaries being aware, to the mutual isolation of the individual colonial districts. Changes in population distribution along the coast were also checked.

Much higher numbers of immigrants compared with former times, especially at the whaling stations during winter, also brought about changes in social structure in the colonies. The fact that assistance could be obtained in bad times by moving to or remaining at the colonies was an important factor. The number of Greenlanders who went to work with the immigrants on long or short terms of employment increased. The heavy manning of the whaling stations when the ships were laid up for the winter prompted the following remarks from Dean Sverdrup: "For besides other transient inconveniences, it was to be feared that the outcome would be the same as is occurring now in certain colonies, viz. each of the crew not only has his maidservant to sew for him and dry his clothes, but also his manservant whose duties often include the most menial tasks." This was detrimental to the trapping, as the men neglected their work as sealers and, where the men did get on with it, the women neglected their flensing work. A check should be kept of who went into service.

The "other transient inconveniences" included the easy availability of hard liquor. It seems that wherever the whalers spent the winter, the cork came out of the bottle more easily than before. Much is heard about brandy in the 1770s, and many complained of "this evil", "this chief source of ruin".

Price increases and the existence of unsatisfied demand also had bad results. In 1778 a Greenlander broke into the Upernavik warehouse and stole "a roll of tobacco" (possibly 14 lb.). The Greenlander was employed in the colony, and the trader in charge requested that he should not be held financially liable for the stolen tobacco as he received only a small wage. Although he was let off, the directors thereafter insisted that all warehouses be secured, which would also prevent accidental shootings through careless handling of ammunition.

A growing sense of insecurity must have been felt in the different colonies; but only at Fiskenæsset did the very zealous senior assistant, Raun, put forward a proposal in *c.* 1776 for a Greenland "police order" of seventeen items. The original is lost, but it appears to have been an attempt at a kind of penal code, including such punishments as an iron collar and "wearing the fiddle" (a violin shaped instrument of punishment made of iron which was worn round the neck, the hands being enclosed in the iron at the same time). Faced with such drastic penal notions, the directors' reaction was that "as regards the Greenlanders, it could not be considered fitting either in view of the country's circumstances or their way of life, not to mention the fact that persons experiencing them would meet with insurmountable difficulties and even be made to look ridiculous". However misguided Raun's proposal may have been, they are nevertheless evidence of an ever-increasing need for order and security, even in such a relatively peaceful place as Fiskenæsset.

A general review was plainly necessary.

23

SETTING UP AND NEW PLANS
1778–1782

The Government's sudden intervention with the order-in-council of 26 March 1779 was probably not the only reason why the Stats-balancedirektion and the directors of the Royal Greenland Trade executed the royal order of 21 April with such haste. Although a royal decision of such importance had to be carried out promptly, it was also vital, once the decision had been taken, to send out the two jurists as inspectors so that they could acquaint themselves fully and quickly with the situation. The order-in-council stated that they were to have access to everything concerning the Greenland trade and whaling.

On 26 April the Statsbalancedirektion addressed letters about the posting to Schwabe and Olrik separately at the same time as the directors of the Trade were informed of the order-in-council and royal order. This undoubtedly made the directors feel they had been by-passed, and treated with much less than full confidence. Nonetheless it was their responsibility to draw up the terms of reference within which the two controllers were to act in Greenland. The purpose of the arrangement emerged clearly from these instructions. They were both to spend the winter of 1779–80 at Godhavn, investigating thoroughly how the trade and whaling operated in this colony, and whether there was enough trade to warrant having a trader and an assistant there, whether the place had been well chosen for whaling, whether the local Greenlanders could catch enough to support themselves or really needed extra European provisions, and whether a suitable number of Greenlanders were living at Godhavn. Always the whaling was to be their concern, "since it is through the success of this whaling that the State stands to derive any real benefit from Greenland, and the King hopes to see all his paternal solicitude for that country rewarded, so it is your duty to study closely everything that will best further this plan."

Although the benefits to the State were stressed and *raison d'état* was emphasized, the Danish autocracy acted in an enlightened way. The principle of reciprocity was evident, as when it was said that the

Greenlanders' "rightful Sovereign and King is alone entitled to permit them to dispose for payment of any of the country's products that they might acquire and not need for their own consumption, just as they for their part are bound to allow the Danish Trade alone to benefit thereby, in return for which they enjoy protection against molestation by foreign nations and help from the Trade should the trapping fail and famine ensue." These sentiments have been heard before in connection with Greenland; here is the traditional fiction of "the King's peace".

The fact that what the Greenlanders could part with after satisfying their own needs was to accrue to the Trade in return for payment was also emphasized in the instructions for Schwabe and Olrik. The concern was to be with material aims alone. Schwabe and Olrik were not to concern themselves with the spiritual side – that belonged to the mission. In an age of rationalism, no connection between these factors in the cultural development of the community could be perceived.

Hence Schwabe and Olrik were called upon to investigate such matters as the whaling masters' maintenance of good order, the diligence and alertness of both masters and crews, the opportunities for other forms of fishing and, finally, the state and adequacy of the stores, materials and buildings. They were to investigate coal-mining, the idea being that this coal should be extracted partly for heating the houses and partly for refining whale-oil in order to rationalize transport; this was why iron cauldrons were sent out to Godhavn and Ũmánaq in 1777, but even by 1779 nothing had been heard as to whether or not they had been used.

The two jurists, of whom Olrik was well known for his economic acumen, were to examine Greenland's economy, particularly to see whether the provisions supplied for the food rations were used by the traders and assistants as intended and not as a means of bartering with the Greenlanders "to their ruin" (spoiling with European food). The maintenance of wives and children of "mixed marriages" was to be investigated – to what extent it was at the expense of the Trade – as well as their housing conditions and "and how far the Greenlander wives are used as whores by the colonists". Their assignment was a highly varied one.

The traders' buying methods were to be investigated, "whether the buying is done fairly, at any rate with proper barrels or measuring tubs provided with a bottom at the end which rests on the ground, and not with bottomless measures placed where there is a hole in the ground". The buying of all kinds of skins was to be investigated, especially the reasons why almost no skins were now being traded in from the Bay colonies – previously quite a quantity had been. A check was to be made "whether such products are now being used as a luxury in the country itself or sold to the ships of foreign nations, or disposed of in some other illegal manner". For the rest the two controllers were to use their own discretion, but Olrik, after a trip to Ũmánaq, was to winter at Jakobshavn and Schwabe in Godhavn after visiting the Bay colonies. Both were to return home in the summer of 1781.

They were apparently not to concern themselves with what lay south of Egedesminde, since the southern colonies were not mentioned. This meant only that any investigations there would have been impracticable, both the trapping and the trade still being on traditional lines. Also, less capital was at stake there than in the Bay with its many whaling stations.

Schwabe and Olrik were to "observe and investigate everything without disclosing their purpose", and thus were not to become involved in any transactions. This good advice has a burlesque touch since the directors simultaneously circularized all traders in the Bay that Schwabe and Olrik would be arriving "to investigate various matters". The Bay traders had never before experienced State control at local level. That was where the blow fell hardest.

Schwabe voiced his uneasiness about being a controller. "Never have I assumed a mask at any time until coming to Greenland; but here I have been obliged to act a part. Notwithstanding this and although I have set about the task as discreetly as possible and never directly interfered in any matter, yet both my colleague and I are mistrusted." They behaved differently from the other Europeans at the trading post and did no minor deals with the local Greenlanders. People were obviously anxious and suspicious. The following year (1780) the two jurists began sending home their reports and journals. It is strange that Schwabe's communications were significant, but not Olrik's.[1] To these can be added Schwabe's personal letters to Ove Høegh-Guldberg with whom he obviously had a special connection.

In almost every one of Schwabe's letters to Guldberg he deferred a more detailed account of the topics touched upon until they could meet face to face on his return to Copenhagen. Some things he only mentioned in his letters to Guldberg, stating explicitly that he was not communicating them to the directors. In the last of his letters to be preserved he wrote of his reports: "I did not think it fitting to write the same to a whole kollegium", by which he meant the directors as well as the Statsbalancedirektion. It is thus tempting to believe that they contained severe criticisms of the directors.

Schwabe's report and letters give an unattractive picture of conditions in the Bay, especially at Godhavn. He and Olrik followed the whalers' activities day by day and noted when they were inactive. The list of their activities which he sent to Guldberg testifies to no excess of effort by the whalers. From December 1779 to mid-May 1780 they went out thirty-eight times, the Greenlanders seventeen times; they caught two whales and lost five. "In my view", wrote Schwabe, "the ship discharged her duty only half-heartedly." The catch had been better within the Bay. In all eight whales had been caught, in addition to which ten were found. It was an unimpressive figure in relation to the investment.

When the Dutch and English ships appeared beyond the ice there was a regular procession out to them. Schwabe's description in the journal gives an impression of complete licence, with drunkenness and sex combined with the illicit trading of skins for tobacco and spirits. Even Sandgreen, the trader, took part in the illicit trading under the very noses of Schwabe and Olrik. Schwabe dealt later with the illicit trade in eiderdown, in which he thought that the captains of the colonial supply ships were the worst offenders. If traders and assistants had a hand in unauthorized deals, it was perhaps because of their low salaries. He therefore suggested improving their wages by means of a percentage commission related to quantities bought. He also touched on the cheating that occurred in bartering: it was necessary to take an excess measure. It was impossible to measure frozen blubber accurately, and if it was to be kept in storage for long before being sent home, it dwindled away appreciably, causing losses for the trader. Schwabe's pronouncements concerning overcharging for barter goods were vague; he did not state outright that an exorbitant profit was being made on sales but nor would he deny it. Hence it occurred to him that a general price list applicable to the whole country and drawn up in Danish and Greenlandic might solve the problem.

Schwabe and Olrik had been instructed to investigate every conceivable problem. Schwabe therefore discussed the curious fact that venereal diseases did not seem a matter for concern although many Godhavn women were known to have intercourse with infected men on both national and foreign whaling vessels. He was surprised that not more children were born, but he had heard that induced abortions were common. He also noted that sexual activity started at an early age and was shocked by the lax morals.

Schwabe also considered the question of whether the unbaptized Greenlanders were more industrious than the baptized. At a time when the baptized had gradually come to be in the majority in most districts from the Bay south to and including Frederikshåb, this problem might seem of minor importance. Nevertheless it gave him the opportunity to air his views as to why a competent breadwinner would not allow himself to be baptized: he would be obliged to forego so much of his former liberty. On certain points, his opinions show a surprising ability to identify himself with the Greenlanders, but for the rest, his journal and letters show a pleasing reserve in making judgments and evaluations. Time and again he emphasized the difficulty of discovering the true facts of any problem.

Schwabe stressed the educational importance for Greenland in having not only missionaries and catechists but also traders and assistants sent out who were upright and capable. He touched on the dissension between traders and missionaries, laying some of the blame on the traders. They and their assistants were over-concerned with their own profit. "Patriotism, unselfishness and diligence should distinguish a capable trading employee and above all a trader. If they do not think on Danish lines, if they do not deal honestly, if they do not themselves possess a spirit of enterprise and the gift of communicating it to others, so encouraging the Greenlanders and winning their respect, then they are certainly of no benefit to the Trade, which will never get on its feet, or reduce its expenses." Here for the first time the Trade's educational or cultural obligation was formulated, though he concluded with a sly acknowledgment of the contemporary requirement that everything and every relationship should have a utilitarian value.

The picture painted by Schwabe and Olrik cannot have been encouraging for Guldberg, let alone the directors. The order-in-council drafted by Guldberg after perusal of the reports seems surprisingly bland; the order contained approval of the directors' plans for the whaling year of 1780–1. But in the preamble Guldberg strongly criticized the whaling-masters: "It is obvious that most of the masters are bad men . . . so that our money is wasted and the authorities' best endeavours are fruitless. Other nations make a catch while we, who have every advantage, achieve nothing." He later ordered "that the wicked man who caught nothing at Godhavn except what he stole from the Greenlanders shall not command any ship of ours again; neither shall the other who did not arrive at Godhavn until 2 June . . ." Proceedings were to be taken against these and other culprits through a special commission, the appointment of which was unpleasant for the directors, as it was customary for chartered companies to have supreme authority over their own affairs. In the case of a royal company, however, the reigning powers could intervene at any time. Guldberg's order-in-council announced that diligence was to be rewarded by the distribution of silver cups worth 16 rigsdaler or silver spoons valued at 4 rigsdaler. It was the local whalers in the Bay, not the whaling masters, who were thus to be rewarded for their services. "This is how we reward people, but now and again we are also obliged to punish."

Retrenchment was now the watchword. H. C. Schimmelmann, whose influence had been omnipresent at the start of the State whaling project, had now vanished from the picture. In the autumn of 1780, some of the Greenland Trading and Whaling Company's buildings were given up; so too were some of the ships. The ground was giving way beneath the directors' feet, but it was they who had to control the landslide. At the same time, it was necessary to make plans for continuing the venture; no one for a moment thought of abandoning the Greenland trade, let alone the mission, but the planning was no longer entrusted to the directors of the Royal Greenland Trade but to the Statsbalancedirektion.

On 20 April 1781 the boards of directors of the Greenland, Finnmark and Faroe Islands trades were informed of the royal intention to transfer the Greenland trade to their trading companies forthwith. From 1 May the Royal Chartered Greenland, Iceland, Finnmark and Faroe Islands Trade would come into existence, its board of directors consisting of Privy Councillor (Gehejmeråd) C. L. Stemann (Senior Deputy for Finance and the Rentekammer), Privy Councillor and Secretary of State Ove Høegh-Guldberg, Councillor of State (Etatsråd) Jon Erichsen (Deputy in the Rentekammer as an expert on the affairs of the trading companies involved), Councillor of State Wilhelm August Hanssen (hitherto managing director of the Faroe Islands Trade, which he continued to control), a managing director of the Iceland and Finnmark Trades and finally Hartvig Marcus Frisch as managing director of the Greenland Trade. Frisch was a new man in the State-operated trading companies; a banker by training, he had risen via the Øresund Customs House. The old directors of the Greenland Trade took up various new posts, none connected with the trade they had once controlled.

Then in July the detailed regulations prescribing in detail the transitional arrangements and future organization were issued. These were more like a charter than a set of regulations, being mainly concerned with the rights and liberties granted to the Trade. This reformed enterprise was very much like a company; the State held the shares, but the right to the fixed assets and the operation of the business was transferred to the Trade for a specific period of thirty years. The regulations provided the guide-line by which Hartvig Marcus Frisch was to administer the Greenland Trade as its sole director. The critical reports of Schwabe and Olrik, and the poor return on the whaling, had brought about the reorganization. Schwabe's ideas and suggestions for future operations in Greenland were yet to make their mark, but implementation of these ideas steered the development of the West Greenland colonial districts away from being almost a matter of chance to one of organization. There had been a growing demand for "order" from the 1720s onwards, but 1781–2 was the year of change. Glancing back over the eighty years or so of development in West Greenland, the significance of chance events is evident. Moreover, we get a strong impression of public lethargy which began with a reluctance to involve the State in what was in many respects a hazardous undertaking.

From being a means of furthering the mission, the Trade became increasingly an end in itself. This was one of the consequences of the clash between Trade and mission which had started on a small scale in Sewerin's time. This partial secularization of "the Greenland *Dessein*" had repercussions, and the breach between mission and Trade generally deepened. The increasing demand for a reasonable reward in those sectors which received State investment in capital and manpower also contributed to the growth of the Trade, and it began to take precedence over the mission in the eyes of the authorities. Since the mission's expenses were a charge on the budget, its organization needed to be efficient. This meant a departure from Hans Egede's fundamental viewpoint.

The century had begun with Vídalín's comprehensive analysis, making reference to the Norse past, and his extremely broad and advanced proposals for a cultural, economic and political effort towards a bright future for Greenland and for the Danish–Norwegian monarchy. Whether or not his plans had any direct significance is immaterial. Hans Egede was responsible for first realizing the idea of resuming the connection with Greenland, and he made its development serve the mission's interests.

The Government gradually came to realize that the Danish–Norwegian King's rights in Greenland and the adjacent seas were not just nominal on the basis of a tradition dating back to 1261. It was important that these rights should be established, but this involved delicate diplomatic problems. The formal rights embodied in the sovereignty over the land and territorial waters might form the constitutional and international basis for carrying through the economic and cultural measures, but the two latter areas of activity formed the true basis. It also became increasingly clear that the Government had to act with due regard to the financial and cultural resources of the monarchy as they were at that time and would be in the long term. Yet by progressive steps the State was drawn into direct economic collaboration, because at no time throughout the period was there sufficient private capital to finance the Greenland Trade and mission. This was bound to lead sooner or later to a deliberate Greenland policy; indeed, such a policy was started in the 1780s and basic principles were established.

The colonization of Greenland society began in the flickering glow of

Last page of Jacob Poulsen's letter to Poul Egede, written in June 1765. (Central Record Office, Copenhagen.)

Hans Egede's lamp, from whose flame candle after candle was lit. The speed with which the Eskimo spiritual tradition collapsed remains a mystery. The Christian faith, as preached by either the Brethren or the royal mission, took root in the West Greenlanders' minds and became a decisive factor for an ever-increasing number of them. Young Jacob Poulsen, whose father Poul Grønlaender was accidentally shot, wrote to Poul Egede in 1765: "I would be grief-stricken over father's death, had not God given us His Word. But the dear Saviour has really saved us, cares for us and loves us. No one loves men more than He who died [for them]. He suffered greatly for our sins so that we might be saved. Through Him we can come to Heaven. Jesus has also given us comfort in the following words: 'He who believes will live although he is dead, and he who lives in the faith will live forever'." The latter is a quotation from St. John's Gospel (11. 25–6) in the Greenlandic version. For him, as for his dead father, those words were the truth, the way and the life.

In a wider context, a fundamental element in the European pattern of culture – in its Scandinavian form – became a decisive factor in the life of the individual in Greenland during the six decades 1721–82. Inevitably, much of the West Greenland Eskimo tradition would be broken and forced to disappear if the new tradition were adopted. Part of the old tradition survived in secret, and in many minds created an awareness of sin peculiar to the Greenlanders, which probably contributed to this particular element in the Christian religion being well understood. Certain reports allude to this all but fortuitous means of furthering the aims of the mission.

The material and economic influence of the colonial culture too were not without an effect on cultural life. Association both with the colonists sent from Denmark with the foreign whalers had its unavoidable consequences – economic, occupational and cultural. Some of the consequences were also biological, at once fortunate and unfortunate in their effect on the growth of society. The unfortunate aspect was the number of illegitimate children born, but it was fortunate that "mixed families" were created by the relatively large number of marriages. Society and the economy benefited from the specialization and greater efficiency brought about by imported implements and weapons, but they suffered from the drunkenness that had crept in, and from the loosening of traditional communal bonds caused by the selling of produce.

The more the trade became not simply an instrument of supply but also a factor regulating production, the more did Scandinavian equipment and economic culture become integrated into the Greenlanders' daily life. It was a long time before this changed their way of thinking and their attitude towards production. The stern demands of daily existence still had to be met, and mostly people were content simply to fulfil these. However, there were now everyday needs which could only be satisfied by selling to and buying from the Trading Company.

At the time interest in Greenland, especially in the mission, was keen among the Danish public. It was felt that Hans Egede deserved to be numbered among Denmark–Norway's great pioneers. In 1777, Ove Malling in his widely-read book, *Store og gode Handlinger, etc* (*Great and good deeds of Danes, Norwegians and Holsteiners*) gave a description of Hans Egede's work. In 1778 the first important biography of Hans Egede was published, the work of Pastor Jacob Lund, who married a granddaughter of the old bishop. A memorial to him by the sculptor Johannes Wiedewelt was erected in Jægerspris Park in 1779. In 1775 a wealthy spinster, Karen Ørsted, who lived in Haderup in the diocese of Ribe, bequeathed 2,250 rigsdaler, invested in six royal debentures, "for the benefit of the Greenlanders".

The integration of Greenland with Denmark was about to take place.

REFERENCES

1. Schwabe's diary does not seem to exist any longer, except for a fragment of six combined sheets in folio, marked as pages 111 to 131. This fragment includes notes from 23 April to 20 May 1780. Schwabe signed page 131 of his diary, which thus seems to be the last page of the diary that he despatched from Godhavn that summer. In a later letter to Guldberg (16 June 1780) Schwabe reported that he had sent sheets 7 to 58 of his diary to the Directors and that he hoped Guldberg would read them. Apart from these fragments, all we have are some letters from Schwabe and Olrik to Guldberg.

NOTE ON THE SOURCE
MATERIAL

The source material for the *History of Greenland 1700–1782* may be divided as usual into two parts, *unprinted* and *printed*, the latter referring to the contemporary books and to some outstanding later ones.

THE UNPRINTED SOURCES

The archives are rather scattered, some of them being private. In former times there was a seemingly lax attitude as to what constituted official documents, documents pertaining to particular official posts and private property. This has caused some confusion, besides the normal official practice of picking out parts of a file required in connection with some other matter; sometimes parts of the files have then disappeared, only to be found again by chance. Furthermore the practice of the record offices and the departmental registries in this century have been far from fixed. Finally some of the archives have been consumed by fire, especially the big fires of Copenhagen. Most of the archives and the library of the Missionskollegium was burned in such a big fire in 1795. Several originals of Hans Egede's and most of the diaries from the missionaries' hands disappeared at that time. Thanks to copies and the above-mentioned lax attitude, parts of it can be reconstructed. The copies and the few original manuscripts are preserved in the Royal Library of Copenhagen, the National Museum of Copenhagen and, last but not least, in Rigsarkivet (the Main Public Record Office), Copenhagen. Besides this, by chance or due to being transferred later from Denmark to Norway, some are in the Norwegian Main Public Record Office, Riksarkivet, and in Deichmanske Library, both in Oslo, or in the local public record office and the town record office of Bergen, Norway; in the latter, for example, are several files concerning the Bergen–Greenland Company.

By far the greater part of the documents and files are in Rigsarkivet in Copenhagen, where the different departmental archives are kept, together with files from Jacob Sewerin's "trading company" (in copies, the originals being kept by the local public record office in Viborg, Jutland), the Royal Chartered Common Trading Company, and the Royal Greenland Trade and Fishery.

The government records are filed according to the administration office pattern, following its alterations. It is useless here to go into details about that, but it may be sufficient to say that the documents have to be gathered from a wide range of departments, which has been done in preparing this text and will continue to be done for the later periods.

THE PRINTED MATERIAL

Some of the source material has been printed. Dr. Louis Bobé has in MoG 55, 3, edited a selection of the most important documents from 1492 to 1814, being more and more selective towards the latter date. It is of course edited in the original languages, far the greater part being in Danish. Quite apart from the editor's lack of accuracy, his selection of documents is insufficient to cover the full range of the history of Greenland in the period concerned. But it must be admitted that Dr. Bobé's selection had a clear aim, just as the Norwegian edition of documents on the period 1721–6: Solberg og Sollied, *Bergenserne på Grønland i det 18. århundrede I*, Oslo, 1932, involved editing almost the same documents as Dr. Bobé had done. In another way the Norwegian edition is useful, introducing several biographical notes which are difficult to gather otherwise.

Besides these two editions of documents, several of the surviving diaries have been printed and edited with notes, all of them in Danish or Norwegian. Hans Egede's *Relations* are printed in MoG 54. Of his own drafting and edition of 1738, reprinted in Copenhagen in 1971, no English edition exists, but only one in German: *Ausführliche und wahrhafte Nachricht vom Anfange und Fortgange der Grönländischen Mission*, Hamburg, 1740. His *Perlustration* was translated into English and edited with the plates in London in 1744 under the title *A Description of Greenland; a new edition With an Historical Introduction and a Life of the Author* was published in London in 1760, and reprinted in 1818. Poul and Niels Egede's continuations of the *Relations* were published respectively in 1741 and 1744, both reprinted in Copenhagen in 1971, and furthermore edited with notes by H. Ostermann in MoG 120, 1939, all in Danish.

David Cranz's *Historie von Grönland*, Barby, 1765, and his *Fortsetzung*, *ibidem*, 1770, have never been translated into English and edited. His "Brüdergeschichte", 1771, however, was translated and printed with the title *The Ancient and Modern History of the Brethren, or a Succinct Narrative of the Protestant Church of the United Brethren, or, Unitas Fratrum*, London, 1780. This comprises some of the history of the Brethren in Greenland, but is far from the detailed narrative in his *Historie von Grönland*.

In English only one more "modern" survey of the history of Greenland exists: Dr. Louis Bobé's, translated from his introductions to *Diplomatarium Groenlandicum*, MoG 55, 1 and 2, printed in *Greenland*, Vol. III, 1928–9. In the same volume a history of the mission is included, condensed by H. Ostermann from his history of the Greenland mission and church, Copenhagen, 1921; this is not translated or published in any foreign language. I do not find it worth mentioning the shorter and more or less "popular" writings about "Greenland, its nature, population and history", or whatever titles they may have, e.g. Wilhjalmur Stefánsson's more or less bungled book, New York, 1942.

Concerning biographies of Greenland personalities who lived in this period, the bookshelves are likewise empty. Only Dr. Louis Bobé's comprehensive biography of Hans Egede is worth mentioning. It is in somewhat abridged form, being translated from his Danish monograph, and published with the title *Hans Egede, Colonizer and Missionary of Greenland*, Copenhagen, 1952.

The printed source material in Danish is very scarce, as are the more comprehensive surveys. In fact this book is the first detailed and comprehensive narrative on the development of Greenland and its background, even in Danish. For the literature on special items in Danish I must refer to the Danish edition of this book. From the book-list there, however, some items in English may be mentioned here:

"Otto Fabricius' Ethnographical Work", ed. Erik Holtved, MoG 140, 2, Copenhagen 1962.

Astrid Friis and Kristof Glaman, *A History of Prices and Wages in Denmark 1660–1800*, I, Copenhagen, 1958.

Chr. Vibe, "Arctic Animals in Relation to Climatic Fluctuations", MoG 170, 5, Copenhagen, 1967.

MoG means *Meddelelser om Grønland*, 1878 ff.

GLOSSARY

Cabinet, the King's private office.

Cabinet order, a Royal Order issued by the King himself, often written by his private secretary, who could thus obtain considerable influence and sometimes actual political power, as happened in 1770–2.

Conseil, or *Gehejmeconseil*, established 1670 as a council to the autocratic King, having for the first couple of years seven, and in the eighteenth century usually four or five members. In the beginning it numbered among its members most of the presidents of the *kollegia* and the two vicegerents of respectively Norway and the duchies of Slesvig and Holstein; later it included only some of the King's intimates, in addition to a few of high rank, chosen among the highest administration officials. It was abolished in 1770, but reorganized as *Gehejmestatsrådet* (*q.v.*) in 1772.

Cordel(*er*), a Dutch term of measure of capacity corresponding sometimes to 2, sometimes 1½ Danish barrels. It seems to correspond with the English hogshead, which is 52½ imperial gallons, a little more than 2 Danish or Norwegian fish-barrels. If it is 1½ Danish–Norwegian fish barrels, it corresponds to the English cran, 37½ imperial gallons, being a little more. It is not quite clear when the cordel is 2 or 1½ Danish–Norwegian barrels. To increase the confusion it seems in the few accounts from 1734–49 to correspond to 2½ Danish–Norwegian fish-barrels, quite near the English quarter, 64 imperial gallons.

Danske Cancelli, organized as a *kollegium*, was the central administration concerned with affairs of the interior and justice, both in Denmark and Norway and adjacent islands, but not the "German countries" (see *Tyske Cancelli*).

Deputy, member of the board of a *kollegium*.

Fanger (pl. *fangere* or *fangers*), one who is occupied with whaling, sealing, hunting mammals and birds at sea and on land, fishing and trapping. In the Eskimo language called *piniartoq*, i.e. one who endeavours to get something.

Føhn wind, warm wind, curiously enough blowing down from the Ice Cap.

Gehejmerådet or *Gehejmestatsrådet*, established in 1772 as a council to the King under his own leadership. Its members, called *statsminister* (*statsministre*) or *gehejmestatsminister*, usually numbered six, besides the King, the Crown Prince (when he was of full age, i.e. eighteen years old) and those of the Royal princes whom the King appointed to it. This council existed until 1848.

The *General Commissariat of the Army*, translated name covering the Danish *Land Etatens Generalkrigskommissariat*, which was formerly called *krigskollegiet* (war *kollegium*), the administration board for war affairs, i.e. the Royal Army.

The *General Commissariat of the Navy* is a translation covering the Danish *Søe Etatens Generalkommissariat*, once the central administrative office for Navy affairs, organized as a board of high-ranking civil and naval officials. The *Admiralty* was the board of admirals in charge, the practical leadership of the Navy. The two boards were later combined into one, *viz.* the *Admiralty*.

Kollegium. The Danish central administration was from 1660 to 1849–50 organized as *kollegia*, which means that every "branch" was directed by a board of deputies of whom one called *oversekretær* (here translated *chief secretary*) or *præses* ("president") was the head. The head of one *kollegium* could be a deputy of the board of another. The chief secretary or president had to refer cases to the King.

Kurantbanken, established 1736 in Copenhagen as a private institution, but with the right to issue bank-notes, which were legal currency, hence the term *courant banque*. It was the only bank in eighteenth-century Copenhagen.

Missionskollegium, established in 1714, organized as a *kollegium* with three or five members, in close connection with *Danske Cancelli*. It was concerned with the Royal missions in Trankebar (India), the Virgin Islands and Finnmarken, and hence later with the Greenland mission.

Overskattedirektion, literally "the Supreme Treasure Management", "treasure" implying the funds, revenues and expenses of the monarchy. The Directors' concern was the budget and main financial policy. Established in 1773, but reorganized a few years later as *Statsbalancedirektionen* (*q.v.*).

(Politi- and) Commercekollegium, a board of officials, at first concerned with affairs of public order (*politi*) and trade in Copenhagen. Developed into the *Commercekollegium*, established in 1736, dealing with affairs of trade for all the King's countries.

President (in the central administration), head of the board of deputies in a *kollegium*.

President (in the city administration) is the town's chief burgomaster in the royally appointed municipal corporation.

Reindeer. Readers in the Western hemisphere, generally, should realize that the Greenland reindeer is wild. It is not the same type as the caribou, hence our use of the word reindeer. Quite recently, in about 1953, tame reindeer were imported from Norway, and reindeer breeding began.

Rentekammer was a central administrative department, established in about 1540, dealing with the State finances and auditing official accounts. It was reorganized as a *kollegium* in 1660 with another name, but from 1680 it was again called Rentekammer, still having the same functions. In 1771–3 it was combined with the General Customs Administration under *Finans-*

kollegiet, but later on again established with its old name besides several other branches of the financial administration under the Overskattedirektion, later *Statsbalancedirektion (q.v.)*

Rigsdaler, mark and *skilling* (abbreviated as rdl., mrk., sk.). The Danish monetary system up to 1874 was 1 rigsdaler = 6 mark = 96 skilling. The value of the mintings changed, so it is difficult to fix the value of exchange in buying. (Reference: Friis and Glaman, *A History of Prices and Wages in Denmark 1660–1800*).

Stationed. This English word is here used terminologically, e.g. *a stationed catechist* is a catechist born in Denmark or elsewhere outside Greenland, and sent out to a post in Greenland as a catechist; he might stay there, but would always have had the opportunity to return home after a certain period.

Statsbalancedirektion, the general board of the Danish financial administration in the 1770s, dealing with the budget and the main finance policy.

Storis or *Stor-is*. The tremendous quantities of field-ice which flow southwards along the East coast of Greenland from the Polar Basin round Cape Farewell and then northwards, usually as far as Frederikshåb, barring access to the coast. It consists of polar field-ice, sometimes packed and pressed together and piled up in fantastically shaped frozen formations, and icebergs calved from the East Greenland glaciers.

Tyske Cancelli, organized as a *kollegium*, concerned with the administration of the King's so-called "German countries" (hence the name), which covered the first department. The second department administered the foreign affairs of the whole monarchy.

INDEX